GRADES K-1
EARLY LEARNER WORKBOOK™

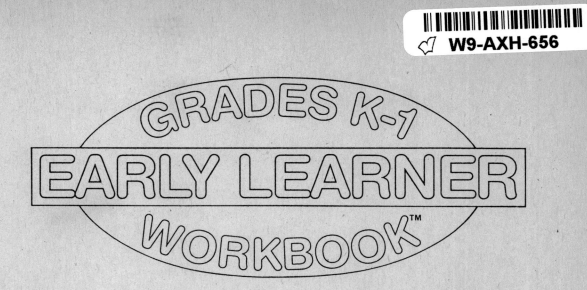

Modern Publishing
A Division of Unisystems, Inc.
New York, NY 10022

Educational Consultant, Shereen Gertel Rutman, M.S.

Copyright © 1990 by Modern Publishing, a division of Unisystems, Inc.

™ Grades K-1 Early Learner Workbook is a trademark of
Modern Publishing, a division of Unisystems, Inc.

® Honey Bear Books is a trademark owned by Honey Bear Productions, Inc.,
and is registered in the U.S. Patent and Trademark Office. No part
of this book may be reproduced or copied without written permission
from the publisher. All Rights Reserved.

Printed in the U.S.A.

All materials © 1988, Educational Insights, Inc.

TO THE PARENTS

Dear Parents,

As your child's first and most important teacher, you can encourage your child's love of learning by participating in learning activities at home. Working together on the activities in this workbook will help your child build confidence, learn to reason, and develop reading, writing, math, language, and perception skills.

Following are some suggestions to help make your time together both enjoyable and rewarding.

- Choose a time when you and your child are relaxed.

- Provide a selection of writing material (either thick or thin pencils and/or crayons).

- Don't attempt to do too many pages at one time or expect that every page be completed. Move on if your child is frustrated or loses interest.

- Praise your child's efforts.

- Discuss each page. Help your child relate the concepts in this book to everyday experiences.

ESSENTIAL SKILLS

The repetitive activities within each chapter have been designed to help children learn to sort, separate, put together, and figure out—the organizational skills so necessary for learning and thinking.

CHAPTER 1   Handwriting Skills
Learning to control the small muscles of the hand (**fine motor skill development**) allows the child to make the precise movements necessary for forming letters, while activities such as **writing from left to right**, **tracing**, and **forming lines** help to refine **eye/hand coordination**. Making **associations**—recognizing what things "go together" (for example, a dog and a bone)—enables a child to recognize that an upper case "A" and a lower case "a" go together.

CHAPTER 2   Colors, Shapes, and Numbers
Looking at familiar shapes helps children notice similarities and differences. Activities in which the child reproduces shapes and/or matches shapes to words, encourages **sight vocabulary recognition** and the ability to make **associations between words and objects**. Grouping things according to common attributes such as color, size, shape, etc. (**classification activities**), encourages development of a child's ability to reason and make **logical connections**. **Recognizing number words, writing numerals**, and **forming sets of objects** all prepare a child for basic math skills.

CHAPTER 3   Basic Math Skills
Becoming familiar with the **order of numbers from 1-10, learning to write those numbers**, and **understanding the connection between a set of objects and its corresponding numeral**, all prepare a child to understand the concepts of addition and subtraction.

CHAPTER 4   Reading Readiness
Determining which items in a group "go together" (**making associations**), and learning to group things according to common attributes (**classification skills**), prepare a child to **notice details**. These skills are necessary for learning to recognize and reproduce the letters of the alphabet.

CHAPTER 5   Phonics Skills I
This chapter focuses on teaching a child **to recognize the initial and final consonant sounds, to learn to write letters and words using these sounds**, and **to understand the association between sounds, symbols, and words**.

CHAPTER 6   Phonics Skills II
Phonics II focuses on training a child to **hear and reproduce the long and short vowel sounds**, as well as the sounds made by combining two letters together to make **consonant blends** and **consonant digraphs**.

TABLE OF CONTENTS

HANDWRITING SKILLS

Trace and color the picture.

Skills: Tracing; Fine motor skill development; Eye/hand coordination

HANDWRITING SKILLS

Trace and color the picture.

Skills: Tracing; Fine motor skill development; Eye/hand coordination

HANDWRITING SKILLS

Trace and color the picture.

Skills: Tracing; Fine motor skill development; Eye/hand coordination

HANDWRITING SKILLS

Trace the broken lines.

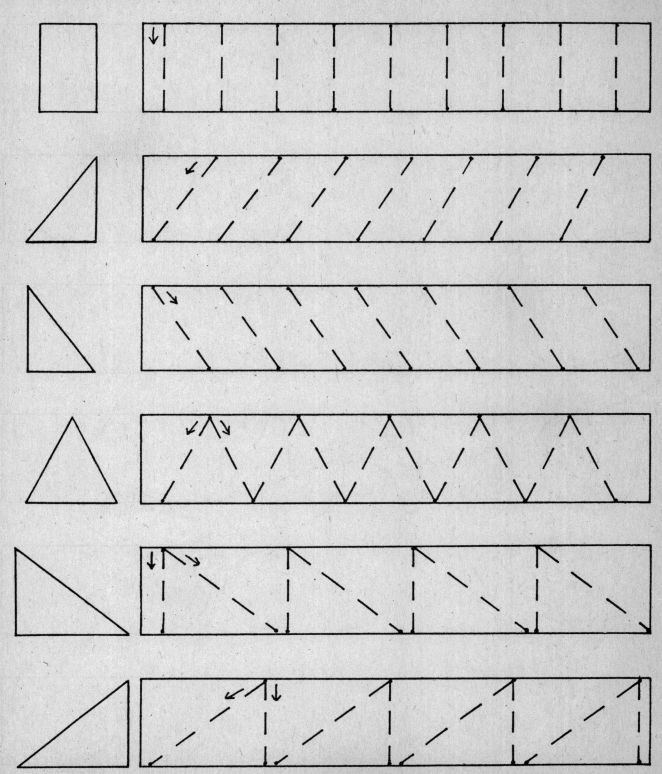

Skills: Fine motor skill development; Forming vertical and diagonal lines; Eye/hand coordination; Corresponding relationships

HANDWRITING SKILLS

Trace the broken lines.

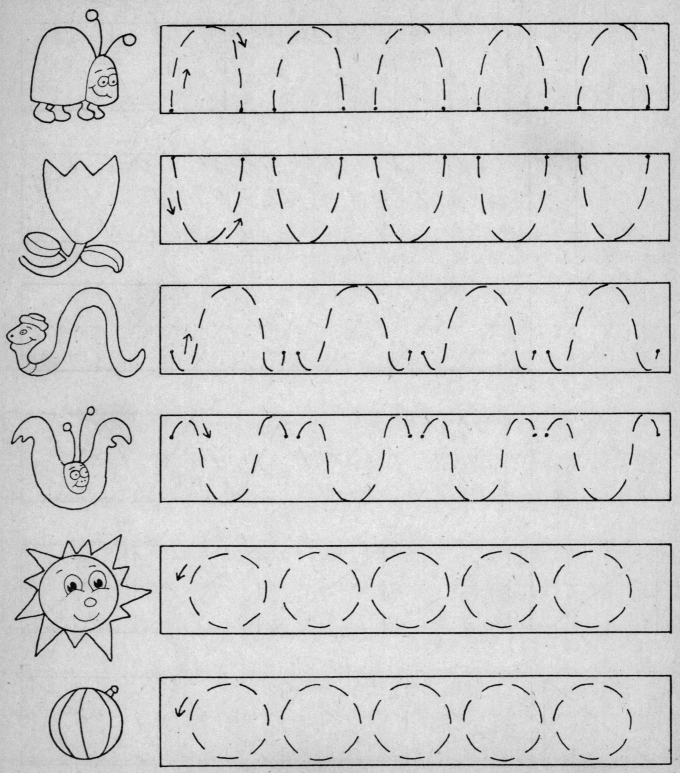

Skills: Fine motor skill development; Eye/hand coordination; Corresponding relationships

HANDWRITING SKILLS

Start at the dots. Trace the broken lines. Then finish the page.

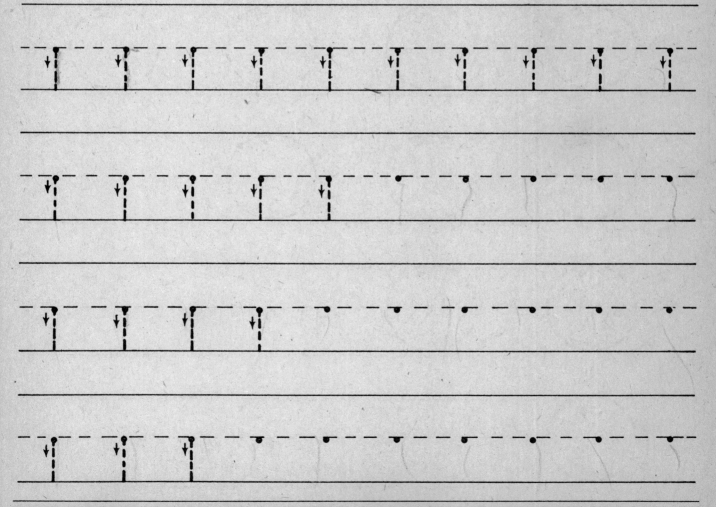

Skills: Fine motor skill development; Eye/hand coordination; Forming vertical lines

HANDWRITING SKILLS

Start at the dots. Trace the broken lines. Then finish the page.

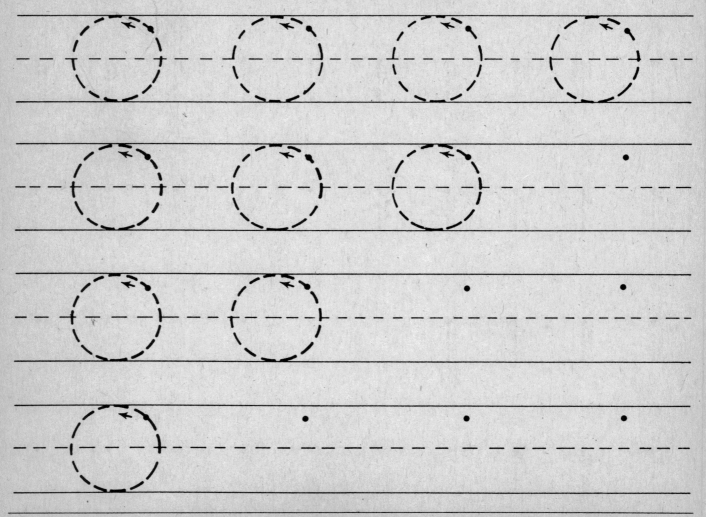

Skills: Fine motor skill development; Eye/hand coordination; Forming closed curves

HANDWRITING SKILLS

Start at the dots. Trace the broken lines. Then finish the page.

Skills: Fine motor skill development; Eye/hand coordination; Forming vertical lines

HANDWRITING SKILLS

Start at the dots. Trace the broken lines. Then finish the page.

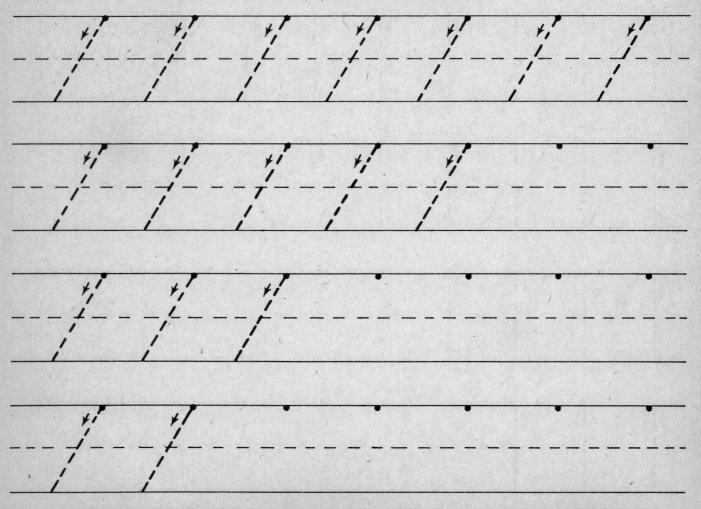

Skills: Fine motor skill development; Eye/hand coordination; Forming diagonal lines

HANDWRITING SKILLS

Start at the dots. Trace the broken lines. Then finish the page.

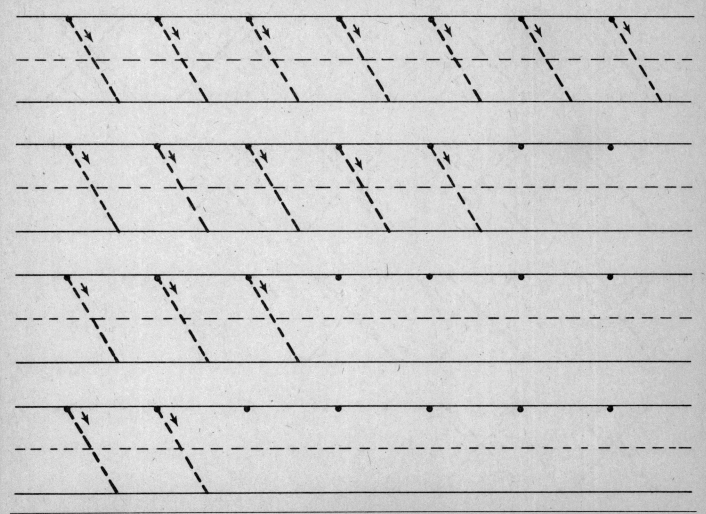

Skills: Fine motor skill development; Eye/hand coordination; Forming diagonal lines

HANDWRITING SKILLS

Start at the dots. Trace the broken lines. Then finish the page.

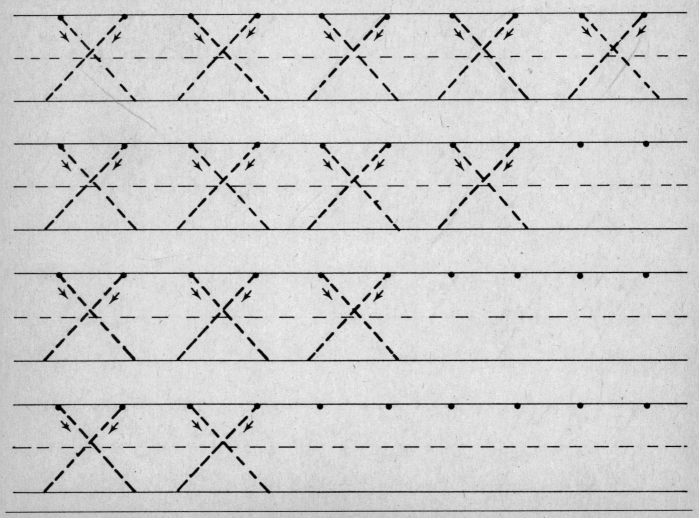

Skills: Fine motor skill development; Eye/hand coordination

HANDWRITING SKILLS

Start at the dots. Trace the broken lines. Then finish the page.

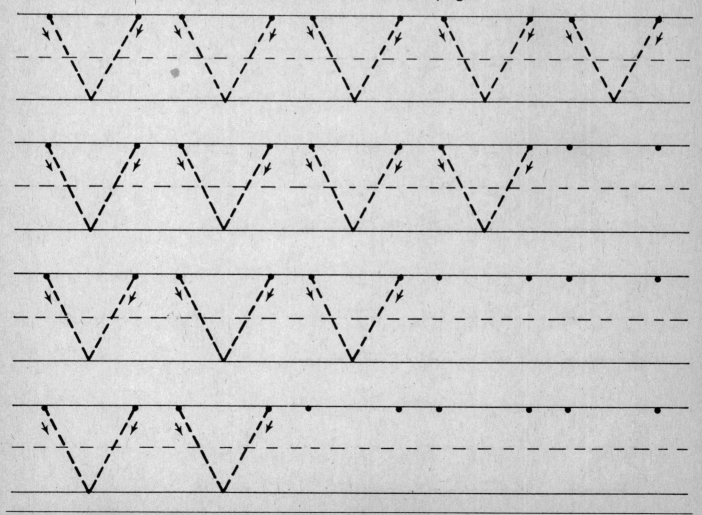

Skills: Fine motor skill development; Eye/hand coordination

Start at the dots. Trace the broken lines. Then finish the page.

Skills: Fine motor skill development; Eye/hand coordination; Forming horizontal lines

Follow the direction of each arrow. Then practice writing each letter.

Skills: Forming upper/lower case "a"; Writing left to right

HANDWRITING SKILLS

Follow the direction of each arrow. Then practice writing each letter.

Skills: Forming upper/lower case "b"; Writing left to right

HANDWRITING SKILLS

Follow the direction of each arrow. Then practice writing each letter.

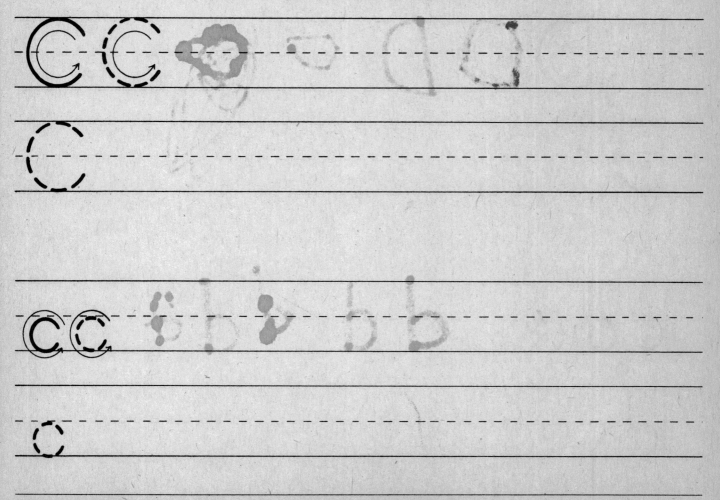

Skills: Forming upper/lower case "c"; Writing left to right

HANDWRITING SKILLS

Follow the direction of each arrow. Then practice writing each letter.

Skills: Forming upper/lower case "d"; Writing left to right

HANDWRITING SKILLS

Follow the direction of each arrow. Then practice writing each letter.

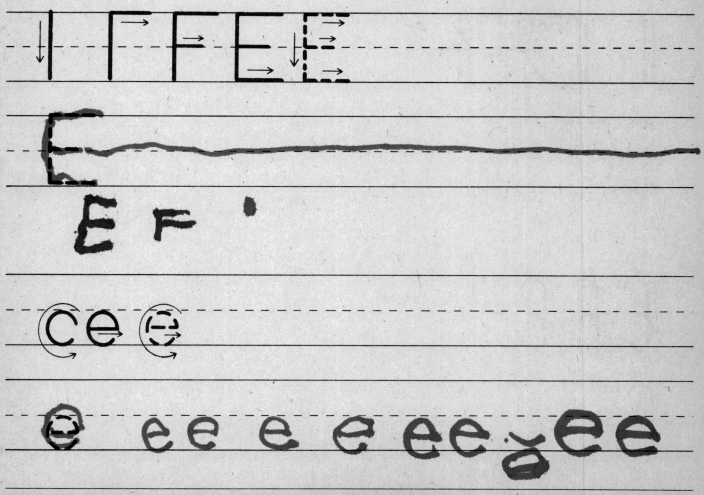

Skills: Forming upper/lower case "e"; Writing left to right

HANDWRITING SKILLS

Follow the direction of each arrow. Then practice writing each letter.

Skills: Forming upper/lower case "f"; Writing left to right

HANDWRITING SKILLS

Follow the direction of each arrow. Then practice writing each letter.

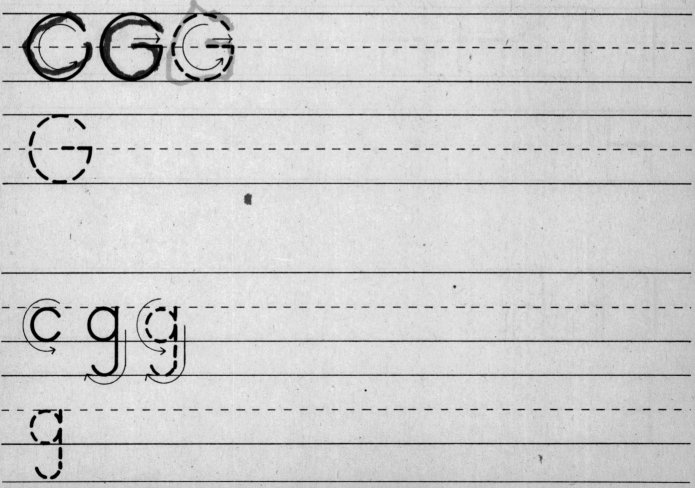

Skills: Forming upper/lower case "g"; Writing left to right

HANDWRITING SKILLS

Follow the direction of each arrow. Then practice writing each letter.

Skills: Forming upper/lower case "h"; Writing left to right

HANDWRITING SKILLS

Follow the direction of each arrow. Then practice writing each letter.

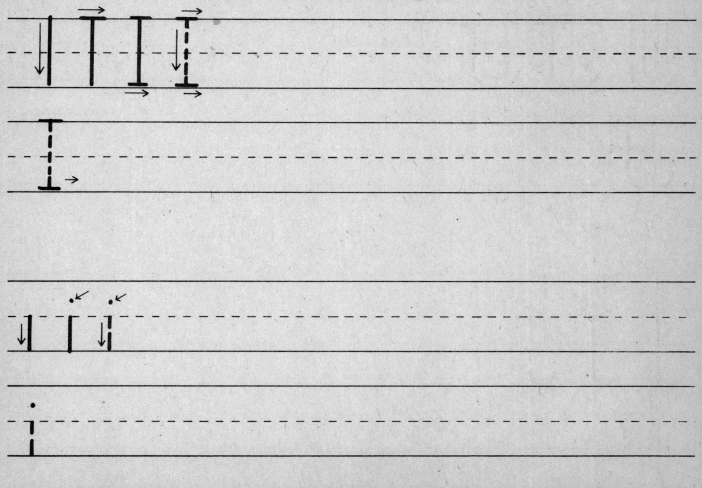

Skills: Forming upper/lower case "i"; Writing left to right

HANDWRITING SKILLS

Follow the direction of each arrow. Then practice writing each letter.

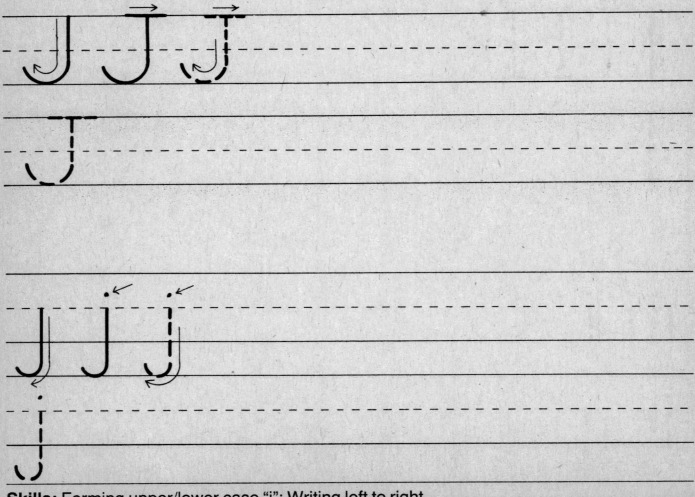

Skills: Forming upper/lower case "j"; Writing left to right

Follow the direction of each arrow. Then practice writing each letter.

Skills: Forming upper/lower case "k"; Writing left to right

HANDWRITING SKILLS

Follow the direction of each arrow. Then practice writing each letter.

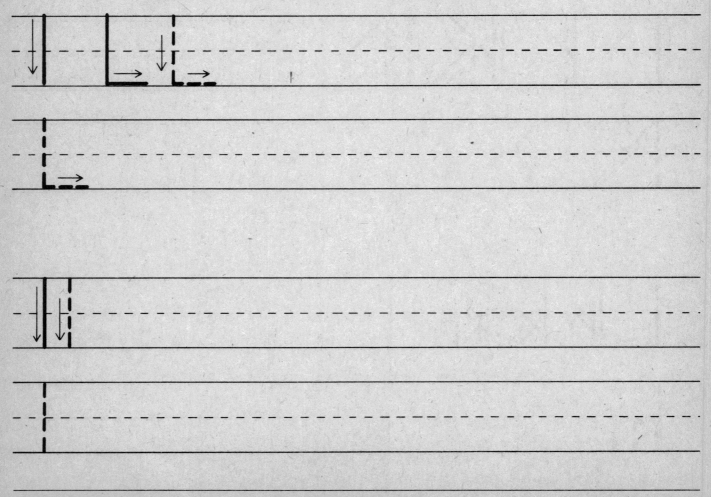

Skills: Forming upper/lower case "l"; Writing left to right

HANDWRITING SKILLS

Follow the direction of each arrow. Then practice writing each letter.

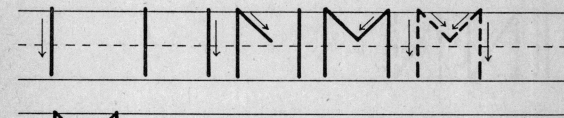

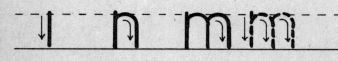

HANDWRITING SKILLS

Follow the direction of each arrow. Then practice writing each letter.

Skills: Forming upper/lower case "n"; Writing left to right

HANDWRITING SKILLS

Follow the direction of each arrow. Then practice writing each letter.

Skills: Forming upper/lower case "o"; Writing left to right

HANDWRITING SKILLS

Follow the direction of each arrow. Then practice writing each letter.

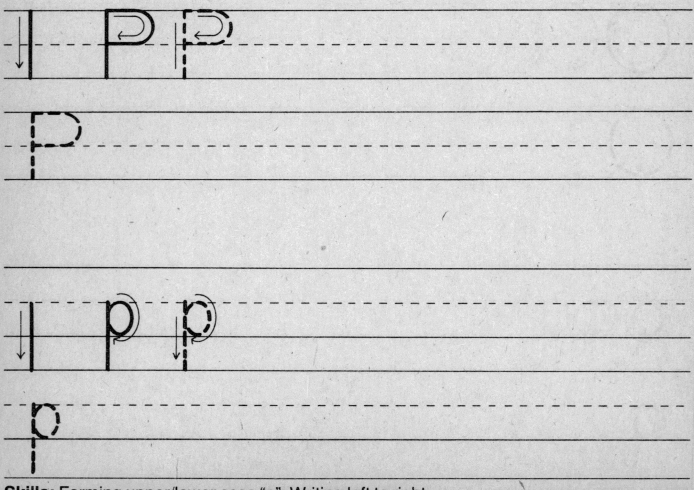

Skills: Forming upper/lower case "p"; Writing left to right

HANDWRITING SKILLS

Follow the direction of each arrow. Then practice writing each letter.

Skills: Forming upper/lower case "q"; Writing left to right

HANDWRITING SKILLS

Follow the direction of each arrow. Then practice writing each letter.

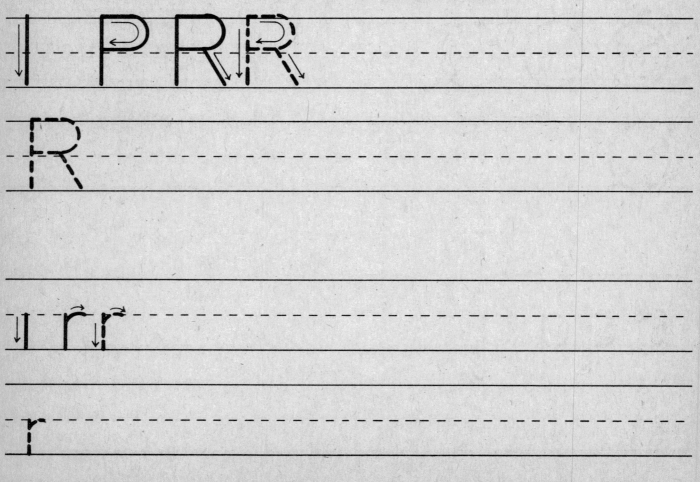

Skills: Forming upper/lower case "r"; Writing left to right

HANDWRITING SKILLS

Follow the direction of each arrow. Then practice writing each letter.

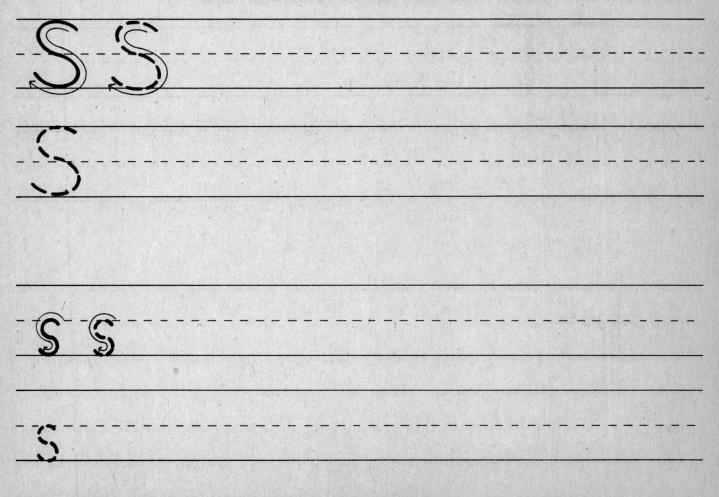

Skills: Forming upper/lower case "s"; Writing left to right

HANDWRITING SKILLS

Follow the direction of each arrow. Then practice writing each letter.

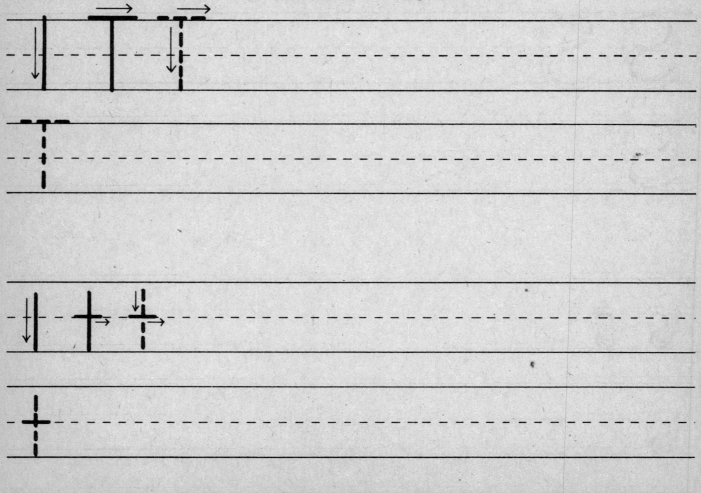

Skills: Forming upper/lower case "t"; Writing left to right

HANDWRITING SKILLS

Follow the direction of each arrow. Then practice writing each letter.

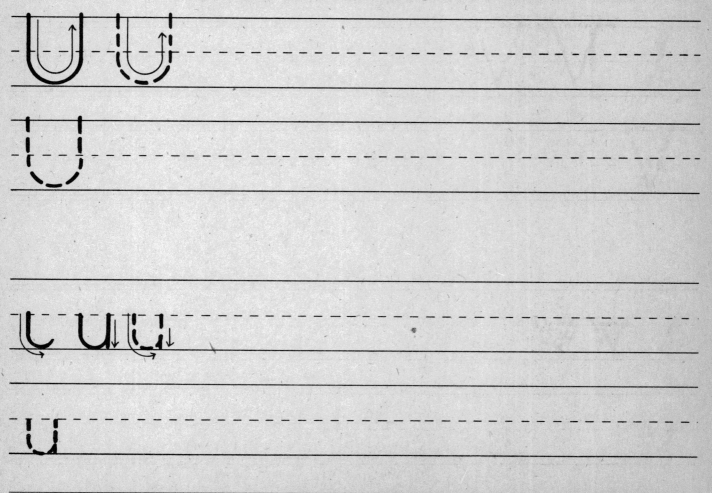

Skills: Forming upper/lower case "u"; Writing left to right

Follow the direction of each arrow. Then practice writing each letter.

Skills: Forming upper/lower case "v"; Writing left to right

HANDWRITING SKILLS

Follow the direction of each arrow. Then practice writing each letter.

Skills: Forming upper/lower case "w"; Writing left to right

HANDWRITING SKILLS

Follow the direction of each arrow. Then practice writing each letter.

Skills: Forming upper/lower case "x"; Writing left to right

HANDWRITING SKILLS

Follow the direction of each arrow. Then practice writing each letter.

Skills: Forming upper/lower case "y"; Writing left to right

HANDWRITING SKILLS

Follow the direction of each arrow. Then practice writing each letter.

Skills: Forming upper/lower case "z"; Writing left to right

HANDWRITING SKILLS

Trace each letter.

Skills: Forming upper/lower case letters; Writing the alphabet

red red r

Color these things that are red.

yellow yellow

y

Color these things that are yellow.

Skills: Distinguishing color; Classification; Word recognition

COLORS, SHAPES, AND NUMBERS

blue   blue   b

Color these things that are blue.

Skills: Distinguishing color; Classification; Word recognition

orange   orange

o

Color these things that are orange.

Skills: Distinguishing color; Classification; Word recognition

purple   purple

p

Color these things that are purple.

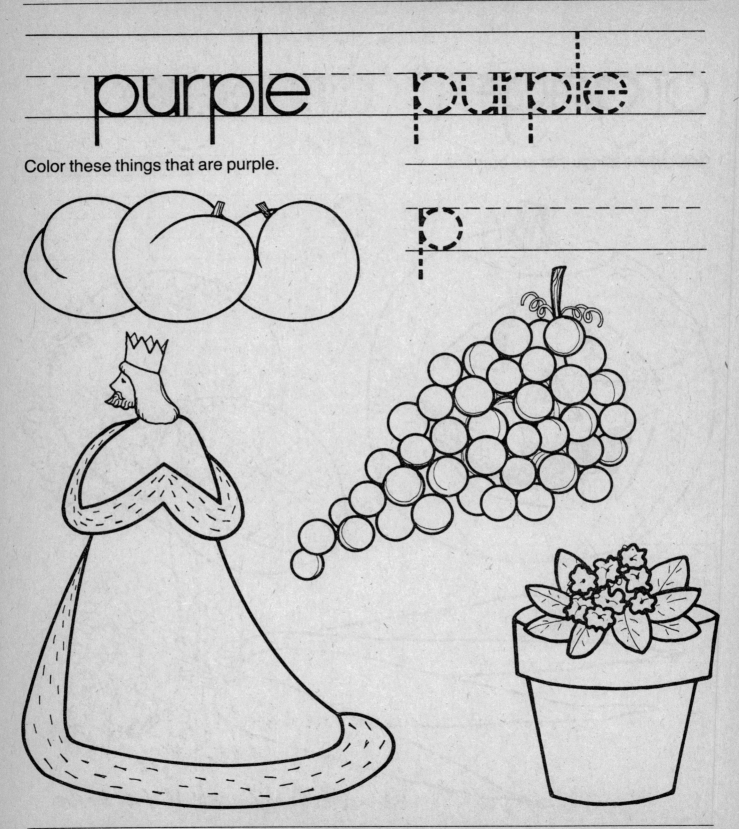

Skills: Distinguishing color; Classification; Word recognition

green green

g

Color these things that are green.

Skills: Distinguishing color; Classification; Word recognition

black   black

b

Color these things that are black.

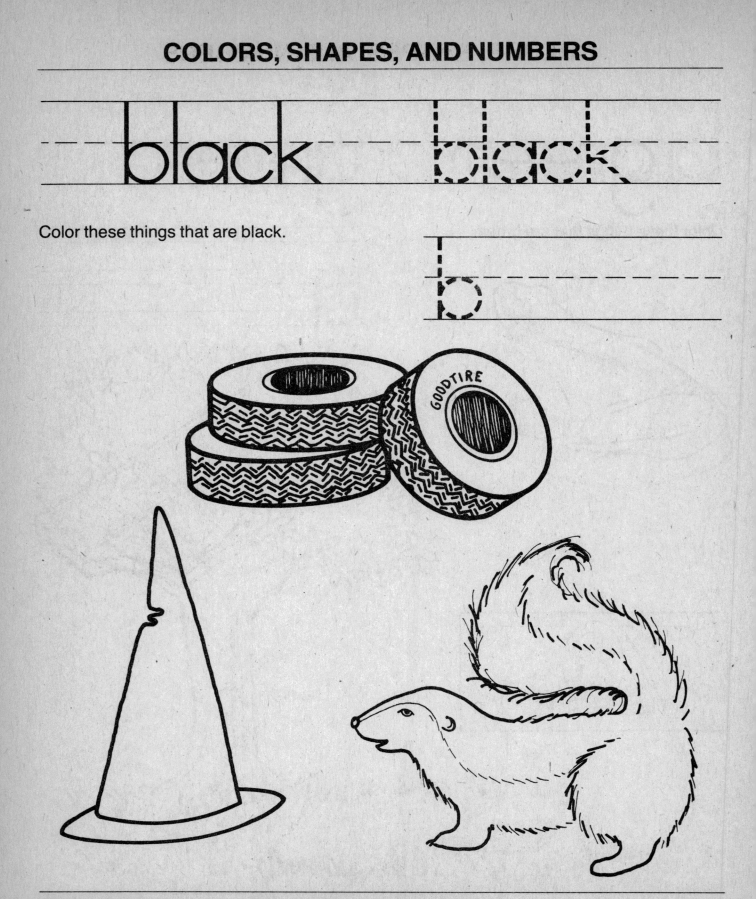

Skills: Distinguishing color; Classification; Word recognition

brown brown

b

Color these things that are brown.

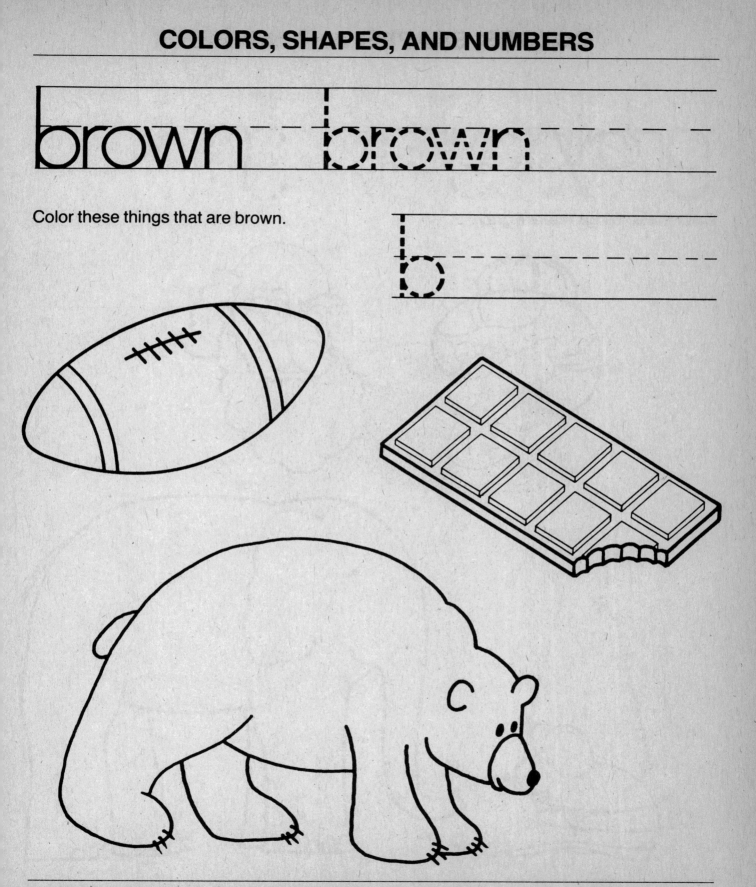

Skills: Distinguishing color; Classification; Word recognition

gray gray g

Color these things that are gray.

Skills: Distinguishing color; Classification; Word recognition

COLORS, SHAPES, AND NUMBERS

Color the target to score a hit.

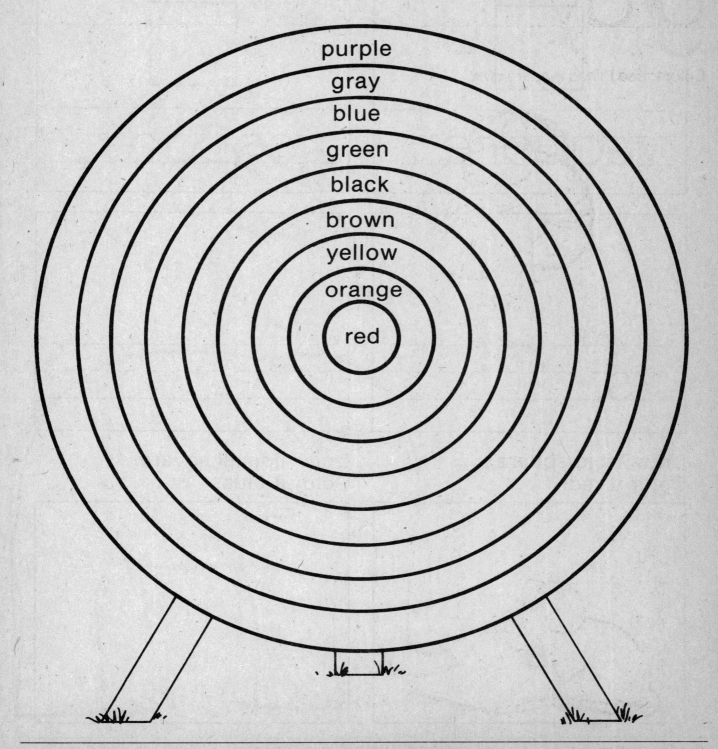

Skills: Visual memory of sight vocabulary; Following directions

COLORS, SHAPES, AND NUMBERS

Look at the square.
Then trace, print, and draw.

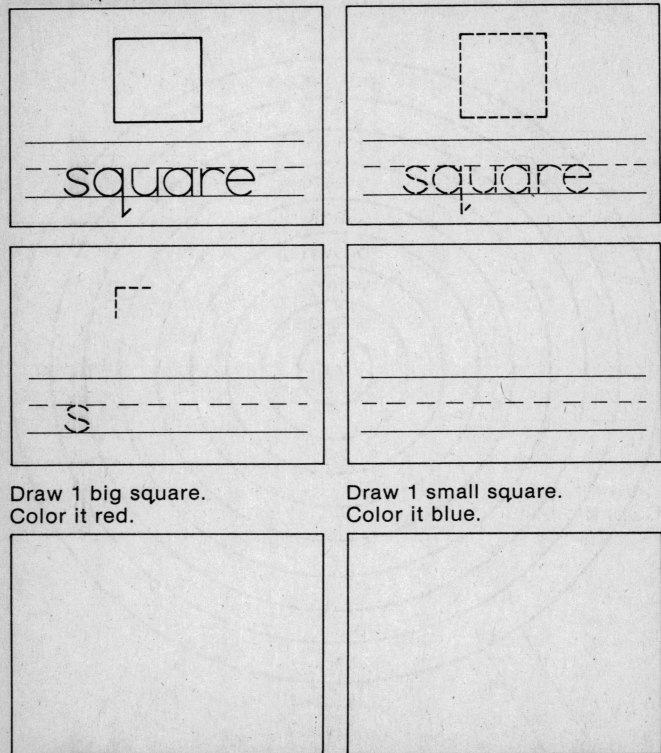

Draw 1 big square.
Color it red.

Draw 1 small square.
Color it blue.

Skills: Fine motor skill development; Sight vocabulary recognition; Association between sight vocabulary and shapes

COLORS, SHAPES, AND NUMBERS

Look at the circle.
Then trace, print, and draw.

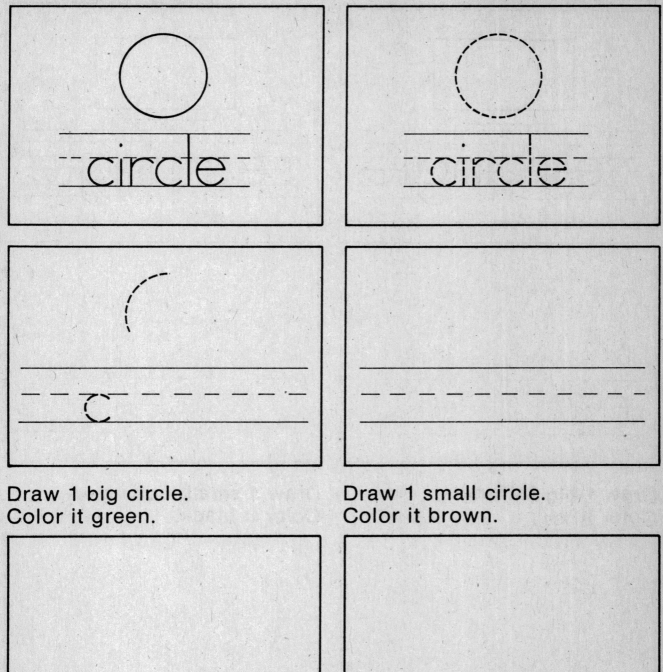

Draw 1 big circle.
Color it green.

Draw 1 small circle.
Color it brown.

Skills: Fine motor skill development; Sight vocabulary recognition; Association between sight vocabulary and shapes

COLORS, SHAPES, AND NUMBERS

Look at the rectangle.
Then trace, print, and draw.

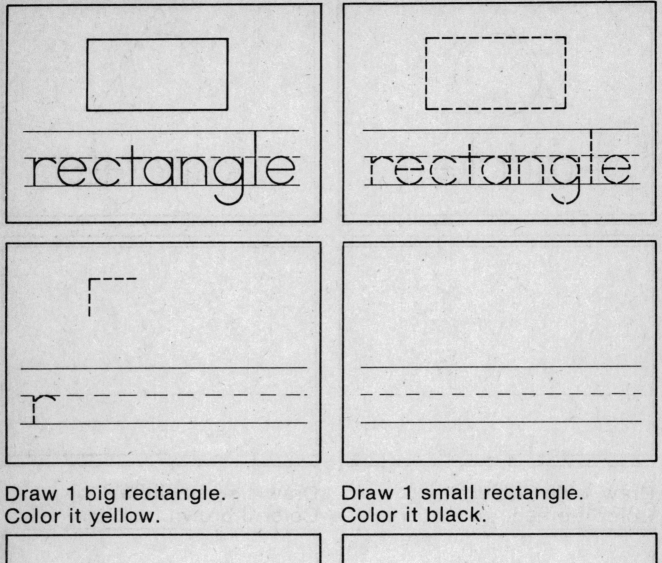

Draw 1 big rectangle.
Color it yellow.

Draw 1 small rectangle.
Color it black.

Skills: Fine motor skill development; Sight vocabulary recognition; Association between sight vocabulary and shapes

COLORS, SHAPES, AND NUMBERS

Look at the triangle.
Then trace, print, and draw.

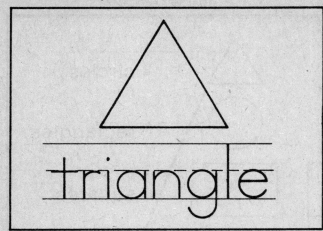

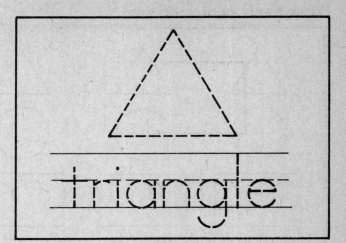

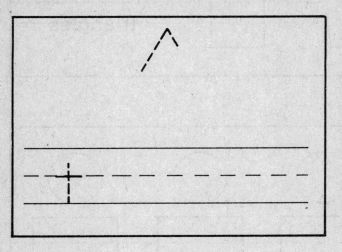

Draw 1 big triangle.
Color it green.

Draw 1 small triangle.
Color it blue.

Skills: Fine motor skill development; Sight vocabulary recognition; Association between sight vocabulary and shapes

COLORS, SHAPES, AND NUMBERS

Match the shapes to the word.

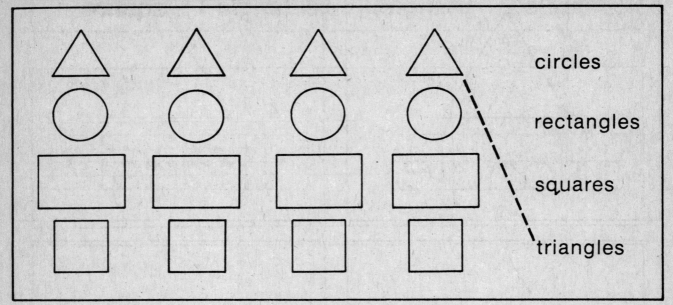

Match the word to the shapes.

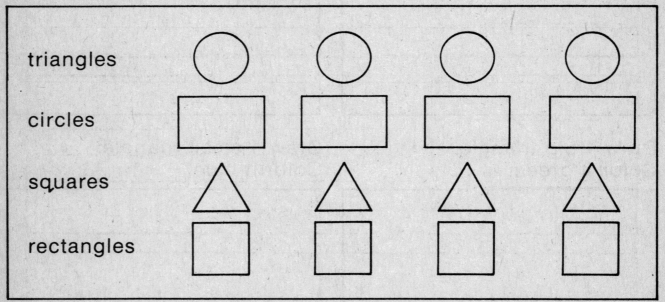

Color the △'s triangles blue.
Color the ○'s circles red.
Color the ▭'s rectangles yellow.
Color the □'s squares green.

Skills: Following directions; Association between sight vocabulary and shapes; Sight vocabulary recognition

COLORS, SHAPES, AND NUMBERS

circle   triangle   rectangle   square

Print the word. Color the shape.

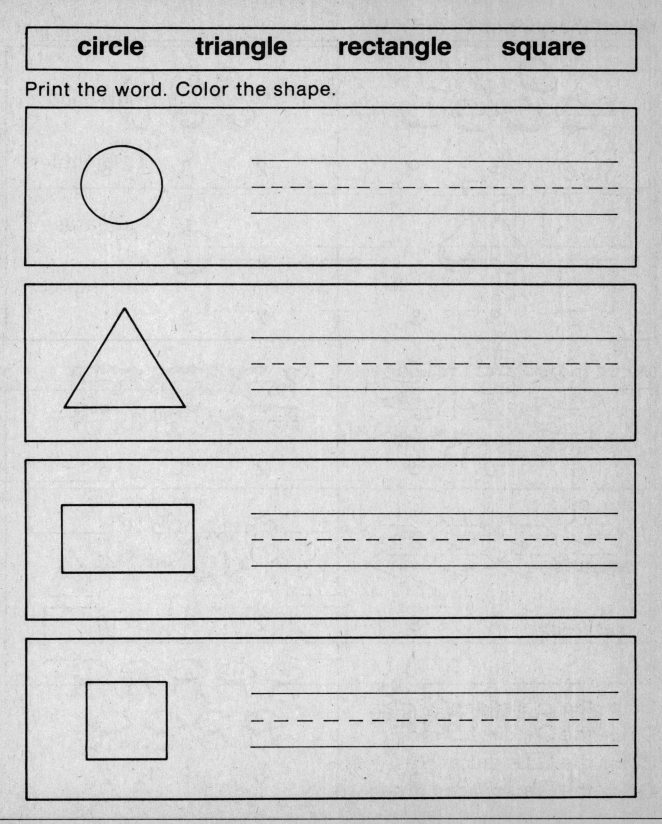

COLORS, SHAPES, AND NUMBERS

Circle the correct numeral.

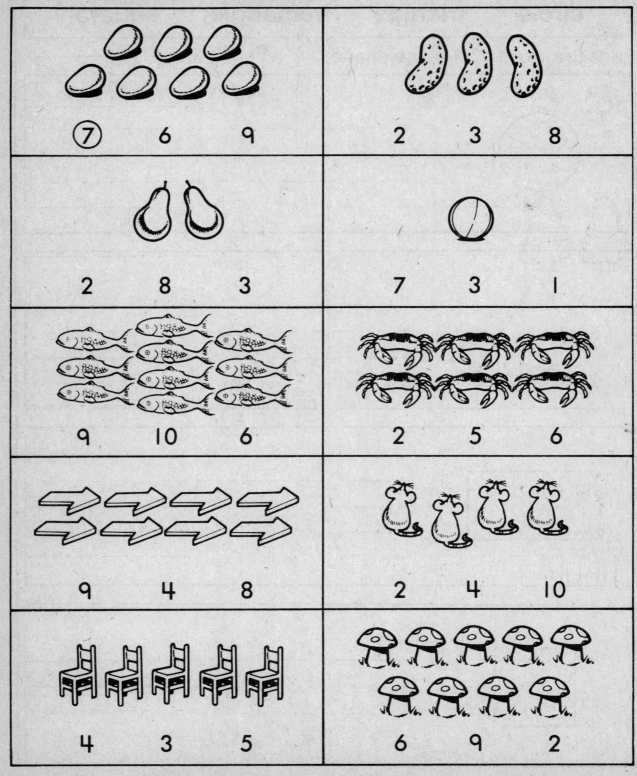

⑦ 6 9	2 3 8
2 8 3	7 3 1
9 10 6	2 5 6
9 4 8	2 4 10
4 3 5	6 9 2

Skills: Recognizing sets of objects and the corresponding numeral; Following directions

COLORS, SHAPES, AND NUMBERS

Print the correct numeral.

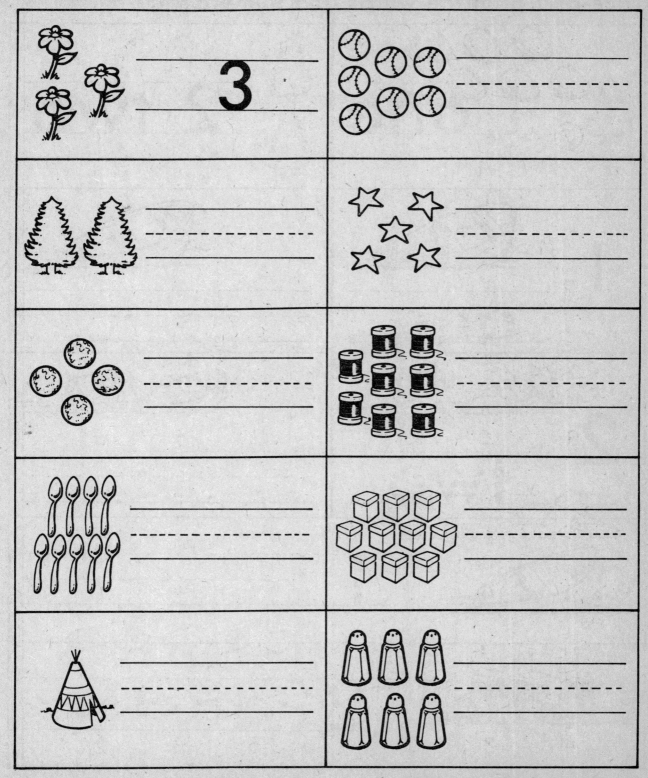

COLORS, SHAPES, AND NUMBERS

Trace and print the words and numerals.

COLORS, SHAPES, AND NUMBERS

Trace and print the words and numerals.

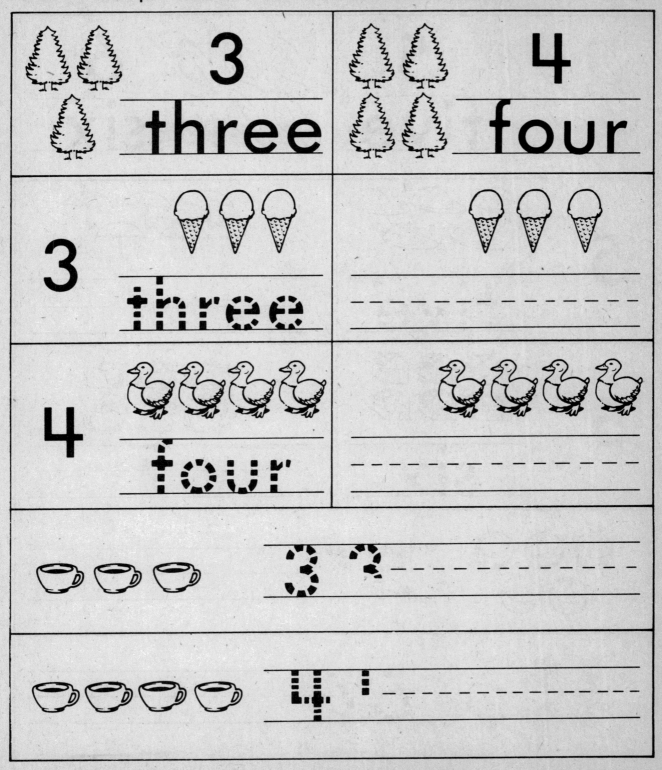

COLORS, SHAPES, AND NUMBERS

Trace and print the words and numerals.

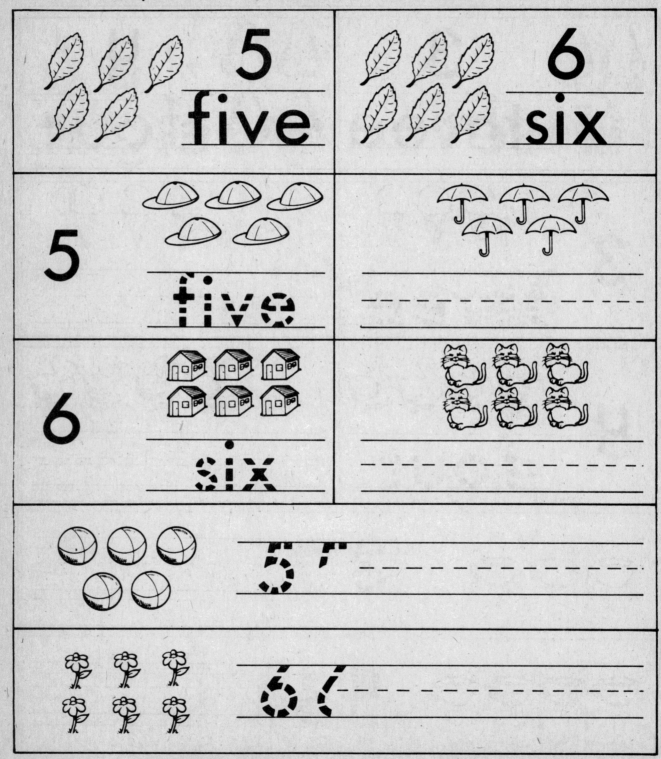

Skills: Recognizing sets of 5 and 6; Association between sight vocabulary, numerals, and sets

COLORS, SHAPES, AND NUMBERS

Trace and print the words and numerals.

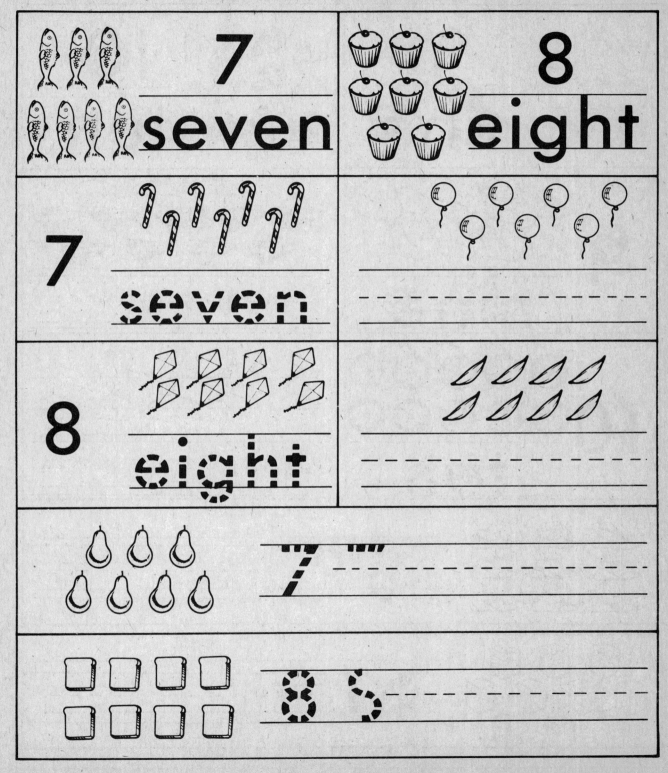

COLORS, SHAPES, AND NUMBERS

Trace and print the words and numerals.

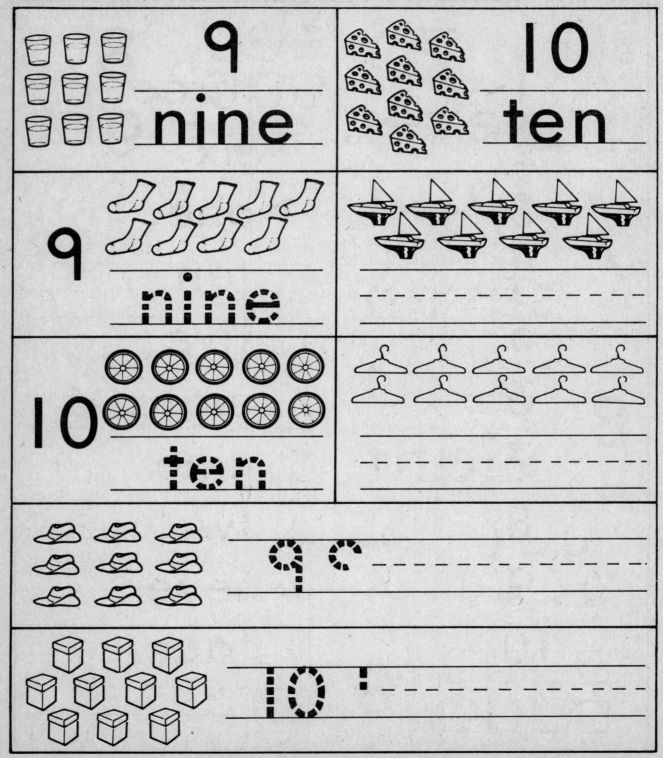

COLORS, SHAPES, AND NUMBERS

Match the numerals and words.

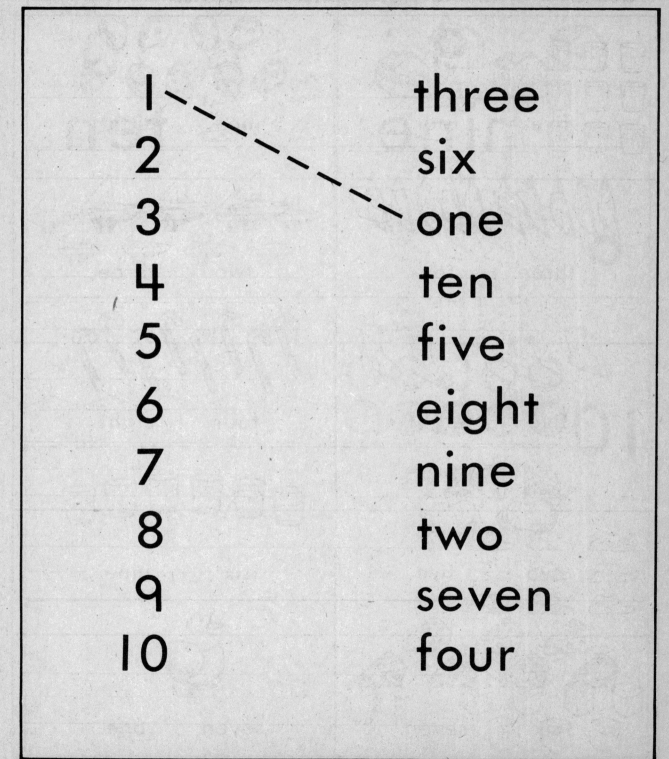

1	three
2	six
3	one
4	ten
5	five
6	eight
7	nine
8	two
9	seven
10	four

Skills: Recognizing numerals and the corresponding number word

COLORS, SHAPES, AND NUMBERS

Circle the correct word.

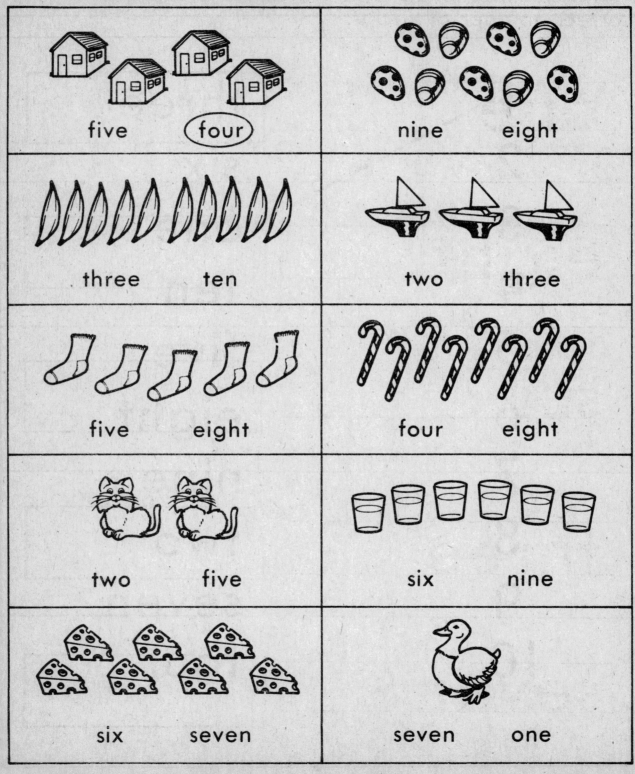

five   (four)

nine   eight

three   ten

two   three

five   eight

four   eight

two   five

six   nine

six   seven

seven   one

Skills: Recognizing sets of objects and the corresponding number word

COLORS, SHAPES, AND NUMBERS

Trace the word. Print the numeral. Draw the correct number of circles.

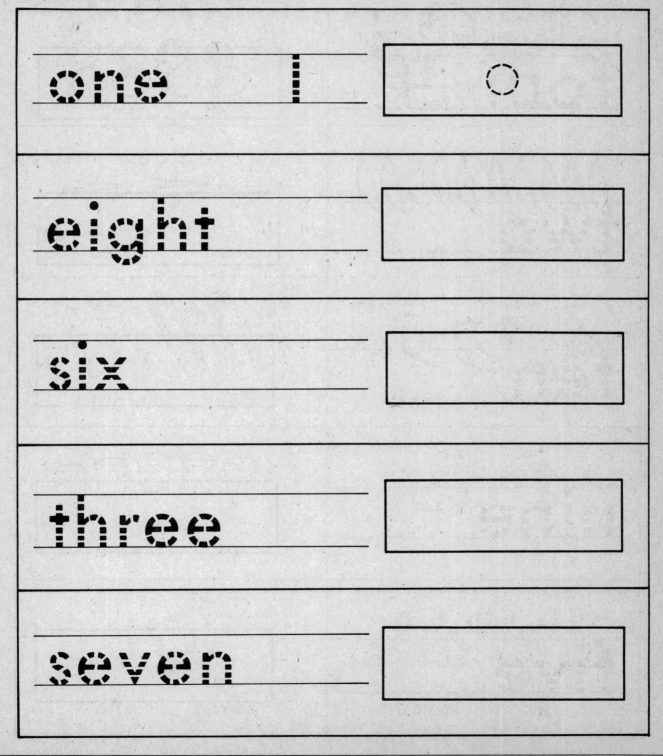

Skills: Recognizing number words and writing numerals; Forming corresponding sets of objects

COLORS, SHAPES, AND NUMBERS

Trace the word. Print the numeral. Draw the correct number of circles.

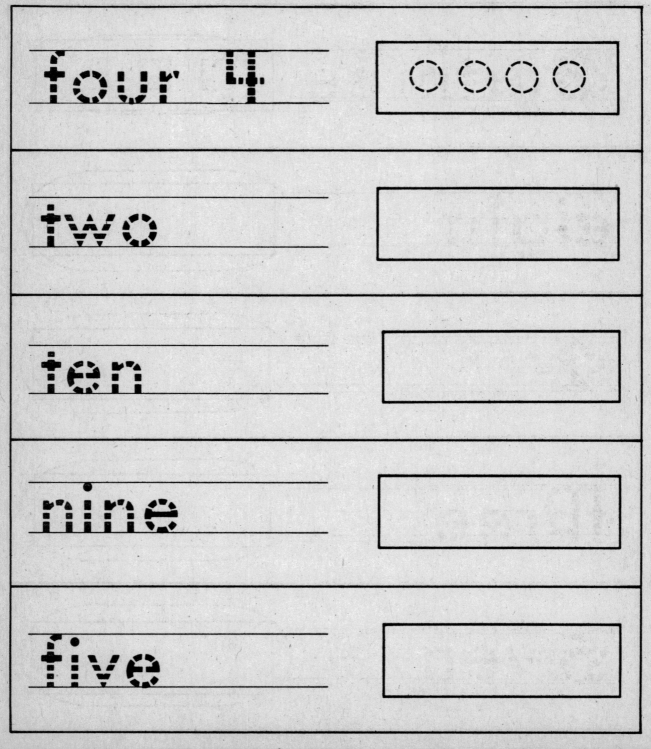

Skills: Recognizing number words and writing numerals; Forming corresponding sets of objects

COLORS, SHAPES, AND NUMBERS

Trace the numeral. Print the word. Draw the correct number of boxes.

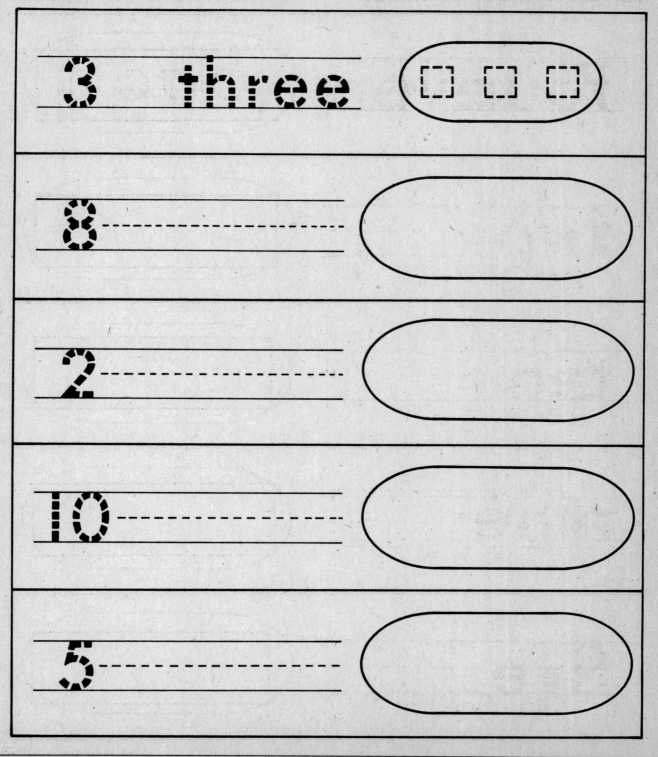

Skills: Recognizing numerals; Writing number words; Forming corresponding sets of objects

COLORS, SHAPES, AND NUMBERS

Trace the numeral. Print the word. Draw the correct number of boxes.

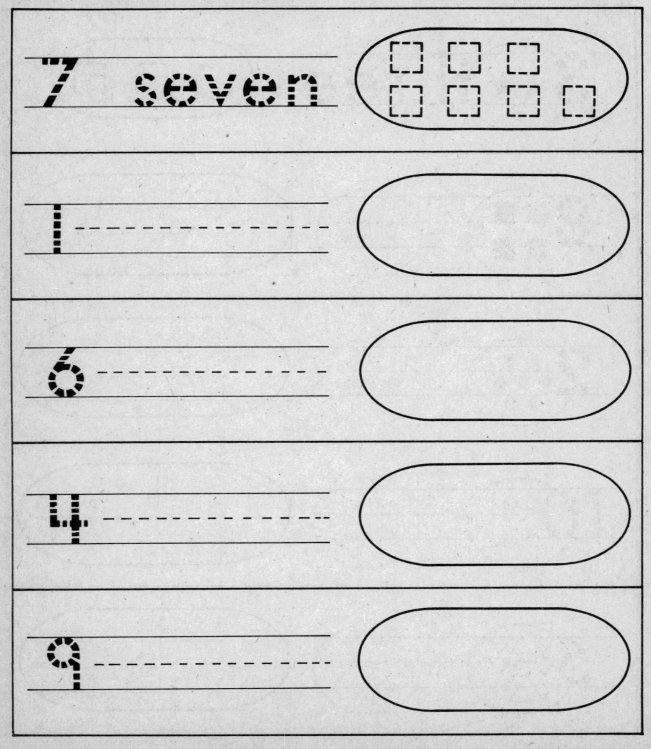

COLORS, SHAPES, AND NUMBERS

Trace the numeral. Match the numeral with the correct number. Print the word.

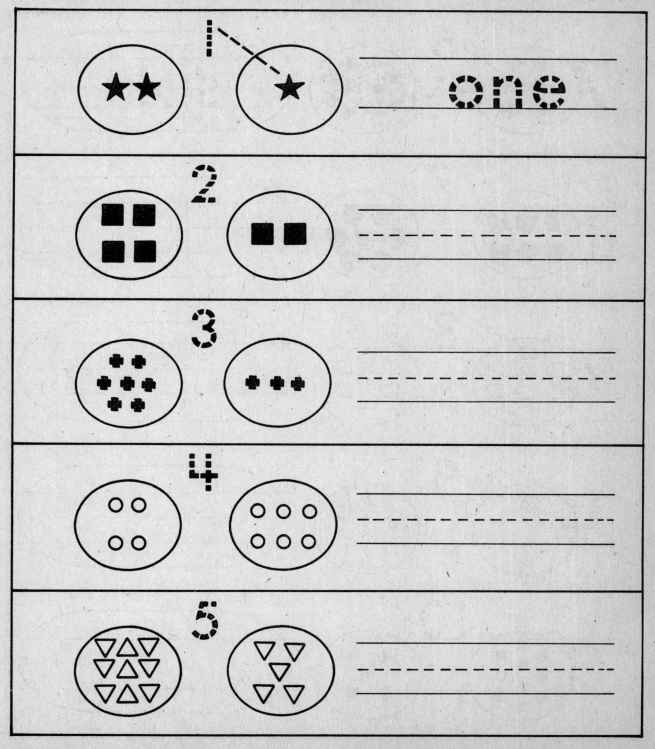

COLORS, SHAPES, AND NUMBERS

Trace the numeral. Match the numeral with the correct number. Print the word.

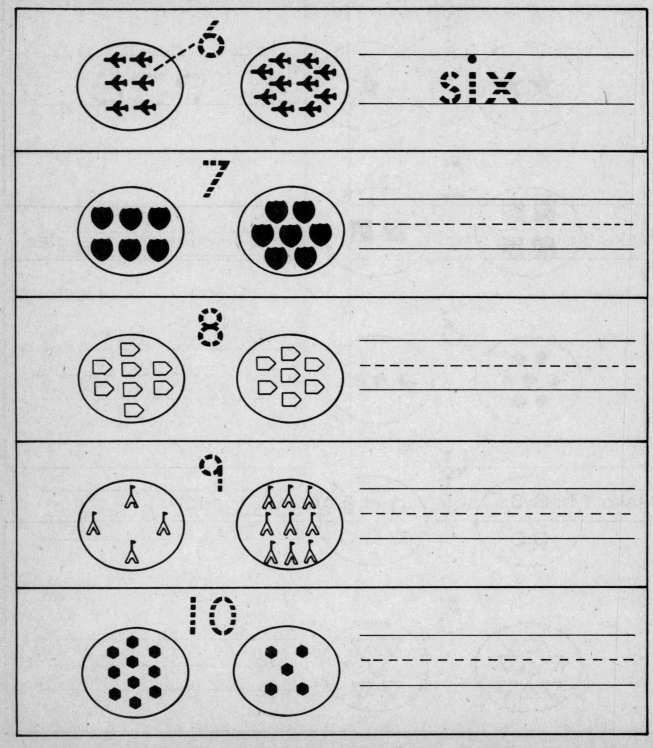

COLORS, SHAPES, AND NUMBERS

Make 1 green ☐ square.

Make 2 red ○'s circles.

Make 3 blue ▭'s rectangles.

Make 4 yellow △'s triangles.

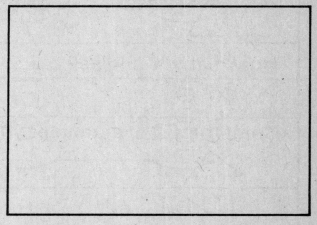

Make 1 brown ☐ square and 2 green ○'s circles.

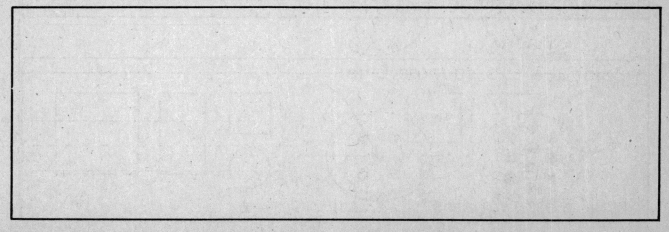

Skills: Following directions; Understanding number, shape, and color; Fine motor skill development

COLORS, SHAPES, AND NUMBERS

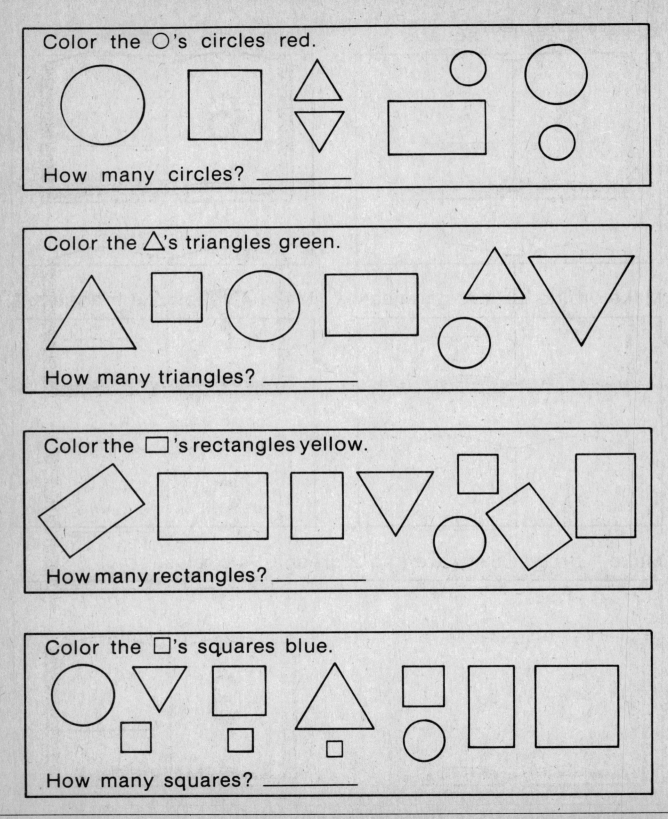

Color the ○'s circles red.

How many circles? _____

Color the △'s triangles green.

How many triangles? _____

Color the ▢'s rectangles yellow.

How many rectangles? _____

Color the ▢'s squares blue.

How many squares? _____

Skills: Following directions; Understanding color, shape, and number; Noticing attributes

BASIC MATH SKILLS

Look at each book.
What number comes next?

8 9 _____   6 _____

2 _____   7 _____

4 _____   9 _____

5 _____   3 _____

Skills: Ordering numbers to 10; Writing numerals

BASIC MATH SKILLS

Look at each group of ice cream cones.
What number comes between?

Skills: Ordering numbers to 10; Writing numerals

BASIC MATH SKILLS

Look at the stars.
Write the missing numbers.

Skills: Ordering numbers to 10; Writing numerals

BASIC MATH SKILLS

Look at each picture.
How many are in the first group?

How many are in the second group?
How many in all?

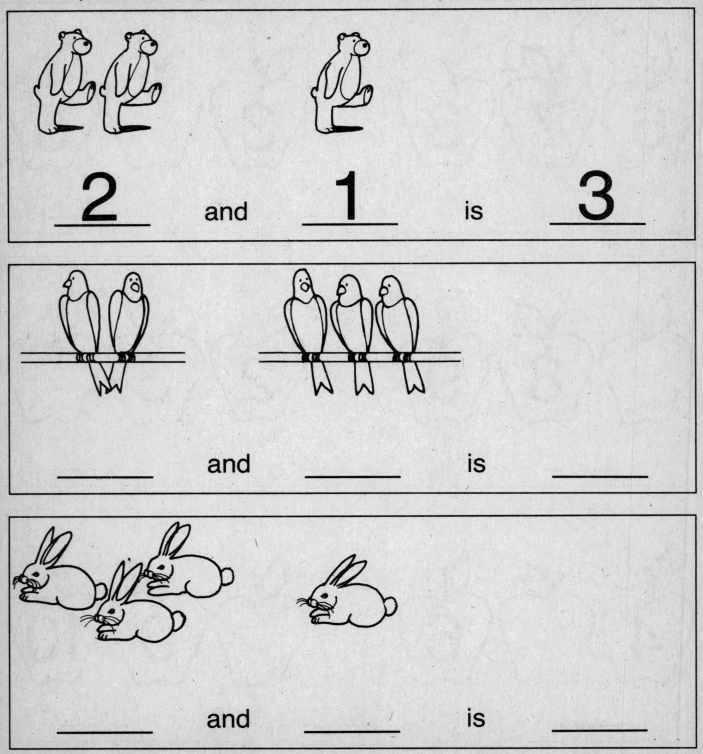

2 and 1 is 3

____ and ____ is ____

____ and ____ is ____

Skills: Recognizing sets of objects and writing corresponding numerals; Adding groups of objects

BASIC MATH SKILLS

Look at each picture.
How many are in the first group?

How many are in the second group?
How many in all?

_____ and _____ is _____

_____ and _____ is _____

_____ and _____ is _____

Skills: Recognizing sets of objects and writing corresponding numerals; Adding groups of objects

BASIC MATH SKILLS

Look at each picture.
How many are in the first group?

How many are in the second group?
How many in all?

$$\underline{3} \text{ and } \underline{1} \text{ is } \underline{4}$$
$$\underline{3} + \underline{1} = \underline{4}$$

$$\underline{\hphantom{0}} \text{ and } \underline{\hphantom{0}} \text{ is } \underline{\hphantom{0}}$$
$$\underline{\hphantom{0}} + \underline{\hphantom{0}} = \underline{\hphantom{0}}$$

$$\underline{\hphantom{0}} \text{ and } \underline{\hphantom{0}} \text{ is } \underline{\hphantom{0}}$$
$$\underline{\hphantom{0}} + \underline{\hphantom{0}} = \underline{\hphantom{0}}$$

Skills: Recognizing sets of objects and writing corresponding numerals; Adding groups of objects; Understanding addition sentences

BASIC MATH SKILLS

Look at each picture.
How many are in the first group?

How many are in the second group?
How many in all?

_____ and _____ is _____

_____ + _____ = _____

_____ and _____ is _____

_____ + _____ = _____

_____ and _____ is _____

_____ + _____ = _____

Skills: Recognizing sets of objects and writing corresponding numerals; Adding groups of objects; Understanding addition sentences

BASIC MATH SKILLS

Look at each picture.
How many are in the first group?

How many are in the second group?
How many in all?

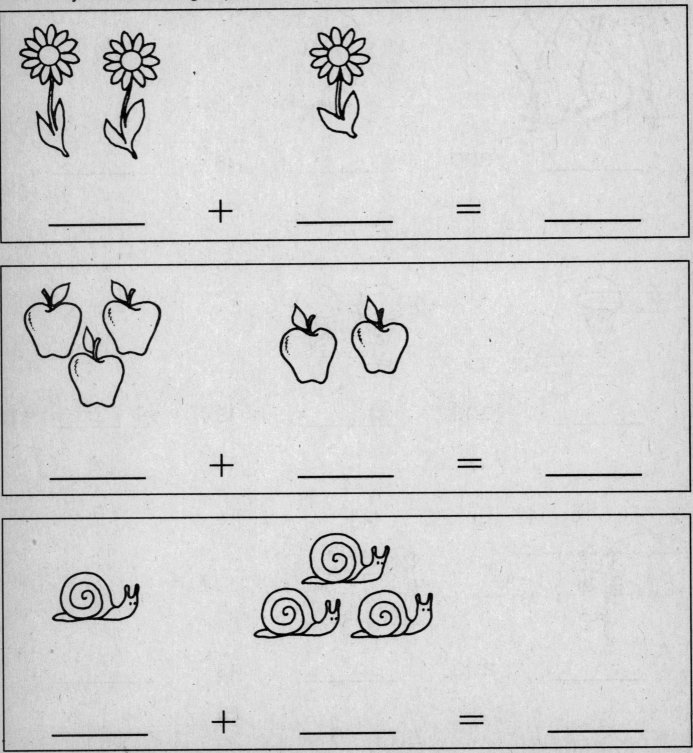

_____ + _____ = _____

_____ + _____ = _____

_____ + _____ = _____

Skills: Recognizing sets of objects and writing corresponding numerals; Adding groups of objects; Practicing addition problems

BASIC MATH SKILLS

Look at each picture.
How many are in the first group?

How many are in the second group?
How many in all?

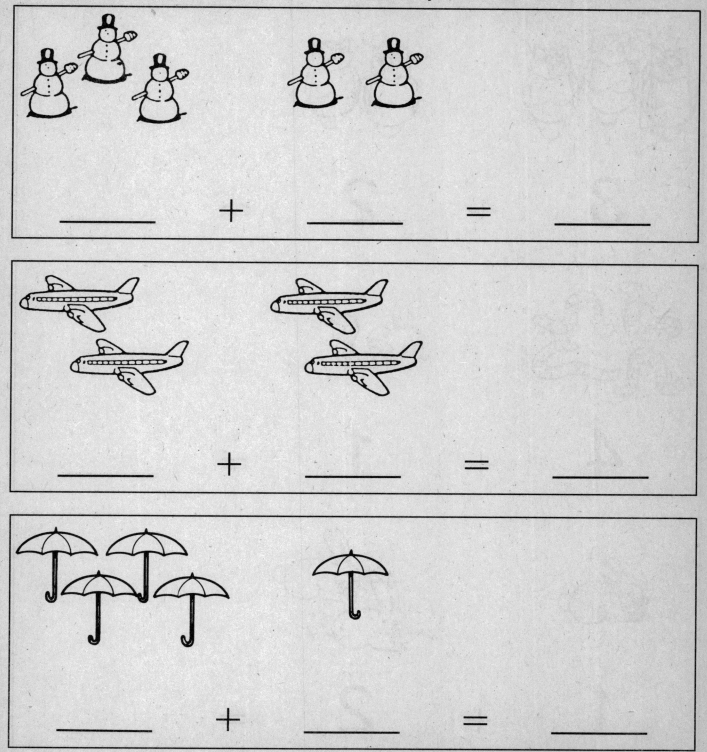

Skills: Adding groups of objects; Practicing addition problems

BASIC MATH SKILLS

Look at each picture.
How many are in the first group?

How many are in the second group?
How many in all?

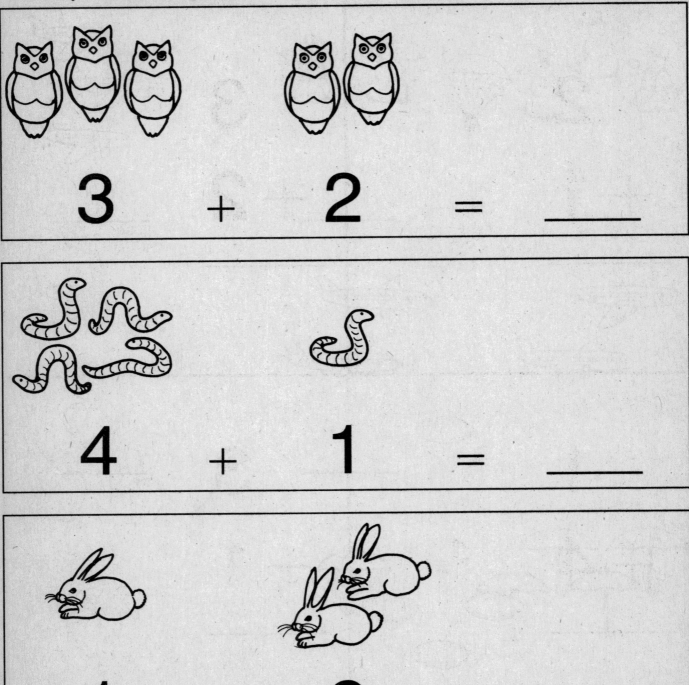

3 + 2 = ____

4 + 1 = ____

1 + 2 = ____

Skills: Adding groups of objects; Practicing addition problems

BASIC MATH SKILLS

How many in all?
Add to find out.

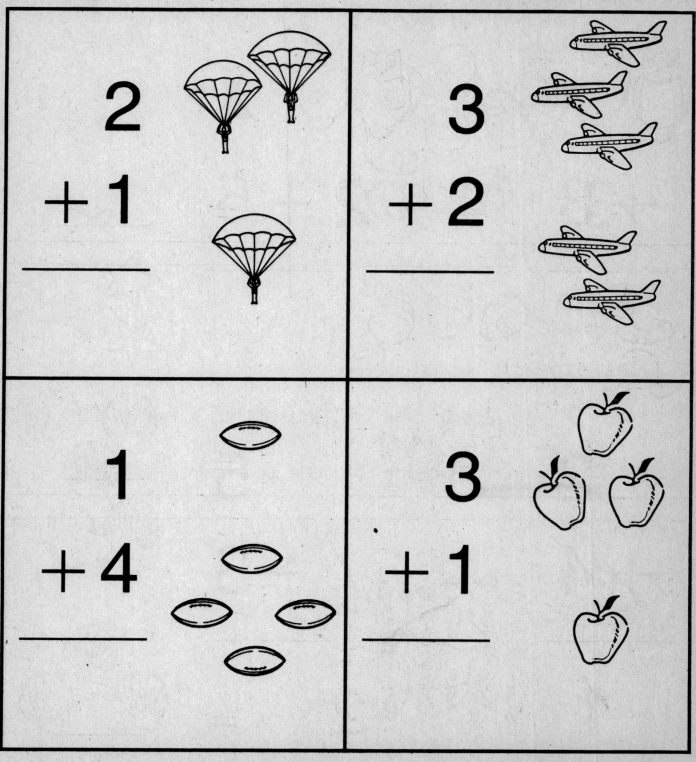

BASIC MATH SKILLS

How many in all?
Add to find out.

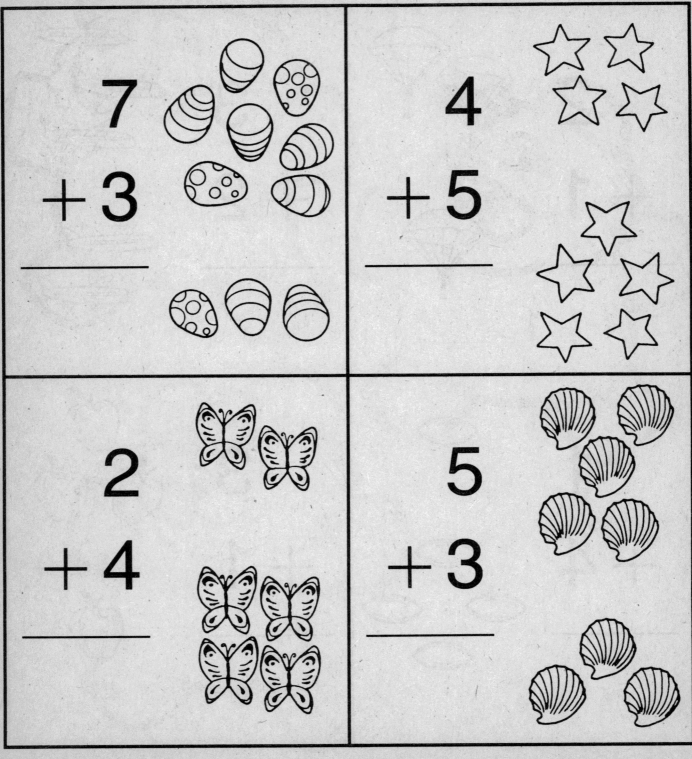

Skills: Solving vertical addition problems to 10; Writing numerals

How many in all?
Add to find out.

$$4 + 1 = \underline{\hspace{2cm}}$$

$$1 + 1 = \underline{\hspace{2cm}}$$

$$2 + 2 = \underline{\hspace{2cm}}$$

Skills: Solving addition sentences; Writing numerals

BASIC MATH SKILLS

Add the numbers in each balloon.
If the answer is 5, color it red.
If the answer is 4, color it blue.
If the answer is 3, color it yellow.

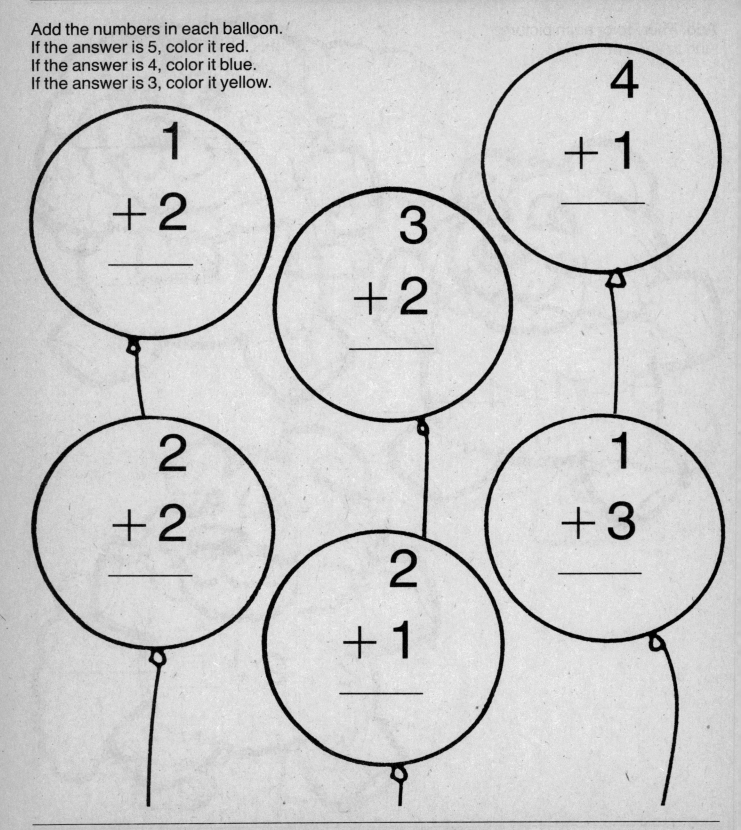

$$1 + 2$$

$$3 + 2$$

$$4 + 1$$

$$2 + 2$$

$$2 + 1$$

$$1 + 3$$

Skills: Solving vertical addition problems; Writing numerals

BASIC MATH SKILLS

Add. Then color each picture.

8 + 2 = _____

7 + 1 = _____

5 + 4 = _____

Skills: Solving addition problems to 10; Writing numerals

BASIC MATH SKILLS

Look at each picture.
How many are left?

__3__ take away __1__ is __2__

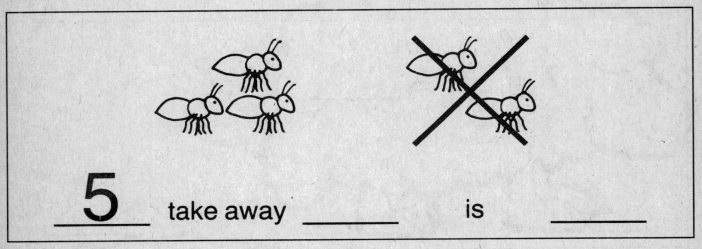

__5__ take away _____ is _____

__4__ take away _____ is _____

Skills: Recognizing sets of objects and writing corresponding numerals; Subtracting groups of objects

BASIC MATH SKILLS

Look at each picture.
How many are left?

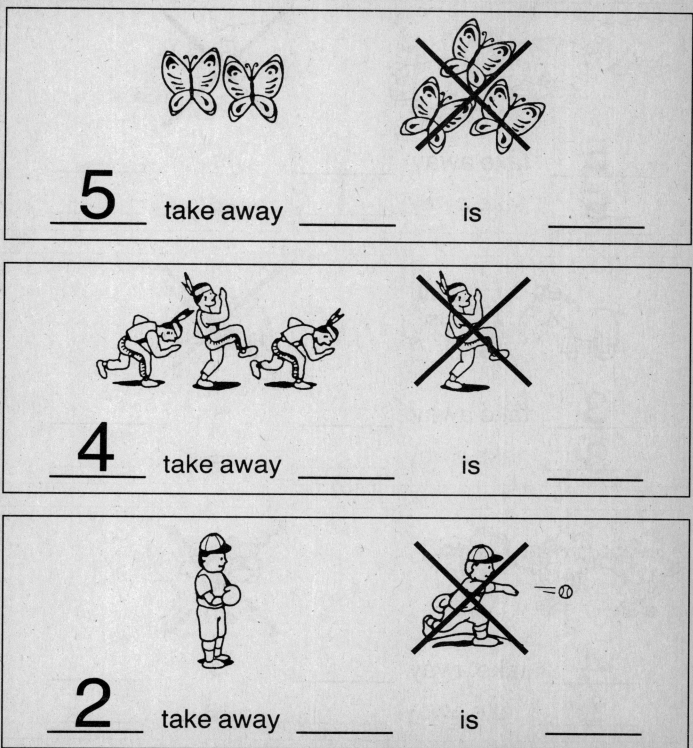

____5____ take away _____ is _____

____4____ take away _____ is _____

____2____ take away _____ is _____

Skills: Recognizing sets of objects and writing corresponding numerals; Subtracting groups of objects

BASIC MATH SKILLS

Look at each picture.
How many are left?

<u> **5** </u> take away <u>   </u> is <u>   </u>

<u> **5** </u>   —   <u>   </u> = <u>   </u>

<u> **3** </u> take away <u>   </u> is <u>   </u>

<u> **3** </u>   —   <u>   </u> = <u>   </u>

<u> **4** </u> take away <u>   </u> is <u>   </u>

<u> **4** </u>   —   <u>   </u> = <u>   </u>

Skills: Recognizing sets of objects and writing corresponding numerals; Subtracting groups of objects; Understanding subtraction sentences

BASIC MATH SKILLS

Look at each picture.
How many are left?

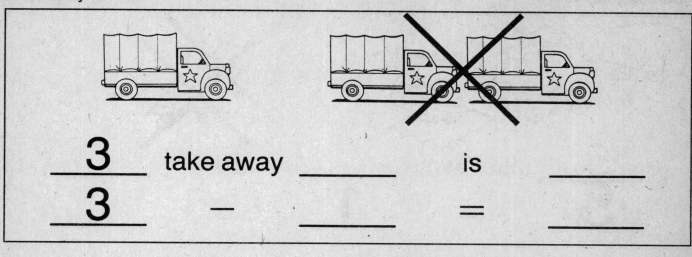

3	take away	_____	is	_____
3	—	_____	=	_____

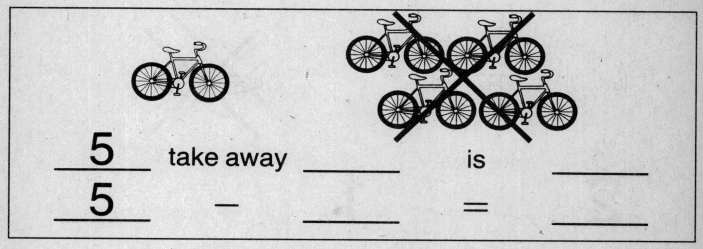

5	take away	_____	is	_____
5	—	_____	=	_____

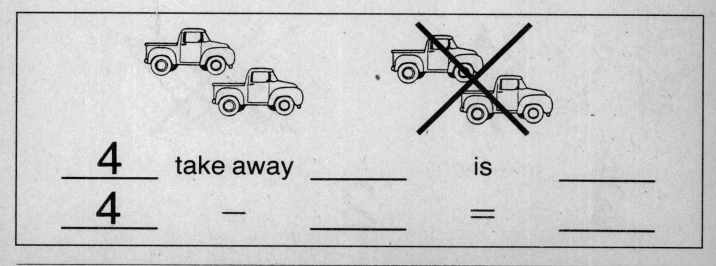

4	take away	_____	is	_____
4	—	_____	=	_____

Skills: Recognizing sets of objects and writing corresponding numerals; Subtracting groups of objects; Understanding subtraction sentences

BASIC MATH SKILLS

Look at each picture.
How many are left?

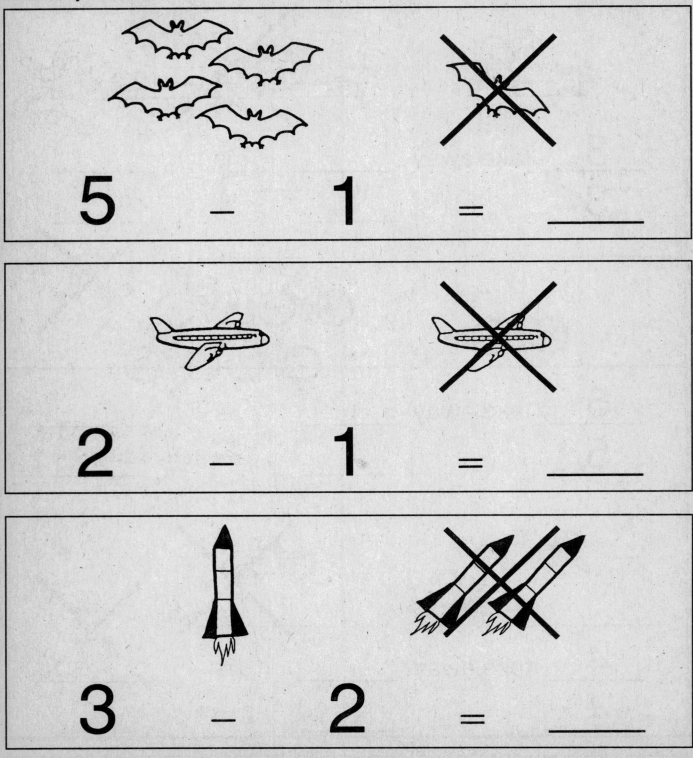

5 — 1 = _____

2 — 1 = _____

3 — 2 = _____

Skills: Recognizing sets of objects and writing corresponding numerals; Subtracting groups of objects; Practicing subtraction problems

BASIC MATH SKILLS

Look at each picture.
How many are left?

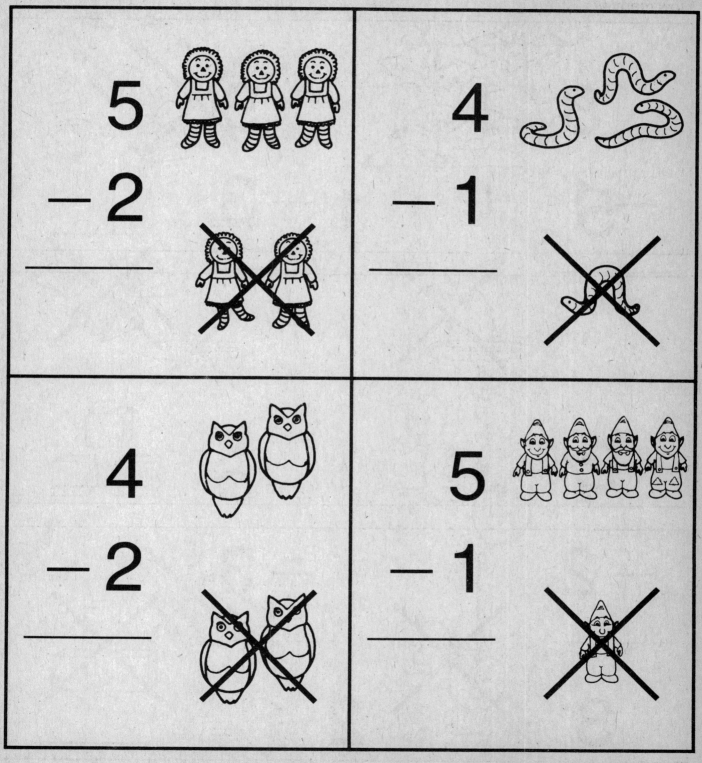

Skills: Solving vertical subtraction problems; Writing numerals

BASIC MATH SKILLS

How many are left?
Subtract to find out.

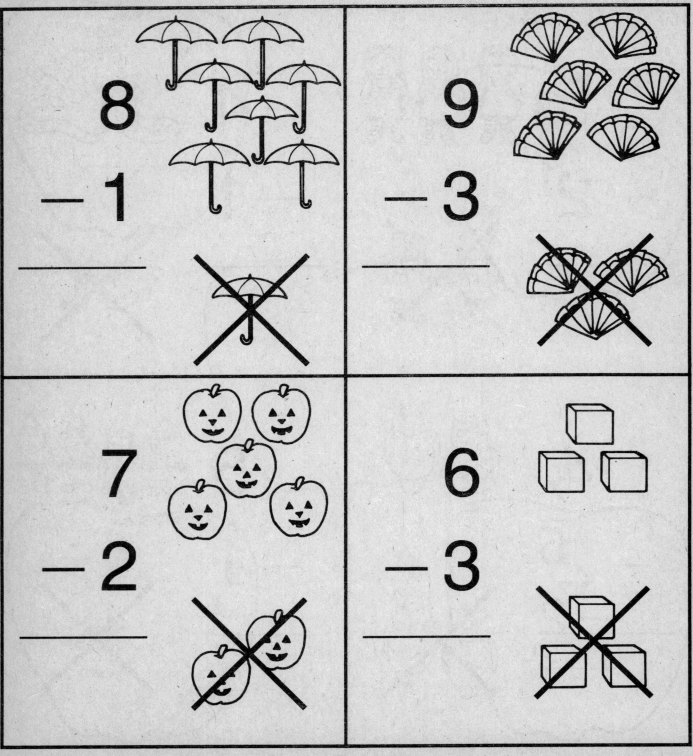

Skills: Solving vertical subtraction problems to 10; Writing numerals

BASIC MATH SKILLS

Subtract the numbers in each apple.
If the answer is 1, color it red.
If the answer is 2, color it yellow.
If the answer is 3, color it green.

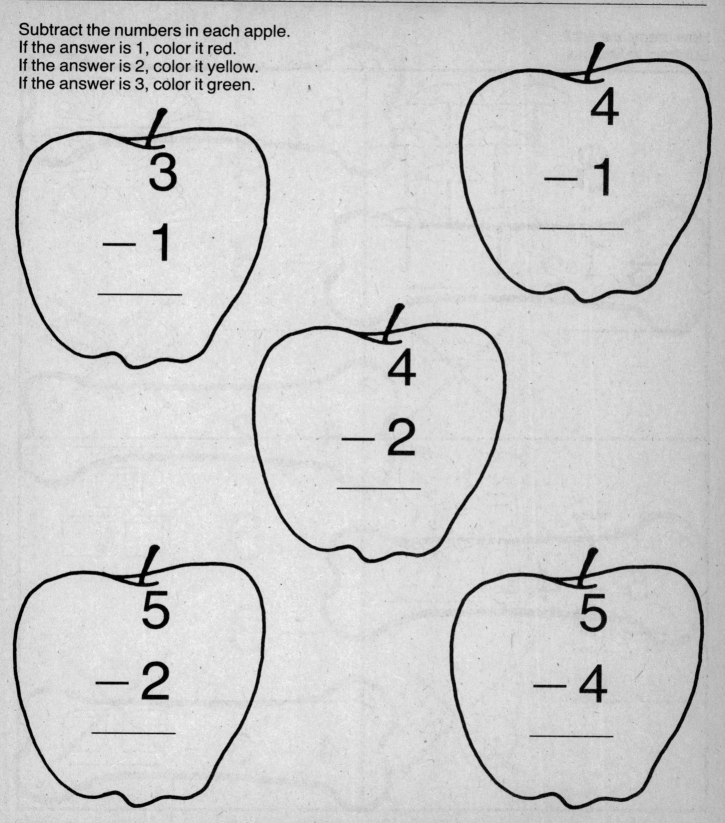

Skills: Solving vertical subtraction problems; Writing numerals

BASIC MATH SKILLS

How many are left?
Subtract to find out.

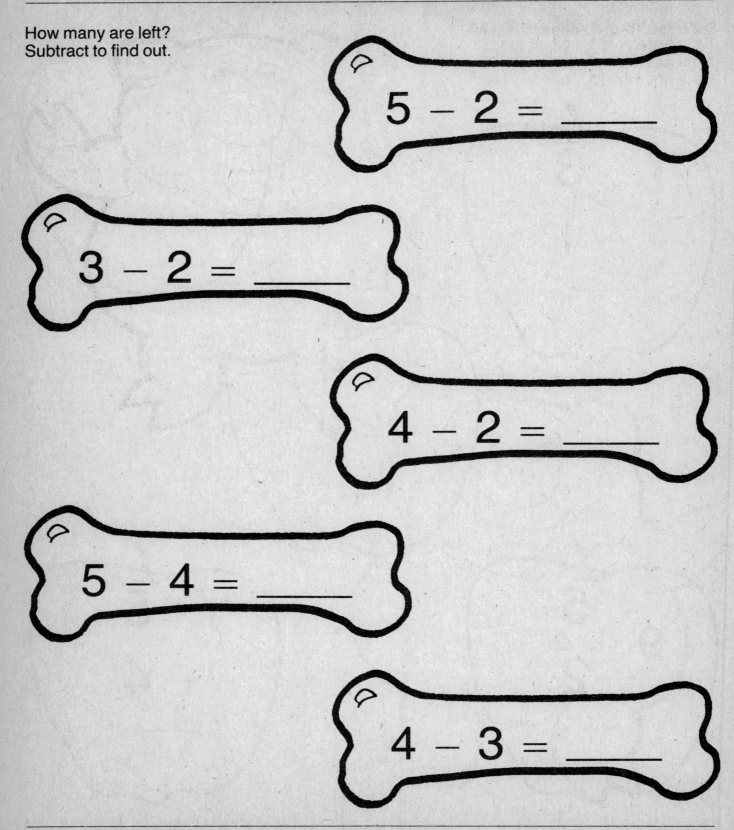

5 – 2 = _____

3 – 2 = _____

4 – 2 = _____

5 – 4 = _____

4 – 3 = _____

Skills: Solving subtraction problems; Writing numerals

BASIC MATH SKILLS

Subtract. Then color each picture.

10 – 7 = _____

9 – 4 = _____

Skills: Solving subtraction problems to 10; Writing numerals

BASIC MATH SKILLS

Follow the dots from 1 to 25 to find a furry friend.

Skills: Order of numerals from one to twenty-five; Following directions

BASIC MATH SKILLS

Look at these baseballs.
Make groups of ten.

Skills: Forming groups of ten; Counting objects to form groups

READING READINESS

Look at each picture.
Draw a line between the things that are the same.

Skills: Visual matching; Classification

READING READINESS

Color the two pictures in each box that go together.

READING READINESS

Look at the pictures in each row.
Cross out the one that is different.
Then color the others.

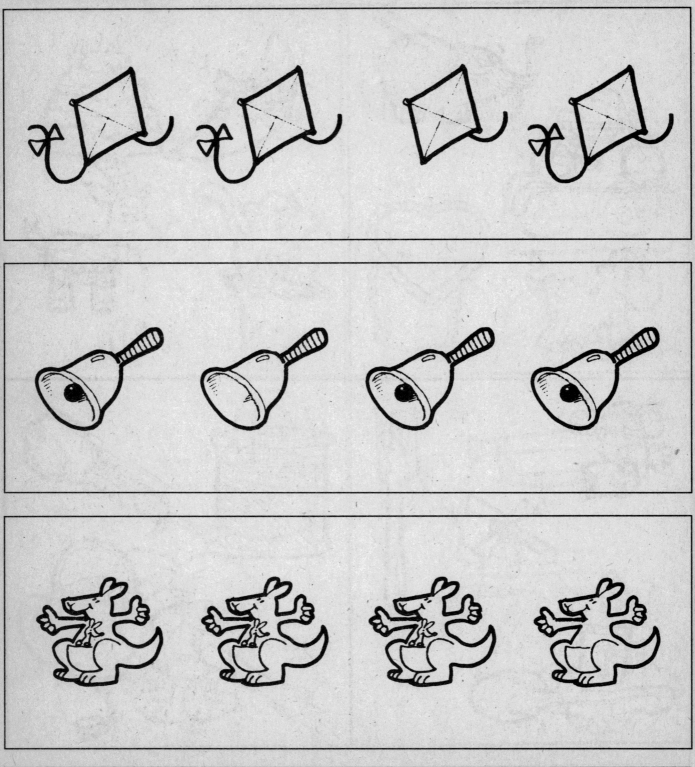

Skills: Visual discrimination; Noticing details

READING READINESS

Which one does not belong?
Cross out the one that does not belong with the others.
Then color the other pictures.

Skills: Classification; Association

READING READINESS

Look closely at each row of pictures.
One of the objects is in a different position.
Cross it out and then color the other pictures.

Skills: Visual discrimination; Noticing details; Spatial orientation

READING READINESS

Look at the large pictures.
Then look at the detail in each small box.

Find the detail in each large picture and circle it.
Then color the pictures.

Skills: Visual discrimination; Noticing details

READING READINESS

Look at the pictures in each box.
Circle the pictures that are facing right.
Make an "X" over the pictures that are facing left.

Skills: Recognizing right and left

READING READINESS

Look at the first picture in each row and say its name.
Circle the picture whose name rhymes with it.

Skills: Auditory discrimination; Reproducing sounds

READING READINESS

Look at each picture.
Draw a line between the pictures whose names rhyme.

Skills: Auditory discrimination; Reproducing sounds

READING READINESS

Look at the pattern in each row.
Draw a line to the picture that continues each pattern.
Then color the pictures.

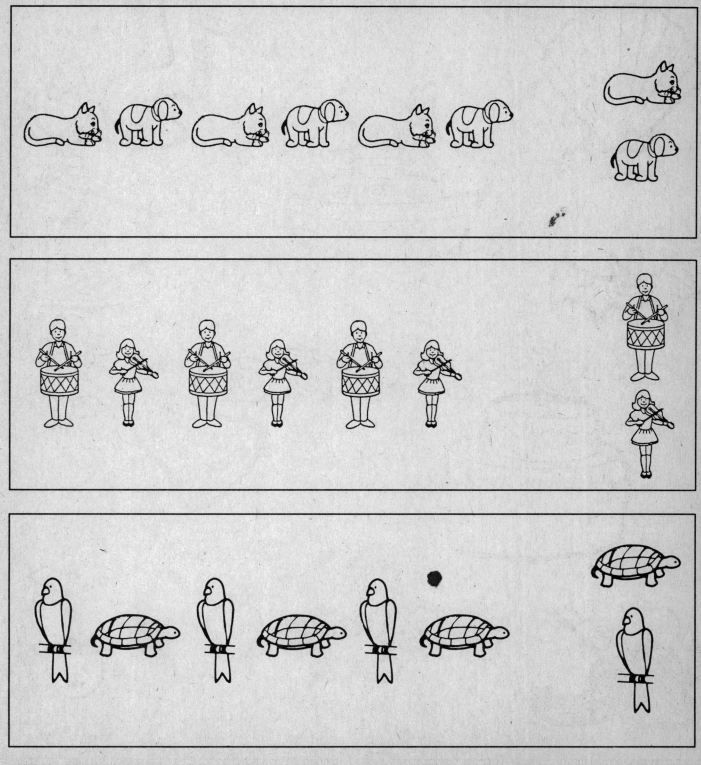

Skills: Observing and continuing patterns; Visual memory

READING READINESS

Look at the pattern in each row.
Draw a line to the picture that continues each pattern.
Then color the pictures.

Skills: Observing and continuing patterns; Visual memory

READING READINESS

Look at the pattern in each row.
Draw a line to the picture that continues each pattern.
Then color the pictures.

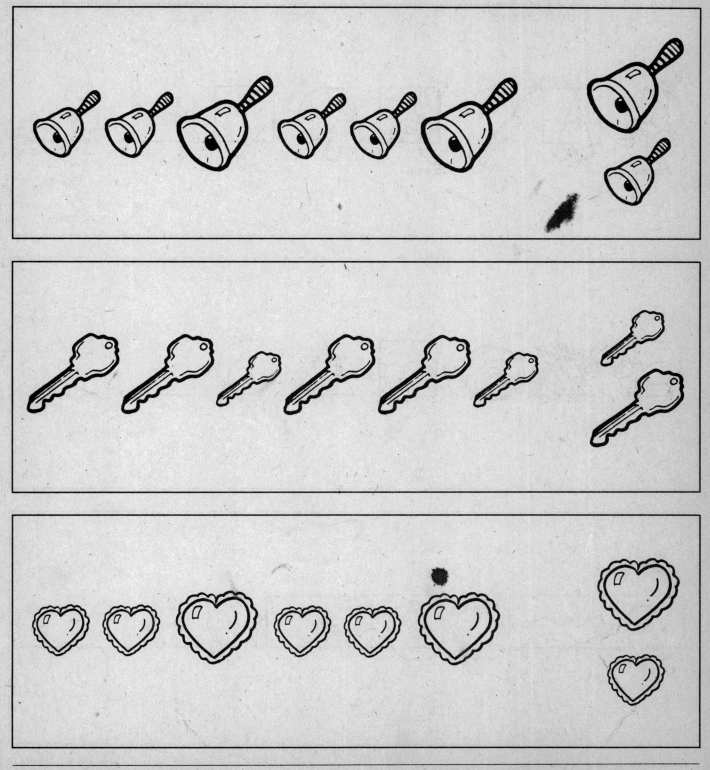

Skills: Observing and continuing patterns; Visual memory; Size discrimination

READING READINESS

Look at the pattern in each row.
Draw pictures to continue the pattern.
Then color the shapes.

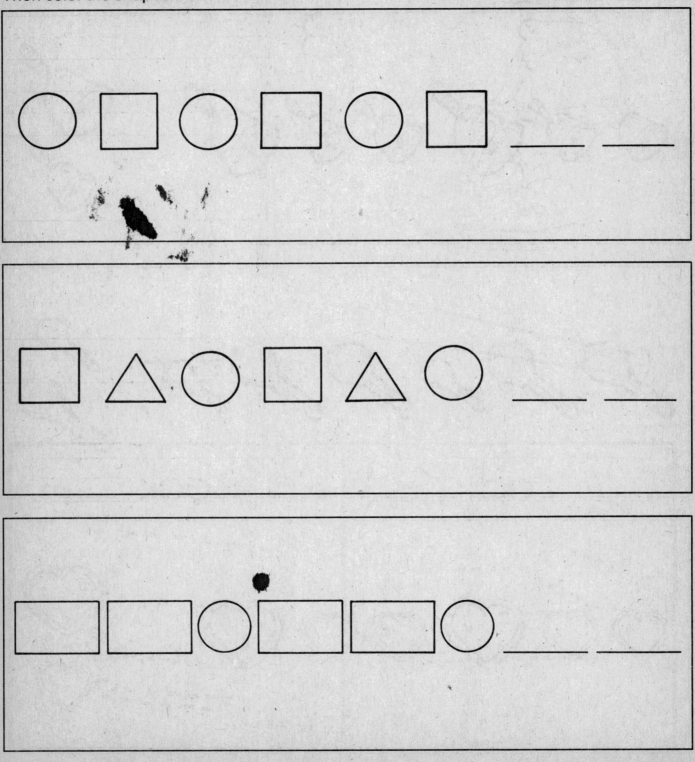

PHONICS SKILLS I

Initial consonant: **b**

Print the letters and words.

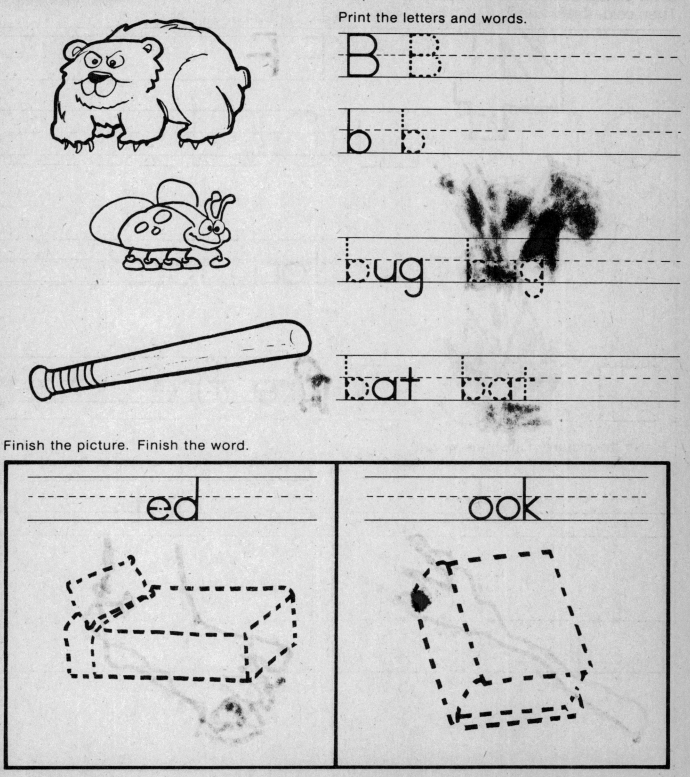

B B

b b

bug bug

bat bat

Finish the picture. Finish the word.

ed

ook

Skills: Recognition of the initial consonant "b"; Writing letters and words; Association between sounds, symbols, and words

PHONICS SKILLS I

Initial consonant: **f**

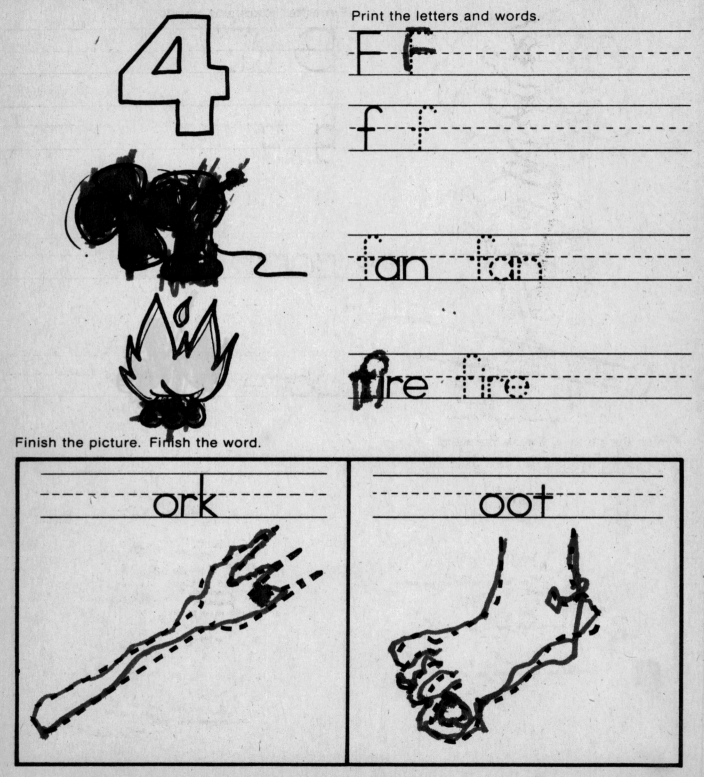

Print the letters and words.

F F

f f

fan fan

fire fire

Finish the picture. Finish the word.

ork

oot

Skills: Recognition of the initial consonant "f"; Writing letters and words; Association between sounds, symbols, and words

PHONICS SKILLS I

Initial consonant: g

Print the letters and words.

G G

g g

goat goat

gate gate

Finish the picture. Finish the word.

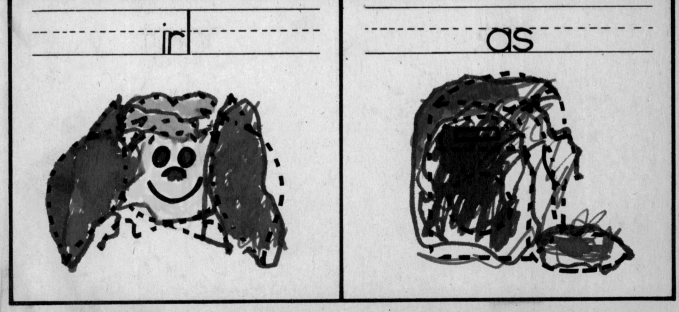

ir

as

Skills: Recognition of the initial consonant "g"; Writing letters and words; Association between sounds, symbols, and words

PHONICS SKILLS I

Initial consonant: **k**

Print the letters and words.

K K

k k

kiss kis

key key

Finish the picture. Finish the word.

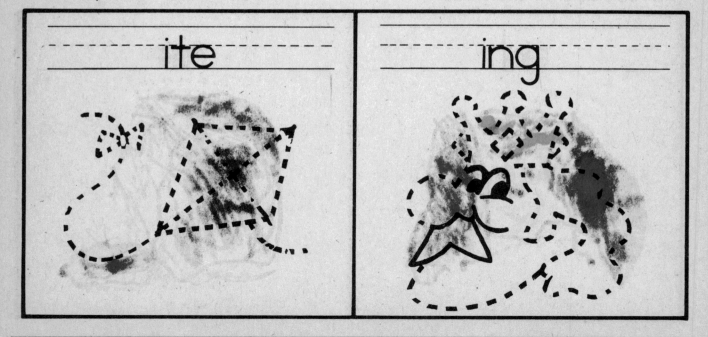

____ ite

____ ing

Skills: Recognition of the initial consonant "k"; Writing letters and words; Association between sounds, symbols, and words

PHONICS SKILLS I

Initial consonant: V

Print the letters and words.

V   V

v   v

vine   vine

van   van

Finish the picture. Finish the word.

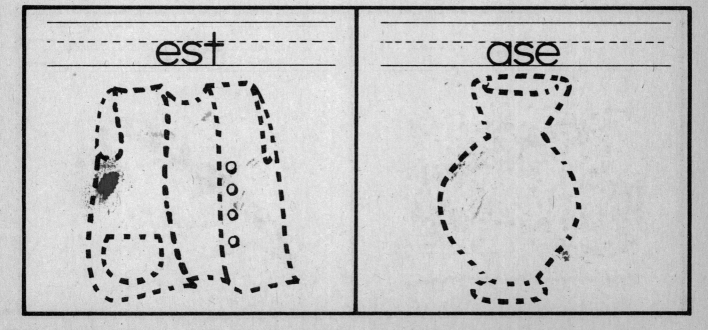

_ _ _ est

_ _ _ ase

Skills: Recognition of the initial consonant "v"; Writing letters and words; Association between sounds, symbols, and words

PHONICS SKILLS I

Initial consonant: **C**

Print the letters and words.

C C

c c

can can

cow cow

Finish the picture. Finish the word.

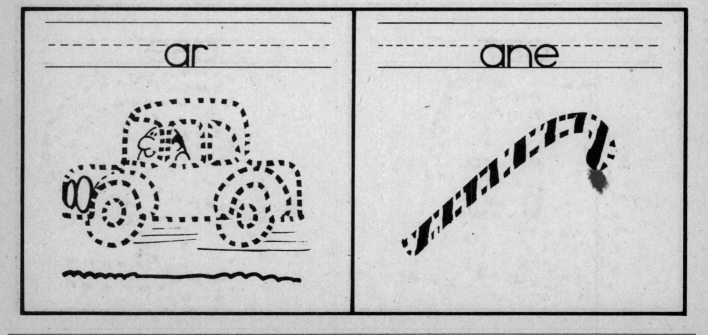

ar

ane

Skills: Recognition of the initial consonant "c"; Writing letters and words; Association between sounds, symbols, and words

PHONICS SKILLS I

Initial consonant: **h**

Print the letters and words.

H H

h h

hive hive

hat hat

Finish the picture. Finish the word.

orn

ose

Skills: Recognition of the initial consonant "h"; Writing letters and words; Association between sounds, symbols, and words

PHONICS SKILLS I

Initial consonant: **m**

Print the letters and words.

M — M — — — — — — — — — — —

m m — — — — — — — — — — —

mitt — mitt — — — — — — — —

mop — mop — — — — — — — —

Finish the picture. Finish the word.

— — — — — oon

— — — — — ap

UNITED STATES

Skills: Recognition of the initial consonant "m"; Writing letters and words; Association between sounds, symbols, and words

PHONICS SKILLS I

Initial consonant: p

Print the letters and words.

P P

p p

pig pig

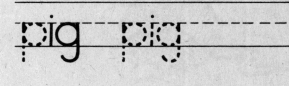

pin pin

Finish the picture. Finish the word.

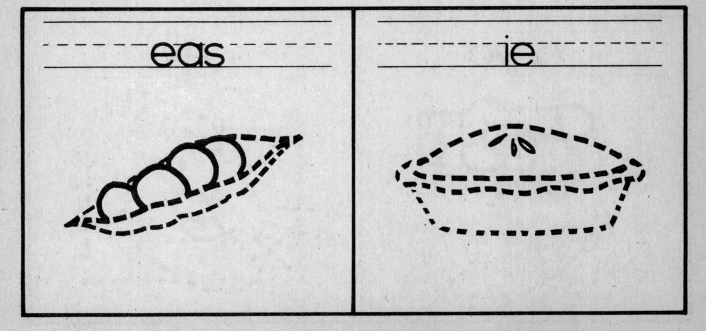

eas

ie

Skills: Recognition of the initial consonant "p"; Writing letters and words; Association between sounds, symbols, and words

PHONICS SKILLS I

Initial consonant: **y**

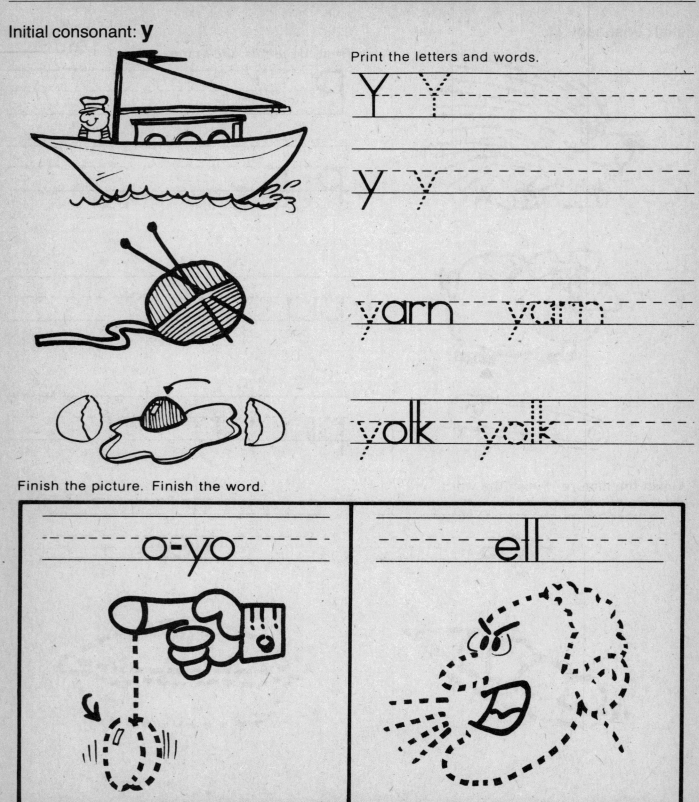

Print the letters and words.

Y Y

y y

yarn   yarn

yolk   yolk

Finish the picture. Finish the word.

o-yo

ell

Skills: Recognition of the initial consonant "y"; Writing letters and words; Association between sounds, symbols, and words

PHONICS SKILLS I

Initial consonant: **d**

Print the letters and words.

D D

d d

deer deer

duck duck

Finish the picture. Finish the word.

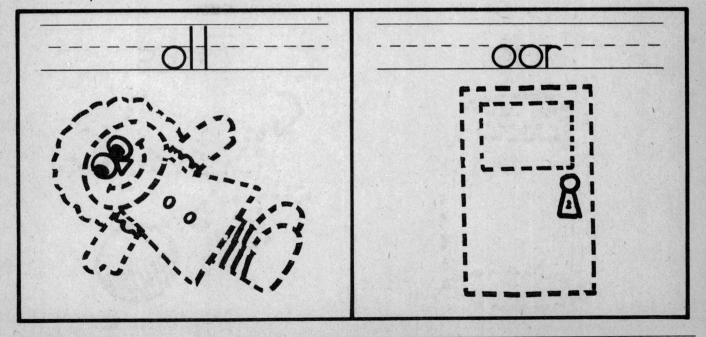

oll

oor

Skills: Recognition of the initial consonant "d"; Writing letters and words; Association between sounds, symbols, and words

PHONICS SKILLS I

Initial consonant: **j**

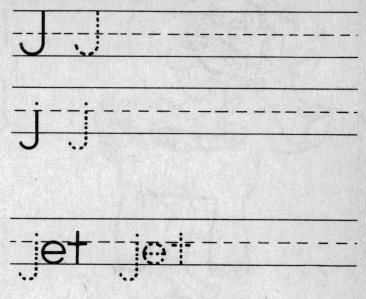

Print the letters and words.

J J

j j

jet jet

jug jug

Finish the picture. Finish the word.

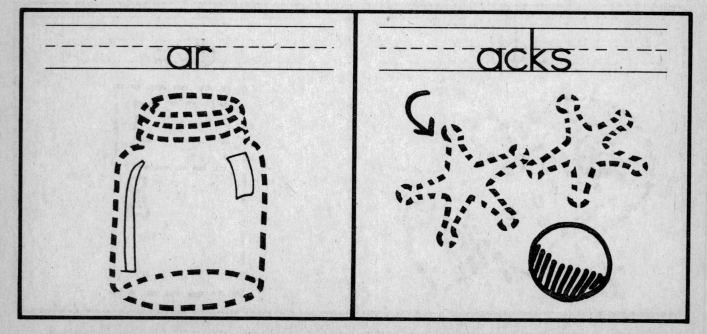

___ ar

___ acks

Skills: Recognition of the initial consonant "j"; Writing letters and words; Association between sounds, symbols, and words

Initial consonant: **l**

Print the letters and words.

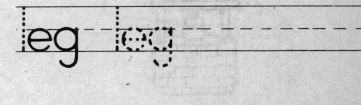

eg eg

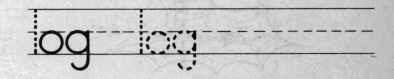

og og

Finish the picture. Finish the word.

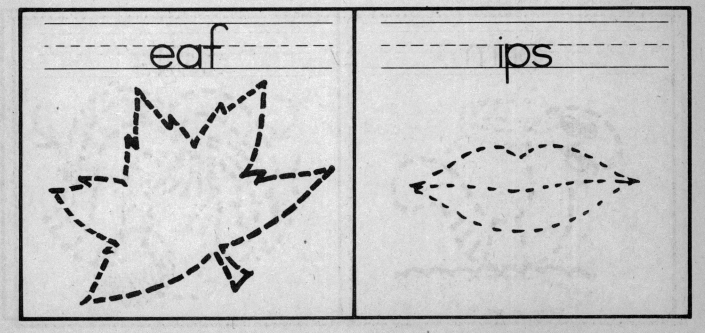

eaf

ips

Skills: Recognition of the initial consonant "l"; Writing letters and words; Association between sounds, symbols, and words

PHONICS SKILLS I

Initial consonant: W

Print the letters and words.

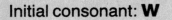

W W

w w

well well

web web

Finish the picture. Finish the word.

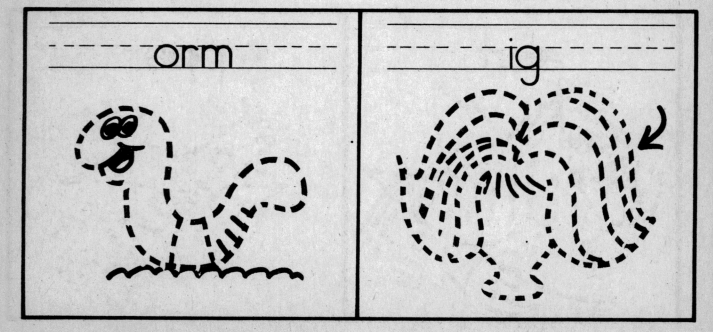

orm

ig

Skills: Recognition of the initial consonant "w"; Writing letters and words; Association between sounds, symbols, and words

PHONICS SKILLS I

Initial consonant: Z

Print the letters and words.

Z Z

z z

ZOO ZOO

zero zero

Finish the picture. Finish the word.

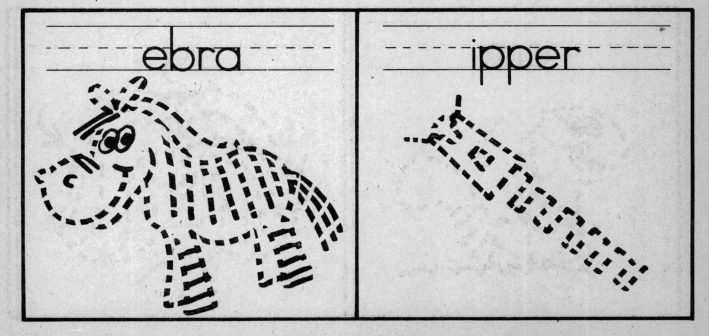

ebra

ipper

Skills: Recognition of the initial consonant "z"; Writing letters and words; Association between sounds, symbols, and words

PHONICS SKILLS I

Initial consonant: **n**

Print the letters and words.

N N _ _ _ _ _ _ _ _

n n _ _ _ _ _ _ _ _

nut nut _ _ _ _ _ _

net net _ _ _ _ _ _

Finish the picture. Finish the word.

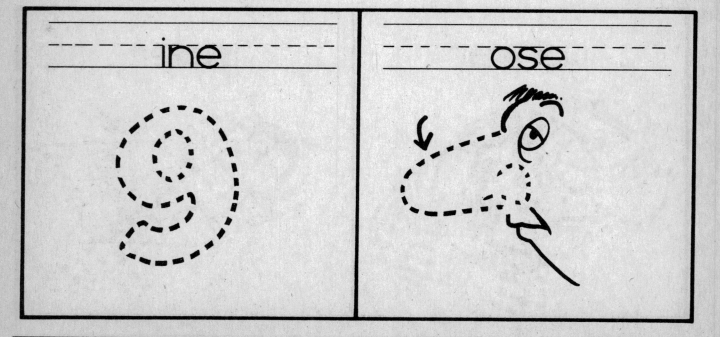

_ _ _ _ ine

_ _ _ _ ose

Skills: Recognition of the initial consonant "n"; Writing letters and words; Association between sounds, symbols, and words

PHONICS SKILLS I

Initial consonant: q

Print the letters and words.

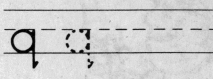

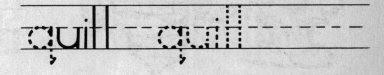

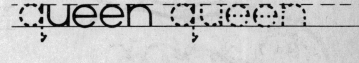

Finish the picture. Finish the word.

uarter

uilt

Skills: Recognition of the initial consonant "q"; Writing letters and words; Association between sounds, symbols, and words

PHONICS SKILLS I

Initial consonant: **r**

Print the letters and words.

R R

r r

ring ring

rain rain

Finish the picture. Finish the word.

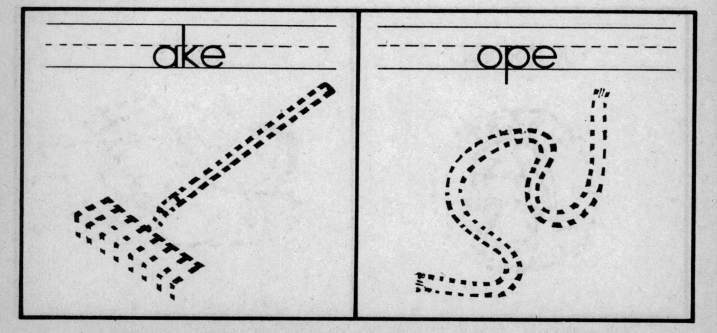

ake

ope

Skills: Recognition of the initial consonant "r"; Writing letters and words; Association between sounds, symbols, and words

PHONICS SKILLS I

Initial consonant: S

Print the letters and words.

S S

s s

seal   seal

sun   sun

Finish the picture. Finish the word.

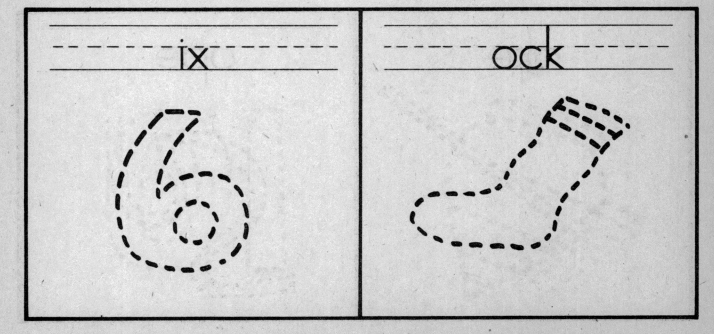

___ ix

___ ock

Skills: Recognition of the initial consonant "s"; Writing letters and words; Association between sounds, symbols, and words

PHONICS SKILLS I

Initial consonant: **t**

Print the letters and words.

tent tent

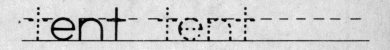

tire tire

Finish the picture. Finish the word.

_ op

en

Skills: Recognition of the initial consonant "t"; Writing letters and words; Association between sounds, symbols, and words

PHONICS SKILLS I

Final consonant: **b**

crab

b

Which ones end with **b**? Color them orange. Color the other pictures blue.

Skills: Recognition of the final consonant "b"; Auditory discrimination; Writing the letter "b"; Sound/symbol association

PHONICS SKILLS I

Final consonant: **f**

chief f – – – – – –

f f – – – – – –

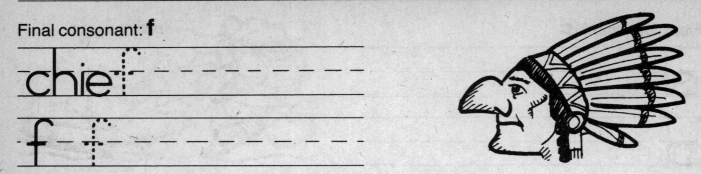

Which ones end with **f**? Color them red. Color the other pictures green.

Skills: Recognition of the final consonant "f"; Auditory discrimination; Writing the letter "f"; Sound/symbol association

PHONICS SKILLS I

Final consonant: **d**

sled _ _ _ _ _ _ _ _ _ _ _ _

d _ _ _ _ _ _ _ _ _ _ _ _ _

Which ones end with **d**? Color them yellow. Color the other pictures red.

Skills: Recognition of the final consonant "d"; Auditory discrimination; Writing the letter "d"; Sound/symbol association

PHONICS SKILLS I

Final consonant: **g**

Which ones end with **g**? Color them brown. Color the other pictures blue.

Skills: Recognition of the final consonant "g"; Auditory discrimination; Writing the letter "g"; Sound/symbol association

PHONICS SKILLS I

Final consonant: **k**

peek

k

Which ones end with **k**? Color them blue. Color the other pictures red.

Skills: Recognition of the final consonant "k"; Auditory discrimination; Writing the letter "k"; Sound/symbol association

PHONICS SKILLS I

Final consonant: **m**

drum

m m

Which ones end with **m**? Color them orange. Color the other pictures red.

Skills: Recognition of the final consonant "m"; Auditory discrimination; Writing the letter "m"; Sound/symbol association

PHONICS SKILLS I

Final consonant: l

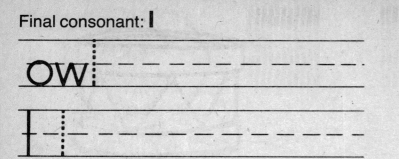

Which ones end with l? Color them red. Color the other pictures blue.

Skills: Recognition of the final consonant "l"; Auditory discrimination; Writing the letter "l"; Sound/symbol association

PHONICS SKILLS I

Final consonant: **n**

lion

n n

Which ones end with **n**? Color them green. Color the other pictures yellow.

Skills: Recognition of the final consonant "n"; Auditory discrimination; Writing the letter "n"; Sound/symbol association

PHONICS SKILLS I

Final consonant: **p**

jeep

p

Which ones end with **p**? Color them red. Color the other pictures green.

Skills: Recognition of the final consonant "p"; Auditory discrimination; Writing the letter "p"; Sound/symbol association

PHONICS SKILLS I

Final consonant: **r**

bea<u>r</u>

r   r

Which ones end with **r**? Color them brown. Color the other pictures green.

Skills: Recognition of the final consonant "r"; Auditory discrimination; Writing the letter "r"; Sound/symbol association

PHONICS SKILLS I

Final consonant: **t**

Which ones end with **t**? Color them yellow. Color the other pictures blue.

Skills: Recognition of the final consonant "t"; Auditory discrimination; Writing the letter "t"; Sound/symbol association

PHONICS SKILLS I

Final consonant: **X**

f o x

x x

Which ones end with **x**? Color them green. Color the other pictures brown.

Skills: Recognition of the final consonant "x"; Auditory discrimination; Writing the letter "x"; Sound/symbol association

PHONICS SKILLS II

Short vowel: ă

Print the letters and words.

A A

a a

bat bat

cat cat

Finish the picture. Finish the word.

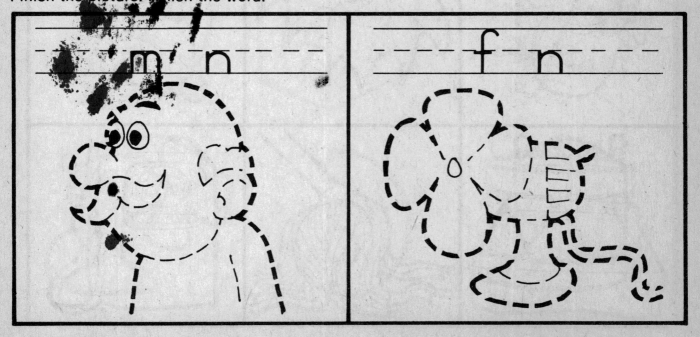

m n

f n

Skills: Recognition of the short vowel "a"; Writing letters and words; Association between sounds, symbols, and words

PHONICS SKILLS II

Short vowel: ă

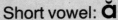

Which ones have the ă sound? Color them blue. Color the other pictures green.

Skills: Recognition of the short vowel "a"; Auditory discrimination; Writing the letter "a"; Sound/symbol association

PHONICS SKILLS II

Short vowel: ě

Print the letters and words.

E E

e e

pen pen

leg leg

Finish the picture. Finish the word.

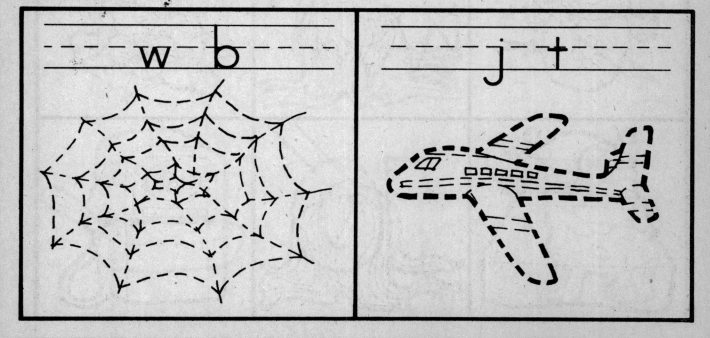

w b

j t

Skills: Recognition of the short vowel "e"; Writing letters and words; Association between sounds, symbols, and words

PHONICS SKILLS II

Short vowel: ĕ

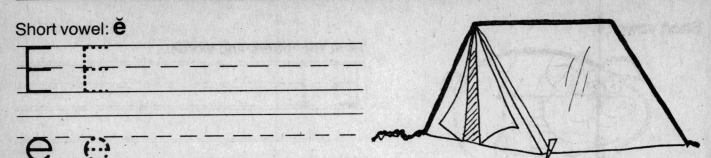

E
e

Which ones have the ĕ sound? Color them blue. Color the other pictures yellow.

Skills: Recognition of the short vowel "e"; Auditory discrimination; Writing the letter "e"; Sound/symbol association

PHONICS SKILLS II

Short vowel: ĭ

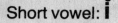

Print the letters and words.

I I

i i

pin pin

six six

Finish the picture. Finish the word.

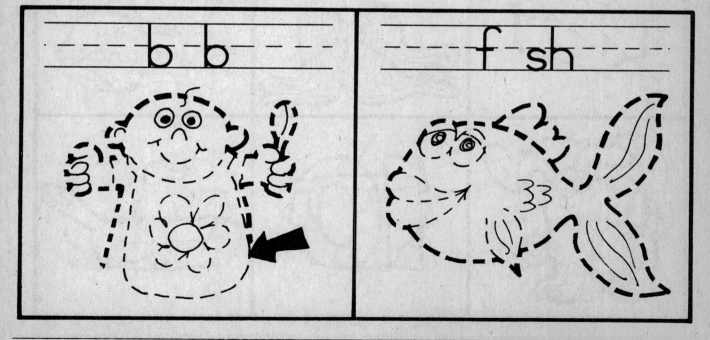

b b

f sh

Skills: Recognition of the short vowel "i"; Writing letters and words; Association between sounds, symbols, and words

PHONICS SKILLS II

Short vowel: **ĭ**

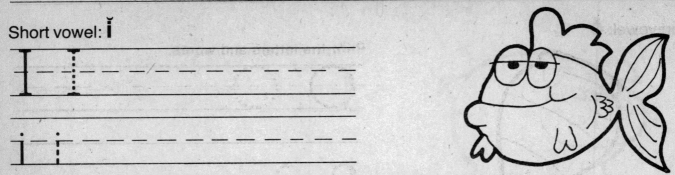

Which ones have the **ĭ** sound? Color them green. Color the other pictures brown.

Skills: Recognition of the short vowel "i"; Auditory discrimination; Writing the letter "i"; Sound/symbol association

PHONICS SKILLS II

Short vowel: ŏ

Print the letters and words.

O -- O⋯ - - - - - - - -

o o⋯ - - - - - - - -

mop mop - - - - -

fox fox - - - - -

Finish the picture. Finish the word.

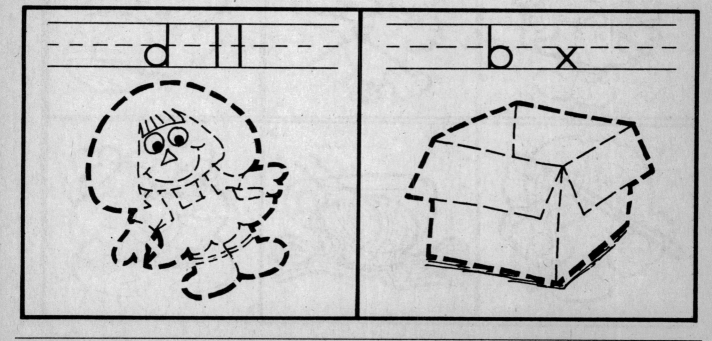

d _ _ t

b _ x

Skills: Recognition of the short vowel "o"; Writing letters and words; Association between sounds, symbols, and words

PHONICS SKILLS II

Short vowel: ŏ

Which ones have the ŏ sound? Color them orange. Color the other pictures green.

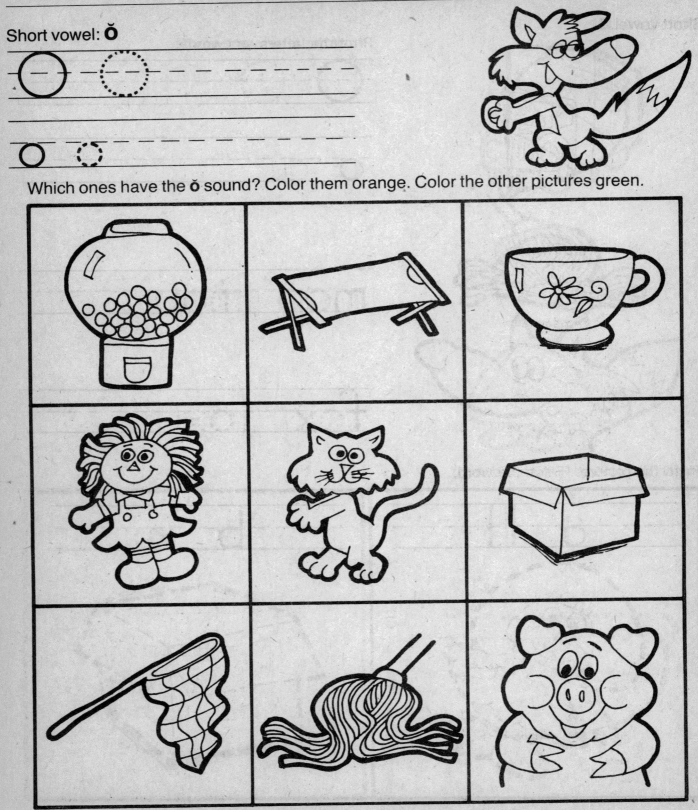

Skills: Recognition of the short vowel "o"; Auditory discrimination; Writing the letter "o"; Sound/symbol association

Short vowel: ŭ

Print the letters and words.

U U

u u

nut nut

bug bug

Finish the picture. Finish the word.

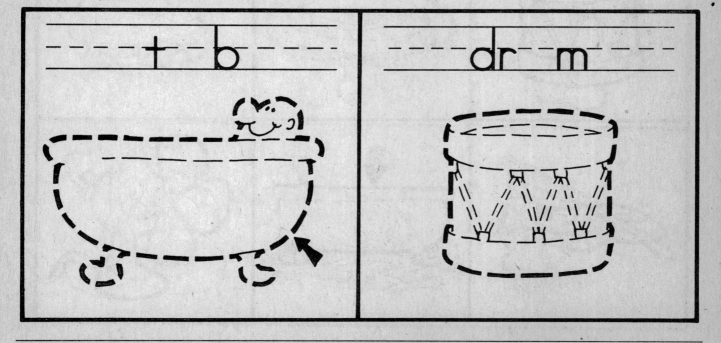

t b

dr m

Skills: Recognition of the short vowel "u"; Writing letters and words; Association between sounds, symbols, and words

PHONICS SKILLS II

Short vowel: **ŭ**

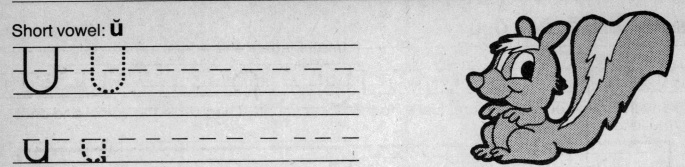

Which ones have the **ŭ** sound? Color them red. Color the other pictures yellow.

Skills: Recognition of the short vowel "u"; Auditory discrimination; Writing the letter "u"; Sound/symbol association

PHONICS SKILLS II

Short vowels: ă, ĕ, ĭ, ŏ, ŭ

a a   e e   i i   o o   u u

Say the name of each picture. Listen to the vowel sound. Then circle the vowel and print the letter.

Skills: Recognition of the short vowel sounds; Writing letters; Auditory and visual discrimination

PHONICS SKILLS II

Long vowel: ā

Print the letters and words.

A A

a a

cane cane

cape cape

Finish the picture. Finish the word.

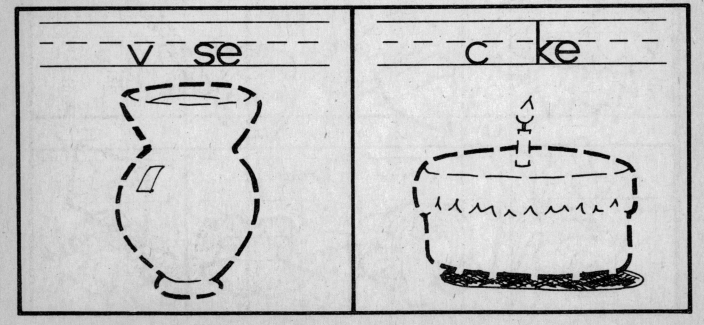

v͞se

c͞ke

Skills: Recognition of the long vowel "a"; Writing letters and words; Association between sounds, symbols, and words

PHONICS SKILLS II

Long vowel: ā

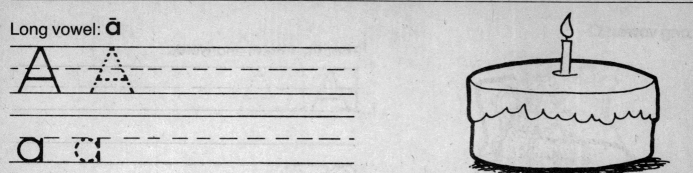

Which ones have the ā sound? Color them red. Color the other pictures blue.

Skills: Recognition of the long vowel "a"; Auditory discrimination; Writing the letter "a"; Sound/symbol association

PHONICS SKILLS II

Long vowel: ē

Print the letters and words.

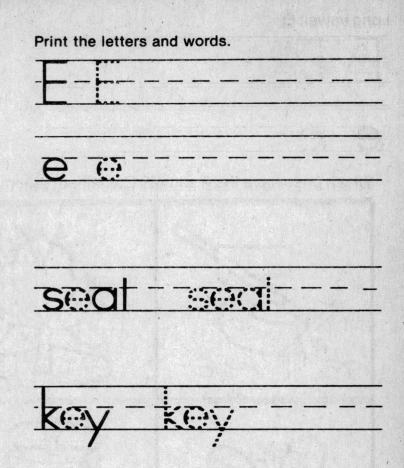

E E

e e

seat seat

key key

Finish the picture. Finish the word.

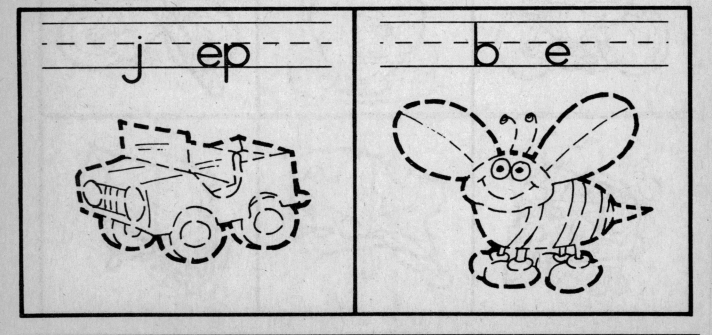

j_ep

b_e

Skills: Recognition of the long vowel "e"; Writing letters and words; Association between sounds, symbols, and words

PHONICS SKILLS II

Long vowel: ē

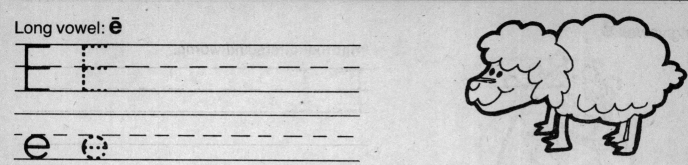

E

e

Which ones have the ē sound? Color them green. Color the other pictures blue.

Skills: Recognition of the long vowel "e"; Auditory discrimination; Writing the letter "e"; Sound/symbol association

PHONICS SKILLS II

Long vowel: ī

Print the letters and words.

I I

i i

pie pie

vine vine

Finish the picture. Finish the word.

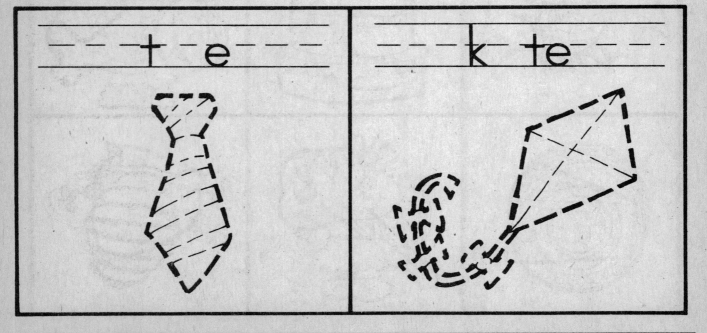

t__e

k__te

Skills: Recognition of the long vowel "i"; Writing letters and words; Association between sounds, symbols, and words

PHONICS SKILLS II

Long vowel: ī

Which ones have the ī sound? Color them yellow. Color the other pictures red.

Skills: Recognition of the long vowel "i"; Auditory discrimination; Writing the letter "i"; Sound/symbol association

PHONICS SKILLS II

Long vowel: ō

Print the letters and words.

O O

o o

toe toe

note note

Finish the picture. Finish the word.

r_be   c_ne

Skills: Recognition of the long vowel "o"; Writing letters and words; Association between sounds, symbols, and words

PHONICS SKILLS II

Long vowel: **ō**

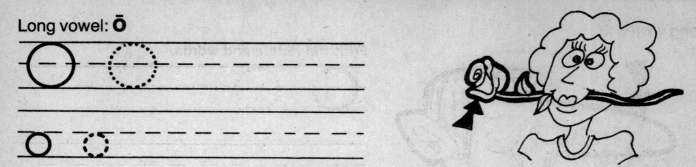

Which ones have the **ō** sound? Color them brown. Color the other pictures blue.

Skills: Recognition of the long vowel "o"; Auditory discrimination; Writing the letter "o"; Sound/symbol association

PHONICS SKILLS II

Long vowel: **ū**

Print the letters and words.

U U

u u

tube   tube

cube   cube

Finish the picture. Finish the word.

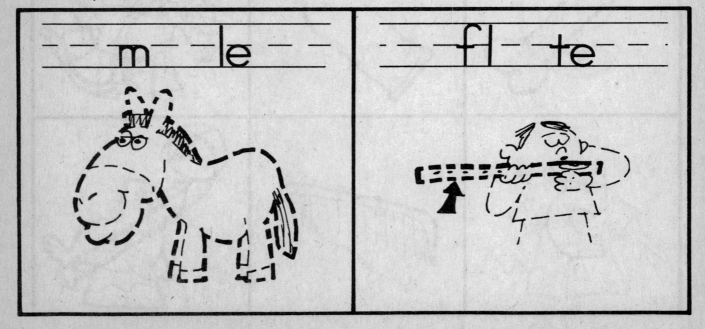

m ___ le

fl ___ te

Skills: Recognition of the long vowel "u"; Writing letters and words; Association between sounds, symbols, and words

PHONICS SKILLS II

Long vowel: ū

U U _____

u u _____

Which ones have the ū sound? Color them green. Color the other pictures red.

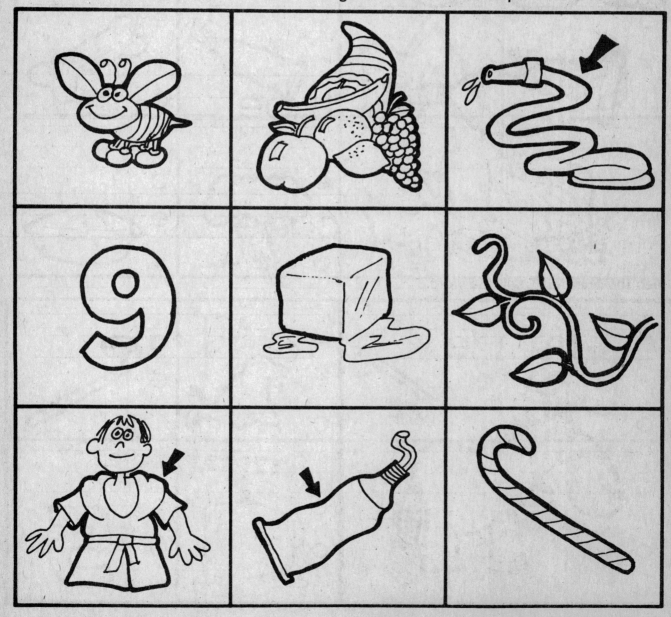

Skills: Recognition of the long vowel "u"; Auditory discrimination; Writing the letter "u"; Sound/symbol association

PHONICS SKILLS II

Long vowels: **ā, ē, ī, ō, ū**

a a c e e i i o o u u

Say the name of each picture. Listen to the vowel sound. Then circle the vowel and print the letter.

Skills: Recognition of the long vowel sounds; Writing letters; Auditory and visual discrimination

PHONICS SKILLS II

Long and short vowel: **a**

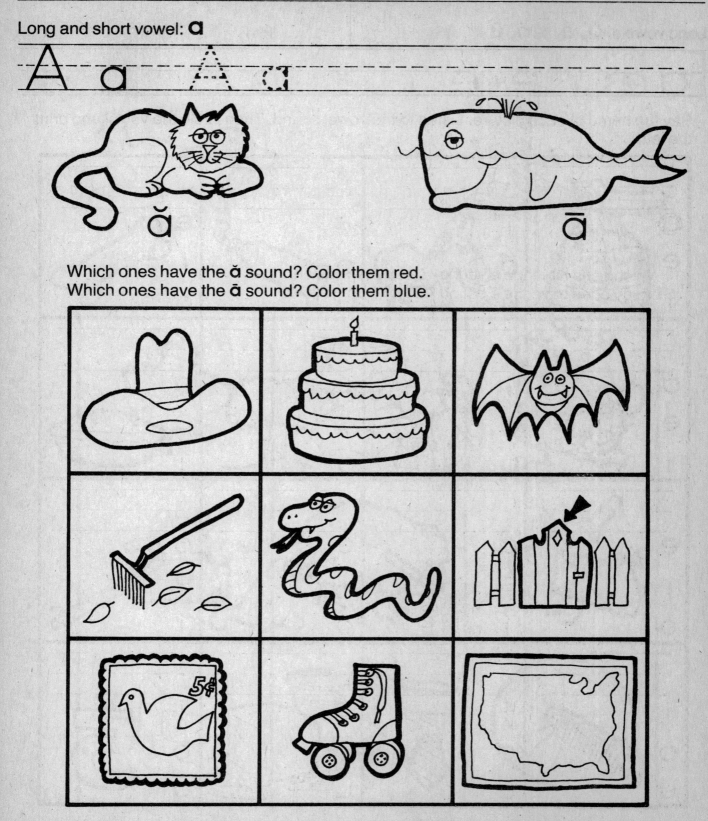

Which ones have the ă sound? Color them red.
Which ones have the ā sound? Color them blue.

Skills: Auditory and visual discrimination; Sound/symbol association; Writing the letter "a"

PHONICS SKILLS II

Long and short vowel: **e**

Which ones have the **ĕ** sound? Color them green.
Which ones have the **ē** sound? Color them yellow.

Skills: Auditory and visual discrimination; Sound/symbol association; Writing the letter "e"

PHONICS SKILLS II

Long and short vowel: **i**

Which ones have the **ĭ** sound? Color them orange.
Which ones have the **ī** sound? Color them yellow.

Skills: Auditory and visual discrimination; Sound/symbol association; Writing the letter "i"

PHONICS SKILLS II

Long and short vowel: **O**

Which ones have the ŏ sound? Color them blue.
Which ones have the ō sound? Color them green.

Skills: Auditory and visual discrimination; Sound/symbol association; Writing the letter "o"

PHONICS SKILLS II

Long and short vowel: **u**

Which ones have the **ŭ** sound? Color them green.
Which ones have the **ū** sound? Color them red.

Skills: Auditory and visual discrimination; Sound/symbol association; Writing the letter "u"

PHONICS SKILLS II

Long and short vowels: a, e, i, o, u

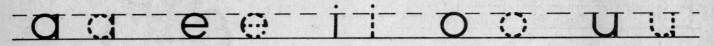

Say the name of each picture. Listen to the vowel sound. Then print the vowel you hear.

Skills: Recognition of the long and short vowels sounds; Writing letters; Auditory and visual discrimination

PHONICS SKILLS II

Initial consonant blends: **cl, cr**

c‑l - - - - - - - - - -

c‑r - - - - - - - - - -

Which ones begin with **cl**? Color them blue.
Which ones begin with **cr**? Color them green.

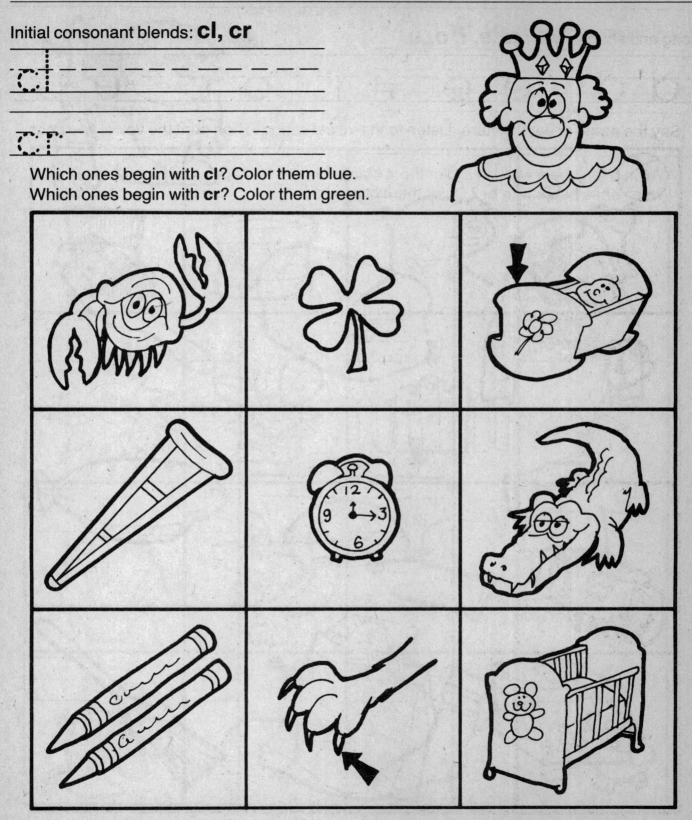

Skills: Understanding that some consonant sounds can be blended together;
Sound/symbol association

PHONICS SKILLS II

Initial consonant blends: **bl, br**

bl

br

Which ones begin with **bl**? Color them black.
Which ones begin with **br**? Color them brown.

Skills: Understanding that some consonant sounds can be blended together;
Sound/symbol association

PHONICS SKILLS II

Initial consonant blends: **dr, tr**

dr

tr

Which ones begin with **dr**? Color them blue.
Which ones begin with **tr**? Color them red.

Skills: Understanding that some consonant sounds can be blended together;
Sound/symbol association

PHONICS SKILLS II

Initial consonant blends: **sk, sl**

s k

s l

Which ones begin with **sk**? Color them yellow.
Which ones begin with **sl**? Color them red.

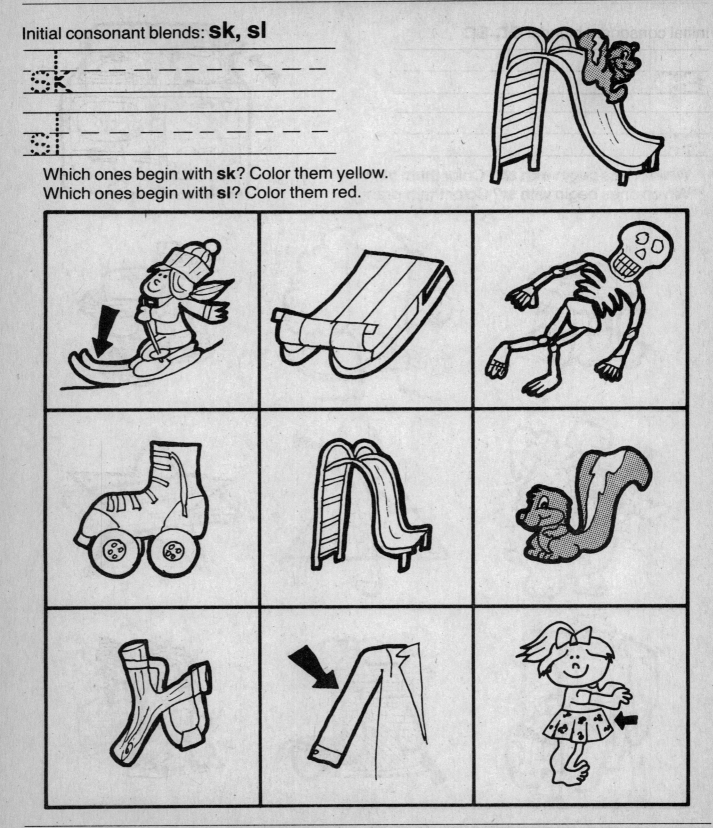

Skills: Understanding that some consonant sounds can be blended together;
Sound/symbol association

PHONICS SKILLS II

Initial consonant blends: **st, sp**

sp

st

Which ones begin with **sp**? Color them yellow.
Which ones begin with **st**? Color them orange.

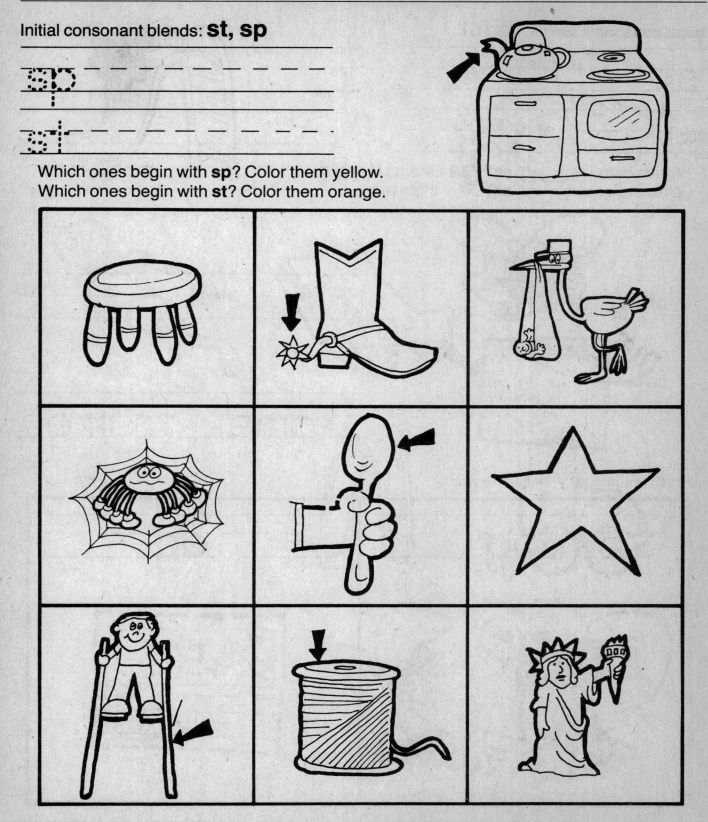

Skills: Understanding that some consonant sounds can be blended together; Sound/symbol association

PHONICS SKILLS II

Initial consonant blends: **fl, fr**

Print the letters and words.

fr fr

fl fl

fly fly

frame frame

Finish the picture.   Finish the word.

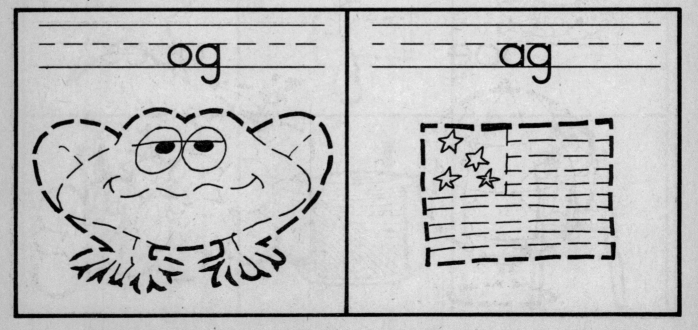

og

ag

Skills: Understanding that some consonant sounds can be blended together; Sound/symbol association

PHONICS SKILLS II

Initial consonant blends: gl, gr

Print the letters and words.

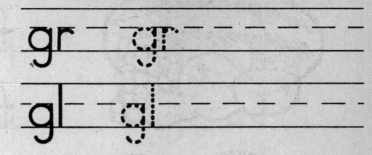

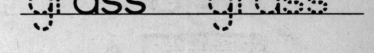

grass   grass

glove   glove

Finish the picture.   Finish the word.

_obe

_apes

Skills: Understanding that some consonant sounds can be blended together;
Sound/symbol association

PHONICS SKILLS II

Initial consonant blends: pl, pr

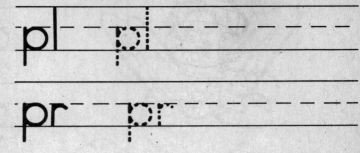

Print the letters and words.

pl   pl

pr   pr

plow   plow

price   price

Finish the picture.   Finish the word.

ug

ize

Skills: Understanding that some consonant sounds can be blended together; Sound/symbol association

PHONICS SKILLS II

Initial consonant blends: **sn, sw**

Print the letters and words.

sn   sn

sw   sw

snake   snake

swan   swan

Finish the picture.   Finish the word.

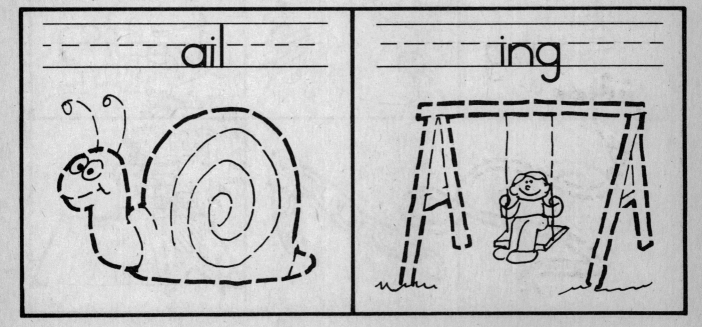

ail

ing

Skills: Understanding that some consonant sounds can be blended together; Sound/symbol association

PHONICS SKILLS II

Consonant digraph: **ch**

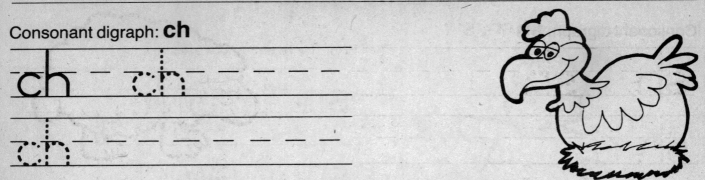

Which ones begin with **ch**? Color them brown. Color the other pictures red.

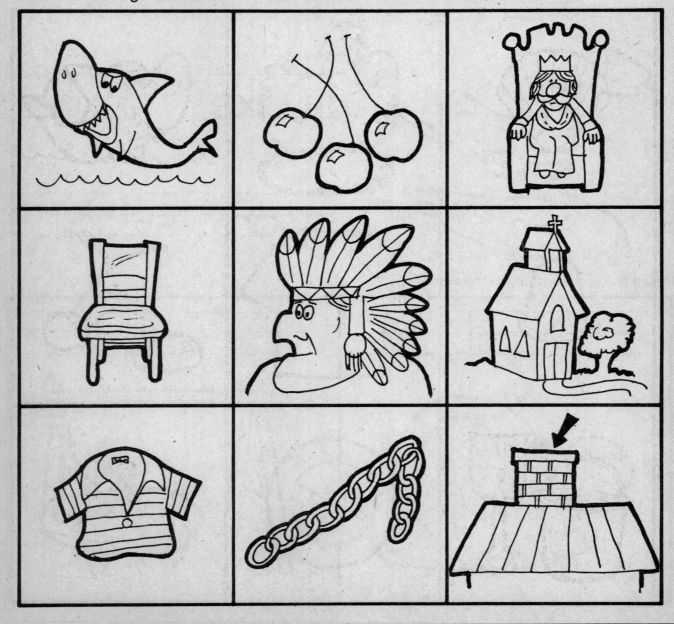

Skills: Recognizing and understanding consonant digraphs; Sound/symbol association

PHONICS SKILLS II

Consonant digraph: **sh**

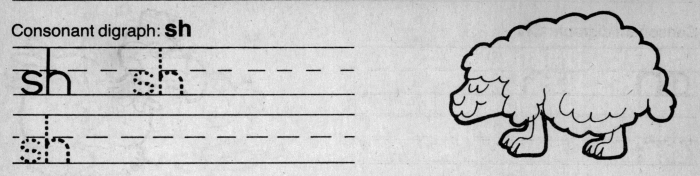

Which ones begin with **sh**? Color them orange. Color the other pictures green.

Skills: Recognizing and understanding consonant digraphs; Sound/symbol association

PHONICS SKILLS II

Consonant digraph: **th**

t h   th _ _ _ _ _ _ _ _

t h _ _ _ _ _ _ _ _ _ _

Which ones begin with **th**? Color them blue. Color the other pictures red.

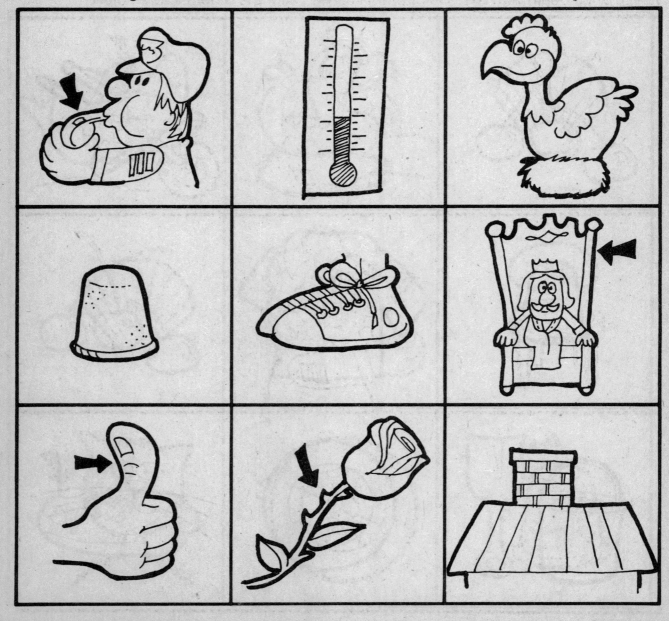

Skills: Recognizing and understanding consonant digraphs; Sound/symbol association

PHONICS SKILLS II

Consonant digraph: **wh**

wh   wh

wh

Which ones begin with **wh**? Color them yellow. Color the other pictures blue.

PHONICS SKILLS II

Consonant digraphs: **ch, sh, th, wh**

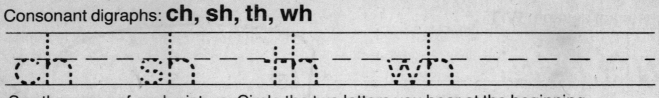

Say the name of each picture. Circle the two letters you hear at the beginning.
Then print the letters.

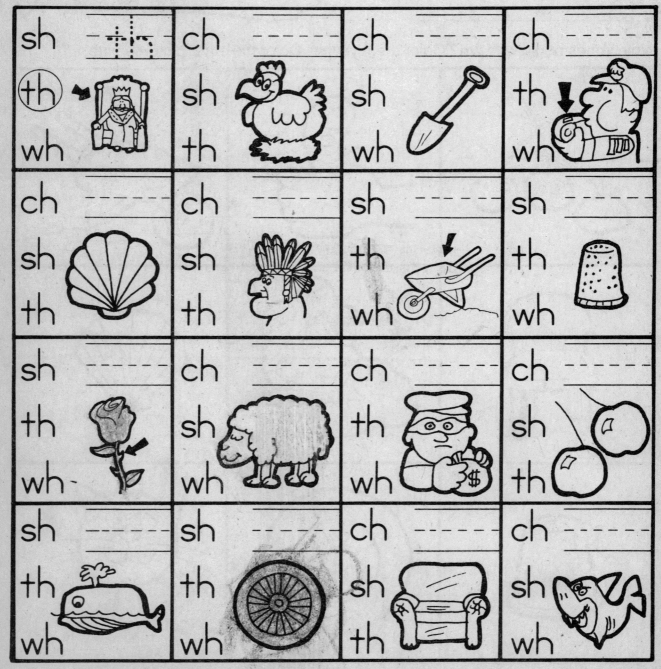

Skills: Recognition of consonant digraphs; Auditory and visual discrimination;
Writing letters

Donated by
The Chester Garden Club
2006

The Essential
Garden Maintenance
Workbook

The Essential
Garden Maintenance
Workbook

Rosemary Alexander

Timber Press

All photographs by Rosemary Alexander, except page 253 by Sheherazade Goldsmith and pages 190 bl and 341 by Peter Kiernan.

All illustrations by Roger Sweetinburgh, except pages 15, 16, 17, 18, 19, 21, 22, 23, 24, 26, 27, 28, 33, 34, 35, 36, 53, 54, 55, 58, 59, 60, 65 bl, 73 l, 76, 77 tl, bl, tr, 89, 97, 100, 102, 138 tl, 142 by Joseph Kent; pages 45, 46, 117, 184, 186, 249, 255, 257 by Rosemary Alexander; pages 252, 253 by Sheherazade Goldsmith.

Garden Log by Kim Bay (pages 114–117); Plant Groupings Profile by Sheherazade Goldsmith (pages 252–53).

Published in 2006 by
Timber Press, Inc.
The Haseltine Building
133 S.W. Second Avenue, Suite 450
Portland, Oregon 97204-3527, U.S.A.
www.timberpress.com

For contact information regarding editorial, marketing, sales, and distribution in the United Kingdom, see www.timberpress.co.uk

Project Editor: Annelise Evans
Design by Dick Malt
Printed through Colorcraft Ltd., Hong Kong

Library of Congress Cataloging-in-Publication Data
Alexander, Rosemary.
  The essential garden maintenance workbook / Rosemary Alexander.
     p. cm.
  Includes bibliographical references and index.
  ISBN-13: 978-0-88192-783-2
  ISBN-10: 0-88192-783-X
  1. Gardening. I. Title.
  SB453.A61 2006
  635--dc22
                      2005038003

A catalogue record for this book is also available from the British Library.

Contents

Acknowledgements

My thanks must first go to Timber Press, in particular to Anna Mumford, for commissioning this book. I am indebted to the project editor, Annelise Evans, whose experience, interest and attention to detail has greatly improved my text, and to Dick Malt for his design creativity.

My appreciation to Joe Kent, who did the original illustrations, to Roger Sweetinburgh for technical illustrations and for his contribution to the text, to Pippa Greenwood for her advice on organic gardening, and to Kim Bay and Sheherazade Goldsmith for allowing me to reproduce some of their excellent course work. I also thank my wonderfully supportive team of lecturers, from whom I continue to learn so much, and, especially for often helping me out at short notice, my small but encouraging management team at The English Gardening School in London.

Having visited many gardens each year, I am grateful to the creators of those illustrated in this book and ask forgiveness of those whose names may unwittingly have been overlooked. Thanks also to Peter Kiernan, for his photographs of me in action, to Janet Bligh, who helped me select the first batch of images, and especially to all the gardeners, past and present, who have worked with me in my gardens.

Our England is a garden, and such gardens are not made
By singing:— "Oh, how beautiful!" and sitting in the shade

The Glory of the Garden
Rudyard Kipling

Introduction

What Makes a Good Gardener?

Many of us long for a beautiful garden, but have little or no idea how to achieve our dreams. The dictionary definition of the word "horticulture" is "the art of garden cultivation", but how do we acquire this art? Good gardens are not simply a matter of choosing plants and arranging them together. More often they are the reward of several decades of hard work, usually by an inspired and knowledgeable gardener or owner.

As well as understanding plants and how to grow them, a good gardener needs to be able to combine many different skills and to call on various fields of knowledge, from planning and design of the garden space and hard landscaping to managing the soil and exploiting texture, form and colour in selecting plants for the garden.

This book aims to give you a deep understanding of horticulture, as well as encourage you through the process of creating or restoring a beautiful and healthy garden. It takes you logically through the various stages, from assessing the garden as it is now and having a vision of its potential, planning out the new design and getting the preparatory work done, for instance to make a lawn or create a new border. It continues through laying out the new structure of the garden and understanding what plants you can grow to creating and maintaining new plantings.

Learning about Plants

Plants can be as variable as people—they have preferences and dislikes, different growth rates, variable times of flowering or fruiting, can be temperamental or accommodating, and may be quick or slow to adapt to a new situation. Plants are also affected by their surroundings: the way they respond to the type of soil and to the local climate will determine what can be grown in your garden. All these factors need to be taken into account when selecting and growing plants, as well as their more obvious charms such as flowers, foliage and scent.

Accordingly, this book will help you to acquire and develop a good knowledge of garden plants. You will learn about the anatomy of plants, the purpose and meanings of their botanical names, and which criteria to use when selecting plants.

There are discussions of the art of planting, including how to create structure, the use of colour and shape, maintaining interest through the seasons and combining plants. Extensive lists of recommended plants will help you make the best choice of plants for your own garden.

Most importantly, you will learn how best to grow, maintain and propagate the plants: every topic, from planting and pruning to plant health and seed sowing is covered.

Structure of this Book

This book sets out to teach you how to develop and care for your garden in a professional and creative manner, taking you step-by-step through the entire process, from initial assessment of your garden to maintenance of your newly planted or renovated creation. Each chapter is self-contained, allowing you to digest and understand it before progressing to the next stage. The text provides some theoretical background and lots of practical advice and is illustrated with many clear and informative drawings as well as full-colour photographs.

At the end of each chapter, projects are provided to reinforce your understanding of the content and to provide you with reference material that you will find useful in the care of your own garden. These projects include a garden log, or diary, photographic records, and a plant portfolio.

You will also be shown how to draw up a plan of your garden and use it to plot out each stage of your work. To help and inspire you, each chapter includes a plan taken from my own garden in Britain at Sandhill Farm House, Hampshire, showing how I tackled the renovation in phases, so that you can trace its development through the book.

More practical information is included in the appendices. The comprehensive gardening calendar guides you through seasonal tasks such as lawn care, staking, pruning, taking cuttings and planting bulbs. Our suggested reading list may be helpful if you need more specific information about a plant or task, and further information is given on plant hardiness and climates.

When to Begin?

Horticultural techniques may be practised in any size of garden, small or large, or you could adopt or borrow a neighbour's garden. It is useful to work and study in the same garden for at least one entire year, so that you can observe and enjoy the way it changes through the seasons. You can begin caring

for your garden at any time of year—there is always something to be done—look in the gardening calendar for a monthly reminder of garden tasks.

In an ideal world, a full year should elapse before beginning work on the garden, seeing the growing season through to discover what we have that we want to keep or dispose of. In this world of instant gratification, this is not easy, but do go carefully—a saw and weedkiller can destroy what may have taken years to establish.

For most of us our gardening has to be fitted in around other activities and finding time to do everything is the hardest part. Remember that some of the best-known gardens have taken many years, sometimes decades, to create, and it is always an ongoing process. I do hope you will have as much enjoyment out of caring for your garden as I do out of mine.

With this book to guide you, your new garden and understanding of horticulture should bring pleasure to you, to your family and to your friends.

Chapter 1
Getting Started

Before embarking on a major project or schedule of work, it is always wise to step back and contemplate the garden and your vision for its future. Achieving it can seem like a daunting task, especially if you are tackling a new or unruly garden. This chapter aims to prepare you for the first steps of making, or restoring, and caring for your garden. It sets out practical steps needed to assess the scale of the task ahead of you, and what points you need to consider before beginning any work in the garden.

The chapter also includes a section on plant names and horticultural terminology, so that you may begin to feel more at ease with the language of the garden centre or nursery or with the books and catalogues at home.

Assessing the Garden

Most of us dream of having a beautiful garden—our own private space for relaxation, enjoyment, outdoor living and, above all, a place for plants. Television and other media bombard us with inspirational ideas and it is all made to look so easy. But still, very few of us know what to aim for, never mind how to achieve it or why.

Basically, most of us seek an attractive yet practical layout that allows us to indulge our taste in plants. The mood or style of your garden should be in tune with your house or the architectural style and the local surroundings, so this may mean anything from, for example, a traditional, formal design or a

romantic retreat to a slick, contemporary setting. If you use the house and the surroundings as the starting point, then you can begin to consider the purpose of your ideal garden and think of the elements that would be needed to create it. A garden should be an enjoyable place and satisfy both the mind and eye of the beholder. It should be a place for relaxation—sitting, pruning, mowing, digging or deadheading—and at the same time, give the opportunity to commune with nature.

It should also be a highly personal expression of your character—formal, relaxed, eccentric or intensely practical—and a place where your family and friends want to linger and appreciate each other's company in attractive surroundings. For most of us, this means a sitting area, a terrace, a lawn, a path and perhaps some water, as well as beautiful plants, but there are many different ways of putting these ingredients together.

Before any planting can begin, it is vital to assess how a garden is going to be used and allocate areas in your plan for each activity, such as relaxation, play, or socializing.

To do this, we should have the painter's eye for composition, the architect's skill for using space, and sufficient botanical and horticultural expertise to cultivate the soil and grow the chosen plants. Few of us possess all these skills and so need to adopt a more practical approach to achieving our ideal. The first step is to look at the garden as it exists now and make some necessary observations.

Before
The zone of visual influence in a town or suburban garden may be extensive. Usually only part of it is intrusive.

After
This shows how the zone of influence may, if desired, be partially screened. The relatively small trees in the foreground to the right help to obscure the most intrusive buildings from certain viewpoints.

Remember that trees may grow much larger; often you can achieve considerable seclusion and screening by using relatively small shrubs close to the point of view instead of big trees farther away.

Your notes on views will help you to decide what to screen and what to frame up or emphasize.

Your Surroundings

No garden exists in a vacuum. Small or large, urban or rural, in reality every garden is part of a larger whole with which it interacts, rather like a single piece of a jigsaw. It will affect and be affected by its environment. When you first consider what to do with your garden, look at the view beyond it—the "zone of visual influence". This may simply be the back of houses in the next street or may extend to woods and hills on the horizon. Think whether you want to screen out or preserve this view, or parts of it.

The façade or architectural style of your property should be the next consideration—go to the boundary of your site and look back at your house. In making a garden, the house should merge imperceptibly into the garden, and in turn, the garden should blend into the surrounding townscape

Before
The boundary makes a very harsh delineation between the garden and the surrounding landscape.

After
The boundary has been made imperceptible except for a gate and the view has been artfully framed by trees, with a tree canopy high enough to let the view be seen underneath it.

or landscape. Too many gardens are made without reference to the zone of visual influence and stand out awkwardly, isolated from their surroundings.

Most gardens fall into one of two categories: introvert or extrovert. An introvert, or inward-looking, garden maintains interest within the site itself—holding the eye perhaps by focusing on a particular feature such as a statue, pool or pergola, while obscuring the boundaries with planting. By contrast, the extrovert site makes use of interesting

features beyond the boundary, such as a distant church or wooded hills. The garden itself may be featureless but, by using flowing lines and shapes, the eye can be carried beyond the boundary, making the site appear to extend into the distant horizon or to a particular feature. The Japanese called this technique the "borrowed view".

In many cases, simply framing a piece of open sky with trees will create a view of classic beauty.

The borrowed view can be accentuated by placing trees, groups of trees or other objects to channel or "frame" the desired or borrowed picture. This exacting and useful technique can be used to frame anything desirable, whether it is a simple group of chimney pots, a distant building or a hill on the far horizon. You could also consider your neighbours and passersby: how will they view your garden? There may be features outside the garden that you could enhance with your planting.

Evaluating the Space

Having considered the surroundings and the house, the garden itself must now be scrutinized. This means being ruthless in defining how you want to use the garden. Then study the space to see whether it is indeed possible to include all your needs, for example a sunny terrace near the door that looks on to the garden or, if that area is in shade, a sunny terrace at the other end of the garden.

An existing garden

Perhaps you have lived with a garden for several years and have only recently decided to improve it. It is much harder to be objective about a place with which you are very familiar because certain features such as an old climbing frame, poorly performing plant, or broken fence will no longer register.

Try to look at your garden with a fresh and critical eye and spot shabby or dull areas and features.

A good way of taking a fresh look at your garden is to take photographs and use them to analyze the virtues and disadvantages of your outdoor space. Ask family or friends also to look at them with you to help decide what should stay and what should go. There is little point in assessing the garden unless you are prepared to make some radical changes, but it is equally important not to rush in and make changes that you might regret later. So much depends on the current state of your garden.

Opportunity for a fresh start

It may be difficult to visualize a building site as an established garden, but this is the most opportune moment to connect house, garden, and surroundings. Too often the garden is a low priority compared with the house; frequently, the majority of the budget has been already spent, leaving little spare cash for the

garden. However, everything does not need to be done at once, but can be phased over a number of years, perhaps beginning with the area nearest the house and leaving work on the less noticeable parts until labour or your budget allows.

Perhaps your intended garden is a vacant field, in which case you may be able to choose the position for the house. The preferred aspect in most countries is open to the southwest, which allows full benefit from long summer days in both house and garden. If the main living rooms and bedrooms face south, they will be bright and cheerful and can lead out on to terraces or paving for easy outdoor living. The other side of the house—perhaps the entrance area—will then face northeast. In relentlessly hot countries, some shade for the main living rooms may be necessary, so the aspect may need to be reversed.

When assessing a blank site, begin by trying to divide up the outdoor space into different areas, allocating some for a terrace, paths, steps, some lawn or grass, as well as areas for planting. Use the main architectural elements of the house, such as prominent corners, doors or windows, as reference points and divide up the garden from these dominant features. If this preliminary work is done while building workmen are still on site, it may save you time and labour costs.

Be generous with each area: make sure that any outside dimensions are in proportion with the surroundings; it is easy to make allocated spaces too tight for people to circulate freely.

Getting to know a mature garden

If you are taking over an established garden, there may well be scope for improvement. Most of us want our home—house and garden—to adapt to our own family's lifestyle. Try to live with the existing garden for the first year before making any radical changes. There may be reasons for certain elements, such as a hedge grown high to protect the garden from strong winds. You may find plants, unfamiliar to you, which

Practical Points

- Ensure any changes in level are comfortable and easily negotiable. Often the transition from interior to exterior is too abrupt. The treads of exterior steps should be wider and the risers shallower, about 10 cm (4 in.), than internal stairs because the surrounding landscape is also on a more generous scale.

Areas next to house walls are often filled with building rubble and rubbish.

Exterior steps should be wider and the risers shallower than internal staircases, to allow you to walk comfortably through the garden.

- Consider the suitability of each part of the space for its intended use. For instance, areas adjacent to house walls are generally dry because they are shielded from rain by overhanging eaves and are also often backfilled with rubble. This situation will not support healthy plant life unless improved.

- The terrace is a critical feature, and should have sun at the times you and your family are likely to use it. Depending on the aspect of your house, this may mean the terrace should be placed at the far end of the garden. How it is accessed from the house will also be a consideration.

- Views are also relevant. Use a camera to record the panorama that will be seen from your property. If possible, try to angle your house so that you make the most of good views. There may well be nearby buildings that need to be concealed and strategic planting can often achieve this.

- Ornamental pools usually need to be placed in a sunny location where their mirror-like reflections will be appreciated, and where the water will reflect light as well as nearby objects. In a shady area where light is not reflected, the effect can be similar to a large puddle.

  Safety is paramount—water is something that children find irresistible and they have been known to drown in even the shallowest of pools. If you must mix children and water, choose a feature that doesn't include any standing water, for example a wall-mounted or bubble fountain.

perform well at a particular time of year; these can be either retained in situ or replanted elsewhere. Paths, lawns and borders or ponds may not be where you want them, but these can also be adapted or altered once you have decided how to use the garden.

An overgrown garden requires additional caution. Begin by removing any dead trees, taking them out by the roots so that the space can be replanted. If the roots are embedded, a tree surgeon can provide a stump grinder, which will rotate within the stump and quickly remove it. Overgrown plants can gradually be reshaped or removed and may reveal paths or steps previously hidden. Diseased or straggly plants may be brought back to vigour by pruning or remedial care. The first year in a new garden is always an interesting learning curve but does require patience.

If the garden is of historical interest, you may wish to restore it to its original state by researching the designer or landscapers and locating the original plans. Alternatively, the old layout can be adapted to a more modern and easily maintained scheme.

Legal considerations should also be taken into account. These can vary from tree preservation orders (TPOs), which ban the felling of trees, to the maximum heights for fences, walls and hedges, to stop them interfering with your neighbour's right to light. Underground services such as drains and cables may be disrupted by heavy machinery or careless workmanship. The law varies in different countries, so, if in any doubt, check with your local authority.

Assessing your Resources

The amount of available space in a garden will vary enormously—but it is often more difficult to implement improvements successfully in tiny gardens than in larger ones where the odd mistake goes unnoticed. In small gardens, there is less room for error and every plant must perform well to earn its keep. Each area—terrace, lawn or border—must be useful and visually pleasing and should work with other areas in the garden to form an integrated space.

Before planning out any changes, make sure that any required resources are achievable. Try to work out a budget for your garden so that you can plan ahead both for developing the garden and for maintenance: consider both financial and labour costs for all elements of your plan. Spend time working out what labour and machinery is needed—initially, it may be better to employ a reliable contractor who knows his job and who has his own machinery, rather than relying on the goodwill of unskilled family or friends and investing in machines and tools that need regular servicing. Equally, money can be wasted on impulse purchases of plants if they are unsuited to your location.

In most gardens, labour is usually in short supply and the initial enthusiasm of family or friends may quickly wear thin. Before your own enthusiasm takes over, consider the vital factor of routine maintenance. Who is going to look after the garden? Even a small plot can take up a surprising amount of time and skilled labour is now hard to find. Ignore this factor and your garden could quickly become a chore instead of a pleasure.

Basically, the different garden spaces can be classified according to the level of maintenance they require (see below). Divide all this up into hours of labour and you will have a more realistic idea of the amount of work involved and who can do it. Sometimes a contractor can be relied upon to cut the lawns and hedges, often saving you hours of regular maintenance, and leaving you free to carry out more creative tasks.

Hard landscaping

This includes all places where inert materials are used. Good-quality hard-landscaping materials are one of the more costly items in making a garden, yet apart from regular sweeping, weeding or spraying they take little looking after.

If you do not have the resources to maintain the entire garden, then consider instead leaving some areas as rough grass until you come to terms with what you have and what you want to do in the future.

Lawns and areas of grass

Although it needs cutting, grass is a relatively inexpensive commodity in the garden. However, a well-tended lawn demands commitment. Grass begins to grow early in the growing season, and from spring onwards it will need mowing once or twice per week, and the lawn edges will need trimming every two or three weeks. The lawn will also require remedial care in spring and autumn. Meadows and areas of longer grass are not as time-consuming, but still need cutting at least twice per year; the cut grass then must be disposed of or added to the compost heap.

Boundary and internal hedges

Depending on how rapidly the hedging plants grow, these will need cutting several times a year. In most cases, you will need ladders and planks, or to stand on a special platform ladder to reach the tops. The hedge prunings usually are taken to the bonfire, shredded or recycled. Some hedging plants, such as *Ligustrum* (privet) grow faster than others, so need cutting more frequently.

Borders or flowerbeds

Caring for beds and borders is the most time-consuming part of gardening. To maintain healthy plants and weed-free soil, most borders need working over every month during the growing season (on average, seven months long). There are other tasks too, such as staking tall plants or tying in wall plants or climbers.

Water features

Unless the water feature is very simple, such as a wall spout or mask, it can be difficult to maintain. Levels may need to be topped up, chemicals may be needed to keep the water clear of algae and free from mosquitoes and, especially in autumn, fallen leaves may need to be removed from filters.

Garden Analysis

Most gardens are a combination of good and bad points. Some can be altered, but other key factors maybe impossible to change. During the first year, you will gradually get to know the advantages and limitations of the local:

- climate and weather
- aspect
- soil.

Climate and weather

This will be a major influence on how the garden is used and what plants can be grown. Individual and regional climates vary considerably, within as well as between countries. Rainfall will differ according to locality. Topography, altitude, exposure and the surrounding landform also govern the local climate. Coastal areas are affected by salt spray but have a better quality of light, and industrial areas often suffer air pollution.

In the temperate, maritime climate of Britain, north is colder than the south and the west wetter and warmer than the east, but the country suffers relatively few seasonal extremes of cold or hot weather. Hardy plants thrive over all the country, and half-hardy or even tender plants can remain outdoors over winter in sheltered areas.

surroundings—for example, sheltering or overshadowing hedges and buildings or the open and exposed areas. Cold air flows downhill and becomes trapped at the bottom, so can cause a frost pocket, which will remain cold until it is dispersed by wind or sun.

Wind is often the most damaging aspect of a local climate. It may affect how the garden is used and what can be grown in it. The direction of the prevailing wind may seem obvious, but can change in different parts of the garden. Surrounding buildings or openings between buildings can cause wind tunnels, which funnel and strengthen the winds, resulting in broken branches and flattened or scorched plants. The cold, drying effect of wind can inhibit plant growth.

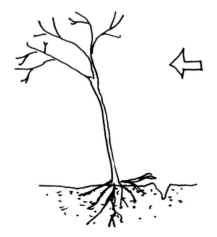
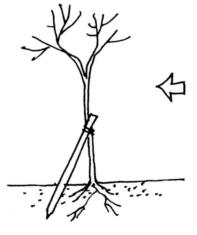

The prevailing wind and lack of protection has rocked this young tree (**left**) until its roots have been dislodged. It can happen to both bare-rooted and container-grown shrubs and trees. Obviously, the roots should be well heeled in at planting, but proper staking helps (**right**). However, in windy sites, some form of protective wind screening will also be needed.

In the United States, as in some other countries, the climate varies much more from region to region, and from season to season, than in Britain. American gardeners rely on the hardiness-zone system (see pages 365–366) to judge which plants may be grown in their zone or locality.

Certain areas of the garden will have their own microclimates created by the immediate

If a garden is affected by wind, the first priority should be to create some shelter. A hedge allows wind to filter through it while reducing its velocity. A wall or fence will interrupt the wind but may cause violent eddying on the leeward side. Hedges take time to grow to a reasonably protective height. If the site is very windy, it may be worth considering putting in a fence with a hedge planted on the leeward side. The fence will protect the hedge while it is becoming established and also help avoid "wind rock". When wind rocks a stem, it loosens its roots, which is often the cause of plants failing to establish quickly. Fences tend to rot at the base (they have a life span of about 10 years), so hedges are a better long-term solution. Walls are expensive to construct and can often appear forbidding, particularly in a rural situation.

Rainfall and drainage will also affect how you use your garden. A high rainfall will encourage lush plant growth whereas, unless suitable plants are chosen, low rainfall may mean installing a drip irrigation system, but local soil conditions, drainage and topography will in turn affect this. Sloping sites drain naturally but, on flat sites, a cross fall or sloping drainage channel may be needed to carry the water away and to avoid puddling.

Aspect

Every garden is affected by its aspect, or orientation—the amount of sun it gets will depend upon whether it faces north, south, east or west. Aspect, light and shade are interrelated and should be assessed before any changes are made to the garden. Use a compass or check on local maps to determine its exact orientation. In the northern hemisphere, a south- or southwest-facing garden is generally considered the best aspect for a garden.

However, provided there is enough light, many plants will thrive in a northerly aspect, particularly early-flowering, scented semi-woodlanders, which are such an asset early in the year. It is also easier to maintain year-round interest in shady areas, so this aspect may actually be preferable. In relentlessly hot countries, some shade may be necessary, so the better aspect for the garden may be northwest. In each circumstance, the choice of plants will be limited to what can survive the climate.

Many plants prefer some sunshine, so sunny areas should be fully exploited. Walls, whether supporting or freestanding, trap the sun's energy and allow more

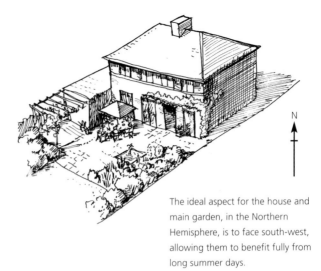

The ideal aspect for the house and main garden, in the Northern Hemisphere, is to face south-west, allowing them to benefit fully from long summer days.

tender climbers, shrubs and other plants to be grown against them. The soil at the base of walls tends to be dry, so either include some method of irrigation or use Mediterranean plants which do not need so much water, planted some distance, say 1 m (3 ft.), from the wall.

Certain areas of the garden will have their own microclimates created by the immediate surroundings, such a sheltered spot or suntrap close to hedges and walls.

It is equally important to be aware of shady areas, particularly in town gardens overshadowed by tall buildings or overhanging trees. Little will grow in dense shade, especially if it is caused by a tree with a heavy canopy, such as the horse chestnut (*Aesculus hippocastanum*), whose roots use up the moisture in the soil beneath. Dappled shade, where light filters through trees or tall shrubs, can be an advantage—it provides variety and welcome relief from bright sunshine and allows you to grow plants that prefer these conditions.

Little will grow in dense shade, especially if this is caused by a tree with a heavy canopy, for example the horse chestnut (*Aesculus hippocastanum*).

The Garden Soil

Most of the soil in a garden is millions of years old and composed of ground-up rock and minerals. Only the rotting remains of organic matter (plants and animals), or what may have been added by the gardener, are recognized as "new" material.

The volume of soil in all but the smallest garden is so vast that you can expect to change or manipulate only the very surface, and then only temporarily. Soils vary enormously from place to place, even in different parts of the same garden. The soil composition will affect which plants will thrive in your garden, and which will not, although most soils in good condition (in "good heart") will support many plants, apart from those with a definite preference for acidic or alkaline conditions. It

therefore pays to find out as much as you can about your soil and its inherent limitations. You can then garden *with* it and not *against* it—deciding which plants to (or not to) grow and what you might do in order to extend the range of plants in the garden or make cultivation easier.

To do this, find a spot where you think the surface soil is fairly typical of the entire garden. Dig out a small sample with a trowel and spread it out on a bench. You are likely to find that it is a mixture of stones, sand or grit, silt, decaying organic matter, and perhaps some clay. To see the particles in greater detail, use a magnifying glass.

Stones

The largest particles in your sample are likely to be stones—ranging from some perhaps quite large stones right down to others only a few millimeters across. Rounded stones indicate that they may have once originated from a riverbed, and sharp, angular ones usually derive from local rocks. Chalk is composed of very finely ground stone so closely compacted together that there is little or no aeration nor any micro-organisms to support plant life. Excavated profiles of chalk with only a thin layer of topsoil may sometimes be seen where land has been cut through for roads or other earthworks.

Some soils appear to contain very few stones while others have many. Stony soil is often well drained and therefore quite dry, although there are always exceptions. A high proportion of stones may mean less of everything else and since they provide little or no nutrition for plants, stony soils are often "poor", or lacking in nutrients. In such a case, certain additives, especially organic matter and nutrients, are likely to improve plant growth significantly.

Sand

As you might be able to see through the magnifying glass, sand is just a collection of tiny stones or grains of rock that, like stones, tend to be rounded or angular (the latter produces "sharp sand"). Soil containing a high proportion of sand often displays the same qualities as stony soil and can therefore benefit from the same additives.

Silt

Silt could be regarded as a very fine grade of sand. Its individual particles are barely recognizable with a magnifying glass; it is almost dust-like and, if you were to rub some moist silt between your thumb and forefinger, it would feel pasty, not gritty or "plastic". The particles can pack together quite densely, particularly on the soil's surface, resulting in poor drainage. While the space between the particles is full of moisture, there will be very little air—this means that root growth and the general health of some plants could be poor, especially during cold, wet winters. Some improvement might be gained from a generous quantity of sharp sand, although its effect is likely to be very localized. Like sand, silt is often nutritionally poor and plants growing in very silty soils respond well to the addition of organic matter and nutrients.

Chalk

Chalk may be recognized as an alkaline (limey) and thin soil which will soak up and leach away large quantities of water and nutrients. It is too hard to allow the roots of plants to penetrate through to access any moisture. A fine and often superficial layer of topsoil is all that is available to maintain healthy plant life. Break up the soil to a depth of about 60 cm (2 ft.), work in plenty of well-rotted compost and organic matter and, even if the soil has a high pH value, many plants should grow well.

Clay

Clay is quite different from the other main components of soil. No longer are the particles rounded or angular, but flat. They are often referred to as platelets. If a soil sample contains a high proportion of clay, it will smear to a shine and feel very smooth and plastic—not pasty. Clay does often have silt mixed into it, but even if it does not smear to a shine, it may be sticky. The platelets trap

moisture in the same way as sheets of glass often do when stacked on top of one another. They are difficult to pull apart (making them seem sticky), but they slide across one another very easily (making wet clay quite slippery). Clay platelets are generally too small to see individually through a magnifying glass.

Unlike chalk, the most important property of clay from a plant's point of view is its ability to attract and hold on to a wide range of nutrients, due partly to the relatively large surface area of each platelet. This means that soils rich in clay are seldom poor. They can, however, bake rock-hard in summer and become wet and sticky in winter, making cultivation quite difficult. Clay may also be poorly drained.

Improving Clay

The addition of garden lime (calcium hydroxide) or gypsum (calcium sulphate) can break up clay by a process called flocculation, whereby the tiny platelets, or at least large groups of them, are encouraged to form larger granules. This causes large lumps of clay to crumble and become easier to cultivate.

If lime or gypsum is sprinkled generously over recently dug, lumpy clay in the autumn, the result can be quite dramatic by spring. Unfortunately, this improvement may last only a year or so and not penetrate very deeply. It does, however, provide a valuable opportunity to create a tilth—an evenly raked bed of crumbly soil several centimetres or inches deep—into which materials such as fertilizers and organic matter can be incorporated.

A tilth also makes it possible to sow seeds or put in small plants. The addition of lime may, however, raise the soil pH levels, making it, at least temporarily, more alkaline (see "Soil pH", page 28).

Test your Soil Type

- Using a trowel, take some soil from 7–15 cm (3–6 in.) below the surface; the lighter the soil, the deeper the hole should be because plants will put their roots down farther in lighter soil.
- Squeeze the excavated soil in the palm of your hand.
- If the soil sticks together in one sticky lump, it is clay.
- If the soil holds together fairly well but is not sticky and shiny, it is loam. Silty loam may feel smooth or soapy; sandy loam slightly more gritty.

To assess the structure of the soil, squeeze a sample from the garden in the palm of your hand.

- If the soil falls apart into gritty crumbs, it is sandy.
- If soil is loose and has white stones in it, it is chalky.

Organic matter

On close examination of your soil sample, you may find partially decayed leaves and other plant debris as well as insects or other small animals. This is humus: it is often present on, or close to, the surface of most soils. In woodland, there is frequently a deep carpet of humus, whereas there could be very little on stony soils. Humus is generally dark in colour and soft to the touch. While it can provide plants with some nutrients (especially nitrogen), its main function is to hold moisture and air in the soil like a sponge, and therefore stimulate root development.

Humus and other organic matter, such as peat, compost, coco fibre or coir, manure, and so on, make up the least stable component in garden soil. In the presence of air, it continues to decompose to virtually nothing, thanks to the action of bacteria. The process does however release valuable nitrogen needed for plant growth (see "Nutrients", page 29).

Organic matter in its various forms can be added to all soils. If incorporated deeply into light, sandy soils, it will act as a reservoir of moisture during drought. It also helps to keep clay separated after the initial flocculation.

Structure of the Soil

The general composition of soil is called the structure, or profile. This describes the depth of the topsoil as well as the type of subsoil, which can have a direct bearing on how well plants grow. In simple terms, the structure is the binding together of the various solid particles with organic matter to form soil crumbs. Generally, the darker the soil the richer it is and the better its structure. Although crucial to plant growth, the actual structure of the soil is often overlooked. To examine your garden's soil structure, dig a fairly deep, clean-sided hole, about 30 cm (12 in.) square, in a part of the garden that has not been disturbed or cultivated in recent years.

You may see a change in colour from top to bottom of the wall of the pit, with the top portion appearing darker than the rest. This is because the top zone contains most of the organic matter. As you go deeper, the colour changes and becomes lighter; this is the subsoil. (On clay soil, you might not see such a clear contrast.)

In areas of poor drainage, the subsoil may smell stagnant and appear to be saturated. This may affect the condition of the topsoil and will need addressing

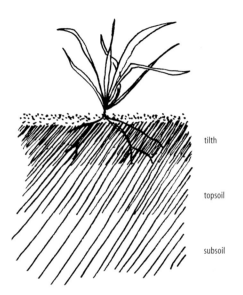

tilth

topsoil

subsoil

will also gradually increase the depth of topsoil and help to improve the vigour of plant growth. This is not as important for trees and shrubs (most of which have relatively deep, coarse roots) as it is for herbaceous plants, annuals and vegetables, especially root crops like carrots and parsnips.

Soil Texture

Most soils are a mixture of all the components discussed above. Those that appear to have a bit of everything are often called loam although, strictly speaking, this term describes soil that occurs under a crop of field grass where the grass roots help to ensure a crumbly texture. Soils with a predominance of clay—but not to the exclusion of everything else—are referred to as heavy, or clayey, loam. Soils with a good deal of sand or silt would be referred to as sandy, or silty, loams.

The most desirable soil for a wide range of plants is a medium (not heavy or light) loam, which often has a good friable (crumbly) texture. Good potting and seed composts are based on sterilized medium loam.

The texture of the soil in a recently acquired garden may well depend on how the garden has been maintained in the past. If the beds and borders have been regularly dug or forked over, air and water will percolate through, resulting in a lighter soil. If the soil has been rarely worked, the soil may be less easy to dig as well as prone to panning or hardening. Such soil may not absorb much air and water and will not therefore be hospitable to the worms and insects that keep soil open and healthy.

because, although plants get most of their nutrients from the topsoil, many will need to grow roots much deeper for moisture and anchorage. The area may have a high water table, in which case the only solution is to install a drainage system or incorporate grit or rubble—deep digging or aerating may only cause more water to fill the worked-over areas.

The structure can be improved—working in plenty of peat, peat substitute, compost, or well-rotted manure will help break up a heavy clay soil. Conversely, in sandy soil, it will hold the coarse particles together so that they better retain moisture. Incorporating humus and compost into the surface of the soil (by digging or using a mechanical rotavator)

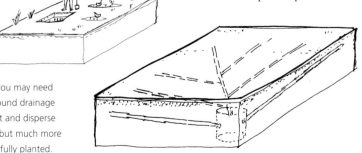

If the soil is very poorly drained, you may need to consider installing an underground drainage system with a soakaway to collect and disperse the drained water. It is a big job, but much more difficult to do once the garden is fully planted.

Even before you consider redesigning any part of the garden, much can be done to improve the soil texture by taking steps to correct any deficiencies, such as adding grit to lighten heavy soils or well-rotted manure to improve soil structure. Gradually, a marked improvement will be noticeable. When undertaking renovations to a large, neglected garden, it is not unusual to spend the first year removing weeds and the second year improving the soil texture, and not replanting until the third year.

Soil pH

Soils are acid, neutral or alkaline and this can have a direct bearing on how successfully plants grow. For example, plants like rhododendrons, azaleas and *Pieris*, which all belong to the Ericaceae family, much prefer acid soil and may eventually die if the soil is too alkaline. On the other hand, *Dianthus* (pinks and carnations) and *Brassica* crops, such as Brussels sprouts and cabbages, do best in neutral or slightly alkaline soils. Cabbages become susceptible to a disease called club root if the soil is too acidic.

The degree of acidity or alkalinity is called the pH scale. For garden soils, this ranges from about 5 (very acidic) through neutral (7) to about 8 (very alkaline). Although peaty soil is nearly always acid and chalky soil is usually alkaline, most other soils could be either; often the only visible clue is gained by noting the types of plants which seem to be thriving, particularly native plants. Wild clematis and *Viburnum opulus* (Guelder rose) usually indicate an alkaline soil, whereas extensive areas of *Rhododendron ponticum* and *Pteridium aquilinum* (bracken) usually indicate acid soil.

Measuring pH

Measuring the acidity or alkalinity of your soil involves taking several samples from around the garden and at different depths; the samples can then be tested in two different ways.

The first involves the use of a special soil-testing kit, which contains a test tube, a powdered chemical (barium sulphate) and a coloured indicator chart. For this only a small amount of soil, equivalent to one or two tablespoonfuls, is needed for testing. Remove the soil with a trowel, and put each soil sample into a separate plastic bag, marking which area the soil came from.

Allow the soil samples to dry out naturally before testing according to the instructions supplied with the kit. Usually, this entails adding a sample of soil and some distilled water to the chemical in the test tube, to produce a coloured liquid. The colour can

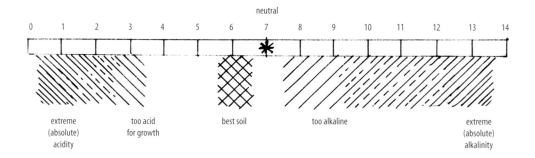

Plants will grow in soils ranging from pH 4 (acid) to 8 (alkaline). The widest range of plants thrive in pH 5.7–6.7; they will not grow in soils with a pH of less than 4 or higher than 8.

then be matched to the indicator chart, to estimate the pH of the soil sample.

A second technique uses a pH meter: a small piece of equipment that has a probe and a calibrated dial. When the probe is inserted into a mixture of soil and distilled water, a needle on the dial instantly indicates the soil pH.

There are also now available soil pH meters, which are simply stuck in the ground, at your predetermined points. The meter needle registers extremes from neutral to give a pH reading—note down each reading accordingly.

Changing the soil pH

It is relatively easy to make soil more alkaline (raise its pH) by adding lime (calcium hydroxide), usually in the autumn when the ground is devoid of flowers and vegetables. It is less straightforward to make a soil more acidic. The addition of manure helps, and it is possible to add sulphur, but calculating the amount of sulphur can be difficult. It is therefore better to try to garden within the natural limitations of your soil.

Nutrients

Plants need a whole range of mineral nutrients to sustain healthy growth. While most soils do contain a reasonable balance of minerals, a soil may be deficient in some of them, which then affects the plants' growth and performance. It therefore helps to know a little about the most significant of these nutrients, so that you can identify deficiencies and put them right in order to improve performance. These deficiencies are often not evident until plants are established, when unhealthy growth or poor performance soon indicate that all is not well.

There are kits available and, better still, laboratories that offer a soil-testing service, giving a detailed analysis of the nutrient content of soil samples. You can also look for symptoms that indicate some deficiencies. This section covers the most common

nutrients, symptoms of their deficiency, as well as organic and inorganic methods of improving the nutrient levels.

If necessary, extra amounts of nutrients can be applied to the soil in two main types of fertilizer:

- Organic: natural, not man-made, substances or products—less potent and much less likely to damage plants if overdosed. An example of a typical organic fertilizer is one made from seaweed.

- Inorganic: man-made and often much more potent, so much so that, if used carelessly, they can burn or even kill plants. Compound fertilizers are mainly inorganic and contain a whole range of nutrients; sometimes one nutrient comprises a higher percentage of the product than the rest. This is the most common (and often the safest) way of administering inorganic fertilizers.

Essential Plant Nutrients

The most common nutrients required by plants are:
- Calcium (Ca)
- Magnesium (Mg)
- Nitrogen (N)
- Phosphorus (P)
- Potassium (Potash) (K)
- Sulphur (S)

A whole range of lesser, "trace" elements are needed, including:
- Boron (B)
- Chlorine (Cl)
- Copper (Cu)
- Iron (Fe)
- Manganese (Mn)
- Molybdenum (Mo)
- Zinc (Zn)

Nitrogen

The nutrient nitrogen is largely responsible for the vigour and size of leaves and stems. In nature, plants get most of their nitrogen from decaying vegetation, animals, and manure. Fresh manure may be rich in uric acid, which is a potent form of nitrogen, although it can easily burn plant tissue; this is why any manure applied in the garden should be well rotted, about two to three years old. All these organic forms of nitrogen have first to be broken down by nitrifying bacteria before a plant is able to use them.

Many "leguminous" plants (peas, beans, clover etc.) are able, with help from bacteria, to fix gaseous nitrogen in special nodules on their roots. Soil in which these crops have recently been grown can therefore become quite rich in nitrogen.

The amount of nitrogen derived from rotting organic matter may not be sufficient. In well-drained, sandy soils, a nitrogen deficiency can soon develop and will need correcting. This can be especially important in lawn cultivation or in the production of leafy vegetables such as cabbages and lettuces.

While nitrogen can be applied on its own (often with dramatic results), it is usually better given in conjunction with some potash, since a plant needs a balance of the two. Here is a good case for the use of a compound fertilizer, containing a relatively high proportion of nitrogen. Too much nitrogen and a plant may develop very lush, soft foliage and stems, which can become susceptible to fungal infections and physical and frost damage. An excess of nitrogen can also inhibit production of flowers and fruit.

On the other hand, if there is too little nitrogen available, a plant may be rather stunted with shorter internodes, harder stems and smaller leaves. If container-grown plants are starved of nitrogen, they often take nutrients from their oldest leaves in order to keep growing. These older leaves then turn brown and fall off.

Nitrogen Fertilizers

Nitrogen is typically added in these forms. Extra-strong nitrogen is normally applied only during spring and summer, seldom in autumn and rarely in winter.

- Organic: hoof and horn or dried blood, either of which will be broken down into available nitrogen after a week or two. Hoof and horn is useful on lawns, although mowing should be delayed until the particles have been washed in.
- Inorganic: sulphate of ammonia (ammonium sulphate) is one of the most common. Although it can produce dramatic results within one week, it does burn soft tissue (for example blades of grass). It must therefore be used carefully and sparingly.
- Compound (mostly inorganic): this is a relatively safe way of giving a plant inorganic nitrogen since it will contain a mixture of several important elements that can work together to produce a well-balanced response. Stick to the recommendations on the packet to avoid overdosing. Some compound products are developed to be especially suited to foliage pot plants, leafy vegetables and for lawns during spring or summer. An analysis of contents listed on the packet will reveal a higher percentage of nitrogen than any other ingredient. When examining compound fertilizers in a local garden centre, see if you can identify one that is high in nitrogen.

Phosphates

Phosphorous compounds (phosphates) are especially important for the development of vigorous seedlings and for strong root growth and are therefore particularly vital for root vegetables. Lawns can be given extra phosphates in the autumn to encourage deeper rooting. Any seedbed, whether it is for flowers, vegetables or grass, should always have a good supply of phosphates.

Symptoms of a phosphorus deficiency may not always be obvious but can include weak or shallow roots, low resistance to drought (in some lawns), a poor response to other fertilizers (because of feeble roots) and disappointing growth in seedlings.

Phosphorous Fertilizers

Phosphate is typically added in these forms.
- Organic: bone- or fishmeal, raked into a seedbed a week or so before seed sowing. It is also traditional to sprinkle some around the roots at planting time, although how much good this does is debatable. Moist peat, a peat substitute or humus would probably be more successful in stimulating new root growth in this case.
- Inorganic: superphosphate (or triple superphosphate) can be raked into any seedbed a week or so before seed sowing. Despite being inorganic, superphosphate is reasonably benign and is unlikely to cause damage. It can be mixed with grass seed to encourage rapid results when repairing worn patches of lawn.

Potassium

Potassium, or potash, works in conjunction with nitrogen to produce well-balanced growth of leaves and stems but, in particular, influences production of flowers and fruit. Plants that fail to flower properly can sometimes be encouraged to do so by the addition of potash. A potash deficiency is often characterized by scorched leaf margins and perhaps a reddish tint in the leaves. Potash is highly soluble, so well-drained, sandy soils can often be deficient.

Potassium Fertilizers

Potash is typically added in these forms:
- Organic: generous amounts of wood ash or fertilizers based on seaweed.
- Inorganic: potassium sulphate (sulphate of potash), but it is seldom used on its own.
- Compound fertilizers: those which have a higher percentage of potash than other nutrients are the most reliable way of administering potash and maintaining a good balance with nitrogen. There are many such products available which claim to boost flower and fruit production, for example tomato plant food.

Trace elements

While all trace elements are important for sustained plant growth, some are more important than others. Two in particular, magnesium and iron, can have a dramatic effect on the growth of certain plants if they are suffering from a deficiency. Some plants have difficulty in taking up certain trace elements if the soil pH is too high or if there is a lot of free lime in the soil.

The most striking symptom is lime-induced chlorosis that shows as a very distinct yellowing between the leaf veins. Tomatoes, roses, and magnolias are a few common examples that can suffer from chlorosis, often because soil conditions are preventing them from absorbing magnesium. Watering a dilute solution of magnesium sulphate (Epsom salts) into the soil sometimes helps.

A more direct way is to spray a very dilute solution of specially formulated foliar feed, which contains a whole range of trace elements, on to the leaves—preferably not in strong sunlight. It is important to avoid a strong concentration: little and often is the safest approach; apply it only on relatively soft, and therefore absorbent, leaves.

A deficiency of iron often shows as a general yellowing of leaves, especially on young leaves. Again, a compound foliar feed can help. In the case of lawns, a direct application of iron sulphate can dramatically "green up" a pale lawn. It is used mainly in the spring and summer, but if it is not applied sparingly enough and not watered in straightaway, it will burn the grass.

Testing your Soil

Even in a small garden, the soil pH, structure, or even soil type may vary. Mark out points in the parts of your garden where you may grow plants, such as in proposed borders, beside house walls or underneath trees. Later you will be able to mark these on your garden plan and the readings will indicate the type of plants that can be grown successfully.

- Use the hand-squeeze test to tell if the soil is sandy, silty, chalky, loamy or clay.
- Gauge the pH (acidity or alkalinity) with a soil-testing kit or soil pH meter.
- Investigate the soil structure by digging out a hole to examine the soil profile.
- Look for evidence of nutrient deficiencies in the existing plants, such as:

Iron—yellowing between leaf veins, especially on younger growth.

Magnesium—yellow or brown patches around margins and between veins of leaves.

Nitrogen—pale leaves and generally unhealthy growth.

Phosphate—poor root development and stunted growth.

Potash—poor flowering, fruiting and berrying; tendency to frost or general winter damage.

Other nutrients—generally poor growth; symptoms may indicate a deficiency of a particular nutrient.

Alternatively, use a good soil testing kit or send your soil samples to a soil-testing laboratory.

Making a Plan of the Garden

Although you may think you know your garden well, it is always best to work to a simply drawn plan before making major changes. A garden is almost bound to appear different on paper to how it looks with the naked eye because perspective distorts the angles and proportions in the garden when you look at it. You can learn a great deal about your garden while measuring up for and drawing a plan.

Drawing up a simple plan does not need to be a complex procedure but will depend on the current state of the garden. Most sites can be measured fairly easily with a minimum of equipment, although overgrown, uneven or sloping sites with awkward angles will obviously pose some difficulties. A starting point could be an architect's plan of the house or a survey from the government or local authority showing the extent of the property. In towns, even a street map can be a useful beginning.

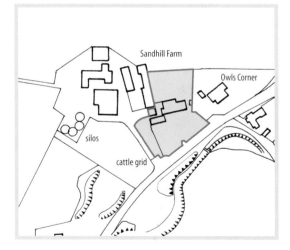

A survey or map of your property makes a useful reference for drawing up an accurate plan.

Equipment Needed to Draw Up a Plan

- Two 30 m (100 ft.) measuring tapes
- 1.8 m (6 ft.) flexible metal tape
- Metal skewer (for fixing tape in ground)
- Ball of smooth, fairly thick string (for setting out any lines too long for the tape measure)
- Wooden pegs or garden canes (to drive into ground to mark specific points)
- Small spirit level
- Clipboard
- A4, A3 or 8.5 x 11 in. sheets of paper (graph paper is helpful), depending on size of garden
- Pencils and eraser
- Coloured, felt tip pens
- Scale rule, 1:50 or 1:100, or imperial equivalent, to coordinate with the measuring system you use
- Compasses to mark out triangulation dimensions

Drawing Up a Rough Plan

Begin by going into the garden and, using a clip board and paper, draw a rough plan, showing the outline of the house and the boundary of the garden. If the site is large or if the house divides the garden into front and rear gardens, draw up an outline plan for each area.

Mark up your measurements on this rough plan and try to keep proportions and relative positions of one element to another fairly accurate. Fixed features such as doors, windows and gates should be relevant to the position and width of borders, paths and lawns, so they also need to be shown on this plan.

The first measurement

To start off, look at your rough outline plan and choose the longest unobstructed line from which all or most of the area can be seen—known as the base-line. Often this will be along the front or rear of the

house, and will extend to the boundary (fence, wall or hedge) on either side. Use pegs, garden canes, a skewer or even a brick to secure your measuring tape at one end of your baseline. Make sure it does not sag or twist and stretch it across in a straight line to the other end of your proposed baseline. Secure it at this end too. Walk back to the beginning of the tape.

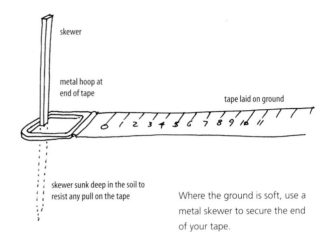

skewer

metal hoop at end of tape

tape laid on ground

skewer sunk deep in the soil to resist any pull on the tape

Where the ground is soft, use a metal skewer to secure the end of your tape.

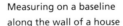

Measuring on a baseline along the wall of a house

secure end of tape with a brick or skewer

brick keeps tape taut while you are measuring

From the start point, read off the measurement on the tape at each point that corresponds to features such as doors, corners of the house, bay windows, French windows etc. These measurements are the "running dimensions". Enter them on your rough plan. Then use your small, rigid tape to measure how far out any of these features project and also mark these on your plan. Having entered all your baseline

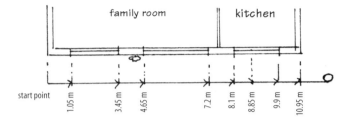

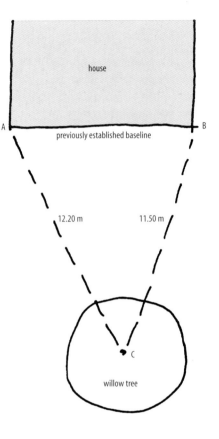

Record the positions of such features as doors and windows and the length of the wall, by reading off the running dimensions.

measurements on your rough plan, label the baseline. The measuring tape can then be rewound.

When entering measurements, always try to write the figures the same way up, running along the line to which they refer. They will then be much easier to decipher later.

Measuring from house to boundary

Unless your garden is small, square or rectangular, the simplest way of measuring the boundary is by a method called triangulation. This means that you use your measured baseline and tapes to form a precise triangle.

Fix the end of your measuring tape to the start point of the baseline, or point A. Keep the tape straight and taut and stretch it out to the farthest point of your triangle (say a corner of the garden). Read off the measurement and label it A–C on your rough plan. Next, measure from the end of your baseline (point B) to point C as before. Label this measurement B–C.

You can use triangulation to measure the relative position to the baseline of many elements in the garden. Make sure that you plot everything you can, such as boundary corners, existing trees, corners of beds, paths or buildings, even if it means that your rough plan will be divided into a series of interlocking triangles. Work this out carefully on your rough plan because it is very annoying to find out later that you have missed out a vital side of a triangle.

Locating a tree by triangulation
We have used a tree as an example here, but the feature to be located could be anything on the site, from a boundary corner to a swing pole. To take a triangulation, you need to measure from two fixed, or previously located, points on an established baseline. Measure the distance between point A and point C (the tree), and then the distance between point B and point C. Record these measurements on your rough plan, as shown.

Position of random features

Another surveying method may be necessary to measure the position and shape of island beds or any feature that cannot be located by triangulation from the baseline. These measurements are taken by "offsets", which are measurements taken at right angles from a baseline. With pegs or canes, mark out regular intervals along your baseline. Check the right angle by using any rectangular object such as a box or piece of cardboard to fix your flexible metal tape

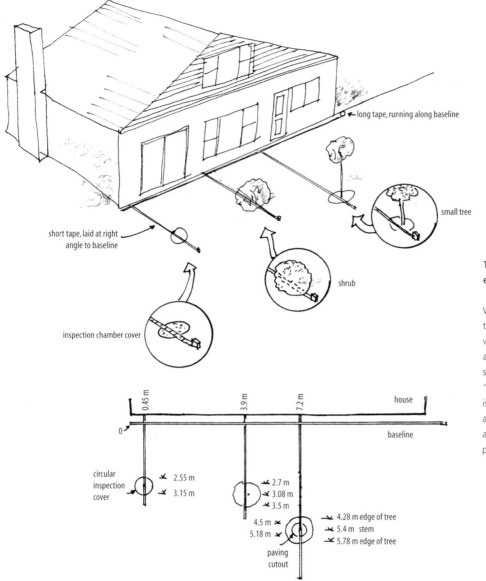

long tape, running along baseline

small tree

short tape, laid at right
angle to baseline

shrub

inspection chamber cover

**Taking offsets to measure
elements close to the house wall**

When taking an offset measurement,
the long tape, laid against the house
wall, is used to measure how far
along the item occurs. The rigid,
short tape is used to measure the
"offset", or how far out the element
is from the baseline. Manhole covers
are particularly important to locate
accurately—they will often affect
paving patterns around the house.

0.45 m   3.9 m   7.2 m   house

0   baseline

circular
inspection   2.55 m
cover   3.15 m

2.7 m
3.08 m
3.5 m

4.5 m   4.28 m edge of tree
5.18 m   5.4 m stem
           5.78 m edge of tree

paving
cutout

or long measuring tape at the baseline. Then run the
tape out to the feature to measure out the offset
dimensions. You can use a triangulation line in the
same way as a baseline to take offset measurements.

Existing buildings can also be plotted from the
baseline or triangulation line, using either

triangulations or offsets. Once you are more familiar
with these two methods, you will be able to decide
which method will be the simplest, quickest and
most accurate. The same approach will apply to other
features—statues, trees, paths or pergolas, or ponds.
Locate them on your rough plan once the main
measurements have been noted.

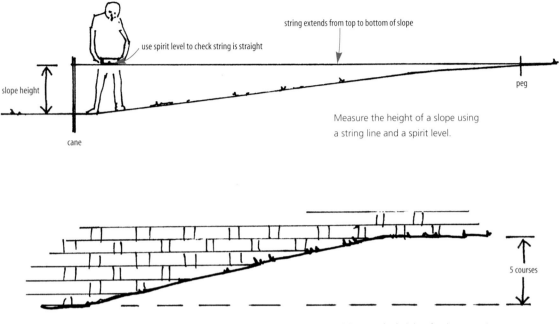

string extends from top to bottom of slope

use spirit level to check string is straight

peg

slope height

Measure the height of a slope using
a string line and a spirit level.

cane

5 courses

Measure the height of a slope running
against a brick wall by counting the
brick courses.

Measuring slopes

If the site slopes, use a ball of string tied to pegs
or canes to set up a level string that runs from the
highest point of the slope to the lowest. Use a spirit
level to check that the line is level and measure it.
If you ran a tape measure along the surface of the
ground on a slope, the measured dimension would
be longer than the actual distance, and the plan
would be inaccurate.

Microclimates and aspect

Once all information is recorded on your rough plan,
walk around the garden and note the immeasurable
aspects, such as the direction and force of the wind,
sunny or wet areas. These too will affect how you
use the garden. Coloured felt-tip pens can be used to
indicate the various spaces, such as blue for a cold
area or yellow for sunny spaces.

Drawing Up an Accurate Plan

Draw the plan up more accurately; if you wish, you
could place your paper over some graph paper so
that the rules show through, to help you draw
straight lines, and provide a grid to help you plot
accurate dimensions using a scale rule. For small
gardens, use a scale of 1:50. That means than all
dimensions will be shown 50 times smaller than in
real life. Larger gardens may be better drawn at
1:100 (100 times smaller than in real life). Using a
scale rule is daunting for some, so if your garden is a
simple shape and not too large, you may be able to
plot it on graph paper using the larger graph squares
as a guide to represent a metre or 90 cm (3 ft.). Most
straight lines can be plotted in this way.

The actual size of the paper—A4 (8½ × 11 in.), A3
(11 × 17 in.) or larger—will depend on the size of
the garden. Try to use paper large enough to make

notes on the right-hand side. Decide on what size of paper is needed by taking the longest dimension: not north to south, or east to west, but across the broadest angle of the site. With your scale rule, measure across an A4 or A3 sheet until you find out what sheet size and scale is most appropriate. You can now transfer all the information from your rough plan and mark it up accurately on the new plan. You will probably need to use your scale rule and compasses to fix your triangulation points accurately.

Remember to note the scale or size to which the plan is drawn, when it was drawn and to indicate the direction of North. On a separate sheet of paper, make a checklist to focus your mind on what you and your family want from the garden. Your simple plan of the existing garden and your requirements should now be complete. It can be photocopied for marking up any further ideas or changes.

Understanding Plant Names

The trouble with "common" plant names is that they are not sufficiently specific. They can describe more than one plant and they are certainly not universal. For example, "quince" is the common name often given to a plant properly called *Chaenomeles speciosa*. It can be grown against a wall, and has pink, red, or white flowers in early spring and small, apple-like fruits in summer. "Quince" is also the common name for *Cydonia oblonga*, a small tree that bears yellowish, pear-shaped fruits. Common names also differ from country to country. Without the Latin name, there is confusion.

Each Latin, or botanical, plant name is unique, describing just one plant. Latin names tell you something about the plant, often including a tiny detail that sets that particular plant apart from the rest. The thought of having to learn hundreds of Latin plant names can be daunting but once learned, these names can be used and understood anywhere in the world.

The Binomial System

Plant naming is based on a binomial system that was devised by Carl Linnaeus back in 1753. Each plant has a name in two parts, a generic and a specific name, denoting the genus and species. They are equivalent, if you like, to your last or surname and first name—in that order. Genus describes a group of closely related plants that share some characteristics. Species defines the specific, individual characteristics of the plant, when reproduced by seed.

Although some publications print the generic name in upper case (capital letters) and the specific name in lower case, the Royal Horticultural Society in Britain insists that the correct form of both is italicized—for example, *Quercus rubra* (red oak). If you are handwriting the Latin name, the convention is to underline it.

For centuries, plant collectors and botanists have gone out into the wild and brought back plants for their beauty, botanical interest, or culinary or pharmaceutical properties. In many cases, the plant has been given a generic name based on the collector's or botanist's own name. The generic name (or genus) *Lewisia* is named after Captain Meriwether Lewis, who found the bitter root plant (*Lewisia rediviva*) in Montana, North America in 1806. The genus *Camellia* is named after George Joseph Kamel, and so on.

A plant's second name—its specific name or species—often describes something about the plant or where it has come from, for example *Camellia japonica* is from Japan. The pond plant *Pontederia cordata* has leaves that are "cordate", or heart-shaped. *Garrya elliptica* has elliptically shaped leaves. Where the context is clear, as in a discussion of various types of oak, the genus name may be abbreviated, as in *Q. cerris* and *Q. robur*.

Variations and cultivars
Some plants have so many variations that they are given a third name. This is their variety or

subspecies. These indicate slight variations that might occur naturally, for example flower colour.

Another part of the name might be the cultivar: this part of the name is always in single quotation marks, starts with a capital letter, and is not italicized. The cultivar name identifies variations in the plant species as a result of cultivation by man. The plant may be found either in the wild as a natural "sport" and then propagated in controlled cultivation, or bred deliberately. Again, cultivar names may tell you more about the plant. *Cotoneaster atropurpureus* 'Variegatus' has pink, green and white variegated leaves. *Hydrangea arborescens* 'Grandiflora' is tree-like (the Latin *arbor* = tree) and has large flowers.

Other divisions and variations
Where the difference between one plant and another is too small to warrant it being called a different cultivar, yet is different enough to attract the interest of keen gardeners, the plants are considered to be in the same "group". An example is the *Acer palmatum* Viride Dissectum Group, which includes several plants that all have similar foliage. Nurseries sometimes sell several of these variations as distinct types to enthusiasts.

Where two species have been cross-pollinated to produce a new specific hybrid, it is shown thus: *Quercus × hispanica* (a cross between *Q. cerris* and *Q. suber*). Where two genera have cross-pollinated, the result is a generic hybrid and is shown as follows: × *Mahoberberis* (*Mahonia × Berberis*).

Most plants, when grafted to one another, keep their own identity even though they are both living off the same root. In rare cases, a true graft hybrid is produced and becomes a mixture of the two as in the case of + *Laburnocytisus* 'Adamii', which was created when *Cytisus* (broom) was grafted on to *Laburnum*. The resulting tree has some yellow laburnum flowers, some purple broom flowers, and others that are a coppery pink.

Many annual and biennial garden flowers (see "Terminology", opposite), as well as vegetables, are constantly being bred from two different species (hybridized) to produce new cultivars. Seed catalogues are full of these. Pure hybrid parents are cross-pollinated to create a new super generation (F1 hybrids) and these in turn may be used to breed yet a further generation (F2), often with amazing results.

There are F1 and F2 antirrhinums, pelargoniums, petunias and others, as well as many F1 vegetables. Some F1 and F2 flowers are double, extra-large, an unusual colour, and possibly dwarf or cascading. The vegetables may be heavier cropping, disease-resistant, larger, or more compact and so on. All this extra breeding has to be paid for and therefore the seeds can be quite expensive. There is little use in saving seed from such plants for the next season since they are unlikely to be "true", that is, the same as the parent plant.

Plant Families

Plant families are groups of different genera (plural of genus), which share the same characteristic, for example a type of flower, fruit, or specialized organs.

- The family Umbelliferae includes the genera *Petroselinum* (parsley), *Daucus* (carrot), and *Foeniculum* (fennel). This is because they all bear flowers in "umbels", which are circular clusters of flowers on stalks around a common centre, like an umbrella.

- The family Leguminosae includes the genera *Genista* (broom), *Laburnum*, *Lathyrus* (pea), and several other plants, all of which have pea-shaped flowers.

There are, however, some families that contain only one genus, like Garryaceae, which has only the genus *Garrya*. The family identification is not usually included when giving the name of a plant.

Terminology

You need to be familiar with these gardening terms to find your way through plant catalogues and the descriptions on plant labels.

- **Hardy annual:** plant that grows, flowers and dies within one growing season (e.g. *Nasturtium*). It is not affected by low temperatures, so can be sown direct into cold ground in spring.
- **Half-hardy annual:** as hardy annual, except it cannot survive very low temperatures or frost (e.g. *Petunia*). As a result, plants usually have to be raised from seeds in the warmth of a greenhouse and cannot be planted out until all danger of frost has passed. Many half-hardies come from warm countries where they may continue to grow and flower for several seasons.
- **Biennial:** plant that takes two years to grow and flower, then dies. The first year is used for growth, with flowering taking place during the second year—for example, common foxglove (*Digitalis purpurea*) and honesty (*Lunaria biennis*).
- **Perennial:** any plant or part of a plant that remains alive during the winter, to continue growing in the following year. The term could also refer to stems or roots.
- **Herbaceous perennial:** in general, plants with perennial roots but annual, often fleshy stems which emerge in spring, grow and flower during the summer, and then die back for winter. Examples include *Delphinium* and *Aster* (Michaelmas daisies). Some herbaceous plants, such as *Bergenia*, *Helleborus* and certain *Euphorbia*, do not die back in winter but remain green all year round.
- **Hybrid:** plant bred from two different species.
- **Shrub:** a plant that builds up, year after year, a system of woody branches without any clear central stem or "apical dominance". The distinction between a large shrub and a small tree is rather blurred, as some large shrubs can grow into trees, like *Sambucus nigra* (common elder).
- **Tree:** as shrub, but with usually one stem and one or more central leaders (dominant shoots) that continue to grow upwards. Some trees have just one main leader (most conifers) while others have several (*Amelanchier*).
- **Conifer:** any shrub or tree that bears cones.
- **Evergreen:** remaining green with foliage throughout the year, like *Ilex* (holly).
- **Semi-evergreen:** some leaves may fall in winter, especially in harsh weather (*Abelia floribunda*).
- **Deciduous:** mainly woody plants that lose their leaves in winter, such as *Philadelphus* (mock orange).

Learning Plant Names

Much of the time you will learn names on your own, and you may find that a specific system will help you. One suggested system is to choose groups of plants with something in common or that can be used for the same purpose. Besides learning the names, this can help you plan your planting for various situations or types of borders. Here are some possible categories to target:

- Groups of plants growing under various conditions—perhaps some you have seen growing successfully against a north-facing wall, in wet, boggy ground, under the canopy of a large tree, or close to the sea.

- Plants that flower in a particular week or month.

- Weeping or fastigiate (narrowly upright) plants.

- Plants suitable for a rock garden.

- Plants that seem to do well in very chalky soil.

Identifying plants

You may have difficulty in finding out the name of a plant in the first place. Apart from asking around, you could take a small piece to a garden centre or botanical garden and see if you can match it up with a named specimen. Never remove pieces from plants without permission. If you are permitted to take away pieces of plants, transport them in a moist plastic bag so that they remain fresh for as long as possible.

Do remember that a garden-centre specimen might show you the leaf shape and flower colour but it probably won't give much idea of how a mature plant looks. Always try to store a picture of the mature plant in your mind so that you can use it effectively in any borders you might plan in the future.

Other tips for learning your plants

It can help for your own personal use to describe the plant in terms you recognize, such as "cabbage-like leaves tight on the ground, then a flower spike rather like a head of purple daisies". This will help you to visualize the plant several weeks later just from the name. Photographs are also useful, of course.

Never throw away these "plant ident" notes. It could be years later that you want to use a plant and need to re-establish it in your mind by referring back to your original description.

You may need to revisit the same plant several times to get a full picture of how it grows and develops during a year.

Using Latin Names

Pronunciation of botanical plant names can vary around the world and even between neighbours! For a few guidelines, see box below. Take care when writing the names. Most people are not familiar with Latin, so if you misspell the name, the reader may not be able to guess or deduce what you mean, as they might with an English word.

Latin Pronunciation

Phonetic version in brackets and any emphasis in bold lettering.

- The consonants *b d f g h l m n p q r t* and *z* are pronounced as in English
- *ch* is usually hard like "k" in English as in *Chamaecyparis* (ka-mee-sy-**par**is) and *Chamaerops* (ka-**mee**-rops)
- *c* is often soft, as in *Cistus* (**sis**-tus) and *Cytisus* (**sy**-ti-sus)
- *j* is usually pronounced as a "y" in English, e.g. *Buddleja* (**bud**-leya)
- *s* is nearly always soft and not like a "z"

Acer (**ay**-ser—note the soft "c").
Brachyglottis (brackee-**glot**tis)
Ceanothus (see-an-**oth**us or kee-an-**oth**us)
Chaenomeles (ky-**nom**-ee-lees)
Cotoneaster (kot-on-ee-**ast**er)
Deutzia (**doyt**-sia)
Elaeagnus (elly-**ag**nus)
Euonymus (you-**on**-ee-mus)
Fuchsia (**phew**-sha)
Leucothoe (lou-**ko**-tho-ee)
Rubus (**roo**-bus)
Stachyurus (sta-kee-**ur**-us)
Teucrium (**too-k**-ree-um)
Weigela (why-**jee**la)

Using Plant References

Common names must be used with caution, as pointed out at the beginning of this section. Many books do, however, include them and you can usually regard those that appear in print as fairly reliable. Books with a separate index of common names can be especially useful because if you know only the plant's common name, the index should give a cross-reference to its Latin name and therefore access to a lot more information. Many nurseries now have websites, allowing you not only to buy their plants by mail order, but also to check up on the botanical and common name of the plant.

The *RHS Plant Finder*

In Britain, serious gardeners and plantspeople use this invaluable paperback book—an "official" list of Latin plant names published and updated annually by The Royal Horticultural Society. This is the authoritative source of correct, up-to-date plant names, recent synonyms, and spellings of names. The *RHS Plant Finder* is also an invaluable source for listing cultivars, and tells you which nurseries supply them. The *RHS Plant Finder* is available on CD ROM.

Project 1

For your first project, you need to assemble a set of plans so that you can continue updating them and building an accurate record of the garden as you work on it. You also could compile the suggested reference material to remind yourself of considerations to focus on, as you proceed with caring for your garden. This project will create an invaluable record of how your garden develops, and will also ensure that you become familiar with your garden before you begin to make changes.

Photographic Records

Keep photographic records of significant features or aspects of your garden—mount these on paper or card for easy reference—to remind you of work that may need to be done.

The photographs on this page show areas of my garden at Sandhill Farm House: as you can see, the rear garden needed some work.

Top left: Rear façade of house—island beds with overgrown conifers make the garden seem smaller than it is, and the conifers spoil the good views. The willow to the right looks sick. The grass is well kept, but worn in some areas.

Top right: Existing shrubs and gravel/stone path—*Vinca major* (periwinkle), old shrubs, trees and prostrate conifers take up much of the space in this part of the garden.

REAR   GARDEN

REAR FACADE OF HOUSE

EXISTING SHRUBS AND GRAVEL/STONE PATH

EXISTING PLANTING AND STONE PATH

DISUSED VEGETABLE GARDEN

FRONT   GARDEN

EXISTING BEECH HEDGE

EXISTING GRAVEL PATH AND CONIFERS

OVERGROWN SHRUBS, APPLE TREES, CONIFERS

TALL UNKEMPT CONIFER HIDING TELEGRAPH POLE

Opposite, bottom left: Existing planting and stone path—the path helps to break up the rear garden into halves. Dense, evergreen planting on either side is backed by overgrown honeysuckle climbing up poles and supporting wires.

Opposite, bottom right: Disused vegetable garden—plastic-covered metal arches spoil the view of fields beyond. The clipped box balls are in good shape, but a conifer is taking up valuable vegetable growing space, and the area needs cultivating.

The photographs on this page show elements of my front garden, which needed renovation.

Top left: Existing beech hedge—although it is useful as a windbreak, the height, 4 m (12ft), of the hedge means that the immediate area behind it is in deep shade for most of the day.

Top right: Existing gravel path and conifers—the path is 2.4 m (8 ft.) wide. The now empty bed alongside was infested with couch grass. The mature conifers, all planted over 22 years ago, give a gloomy mood to this part of the garden.

Bottom left: Area of paths through shrubs—having been left unpruned for the past few years, the shrubs and herbaceous plants have converged over the paths. The apple trees in the distance seem out of keeping, do not yield much fruit, and are underplanted with grass and wild flowers.

Bottom right: Tall, unkempt conifer hiding view of a telegraph pole—these unattractive conifers, now mature, block light from the boundary hedge, preventing it from putting on much growth. The conifers' greedy roots make the soil beneath them very dry. The tree to the right is a flowering Sheraton cherry—*Prunus* 'Kanzan'

Make Reference Lists

1. Compile a checklist of family requirements for your new/improved garden.

2. List the existing plants and trees (using botanical Latin), and their condition. List the plants, preferably alphabetically, under headings by type and also by area, for example:

   List One
   > Trees
   > Shrubs
   > Perennials, grasses, ferns
   > Annuals and biennials
   > Bulbs, rhizomes and corms
   > Roses (name if known)
   > Climbers

   List Two
   > Border beside house
   > Border in front of shed
   > Plants around pool
   > Trees and shrubs at the far end of the garden.

Draw Up Plans

1. Draw up a rough, and then an accurate, simple plan of the existing garden.

2. Note the results of your soil tests, showing on your plan where they were taken.

Opposite: These rough plans of my rear and front gardens at Sandhill Farm House show all the existing features and also show where soil samples were taken, with their pH values. Soil samples are noted on the plan thus: SS–F (pH 6.5).

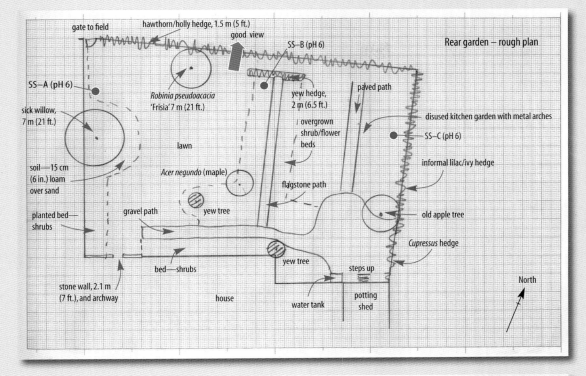

Rear garden – rough plan

gate to field

hawthorn/holly hedge, 1.5 m (5 ft.)

good view

SS–B (pH 6)

SS–A (pH 6)

Robinia pseudoacacia 'Frisia' 7 m (21 ft.)

yew hedge, 2 m (6.5 ft.)

paved path

sick willow, 7 m (21 ft.)

overgrown shrub/flower beds

disused kitchen garden with metal arches

SS–C (pH 6)

soil—15 cm (6 in.) loam over sand

lawn

Acer negundo (maple)

informal lilac/ivy hedge

planted bed— shrubs

gravel path

yew tree

flagstone path

old apple tree

bed—shrubs

yew tree

Cupressus hedge

stone wall, 2.1 m (7 ft.), and archway

house

water tank

steps up

potting shed

North

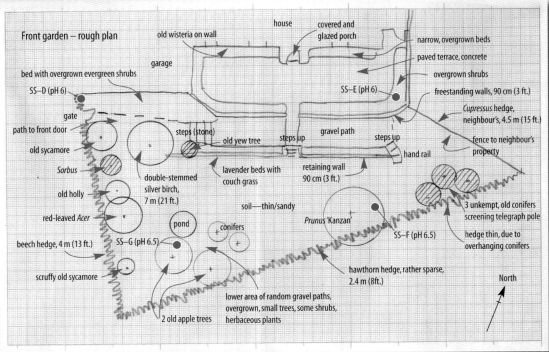

Front garden – rough plan

house

old wisteria on wall

covered and glazed porch

narrow, overgrown beds

garage

paved terrace, concrete

bed with overgrown evergreen shrubs

overgrown shrubs

SS–D (pH 6)

SS–E (pH 6)

freestanding walls, 90 cm (3 ft.)

Cupressus hedge, neighbour's, 4.5 m (15 ft.)

gate

path to front door

steps (stone)

old yew tree

steps up

gravel path

steps up

fence to neighbour's property

old sycamore

hand rail

Sorbus

double-stemmed silver birch, 7 m (21 ft.)

lavender beds with couch grass

retaining wall 90 cm (3 ft.)

old holly

soil—thin/sandy

3 unkempt, old conifers screening telegraph pole

red-leaved Acer

pond

conifers

Prunus 'Kanzan'

SS–F (pH 6.5)

hedge thin, due to overhanging conifers

beech hedge, 4 m (13 ft.)

SS–G (pH 6.5)

scruffy old sycamore

hawthorn hedge, rather sparse, 2.4 m (8ft.)

North

2 old apple trees

lower area of random gravel paths, overgrown, small trees, some shrubs, herbaceous plants

Here is the accurate plan, drawn up from the two rough plans, of my garden. The original was drawn on A3 (11 × 17 in.) paper at a scale of 1:200.

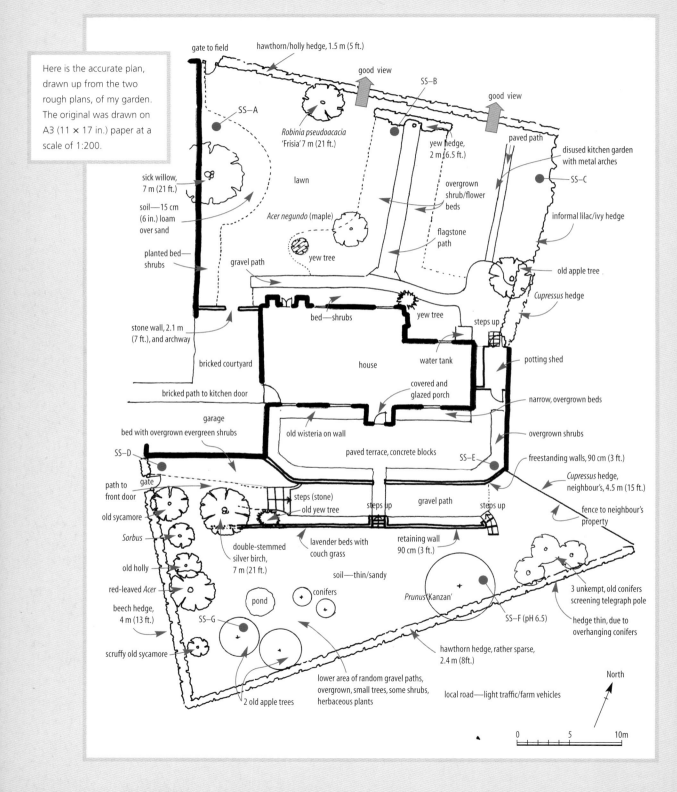

Above: This seating area is shaded by woven bamboo slats, supported by metal uprights; the slats are easily removed when not required.

Above: Seating areas should be planned into the garden design. The extension of this colonial-style house provides a shaded outdoor seating area and a good view of the garden.

Below: Gardens designed by interior decorators tend to reflect the style used in the house. In this case, clipped trees and shrubs repeat details of the interior, creating a small but highly formal garden.

Above: Formal style—in this sunken garden, stone paths converge on an ornamental pool and the beds are sharply pointed and filled with annuals.

Above: Cottage-garden style—a plethora of closely planted herbaceous plants leave little room for unwelcome weeds and accentuate the informality of the garden.

Above: The formal shape of this central pool holds the other elements in this design together. The low stone wall, edged with slate, doubles as a seating area.

Above: In a rural setting, a timber deck suspended over a naturally styled water feature affords a place to relax and a close view of the wildlife. It is a good idea to erect safety rails on such a deck.

Above: Mirrors can be used to introduce more light to an outdoor space, but need to be positioned carefully. In this case, the tree seems to emerge from above the wall, creating a discordant note and spoiling the view.

Left: Framing a view with an arch channels the eye to the scene beyond. Ideally, for a more balanced view, the stone path should be centred within the archway.

Right: Focal points are important in a formal garden. Backed by a curved yew hedge, this statue is emphasized by spiral and ball forms of clipped box.

Below: The white garden at Sandhill Farm House—before renovation, with misshapen, overgrown shrubs.

Above: The white garden at Sandhill Farm House—after renovation, with clipped-box hedging, white *Tulipa* 'Spring Green', *T.* 'Maureen', and a scented, standard *Elaeagnus* 'Quicksilver'.

Left: Sandhill Farm House—in the recently planted Red Border, a relocated, upright conifer creates a vertical accent and draws attention away from the change in pitch of the roofs.

Left: Sandhill Farm House kitchen garden—a new sloping path was put in to the approach to the garden, but it still needed replanting to continue the renovation.

Left: Sandhill Farm House kitchen garden—the same area two years later, with the summerhouse as a focal point, additional box balls, and seasonal tulips such as the terracotta-orange *T.*'Dillenburg'.

Chapter 2
Shaping It Up

This chapter goes through the vital practical steps you will need to take before you start thinking about undertaking any planting in your garden.

Whether you are starting on a virgin site, clearing an overgrown jungle, restoring an old garden, or adapting an existing one to your new needs, you will probably have identified some structural problems that need to be addressed. These may include the layout of the garden, state of the hard landscaping, or changes in features such as arches or water features. Tackling these problems now will save time, effort and probably expense later.

Another crucial task at this point is to bring the condition of the garden up to scratch. Almost certainly you will need to tackle annual and perennial weeds, clear the site of unwanted plants, and thin out or renovate the remaining plants. You must make sure that the soil is in good condition and will need to know how to improve it. If you have a lawn, it will probably need some remedial treatment.

All these steps require a good deal of time and effort, but the importance of such preparation cannot be overestimated—the investment you make at this stage will be repaid many times over in future years. You want to give the garden a chance to work for you in every way—as a practical, enjoyable space full of healthy plants.

This is also the time to start keeping a Garden Log— it will serve as an invaluable record of how the garden develops and a reference for future maintenance.

Where to Begin?

In a new garden, rubbish may have been left over by the workmen—half-used bags of cement, unused bricks or timber and other debris. A plot that was previously a vacant field may harbour rotting tree trunks, old drinking troughs or baths, and wire

netting. Older gardens may have a general air of dereliction with anything from old mattresses and discarded bottles to broken paving and cracked walls. Weeds and overgrown shrubs may render it an impenetrable jungle. Before considering anything new, an initial clearance of rubbish and weeds will be necessary so that you can see exactly what you have.

We've got to begin somewhere…

With most new properties, the first priority is usually the house. However, clearing debris from the garden while you have men and machinery on site to work on the house may save you extra disposal charges. It will also save you precious time in the future. You may need to hire a skip or using a local contractor to remove heavier items from the garden.

If the workmen have left ruts and humps, the contractor may be able to bring in a rotavator to level and cultivate the soil. Areas of concrete or hard standing may need to be broken up with a drill and carted off site before you can assess the condition of the underlying soil. Too often the soil is full of rubble or stone, and will need to be removed and replaced with some decent topsoil.

Occasionally, there maybe an unwanted pond into which bricks and other suitable material can be dumped and covered with an 45 cm (18 in.) layer of

An old, leaking pond may be used as a dump for rubble.

topsoil. Alternatively, some of the unwanted material could be reused as hard core beneath new paving or a base for a new greenhouse or potting shed. Left-over wooden pallets could also be recycled: flat ones make excellent walls for large compost bins and box pallets can be converted into leaf-mould bins by lining them with wire netting.

Clearing Undergrowth

In a long-neglected garden, attacking the impenetrable mass of brambles, tree seedlings, suckers and overgrown shrubs to clear the space can be a very satisfying way of using up surplus energy or frustration. Only then can you begin working on the new layout. The objective is to restore some order without destroying a sense of maturity. It is best to proceed slowly, frequently standing back from your labours to look and make sure that the better and most established plants are retained. It is quicker and easier to pull out young trees or seedlings with the aid of a pick axe and leverage than to cut them down and spray or dig out the roots later.

If possible, set aside a place for a bonfire—a place where the windblown smoke will not annoy your neighbours. The rubbish can then be burned gradually as work progresses, to save the effort or expense of having it carted off site.

Which Plants Must Go?

Most of us inherit plants chosen and grown by previous owners. They may not be to our particular taste, or we like them but not in that particular place, or perhaps they have outgrown their original planting positions. Initially, the gardener usually enjoys each plant for its individual beauty or character, but the success of the garden as a whole depends much more on the arrangement and combination of all the planting than on the charms of individual specimens.

Plants grow at different rates so, as time goes by, the garden changes. Some plants grow vigorously and smother slower and lower-growing varieties, which then may die because they no longer have access to

Overgrown plants by paths may become a nuisance; either get rid of them or move them to a more suitable position.

light. Other plants so engulf lawns and paths that the original layout of the garden is no longer apparent. All too often botanical thugs take over and then the garden becomes a Victorian hangover of suffocating shrubs and overgrown trees.

Some tough decisions have to be made. But beware! To try to keep matters under control, new garden owners often indiscriminately cut back all the shrubs to a uniformly tall, rounded shape, completely destroying the intrinsic beauty of each plant's natural growth habit or outline. A shrub pruned in such a way can become very overcrowded as individual stems fight it out for light, air and space.

If the garden is overgrown, it is far better to take out a few entire plants, giving room to the remaining specimens so that they can thrive in their most graceful, natural or elegant form. First, take out what you don't want to keep; then reduce the size of any worthwhile overgrown specimens that remain by renovation pruning (see pages 76–85) and move any that are in the wrong place (see page 86).

Of course, I'd like to get next door's plants into shape too!

Using your Plan

Begin to get to know your garden by using your plan to note things that you like or dislike—not only the plants but also the general layout. If possible, do this during the growing season—late spring until early

summer—otherwise many plants will be without their leaves or have disappeared below ground. Tie anything destined for removal or rubbish with a piece of red tape, marking plants that may possibly be kept with green or blue tape. You will then be able to stand back and imagine the consequences of their removal. By not being too hasty, you may perhaps discover that some plants or features are screening something that is best left hidden.

Perhaps a previous owner can give you the names of some of the plants so that you can label them, or you may photograph them to create a "before" and "after" record. The simplest way of labelling the plants is to buy some white plastic labels (which often come in a packet complete with marking pencil) and stick them into the soil beside the plant. However, these sometimes get moved by accident or pecked out by birds. For more permanent labelling, use black plastic labels that can be engraved with the plant name; these either have a hole punched into them so that they may be tied on to the tree or shrub or supplied with a black metal holder on an 20 cm (8 in.) spike. There are many other types of labels, from simple to ornate, but the main thing is to be able to identify the plant.

Assessing the Trees

Through age, neglect or abuse, some of the trees in the garden may be in a distressed state. A tree surgeon, or in Britain, your local council arbori-cultural officer, will usually make a brief report on the state of the trees free of charge—in the hope that they will later be paid to do any remedial work. This sort of job is highly skilled and often dangerous, so make sure that you employ only people who are suitably qualified; some rogues may be more intent on reselling the timber than on saving your tree.

Your property may be in a conservation area. In Britain, this usually restricts you from removing trees without permission from the local council. Some trees may be governed by tree preservation orders

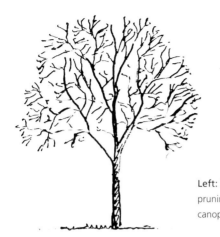

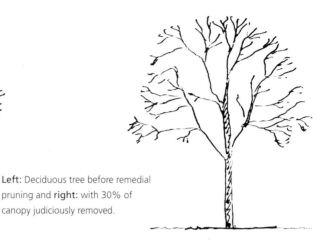

Left: Deciduous tree before remedial pruning and **right:** with 30% of canopy judiciously removed.

(TPOs), which forbid the removal of any branches or felling without permission from the local authority—failure to do so may result in a heavy fine or, in extreme cases such as felling a wood, imprisonment. If remedial work is needed, you must apply for permission. Usually permission is granted if a tree or its limbs are dead, dying or dangerous. On older deciduous trees, it is quite usual to be granted

permission to remove or reduce up to 30% of the tree canopy, in order to allow light and air to circulate through it and bring the tree back to health.

Coniferous trees are less easy to rejuvenate because they don't regrow from the main stem. Yew, however, is an exception: it should be cut back to the "quick", or main stem; activated by increased exposure to light, the old stem will put on new growth within a few months. Some other conifers can be reduced in height if they become too lanky. The popular—or infamous—Leyland cypress (× *Cupressocyparis leylandii*) or *Cupressus macrocarpa* (Monterey cypress) can be "topped", but they will not regenerate from the main stem.

Stumps and waste timber

Smaller, dead or dying trees are relatively easy to remove by hoisting them out with a winch or by digging out the roots. Large ones however will require a stump grinder to eradicate the stump so that the resulting space can be replanted. A stump grinder can reduce a large tree stump to a pile of wood chips in under an hour. It may be possible to hire one for the day and remove several stumps at once.

Alternatively, leave the stumps to rot—the process can be speeded up by boring a few holes into the

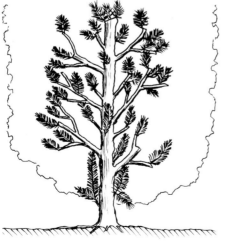

Unlike most conifers, *Taxus* (yew) species can be cut hard back into old wood to make them regenerate.

Stump killing
Drill holes in the cut surface around, and close to, the perimeter of the stump (**left**). Alternatively, use a chain saw to "dice" the surface (**right**). Then put a suitable poison into the holes or into the diced surface.

live tissue of the stump (the cambium) and then sprinkling it thickly with a weedkiller product such as concentrated glysophate. If the stump throws up fresh shoots, these too can be treated with weedkiller but remember to protect any nearby plants. The alternative is to dig out the stump by hand but this can easily take days of hard labour.

Tree trunks and other debris can be carted off site, used as logs for edging paths or for the fire, or burned with other general rubbish (garbage). The timber from rarer trees may well be sought by woodcarvers or craftsmen, provided that it is left in long lengths rather than short logs, which are useless to woodturners. Most hardwoods burn well as logs for the fire, but burning coniferous wood, which spits and crackles, is best avoided.

Neglected fruit trees
Gnarled, old fruit trees give character to a garden and are often worth keeping for appearance alone. A single specimen can act as a pivot for the rest of the garden, perhaps with a circle of brick or stone paving, or a circular seat, beneath its boughs. Old fruit trees can also double as hosts for climbing roses, honeysuckle or clematis, which looks more natural than training them up a timber tripod.

An old tree can be brought back into productivity by feeding it and carrying out renovation pruning (see page 288) but, unless you like and can use the fruit,

there is little point—you will only spend time clearing up windfall apples, which attract wasps. If the tree flowers but does not fruit, it probably lacks a suitable cultivar nearby to pollinate it, such as the crab apple *Malus* × *zumi* 'Golden Hornet'. Most apple trees need to be pollinated by another tree that flowers at the same time of year. Try to find out what variety of fruit you have, so that you can ask your local nursery for advice on a suitable pollinator to plant in the garden.

New fruit trees, like roses, will not thrive in ground where similar cultivars have recently been grown. If you are planning an orchard, or replacing an old fruit tree, either plant in a different part of the garden or grow an alternative crop, such as potatoes, in the ground for three years before replanting.

Hedges

Perhaps the boundary of your garden is formed by an old hedge. Unless you particularly dislike it, try to rejuvenate or improve it; this will probably save you

When growing conifers for a hedge or screen, wait until the main body of each conifer has reached the desired height before taking out the top.

time and money. Hedges filter noise and wind and, in the long term, are usually more sympathetic to the surroundings than walls or short-lived fences.

Grass, ivy or weeds colonizing the ground around the roots of a hedge will hinder its healthy growth. Clear out the undergrowth, water and feed the hedge, and you will help it to regenerate. Where there are gaps in a hedge, perhaps due to shade from a previously overhanging tree, buy some new plants of the same type as infill.

If the hedge is too tall, cutting it back will stimulate growth at the base and sides. If the desired height is not yet reached, clip only the sides of the hedge until it is. Cut the tops of conifer hedges only when the bushy part reaches the height you want—branches of conifers do not regrow from cut stems.

If parts of the existing hedge are unhealthy, the reasons may be more serious—the hedge may have been planted to take the place of a line of trees whose roots have been left in situ after felling. In turn, these roots may have developed honey fungus, identifiable by black "bootlace" growths at the bases of infected plants, and this may in turn infect the hedging plants. There are various ways of approaching this problem, see "Honey Fungus", page 328.

Improving the Hard Landscaping

Unless the general layoutof the garden is appropriate and works for your family needs, you will never be satisfied with it. The hard landscaping, or the inert part, of the garden should blend with the property and by doing so will help to set off the planted areas. Hard landscaping is often the most costly part of developing a garden and should be seriously considered when doing any renovations. Too often the previous materials used are cheap and the workmanship poor and it will always irritate you. It will be less expensive and less disruptive in the long run to change or install the hard landscaping at this

early stage. When choosing any hard landscaping material, remember to consider whether it is practical and visually appropriate to the garden, as well as within your budget. It often helps to make a list of all existing hard-landscaping features, their condition, and what it will take to repair or replace them.

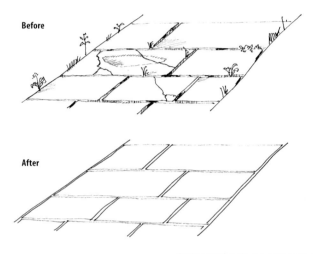

Before

After

Paving can be given a new lease of life if it is cleaned up and repaired.

Paving

The paving may be inadequate, either in size, situation or style. If the paved space is too small for your family needs but is basically sound, it may be possible to extend or improve it inexpensively by using some of the existing material and interspersing it with other material such as brick or stone that will relate it to the house. Perfectly good materials may look shabby because of occasional cracks or deteriorated joints. Individual cracked slabs can be replaced and loose mortar can be raked out and joints repointed.

When installing paving, aim for well-constructed, clean and simple outlines and generous proportions—tables, chairs and people usually seem to take up more space outdoors, since they are less confined. Remember to leave space around a table for chairs to be pushed back.

Making Changes

Almost every garden owner makes changes to an existing garden. It may be too simple, dull or boring, or too complex with over-fussy planting that demands high maintenance, or it may simply not suit your requirements for your family. You may have decided to change the style or theme to suit your own taste. Keep in mind a few simple principles.

- The house and garden should appear united. Your property will seem larger if both appear to be one cohesive unit.
- The garden should complement the house and be appropriate to your locality and surroundings—an old stone house, for example, might look strange surrounded by new brick walls. An old, clapboard country retreat might look out of place in a garden with contemporary materials and architectural planting; in this case, a country style would be more suitable.
- The interior of your home reveals your taste, personality and favourite colours— reflect the same style and colours in your garden design.
- Any garden is a combination of mass and void. Anything above eye level, such as plant material, is mass; anything below eye level, such as paving, a lawn or pool, is void. As a general rule, try to use two-thirds of mass to one-third of void in the garden, or the opposite. The two-thirds/one-third principle is easy on the eye and helps to connect the vertical bulk of the house to the horizontal plane of the garden.
- Use architectural elements, such as corners or projections of the house and door and windows, as reference points to divide up the garden into a series of interlocking spaces connected by paths, steps, walls, pergolas and other features.

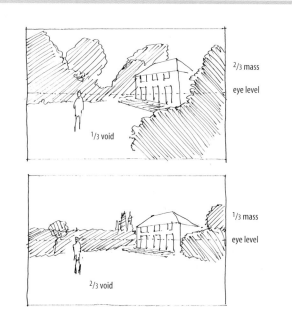

Below: corners or projections of house and garage, doors, gates, and piers in a wall can all serve as reference points for dividing the garden up into a series of interlocking spaces. The garden can then be designed using this underlying geometry, so that the terrace, walls, raised beds and other features all have a relationship with the forms of the architecture and walls.

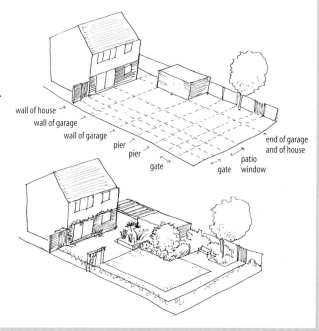

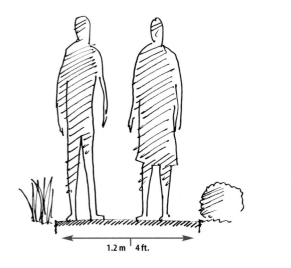

Consider whether the paths in your garden need to accommodate more than one person at a time. A path at least 1.2 m (4 ft.) wide allows two people to walk side by side (**far left**); anything narrower forces one person to walk in front of the other (**left**).

1.2 m   4 ft.

90 cm   3 ft.

If the paving looks too harsh, lift a few randomly spaced stones, remove the subsoil beneath and replace it with good garden soil. You can then use this planting pocket for *Dianthus* (pinks), chamomile, thymes, or other creeping plants. There is still a tendency for cracked paving stones to be used as crazy paving, but this now looks dated and second-rate.

Paths

Paths are the arteries of the garden and provide an easy way of accessing different areas without getting wet or dusty feet. An average width of 1.2 m (4 ft.) allows two people to walk side by side, whereas 90 cm (3 ft.) is sufficient for one person to walk slightly ahead of the other but still carry on a conversation.

Paths can be of stone, brick, wood chippings or of many other materials. Unless they are well constructed, brick or stone paths may have cracked pointing or uneven levels and the bricks may be shattered or cracked due to the action of frost. The only answer is to lift and re-lay them or replace them with a longer-lasting or tougher material.

Grass paths can cut the cost of hard landscaping and allow you to change the route of the path from year to year, but can easily become worn, especially in

Practical Tips on Gravel

- Choose a gravel that is in keeping with the local stone in your area.
- Gravel should be laid on a compacted base or subbase, such as hardcore.
- Lay hardcore to falls for drainage and compact it with a roller to lock the aggregate together. A normal thickness is 5–7.5 cm (2–3 in.), laid in a single layer.
- To prevent the gravel from sinking into the ground, or weeds from going deep into the base or subbase, a layer of geotextile matting or fabric may act as an interface between the base and the gravel. The fabric needs careful laying and pegging down so that it does not show.
- The depth of gravel for comfortable use is 7.5 cm (3 in.). The gravel size should be around 1–2 cm ($3/8$–$3/4$ in.); if the stones are much smaller, cats may mistake the gravel for a large litter tray.

areas that are used regularly. Some species of grass are more resistant than others, so it is worthwhile making sure you start off with a suitable grass seed mix or turf (see pages 65–67). However, they do need to be mown regularly throughout the growing season, so are quite high maintenance. Whenever possible try to make the grass path no wider than the width of the mower, or multiples thereof—trying to mow a narrow left-over strip is very time-consuming.

Today gravel is the most usual choice because it is inexpensive and easy to spread. A gravel path should be bounded on either side by narrow, pressure-treated timber boards, pegged into place at 90 cm (3 ft.) intervals, to separate it from the adjacent soil or lawn. The gravel will need regular raking and can be topped up every two or three years when it begins to sink into the hard core (the rubble or compacted stone and sand used as a base by landscapers) or subsoil beneath. Usually a 5 cm (2 in.) layer of gravel is sufficient—any deeper makes for heavy going. A disadvantage is that modern footwear such as trainers (sneakers) can carry it indoors. A gravel path can also be interspersed with paving stones laid in the directional flow (the direction in which one would walk, as opposed to across), which may make walking easier.

Although inexpensive and easily laid, the downside of using gravel is that walking on it can be noisy. However, this may increase your sense of security, making it difficult for anyone to walk up a path without being heard, for instance. The progress of wheel chairs, pushchairs (strollers) and wheelbarrows is slow on gravel and the ensuing ruts and grooves may be a nuisance to rake over.

Steps

Some steps in the garden may need repointing and there may be other details to consider. Proportions of internal dimensions such as a flight of stairs will appear mean when transferred to the outdoors, so the width, treads and risers need to be more generous.

To be comfortable for outside use, the height of the riser should be about 10 cm (4 in.), the width of the tread no less than 25 cm (10 in.), and the breadth of the steps about 90 cm (3 ft.). Make sure that the heights and widths of the risers are uniform; if the flight consists of more than about eleven risers, consider an occasional landing.

Occasionally, where space is limited, particularly in town gardens, the risers may be steeper and the treads shallower than is really comfortable, but in an enclosed space it may not be so noticeable. Wider steps may double as seating areas or as places to display pots, whereas narrow ones can create a feeling of tension.

Walls

The garden may already possess walls, or you may consider building a wall to replace a hedge or fence. Newly acquired properties are often bounded on all sides by walls or a mixture of walls and fences, all too often in a dilapidated state. Any refurbishment of the walls will make a substantial difference to the garden.

Before deciding on any action, you need to establish who owns the boundary division. Find out who has responsibility for their upkeep from your local town council, from title deeds or from previous owners. If repairs are needed, try to negotiate with your neighbours since their garden may be affected by any reconstruction. Plants that have grown against the wall may need to be cut back or removed before any rebuilding takes place.

If you already have freestanding or retaining walls within the garden, it makes sense to do any repairs, such as repointing, before beginning work on the planting. It will be easier to get to the wall, and since many workmen lack respect for plants, you will avoid the likelihood of damage to nearby plants, particularly smaller, newly planted specimens.

Boundaries

From the very earliest times, some form of boundary demarcation around our gardens indicates that what lies within is private and belongs to us. The main reasons for this are:

- Protection—to keep out the casual offender.
- Seclusion—to prevent others from seeing what goes on within our private space.
- Shelter—usually from the climatic effects of wind and rain.
- Noise—to reduce undesirable noise such as that of traffic or children's playgrounds.

Most established properties will already have some type of boundary, but if there is the opportunity to start from scratch, the first consideration should be visual. Beautiful views over surrounding countryside might be alienated with the straight line of a hedge, wall or fence. In a small town garden, similar demarcation lines can exclude valuable light and circulation of air.

Boundaries do not need to be obvious; indeed, one of the objects of planting can be to disguise a hard perimeter line. A sense of privacy does not necessarily depend on a forbidding barrier.

On the other hand, in some circumstances, a formally planted boundary is a great asset to the garden. It can provide a stylish backdrop to planting on one side, or create an inviting sense of mystery from the other. Used imaginatively, trees, hedges and topiary are more rewarding than inert structures such as walls or fences.

Choosing a Fence

- Do you prefer a traditional or contemporary and imaginative design? Consider having fencing made out of pressure-treated hardwood to your own design.
- The majority of fencing panels are made from timber, often preconstructed, but they can be made of chain link, or other metal. Flimsy, "closeboard" or "larchlap" panels have a life span of less than ten years, so are a short-term solution.
- Most hardwoods—larch, oak, red cedar and sweet chestnut—need no maintenance. Ash, beech, elm, pine and sycamore need to be treated with a preservative.
- Woven willow hurdles or wattle poles are now popular; they provide a welcome, softer alternative to traditional fencing, but are not as durable, usually collapsing after three to five years. Rolls of bamboo to create a relaxed mood and as a background to modern plantings are very inexpensive, but quickly look faded, and may splinter.
- Vertical uprights, usually square timber posts, should be bought already treated. (This is done by immersing them in cold creosote, which is then heated to allow the timber to absorb it over a period of time.) Check that the posts are treated to a height that will be at least 30 cm (12 in.) above ground level, once erected. Brushing, spraying or dipping timber with preservative gives only surface protection, and can in turn leach into the soil, stunting plant growth. Supporting uprights should be set in the ground and either buried into concrete or set into a type of metal "shoe" or post-holder for stability.
- If security is part of the reason for fencing, make sure it is difficult to climb, or stretch wires along the top to give added height.

Fences and trellis—repair or replace?

Previous owners may have used fences to delineate your boundary or other areas of your garden. Unless they are particularly strong, most fences have a life expectancy only of up to ten years. Uprights tend to rot at the base or flimsy panels tend to break through misuse.

Before rushing to replace or renew an existing fence, consider whether it is really necessary and whether you like it. Perhaps it could be replaced with a more long-term solution such as a hedge.

If a boundary is really necessary, a fence is usually the least expensive, and quickest, short-term boundary. A staggered fence is less threatening than a straight one and can double as a backdrop and shelter for plants. For a less claustrophobic effect, trellis is useful; it is not so solid and plants may be trained against it, although they may need to be taken off or pruned back if the trellis needs repainting.

Avoid spraying fencing or trellis with wood preservative after it is in place because the spray may fall on to the soil and kill nearby plants.

In exposed areas, fences and trellis can provide protection for plants. If removing a fence, check that nearby planting is sufficiently hardy to cope with the sudden exposure to the elements. If the fence has been close to established shrubs or hedging, plants growing very near to it will have suffered from shortage of light, so that the lower stems, on the fence side, will be bare. You will probably have to plant "infill" shrubs to disguise the bare stems.

Arches and Pergolas

In most gardens, some form of vertical structure such as an arch or a pergola is needed either for shade or to connect one part of the garden to another. Most vertical structures make strong visual statements in the garden and can usually also be seen from the house, so they should be decorative and in scale and harmony with your surroundings.

A flimsy timber or metal trellis may best be replaced with something more robust and appropriate to your area, such as brick pillars or heavy-duty timbers. To allow people to walk comfortably beneath, the uprights should be 2–2.5 m (6½–7 ft.) in height and set about 1.5–2 m (5–6½ ft.) apart, and will need either secure foundations similar to a fence or to be supported on a solid plinth. Crossbeams are usually of timber, must be securely fixed to the uprights, and for the sake of appearance should project beyond the uprights. Longitudinal beams require similar fixing. Both beams are necessary to support the weight of plants, and the overhead space between the uprights and crossbeams can be filled with wire or sheep netting stretched across to prevent plant stems from falling through.

Arches and pergolas are also available in metal or timber kit form. The metal ones sometimes are plastic coated; in a hot climate, the metal will absorb heat and, if in contact with the plant, may deter growth. Mature climbing plants can also easily swamp and break lightweight structures, so be careful not to choose a rampant variety, and plant at reasonable distance, say 50–60 cm (20–24 in.), away from the foundations.

Lawns and Grass

In most gardens, probably a larger area is devoted to lawn than all the borders and paving put together. On the whole, lawns are relatively easy to look after once established but if something goes wrong, it affects a large and very obvious part of the garden. A neglected lawn does nothing for your morale and when taking over a new property, improving the lawn is often the first priority. Any restoration work should begin as soon as possible: spring is the best time to start mowing.

If mowing has been overlooked and the grass is unruly, the lawn may need to be cut for the first few times with a rotary mower. Gradually reduce the height of the cut until a cylinder mower can be used. Regular mowing—at least once a week in the growing season—will weaken coarser grasses and encourage the finer-leaved varieties. All surface debris should be raked off beforehand and the collected mowings burned, not composted, because at this stage they may contain grass and weed seeds. Once the lawn is edged, it may look quite presentable and then routine maintenance such as scarifying, spiking and feeding (see pages 73–75) can be practiced as usual, depending on the desired degree of perfection.

If the lawn is in a very bad state—more moss than grass, with worn patches or simply a proliferation of weeds—you may be encouraged or tempted to returf or seed the area (see page 67). Unless there is little grass left, reclaiming a neglected lawn is usually more cost-effective than starting from scratch and, in most cases, a renovation programme will restore the lawn in one growing season. Renovation work can be time-consuming and monotonous, but the end results are very gratifying.

Rescuing an Old Lawn

- First, cut down closely all the tall grass and weeds, raking off all the cuttings, then brush the surface. Remove any stones that might damage a mower.
- Mow with the blades set as high as possible, and trim the lawn edges. Then mow at weekly intervals, progressively lowering the height of the cut to about 2.5 cm (1 in.).
- Feed and weed the lawn in early summer with a combined lawn dressing.
- Water the lawn in summer, especially during dry weather, and feed it again in autumn. If the turf looks pale, use a low-nitrogen lawn fertilizer in early autumn.
- Autumn is a good time to level out bumps and hollows or repair torn edges.
- Also in autumn, scarify and spike, or aerate, compacted areas, and seed any bare areas with an appropriate grass mix.
- Next spring, begin an annual lawn management routine.

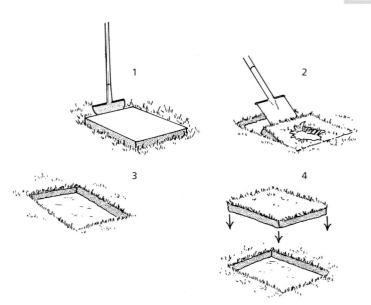

Patching a lawn with turf

1 Use a wooden block (or something similar) that is slightly larger than the damaged area to use as a template. Cut all round it with an edging iron.

2 Working from the centre outwards, use a spade or a "turfing iron" to lift out the damaged turf. This will prevent the edges of the patch from being crushed.

3 Neaten up all four edges and the base of the excavation.

4 Using the same block and tools, cut an identical piece of turf from the nursery area and carefully fit it into the excavated patch. Firm in the new turf and brush in a little compost or fine soil along the cracks.

Often only part of your lawn is in a poor state—perhaps under a dripping tree, below a child's swing, at the beginning of a grass path, or where it has been sprayed with bitch urine. With small areas, such as these, the best solution is to clear away any top growth of weeds and either reseed or turf them.

If returfing, remove the dead grass by slicing under it with a spade to a depth of about 5 cm (2 in.) and square it up. Break up the soil surface with your fork. Cut the new turves to size and place snugly into position. Fill in any cracks with sifted soil. If reseeding, disturb the existing surface by pricking it over with a fork. Then rake it over, removing any debris, to form a seedbed. Sow with seed and cover the area with a thin layer of soil. Protect the area from birds and keep it watered.

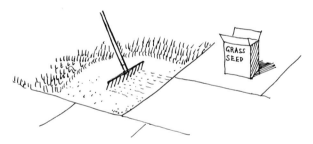

To repair a bare patch in a lawn, sow grass seed into the prepared soil and lightly rake in.

Types of Grass and Turf

Not all grass is suitable for lawns and for both seeding and turfing, the quality of your lawn will depend on your chosen seed type. Suppliers of grass seed sell special blends of grasses which produce grassed areas for various purposes: hardwearing, fine in appearance, or suited to different sports and so on. The grasses in each mix are chosen for their appropriate type of growth.

Rye grasses and various meadow grasses are generally quite tough, but do not grow very densely and therefore appear thin if cut too close. They are

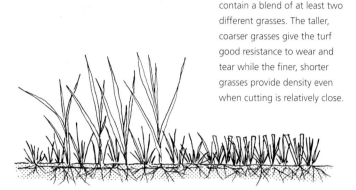

Many lawn-seed mixtures contain a blend of at least two different grasses. The taller, coarser grasses give the turf good resistance to wear and tear while the finer, shorter grasses provide density even when cutting is relatively close.

often included in sports turf where a good resistance to hard wear is required. Fescues and bents on the other hand are not as hardwearing. They grow more densely and closer to the ground and can therefore cope better with close mowing. These are associated with very fine, close-cut lawns and manicured sports surfaces, such as golf greens, that are not likely to suffer abuse. A blend of these two major types of grass is used to achieve a combination of durability and fine quality.

The selection and proportions of grass species can therefore be varied to produce a range of surfaces. At the extremes could be a blend of mostly rye grass for a football pitch and a mix of fescues and bent for a bowling green. A good hardwearing lawn will lie somewhere in-between. Companies who supply seed will offer a reliable selection of blends for you to choose from.

Cultivated turf

Turf has become big business and there are various types and thicknesses, which can be rolled out rather like a carpet. Shop around for prices, ask to see a sample of the turf before you order, and make sure, whether you use a reliable contractor or do it yourself, that it is laid with care (see pages 68–69). Cultivated turf is supplied as rolls of cut turf that has been raised from a special blend of seeds and therefore grown for a specific purpose. There are many types available. Overall, cultivated turf is

Typical Mixes of Grass Seed for Different Purposes

Purpose	Soil	Name	Species	Proportion %
Utility lawn	Medium	Perennial rye grass	Lolium perenne	25
		Smooth-stalked meadow grass	Poa pratensis	25
		Rough-stalked meadow grass	Poa trivialis	25
		Crested dogstail	Cynosurus cristatus	25
		OR		
		Sheep's fescue	Festuca ovina	25
Fine ornamental	Light	Browntop bent	Agrostis capillaris (syn. A. tenuis)	30
		Sheep's fescue	Festuca ovina	40
		Fine-leaved sheep's fescue	Festuca ovina subsp. tenuifolia	20
		Creeping red fescue	Festuca rubra subsp. rubra	10
Rough sports and games	Heavy, moist	Perennial rye grass	Lolium perenne	50
		Rough-stalked meadow grass	Poa trivialis	30
		Creeping bent	Agrostis stolonifera	20

probably the best value for money. It gives a predictable and uniform product, which is most important for an area of lawn. However, other less expensive types of turf include:

– Meadow turf—cut from meadows. It may contain some weeds and even cow dung. This turf is usually made up from coarse (but relatively hardwearing) grasses.

– Downland turf—cut from hillsides. It also may contain some weeds but the grasses are likely to be finer than those in meadow turf. Downland turf is therefore regarded as better quality.

– Sea-washed turf—usually cut from areas close to the sea. Whether pre-sown or natural, it usually contains mainly fescues and bents and the sea air helps to keep out the coarser grasses. This turf is often used for bowling greens or very special lawns. Unfortunately, coarser grasses do begin to creep in once the turf is brought inland and fungal diseases often plague the fine turf.

Creating a New Lawn

If starting a lawn from scratch, you have a choice of seed or turf, but whichever you use, you need to prepare the ground first. Remember that the lawn will be cut by a machine that operates best over a smooth (or gently undulating) surface. Preparation for turf and seed is similar, although seeds need a fine seedbed with a good tilth and an absence of large stones.

The topsoil should be cultivated down to a depth of at least 10 cm (4 in.), preferably more. The subsoil should be decompacted well below this depth to guarantee good drainage. Where topsoil is spread over heavy clay, water can build up to make it waterlogged and therefore unsuitable for seeding (or turfing) until it has time to dry out.

Compacting topsoil

Despite the dangers of over-compaction, the freshly cultivated topsoil must be raked smooth, then thoroughly and systematically "trodden in" with the heels of your boots. This may sound arduous, but it is a very effective way of finding the soft spots and ensuring that the ground is evenly compacted.

Seed or Turf?

Seed

- Much less expensive than turf, although need a more thorough ground preparation and patience.
- Can be slow to establish and is best sown in the spring.
- Difficult to establish on banks steeper than a 30 degree incline.
- Allows a wide choice of grass species.
- May develop a weed problem during its establishment period.

Turf

- More expensive than seed.
- Instant—turf can be laid at almost any time of the year as long as the ground is not frozen or dust dry. In summer months, it is unwise to lay turf unless you are prepared to irrigate it until the turves have set together.
- Better on banks and shallow soils than seed.
- Fewer choices of grass species, with the exception of cultivated turf.
- Can be supplied as "weed treated" so it remains free from weeds for many weeks or months.

After the first treading, the soil should be raked and trodden for a second time, so that you end up with a smooth, stable tilth. Large stones must be raked up and removed, but small ones can be removed once the seeds have germinated. Turf can be laid over small stones.

Seeding a new lawn

The ideal time to sow grass seed is in the spring once the soil has begun to warm up. This is also a time when there is usually ample moisture to ensure successful and sustained germination. If the weather is dry after sowing, the seedbed must be kept moist until the seedlings have become established.

An autumn sowing is also possible, but if it is followed by cold, wet conditions, the seeds may germinate and then fail to develop before the onset of winter. This poorly developed area of grass may then take weeks to start growing again in the spring. An autumn sowing should therefore be carried out as early as possible.

Sowing can take place at any time during the summer but only if irrigation is available. Where the ground is thought to be full of annual weed seeds, the seedbed could be prepared early and left for the crop of weeds to germinate. These can then be killed off with a non-residual herbicide such as glyphosate. Having reduced the potential weed problem, the grass can then be sown after a day or two.

Where a whole new lawn is being created, the seedbed should extend 30 cm (12 in.) or so into the surrounding borders. This will mean that the area of grass will, initially, be larger than required. Once the lawn has become established (and the soil is quite firm), the shapes of the borders can be marked and cut out, using an edging iron. Any unwanted grass is then either dug in or skimmed off.

The first cut on a newly sown lawn is usually done with a hover mower or a rotary mower on a fairly high setting. A cylinder mower often has the

After raking the area level, it is vital to compact it thoroughly by treading it with your heels, up and down in rows. The ground can then be raked again before being trodden over for a second time.

Sowing Grass Seed

- Density varies according to the type of seeds. Fine grasses have more seeds per gram weight than coarser grasses, so, from a weight point of view, sowing rates will vary between 18–45 g per sq. m (1/2–1 1/2 oz per sq. yd.). The lower rates mostly apply to the finest grasses such as fescues.
- The seeds should end up about 1 cm (1/2 in.) apart on the ground. You could scatter it by hand, or apply it with a suitable seed or fertilizer mechanical distributor (see page 74).
- After sowing, lightly rake the seeds into the surface. On light sandy soils, you could then lightly roll it to make sure that the tilth does not dry out too quickly and the seeds do not blow away.
- From now on, the seedbed must not dry out until the young seedlings have begun to develop their second leaves. Fine grasses may take two weeks or so to germinate, while coarser ones like rye grass may take only 10–14 days.

Use an edging iron to neaten the shape of the new lawn.

advantage of a weighted roller but unless the cylinder is properly adjusted for a sharp cut, this type of mower can sometimes pull or rip up young grass, or cut it too close.

Laying turf

So long as the tilth is not powder-dry or frozen, turf can be laid at any time of the year. In hot, dry weather, newly laid turf must be irrigated for two or three weeks, otherwise the turves are likely to shrink and die off around the edges.

Turf will normally store for two or three weeks during winter or in cold weather without any significant deterioration but, in high temperatures during spring and summer, it will begin to turn

yellow after just a few days. All folded turf must therefore be kept cool and shaded and not stacked more than, say, six pieces high. It should also be sprayed over in summer—*not* covered over, which might make it heat up. If laying of the turf is delayed by more than a few days, it must be opened out so that light can reach the grass before it goes yellow.

Turves usually measure 1 sq. m (3 × 1ft.). Turf is first laid around the edges end on end and bent to a curve where necessary. On no account should you tread on the prepared bed or directly on the turves, so the edging turves should be laid either by standing on the adjacent border or path, or on planks of wood. A heavy wooden block on the end of a pole (often called a "punner") can be used to bang down the turves so that they are firmly bedded on to the tilth beneath.

Once the edges are in place, planks are laid out at one end and the first full row of turves are laid so that they fit tightly end-to-end. Where the end of a turf strip meets one of the edging turves, it is laid so that it overlaps the edging turf. A neat fit can be achieved by cutting around the end of the turf strip and into the edging turf (underneath), discarding the cut-out section of edging turf and dropping the turf strip into the resulting space.

Lay the walk boards over this first row of turf, so that you can stand on them to lay the next. All the joints must be tightly butted together with no grass

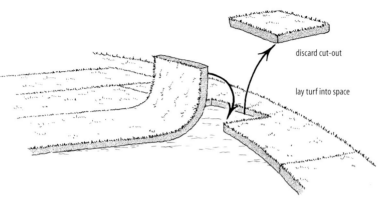

Fit the end turf into an edging strip.

discard cut-out

lay turf into space

Turfing a Bank

Take these measures to keep turf in place while it takes root.

- Make sure that the surface of the bank is moist before the turf is laid, otherwise rooting might take several weeks or the turf may dry up and die.
- Lay the turf diagonally up the bank.
- Use pegs made from bamboo, wooden dowels or steel to keep the turves in place.
- Either knock the pegs right in to stay there permanently or knock them part-way in so that you can remove them once the turf has rooted and is ready for mowing.

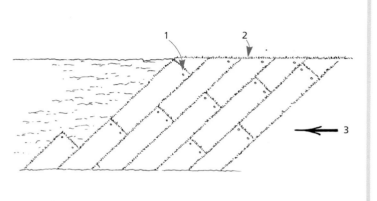

1 pegs
2 turf continues over brow of the bank
3 direction of progress

---

trapped between. Turves are traditionally laid in a staggered fashion, like bricks in a wall, so that the "vertical" joints at least do not line up. As work moves forward, it is important to tread only on the boards. With the help of your weight, they will flatten the newly laid turf. Once turfing is complete, brush some fine soil or compost lightly into the joints and compact any loose turf using the punner. Irrigation may be necessary from now on.

The same rules apply to the first cut of turf as for a seeded lawn. The turf is considered established and safe to cut with a cylinder mower when at least two-thirds of it cannot be easily pulled up (i.e. the roots have grown into the soil).

Edging a lawn

The shaping of a lawn can often be one of the corner stones of design, so maintaining good clear edges over the years is very important. Whether you are laying a new lawn or restoring an old one, clean edges will bring an immediate sharpness and neatness to its appearance. The soil on the lawn side of the edging must be well compacted so that the lawn does not subside and leave the edge sticking up (proud), which could cause problems when mowing. There are several types of edging available: the following are good, durable options.

- Timber: pressure-treated, timber edging concealed beneath the edge of the lawn is one of the most effective permanent edges; it can remain sound for 15–20 years. It is, however, easier to install around the edge of a new lawn than an existing one. This type of edging is not suitable for newly seeded lawns unless the edges have been turfed.

– Steel—lengths of steel with steel pegs welded at regular intervals can also be used in a similar way to timber. The lengths are usually 2–3 m (3–10 yd.) long, about 75 mm (3 in.) wide and 3–5 mm thick and are sometimes supplied with spikes that hold the lengths securely in the soil. The steel will need thorough priming and painting against corrosion; the most effective colours are matt black or brown.

– Brick or block paviors—only stock bricks that are frost resistant should be used. They should be set about 5 cm (2 in.) below the surface of the lawn so that the mower can pass easily over the top. This type of edging may look too wide and clumsy for a small lawn and it is difficult to lay them in tight curves.

– Stone edging—installed in a similar way to brick and block edging or, if large pieces of stone are being used, simply set into the lawn without any foundations. This nearly always ends up wider than a brick edging. It is especially useful alongside herbaceous borders where it acts as a mowing strip, allowing the plants to flop over on to the stone rather than killing the grass.

Mowing the Lawn

Mowing the grass is one of the first steps you will take in caring for the garden, whether it is to begin restoration of an existing lawn, or in the maintenance of a fine new sward. The majority of lawns are cut on a regular basis. Some are allowed to grow as a "meadow", containing wild flowers and species bulbs, but even these are cut down at least once each year. This is done usually in the autumn, once the flowers have set seed. When buying your mower, consider the size of the lawn as multiples of the width of a mower, to work out which width of mower would be best. A small, left-over width of grass is irritating to mow, especially as it will need to be done at least once a week in the growing season.

Brick or block edging

1 stock bricks or block paviors
2 mortar haunching
3 mortar bed
4 compacted layer, approx. 75 mm (3 in.) deep, of scalpings
5 soil
6 turf

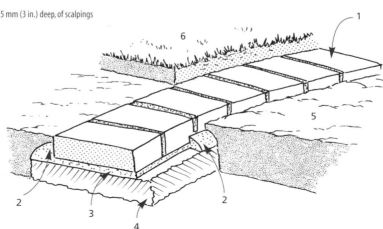

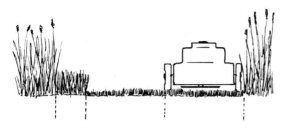

This grass walk was originally cut to a width that is just a little over two mower widths, so a third pass is needed to complete the cut every time the path is mown.

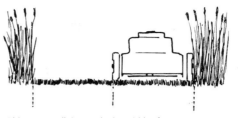

This grass walk is exactly the width of two mowers, making it relatively quick and simple to cut.

Mowers

All mowers are dangerous. Ideally, you should wear steel toe-capped boots when operating rotary or hover mowers. Always switch off the ignition before working on a petrol mower and use a circuit breaker with electric models. There are three main types of mower:

– Cylinder mower—this has a series of slightly twisted, steel blades. These rotate at high speed on a cylinder, pass across a fixed blade called a sole plate and, provided that contact is just made, the grass is cut in a scissor action. The position of the sole plate is adjustable and critical. The number of blades on a cylinder varies; the higher the number of blades, the finer the cut.

Cylinder mowers usually have a roller front and back and it is this rolling action that can give a lawn its stripes. These mowers are designed for relatively close cutting on fine, flat lawns and are widely used on bowling greens. They are not suitable for rough "orchard" grass or bumpy ground. The grass cuttings are collected in a front-mounted grass box. Cylinder mowers are usually petrol-driven; some of the larger models can be fitted with seat attachments to convert them into "sit-and-ride" machines. Some cylinder mowers also have attachments for scarifying.

– Rotary mowers—usually have a horizontally mounted blade, rather like a propeller, which rotates at great speed (under a steel or plastic cover) literally to swipe off the blades of grass. Wheels are more usual than rollers, although some do have a relatively thin roller either at the back or the front. These machines are designed to cut rough "orchard" grass as well as lawns, but do not produce such a fine or close cut as a cylinder mower. They cope well with undulating ground and are often used to cut down areas of "meadow" grass and wild flowers at the end of the summer. These mowers are nearly always petrol driven and are available as "push" or power-driven models. Grass cuttings can be collected in a rear-mounted box or bag. Many of the larger rotary mowers are "sit-and-ride" types with a facility to collect up fallen leaves.

Cylinder mower

1 adjustable handle
2 heavy roller
3 engine
4 cutting cylinder

5 adjustable front roller
6 grass box
7 adjustable sole plate

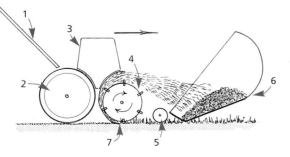

Rotary mower

1 adjustable handle
2 engine
3 protective cover

4 rotating blades
5 adjustable wheels, or roller

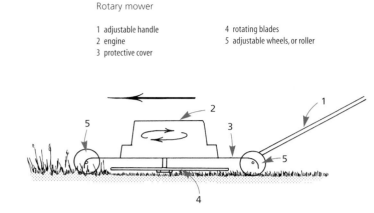

Strimmer

1 long handle with controls at top
2 motor
3 protective casing
4 rotating, nylon cutting line
5 rotating hub and housing for nylon coil

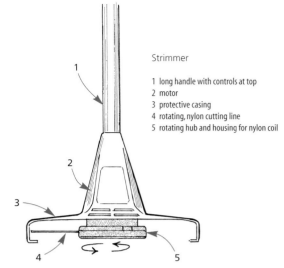

- Hover mowers—operate in the same way as most rotary types, but travel on a cushion of air rather than on wheels or rollers. This makes them ideal for steep banks where they can be lowered down and swung on the end of a rope. However, if the top of the bank is too abrupt, the mower may momentarily lose its cushion of air and scalp the grass.

Strimmers

These cut the grass by means of a length of nylon line rotating at great speed. As the line wears down, it is automatically replaced from a sprung spool, but it will eventually need changing. Strimmers are very useful if you need to cut grass neatly up against walls, steps, into awkward corners or anywhere else that a conventional mower cannot reach. Strimmers are not efficient tools for cutting large areas of grass however. Many of the smaller domestic mowers and strimmers are powered by mains electricity (or sometimes by battery).

Recommended Mowing Techniques

- Dry grass cuts much better than wet.
- To mow in a perfectly straight line, start by fixing your eye on an appropriately placed distant object, then mow towards it without taking your eye off it. This will give you your first straight line. Use this as a guide for the following lines.
- Make sure that you set your mower to an appropriate cutting height.
- If using a cylinder mower, check that the sole plate is correctly adjusted for a sharp cut. There are adjustment points for these.
- Do not cut a fine lawn closer than about 2 cm (³/₄ in.), otherwise the grass could be

weakened, which will encourage the growth of weeds and moss.
- Always collect the cuttings (in a grass box or bag) from a fine lawn—there is no case for leaving them on the lawn. With areas of rougher, longer grass, this task is not so important.
- Mow whenever the lawn needs it—summer and winter (as long as conditions allow).
- Never mow (or walk across) grass that is frozen because the frozen blades of grass will easily fracture. They then go yellow and die when they thaw out.

Lawn Maintenance

To keep a lawn in good order, there are several maintenance tasks that need to be undertaken each year, and that are especially useful in the initial renovation of neglected lawns. Even if the lawn is already in good condition, you will need to spend some time every year on caring for your grass to keep it looking healthy.

Controlling weeds in lawns

Most weeds that grow in lawns can be successfully controlled using a systemic "hormone" herbicide (see page 95). A few, including *Oxalis* species (a tiny, creeping sorrel with small, yellow or purple, trifoliate (three-part) leaves and tiny, yellow flowers) may prove resistant, so where an infestation is not too extensive, it is often best to fork them out by hand. Larger, individual weeds like dandelion and plantain can be spot treated with a weed "stick", which contains a suitably potent herbicide. Push it firmly down on to the centre of each weed.

Spot treat and dig out large weeds with a trowel or small fork.

Moss control

The spores of moss are everywhere and, given the right conditions, they will germinate and grow. Lawns offer the perfect environment for some mosses, many of which can become a serious problem and stifle the grass to extinction. Although green—and quite attractive—most of the time, mosses often die and go brown under very dry conditions and are not in the least hardwearing. They are therefore unsuitable in a lawn and need controlling. Moss killers are available in garden centres; these are usually applied during autumn or spring. Within three weeks of application, the dead moss will turn black or brown and, once completely dead, should be removed using a scarifier or a rake. Unfortunately, moss killers do not kill the spores nor do they radically change the conditions, usually poor drainage and aeration, that helped the moss to thrive in the first place.

Use a wire, spring-tined rake to scarify the lawn.

Scarifying the lawn

This is carried out in the autumn or spring. Moss often develops in the very early spring, so the most fruitful time to carry out scarifying is in the late spring. Only scarify a lawn if there is a good scattering of grass throughout the moss. Once the moss has been removed and some fertilizer applied, the grass should soon spread and thicken up. Using a wire "spring-tined" rake is the traditional, although rather backbreaking, method way of raking moss from a lawn, but there are many motorized devices that do an excellent job and make it relatively easy. Some of the most effective types are those that use rotating wire tines.

It is important to work a scarifier in several directions and to keep going until bare soil is just visible between the blades of grass. The grass is seldom damaged. The action of a scarifier disturbs, removes and destroys most of the moss, irrespective of whether or not it has been previously treated with a moss killer. It also helps to introduce better air circulation into the lawn, making it less hospitable to moss growth—at least until the following autumn. To reduce the drag on the scarifying machine, mow the lawn before scarifying. The grass will also need mowing afterwards because scarifying pulls strands of old dead grass (thatch) to the surface. If scarifying is carried out in the spring, it can be followed by an application of a high-nitrogen feed.

It may prove very difficult and therefore unrealistic to grow a satisfactory sward of grass beneath large trees (especially conifers). If there is a good covering of moss and virtually no grass at all, it is probably best to leave it unscarified. It will look attractive for much of the time and grass is unlikely to do any better.

Away from the overhang of trees, if there is at least 50% moss and only isolated patches of grass, it is often best to destroy both the moss and the grass, cultivate the ground and re-establish a completely new area of lawn with turf or seed. Another possibility is to scarify and lightly cultivate the mossy areas, then spread about 2.5 cm (1 in.) of lawn top dressing, mixed with seed, over the whole area. This must then be rolled lightly and kept watered until a new sward of grass has become established.

Aerating a lawn

The surface of some soils—especially silt—may become blocked, waterlogged and therefore poorly aerated. This can have a detrimental effect on the growth of the grass. A simple garden fork may be used rather like a pogo stick and inserted up to a depth of 15 cm (6 in.) and is sufficient for a small lawn. Various tools and machines, called aerators, are also available: these may be used to make holes or slits over the entire surface at about 45 cm (1½ in.) intervals and range from large, petrol-driven machines to simple, manual implements.

Solid tines, like those of a fork, merely push holes into the surface while hollow tines actually remove a core of soil. The cores can be collected up and a top dressing of sharp sand and compost brushed in to fill the holes. This is obviously a better and more permanent solution than the one provided by solid tines. It is important to remember that any of this is only "skin deep". Unless the holes or slits connect with better-drained soil or some form of drainage just 7.5 cm (3 in.) or so below the surface, the benefit of aerating could be rather limited.

Top dressing and feeding

A well-sieved mixture of loam, peat and sharp sand, often mixed with some fertilizer and sometimes grass seed can be used to fill in low spots, small, denuded

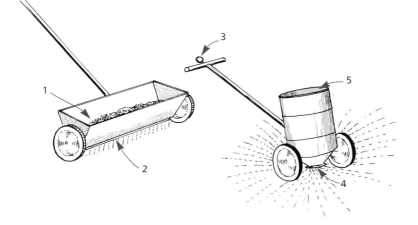

A box-type spreader (**far left**) dispenses seed or fertilizer using a roller bar or belt which rotates. A cyclone-type spreader (**left**) does the same job by means of a rotating plate.

1 hopper
2 roller bar or belt
3 shutter (on/off) control
4 rotating plate
5 hopper

patches made when treating a lawn for moss (see above), or to replace the cores removed by using a hollow-tined aerator.

Most lawns respond well to fertilizers, especially those applied during the spring, summer and autumn. It is very important to apply fertilizers evenly over the surface; otherwise the result can be very patchy and possibly unsightly. You can apply them either as granules applied through a wheeled spreader, or as a liquid to be watered in. Be careful

---

Applying fertilizers

- Little and often is better than occasional heavy dressings.
- Use high-nitrogen compound fertilizers in the spring and summer, but high-phosphate feeds in the autumn. There are many fertilizers on the market specifically labelled as spring, summer and autumn lawn feeds.
- Never apply a granular fertilizer to grass that is wet (from dew, rain, or irrigation), unless you can irrigate immediately afterwards, because the fertilizer is likely to dissolve into small globules of acid and burn the grass if it is not washed off straightaway.
- Under drought conditions, it may be better to use a liquid rather than a granular feed.
- Use a cyclone type of spreader rather than the box and roller type. A cyclone spreader gives a much more even spread and does not leave stripes of under- or overfed lawn.
- Use garden canes to mark out small areas sequentially, about 1 m (3 ft.) wide and 6 m (6 ft.) long, in which to apply the dressing, so that you do not overrun or miss out any areas.

---

not to overdose with fertilizer. Any existing moss may turn black, but let it die off completely before you rake it out.

Alternatives to Grass

If the prospect of mowing and regular care does not appeal, you could plant a lawn with other low-growing plants. They will not be as hardwearing as grass, so are not effective in frequently walked-over areas; they may also look unattractive in winter because not all are evergreen. Grass alternatives include those listed below.

Trifolium repens

One of the benefits of a white clover lawn is its crop of flowers. They often attract great numbers of bees during the summer. Clover is quite tall when it flowers, perhaps 15 cm (6 in.), so a clover lawn is not normally kept short like a grass lawn but allowed to grow more like a meadow. It may prove difficult to control weeds in a clover lawn since the usual herbicides are likely to damage the clover. In winter, a clover lawn can die back and look messy.

Chamaemelum nobile

The best form of lawn chamomile to grow is 'Treneague', which does not flower and remains reasonably compact. Even so, chamomile grows to a height of several centimetres (inches), so cannot normally be kept as short as a conventional lawn. It seems to thrive best in soil which does not dry out too often or in dappled shade, although it will grow well between paving stones in a sunny place.

Chamomile smells pleasant when crushed under foot and its feathery foliage is a fresh green. It is not hardwearing and it may almost disappear in winter, which makes it more suited to small, selected areas rather than for a whole lawn. It can be grown in with grass but the cutting height of the grass must then be raised to accommodate the chamomile, and the effect tends to look messy. It is not possible to use a selective herbicide, so invading weeds will need to be removed by hand.

Bellis perennis

For many years, the Perennial lawn daisy has been banished from lawns as a result of using herbicides. This has been so successful that it is now relatively rare to see lawn daisies—so much so that there is a move to re-introduce them! One of the most effective ways of doing this is to develop a winding path of daisies (and grass) through an otherwise daisy-free lawn. When they are all in flower, the effect can be very attractive and it is not difficult to prevent their spread with a hormone herbicide.

Whenever you prune a plant, keep standing back at intervals to check the outline.

Renovating the Trees and Shrubs

The shrubs or small trees in the garden may have grown too large or leggy to be moved, but would look out of proportion with your planned planting. Depending on the type of plant and speed of growth, the woody plants, whether trees, shrubs, or hedging plants, can be reduced in overall size by about one-third, or in some cases pruned hard back, to bring them back into scale with new planting. Some small trees or evergreen shrubs, such as *Laurus nobilis* (bay), *Buxus* (box), *Ilex* (holly), or *Taxus* (yew), can be topiarized or clipped to form a focal point or feature.

Good pruning is a skilled job, and too often irreparable damage may be done in ignorance to choice plants inherited from previous owners. If you are a complete novice, you may (wisely) be nervous about pruning plants whose growth habits are unknown to you. Even an experienced contract gardener is likely to give your plants a rough short-back-and-sides or rounded treatment—it is quicker, easier and does not involve standing back frequently to check the plant's outline.

However, despite inexperience, if you take the trouble to learn the basic principles of pruning and

Many old shrubs will, when cut back to about one-third of their original size, produce a mass of new growth (**left**). Where this is not possible, new, young plants (**right**) will be needed to regenerate some areas of old borders.

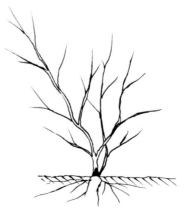

follow the few guidelines detailed below, you should be able to perform a superior job yourself. You will need to understand the different growth habits of woody plants and how they can be modified. More details of pruning techniques for specific plants, and routine maintenance pruning, follow in Chapter 5 (see pages 280–291).

The Correct Way to Prune

The way a plant reacts to pruning can usually be predicted: when growth is removed from one part of the plant, new shoots will be produced elsewhere. Every plant has a genetic desire to try to reach a certain size. For example, cutting off the tip of a shoot will stimulate the sideshoots to sprout lower down. Removing one or two old branches that have stopped flowering or fruiting will encourage new, more productive shoots to appear. Cutting off a lot of older growth may trigger a surge of new growth, while moderate pruning provokes a less dramatic response. Don't forget: the harder you cut the plant, the more vigorous the response is likely to be.

Cutting a shoot

When making a cut on any plant, always use the same basic technique. The cut should be made immediately above a bud (or pair of buds). Whether this cut should be sloping or straight probably does not make any difference, but it is usual to cut to a slope away from the bud, in the hope that any moisture will not sit on the bud and cause it to rot. Avoid leaving a snag or length of stem without a bud at the top because this could become diseased, die back and infect the rest of the shoot.

The direction in which a new shoot will grow can be predicted by looking at the buds just below the intended cut. Buds will produce shoots that grow in whatever direction the buds are pointing, which is useful for example if a lax, sprawling habit is to be corrected by training upward stems to grow flat against a wall.

Left: Incorrect cut— the snag left above the bud could die back and infect the shoot.

Right: Correct cut— immediatley above and sloping away from bud to prevent water from collecting above it.

Dead, damaged or diseased branches

This essential work carries very little risk of harming the plant, and should always be done whether you are pruning a plant to renovate it or as part of its annual maintenance. You may well find that neglected woody plants have a lot of unhealthy growth crowding the plant, and cleaning it out will let light and air into the centre and encourage new, vigorous shoots to be produced. The ideal time for pruning most woody plants is in the winter months when there is no active growth, but it can also be done in the spring or summer, especially for evergreens. It is best to leave cherries and plums (*Prunus* species) until late spring, otherwise the airborne disease silver leaf might enter through the fresh wounds to infect the trees.

Pruning Tools

- Bypass secateurs (pruners)—where one curved blade slices past the other, static curved "blade" and cuts in a similar way to a pair of scissors. The moving blade should actually touch the static blade and make an audible swishing noise as it slices past. The fact that the blades are curved helps to stop the branch sliding out. This type of secateur is preferred by most gardeners.

Bypass secateurs (pruners)

- Anvil secateurs (pruners)—a straight blade meets an "anvil" blade (with a broad, flat edge) in a chopping motion. If the straight blade is blunt, it might crush the branch before cutting it. If your grip is not very strong, you could try using secateurs that have a ratchet or lever system, making them easier to operate.
  There are several types to suit the size of your hand and the type of pruning to be tackled. The anvil can be replaced when it is worn.

Anvil secateurs

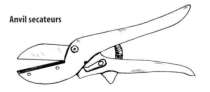

- Long-handled pruners—are, in effect, secateurs with long handles, often up to 60 cm (2 ft.). They can be either bypass or anvil types and may be fitted with a ratchet or lever system, which is an advantage when cutting thicker branches because it requires less strength to operate them.

- Shears—choose a pair which allow you to adjust the blade tension by hand for a finer cut. Clean and oil them after use.
- Tree pruners or loppers—these have a cutting head on the end of a long pole. You pull a rope, or metal rod, to make the blades cut. Loppers are very useful for reaching the tops of small trees and very tall shrubs.
- Folding pruning saw—a fairly narrow, curved saw-edge blade, with a wooden or plastic handle, also called a Grecian saw. The coarse teeth are designed to cut on the backward stroke, so most of the cutting is done as you draw the blade towards you. This is especially useful when you are working on thick branches above your head.

Grecian saw

- Bow saw—named after a bow and arrow, this tool has a coarse blade held in a bow-shaped, metal frame. An ordinary bow handle can be rather cumbersome but a small bow saw, with a handle that narrows to a point at one end, is useful in a confined space.

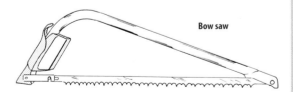

Bow saw

- Pruning knife—this has a sharp, curved blade and is used for trimming or cleaning up any rough cuts. It can also be used, with care, for very small pruning jobs, especially on very soft plants, but it does take some practice to make a good, sharp cut.

- Hedgetrimmers—powered by petrol, mains electricity or rechargeable batteries, these come with a variety of blade lengths to suit different needs. All should come with a number of safety features such as safety guards and a mechanism that quickly cuts out in an emergency.

It is important that all tools are sharp. Blunt tools can leave snags of bark and wood that may eventually allow disease to enter the cut and infect the plant. The blades of all pruning tools should be wiped clean after every use and pruner and knife blades will also need to be sharpened regularly.

When pruning, first look for any dead, diseased or damaged shoots on the plant and remove each by going at least one node (joint or place upon the stem where the leaves are attached) farther back into healthy wood. The wood can be tested by scraping its surface with your thumb nail—if there is a sign of green growth beneath the surface, the plant is alive; if there is no sign of green, some of the plant may well be dead.

Either way, cut back to a good, strong bud or an existing shoot or branch. Choose one from which the new shoot will grow in the most appropriate direction, often in the same direction as the removed branch, or outwards from the centre of the plant. To achieve this, the cut may need to be made farther back along the branch, at the first bud pointing in a suitable direction.

As one of the objectives of pruning is to open up the shrub to allow more circulation of light and air, remove any crossing branches that may rub and disfigure another—chafing wounds allow disease to enter the plant.

Removing branches from a tree

The main problem with this job is the weight of the branch to be removed. Unless you are very careful, before you finish cutting the branch, it will tear the bark and part of the stem that you want to keep, which could cause problems with rot or disease later. You will need a folding pruning saw, or for larger branches a bow saw, to make several reducing and

one final, clean cut (close to an adjoining branch), as illustrated, in order to remove the branch without damaging the rest of the plant.

Branches thicker than about 15 cm (6 in.) should be removed by a qualified tree surgeon.

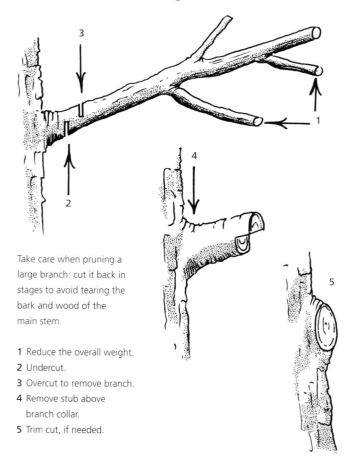

Take care when pruning a large branch: cut it back in stages to avoid tearing the bark and wood of the main stem.

1 Reduce the overall weight.
2 Undercut.
3 Overcut to remove branch.
4 Remove stub above branch collar.
5 Trim cut, if needed.

First, shorten the branch to leave a short length above where the main cut has to be made. Remove this using an undercut and overcut to prevent any tearing, then make the final cut. Aim for a clean cut close to the main stem, but just above the "branch collar", the slightly ridged ring at the base of the branch. Trim or bevel the bark around the edge of the cut with a sharp pruning knife and the branch collar will eventually heal or "callus" over. It is unnecessary to paint the cut surface with wound paint because this hinders the natural healing process.

Recognizing old wood

When pruning, you will need to recognize the difference between old wood and new. If you look into the heart of a well-established shrub, you should be able to see that older branches deep inside (especially close to the ground) are dark in colour and quite gnarled, whereas those newer branches outside are smoother and lighter. New growth is also more flexible.

Reducing the Size of a Plant

If a plant has grown too big for the allocated space and it is not a plant that is usually pruned annually, pruning may be only a temporary solution. Cut large specimen shrubs back with secateurs—a little smaller than the desired size to make allowances for vigorous growth after pruning. As long as the pruning is not severe, it is unlikely to harm the plant. When reshaping trees and shrubs, the aim should be to allow more light and air through the plant.

Some grafted trees or shrubs may have produced suckers, or shoots growing strongly from the rootstock of the plant, below the graft union. If left in place, suckers spoil the outline of the plant and draw energy from the top-growth. They also look different, often coarser, to the rest of the plant because they are produced by the rootstock, which is not the same species as the ornamental plant grafted on to it.

Remove unwanted shoots or suckers from the base of the tree or shrub. Dig down to expose the base of the sucker, then pull it off if you can or cut it off close to the main stem, to prevent regrowth.

If the plant is neglected or severely overgrown, it is best to undertake some remedial pruning in the winter. However, unless you prune at the appropriate time of year for particular plants, it may mean going without flowers or fruits for a season. To avoid this, try to prune just after flowering or fruiting has taken place. In some cases, it will be obvious that flowering is about to occur but in others you will need some knowledge of the plant's flowering habits. For example, trimming back a lavender hedge in early summer would mean cutting off all the shoots that are due to flower in mid- to late summer.

An opposite technique is adopted for hedges (including lavender), where as little as possible is removed with shears to produce a dense growth at the tips of the stems. This method keeps the plants relatively small and compact for many years, but is unsuitable for specimen shrubs.

Trees and Shrubs—Growth Habits

There are four principal types of growth habit in trees and shrubs.

Mounded

These trees and shrubs tend to flower at the tips of their shoots. Then several new shoots usually spring from below the old flowerhead, growing at a wide angle from the old stem. These new shoots will flower and in turn produce further new growth until the plant becomes a mass of flowers over the rounded surface, as in *Choisya ternata* and *Hebe*.

Arching

Plants with arching habits usually flower all along the shoots on short side-growths, or spurs. These shoots generally appear from the centre of the plant, growing straight upwards to reach the light. When mature, these shoots become weighed down as they produce spurs and flowers along their length, resulting in an arching form, for example *Exochorda*, *Forsythia*, and *Spiraea*.

Pyramidal

These plants are usually conifers. The main shoot is the dominant one, but it produces lateral, or side, branches from the main stem on a forked, but tapered trunk. This gives each plant an elegant shape. Unlike most shrubs and trees, conifers have no clear nodes (joints) and internodes (spaces between joints). To the untrained eye, they appear to be a mass of needle-like growth. However, if you look closely at conifer branches, especially those of prostrate (flat-growing) types, you will see that they grow in layers.

Fastigiate

Such plants, with narrow, upright shapes, are mostly conifers, and therefore do not regenerate when cut hard back. The outer layer of attractive, green foliage usually conceals a dead, brown interior. A few conifers, such as *Taxus baccata* (yew) or *Juniperus communis* 'Hibernica' (Irish juniper), however, can be reduced in width. There are also a few deciduous species such as *Fagus sylvatica* 'Dawyck' (upright beech), *Liriodendron tulipifera* 'Fastigiatum' (tulip tree) and, for small gardens, the popular *Prunus* 'Amanogawa' (Lombardy poplar cherry). All are useful as vertical features to draw the eye upwards and to cast intriguing shadows.

Some plants, especially old specimens, resent hard pruning and seem unable to regrow from old branches. These include many of the shrubby herbs, including conifers, hebes, heathers, *Salvia* (sage), *Santolina*, and *Artemisia* (wormwood), where pruning should be limited to trimming off old flowerheads with secateurs or shears. On very old plants, it is safest to prune back part of the plant to start with and then, when the sap is rising in the growing season, cut it back farther. If the plant is very old and bare and knotty at the centre, it might be worth taking some cuttings (see pages 300–310) to raise new plants to replace it.

Reshaped Plants

Any severely pruned plant will try to react to the shock by producing a mass of new growth. All will benefit from a good watering and feeding to help them recover. If too many new shoots appear, either cut them off at the base or thin them out—this will help to channel energy into the growth that you do want from the plant.

Reducing Mounded and Arching Plants

There are two pruning methods that can be used on mounded and arching plants. Many shrubs such as *Hebe* 'Midsummer Beauty' or *Ligustrum* (privet) can be carefully reduced both in height and width without looking ungainly, but if a more radical approach is needed, the plant may have a rugged outline for the first two years.

Method 1

- Remove all the lower branches from the trunk, or thin out the main mature stems, to give the plant a small, tree-like shape.

- Cut back to the stem the less vigorous lateral, or sideways-growing, shoots—work from the ground level upwards, until you achieve a clear canopy.

- Now step back to have a look at the basic structure of the plant. Remove any remaining branches that make the canopy look overcrowded.

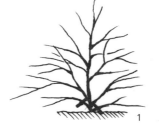
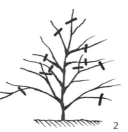

Method 1
1 Cut out lower stems.
2 Shorten weaker laterals.
3 Prune out any other overcrowded shoots.

Method 2
4 Thin out all the shoots after cutting down the leader.
5 Leave an open, smaller canopy.

- In the following growing seasons, remove any new shoots that appear on the clean, main stems so that they in turn do not overcrowd the opened canopy.

Method 2

- Work from the top of the plant downwards: start by removing completely the tallest stem, or leader, tracing it back to just above a node and some sideshoots to make the cut.

- Cut out the leader cleanly above the shoots you wish to keep.

- Gradually thin out some of the remaining shoots until the canopy is more open, but reduced in bulk.

Hard pruning of evergreens

Many of the larger-growing rhododendrons eventually spread too far and become quite bare in the centre. Once every 10–15 years, they can be cut hard back to woody stumps, or to short lengths of stem, immediately after flowering. Since rhododendrons are shallow rooting, if required they can also be moved to new positions once their branches are drastically reduced. The reduction encourages them to produce a completely new set of branches, but it may take two or three years before they resume flowering. Other shrubs respond well to this form of pruning.

Moderate pruning of evergreens

Not all evergreens can tolerate drastic pruning, but may still need occasional rejuvenation. This can be achieved by pruning the entire shrub back by one-third to a half of its size. This pruning would normally be carried out in the spring.

Gentle pruning of evergreens

Some evergreen shrubs, for example *Cytisus scoparius* (broom), can tolerate only gentle pruning if you need to bring them back into shape. All the previous year's growth can be cut back by about a half immediately

---

Pruning Evergreen Trees and Shrubs

Hard prune:
  Prunus laurocerasus (laurel)
  Ilex (holly)
  Laurus nobilis (bay) in mild localities
  Rhododendron

Moderate prune:
  Aucuba
  Camellia
  Cistus (rock rose)
  Choisya (Mexican orange blossom)
  Elaeagnus
  Euonymus japonicus (Japanese spindle)
  Osmanthus
  Prunus lusitanica (Portugal laurel)
  Viburnum—most evergreen species

Gentle prune:
  Convolvulus cneorum
  Cytisus scoparius (broom)
  Phlomis
  Rosmarinus
  Salvia (sage)
  Santolina (cotton lavender)

---

after flowering in late spring. Avoid going back into old wood, and begin this pruning regime when the plant is only two or three years old. As a general rule, prune weak specimens lightly to start with, in order to see if how they respond. If their vigour increases, then pruning in future years could be more severe.

Cutting hard back

This radical pruning is done on shrubs that are grown mainly for their ornamental foliage or stems, or on those shrubs that flower in late summer on branches produced as a result of hard pruning. These are mostly deciduous shrubs and they are pruned in this way usually in winter or very early spring. In cold districts where new shoots could be damaged by frost, delay pruning until the hardest frosts have passed. It is best to start this pruning regime while

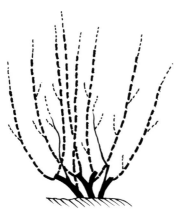

1 Cut all the previous year's growth hard back to within 3 or 4 buds.

2 The remaining stump, or stool, will regenerate very quickly in the spring.

3 New shoots, full of vigour, are produced during the following year.

the plant is only two or three years old but, if the tree or shrub has been allowed to grow unpruned, be less ruthless and prune it back gradually over two or three years. Occasionally, the current state of a plant may mean that it is worth cutting it down to the ground, and taking the risk that it will regenerate.

Cut all the previous year's growth back to the old stump or "stool" (often close to ground level). This usually results in a considerable crop of new shoots,

often with larger, more brightly coloured foliage or perhaps a good crop of flowers at the tip of each shoot in late summer.

Reducing Pyramidal Trees and Shrubs

These are usually conifers—each tends to have its own individual outline—and they are not easy to reduce gracefully. Often the lower branches are overshadowed by those higher up the tree and tend to die off, leaving an ugly, lower main stem. In other cases, shade causes entire branches occasionally to die off; because these branches will not regrow, the plant then looks unbalanced.

Cutting Hard Back

Buddleja davidii (butterfly bush)—other
    Buddleja should be pruned less drastically
Caryopteris
Catalpa bignonioides 'Aurea' (Indian bean
    tree)—sometimes grown as a shrub
Ceratostigma
Cornus alba (dogwood)
Corylus (hazel)
Eucalyptus gunnii—tree sometimes grown
    as a shrub
Fuchsia—hardy species
Hydrangea paniculata
Salix alba var. *vitellina* (golden willow)
Sambucus
Spiraea japonica 'Bumalda'

To replace a damaged conifer leader, first cut it down to just above the replacement shoot (**left**). Tie in the new leader to train it upwards (**right**).

If the plant is growing too tall, attempting to cut out the growing tip will spoil the symmetrical shape, as is often seen with fast-growing conifers such as *Cupressocyparis leylandii* (Leyland cypress), and it will always look strange. Better to remove the tree altogether, but this means roots and all so it could be expensive.

If the central leader has been accidentally damaged, perhaps in a storm, thin out the upper part of the plant until you find a strong, upright growth to form a replacement leader. Train this new leader by tying it to a stake or cane until it grows straight naturally and takes over from the damaged one.

The breadth of spread of pyramidal plants can be reduced slightly by pinching back the soft, new growths made each spring. If you need to prune an oversized conifer more significantly, it is possible if you take care.

- Take hold of a small branch that you want to remove and trace it back into the conifer, to where it projects from an older branch.

- Using your secateurs, cut back the small branch next to the older branch, so it comes away "invisibly", leaving the conifer looking quite untouched but slightly smaller.

- By doing this repeatedly, you can make the plant considerably smaller without it appearing to be clipped.

- Obviously the more growth you remove, the more impact, but always stop short of cutting back into old, brown wood because the plant is usually unable to regenerate from old wood.

- Avoid using shears unless you intend making the conifer into a hedge.

Reducing Fastigiate Plants

Fastigiate, or upright, trees and shrubs cannot generally be pruned without spoiling their appearance, but they can be given a treatment for a denser, more defined shape. To maintain the shape, you may need to carry out this task every year.

Tie in a fastigiate plant to obtain a more refined shape.

- Clear out all the dead debris or leaves from within the plant.

- Tie in the branches tightly with stout, natural-coloured string or yachting twine. Do not use wire because it cuts into, and damages, the stems.

- Foliage will grow over and disguise the twine.

Fastigiate plants can also be reduced in height simply by removing the top metre or so (2–3 ft.), making sure that the cut is level. Tie in the new growth with twine or string. Reduce conifers such as *Taxus baccata* (yew) or *Juniperus communis* 'Hibernica' (Irish juniper) in width by lightly clipping them over with shears.

Dwarf conifers should be dealt with in the same way as fastigiates, but they tend to outgrow their positions quite quickly.

Spreading Juniper

Juniperus horizontalis (spreading juniper) and its cultivars are often used to disguise manhole covers or eyesores. A plant will eventually cover 3–4 metres (3–12 ft.) of ground and needs to be carefully shaped. Pruning off some of the lower branches flush to the main stems should allow others to grow over the area. These plants need replacing after about ten years because their spread and scale usually makes them out of proportion with other plantings.

Transplanting a Shrub

- Decide where the plant is to be moved to, and dig a hole large enough to allow the roots to spread out when replanted. Fill the hole with water and allow it to drain away.
- Tie up the branches so that they are not damaged in the move.
- Dig a trench around the shrub, at a spade blade's depth, in a circle 60–90 cm (2–3 ft.) wide.
- Gradually cut into the rootball at about 45 degrees to the bottom of the trench. Cut through any thick roots, if necessary.

- When you have freed the rootball, ease some sacking or hessian underneath it.
- Tie the ends of the hessian round a pole, if possible, so that two people—one at each end of the pole—may lift the plant. The wrapped, rootballed shrub should not be left unplanted for more than one or two days, particularly if windy conditions are likely to dry out the roots.
- Replant the shrub in the new position and water it well.

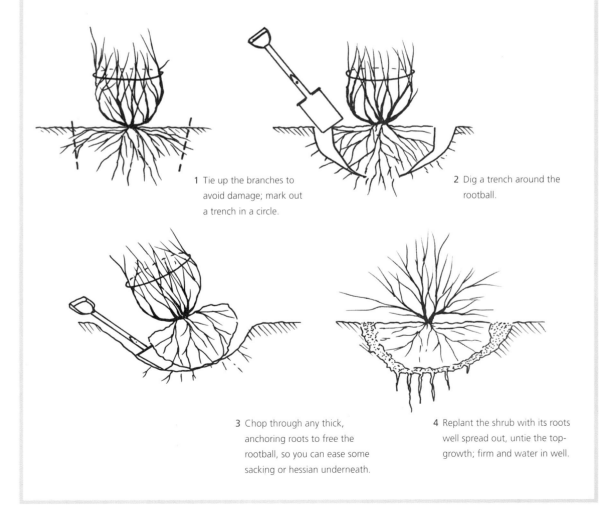

1 Tie up the branches to avoid damage; mark out a trench in a circle.

2 Dig a trench around the rootball.

3 Chop through any thick, anchoring roots to free the rootball, so you can ease some sacking or hessian underneath.

4 Replant the shrub with its roots well spread out, untie the top-growth; firm and water in well.

Moving Shrubs

You may decide that some of the shrubs that you want to keep are in the wrong place, that they might grow better in changed conditions, or that rearranging them might improve the look of the planting.

As long as the shrub is not too large, and its roots are not inextricably entwined with those of another, moving it in the dormant season is quite feasible. You should aim to extract as large a rootball as possible to give it the best chance of recovery. Having dug the new hole for the transplanted shrub, fill the hole with water and plant only once the water has drained away. This will help get the shrub off to a good start by allowing the roots to search for and find moisture immediately. After transplanting a shrub, keep it well watered. Spray the plant overhead twice daily with a hose if the weather is very dry and sunny; this helps to avoid too much transpiration of water from the leaves.

Renovating Borders

In the early stages of developing a garden, a holding bed is a useful repository for storing plants. It can be an old border, vegetable garden or in fact almost any open area of soil free from plants and weeds. In many regions, a western aspect is preferable—this will receive the late afternoon sun, whereas a southerly aspect will tend to be too hot and dry out the plants. A northerly aspect may be too cold, windy or shady for the more tender or sun-loving plants. Plants in the garden that you like, but want to move, can be planted temporarily, or "heeled in", until you are ready to replant them in their permanent sites. The holding bed can also be a useful reception area for storing plant gifts, impulse buys or plants that you may have brought from a previous garden. These will probably be in pots; if you sink them into the soil in the holding bed, they will need less watering and are less likely to dry out. Once the holding bed is ready, the herbaceous borders can be cleared or improved.

Tackling the Herbaceous Plants

Too often the existing plant material in a bed or border may at first look interesting but then yields only plants such as *Solidago* (golden rod) or *Acanthus* (bear's breeches), both prolific spreaders and not easy to eradicate. It is much more difficult to improve an existing border than to start from scratch, particularly if the border is infested with weeds. In the long term, it is usually quicker and easier to empty the bed completely, heeling any desirable plants into the holding bed temporarily until you decide on a permanent place for them. Any trace of weeds must be carefully removed before heeling in; in severe cases, this may mean washing all the existing soil out of the roots before replanting.

The herbaceous bed can then be thoroughly weeded or sprayed, and dug over. If the weeds are pernicious, a sheet of heavy-duty black plastic should be pegged down firmly over the soil for the whole of the next growing season. Starvation of light and air should help eradicate most pernicious weeds (see also "Weeds", pages 89–97).

Other plants may over the years have grown into large masses—which indicates that they spread easily or can become thugs. Many of these large clumps

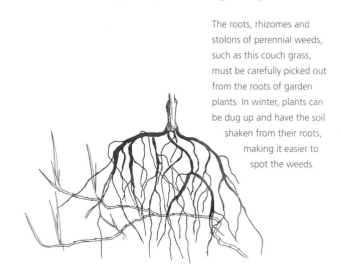

The roots, rhizomes and stolons of perennial weeds, such as this couch grass, must be carefully picked out from the roots of garden plants. In winter, plants can be dug up and have the soil shaken from their roots, making it easier to spot the weeds.

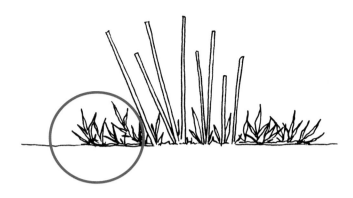

Herbaceous plants can be split up to regenerate an ageing border. Remove the young growth from around the edges of old clumps (**left**). Use divisions with good roots (**below**) to pot up or replant directly into the garden.

will have clusters of new plants emerging from an older centre, with one new plant frequently stifling another. These should be carefully teased out, separated and divided into a dozen or so plants that will take up little space in the holding bed. They can be planted in useful clumps later, but remember to use fewer rather than more divisions of such vigorous plants, because they have already proved that they increase easily.

Plants such as peonies and hellebores that have tough rootstocks will need to be divided into individual plants, by separating them from the main plant with a sharp knife. Some plants are easier to divide than others; by working through the border, you will soon begin to understand each plant's growing pattern.

If digging up and heeling in all the herbaceous plants sounds too radical, a few special, deep-rooted specimens such as hellebores, which are long-lived but slow to increase, can remain in situ and be worked around.

If you know the names of the plants, each should be carefully labelled. If not, you will need to wait until the next growing season to see how they perform and whether they may be suitable. Make a list of the reclaimed plants so that you can consider new positions for them later. In this way, an inexpensive

collection of reclaimed plants can be used to infill among other new, and more choice, varieties selected specifically for leaf form, colour or flower.

Water

Although the most seductive element in a garden, there are so many different ways of using ornamental water that is hard to decide how it should be included and how dominant the feature should be. Simple solutions are usually best, and can vary from a wall-mounted mask and basin to large formal or informal water features with fountains, rills or cascades.

Whether still or moving, the water will be highly noticeable and unless you have a natural flow, it will need careful positioning. To create a naturalistic pond or stream, place the water where it may seem natural in relation to the surrounding landscape. Normally water occupies the lowest level, creating a datum to which everything else relates, so setting it on high ground will be unconvincing, especially if the ground is sloping. The pool itself may appear as a natural contour line, so the relationship of any surrounding contours must also be considered.

The colour of the water is important and will depend on the choice of lining material, usually tiles or a heavy-duty plastic membrane. Black produces the best reflection and, even in a shallow pool, can give the appearance of limitless depth while also hiding elements such as pumps or planting baskets. The level of water is also crucial—if it is set too low, the first element to be reflected will be the side of the pool itself. This will make the water level seem to be twice as deep as it really is, so try to keep it as close to ground level as possible. Proximity also makes it easier to touch the water; wildlife enjoy it and birds may use shallow pools as birdbaths.

Sound is an important property of moving water. Submersible pumps can be easily fitted but the sound may be too dominant, sometimes precluding conversation and disturbing sleep, so adjust the pump until the pressure is suitable. If installing a fountain, experiment with the height of the jets to find out if a strong wind might drive the water beyond the circumference of the pool.

Restoring Water Features

Existing pools and ponds are notoriously difficult and fickle elements to improve. Even if you approve of the design and siting of the feature, you may still have some problems. A low water level may indicate a leak—try refilling it and if it drops again to the same level, the leak is at (or just above) this level. If the pool leaks, it will need emptying and repairing. Even if there is no leak, and you wish to keep the pool, it will almost certainly need to be cleared and restocked.

Restoring a pond is a task best carried out in winter or spring to avoid mosquito bites. Empty it with a slurry pump or bucket and spade, and then pressure-hose it clean or give it a thorough scrubbing. If there is a leak, it will either need a simple repair using a patching kit, resurfacing with either a waterproofing compound painted on to the existing concrete or a flexible, reinforced butyl liner cut to size. Soil may be spread over the bottom before the pond is refilled with water. Aquatic plants, including oxygenating

types, can be inserted into soil on the bottom or in plastic-mesh baskets, which should then be submerged. Leave a couple of weeks for the plants to settle down before adding fish and snails to create a balanced and easily maintained community. Many specialists and magazines will give you ideas and names of suppliers.

If algae is a problem, a black dye is now available, which stops light entering the pond and starves any algae of the light necessary for it to grow. The dye is safe for pets and other visitors such as frogs and newts but should not be used in ponds with fish because the water will have turned completely black.

Weeds

Every gardener complains about weeding at some time or another, so is it really necessary to spend so much time battling against the weeds in our gardens? Whatever your own definition of a weed might be, it could be summed up as any plant growing where it is not wanted. For instance, wild flowers may be highly sought after to create a natural effect in a meadow planting, but are not wanted in the herbaceous border. Most weeds are, of course, members of the local flora and they can be good indicators of the inherent fertility and pH of the local soil.

Weeds… from where cometh my salvation?

Apart from the fact we might not like the look of them, weeds interfere with the ornamental and crop plants we want to grow by:

- Competing for light and moisture

- Taking valuable nutrients out of the soil

- Attracting and harbouring a wide range of garden pests and some diseases

- Swamping small plants and seedlings.

For these reasons, it is crucial never to plant or sow into weed-infested soil. The ground must be cleared of weeds first. Weeds also must be removed before you can get to work on improving the soil.

Types of Weed

There are two main types of weed—perennials and annuals. You will need to identify the group in which any particular weed belongs because the method of control differs.

Perennial weeds usually have perennial roots, and stems in the form of runners or stolons. If you simply pull or cut off these stems, you will not eradicate what is underground. Some also reproduce from their stems and roots. Churning up the ground with a

---

Common Weeds

Perennials
- Bindweed (*Convolvulus arvensis*)
- Bracken (*Pteridium aquilinum*)
- Couch grass (*Elymus repens*)
- Creeping buttercup (*Ranunculus repens*)
- Creeping thistle (*Cirsium arvense*)
- Dandelion (*Taraxacum officinale*)
- Dock (*Rumex* spp.)
- Greater plantain (*Plantago major*)
- Ground elder (*Aegopodium podagraria*)
- Horse or mare's tail (*Equisetum arvense*)
- Perennial nettle (*Urtica dioica*)
- Sorrel (*Rumex* spp.)

Annuals
- Annual meadow grass (*Poa annua*)
- Annual nettle (*Urtica urens*)
- Chickweed (*Stellaria media*)
- Groundsel (*Senecio vulgaris*)
- Hairy bittercress (*Cardamine hirsuta*)
- Shepherd's purse (*Capsella bursa-pastoris*)

---

mechanical cultivator/rotavator will merely chop up the stems and roots and, in effect, encourage them to multiply!

Annual weeds have no perennial underground parts but they do usually produce huge numbers of seeds.

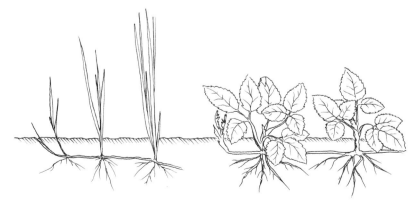

couch grass (*Elymus repens*)   ground elder (*Aegopodium podagraria*)

Pulling up the plants or picking off the flowers before the seeds form will prevent a new generation from being produced. The mature plants left without flowers or seeds will eventually die after a few months, as long as any further flowers are removed. Unfortunately, weed seeds can travel great distances, so no matter how carefully you control your own annual weeds, more are bound to come in from other gardens or nearby fields. Many annual seeds can survive in the soil for several years, even decades, before germinating, so you will almost certainly find that as you begin to cultivate the soil, fresh crops of weeds will spring up and will need to be removed.

Weeding Tools and Mulches

Apart from the essential hoe, here are many hand tools for controlling weeds and cultivating the ground, most in the form of claw or twist cultivators. Although these can be useful in soft soils, they must be used with caution between rows of seedlings and other vulnerable young plants. Once areas of the garden are cleared of weeds, the best way to stop them recurring is to use a mulch or weed mat.

Hoes

A draw hoe is used literally to hack weeds out of the ground. Standing astride the weeds, bring down the hoe in a shallow, chopping action. Don't chop too deep, otherwise too much soil will come up with the weed roots and they will not die. On a dry, windy day, many of the hoed weeds will die but if it rains soon afterwards, many will re-root and continue to grow. Draw hoes are used mainly on weeds that have already become well established but have not yet set seed. If seeds are present, then inevitably, some will germinate afterwards.

A Dutch hoe is used in much the same way as a draw hoe, but the design of the hoe varies considerably. For the hoe to be effective, the surface of the ground must be quite smooth and have (potentially) a good tilth. The weeds should still be at the seedling stage or at least quite small. The hoe is pushed forwards in

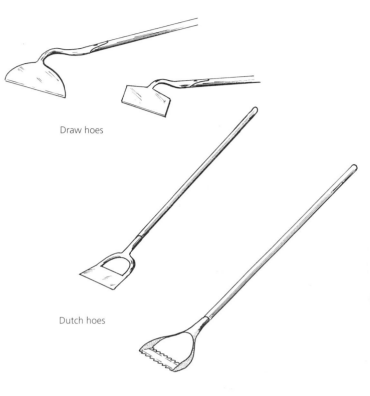

Draw hoes

Dutch hoes

fairly short, repetitive movements, as shallowly as possible so that the blade slips just beneath the weeds and therefore undermines them. On a dry day, they will soon die and fade away.

As hoeing progresses, you walk backwards to avoid treading the weeds back in again. Even if there are very few weed seedlings showing, it is still well worthwhile running the hoe through the ground on a good, dry day because there are bound to be many weed seeds germinating just beneath the surface. This technique will significantly reduce the potential for subsequent crops of weeds and is especially useful between rows of crops in the kitchen garden.

Beware: if you use any type of hoe carelessly, you could undermine the roots of your plants and crops and kill them. Hoes must therefore be used at a safe distance away from any small plants. Leave weeds growing close to crops to be pulled out by hand as soon as they are large enough to be gripped.

Mulches

A layer of organic matter, or an inorganic substance such as plastic or matting, laid on the surface of the soil, is called a mulch. The surface of the ground must be clear of weeds, and be smooth and free from clods of earth, so that the mulch can be laid in a sufficient depth, i.e. at least 7.5 cm (3 in.). It is important to appreciate that while a mulch can suppress many annual weeds and their seeds, perennial weeds can often survive and grow through the more granular forms of mulch. Some commonly available granular mulches are:

- Shredded bark/ bark chippings

- Cocoa shells

- Spent hops

- Mushroom compost

- Well-rotted garden compost

- Well-rotted stable manure.

These are all effective if used thickly. Most of these mulches oxidize away after about a year and will need topping up. Bark is more expensive and lasts longer; in heavy clay soil, the soil texture will be improved as the bark begins to break down.

Small, soft plants such as flowering herbaceous plants and young vegetable plants may be damaged by the thickness of granular mulches; they are usually best kept weed-free by regular hoeing. If perennial weeds come up through the mulch, the mulch must be carefully pulled to one side, and the weeds dug out. The soil can then be put back and smoothed over before the mulch is replaced.

Weed mats

Weed mats can be laid over ground that has already been cleared of weeds to act as a physical barrier to stop new weeds breaking though. Where weeds already exist, they can be suffocated by a weed mat. The mat can be "bulked up" and made more aesthetically acceptable by having a more attractive, thick, granular mulch spread over the top. Mats can also be used under areas of gravel (black plastic is the most effective here), but only if the gravel is being used as ornamental mulch rather than as a busy path. With heavy foot traffic, the weed mat will often ruck up and come to the surface. Weed mats include:

- Black plastic

- Geotextile matting or fabric

- Old carpet.

Plants grow through openings made by cutting crosses into the mat. The flaps of the cross are pulled back to allow for planting and then folded back

A mulch can be at least 7.5 cm (3 in.) thick around shrubby plants (**right**), but much less around small, soft plants (**far right**) to avoid the risk of rot.

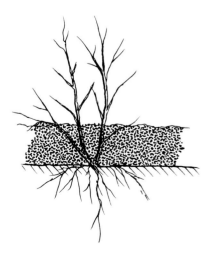

To plant through a weed mat, cut a cross in it and fold back the corners (**left**). After planting (**below**), push back the flaps and spread a mulch over the top to weigh the mat down.

towards the stem once the plant is in place. It is much more difficult to do this with old carpet, which is used more as a total and suffocating blanket over an area already infested with weeds. All weed mats need to be anchored down securely with galvanized pegs to prevent light getting through to the weeds underneath. Light mats have to be weighed down to prevent them from being lifted by wind.

Controlling weeds without chemicals

Non-chemical methods pose no threat to plants around the garden nor to wildlife and are highly effective, especially when used a little and often rather than in a blitz fashion. If you do not weed regularly, vigorous weeds may quickly swamp other plants, becoming so infiltrated into the roots of ornamental plants that it becomes very difficult to get rid of them. There are several common types of weeding problem that you may have to tackle.

Perennial weeds growing in empty ground

– Using a garden fork, work methodically in rows and dig deep enough to find all the roots and stems. Tease these carefully from the clods of soil, leaving nothing behind. Although this is a painstaking task, it can be very effective, if not always 100% successful.

It can be especially difficult in heavy clay and may not be practical for the deepest-rooting weeds, especially mare's tail.

– Burn all the roots and stems. NEVER put them on the compost heap.

– Use an inorganic mulch—for example thick black plastic, weed matting or old carpet. This cuts off the light and will eventually kill the weeds, although it can take a whole growing season. The tops of the weeds may have to be cut down to ground level by strimming before it is possible to lay a sheet mulch flat over the area.

– Isolate the weeds from neighbouring areas of infestation. There is little point in carrying out either of the previous techniques if, after a few weeks, more underground stems and roots emerge in surrounding areas. Hedges can be a particularly common source of infestation. The shallower-rooting perennial weeds such as ground elder, sorrel, bracken, and possibly couch grass, can be kept out by putting a thick, continuous vertical membrane (for example plastic) as a physical barrier into the soil at the perimeter of the area. This is

A continuous, vertical barrier (e.g. PVC) set into the ground, well below the root zone of perennial weeds, will prevent them from re-infecting recently cleared ground.

especially successful if shallow topsoil lies over very hard subsoil, because many of these weeds will tend to stay in the soft, upper zone of the soil. This barrier would usually have to go at least 40 cm (16 in.) deep.

- An alternative to a plastic barrier in the soil is to cut a deep trench or ditch around the area but this may not always be convenient, especially if the threat of invading weeds comes from a nearby lawn.

Annual weeds growing in empty ground
- Once again, using a mulch can be effective.

- Dig them in—annual weeds can be "turned over" or dug in by hand, using a spade or a rotavator. Although the uprooted weeds can look messy, especially after rotavating, most of the weeds soon die and fade away. There will be little risk of these particular weeds leaving behind a legacy of seeds but turning over the soil will, inevitably, bring to the surface seeds from previous generations, and these will soon germinate to produce a new carpet of seedlings. At this point, the ground should be raked level so that a hoe can be used from then on to eliminate the weeds. This raking will disrupt quite a lot of these seedlings, which will die within a few hours on a dry windy day.

Annual weeds in-between other plants and in empty ground
- Hoeing is the most widely used method of controlling annual weeds without chemicals. The two basic types of hoe—draw and Dutch hoe—are used in quite different ways, so try them out and choose the method and tool that suits you best.

- Pull the weeds out by hand, using a small hand fork. This is the easiest, but back-breaking, way of keeping a small bed free of weeds.

Perennial weeds growing among annual weeds
- If there are only a few perennial weeds, place markers next to them before tackling the annuals, then return to dig out the perennials carefully, leaving no pieces of root behind if possible.

- If the perennial and annual weeds are thoroughly mixed, treat them all as perennial weeds.

Perennial weeds growing among the roots of other plants
- If possible, wait until winter before digging up the existing plants. Sift right through the root system (and the surrounding soil), removing all the weeds by hand.

- You may need to rinse the plant roots out under a tap or hose to ensure that all vestiges of the weeds are removed.

- Replant or discard the plant, depending upon how much damage has been done to the plant's roots.

Chemical Control of Weeds

Although chemical control of weeds is useful, it is best reserved for situations that have got out of control. There are various groups of herbicides available and it is important that you know the differences between each, so that you use the correct herbicide for the job.

- Residual herbicide—applied to and stays in the ground for a significant length of time, possibly months. In most (but not all) cases, it will kill virtually all those weeds present and, since it lies on the surface of the ground, it will prevent any regrowth. Some of these chemicals are so potent that they can kill shrubs and flowering plants too. Most of these herbicides are therefore regarded as total residual herbicides and are used on paths, patios, and driveways rather than planted borders.

- Non-residual herbicide—decays rapidly or is neutralized when it comes into contact with the soil and therefore does not poison the soil in any way. It usually kills weeds on contact or as it works through the plant system (systemically).

- Systemic or translocated herbicides—are absorbed through the leaves or taken up by the roots. They are then transported to every part of the plant, so they are particularly effective in treating perennial weeds and their persistent, underground parts.

- Selective and non-selective—a selective herbicide can differentiate between a weed and a "crop", thus killing the weeds and leaving the crop unharmed. A non-selective herbicide cannot differentiate and is, in effect, a total herbicide.

It is important to bear in mind that all herbicides are dangerous and should be handled with care. When handling the concentrate, protect your skin and eyes from splashes and noxious fumes. Many have to be diluted in water and applied with a sprayer or a dribble bar; some are already diluted and are sold in a hand spraygun; others are applied as granules. Always clean out watering cans or sprayers thoroughly after use and label them "WEEDKILLER" so that they are never used for anything else. Store the chemicals in a metal, padlocked cupboard or chest, well out of the reach of children.

Sprayers and dribble bars

Many herbicides are applied with either a sprayer or a dribble bar. For general garden use, pump-up or pressurised sprayers are ideal but for larger-scale work, backpack sprayers are more convenient because they do not need to be filled so often. With any spray, there is always a danger of the liquid accidentally drifting on to leaves and nearby plants. This can be a serious problem on windy days. Some sort of protective guard or even an inverted box may prevent some spray drift, but it is best to spray only when there is no wind.

Where residual herbicides are being applied to the surface of a driveway, path or patio, it is best to set the spray to deliver relatively large water droplets, in a coarse spray, so there is little danger of drift. On the other hand, when translocated or contact herbicides are being applied to the weed's foliage, a much finer spray is needed in order to coat each leaf with chemical without any wasteful run-off on to the ground. This too would be a particularly unsuitable operation for a windy day.

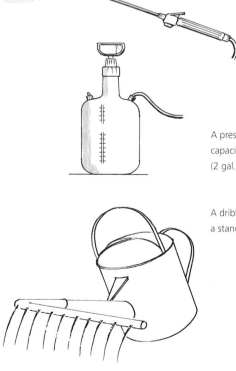

A pressurized sprayer with a capacity of around 7.5 litres (2 gal.).

A dribble bar can be fitted to a standard watering can.

A dribble bar is attached to the spout of a watering can and dribbles the herbicide out from holes in the bar. This helps to avoid the problem of drift and is ideal for residual herbicides, but is very wasteful when it comes to applying translocated or contact herbicides.

Which Herbicide to Use?

When using powerful chemicals in the garden, it is important to use the appropriate herbicide, always diluted as recommended by the suppliers, for the situation and type of weed, otherwise you may end up causing long-term damage or even losing some of your prized plants.

Paths, driveways and patios

A total, residual, non-selective herbicide can be used on these sites for long-term eradication and control. Some of the products sold also include a contact herbicide to kill off any existing weeds. This treatment is most effective if applied in early spring before most weeds have begun to grow and should prevent weeds from appearing for about four months. Remember that these herbicides are potent and could also kill many types of ornamental plants, especially if they happen to be growing between paving stones.

Established weeds in the garden

Non-selective contact and translocated herbicides kill leaves and shoots of annual and perennial weeds on contact. They must be kept away from ornamental plants, although the more robust shrubs can usually withstand a certain amount of damage. The two most common chemicals used are paraquat and glyphosate; the latter is the most effective against perennial weeds. Spraying should not take place on windy days, nor when rain is expected within 48 hours. Treatment is less effective during the winter when weeds have virtually ceased growing.

Weeds between shrubs and trees

In addition to non-selective contact and translocated herbicides, there are some granular products available to deal with annual and perennial weeds in this situation. The correct dose is critical since it is more a case of the survival of the fittest: the chemical takes out the weakest plants—which are the weeds—but if the dose is too strong, it will affect the shrubs.

Chemicals can be used (usually during spring or summer) and are especially effective against ground elder if applied just as the weeds are emerging in early spring. All these products poison the ground and are, to varying degrees, residual so they are not recommended for use between shallow-rooted and herbaceous plants.

Weeds in lawns

There are several so-called "hormone" herbicides available which can kill many lawn weeds without damaging the grass. They are sometimes combined, in a granular form, with fertilizers but are better used on their own in a liquid preparation as and when they are required.

Isolated weeds, especially in lawns, can be spot-treated, using a small hand sprayer that contains a suitable herbicide.

Unfortunately most of these products give off noxious fumes that can damage extension growth—the tender, new shoots—on shrubs, flowers and any young plants, especially kitchen-garden crops. To minimize this, extensive spraying should not take place on windy days and especially not in the spring or early summer, when the garden could be full of plants with vulnerable extension growth. Instead, any extensive treatment is safest done in the early autumn when extension growth on most plants has virtually ceased.

During the spring and summer, isolating individual weeds with a spot treatment is safer and unlikely to cause any significant damage. A number of products are available to tackle the more difficult lawn weeds, especially clover (*Trifolium repens*).

Woody weeds and tree stumps

Herbicides to tackle these problems are usually termed "brushwood killers" and are especially potent. Some are translocated herbicides, others are effective on contact and all are non-selective. Glyphosate can also be quite effective if used at a suitably high dosage.

Cultivating the Soil

In the initial assessment of your garden, you will have already determined what type of soil you have, what fertilizers are needed to correct any nutrient deficiencies and substances required to improve the soil texture, as well as any action you may want to take to affect the soil pH (pages 24–32). Now that you have cleared the garden and are ready to tackle the soil, you must be prepared also to undertake the crucial, mechanical processes of conditioning the soil. You will give your plants the best chance of thriving if they are planted in well-conditioned soil. It is a waste of time trying to make plants grow in hostile conditions.

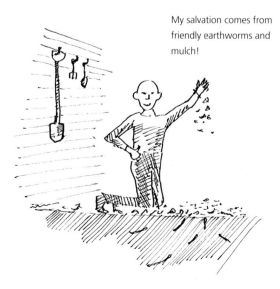

My salvation comes from friendly earthworms and mulch!

Most gardens benefit if in early spring they are mulched with, or have dug in, plenty of well-rotted manure. If the soil is particularly heavy, the plants will probably not die but their roots will take ages to get down into the soil, preventing the plant from putting on healthy growth, so this is a good time to incorporate sand or grit. On the other hand, lighter, sandy soils may drain too quickly or have become so thin that they no longer hold water. These too can be improved by digging in well-rotted manure and other organic matter to bulk up the soil.

To Dig or Not to Dig

There are two types of gardeners—some prefer not to dig the soil, claiming that it is not necessary because nature does it in her own way, using earthworms and other organisms. Others hold the opposite view, spending a great deal of time turning over the soil between plants so that they can introduce additional humus and fertilizer. Where the texture, general composition and drainage of the soil appear to be perfectly satisfactory, then there probably is no reason to dig. However, many soils are lacking in the organic matter that is needed for moisture retention, root growth and some nutrition. Others are over-compacted and poorly drained. Both conditions will hinder the growth of many plants, especially crops in the kitchen garden.

Hand digging the soil can create the opportunity to incorporate organic matter (well-rotted manure or garden compost) as well as to improve drainage. Rose, shrub and herbaceous borders, once planted, tend to remain uncultivated to any depth for a number of years, so it makes sense to dig in as much organic matter as you can and generally improve the soil while they are empty.

When to dig

Digging can be done at any time of the year on most soils, but heavy and clay soils are best dug in late autumn. This allows the frosts to break up the clods before spring. Sprinkling garden lime or gypsum over clay clods in the autumn will dramatically improve the chances of producing a tilth by the following spring.

The Best Type of Spade

The best spades generally are those with a footrest welded on to the top of the blade. Since you tend to push the spade into the ground with your foot, this footrest helps to prevent the top of the blade from cutting into your shoe or boot. Spades are stronger if the steel haft comes well up the wooden shaft. A D–shaped handle is far better than a T–shaped one because the hand slips round it more easily, and will not get so sore. Long-handled spades may be more suitable if you are taller or have a weak back.

Take time to try out different spades before you buy—it is important to use one that you find comfortable if you want to avoid an aching back. Buy the best-quality spade you can afford because it is one of the tools you will use most in years to come. For sticky clay, a chrome-plated or stainless-steel blade is best since the soil will not stick so easily. It will take longer to clog up and will not be such heavy work. Ideally, steel toe capped boots should be worn in case the spade blade slips across your feet.

1 comfortable, plastic handle
2 strong, wooden shaft
3 generous, steel shank
4 foot guards
5 rigid blade—not too springy

Methods of Digging

There are two main ways of digging: single and double digging. They are similar but double digging goes deeper and provides the opportunity to incorporate plenty of organic matter or other soil improvers such as grit. Both types of digging require a spade; double digging also demands a fork. Digging is carried out in rows (rather like knitting!) and both techniques start by creating a straight trench at one end of the area to be dug, running across the entire width of the plot.

Single digging

You will need to start by digging a trench about 20 cm (8 in.) wide along the width of your plot. It should be as deep as the spade's blade, known as one spit, that is, 18 cm (9 in.) deep. Take the soil from this trench and stack it next to where the last row of digging is likely to take place. You can then start digging across the plot, one trench at a time, as illustrated (see opposite).

As you dig, don't be too ambitious—if the clods of soil are too big, they may break up or be too heavy to lift. The twisting action needed to flick each clod into the adjacent trench also takes some practice; sometimes the clod falls in pieces rather than in one lump. This may be because you have taken too much soil out in one go. If there are roots and runners of perennial weeds in any clods or uncovered earth, they must be carefully picked out before the next clod is cut.

Once each row is complete, you should have a neat row of upturned clods with a new trench running along in front. This trench will probably need cleaning and widening just a little before you begin the next row of digging. You can see from the illustrations that you work your way backwards across the plot. The last trench is filled with the soil that was set aside from the first one.

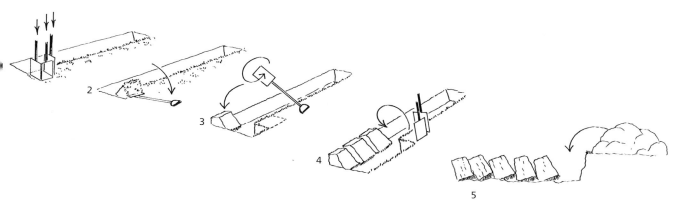

Single digging

Start at one end of the area to be cultivated by digging out a trench a spit deep and about 20 cm (8 in.) wide across the entire width of the plot. Barrow the soil from this trench to the other end of the plot.

1 Start at one end alongside the first trench and cut out the first clod by stabbing the spade down on all three sides to a spit deep, to make a clod about the width of the blade, or 20 cm (8 in.).

2 Push the spade right down to its full depth (with your boot) on the third side. Lever the spade back and carefully lift the clod of soil well clear of the ground.

3 With a quick twist and flick of the spade, turn the clod upside-down against the far side of the adjacent trench. Any surface weeds should now be underneath the clod, so will be buried 20 cm (8 in.) deep.

4 Continue along the row, starting each subsequent clod with two stabbing cuts of the spade before digging in deep, then lifting and twisting it on to the far side of the adjacent trench. When you have finished this row, you can then dig out another, turning the clods into the trench you have just created, and so on across the plot.

5 The final trench is filled in with soil taken from the first.

Double digging

The main difference between single and double digging is that in double digging, the trenches often go down into the subsoil and therefore well-rotted manure or compost is added to provide bulk and nutrients. Each trench is two or three rows wide and manure or compost is forked into the bottom of the each trench before rows of clods are turned into it. Each new, wide trench will need cleaning out to make sure that it is full width before more manure is forked into the bottom.

As with single digging, you continue this process in rows, working backwards until you reach the point where soil from the first two rows is stacked ready to fill in your final trench. Your digging should end up lumpy but fairly level.

Double digging

1 Start by digging out the first trench one spit deep as in single digging, but make it 2–3 spade blades, or 60 cm (24 in.), wide. Dig well-rotted compost or manure into the bottom of this trench to the full depth of the tines of a garden fork.

2 Turn over 20 cm (8 in.) clods from two or three more rows to cover this composted zone and to expose another wide trench. More compost is added and forked in to the base of the new trench.

Forking the Soil

Turning over the soil with a garden fork does not achieve the same results as digging. It is seldom possible to dig out clods of earth and therefore it is not possible to bury the weeds or to incorporate organic matter in quite the same way. However, forking does break up the surface to improve the general aeration of the soil and to dig out roots and runners of perennial weeds. There are also many hand cultivators available, such as three- and five-tined cultivators, which do a similar job.

Rotavating the Soil

A rotavator is a motorized machine that turns over the topsoil (in a churning or mixing motion) and incorporates organic matter that has been laid on the surface. This is not as thorough as digging but does require less effort. It is relatively quick and is therefore used widely by nurserymen and landscape contractors. It is also widely used in domestic gardens but there are two disadvantages that need to be considered:

- The roots and runners of perennial weeds will be chopped up and will readily multiply.

- The constant use of a rotavator means that the soil is always cultivated to exactly the same depth each time. Over many years and under some circumstances, a hard "pan" or layer of compacted soil can develop at that depth—a problem in silty and sandy soils. A pan will impair drainage in the soil and in the development of deep roots. Double digging from time to time would prevent this from happening.

The Potting Shed

For many gardeners, the potting shed is the hub of the garden, providing the space to do basic jobs such as potting up plants, taking cuttings and cleaning seeds. It is also the place to store bulbs, tools, and equipment. If the garden has already got a potting shed, it may need replacing or you may want to move it to a more suitable site. If there is no shed, now is the time to consider the most suitable place for it. It may be possible to use a downstairs room in the house (or part of the garage) instead of using up valuable garden space, but if you decide to purchase a shed, there are a number of points to consider (see below).

Positioning the Potting Shed

- Find a site in the shade rather than in the sun, but avoid the deep shade of tall buildings or overhanging trees since you will still need plenty of light when working in the shed. The sunny areas of the garden should be kept for the plants!

- The potting shed should be convenient to both the house and the kitchen garden, part-way down the garden being more convenient than at the farthest end. It can be screened with planting, if necessary.

Will it all fit in?

- Check that the shed will be served by good paths from the house, the greenhouse and the kitchen garden.

- The shed should be as close as possible to the greenhouse (without casting a shadow on it), so small seedlings and other tender plants do not have to travel far in cold air when being moved from one to the other.

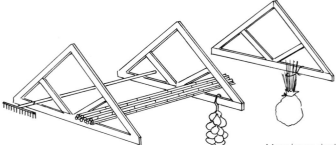

Many larger sheds have horizontal roof joists; these can be useful for storage of tools and canes, and for hanging onions, seeds and so on to dry.

What Size of Shed?

This will obviously depend upon how much equipment you need to store and how much work you plan to do in the garden. Before making a decision, make a list of all the tools, bulk materials such as fertilizers and composts, chemicals, and other equipment that you think you will need, then work out how best to arrange them. You may feel that you need two sheds—one for large pieces of equipment such as mowers, the other as a working potting shed.

- Larger tools—these can hang on hooks to save space and others may rest on joists in the roof space.

- Safe storage—a lockable, steel cabinet is best for keeping chemical pesticides and any other poisonous substances such as weedkillers.

- Bulk storage—a series of plastic boxes, dustbins (garbage cans) or smaller flip-top bins will be useful for storing composts, peat, sand, and so on.

- Small items—an old chest of drawers can be used for storing all manner of small tools and gadgets, labels, bulbs, seeds and so on. Dormant bulbs can be stored in boxes of dry peat, humus, or wood shavings during winter; most prefer to be kept cold, but not frozen. A few bulbs, such as amaryllis, should be kept at about 10°C (50°F) and if the shed is too cold, somewhere in the house might be better.

Potting bench

Potting benches are available in many different styles and materials: you could also build your own from scratch, or from a kit. The bench must be a comfortable height for you to work at. A flat surface with edging boards to the back and two sides is needed for the potting bench, so that potting compost does not fall off on to the floor. If space will be limited, the potting bench could be installed to fold down against a wall or it could be put on wheels so that it can be moved outside on dry days.

Potting bench

1 edge at least 10 cm (4 in.) deep to prevent compost from spilling over the edges
2 smooth, preferably seamless surface (e.g. exterior ply)
3 large, shallow drawers (more useful than smaller, deeper ones)
4 sides blocked in
5 sturdy framework
6 shelf (possibly slatted) for pots, storage and perhaps as a footrest

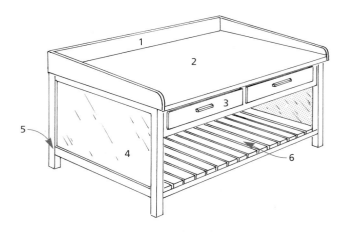

What Type of Shed?

Most sheds are made from timber; a timber floor is more common than solid concrete and, on balance, is probably the better of the two because it is relatively warm and dry. There should be at least one opening window to provide some ventilation in hot weather. The timber must be treated with wood preservative to protect it against decay. If it has not been supplied ready-treated by the manufacturer, it must be thoroughly coated with preservative before the sections are bolted together, especially on the underside of the floor.

If you get one large shed, it can be helpful to have a door at each end or one central door in one side, so that you can take out and put away tools without having to go through the middle of the potting workspace. You could also have double doors. A clear, corrugated perspex roof will allow your shed to double as a cold greenhouse.

Most shed floors are made from planks nailed down on to joists. It can be useful to fix sheet flooring such as all-weather plywood over the top so that it is easy to sweep clean; this also prevents drafts. A concrete floor can be prevented from producing cement dust whenever it is swept by treating it with sodium silicate—an anti-dusting agent—or by painting it with masonry paint.

Rodents can be a problem since they will steal or eat bulbs and seeds. It is not easy to keep them out of a garden shed unless it has been lined with fine mesh wire netting. Mousetraps should always be kept set and ready!

Installing the Shed

Wooden floors are usually set on a series of level, concrete blocks but it is vital to have a piece of damp-proofing membrane between the blocks and the joists, to prevent rising damp from causing decay of the timbers. Solid concrete floors must have a continuous sheet of damp-proofing membrane incorporated into them, again to prevent rising damp. Many tools and materials will be stored directly on the floor and damp would spoil them.

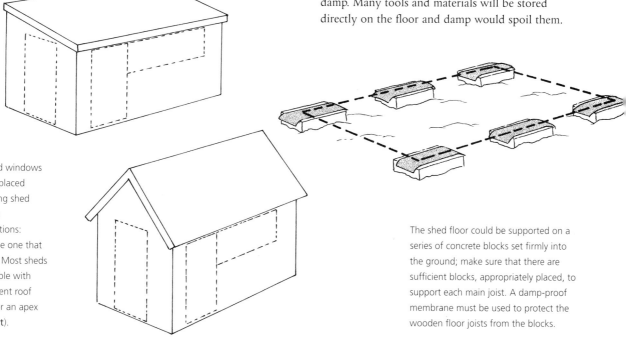

Doors and windows could be placed in a potting shed in various configurations: choose the one that suits you. Most sheds are available with either a pent roof (**above**) or an apex roof (**right**).

The shed floor could be supported on a series of concrete blocks set firmly into the ground; make sure that there are sufficient blocks, appropriately placed, to support each main joist. A damp-proof membrane must be used to protect the wooden floor joists from the blocks.

Any liquids and plants stored in the shed must not freeze, so it is wise to insulate the shed so that it is reasonably frost proof. Heaters with a thermostat-controlled frost setting can also be helpful.

Services you might consider installing in the potting shed to increase its usefulness might include:

- Electricity for heating, lighting and rechargeable tools

- Water (and a sink) for watering plants and washing pots, boxes etc.

- A nearby water butt, connected to the roof gutters of the shed, to collect non-alkaline (soft) water. This is essential for lime-hating (ericaceous) plants.

- An intercom, to connect with the house.

Gardening under Glass

While you are considering where to put the potting shed, you should also think about whether you want a greenhouse in the garden. If you are limited by space, it is possible to make do with smaller types of glass protection. These will allow you to raise a few plants under glass throughout the year or provide temporary protection to less hardy plants, if necessary, during the cold months of winter. However, a greenhouse dramatically increases the range of plants that you could grow or raise.

Cloches

These are usually portable, metal or plastic frames into which sheets of glass or clear polycarbonate are fixed and come in many styles and sizes. A cloche is light enough to be picked up and placed over seedlings or young plants in the garden, to create a warmer microclimate, or it can be used to keep winter rain off alpines and other sensitive plants.

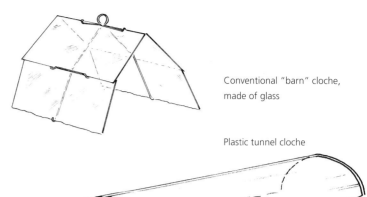

Conventional "barn" cloche, made of glass

Plastic tunnel cloche

Glass and plastic versions of old-fashioned "bell jars", which covered individual plants, seedlings or cuttings, are now available.

Cold Frames

A traditional cold frame is a box-like structure made from timber, bricks or concrete blocks. The top slopes and supports sheets of glass (called "lights") held within a robust, hinged frame. In general, a typical cold frame would be 75–90cm (2½ –3 ft.) wide, no deeper than about 45 cm (18 in.) and virtually any length. Long cold frames are covered by a series of glass lights, which may be propped open during the day and replaced at night. Modern cold frames tend to be made with aluminium or plastic

Traditional cold frame

frames and have glass or clear polycarbonate sides, as well as lids. They are much lighter and more portable than traditional cold frames, but may not be quite so long-lasting.

Cold frames are seldom heated and are used mainly during the winter and spring for crops such as winter lettuce that need protecting from hard frost. They are also often used for "hardening off" plants, such as half-hardy annuals, which have come from a heated greenhouse and will eventually spend the summer out in the garden.

Siting a Greenhouse

In general, a greenhouse should be well away from overhanging trees, in full sun for as many hours of the day as possible and, if it is a freestanding type, not close to a wall or fence (there has to be room to fit or replace glass from the outside). If a site in constant sun is not possible, then a location where the sun is present until early afternoon will suit most crops. If plants are to be raised from seed early in the year, the greenhouse must receive as much sun as possible from early spring through to early summer. The amount of sun is less critical if the greenhouse is being used mainly to overwinter plants.

The ideal orientation for a greenhouse is to have the ends pointing east/west so that the sun passes across and shines between the glazing (sash) bars. When the sun shines directly down the length of the greenhouse from one end to the other (orientation south/north), the glazing bars create more shade—especially in a wooden greenhouse and when the sun is low in the sky.

Services such as water, electricity and good access paths are all important to the usefulness of the greenhouse, so it should not be too far from the house or the potting shed.

Types of Greenhouse

Aesthetically, wooden greenhouses are often preferred to metal ones. The wood is usually either cedar or pressure-treated softwood (pine), so all types are reasonably durable. Most metal greenhouses are made from silvery grey aluminium. The frames of metal or wooden greenhouses may be painted or coated green or white. Metal types let in more light because their frameworks are thinner.

There are many styles of greenhouse available these days, including octagons, hexagons, domes and even pyramids. Although these unusual shapes may fit well into a modern garden, the space inside might not prove quite as useful as that inside a conventional greenhouse. Choose the largest greenhouse you can accommodate and afford to heat. There is never enough room in a greenhouse at the height of the growing season.

Apex greenhouses

The majority of greenhouses are this shape although proportions vary considerably. In many cases, the glass goes right down to the ground, but in others there may be a low wall or solid panels around the base. Where crops are likely to be grown directly in the soil inside a greenhouse, it is advisable to have fully glazed walls.

Apex greenhouse

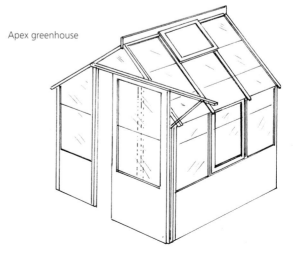

Lean-to and cupboard-style greenhouses

Most of these types require a wall to lean against. The majority of lean-to greenhouses are large enough to stand up in, so the supporting wall has to be at least 2 m (6 ft. 6 in.) high. However, nearly all of the cupboard types are too small to work inside comfortably: they are accessed by sliding doors on the front, so a lower wall, perhaps only 1.5 m (5 ft.) high, can be utilized.

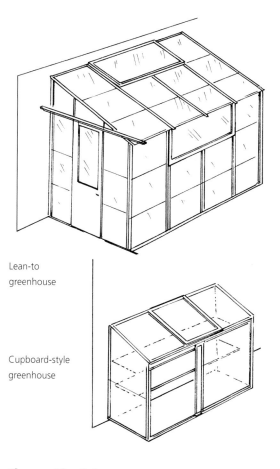

Lean-to greenhouse

Cupboard-style greenhouse

Glass or Plastic?

Most greenhouses are fitted with glass panels, many of these being second-grade horticultural glass which often has slight imperfections but is perfectly adequate. Plastics are generally far less breakable and are therefore useful if safety is a consideration. Another option is clear acrylic which, although expensive, has excellent light transmission and good thermal insulation properties but does eventually become scratched from cleaning. If safety is not an issue, glass or toughened glass is probably the most realistic option for all but the smallest greenhouses.

Choosing a Greenhouse

Having decided on the type of greenhouse, there are several options and features that need to be considered. The most important is ventilation. Plants keep cool by evaporation and some crops are damaged by excessively high temperatures—leaves can scorch, tomato flowers may drop off, cyclamen could fail to flower and so on. So it is vital, on hot, sunny days, to have a good and brisk circulation of air throughout the greenhouse. There should, ideally, be both top and side vents built into the structure, in addition to the door. One small roof vent is not enough. There are various types of automatic vent, which save you the trouble of having to open and close the vents daily during warm weather. Many operate using a hydraulic system that simply expands and opens the vent as it heats up; more elaborate systems rely on an electric motor and thermostat.

Shelves and staging

These can be permanent or temporary, fixed or freestanding. Most are slatted to allow free passage of water. Some greenhouse staging has large trays that can be lined with irrigation matting or a layer of

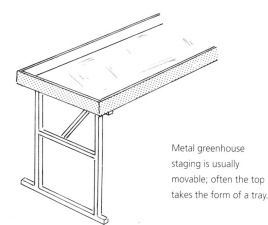

Metal greenhouse staging is usually movable; often the top takes the form of a tray.

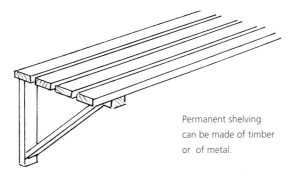

Permanent shelving can be made of timber or of metal.

sand, so that the plants can draw water up through the bases of the pots (sub-irrigation). Where crops are to be grown on or in the floor of the greenhouse, removable shelving is required.

Disabled access

Most greenhouse doors have a threshold, which can be a nuisance for anyone in a wheelchair or with mobility problems. Some manufacturers produce greenhouses that have a slightly wider doorway and no threshold or some other arrangement that allows easy access by wheelchair.

Shading

It is better to have a greenhouse in full sun, and to add shading when needed, rather than have some element of permanent shade that may not give any options at certain times of the day. There are two main ways of shading a greenhouse:

- Painting the outside with a suitable product— laborious but cheap.

- Installing adjustable blinds internally or externally—the best option, but only if you are there to make adjustments when necessary. Although expensive, blinds last several seasons.

Installing a Greenhouse

A strip foundation of bricks or concrete will allow the greenhouse to have an earth floor. Concrete slabs can be put down to form a path and crops grown in the soil on either side. An earth floor will help to keep the humidity relatively high, but could encourage certain pests and diseases. A concrete "raft" foundation will require all the greenhouse plants to be grown in pots or grow-bags, but overall hygiene is likely to be better than with an earth floor.

Electricity

A greenhouse is not a safe place for electrical appliances, so special waterproof sockets and a circuit breaker (RCD or residual current device) are essential in order to cut off the power should anything go wrong. Electricity might be needed for lighting, heating, soil-warming cables, a mist propagation unit, ventilation or other helpful gadgets.

Heating

If a thermostat can be incorporated, the best method of heating is electrical. Many electric heaters use a fan to distribute warmed air evenly. However, electrical heating tends to dry out the atmosphere so the air may need to be humidified by leaving an open container of water in the greenhouse or by regular damping down of surfaces. Paraffin heaters are useful if there is no electrical supply but, if they are not adjusted properly, exhaust gases can inhibit the plant growth. Thermostatic control is not possible with paraffin, so temperature control is also unreliable.

Water

In general, it is an advantage to have a supply of tap water in the greenhouse. It is clean and plentiful and does not carry certain fungal infections that might damage seedlings or cuttings, so should be used throughout the greenhouse. The main exception is when watering acid-loving plants: tap water is often quite alkaline, which is damaging to these plants, so instead rainwater should be used. The only other disadvantage of tap water is that it may leave a chalky deposit on the leaves of some plants, but this takes quite some time to build up and can easily be removed by washing the leaves.

Safety in the Garden

- Protect yourself by using appropriate clothing when using chemicals, sharp tools or machinery.
- Handle all garden chemicals with care. Shield plants and animals from the unwanted effects and avoid spraying on windy days. Always clean out watering cans or sprayers thoroughly after use and label them clearly, so that they are never used for anything else. (For more details on using chemicals safely, see "Chemicals and Safety", page 317.)
- Store any hazardous equipment or chemicals locked well out of the reach of children.
- Use a circuit breaker (RCD or residual current device) when using electrical appliances.

Irrigation

All plants need water to survive and grow healthily. The surfaces of leaves can reach a very high temperature in full sun so, to avoid shock to the plants as well as wasting the water through evaporation, watering is usually best done in the early morning or evening. Dry areas at the bases of house walls, where overhanging eaves prevent rainwater from reaching the soil, are particularly prone to drying out.

Watering the garden by hand can be a time-consuming chore, so consider installing some form of irrigation system while you are creating and restoring beds and borders. Not all parts of the garden may need watering—some drought-tolerant plants such as lavender or *Cistus* (rock rose) positively resent it, so first work out where you need to water, and how often. Then decide which of the many systems available may be most appropriate.

Most of them can be operated manually direct from a garden tap or through a sophisticated, battery- or mains-powered, electronic control system. Although initially expensive, such a system enables water to be applied at the correct time, and by operating at night, reduces evaporation; some systems also allow nutrients to be added. Large gardens may need a complex system and expert advice from a specialist company may be needed, but simple irrigation systems include:

- Perforated pipe irrigation—this system uses an unobtrusive, dark-coloured hose, often made of recycled tyres. The hose is punctuated with holes of a specific size and spacing. It can be threaded around the base of plants, is easily moved, and can be lightly covered or disguised with a mulch or thin layer of topsoil. When activated, the water seeps gently into the soil. Some types of hose rot or degrade in sunlight, so check the manufacturers' guarantee.

- Mini-sprinklers—these are individual units whose height and location can be adjusted to the size and grouping of your plants. If spaced carefully, they can cover every area of planting although dense, upright or spreading foliage can prevent the water from reaching smaller plants below.

- Pop-up sprinklers—these use water pressure to force the watering heads to pop up out of the lawn or planted beds. When not in use, the heads retract below the surface, out of sight.

Project 2

You now need to make an action plan for carrying out the preliminary work in the garden before getting to grips with the next stage—planting. If you draw up a programme setting out such details as work start and end dates, materials needed, who is available to do the work and anticipated costs, it will help you understand what you are taking on. If necessary, you could plan the work to be carried out over several seasons or you can concentrate on specific areas of the garden. Taking on more than you can cope with or afford is very discouraging, and making up this type of schedule will help put matters into perspective and alert you to any potential problems. This is also the time to update your garden plan and start your Garden Log.

Make Up a Schedule of Work

Prepare a worksheet to describe the practical steps you intend taking before you consider new planting. Your worksheet can be illustrated with photographs, diagrams or drawings. Suggestions for the layout are as follows.

- Work up a schedule for site clearance, indicating the different stages and prorities. It may be helpful to divide your garden into different areas for easy reference. Who will do the work, when, and how long will it take?

- Describe how you intend to improve the soil (if necessary).

- Describe what should stay and what should go, noting which method, tools and chemicals are to be used to remove any unwanted plants.

- State what action, if any, you will use to improve the appearance or growth of plants that you want to keep.

- Describe your intentions on hard landscaping, including materials and repairs needed, possible contractors and when the work should be done.

- List tools and equipment you will need to store in your potting shed.

- Using a copy of your simple plan, write on it in note form showing what needs to be done at this stage, and where. This will provide an interesting record for the future.

Update Your Simple Plan

Use a copy of your garden plan to indicate any changes that you want to make.

- Cross out any trees and shrubs that have been removed.

- Mark the position of any new water features.

- Mark where the potting shed, compost bins, water butt and greenhouse (if needed), will go.

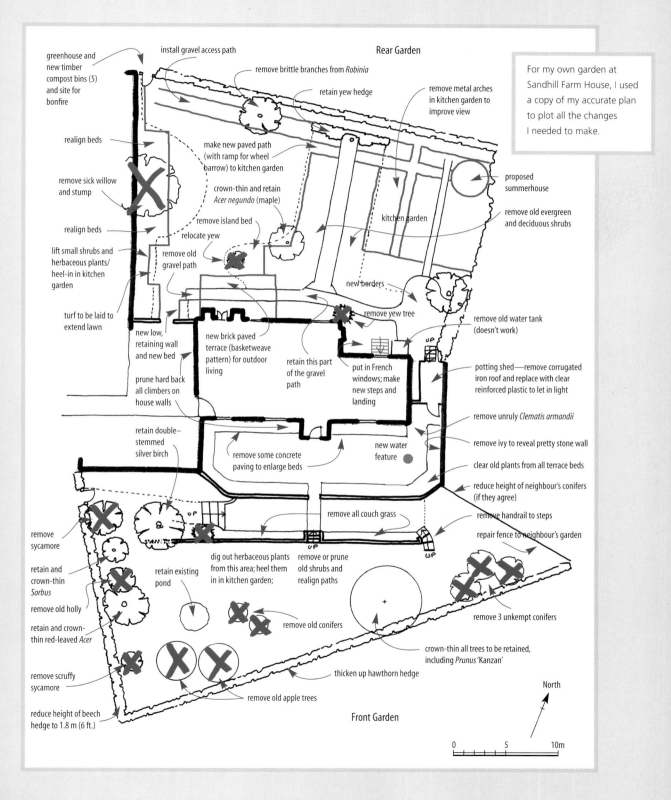

Rear Garden

For my own garden at Sandhill Farm House, I used a copy of my accurate plan to plot all the changes I needed to make.

greenhouse and new timber compost bins (5) and site for bonfire

install gravel access path

remove brittle branches from *Robinia*

retain yew hedge

remove metal arches in kitchen garden to improve view

realign beds

make new paved path (with ramp for wheel barrow) to kitchen garden

proposed summerhouse

remove sick willow and stump

crown-thin and retain *Acer negundo* (maple)

remove old evergreen and deciduous shrubs

realign beds

remove island bed

relocate yew

kitchen garden

lift small shrubs and herbaceous plants/ heel-in in kitchen garden

remove old gravel path

new borders

turf to be laid to extend lawn

remove yew tree

remove old water tank (doesn't work)

new low, retaining wall and new bed

new brick paved terrace (basketweave pattern) for outdoor living

retain this part of the gravel path

put in French windows; make new steps and landing

potting shed—remove corrugated iron roof and replace with clear reinforced plastic to let in light

prune hard back all climbers on house walls

remove unruly *Clematis armandii*

remove ivy to reveal pretty stone wall

retain double– stemmed silver birch

remove some concrete paving to enlarge beds

new water feature

clear old plants from all terrace beds

reduce height of neighbour's conifers (if they agree)

remove all couch grass

remove handrail to steps

remove sycamore

repair fence to neighbour's garden

retain and crown-thin *Sorbus*

retain existing pond

dig out herbaceous plants from this area; heel them in in kitchen garden;

remove or prune old shrubs and realign paths

remove old holly

retain and crown-thin red-leaved *Acer*

remove old conifers

remove 3 unkempt conifers

remove scruffy sycamore

crown-thin all trees to be retained, including *Prunus* 'Kanzan'

thicken up hawthorn hedge

remove old apple trees

reduce height of beech hedge to 1.8 m (6 ft.)

Front Garden

North

0   5   10m

Start a Garden Log

Keeping a garden log is a valuable exercise for any gardener. It can provide an essential record of how your garden develops and your seasonal activities, as well as your observations and thoughts as you progress. The log will also serve as a useful reference for successive years, reminding you of plant performances in past seasons, weather patterns, and when and how you performed various tasks. It will enable you to learn from your successes and failures and provide a basis for you to experiment as you gain in confidence. The process of compiling it should also improve your powers of observation.

The format

Although your log is your own, personal record, it should be recorded logically to be most useful. The templates on the following pages are provided as a guide on how to arrange your log. You could first break down your log into three main categories:

A Maintenance and development
B Observations
C Orders and purchases.

Within each category on the templates, there are suggested subheadings for different areas of the garden or types of task. The space allotted for each section could be altered to suit the balance of features in your garden. For example, if you do not wish to grow fruit and vegetables, omit that section.

It would be easier if you started a fresh page for each category and included the relevant subheadings as listed on the sample sheets provided. You will find that you will probably need to make a fresh record for each month. Try to note correct botanical Latin plant names in full, to save confusion later. You can save space by abbreviating the names when repeated, for instance *Lavandula angustifolia* becomes *L. angustifolia*. If you are handwriting, it is conventional to underline the Latin name.

The introduction

You will find it very useful to add a short introductory section to the log that describes your garden as it is now. Record the size, shape, aspect, soil type, location, how long you have lived there, how mature it is, whether you have help, and so on. You could use an annotated plan (from a copy of the simple plan you made after assessing the garden) to record these details; remember to include scale and aspect.

Other log entries

It is important that the log serves you, so you may wish to develop other sections of your log. For example, you might want to compile gradually a calendar of tasks that you will need to perform on an annual basis—to do this you may want to adapt the garden calender included in this book (see pages 343–362). Perhaps you might want to include an appendix which lists all your plant purchases and where they are planted. You could also develop a section for forward planning in which, for example, you list tasks for the future, or detail planting changes you may want to make in future seasons.

Month:

Maintenance and Development

Hard Landscaping (paths, terraces, drives, fences, walls etc.)
Weed control
Cleaning
Safety
Maintenance/treatment

Water Features
Cleaning/servicing/repairs
Fish

Tools and Equipment
Servicing/replacement
Cleaning/preparation
Repairs
Sharpening
New equipment for future

Projects
New borders/new lawn
Erecting and equipping greenhouse

Month:

Observations

Weather (rainfall, temperature etc.)
Minimum and maximum temperatures
First/last frost
Deviation from the norm—gales, drought, floods

Plant interest (flower, fruiting, leaf fall etc.)
Peak performance times; unusual performance
Good plant?
Descriptions

Wildlife (bees, birds, other insects and animals)
Hibernation/nesting
Breeding/populations
Feeding
Conservation

Month:

Orders and Purchases

Fruit and Vegetables

Ornamental Garden

Lawns and Grass

Hard Landscaping

Water Features

Tools and Equipment

February 2005

Maintenance and Development

Allotment

3 February:

Laid out the seed potatoes for chitting in unheated front room.
4 varieties: 'Charlotte', 'Pink Fir Apple', 'Nicola', 'Maris Peer'.

15 February:

A quick visit to check on things and I found that buds have appeared on the transplanted blackcurrant, and the new apricot tree. Some of the barn cloches are hopefully warming the soil up, although the weather has been rather cold. Andrew & I discussed cutting the blackberry down to the ground, then training new shoots into a manageable arrangement, otherwise it will just grow into the vicious beast of the last years. Alternatively, take it out altogether!

> Here is an example of a Garden Log, written by one of my students in London, about her own garden and allotment (community garden).

20 February:

I had planned today to plant out the shallots and garlic, and move some lavender to the allotment, but discovered that the ground was frozen solid, so this was put on hold. Instead, Tim and I went along and did some hoeing, reassembled the rest of the cloches, and placed them in 2 rows to warm the soil up where I plan the shallots to go. Tim noticed that bindweed is already appearing, so it is time to think about our perennial weed management. He dug out a few dandelions that were growing in the paths. The 'Maris Peer' seed potatoes are streaks ahead of the other 3 varieties, with 'Pink Fir Apple' showing almost no chits.

My garden

7 February:

Looking at past garden photos has persuaded me that the old rose would benefit from more dramatic pruning. I can see that, already, shoots are appearing from the base, and from the old stems, which have not had shoots before. So I cut the long stems right back. Unfortunately, it was then forecast to be frosty, so I covered it with fleece. I looked in the A—Z Encyclopedia for the pruning details for all of the *Clematis* (that I can identify), and gave them a tidy-up. They are all producing fat buds. I had also decided that it was looking very dry, after hardly any rain over the last month, and so I watered, particularly well around the tree ferns and apple tree. Naturally, it then rained in the night!

14 February:

I planted some *Galanthus nivalis* 'Flore Pleno' under the apple tree, as there seem to be fewer snowdrops than there should be. I also added some *Cyclamen coum* in with the *C. hederifolium* to extend the flowering interest. I filled a large terracotta planter with ericaceous compost, and then transplanted the sickly, chewed *Rhododendron* into it, placing it by the back wall. Lastly I got the scrubbing brush out and washed out all the seed trays ready for planting; a job I was putting off.

18 February:

Cleared the decks in the conservatory for the multitudes of seed trays and set up the new heated propagator. Filled the modules with seed compost, and then had a look in my various vegetable-growing tomes. Although I had watered the compost with warm water, I then read that the compost should be warm before planting seeds. Mine definitely wasn't, so I set out the prepared trays to acclimatize. I also read that last season's compost should not be used;

however, it was too late by then as I had already used some old and some new, and I wasn't prepared to start again!

19 February:
With the help of <u>The Allotment Handbook</u>, Dr Hessayon, and the <u>Organic Gardening</u> magazine seed packets, I sorted out which seeds to plant. I ended up sowing tomatoes, artichokes, 4 varieties of basil, parsley, oregano, *Heliotropium*, *Lobelia*, *Cobaea scandens*, plus 2 kinds of peppers from seed extracted fresh from supermarket peppers (pointy red and mini sweet orange) as an experiment, and 3 varieties of aubergine. I have decided to have a go at growing peppers and aubergines at home, rather than the allotment, where I will be pushed for long-term space as it is. I can have a select few plants in the conservatory or outside in the sunny part of the garden in pots. They are quite decorative after all. I also planted up some *Allium aflatuense* and white begonias into pots, and brought them into the conservatory while the weather is very cold. I will put the alliums into the cold frame later. A bit disappointed to read in <u>The Vegetable Expert</u> that the purple globe artichoke rates poorly for flavour.

21 February:
Planted out a trio of *Leucojum vernum* bulbs, rescued from class, under the apple tree.

28 February:
The basils had sprouted after 4 days. The oregano, artichoke, *Lobelia* and *Heliotropium* after 5 days. After 7 days, apart from the tomatoes, there were seedlings of every kind of seed I had sown, although not every seed had sprouted. Most notable, the sweet peas, which were free, and possibly not very fresh, have not sprouted at all. I may experiment by soaking a batch overnight,

and by taking a notch out of another batch, before sowing, to see if germination is easier. I have moved the tomatoes to a warmer spot, and 3 seedlings (of 20 seeds sown) have appeared. There is a mouldy look to some of the peat pots; this method is new to me, so I hope it is not a bad sign. The potatoes had to be moved, and unfortunately I do not now have a cool, light place, so they are on the conservatory floor by the door, covered, where it is pretty cool. Not very optimistic about an optimum result for the chits. The 'Pink Fir Apple' are lagging behind the others, with 'Maris Peer' way ahead.

Conservatory
4 February:
The bigger of the two *Amaryllis* has opened. Whilst watering I noticed that the *Stephanotis* was harbouring scale insect. They must have moved quickly, but luckily they had only encroached about 12 in. from the base. I removed the ones I could see with a soapy cloth, and wiped the dust off the old leaves. I know that there will have been tiny creatures that I missed, so I will keep an eye on it.

21 February:
The oldest orchid is still covered in flowers—a pleasure at this time of year.

February 2005

Weather and Observations

Very cold from Valentine's Day onwards with some rain (mostly drizzly) and strong biting wind in the third week. On the 19th, there were brief snow flurries, and on the 20th, the ground & pond froze solid. There followed a week of very cold weather with snow flurries most days, the heaviest being overnight on Thursday and Friday am, the 25th. Heavy frost again on Sunday 27th.

Plant Interest

6 February: visit to Isabella Plantation

I thought that there must be something to see here by now, and the notice at the gate helpfully pointed out plants of interest. These were some very large *Hamamelis* and *Lonicera purpusii*; both smelled amazing. *Rhododendron* 'Christmas Cheer' jumped out of the green surroundings, covered in pink/white flowers. The heather area was awash with colour. I was pleased to find that some plants have labels, if you look hard enough.

7 February: My garden

I noticed that I have a lot of greenfly in the garden. I imagine this is due to the mildness of the winter so far. Early February plants of interest in the garden are the few snowdrops, yellow *Narcissus*, *Daphne odora* 'Walberton', hellebores, *Clematis armandii*, and a few primroses.

14 February: My garden

The snowdrops have been joined by some purple *Crocus* under the apple tree, and several clumps of daffodils (*N.* 'February Gold', *N.* 'Jetfire' and *N.* 'Tête-à-Tête'). There are plenty more coming through. The aquilegias are beginning to form leafy clumps, and the white azaleas are covered in buds. The new snowdrops and *Cyclamen* look very pretty. I spotted a dwarf *Syringa pubescens* subsp. *patula* 'Miss Kim' at the garden centre, which I had to stop myself from buying (for now!).

21 February: visit to Royal Botanic Gardens, Kew

Cold, with potential for snow, but sunny, so I went to see if crocuses, daffodils, early rhododendrons and camellias were flowering. The Princess Walk was a glorious sea of all shades of purple; unfortunately most of the crocuses were closed but a few were peeping out in sunny spots. The main walk has been newly planted en masse with *Narcissus* 'February Gold', which were just beginning to open. Most of the *Chimonanthus*, *Viburnum* x *bodnantense*, *Lonicera* and *Hamamelis* were practically over. I went to see the beds by the main gate with the lovely group of *Callicarpa bodinieri* var. *giraldii* & aconites, but found that the whole lot has been cleared! I found that the grass garden has had some serious deadheading, with the *Cortaderia* almost unrecognizable. There wasn't much happening in the *Rhododendron* walk, but I found the Temperate House very interesting at this time of year. Lots of tender rhododendrons were in full bloom, some scented (as in *R.* 'Fragrantissimum'!).

28 February: My garden

The *Clematis armandii* is in full flower now and making lots of vertical shoots. The old rose is making shoots from the base. The early daffodils are all at their best, with the later ones a few weeks away yet. Now that things are beginning to flower, I am itching to get out and start moving plants around. Especially since the lecture on Garden Design, and the day on spring-interest plants. However, it has been too cold, and the visit to Sandhill Farm House is coming up, which should provide plenty of inspiration.

February 2005

Orders and Purchases

Membership HDRA (Henry Doubleday   £16.00
Reseach Association)

Seeds
 Artichoke Purple Globe 'Romanesco'   £1.41
 Carrot 'Parabel'   £1.24
 Watercress   £1.34
 Courgette 'Rondo di Nizza'   £1.58
 Cucumber 'Crystal Lemon'   £1.52
 Garlic 'Printator'   £3.95
 Mange tout pea 'Norli'   £1.70
 Shallot 'Longor'   £3.45
 Sweetcorn 'Minipop'   £1.58
 Sweet pea 'White Supreme'   £1.99

Plants
 Eranthus cilicus x 5   £4.95
 Cyclamen coum x 2   £5.98
 Galanthus 'Flore Pleno' x 2   £3.38
 Sarcococca hookeriana var. *digyna* x 2 £19.00
 Chaenomeles speciosa 'Moerloorsei'   £12.95
 Helleborus niger Harvington Hybrid   £7.25

Hard Landscaping
 Terracotta large square planter   £20.00
 (for the pink *Rhododendron*)

Tools and Equipment
 Steel-toe boots   £69.95
 Wellington boots   £42.00
 Root trainers   £9.99
 Window thermometer   £4.60
 Gloves, leather   £12.99
 Vermiculite   £2.70
 Peat pots   £5.99

Books
 RHS Growing Vegetables by Tony Briggs   £8.99
 Discovering The Folklore of Plants by   £5.99
 Margaret Baker
 100 Flowers and How they Got their Names £12.99
 by Diana Wells

Total   £287.45

Above: Clearing overgrown areas allows you to get to know your garden. Mark any plants to be saved with brightly coloured twine in case helpers are over-enthusiastic.

Above: Consider using local materials for fencing. Driftwood provides an informal, imaginative and inexpensive alternative, if suited to the surroundings.

Above: Hard landscaping can be adapted to existing features in the garden. Here, a mature olive tree provides shade for this terrace: the stone paving stops short of the main stem, allowing water to reach the roots.

Left: Sandhill Farm House—especially suited to an informal situation, gravel is inexpensive and easy to spread. Timber boards could be used to define the edges, but here plants are used for the same purpose.

Above: A curved grass path is broken up by treated timber inserts, which make the path more hardwearing. The turf level is higher than the timber so that the path can be mown easily without damage to the mower blades.

Above: Paving stones laid slightly below the level of the turf provide a mowing strip between lawn and borders, allowing the plants to spill out of the beds without damaging the grass.

Above: In an orchard, a mown grass path can be used to define the edge of the meadow area or as a way through the wildflowers. Meadow plantings must be left unmown until the flowers have set seed.

Below: Renovating a hedge—light will soon activate the main stem into regrowth. This renovation method is only successful with yew or some deciduous hedging; other conifers will not regrow from old wood.

Above: Renovating a hedge—overgrown *Taxus baccata* (yew) hedges can be renovated by cutting back severely to the "quick" or the bases of the branches on one side of the hedge. The other side should be similarly pruned in the following year.

Above: Sandhill Farm House hedge—although vital for filtering strong winds, tall hedges can overshadow a garden. *Fagus* (beech) leaves remain on hedges until the spring, when rising sap and new emerging foliage pushes them off.

Above: Sandhill Farm House hedge—the height of the beech hedge was reduced by several feet to allow more light into the garden. The arch giving a glimpse through to the garden was preserved at its full height.

Above: Specimen trees may have taken many years to mature. Before replacing any, consider pruning to give the existing tree a better outline and allow more light and air through to create dappled shade.

Left: Renovating bush roses by removing some of the older and crowded branches will allow light and air through the plant, prompting vigorous new growth and helping prevent fungal disease.

Right: Hazel can be coppiced or pruned to provide pea sticks for staking. Natural materials such as these are less obtrusive than commercial offerings; use them to support herbaceous plants in late spring.

Above: Sandhill Farm House front garden—many conifers and overgrown plants made this small woodland area gloomy, dark and overshadowed the existing hawthorn hedge.

Above: Sandhill Farm House front garden—removing the conifers revealed gaps where they had overshadowed the boundary hedge. A new bed, with a semi-circle of peat blocks edged with *Carex* (sedge) gives a purpose to the space and draws the eye away from the hedge. The stake marks the need for a focal point.

Left: Sandhill Farm House front garden—a decorative, semi-mature tree provided the focal point. Digging a deep hole in order to accommodate the large root ball and planting it required strength!

Right: When renovating a garden, find a suitable place to use as a "holding area", where plants that are potted up can be kept until decisions are made on where to plant them permanently.

Above: The position of new borders can be marked out with garden canes and sand. Study the proposed beds from all angles and from inside the house before deciding on width and shape.

Above: Plants will soon fill up a newly planted border, so leave enough space for them to develop. Regular, neat lawn edges, trimmed once or twice a month during the growing season, help to set them off.

Above: Bindweed—tackling persistent weeds needs determination. To get rid of bindweed, push a garden cane into the soil beside the plant, at a 45° angle, then encourage the bindweed to grow up a cane until it almost reaches the top.

Above: Bindweed—place a bottomless vessel (I used a broken pudding basin) over the cane and trained bindweed. Remove the cane and push all the bindweed into the bowl, bruising the leaves as you go so they will absorb more herbicide. Spray the leaves carefully with herbicide inside the bowl so the bowl stops any spray drifting over other plants. Lift off the bowl and leave the foliage to die back.

Left: Even a small greenhouse will prove invaluable to the gardener. Keeping your greenhouse pristine will help to prevent disease. A water supply and means of shading the plants from strong sunlight are essential. A hard surface flooring is easy to sweep clean.

Left: Larger greenhouses or conservatories have space for ornamental planting. Metal columns support climbers such as *Passiflora* in this greenhouse.

Above: Soil structure and texture is critical for healthy plant life. To improve the soil, spread well-rotted manure or compost to a depth of 7.5 cm. (3 in.) in late autumn or early spring. The worms will soon take it into the soil.

Right: Compost bins can be made with timber or concrete uprights. Slatted boards at the front can be removed from the uprights to empty each bin or to turn the compost. Cover the top surface of the compost with old carpet or a plastic sheet, to increase the heat within the pile while also keeping out light and airborne weed seeds.

Chapter 3
Planning New Plantings:
Woody Plants

The first chapters of this book gave you guidance on what plants need and how to prepare the ground for them, so now you are ready for the creative part of gardening. Planting is for many of us the most exciting, interesting and challenging part of planning a garden. Whether you have inherited an existing garden, are starting from scratch or simply making a few changes, you should choose plants not just for occasional seasonal interest or colour, but for their ability to help combine the house, garden, sky and garden floor. In this chapter, we concentrate on what to look for when choosing plants in general, then consider buying and planting woody plants in particular.

Before you rush out and buy any plants, it is important to learn a few basic principles about designing with plants, such as how to choose, combine and plant them for an overall result that will live up to your expectations. As well as aesthetic considerations, you also need to take into account practical issues, such as the conditions in your garden and each plant's needs, otherwise the plants in your design may fail to perform as expected.

Planting for structural effect is crucial: the permanent planting creates the "bones" of the garden: bones provided by the woody plants, that is trees, shrubs including roses, and woody climbers. This long-term structure provides a permanent backdrop against which the more ephemeral decorative or edible elements provide seasonal relief. For a large part of the year in a temperate climate, you may look at a wintry scene that is dependent on the shape and form of your plants rather than on flowers.

Woody plants form the structure of the garden in many ways. Some trees and shrubs may be planted as living boundaries, other shrubs or climbers used to make divisions within the garden, or they may be used as specimen plants. Small urban courtyards may require only some wall shrubs and climbers or low box hedging to provide the long-term planting, whereas exposed country acres may need shelter belts and windbreaks. Consideration is given to the use of climbers to supply vertical interest—whether against buildings, or on artificial supports, such as pergolas or obelisks.

There is an enormous range of plants now available to the gardener, so this chapter also contains suggested plant lists. The suggestions are by no means exhaustive, but are intended to fire your imagination. They include extremities of size and shape, from tall trees like *Pinus sylvestris* (Scots pine) and *Taxus baccata* (yew) to low-growing shrubs such as *Santolina chamaecyparissus* (cotton lavender), so should help you to check on the performance and maintenance of individual plants.

General Principles for Choosing Plants

You should by now appreciate the importance of ground preparation and maintenance, and be keen to begin buying and growing some new plants. Too often, however, the results are disappointing. Most people rush to the garden centre or nursery and are seduced into buying many plants—mostly those in flower—on the spot, without regard for whether they will suit the conditions in their own garden or without understanding how to group or arrange them in the garden.

Learning to Look at Plants

Skilful planting cannot be learned from books or catalogues. The best plantspeople train their eyes by studying plants, noticing the distinguishing elements of each one and planning plant groupings so that the characteristics of the individual plants enhance each other. Try to train yourself by doing the same thing. Aim to look at plants critically so that you can identify what you like about them and why. Learn to assess their strengths and weaknesses against key criteria such as height, spread, outline or form, and texture of foliage, imagining how a specific plant grouping could be improved by exchanging one plant for another to intensify the combination.

Spend as much time as possible visiting gardens; most countries have publications that tell you what is open and when. Many public gardens have well-maintained and labelled beds from which a great deal can be learned, and will help you to become acquainted with the botanical names of many plants. Get into the habit of carrying a notebook; a camera is also useful for recording particularly effective plantings or plants that you might want to have in your own garden. Write down the name of the garden, the date of your visit, the botanical names of the plants that you like, and also the names of plants nearby that help to set them off. Revisit the same place several times a year to note any seasonal changes in the plantings. Gradually you will build up a repertoire of different seasonal groupings that you could repeat in your own garden.

Keep a notebook to record sightings of plants that you might like to use in your own garden.

Some Useful Plant Terms

These terms are widely used to describe the nature of a plant.

Prostrate Growing flat, or almost flat, across the ground, as with *Juniperus horizontalis* 'Blue Chip'.

Fastigiate Growing with tightly ascending branches to produce a column of growth, for instance *Taxus baccata* 'Fastigiata' (Irish yew).

Pendulous Having branches that grow down to the ground, creating a weeping habit.

Feathered Describing a very young tree with one main stem and several small lateral (side) shoots or branches.

Alpine Strictly speaking, any plant that grows in the mountains, like many *Gentiana* (gentians). Most will grow happily in the garden and are often used in rock gardens.

Aquatic Any plant that will grow wholly or partly in water, for example *Elodea canadensis* (Canadian pond weed).

Studying the gardens in your neighbourhood is also very rewarding. You can observe which particular species seem to thrive in the local conditions, note which types of trees and hedging shrubs are used in boundaries and compare the habits and merits of different plants. Look for creative ideas on dividing different areas of the garden with planting, using climbers and on drawing the eye by using some species for accents or vertical markers.

Practicalities of Plant Selection

In the preceding chapters, many practical factors have been considered and these must be remembered when choosing plants. If plants are to thrive, they need conditions that suit them. Most plants have a strong desire to live and even if placed in inappropriate conditions, they may not actually die.

The Meaning of Some Specific Names

The specific part of Latin botanical names usually describes something about the plant. If you get to know these terms, even when faced with an unfamiliar name, you may be able to recognize one of the plant's identifying characteristics.

Some specific names indicate which part of the world a plant comes from:

australis from southern parts
europaeus from Europe
hispanica from Spain
japonica from Japan
nipponica from Japan
sinensis from China.

Some indicate habitat:

arvensis of the fields
campestre from the plains or flat lands
littoralis from the sea shore
palustre from swamps and marshland
sylvatica from the wood.

Some describe habit or mode of growth:

fastigiate with erect growth
fruticosum shrubby
horizontalis low and spreading
humilis low-growing
nana dwarf
pendula weeping
procera very tall
procumbens prostrate
repens creeping
suffruticosa woody at the base.

Others describe leaf shape:

angustifolia with narrow leaves
arguta with sharp leaves
glabra without hairs
integrifolia without teeth
heterophyllus has leaves of various shapes
hirsutum hairy
laevigata smooth, glossy
mollis soft
sempervirens always green
parvifolia small-leaved
picta coloured, speckled
reticulata veined with a net-like covering
tomentosa covered in short hairs.

Some describe the flowers or their colour:

alba white
argentea silvery
aurantiacus orange
aurea golden
caerulea blue
cinerea ash grey
coccinea scarlet
discolor two-coloured
flava pale yellow
floribunda free-flowering
lactea milky white
lutea yellow
macropetala with large petals
nutans nodding
parviflora has small flowers
plena plentiful (sometimes double)
puniceus crimson
sanguineum blood-red
viridis green.

They will simply sulk, fail to put on any healthy growth and not give of their best. There are plants for every situation and the successful gardener learns to be discriminating, choosing those best suited to both site and climate. Avoid buying any plant unless you have a suitable position for it in the garden. The lists in this—and the following—chapter will help you to make a sensible choice.

Practical Considerations

Ask yourself if the plant will be suited to these conditions in the garden:

- Climate
- Rainfall
- Soil pH, texture and drainage
- Dry or damp soil conditions
- Sunny or shaded site
- Level of exposure to wind
- Pollution levels.

Hardiness Ratings

Plants are categorized according to their ability to survive different temperature ranges. In Britain, they generally fall into four categories:

- Hardy plants are able to cope with temperatures as low as –15°C (5°F)
- Frost-hardy plants tolerate –5°C (23°F)
- Half-hardy plants survive in temperatures above 0°C (32°F)
- Frost-tender plants may be threatened by temperatures below 5°C (41°F).

For a guide to the more varied hardiness zones in the U.S.A., see pages 363–366.

Climate

This is a major factor in considering what plants we can grow in our gardens. The primary influence will be of your region, for example in the northern hemisphere northern areas are colder than the south, and the west coasts of Britain and the United States are warmer than the east. Your garden may have one or more microclimates, created by the immediate surroundings such as buildings, hedges or the lack of them. The microclimate is also determined by altitude and air currents. Cold air flows downhill, and if it becomes trapped at the bottom, for instance by a wall or hedge, it will cause a frost pocket that will remain until it is broken up by wind or sun. So you may have areas in the garden where you could plant tender plants, and others where all plants must be hardy. Always check the hardiness of a plant to decide whether it will survive the extremes of your local climate.

Rainfall will also affect how you use your garden: in areas of low rainfall, you may need to choose drought-tolerant plants. High rainfall can encourage lush plant growth, but the drainage properties of the soil and the topography will in turn affect this. Sloping sites drain excess water naturally, but on a flat site, or on one with poorly draining soil, the conditions may be too wet, especially in winter, for some plants to thrive. A cross fall drainage system may be needed to carry the rainwater away.

Soil

Consider also if plants are suited to the pH, texture and drainage of your soil. Some plants such as *Camellia* or *Acer* (maple) have a distinct preference for an acid (pH 4.5–6.5) soil, whereas *Choisya* and *Philadelphus* prefer an alkaline (pH 7.5–8) soil, but the majority of plants will grow happily in more neutral soil with a pH of 5.5–7.5.

The most desirable soil is a medium loam, which has a moisture-retentive, friable (crumbly) texture with good drainage and yet sufficient nutrients to support healthy plant growth. Such a soil will allow you to grow the widest range of plants. If you have a heavy, clay soil or a light, sandy or silty soil, the best course is to choose plants that are happy in those conditions, although by incorporating humus, well-rotted manure or compost, or any organic matter into the soil to improve its texture, you could increase the plants that might be grown.

Most plants are very particular in their preferences for dry or damp soils, and their wild origins will give you a clue as to whether they will be happy in your garden. Some, like *Lavandula* (lavender) or *Cistus* (rock rose) originate from dry and stony, Mediterranean areas; *Salix* (willows) and *Cornus* (dogwoods) thrive in damp conditions similar to their woodland habitats. If possible, try to match conditions for your plant to its natural habitat.

Aspect

Most plants have a leaf structure or some other feature that renders them able to cope best with sun or shade. The sun-lovers may have silvery grey foliage, which on close examination is seen to have a covering of tiny hairs that cut out the scorching effects of strong sunlight. Other plants have delicate, thinner leaves, which need the shade of overhanging trees or shrubs to protect them. Dappled shade, where light filters through trees or large shrubs, can be beneficial in providing a welcome relief from bright sunshine, so allowing many more plants to be grown.

Exposure to wind can have a very damaging effect on any plant, especially when young leaves are emerging. Not many plants can withstand being placed in a wind funnel—the force of the wind channelled between buildings usually results in broken branches and scorched foliage. In this position, or on an exposed site, there is little point in creating a garden unless some steps are taken to break or filter the wind, such as planting boundary hedges or trees. Coastal winds are salt-laden so this again affects what can be grown.

Pollution

You only have to look at the planting beside motorways or city streets to see how petrol fumes affect plant growth. Few plants will put up with constantly being bombarded with noxious gases and while many will not actually die, they will be unable to photosynthesize, remaining static and not putting on any significant growth. Landscape architects responsible for motorway planting know this and use pollution-tolerant species that can cope with these conditions. Previous workings in the area can also affect your soil by contamination, such as toxic waste from previous minings. Taking soil samples should reveal if this is the case and, in dire cases, the soil may need to be removed and replaced before planting new stock.

Aesthetic Qualities of Plants

Apart from their suitability to the site, the main qualities to look for in choosing plants are outline or shape and foliage texture, as well as their height and spread as they grow and mature. Flower colour is usually a high priority, but generally the foliage is what we see for most of the growing season, so consider how the flowers may be enhanced by a backcloth of foliage.

Your garden should reflect your personality, so consider not only what textures and colours you wear and what suits you, but also those used in decorating your home. Aim to reflect your personal taste in choice of plants, and try to harmonize the style of the garden with that of your home to avoid a jarring transition from house to garden, probably making the garden seem larger and more restful. So if your taste is for clean lines and contemporary furnishings, traditional cottage plants may not be the most appropriate choice.

Aesthetic Considerations

These factors should influence your choice of plants for the garden.

- Plant height, spread and habit
- Season of interest
- Foliage qualities—form or shape, colour and texture
- Flower colour and shape
- Sensual characteristics—sight, sound, touch, smell
- Personal preference

Planting and the Senses

Our response to the pictures created by plants is much the same as our reaction to music, poetry, art or food. Most of us have five senses—sight, sound, touch, smell and taste—all of which come into play when we observe gardens. Sight is obvious, but it becomes more intense if you appreciate what you are looking at, such as the contrasting textures or sizes of a foliage grouping. The sound of birds or a breeze rustling through a stand of bamboo can arouse emotions. The tactile effect of felted-leaf shrubs or silky grasses can be sensual; so can the heady scent of early spring flowers or old-fashioned roses. And although we must be discerning about what we eat in our garden, certain plants such as rosemary or sage excite our taste buds even when not confined to the kitchen garden.

Planting and Time

The skill of arranging plants in a garden is very similar to an artist creating a three-dimensional painting, although gardeners have to work with the added dimension of time. Our palette consists of plants that mature, fade, die or reappear with the next growing season in an ever-changing tableau. Think therefore of how the new plants will look together as they develop—will they flower at the same time or will one plant become much larger and overshadow another? Do you want a plant to perform long-term or just for a temporary effect over one or two seasons?

In an ideal world, an entire year should pass so that you can observe the seasonal effects of the existing planting before you make any changes. Good gardeners require patience but, on the other hand, there is a danger that you will become so accustomed to the planting that you will no longer see it with a critical eye. Deciding on your prorities and discussing them with a friend or neighbour often makes you see a familiar scene more objectively.

The Well-balanced Border

With the huge diversity of plant material now available, it is very easy to go to considerable expense, buying one of this and three of that, and still not have a beautiful garden. Take time to think about how the plants will look when combined in a border and choose them for their contribution to the overall effect.

In most borders, and particularly if the shrubs are evergreen, shrubs provide a solidity of form and texture and a foliage effect over several seasons. To balance the planting, break up the line of a hedge or wall, or to link strong, vertical lines of the house with the more horizontal lines of the garden, an occasional, small tree may also be necessary, but may cast shade and limit what can be grown beneath. Climbers or wall shrubs also link the vertical and horizontal planes, and can be used to clothe walls. Many otherwise tender plants can be grown with the protection of a warm wall. Mix plants with different habits and forms; for instance, contrasting a plant with architectural or spiky leaves with one with a softer, rounded shape makes both look more interesting. Climbing, rambler or shrub roses are useful in most borders, but there are so many that it can be difficult to choose unless you understand their different characteristics.

Herbaceous plants are usually used to contribute colour with their flowers, but the effects of leaves are equally important. Plants such as *Hosta* and *Bergenia* will help anchor the herbaceous plantings, and are particularly useful near the front of borders to set off the shrubs. Some grasses and ferns last well into winter and their leaves or fronds look beautiful in frost.

Seasonal changes can be extended and intensified by using bulbs, half-hardies and annuals. Herbs, fruit and even vegetables can occasionally be used among flower borders—for instance, parsley has a very decorative leaf and can last for two years, provided that it is not allowed to run to seed.

Placing your plants

The professional garden designer or landscaper will draw up a plan, choosing plants both for outline shape and for height and spread, trying to achieve a balance of shapes to occupy the available space. Sometimes they will draw up an elevation to check that the composition is effective from all angles. The same effect may be achieved in a border by an imaginative amateur.

Work out where to position plants within the border by using a combination of garden canes to indicate trees or taller shrubs, upturned plastic pots to represent shrubs and sand or flour to outline the herbaceous areas. The canes and upturned pots can be regrouped until the balance and juxtaposition is satisfactory. This will also help you decide how much space each plant should take up and therefore you can work out how many you need. Much will depend on the age or size of the plants that you buy, and on local conditions, which will determine the rate of growth.

Canes and pots can be used to experiment with the sizes, shapes and number of plants in a border.

Living Boundaries

Living boundaries can be made with suitable species of shrubs and trees and include mixed hedges, evergreen and deciduous species, or even pleached trees and topiary. They can be used for protection from the elements, seclusion, screening, shelter and noise reduction, or as shelterbelts. Boundary plants will form a major part of the structure of your garden and should be chosen with care. Height and density are two important considerations, as are spacing, together with maintenance requirements such as clipping and pruning.

A formal, or informal, living boundary to the garden not only blends into its surroundings but, in the case of deciduous plants, changes with the seasons. Even when the plants are leafless in winter, they still perform the function of delineating your private space and keeping most intruders out. They also provide some structural interest until they spring to life again as the weather becomes warmer in spring.

Evergreens can be useful structural plants, but too many of the same shade of green can look very monotonous so vary the colour, shape and texture of their foliage.

Boundary Hedges

Choice of species is of utmost importance when buying plants for a hedge—look around your locality for plants that are growing healthily in gardens or naturally in hedgerows. That will be a good guide to the prevailing soil conditions, and will help you to choose one or more suitable species.

There are other practical considerations. In the 20th century, *Ligustrum ovalifolium* (privet) used to be popular as a hedge in suburban gardens because it is remarkably resistant to pollution. Other suitable species tolerant of urban poisoning would include *Aucuba japonica* (spotted laurel) or *Buxus sempervirens* (common box). Prickly hedges such as *Berberis* or *Pyracantha* (firethorn) may deter unwanted animals from trying to scramble through.

Aesthetic considerations are important too; there is a very wide choice of colour, for example *Fagus sylvatica* Atropurpurea Group (copper beech), *Forsythia* or *Salix* (willow), and of leaf size, such as *Prunus lusitanica* (Portugal laurel) or *Lonicera nitida* (box-leaved honeysuckle). Some species are more or less adaptable to formality or informality, such as the fast-growing *Rhamnus alaternus* 'Argenteovariagata' which can be left shaggy or tightly clipped and tied into an upright shape. Buxus sempervirens (evergreen box), if left to its own devices, will grow into a loosely shaped shrub, but may also be pruned or clipped to form a ball or a cone.

Evergreen Hedging Plants

If the boundary hedge is to be a purely architectural feature surrounding the garden, an evergreen, dark green can provide an excellent screen. It also serves as a perfect backdrop for other plants. *Taxus baccata*, with its small, evergreen needles, will clip to a firm, neat shape; the foliage is light absorbent (rather than reflective) and forms a matt backcloth. It filters noise successfully too. The fallacy that it is slow-growing is not borne out, if the plants are regularly watered when the soil is dry and they are given an annual feed in spring.

A glossy or light-reflective alternative is *Ilex* (holly). There are good cultivars raised from cuttings, such as the non-prickly, free-berrying, moderately broad-leaved *Ilex aquifolium* 'J.C. van Tol' or the sturdy, dark green, broad-leaved *Ilex* × *altaclerensis* 'Hodginsii'. The latter is a male form and it does not bear berries. If well cared for, both yew and holly can be expected to put on about 30 cm (12 in.) of growth every year after the first season. Holly should be kept to shape by trimming the stems with secateurs rather than clipping the foliage with shears, which would scar the glossy foliage.

A brighter green alternative to yew or holly is *Thuja plicata* (western red cedar); some excellent cultivars are raised from cuttings. For a taller hedge, consider a form of *Chamaecyparis lawsoniana* (Lawson cypress). A hedge of × *Cupressocyparis leylandii* (Leyland cypress) or other fast-growing evergreen plants can quickly cause disputes between neighbours, usually when an inappropriate variety is planted too close or when regular, careful pruning and maintenance is discontinued. New legislation in the United Kingdom requires that boundary hedges should not normally exceed 2 m (6½ ft.) unless incorporated into planning permission—check with your local authority before planting a new hedge.

Deciduous Hedging Plants

Conventional hedging plants such as *Fagus* (beech) or *Carpinus betulus* (hornbeam) are suitable for a tall but narrow hedge. Both plants retain their dead leaves through winter until the rising sap in spring pushes them off. In winter, beech leaves are bright russet and the hornbeam a sadder brown. Both usually need clipping (with shears) only once a year. In country situations, avoid using *Fagus sylvatica* Atropurpurea Group (copper beech) because it will be out of context with the country landscape. It can, however, be very effective in towns.

Hedges for Boundaries

Deciduous Hedging Plants

Shrub/tree	Common name	Soil	Maximum height m (ft.)	Planting distance cm (in.)	Foliage	Notes
Acer campestre	Field maple	Dry/Moist/Chalk/Clay	5–10 (16–33)	40 (16)	Large	Autumn colour, native, colonizes quickly.
Alnus glutinosa	Common alder	Moist/Not waterlogged	25 (80)	75 (30)	Medium	Shiny, green leaves.
Berberis thunbergii	Barberry	Clay	1.5 (5)	40 (16)	Small	Thorny, therefore deterrent.
Berberis thunbergii f. *atropurpurea*	Barberry	Clay	1.5 (5)	40 (16)	Small	Reddish leaves, prickly, semi-evergreen.
Carpinus betulus	Hornbeam	Chalk/Moist	5–10 (16–33)	40 (16)	Medium	Autumn colour. Holds leaf. Tolerates shade and heavy soils.
Cornus alba	Dogwood	Moist/Clay	3 (10)	30 (12)	Medium	Variegation in cultivars. Coloured stems, especially when pruned.
Corylus avellana	Hazel	Moist/Clay	5 (16)	40 (16)	Medium	Catkins in winter.
Crataegus monogyna	Hawthorn	Any/Wet/Extreme	10 (33)	40 (16)	Small	Autumn colour, flowers and berries. Tolerates shade.
Euonymus europaeus	Spindle	Any/Clay/Chalk	5 (16)	50 (20)	Small	Green stems. Native. Attractive fruit.
Fagus sylvatica	Beech	Sandy/Chalk/Not too wet or heavy	5 (16)	40 (16)	Medium	Copper/brown foliage. Holds leaf till spring.
Prunus cerasifera	Cherry plum	Any	3 (10)	100 (39)	Medium	Cultivars with bronze, red, purple leaves. White flowers, followed by fruits.
Prunus spinosa	Blackthorn	Any	3 (10)	60 (24)	Medium	Spiny branches, masses of small, white flowers, then fruits.
Rhamnus alaternus	Buckthorn	Any	5 (16)	60 (24)	Small	Dark green, semi-evergreen.
Rosa rugosa	Rose	Any/Light/Acid	1.8 (3)	100 (39)	Medium	Good flowers and hips. Avoid shade.
Salix lanata	Woolly willow	Moist	1 (3)	45 (18)	Small	Grey, woolly foliage.
Viburnum opulus	Snowball tree	Moist	5 (16)	45 (18)	Medium	Glossy foliage.

Hedges for Boundaries

Evergreen Hedging Plants

Shrub/tree	Common name	Soil	Maximum height m (ft.)	Planting distance cm (in.)	Foliage	Notes
Aucuba japonica	Laurel	Any	3 (10)	45 (18)	Large	Shiny leaves.
Berberis darwinii	Barberry	Any/Not too wet	1.5 (5)	60 (24)	Small	Prickly. Golden flowers, purple berries.
Berberis x stenophylla	Barberry	Any/Not too wet	1.5 (5)	60 (24)	Small	Thorny. Yellow flowers. Purple berries.
Buxus	Box	Any/Well drained	1.5 (5)	15–20 (6–8)	Small	Neat for clipping to formal shapes.
Chamaecyparis lawsoniana	Lawson cypress	Acid	5 (16)	90 (36)	Small	Fast-growing, green, dense.
Elaeagnus x ebbingei		Not chalk	2–3 (7–10)	30–40 (12–16)	Medium	Fast-growing, leathery leaves. Dense.
Escallonia		Any	2–3 (7–10)	30–40 (12–16)	Small	Semi-evergreen, small flowers
Fuchsia		Any	2–3 (7–10)	50 (20)	Medium	May be cut to ground by hard frost.
Genista	Broom	Any/Dry	1–2 (3–7)	40 (16)	Small	Wiry branches, yellow flowers.
Griselinia littoralis		Any	2–3 (7–10)	30–40 (12–16)	Medium	Leathery foliage.
Hippophaë rhamnoides	Sea buckthorn	Any/Not wet	2–3 (7–10)	90 (36)	Narrow	Grey–green. Good by the sea.
Ilex	Holly	Any	3 (10)	50 (20)	Medium	Slow-growing, glossy green foliage.
Ligustrum ovalifolium	Privet	Any	1.5 (5)	50 (20)	Medium	Fast-growing, therefore needs regular clipping.
Lonicera nitida	Box-leaved honeysuckle	Any	1–3 (3–10)	50 (20)	Small	Bushy, can be used instead of box, but shorter-lived.
Pittosporum tenuifolium		Any/Well drained	2–3 (7–10)	30–40 (12–16)	Medium	Needs shelter and light soils.
Prunus laurocerasus	Common laurel	Moist/Not chalk	3 (10)	50 (20)	Large	Fast-growing. Shiny leaves.
Prunus lusitanica	Portugal laurel	Moist/Not chalk	2.5 (8)	50 (20)	Large	Darker green, smaller leaves.
Pyracantha	Firethorn	Not chalk	3 (10)	50 (20)	Small	Thorny, good flowers and fruit.
Quercus ilex	Holm oak	Any	3 (10)	50 (20)	Medium	Tall, dense, good for shaping.
Rhododendron ponticum		Acid	3 (10)	50 (20)	Large	Dark green leaves.
Tamarix	Tamarisk	Any/Well drained	2–3 (7–10)	30–40 (12–16)	Fine	Pink flowers.
Taxus baccata	Yew	Any/Not wet	3 (10)	75 (30)	Fine	Shade-tolerant, dense. Good background.
Thuja plicata	Western red cedar	Any/Chalk	3 (10)	50 (20)	Fine	Superior alternative to *Leylandii*.
Ulex europaeus	Gorse	Poor	1.5 (5)	40 (16)	Small	Very spiny, yellow flowers.
Viburnum tinus		Any	2 (7)	50 (20)	Medium	White flowers in winter. Dark, evergreen foliage.

Being uninteresting in colour, form and texture, *Ligustrum ovalifolium* seems to have fallen out of favour. However, since privet will survive under the shade of trees, in some cases it is hard to find a substitute. It grows quickly and can be made more interesting by clipping it into a hedge that is either tall and tapering, low and wide or even shaped into an undulating line. Privet needs clipping every six weeks or so during the growing season, so it is fairly high-maintenance.

In a rural landscape, an interesting field hedge may be planted comparatively cheaply by mixing indigenous species. For example, in Britain, use:

- *Acer campestre* (field maple)

- *Alnus glutinosa* (common alder)

- *Corylus avellana* (hazel)

- *Euonymus europaeus* (spindle)

- *Prunus spinosa* (blackthorn)

- *Viburnum opulus* (Guelder rose).

Decorative forms of holly and *Crataegus* (hawthorn) can be mixed in to create a tapestry effect, and the hedge will blend with the landscape. Inevitably, in a mixed hedge the different species grow at different rates, but it is a fairly simple task to clip the hedge over when some varieties begin to look leggy.

Used more in milder regions are wild *Fuchsia magellanica* hedges. They flower profusely and are inclined to spread, but are suited to most soils. The thorny (and therefore vandal-proof) *Pyracantha* will not grow too tall, but produces both berries and flowers. *Rosa rugosa* is also effective as a hedge—it too forms an impenetrable barrier and flowers and fruits, but is rarely used except beside motorways. In coastal areas where salt spray is a problem but where the climate may be warmer, *Hippophaë rhamnoides* (sea buckthorn) may be useful in a hedge.

Planting and Maintaining Hedges

Every hedge is a living barrier composed of closely spaced plants that are set out along a defined, but not necessarily straight, line. Many of the plants would by nature mature into quite large trees. Although the top-growth is curtailed by clipping, the roots continue growing. If the individual plants are too close together, some may become stifled. They will not receive enough moisture and will die, leaving awkward gaps.

Single row planting gives the plants the best chance of thriving, but if a thick hedge is needed, use a staggered, double row. Hedges are best planted in the dormant season, i.e during the winter months, provided that the ground is not frostbound.

- Dig a trench both deeper and wider than the rootballs of the plants, removing the topsoil.

- Loosen the subsoil with a fork to allow the hedging plants' roots to penetrate it.

- Fork in about 20 cm (4 in.) well-rotted manure or compost to the bottom of the trench.

- Add some of the removed topsoil and position each plant so that its pot, or rootball, is level with the soil surface.

- Infill with the rest of the topsoil.

- Tread plants in firmly.

- Water in thoroughly.

- Stake each plant, if necessary.

Clipping and pruning

Clipping of hedges is usually carried out in late summer or whenever the hedge is becoming shaggy. Clip to a slight taper or "batter", leaving the hedge wider at the base and slightly narrower at the top. This will enable light to reach the lower branches and makes it less likely that snow will settle on top and perhaps weigh down and split the hedge. The clipping may be done with either a powered hedgetrimmer or hand shears. The line may be judged by eye, or you can use a length of garden twine tied between stakes or canes—check the string with a spirit level.

Interesting effects can be achieved with gentle undulations or stepped curves in hedges. To achieve a lengthening of perspective, "pillars" of differing heights could be cut into the hedge at each end, with the hedge forming a shallow serpentine or S-shape between them. This treatment suits smaller-leaved, evergreen species which respond well to close clipping.

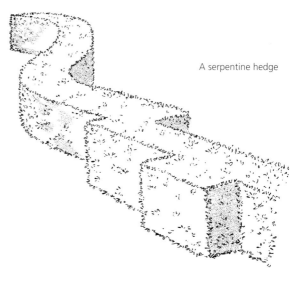

A serpentine hedge

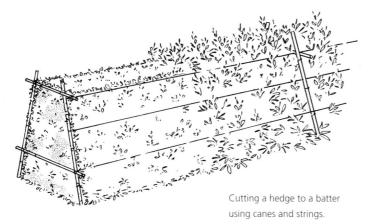

Cutting a hedge to a batter using canes and strings.

Informal, native hedges need less attention, whereas flowering hedges must be pruned at the appropriate time after flowering to avoid destroying next year's flowerbuds. As a general rule, if the plant flowers on the previous season's wood, prune it directly after it flowers; if the plant flowers on new wood made during the current growing season, prune it in spring.

Rose hedges need little trimming, particularly as many of them have flowers and hips. Cutting out some of the older stems in their entirety may be enough and will allow other stems to produce flowers followed by rosehips later; if you deadhead them, you will remove the future hips. Some informal hedges need no regular trimming at all. Many grow quite slowly, such as *Skimmia japonica* and *Berberis thunbergii* f. *atropurpurea*. All they require, if growth is untidy, is an occasional trim in spring or autumn.

Internal Divisions

Unless it is to be bland and boring—perhaps a stretch of lawn bordered on either side by a few shrubs and perennials—even the smallest gardens need some internal divisions to give them structure and form. However restricted the space, we usually have a desire to grow a wide range of plants, some of which are suited to different areas such dry shade, damp shade, full sun or perhaps a bog or waterside garden. Quite small spaces within a larger space can each have their own identity or type of planting. In a building, walls divide up the internal space into different rooms. In a garden, hedges, walls, fences and trellis are used to the same effect.

Even in a very small garden, some form of living structure, for instance a clipped box square, yew

Pruning Times for Informal Hedges

Early spring—cut back flowering shoots by two or three buds:

Acer negundo

Fuchsia

Hydrangea

Hypericum

Olearia × haastii

Potentilla fruticosa

Rosa rugosa

Spiraea japonica.

Early spring—cut back hard:

Buddleja

Sambucus nigra.

Early spring—clip over top 2–3 cm (3/4–1¼ in.), avoiding cutting into old wood:

Lavandula

Santolina chamaecyparissus.

Summer—after flowering, trim to shape and cut out any suckering shoots close to the base:

Amelanchier canadensis

Berberis darwinii

Berberis x stenophylla

Buddleja alternifolia

Ceanothus dentatus

Chaenomeles japonica

Deutzia

Hippophaë rhamnoides

Mahonia aquifolium

Osmanthus delavayi

Philadelphus

Prunus cerasifera

Ribes sanguineum

Rosa moyesii

Sarcococca var. digyna

Spiraea thunbergii

Viburnum opulus

Weigela.

pillar, or terracotta urn, will help to define the end or beginning of a border. This is particularly necessary in winter when many plants disappear below ground. A single vertical element—perhaps a conical bay tree—can act as an exclamation mark or, at a lower level, a box ball can act as a punctuation stop. Each garden room, or the vertical elements used to create it, may interconnect with another by means of arches, pergolas or arbours, which double as supports for climbers.

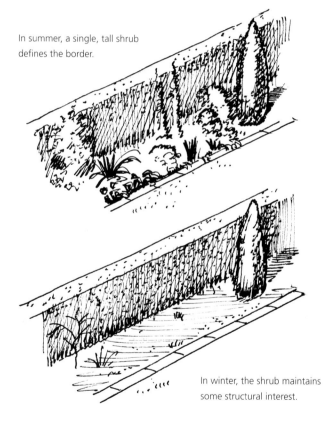

In summer, a single, tall shrub defines the border.

In winter, the shrub maintains some structural interest.

Choosing structural hedges

If chosen with care, internal hedges will become part of the "bones" of the garden. Bear these principles in mind when selecting the plants.

- Use them to divide up or accentuate different areas, keeping in mind the primary needs of the overall garden layout.

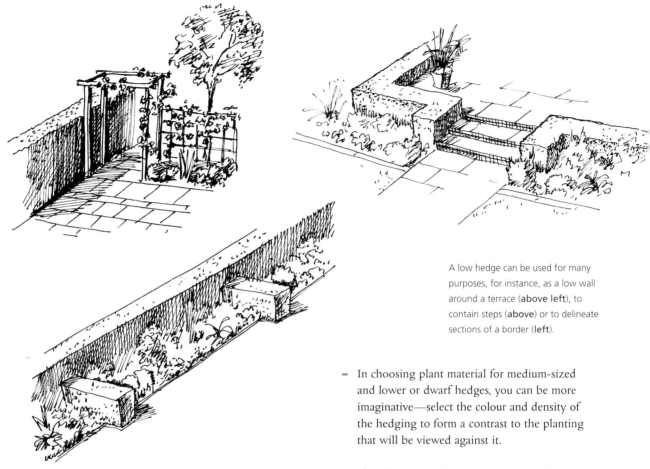

A low hedge can be used for many purposes, for instance, as a low wall around a terrace (**above left**), to contain steps (**above**) or to delineate sections of a border (**left**).

– Decide first on the shape, colour or texture needed to harmonize with the style of the garden.

– Consider what mature size the plants should reach and how long you are prepared to wait for them to reach that size.

– Choose the plant that is closest to this specification; try to avoid being diverted by flowers or foliage.

– Structural planting is often used as a background, so the plants should not compete with decorative shrubs or perennials that are in front of the hedge.

– In choosing plant material for medium-sized and lower or dwarf hedges, you can be more imaginative—select the colour and density of the hedging to form a contrast to the planting that will be viewed against it.

– If a tall internal division is needed, perhaps 2–3 m (6–9 ft.) tall, consider the same species as discussed for boundary hedges (see pages 33–34).

– Use a low hedge to delineate corners of borders and hold the border planting together visually.

Plants for Internal Hedges

Buxus sempervirens

Yew is closely followed for classical style by box, with its luxuriant green leaves. It grows in any soil including chalk. Box is usually kept to a height of 30–60 cm (1–2 ft.) but in time it can, if fed and watered and not heavily clipped, reach over 2 m (6½ ft.). Recently, exuberant "cloud" hedges of box have been seen in gardens and at major flower shows. These are usually formed from very old plants, perhaps grown in the wild as single specimens that have been replanted to form a hedge. They are then clipped to shape following their natural outline—hence the billowing, or cloud, effect. Their age and size make them very expensive.

A cloud hedge makes a graceful backdrop to herbaceous planting.

Unfortunately many gardens which depend on box for their structural planting are now suffering from a pathogenic fungal infection specific to box. This is called *Cylindrocladium*, or box blight, which causes the plant to lose its leaves and eventually die. It infects the leaves, causing spots that initially look similar to a cigarette burn; these soon lead to defoliation and rapidly move to the stem tissue, causing dieback in the smaller branches. Patches of greyish fungus may also be seen on the undersides of the leaves. Box blight is extremely virulent and capable of defoliating mature plants in a matter of weeks. There are as yet no chemical remedies and the fungus remains in the soil only to infect any new box plants that are planted to replace those lost. Since investments in box plants often represent large amounts of time and money, always buy box plants from a "clean" or disease-free source.

Euonymus fortunei
Variegated plants are usually too visually demanding to be effective as internal divisions but *Euonymus fortunei* 'Emerald Gaiety' and *E. fortunei* 'Emerald 'n'

Gold' are variegated evergreens which, when clipped hard, can be trained into small hedges. They are easily propagated. Since they are both naturally scrambling plants, they need regular attention to prevent the hedge from looking untidy.

Hedera helix
In Victorian times, common or English ivy was popular for hedges and edging. It is more versatile and faster-growing than box. The pliable shoots can be trained over wire frames to form quick-growing architectural shapes and topiary.

Lavandula
For a low, blue-grey, semi-evergreen effect, scented lavender is always a good choice. *Lavandula angustifolia*, the traditional, old English lavender, is the most scented, and grows slightly taller and wider than most other cultivars. *Lavandula* 'Hidcote' is the deepest blue and slightly lower-growing. Both should be clipped in spring, and then pruned back after flowering to encourage new growth—don't cut back into the old wood. Lavender hedges smell delicious when brushed against, but they need replacing every eight to ten years because they become leggy as they age.

Lonicera nitida
Used as an alternative to box, the box-leaved or shrubby honeysuckle will quickly establish to form a low, evergreen hedge but it needs more frequent clipping than box to keep it tidy and compact. For a bright, yellow contrast, perhaps for a knot garden, *Lonicera nitida* 'Baggesen's Gold' propagates easily from cuttings and can be trained into standards, balls or pyramids.

Potentilla
In a narrow or bare area, perhaps between a path and the base of the wall, a flowering hedge can be effective. The shrubby *Potentilla fruticosa* 'Primrose Beauty' has a dense, picturesque habit, and greyish-green, downy foliage with exceptionally long-lasting, primrose-yellow flowers. Less formal in

Recommended Plants for Internal Hedges

Plant	Soil	Height cm (in.)	Planting distance cm (in.)	Characteristics
Berberis darwinii	Chalk/Clay/Dry	200 (72)	70–80 (28–32)	Dark evergreen. Orange or red flowers in spring. Prickly, forming dense, impenetrable barrier. Pollution-resistant.
Berberis thunbergii 'Atropurpurea Nana'	Any/Not wet	45–60 (18–24)	35 (14)	Dwarf, semi-evergreen. Small, reddish-purple leaves. Prickly.
Buxus sempervirens	Chalk/Clay/Moist	30–50 (12–20)	15–20 (6–8)	Many cultivars. Pollution-resistant. Formal.
Escallonia	Chalk/Clay	150–200 (60–72)	50 (20)	Pink and white flowers in summer. Small, glossy leaves. Good by the sea.
Euonymus fortunei	Any/Moist	50 (20)	30 (12)	Exposed areas. Fast-growing, adaptable.
Griselinia littoralis	Any	150–200 (60–72)	50 (20)	Coastal areas. Fresh, evergreen leaves.
Hebe rakaiensis	Any/Chalk	50 (20)	30 (12)	White flowers, light, evergreen leaves. Small, rounded form—can be clipped into balls or quickly establish as low hedge.
Hebe 'Midsummer Beauty'	Any/Chalk	60 (24)	30 (12)	Coastal areas. Blue flowers, evergreen.
Hedera helix	Any	50 (20)	15 (6)	Train up netting until established, then clip.
Lavandula angustifolia	Any/Not wet	75 (30)	45 (18)	Coastal areas. "Old English" style.
Lavandula angustifolia 'Hidcote'	Any	50 (20)	30 (12)	Violet flower spikes, compact form. Coastal areas.
Lonicera nitida	Chalk/Clay/Dry	30–45 (12–18)	30 (12)	Much larger, 2 m (7 ft.), if unclipped. Suitable for heavy shade. Tends to be untidy after 10 years.
Osmanthus x burkwoodii	Clay/Dry	100–150 (40–60)	50 (20)	Can grow to 2.5 m (8½ ft.). Early, fragrant, white flowers. Lustrous, dark, evergreen, pointed leaves make good foil for bright or pale border flowers. Pollution resistant.
Pittosporum tenuifolium	Any/Not wet	150–200 (60–72)	50 (20)	Evergreen with unusual, bright, undulate (wavy-margined) leaves on black twigs. Unsuitable for very cold areas.
Potentilla fruticosa 'Primrose Beauty'	Any/Chalk	100 (40)	60 (24)	Grey-green foliage. Long-lasting, yellow flowers.
Prunus x cistena	Any/Chalk	120–150 (48–60)	60 (24)	Deep crimson leaves, blood-red growing tips. White flowers in spring—trim after flowering. Purple fruits.
Rosa gallica 'Versicolor'	Chalk/Clay	120–180 (48–72)	70 (28)	Semi-double, rose-red flowers, with white stripes.
Rosa 'Fru Dagmar Hastrup'	Chalk/Clay	150 (60)	80–150 (32–60)	Rose-pink flowers, dense, rounded habit. Large, globular hips.
Rosa 'Roseraie de l'Haÿ'	Chalk/Clay	200–250 (72–98)	80 (32)	Pointed purple buds, red flowers with cream stamens.
Rosa 'Blanche Double de Coubert'	Chalk/Clay	200 (72)	90 (36)	Semi-double, white flowers, very fragrant. Perpetual.
Rosmarinus 'Miss Jessopp's Upright'	Chalk/Any/Well drained	120–108 (48–64)	60 (24)	Very erect, must have sun. Small, blue flowers, aromatic.
Santolina chamaecyparissus	Any/Well drained	50 (20)	22 (5)	Finely divided, grey-green foliage. Button-like, yellow flowers if untrimmed. Good for coastal areas.
Santolina rosmarinifolia subsp. rosmarinifolia	Sandy	50 (20)	22 (5)	Coastal areas. Dwarf, vivid green foliage.
Sarcococca confusa	Any/Chalk	50 (20)	30 (24)	Fragrant flowers in winter, black berries. Shade-tolerant, evergreen.
Teucrium chamaedrys	Any/Well drained	30 (12)	20 (8)	Aromatic, must have sun.
Taxus baccata	Any/Chalk/Clay	150–300 (60–120)	50–75 (20–30)	Versatile, needs good drainage. Classical backcloth.
Viburnum tinus	Any/Clay	100–150 (38–60)	40–50 (16–20)	Several cultivars, most with dark green leaves and white or pink flowers in winter. Provides good cover in shade.
Viburnum tinus 'Gwenllian'	Any/Clay	1–2.4 (3–8)	50–60 (20–24)	Very free-flowering cultivar, pink flowers from deep pink buds.

shape, it needs only to be lightly clipped over after flowering. More upright is *P. fruticosa* 'Goldfinger', which has greener foliage and deeper yellow flowers.

Rosa

Some roses can be excellent as informal hedging. *Rosa gallica* 'Versicolor' (formerly called *R. mundi*, the gallica rose) was cultivated prior to the 16th century, and produces quantities of large, semi-double, brilliant crimson flowers that are striped white. It flowers in a single flush. Careful pruning between mid-autumn and late winter can keep it to a compact 1.2 m (4 ft.); later pruning may result in new flowering shoots being sacrificed. *R.* 'Fru Dagmar Hastrup', the rugosa rose, is slightly taller and has single, flesh-pink flowers with pointed buds that turn into hips later in the season—provided that the flowers are not deadheaded. The same applies to another good, but even taller, rugosa rose: *R.* 'Roseraie de l'Haÿ', with rich wine-purple, elongated buds and crimson-purple, strongly perfumed flowers. Taller again, but with pure white, open, semi-double flowers of almost paper-like texture, which flower continuously rather than in one flush, is *R.* 'Blanche Double de Coubert'. It is highly reliable and early to come into flower.

Santolina chamaecyparissus

The cotton lavender is also an evergreen, with blue-grey leaves, but because it is quick-growing it soon becomes untidy and woody, and needs replacing every five years. Clip it in early summer to stop it flowering, which would weaken the plant. There is also a bright green version, *S. rosmarinifolia* subsp. *rosmarinifolia* (a small plant with a very big name!), that has thread-like foliage and grows slightly taller.

Sarcococca confusa

The sweet box can be used to make an evergreen, dwarf hedge about 45 cm (18 in.) high. It produces deliciously scented flowers from midwinter to early spring. Clip it over once in late spring—clipping later would mean losing some of the flowers for the following year.

Taxus baccata

For a dark to mid-green backdrop with a dense, matt effect, coniferous yew is the classical and most elegant choice. It dislikes waterlogged soil, but will tolerate most conditions, including dry, chalky soils. Contrary to its reputation, yew grows quickly provided that it is fed and watered regularly, especially after planting. Female plants produce bright red fruits in autumn. All parts are toxic.

Teucrium chamaedrys

This evergreen subshrub, germander, has deep green leaves and will quickly form a 30 cm (12 in.) low hedge. It needs to be pruned hard regularly to keep it to a tight shape and to encourage new growth. Often a short-lived plant, prone to die back, it usually needs replacing every four to five years.

Trees in Garden Boundaries

A boundary can be delineated by trees but, since most mature deciduous trees have a clear stem or trunk, they do not really fulfill the screening objective. However trees may be useful in defining an area beside a driveway or disguising a car parking space. The choice of species will depend on the required boundary height and width. Farm vehicles, trucks or buses may make it impractical to have a wide, overhanging tree canopy.

Trees planted in a single line, 3–6 m (9–20 ft.) apart will give some protection, but a double, staggered line would be even more effective. Even if there is only space for a straight line of trees, they will form an important structural boundary. The best trees for screening purposes are:

- *Acer campestre* (field maple)

- *Acer platanoides* (Norway maple)

- *Carpinus betulus* (hornbeam) tolerates heavy, moist soils

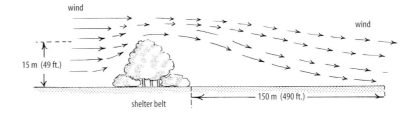

wind

wind

15 m (49 ft.)

shelter belt

150 m (490 ft.)

- *Crataegus* (hawthorn)

- *Euonymus* (spindle)

- *Fagus sylvatica* (beech) is good on lighter soils

- *Sorbus aria* 'Lutescens' (whitebeam)

- *Sorbus aucuparia* (mountain ash or rowan)

- *Tilia* (lime).

The smaller trees such as *Crataegus* or *Sorbus aucuparia* will take up less space. They should be planted at 3–5m (10–15 ft.) intervals to allow the spreading canopies to meet when mature.

Evergreen boundary trees

Because of its rapid growth, the most used evergreen tree for boundary purposes is the much-maligned × *Cupressocyparis leylandii* (Leyland cypress). It is a good, dark green but, if it is to be kept in shape, the speed of its growth demands regular clipping in late spring and in autumn. If this is overlooked—and it often is—the result is a tall, lanky hedge, which robs you or your neighbour of light and uses up any available moisture in the ground.

Of slightly slower growth is a form of *Chamaecyparis lawsoniana* (Lawson cypress), but this is often raised from seed and is extremely variable. A form known as *C. lawsoniana* 'Green Hedger' is of excellent uniform growth and a slightly brighter green. Another alternative is *Thuja occidentalis*, which is similar to *Chamaecyparis* in its bright green foliage and thrives in any well-drained soil. *Quercus ilex* (Holm oak) is useful by the coast; *Arbutus unedo* (strawberry tree) is a smaller tree and grows quickly in town or country.

Shelter belts

Large, exposed gardens may need a shelter belt—a barrier of planting to protect the garden from the prevailing wind. If at least 15 m (50 ft.) wide, the trees in such a belt will reduce the wind by about 50% over a distance approximately 10 times the height of the trees. A shelter belt should generally consist of one dominant native species that is particularly suited to the landscape and the soil, such as *Fagus* (beech) for chalk, *Betula* (birch) for light, sandy soil, or *Quercus* (oak) for clay. The dominant species should be augmented by two supporting species (one evergreen and one deciduous) in the centre of the belt, and a fringe planting of smaller trees and shrubs. For a natural effect, the different species should be planted in groups, rather than being dotted about at random.

Pleached Trees

Pleaching, or making a "hedge on stilts", involves removing all the lower branches from a line of trees and intertwining carefully selected upper lateral, or horizontal, branches until the canopies knit together into a hedge. The trees should be planted approximately 1.8 m (6 ft.) apart, and then the clipped and interwoven branches should be trained along wires, or horizontal bamboo canes, until they can be intertwined.

Pleached trees with naturally upright, yet young and therefore still pliable, main branches such as *Fagus* and *Crataegus* give a strong linear emphasis to a design. They hold their leaves well into winter, until wind (or the rising sap in spring) causes them to

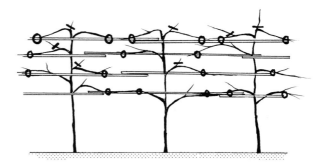

drop. In towns, *Tilia × euchlora* can be very effective; unlike other limes, it does not attract aphids, so does not drip with their honey dew. Now that pleached trees have become popular, nurseries specializing in larger stock often provide them with the laterals trained against bamboo frames.

It is perfectly possible to create an unusual, two-tiered effect with a hedge and row of pleached trees behind it. Such a screen is still functional but with a rather intriguing space between the two layers. Visually, it is probably best to use the same material—beech on beech or hornbeam on hornbeam—rather than two separate species. In this case, the trees should be planted first and, if possible, slightly deeper in the soil than the proposed hedge. If the pleached "hedge on stilts" casts too much shadow and takes up too much moisture, the lower hedge may suffer.

Trees suitable for pleaching

Traditionally, pleaching was done with *Tilia × euchlora* but there are many other deciduous trees that are equally suitable. Look for a species or cultivar that has fairly flexible or pliable branches, because the three main lateral branches need to be trained and tied together to form the framework. *Fagus sylvatica* (common beech) can be trained in this way but will need to be planted slightly closer together. This is because the branches are stiffer and less easy to manipulate than on other trees, particularly when it is mature.

Pleaching requires young trees of species such as limes or hornbeam (**left**). The lateral branches are trained horizonally by tying them in to wires or bamboo canes (**right**).

For a two-tier boundary, plant hedging plants and clip them in the normal way, but intersperse pleached trees. The trees are most effective if they are of the same species and pleached at 1.5 m–1.8 m (5–6 ft.) above the mature height of the hedge.

Topiary

Boundary trees can also be topiarized, which means clipping them into ornamental shapes. Topiary is an art much practiced by French gardeners. Almost any tree can be topiarized, but this technique is more successful on subjects that naturally have a dense habit and do not grow too rapidly. Traditionally, topiary is carried out on *Taxus baccata* (yew) or *Buxus*

Trees topiarized into cube shapes can create the same effect as pleached trees.

marks, allowing the eye to pause. They can also act as a pivot to direct you around corners or to draw your eye to a certain point.

Almost all small, ornamental trees can hold the eye, but usually we think in terms of upright or columnar shapes such as *Taxus baccata* 'Fastigiata' (Irish yew) with deep green foliage. It can be used as a "dot plant" or planted in a series to flank a vista. Other fastigiate, or narrow columnar, forms of ornamental trees can also be found, for example of *Chamaecyparis* (cypress), *Juniperus* and *Ilex* (holly).

Use accent plants to emphasize the dominant shapes of borders and to break up a straight line. For instance, a long and fairly wide border could have three vertical accents, provided by fastigiate Irish yews; at the corners of the border, four *Buxus sempervirens* could be planted in a square, quite close together. Each one of the box shrubs could then clipped so that they form a box "table".

Low-growing shrubs, such as *Berberis thunbergii* 'Atropurpurea Nana' or *Santolina chamaecyparissus* (cotton lavender), may also be used as accent points to identify the beginning and end of a planted area.

(box); many varieties can be cut into cubes, lollipops or mopheads to add an unexpected touch of animation and humour to the garden.

The Japanese technique of "cloud pruning" has recently become popular. The majority of the growth along the main branches is removed, allowing the remaining growth to form a rounded shape or "cloud". Other trees that can be topiarized include:

- *Acer pseudoplatanus* (sycamore)

- *Crataegus* (hornbeam)

- *Fagus sylvatica* (common beech)

- *Prunus lusitanica* (Portugal laurel).

Using Woody Plants as Accents

Strongly vertical elements in a garden allow the human eye to rest on them, then refocus, rather like a camera does, to take in more intricate planting in the borders. All this is quite subconscious, but a garden without any vertical elements is not restful or relaxing; the eye tends to scan the garden looking in vain for something on which to settle. Vertical elements give perspective, balance, and height and sometimes provide a backcloth. They are punctuation

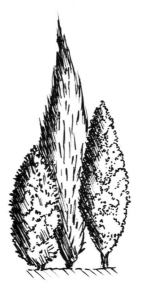

A group of conifers may be used to link the vertical lines of buildings with the horizontal, or flat, plane of the garden.

Recommended Accent Plants

Plant	Soil	Height cm (in)	Characteristics
Agave	Dry	200 (72)	Rosette of sharp, pointed, sword-like leaves. Not hardy.
Berberis thunbergii 'Atropurpurea Nana'	Any/Not wet	60 (24)	Rich purple-red leaves. Dwarf shrub, semi-evergreen. Prickly.
Berberis thunbergii 'Helmond Pillar'	Any/Not wet	150 (60)	Erect, with large, round, reddish-bronze leaves. Prickly, semi-evergreen.
Ilex aquifolium	Any	150 (60)	Many cultivars, with different foliage characteristics. Suitable for topiary, but slow-growing.
Laurus nobilis	Any/Well drained	250 (98)	Leaves excellent for cooking. Erect, well-branched stems. Can be trimmed to pyramids for accent. Prune hard if too large.
Lonicera pileata	Any	100 (38)	Neat, spreading habit. Good for horizontal accents, box-like leaves.
Perovskia atriplicifolia	Any	120 (48)	Subshrub or herbaceous perennial. Spires of violet or mauve flowers. Grey foliage with sage-like aroma.
Phormium	Moist	120 (48)	Spectacular, upright spikes of sword-shaped leaves. Many cultivars available in range of foliage colours and variegation.
Santolina chamaecyparissus	Dry/Sandy	60 (24)	Silver-grey foliage. If allowed to flower, foliage becomes straggly. Loses shape.
Viburnum davidii	Any/Moist/Chalk	150 (60)	Low-growing evergreen. Superb ribbed foliage. Small, white flowers.
Yucca filamentosa	Dry/Well drained	100 (38)	Stiff, erect, pointed leaves. White flowers in plumes.

Conifers

Plant	Soil	Height m (ft.)	Characteristics
Chamaecyparis lawsoniana 'Pembury Blue'	Any	2 (7–8)	Blue-grey foliage is neat foil for other green plants.
Cupressus sempervirens	Well drained	2–30 (7–98)	Italian cypress. Narrow tree, erect sprays of dark green leaves.
Juniperus scopulorum 'Skyrocket'	Well drained	2–7 (7–22)	Exceptionally narrow, 30 cm (12 in.), blue-grey column.
Metasequoia glyptostroboides	Acid	7–40 (22–130)	Deciduous, neat, conical shape. Feathery foliage. Suitable for large gardens only.
Picea omorika	Neutral/Acid/Moist		Beautiful conical shape with upturned branches. Spectacular.
Taxus baccata 'Fastigiata'	Any/Not waterlogged	2.4 (8)	Great garden value to use as a "dot" plant or to flank a vista.
Taxus baccata Fastigiata Aurea Group	Any/Not waterlogged	2–20 (7–70)	Upright form of golden Irish yew. Striking, old gold foliage in sunny position.

Using Trees in the Garden

As well as in boundaries, trees may be planted as specimens—individually—to show off their attributes or outlines. They may also be used as markers, perhaps to indicate where a path twists or turns, to create interesting focal points or perspectives and to give height when combined with other lower plantings.

Most gardens are too small to grow forest trees such as beech or oak. Instead opt for smaller, decorative trees. Avoid deciding on a flowering crab apple (*Malus* spp.) or cherry (*Prunus* spp.) simply because of the blossom—that usually lasts a mere week or ten days in an average spring and there may be little else to recommend the tree for the rest of the year. To earn a place in your garden, a tree ought to have several points of interest, so try to choose one that fulfils as many as possible of the criteria listed below.

round-headed

conical or pyramid

> ### Tree Selection
>
> These are the points to consider when choosing a tree.
> - Plant needs, such as soil and aspect
> - Outline or form (if deciduous, even in winter)
> - Speed of growth
> - Bark
> - Evergreen or deciduous
> - Leaf texture, size and autumn colour
> - Flowers and fruit
> - Scent.

Choosing a Suitable Tree

The first factor to consider is the plant's needs and whether it will thrive in the intended position in your garden. In common with other plants, trees have preferences for particular soil types and conditions as well as aspect and climate—check that the conditions that the plant needs do match those available in the garden. Trees will endure longer than shrubs; their roots go deeper into the soil to seek moisture and nutrients from the subsoil. If there is a risk of waterlogging, some trees such as yew may fail, whereas others such as willow will thrive. Make sure the soil drainage is adequate for your choice of tree.

Think about whether the site is exposed to wind. Most fast-growing trees, such as *Robinia pseudoacacia* (false acacia) and some willows, tend to have brittle branches that may become damaged by wind. Evergreen trees are particularly vulnerable in winter gales; they tend to be top heavy and wind cannot filter through them, as it does through deciduous trees when their branches are leafless.

Outline or form
Most tree canopies will fall into the rounded category but others form spires, columns, or weeping shapes or outlines. In choosing a deciduous tree, the outline or form should always be the first concern

upright—broadens with age

columnar or fastigiate

weeping or pendulous

because this gives the tree its character. Some trees, such as *Betula* (silver birch) are naturally elegant even when leafless, whereas *Fraxinus* (ash) has more densely packed twigs and a more stumpy outline.

Evergreen or deciduous?

This is a fairly momentous decision because it will affect the balance of your borders. Most evergreens, of course, retain their leaves during winter, whereas deciduous plants may spend five to six months in a naked state. If you decide to use an evergreen, consider a conifer for a vertical accent (see page 144) or a broader conifer as a specimen.

Hardy examples of non-coniferous, evergreen trees, such as *Quercus ilex* (evergreen or holm oak) and *Lyonothamnus floribundus* (ironwood), are fairly scarce commodities because many are not hardy in colder areas, but they are suitable for warmer climes such as southern U.S.A. Just to confuse you, there are also a few deciduous conifers such as *Ginkgo biloba* (maidenhair tree), much used as a street tree in the U.S.A., and *Larix decidua* (European or common larch), whose leaves turn gold and drop off in the late autumn.

An evergreen tree is viewed mostly as a solid block, and the actual shape and texture of the foliage is less apparent than on deciduous trees. The darker the leaf, the greater will be the seeming density of the evergreen's shape. Choose varieties for their light-reflecting or light-absorbing qualities of foliage, avoiding plants with too much dark or dull green, which would make the garden seem leaden and heavy. The *Ilex* (holly) family, for instance, has glossy and prickly leaves, whereas *Eucalyptus gunnii* (cider gum) has sickle-shaped, matt, sage-green leaves when it is mature.

Deciduous trees are seen as a solid block only while they are in leaf. Devoid of foliage in winter, their outlines vary considerably. Some such as *Amelanchier × grandiflora* 'Ballerina' has an elegant rounded crown even when leafless, whereas *Gleditsia tricanthos*

'Sunburst' is broadly conical and, because its branches are brittle, has an unbalanced appearance when leafless. Despite being able to see through their winter canopies, your eye rests on them instead of taking in any less favourable scene behind them because they interrupt the middle distance.

Leaf texture, size and autumnal colour

The leaves on each plant—tree, shrub or herbaceous plant—have their own textures. They may be fine or coarse, absorb or reflect light, hold or reject shadows. Foliage can be likened to furnishing or dress fabrics—they may resemble fur, velvet, wool, suede, metal or even plastic—and this quality is totally separate from the colour.

There are also many different shapes and sizes of leaf (see page 148). Some leaves may be palmate (hand-like) as with *Acer platanoides* and others may be lanceolate (long and slim) like the contorted, narrowly tapering foliage of *Salix babylonica* var. *pekinensis* 'Tortuosa'. Leaves may be very small and delicate such as in *Sorbus aucuparia* 'Aspleniifolia' or large and leathery, as with *Catalpa bignonioides*.

The leaf margin, or edge, may be smooth, serrated or jagged. In addition, many trees provide autumn interest because their foliage turns into striking gold, red and copper shades, especially on acid soils.

Flowers and fruit

All trees must produce some type of flower if they are to reproduce, but on many trees the insignificant flowers are hardly noticeable. Other trees, like *Malus* (crab apple), *Prunus* (cherry) and *Crataegus* (hawthorn), have the bonus of pretty, albeit transitory, blossom. When the blossoms fade, the seedheads, often in the form of berries, fruits or hips, appear and are a huge asset until the winter frosts, when birds search for food and deplete the trees. The *Malus*, *Sorbus* and *Crataegus* families make particularly attractive trees in autumn with their brightly coloured, glossy and cheerful berries.

Examples of leaf shapes

palmate

ovate

oval

lanceolate

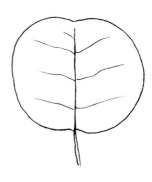

orbicular

entire margin

pinnatafid

serrate

serrulate

pinnate

trifoliate

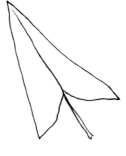

sagittate

Scent

Often this quality is overlooked when searching for a suitable tree. Occasionally, it is the foliage that is scented and this is most intense if the leaves are broken and rubbed between the fingers, as with *Laurus nobilis* (bay) and *Populus balsamifera* (balsam poplar). The balsam-scented *Elaeagnus* 'Quicksilver' is a small tree or large, spiny shrub with fragrant flowers in midsummer and silver-grey, willow-like leaves. Grown as a small tree or shrub, the evergreen *Azara microphylla* produces creamy yellow, vanilla-scented flowers on the undersides of its twigs in early spring.

In midsummer, *Tilia × europea* (common lime) produces fragrant, creamy yellow clusters of flowers that are toxic to bees. Sticky honey dew produced by aphids is a problem with some lime trees. It drops on to any foliage or plants below, and sooty mould then grows on the dew, so that the underlying plants become covered in unsightly black "soot". This is a particular problem in towns, where the air is more polluted. To avoid this, use *Tilia × euchlora*, a clean lime, since it is aphid-free.

Bark

Although the bark of trees is always on view, its texture and colour is often ignored, probably because the bark is not usually sufficiently developed to be remarkable on young trees in the nursery or garden centre. In older and forest-type trees, such as *Quercus* (oak) or *Fraxinus* (ash), the bark can become a sculptural feature. In smaller, ornamental trees, the bark develops more quickly and should be a determining factor in making a choice. Many of the more unusual varieties of *Betula* (silver birch) have eye-catching, pale or pinkish bark. Some of the *Prunus* family, such as *P. serrula* (Tibetan cherry), have polished, red-brown mahogany bark. The bark of *Acer griseum* (paperbark maple) flakes and curls back to reveal cinnamon-coloured underbark. Distinctive bark is especially valuable in winter, when there is little else of interest in the garden.

Speed of growth

Like children, plants grow at different rates and trees are no exception. Consider how long you are prepared to wait for the tree to mature; will an immature sapling look lost if surrounded by other plants? Climate and soil conditions will affect their growth rates, particularly if the site is windy. Most trees are supplied as young saplings, so you will usually have to wait several years before the tree begins to make a significant impression.

Most of us tend to be impatient and want an instant effect; there are many landscaping firms who supply, at a substantial cost, large, mature trees. There are, however, drawbacks to large specimens. They are supplied either containerized or rootballed, so their access to the garden through a house or narrow passageway can be a problem. A mature tree will also extremely heavy to lift, needing a forklift truck and two strong helpers to lever it into place. The planting hole should be prepared in advance so the tree can be eased into position when it is delivered or as soon as possible. It may then need support and regular watering until it is established; the nursery or suppliers will usually advise on the most appropriate method.

Buying and Planting Trees

Rather than going to your local nursery or garden centre, which may have a limited stock, it is often better to choose your trees from a specialist tree nursery. There are so many variations in height, trunk shape, and canopy size and outline between plants of the same species. Try never to buy a tree unseen, but make an appointment with a member of staff in the tree nursery to walk you round, showing you the different varieties. The trees may be growing in open ground (later to be lifted by special machinery) or they may be containerized. If you are choosing plants for an avenue or line of trees, it is particularly important that the trunk and canopies match each other as much as possible. A good tree nursery will tag your chosen trees for you and keep them until you are ready to plant.

Tips on Buying Trees

- Examine both the shape of the tree and the root ball. Often trees are raised close together in polytunnels and the lack of space makes them leggy and unshapely. If they have been left lying around the nursery for a long time, they may be potbound, with their roots twisted together in a spiral so that they may never unravel to get a grip in the soil.
- Remember to look at the size of the root ball to make sure you can get it through any gate or entrance to your property.
- Look at the base of the trunk and avoid any plant that shows signs of suckering at the base.
- If the tree has been grafted on to nursery stock, study the graft to make sure that it is well done and not ugly. The graft line will get bigger and more noticeable through time as the tree matures.
- Consider the leader, or main stem. Occasionally it will have been cut back to prevent the tree from growing taller; such a tree will never achieve a natural outline when mature.

Trees are supplied in various sizes, starting from whips at 125–175 cm (4–5 ft. 9 in.) tall to extra-heavy standards at 4.25–6 m (14–20 ft.) with girths of 14–16 cm. (6–6¼ in.).

Unless trees are firmly staked, windrock will stop the roots becoming established in the soil, inhibiting plant growth. It is best to buy tree stakes and tree ties from the suppliers of a tree, if possible, because they should know what is needed. If the site is very exposed, plant smaller stock, which may escape the full brunt of the wind. In regions with extremes of cold or heat, help its new roots settle in by planting a tree in a mound where the soil is very waterlogged or in a dip where it is very dry (see also page 156).

Newly planted trees need regular watering during their first year to help the roots to establish. One way of making sure water gets to the roots is to install a watering tube at the time of planting. When you infill the soil, create a watering "basin" by leaving the surface of the planting hole slightly lower than the surrounding soil.

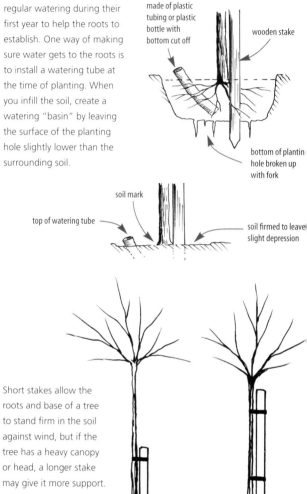

watering tube made of plastic tubing or plastic bottle with bottom cut off

wooden stake

bottom of plantin hole broken up with fork

soil mark

top of watering tube

soil firmed to leave slight depression

Short stakes allow the roots and base of a tree to stand firm in the soil against wind, but if the tree has a heavy canopy or head, a longer stake may give it more support.

Most tree ties are designed to form a "figure-of-eight" to prevent the stake from rubbing against the bark and wounding it. Check the tie at least a couple of times each year and loosen it as necessary.

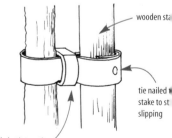

wooden sta

tie nailed stake to st slipping

typical plastic tree tie

Using Shrubs in the Garden

Shrubs, particularly the evergreens, often form the "backbone" of the garden. Other planting, such as a small tree acting as a focal point, or an herbaceous border that enhances seasonal variations, are incidents set against the structural, shrubby planting.

Shrubs form the backbone of the garden, giving structure to the borders all year round.

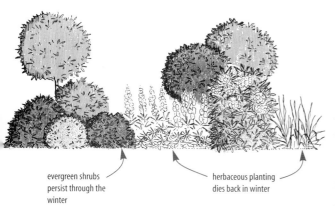

evergreen shrubs persist through the winter

herbaceous planting dies back in winter

Shrub Selection

Consider these factors when choosing a shrub.

- Plant needs
- Evergreen or deciduous
- Outline and form
- Height and spread
- Foliage—texture, size and seasonal colour
- Flowers—colour, form and season
- Fruits—colour and season
- Bark
- Scent
- Numbers needed for structural planting
- Good performers

Over the last century, skilled help in gardens has decreased hugely. Most of us are short of time and may rely on occasional, and not necessarily skilled, labour. Apart from occasional pruning, shrubs are virtually trouble-free and also are low-maintenance. They provide attractive foliage and flowers in return for little more than appropriate soil conditions and aspect and the occasional feed. When choosing shrubs, as for trees, remember to match the plant to soil type, aspect, and the amount of light or shade they will receive. Shrubs are a longer-term investment than herbaceous plants, so take care to site and plant appropriately.

Evergreen or Deciduous?

As a general rule of thumb, the balance of evergreen to deciduous shrubs should be about one-third of evergreens to two-thirds deciduous plants. The evergreens provide the structural backbone of the garden; however, too many evergreens make the garden seem heavy. The process of choosing shrubs is not simply a matter of heading for a nursery or garden centre and filling up a trolley with plants. A successful mixed border is created by teamwork between the plants, each one playing a supporting role to another, so they must be chosen carefully, as much for their compatibility with each other as for their individual attractiveness. Begin by first choosing the shrubs for the evergreen framework, then follow with the deciduous shrubs.

Size and Shape

In most teams, there is a leader or a star player. In the shrub border, this could be a strong vertical, such as *Berberis thunbergii* 'Erecta' with good autumn colour or *Hamamelis mollis* (witch hazel), which has upwardly spreading, zig-zag branches and flowers in late winter—then it retires while the other players take up the baton. Choosing an appropriate "star" of the shrubs is very important, since the rest of the planting will be viewed against it. Usually it is chosen for its outline shape in the same way as for

Hummocky shape of *Ceanothus* 'Blue Mound'

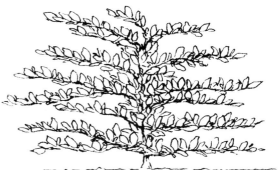

Open, spreading *Viburnum plicatum* f. *tomentosum* 'Mariesii'

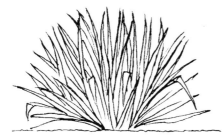

Spiky *Yucca*

Rounded outline of *Choisya ternata*

trees, but if the plant outgrows its space, it may need hard pruning to contain it, thus losing the very shape for which it was chosen. So always check the height of the mature plant before you buy and try to give any star player in a border sufficient room to develop its mature shape without being overcrowded by its immediate neighbours.

Plants vary in their performance depending on how they adapt to where they are grown. Some plants, like *Ilex* (holly) are slow growing whereas others, like *Sambucus nigra* (elder), grow so fast that they need to be controlled by severe, annual pruning. Often faster-growing shrubs crowd out the slower ones, putting them into deep, airless shade that distorts their natural form. To avoid this, make sure that you give each shrub enough space to develop to the anticipated ultimate height and spread.

If the area between young shrubs looks bare, interplant with quick-growing ground cover, perhaps a spotted-leaved *Pulmonaria* (lungwort), which can later be split up and used elsewhere when the shrubs begin to mature. It usually takes about three years for the roots of shrubs to get down into the soil, put on a growth spurt and begin to look substantial.

The Importance of Foliage

As well as for form and growth habit, most shrubs should be chosen for their foliage; the flowers are more transient so are really an added bonus. It is easy to get carried away over the flowers but these rarely last for longer than a few weeks, whereas the leaves last for months. A variety of texture, from shiny (light reflective) to matt (light absorbent), and of foliage colour, including shades of green, should also influence your choice.

Structural Planting

When planning to purchase shrubs for the evergreen backbone of the garden, you need to consider how many plants of each type will be needed, according to their function in the design. Structural plants should be planted in groups of threes or fives, which then unite to make a block to be read as one unit instead of restless, individual mounds. The groups could be increased to sevens or elevens, depending on the available space and sizes of the plants. Odd numbers look more natural in the landscape and are easier to merge with other groupings, while even numbers tend to appear stiff and more formal.

Single shrubs such as *Phormium* (New Zealand flax) may be planted for structure or as a focal point. A star plant, perhaps the early spring-flowering *Magnolia stellata*, differs from a structural plant in that only one plant is needed, giving a spectacular but relatively short performance, then this merges into the background with the support group or rest of the plantings.

Repetition of groups of plants through a border gives rhythm and unity to the planting, whereas a row of different plants creates a restless effect. Repetition does not necessarily require continuous use of the same plant, but a selection of plants that have similarities of form and colour.

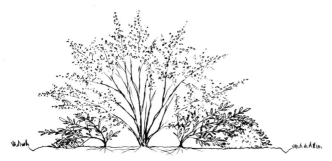

Too often, fast-growing shrubs and shrubs planted too closely together crowd out the slower-growing ones.

Another classic technique in planting shrubs is to create a group that consists of one tall plant, such as the evergreen *Juniperus scopulorum* 'Blue Arrow', a rounded shrub such as *Buxus* (box) and then a spreading plant such as *Cotoneaster horizontalis*, to link the uprights with the horizontal ground plane.

Using shrubs to emphasize the outline of a border, or marking the corners by planting repeat groupings of five, seven, or nine shrubs, provides a foil to the rest of the planting. For instance, in a sunny and well-drained soil, *Lavandula* 'Hidcote' (lavender) can be very effective, whereas the tough and densely mounded *Viburnum davidii*, a distinctly veined semi-evergreen, is less particular and will prevent people from cutting across corners.

Emphasize the outline of the garden design by repeating the shape of the design in your arrangement of plants.

Good "Doers"

When selecting shrubs for the permanent, evergreen framework of the garden, there are a few shrubs that really do well, earning their keep in almost every garden. These are indispensible for playing supporting roles to the occasional star, or more demanding, plant. Successful planting schemes usually depend on each plant having characteristics that contrast with or complement the attributes of other plants around it.

Shrubs with evergreen leaves have the added value of being enjoyed all year round, and should be strategically distributed through the deciduous plants. The choice for framework planting is considerable, but take care to combine only about three different foliage effects in one area or the effect will be disjointed and restless. The many types of foliage available include leaves that are:

- Shiny or light reflective

- Matt or light absorbent

- Silver or grey

- Blue or glaucous

- Red or bronze

- Variegated.

For a subtle contrast of greens, combine shiny-leaved plants with matt foliage. Silver foliage brings light and life to a border of mainly green plants, although it can form a harsh contrast if combined with variegated or golden-leaved plants. However, silver looks marvellous when combined with the comparatively rare evergreens that have glaucous foliage. Coloured foliage, such as red or bronze, can be used to echo the hues of seasonal blooms in the border, or provide a contrast to them. Use variegated shrubs with restraint —too many types of variegation could look chaotic.

Shrub Star Performers

Shiny leaves

Choisya ternata (Mexican orange blossom)
A distinctive, shiny evergreen that flowers spasmodically during most months of the year. Despite its origin, it will survive in most sites apart from very cold or windy areas. Its golden relative, *C. ternata* 'Sundance' is lower, slower-growing, and its yellow foliage can look jaundiced, but will appear duller if grown in shade. The elegant *C.* 'Aztec Pearl' has smaller, more dissected, bright green leaves. It flowers profusely in late spring, then again in late summer.

Magnolia grandiflora 'Exmouth'
Has handsome, leathery foliage, covered underneath with thick, felty, brownish down. The large, richly scented, creamy-white flowers appear mainly around midsummer, but also spasmodically at other times. It needs careful siting, with protection from cold winds, but can grow fast against a warm wall.

Mahonia × *media* 'Charity'
Hard to beat for architectural value—the luxuriant, slightly shiny foliage is pinnate, with many leaflets, and sets off racemes, or flower spikes, of fragrant, lemon-yellow flowers from midwinter onwards.

Prunus laurocerasus 'Otto Luyken' (cherry laurel)
Grows quickly, eventually becoming a large shrub or small tree. It has dark green leaves, white, candle-like flowers and will withstand heavy shade and drip from trees.

Sarcococca confusa (sweet box)
A scented, winter-flowering delight. Its creamy-white flowers show up well against dark, glossy leaves. The variety *S. hookeriana* var. *digyna* has narrow, paler green leaves, and increases by suckers.

Viburnum davidii
Eventually forms a dense, low mound, with handsome, deep green, distinctly veined foliage. Female plants carry white flowers in early summer and bright turquoise berries in autumn. Plant this viburnum in mixed groups, of female and male plants, to ensure cross-pollination for the flowers and berries.

Matt foliage

Bupleurum fruticosum
Not commonly known but has an unusual, bluish tinge to its green-grey foliage. It quickly forms a loose, rounded shrub and bears yellow-green flowers from midsummer to early autumn.

Ceanothus (Californian lilac)
Has various evergreen forms and will be happy at the back of a sunny border on any well-drained soil. C. 'Autumnal Blue' has china-blue flowers from midsummer onwards, while C. 'Cascade' has a more arching habit and powder-blue flowers. Taller Ceanothus tends to be short-lived, rarely surviving in good shape for more than ten years. For the middle of the border, use the quick-growing C. thyrsiflorus var. repens (creeping blueblossom), which will form a dense mound of mid-blue flowers in late spring. Give it plenty of space because it can spread to 2 m (7 ft.) or more.

Euonymus fortunei
Versatile shrub that can either scramble up or along a bank, or be clipped loosely to form a freestanding shrub. Will tolerate dry, deep shade, and is available in forms with different foliage, variegated in gold or white.

Hebe 'Autumn Glory'
Has dark, purple-green foliage and produces deep blue flowers continuously from early summer to late autumn. Evergreen, although not completely hardy in colder districts.

Hebe 'Midsummer Beauty'
Taller-growing cultivar, with short, blue-mauve flowers set off by leaves that are dark green with red undersides.

Silver or grey foliage

Brachyglottis 'Sunshine Improved'
Formerly known as Senecio. It is tough with slightly felted foliage and forms a dense mound. The yellow, daisy-like flowers are quite strident—cut them off if they do not fit into your colour scheme.

Convolvulus cneorum
Small but choice aristocrat for sheltered, well-drained areas, perhaps at the foot of a warm wall. It is a soft, silvery evergreen, with foliage covered in silky hairs that perfectly offset its funnel-shaped, white, flushed-pink flowers.

Lavandula
The obvious choice for a sunny area with poor soil. There are now many new Lavandula cultivars, including some with white or pink flower spikes, which makes choosing one variety all the more difficult. L. stoechas (French lavender) has fragrant, purple flowers but it and its cultivars are not as hardy as L. angustifolia (the traditional, Old English lavender). This latter species and the smaller, but more intensely blue-flowered L. angustifolia 'Hidcote' are both highly scented and hard to beat. Lavender becomes leggy, eventually losing its shape, and needs replacing after eight to ten years.

Rosmarinus officinalis (common rosemary)
Rather similar to lavender in form, but with a more upright habit. It is bushy with narrow, dark green, aromatic leaves. R. 'Miss Jessopp's Upright' is more erect and can be used for a low hedge. Another fast-growing, but short-lived, shrub, it is useful for infilling until slower-growing shrubs take up their allotted space.

Shrub Star Performers (continued)

Santolina (cotton lavender)
Has dainty, feathery foliage. The yellow flowers need to be pruned off to avoid the foliage becoming dull and the shape spoiled.

Blue or glaucous foliage

Coronilla valentina subsp. *glauca*
Has rich yellow, pea-shaped flowers and a rather rounded form.

Ruta graveolens 'Jackman's Blue' (rue)
Similar to *Coronilla valentina* subsp. *glauca*, compact and equally admirable, with filigree foliage and a pungent smell.

Red or bronze foliage

Berberis thunbergii f. *atropurpurea*
Its red, semi-evergreen leaves make for an enjoyable combination against a brick wall or with a backdrop of grey or yellowish stone. It is a very spiny shrub, so is ideal under windows to deter burglars. Of this species' cultivars, the smaller 'Atropurpurea Nana' is excellent for framing borders, 'Dart's Red Lady' has dark purple, almost black leaves and a low, semi-spreading habit, and 'Harlequin' has small, purplish-pink leaves with white speckles.

Photinia × *fraseri* 'Red Robin'
Has a fairly dense habit, with sharply toothed leaves that are brilliant red when young and turn dark green when mature. It produces colourful new growth in late autumn, which is held through winter and spring, ageing to bronze in summer.

Variegated foliage

Elaeagnus pungens 'Maculata'
Fast-growing, golden variegated evergreen, very popular for the splash of brightness it brings to the garden in winter. Any branches bearing leaves without yellow variegation should be removed promptly to stop the plant reverting to plain, dark green foliage.

Yucca gloriosa 'Variegata'
With its long, sword-like leaves striped in cream, gives an exotic effect to borders and punctuates the planting.

Planting in Problem Soils

In severe climatic zones, on poorly drained, heavy clay, roots of newly planted shrubs, especially *Rhododendron*, may rot. To avoid this, mound planting can be useful—raising the root ball above the soil surface by 5–7.5cm (2–3 in.) when you plant it and mounding the soil around it. This allows the roots to settle into a freedraining site. The shrubs must be watered every 7–10 days in dry spells in the first year after planting, until a hard frost, and kept moist in the following year. If the soil is very dry, plant the shrub in a dip, 5–7.5cm (2–3 in.) below soil level; when watered, the dip will hold a puddle of water that can drain on to the new roots.

Deciduous Shrubs

Once the evergreen framework is in place, the deciduous shrubs can be arranged around them, taking their lead from the foliage texture and form of the evergreen shrubs. Height is also crucial—an interplay of varying heights is easier on the eye than serried ranks of uniformly sized plants. For a long period of flowers, include in your choice of shrubs plants that bloom in different seasons as well as offer a flourish of autumnal foliage and berries.

Flowering Shrubs for Each Season

Winter and early spring

Corylus avellana (hazelnut)
A British native and loved for its long yellow catkins, produced in late winter.

Daphne mezereum
Has shapely, stiffly erect branches, is slow-growing and delights with its heavily scented, purplish-red flowers that are borne in dense clusters during early spring.

Lonicera fragrantissima
The winter-flowering, bushy form of honeysuckle. It is a twiggy plant and produces creamy-white, bell-shaped, strongly fragrant flowers from midwinter to early spring.

Viburnum farreri
An old favourite, it is tall, upright and fairly slender and matures quickly. It produces deliciously scented, pale pink buds and white flowers, which emerge intermittently from late autumn throughout winter before the pale green leaves. Stands up to –23°C (–10°F) degrees of frost.

Viburnum × burkwoodii 'Anne Russell'
Has round trusses of pink buds followed by sweetly scented, white flowers on upright stems. Many other later-flowering viburnums are also well worth growing.

Early and midsummer

Buddleja davidii 'Black Knight'
Has long, sweetly scented panicles or flowerheads, which are attractive to butterflies. This shrub is fast growing and invaluable if a quick, colourful effect is required. Other good cultivars are 'Pink Delight', *B. davidii* 'Empire Blue' and *B. davidii* 'Royal Red'.

Philadelphus 'Belle Etoile'
Semi-arching, broad shrub with exquisitely scented, large, single, white flowers. The smaller, bright yellow-leaved *P. coronarius* 'Aureus' needs some shade to prevent its leaves from becoming scorched by the sun.

Late summer and autumn

Hydrangea species
Perform well in autumn, if given well-drained and manured soil and a moist root run. The oak-leaved variety, *H. quercifolia*, has pyramidal, white flower panicles and scalloped leaves that turn crimson and purple in autumn. *H. arborescens* 'Annabelle' has large, showy, white flowers on compact but loosely arranged branches.

Indigofera hetrantha
Thrives in hot, well-drained sites. It has luxuriant foliage with many leaflets and terminal racemes or flower spikes of rosy, pea-shaped flowers. These appear from early summer to mid-autumn.

Potentilla fruticosa 'Tilford Cream'
Has a wiry, twiggy habit and creamy-yellow flowers. It can be used as a flowering shrub or as a low hedge and is invaluable for its long flowering period.

P. fruticosa 'Abbotswood'
Has white flowers shown off against greyish foliage.

P. fruticosa 'Red Ace'
Has vermilion flowers.

Fast-growing Shrubs

Patience is a great virtue in a gardener but, in today's world of instant gratification, it is hard to wait for several years before our carefully chosen shrubs begin to bulk up and show their true form. It usually takes about three years for the roots to delve down and become firmly locked into the soil, after which point the plants respond by increasing their growth and develop a mature outline.

Fast-growing Shrubs

Ceanothus
Whether it is an evergreen or deciduous form, matures quickly, but the foliage is very susceptible to scorch by cold winds, so the protection of a warm wall is advisable.

Cytisus battandieri (pineapple broom)
An early summer-flowering shrub, suitable for milder areas. It is an unusual, rather lax plant with silvery, silky down on the leaves and upright, golden yellow, pineapple-scented flower spikes. Pineapple broom is very decorative, but needs the protection of a warm wall.

Ligustrum lucidum (Chinese privet)
A 1.8 m (6 ft.), erect evergreen with handsome panicles of white flowers in late summer; some varieties have variegated or mottled foliage.

Pyracantha rogersiana 'Flava'
Very dark green, small, oblong leaves with clusters of bright yellow fruits in autumn. Often used as a climber, but equally good as a freestanding shrub.

Sambucus nigra 'Aurea' and *S. nigra* f. *porphyrophylla* 'Guincho Purple' (syn. 'Purpurea')
'Aurea' has golden yellow foliage; 'Guincho Purple' has purplish-green leaves. Both are elders that produce plentiful and handsome growth within the first three years. In fact, if not pruned each spring, the shrubs rapidly become woody and uninteresting—the leaves become smaller, and golden varieties tend to scorch in full sun.

S. nigra 'Eva' (syn. 'Black Lace')
Has dark purple leaves and rose-coloured flowers.

Symphoricarpos × doorenbosii (snowberry)
Has large, pink-tinged fruits in late summer. It will grow almost anywhere including under trees in dry shade. Tends to sucker and may become invasive.

Tamarix tetrandra
Graceful, open shrub with dark foliage and contrasting pink racemes (flower spikes) in early summer on branches from the previous year. Tolerant of salt spray in coastal gardens.

However, if speed is essential, perhaps to hide an unsightly oil tank or rubbish bins, there are a few fast-growing shrubs that will be useful. They need regular pruning, or annual removal of about one-third of the older branches, because of their rapid growth; otherwise they may not retain an open habit.

Autumnal Interest

Just when the days are shortening, when early morning mists arrive (a result of cold air flowing downhill), colourful autumn foliage ends the growing season in a blaze of glory. Leaves turn to red, gold, or yellow before the sap ceases to rise and causes them to drop off, leaving only a tracery of branches. Some shrubs also provide a bonus of colourful berries. If strategically placed so that their autumn leaves stands out against a backdrop of green foliage plants, these shrubs will lighten up the garden as the days draw in.

Shrubs with Autumnal Interest

Acer palmatum 'Bloodgood' and
A. shirasawanum 'Aureum'
Two Japanese maples that provide the most colourful display—check on your soil type before planting maples because they need acid soil. Generally, plants that have a preference for acid soil conditions show good autumn colour.

Amelanchier lamarckii (snowy mespilus)
A hardy, small tree or multistemmed shrub. Clouds of starry, white flowers in spring; the foliage colours to orange and red in autumn. Best on well-drained, neutral or lime-free soil.

Berberis aggregata and *B. wilsoniae*
Both very useful and easily grown varieties for fruiting and autumn colour. They have arching, spiny stems and form rounded mounds. *B. aggregata* has twiggy and dense branches with small green leaves that colour orange-red in autumn. *B. wilsoniae* is a small to medium-sized shrub with interesting pink and orange berries.

Callicarpa bodinieri var. *giraldii* 'Profusion' (beauty berry)
Produces large clusters of small, bead-like, violet fruits, shining out against the fading purple leaves.

Ceratostigma willmottianum
One of the jewels of the autumn, with true blue flowers contrasting dramatically with yellow autumn foliage; it also has a fast growth rate.

Cornus florida (North American flowering dogwood)
Spectacular, orange-red autumn foliage; provides a contrasting backdrop to perennials such as the clear blue-flowered *Aster* × *frikartii* 'Mönch', or to intensify the brilliant hues of dahlia blooms. Prefers neutral to acid soil.

Cotinus coggygria (smoke bush)
Round, bushy habit, with leaves turning bright yellow in autumn. Colours best on sandy loam and may be underplanted with autumn-flowering crocuses or cyclamen to double the impact.

Cotoneaster
Berries prolifically in most of its forms. The prostrate ground cover, *C. dammeri*, has shoots that root where they touch the soil, so is particularly useful on banks, where the growth creeps downwards. Its bright red berries last well into winter. *C. frigidus* 'Cornubia' makes a superb, tall, arching shrub, with abundant, rich green leaves setting off large, bright red berries. *C. salicifolius* 'Rothschildianus' has yellow berries, borne singly along the twigs, and lighter green leaves. *C. lacteus*, a tall evergreen, has red berries.

Diervilla sessilifolia
An attractive, medium-sized, summer-flowering shrub with purple-red, autumn foliage.

Shrubs with Autumnal Interest (continued)

Euonymus europaeus (common spindle)
Has fascinating, pendulous, pinkish-red fruits that open to display bright red seed capsules in autumn.

Mahonia aquifolium
A useful, ground-covering shrub; the leaves turn purple-red in autumn and winter.

Photinia davidiana (syn. *Stranvaesia*)
Has long, leathery leaves, some of which turn bright red in autumn.

Skimmia japonica 'Veitchii'
Has broad, but tapered leaves and brilliant red fruits in autumn. The most conspicuous fruits are produced on female plants. One male is able to pollinate three females, so make sure that you have both sexes, otherwise no berries will appear. This shrub thrives in shade or partial shade, but full sun tends to bleach the leaves.

Ornamental Bark

Colourful or interesting bark is usually associated with trees, but several shrubs also fall into this category and can be a joy to carry you through the dreary winter months. The bark of both *Cornus* and *Salix* colour best if the old stems are coppiced, or cut back hard, in early spring. Unpruned shrubs lose some stem colour but do flower and fruit, whereas pruned shrubs do not. By pruning back only half the stems every year you have a less spectacular display of winter colour, but the uncoppiced stems will still flower and fruit.

Shrubs with Ornamental Bark

Acer palmatum 'Senkaki'
Distinctive, bright coral-red stems in winter.

Cornus alba 'Elegantissima' and *C. sericea* 'Flaviramea'
The former has bright red stems, the latter has butter-yellow shoots; they are perhaps at their best when leafless in winter, particularly if planted in groups in a border or beside water.

Myrtus communis (common myrtle)
Evergreen; when mature, the small, dark green leaves stand out well against its amber-brown bark.

Rubus cockburnianus
The white-stemmed bramble has ferny leaves and ghostly, white winter stems. Becomes very spreading with age and tends to sucker.

Salix alba var. *vitellina* 'Britzensis'
Grown mainly for the bright, orange-scarlet, winter colour of its young shoots.

Salix 'Erythroflexuosa'
Produces reddish-brown wands.

Salix gracilistyla 'Melanostachys'
Forms a round shrub with purple-brown twigs, and before the leaves appear, produces black, male catkins with brick-red anthers.

Using Roses in the Garden

The best known and most loved of garden plants, the rose, is much travelled and has been grown by many civilizations across the world, some species going back for more than two thousand years. Roses were first valued for their perfume, for the lasting scent of the dried petals, for the distillation of rose water from the flowers, and finally for their beauty. Nevertheless, only relatively few of the myriad roses cultivated over the last 200 years have become popular in the horticultural trade. Roses, if appropriately chosen, can be used in borders, in open spaces and wild areas, to carpet the ground, to scramble up banks or tumble over low walls. They blend well with other flowers and foliage and don't need to be confined to a traditional rose bed where there is little else to set them off.

Buying Roses

Until fairly recently, roses were supplied only during winter months as bare-rooted stock, which means they were dug up from the grower's field and packaged without soil, making them lighter and easier to send by post. The popularity of roses has changed this and they are now available in the following forms.

- Bare-rooted—usually the cheapest, but available only during their dormant season, from late autumn until early spring.
- Containerized—dug up from the grower's field and recently potted up to make transporting them less hazardous than for bare-rooted plants.
- Container-grown—have been grown on for some time in a container. Are available and may be planted all year round.

Most roses begin blooming from early summer to late summer. Shades through from pink to purple are the most plentiful, and therefore such roses offer more choice of plant height and flower form, hue and size. However, the first criterion for choosing a rose must be height and spread, so that it is suitable for the available space, although the ultimate sizes of many roses may be controlled by pruning (see pages 282–285). To get really good plants, it is wise to order roses early from nurseries—order in the early autumn for planting next spring.

Types of Rose

Different types of roses could be exploited in many situations in the garden, so it is useful to learn how the various forms of rose grow and how much space each may take up. Garden roses range from 60 cm (2 ft.) to 3.6 m (12 ft.) in height. The flowers also show great variety, in flower form and in size, ranging from 2.5 cm (1 in.) to 15 cm (6 in.) in diameter. Roses can be divided into six main categories:

- Shrub roses

- Bush roses

- Ground-cover, or patio, roses

- Standard roses

- Wild roses

- Climbing and rambler roses (see pages 177–179).

Shrub roses
These include the old roses of early European origin as well as modern shrub roses, many of which are crosses between modern bush roses and other strong species of climbing rose. This group also includes the relatively new 'English' roses and the wild roses.

Old shrub roses are invaluable as garden plants, mixing well with other border plants to create a delightful, old–English, cottage garden style. The true old roses are extremely tough, live almost indefinitely, require little pruning, and usually have a wonderful scent. They are subdivided into different groups, such as gallicas, damasks, albas and centifolias, and China roses: each group has its own characteristics.

Their old-fashioned blooms come mostly in sumptuous pink, crimson, purple or mauve hues. Many of them flower only once in the season, but are still well worth growing, for both their heady scents and beautiful flowers. Other shrub roses are repeat-flowerers, producing some blooms sporadically after the main flush.

A few species shrub roses come into their own in late spring. Most of these (*R.* 'Helen Knight', *R. primula*, and *R. xanthina* 'Canary Bird') are yellow, and need regular pruning immediately after flowering so they have time to produce flowering shoots for the next season. These roses can be grown as feature plants among other early-flowerers such as *Brunnera*, *Ceanothus*, *Myositis* (forget-me-not) and *Pulmonaria*.

Among the older roses, there is less choice in the yellow shades, which can range from pale lemon through to deep apricots. The valuable hybrid musks are good border shrubs, flowering profusely in early summer and intermittently later. Old roses such as the large, opulent, rich crimson *R.* 'Charles de Mills' is so spectacular that it can be forgiven for flowering only once in the season. The very showy *R. gallica* 'Versicolor' (rosa mundi) has pale pink flowers painted wonderfully with dark pink stripes; it is best planted in groups of three to five or as a low hedge.

The madder-crimson and very fragrant bourbon rose, *R.* 'Madame Isaac Pereire' has heavy, rather open growth, so often needs some support in the form of stakes or canes. Prune it hard every spring and deadhead it weekly so that later flushes of growth are strong enough to provide plentiful flowers.

Some Choice Old Roses

'Blanche Double de Coubert'
Rather lax, but reliable whether grown in the open or against a wall.

'Boule de Neige'
Has camellia-like, pure white, semi-double flowers early in the season that repeat quite well.

'Buff Beauty'
Has large trusses in warm apricot shades; the young foliage is reddish-green.

'Céleste' (also known as 'Celestial')
Has a strong, tidy growth habit, with vigorous, disease-resistant, grey-green foliage and transparent shell-pink, sweetly scented blooms.

'Cornelia'
Vigorous plant with good, dark green foliage and copper-apricot flowers that fade to pink.

'Fantin-Latour'
Shapely rose, bears beautifully formed, full-petalled flowers in shell-pink that have a delicate scent.

'Madame Hardy'
An old damask; it has perfectly formed, double flowers with a hint of lemon in the fragrance. It would suit a white border or a spot where pale shades are needed, perhaps where it could be appreciated in early evening.

'Penelope'
Similar to 'Buff Beauty', but with creamy-pink flowers.

'William Lobb'
Old velvet moss rose, a fascinating rose, best at the back of a border because of its tall, lax habit; its blooms are violet-purple with a rich perfume.

Modern shrub roses

This category used to include roses from widely diverse origins, and produced some of the best shrub roses—strong, robust, very free-flowering and blooming intermittently during summer. Popular *Rosa rugosa* cultivars are included in this group.

Among the modern shrub roses, the excellent, large, early summer-flowering *R.* 'Frühlingsgold' has pale yellow, almost single flowers and grows in height and spread to 2 m (over 6 ft.). With unfailing continuity and large, single, yellow flowers, *R.* 'Golden Wings' requires a smaller space, only about 1.5 m (5 ft.) square, and looks best when grouped. In the English rose section, *R.* 'Graham Thomas', named after the influential rosarian, has unusually rich yellow blooms, glossy, pale green foliage and a rather stiff, upright habit.

For a large arching shrub, *R.* 'Nevada' with semi-double, creamy-white blooms and later intermittent flowers, is hard to beat. *R.* 'White Pet' is a lower-growing but vigorous, spreading bush, and forms a delicately fragrant, low mound; the tiny flowers can be laborious to deadhead.

English roses are a comparatively new group, which first came to prominence in the 1970s; they originated from crosses made between certain old roses, modern hybrid teas and floribundas. They combine the delicate charm and scent of an old rose with the colour range and summer-long flowering of a modern rose.

Bush roses

These were once hugely popular and commonly known as hybrid tea and floribunda roses. They are stiffer in form than the shrub rose. Therefore they do not blend so well with other plants in the mixed border, but are suitable for a formal rose garden or in part of a kitchen garden as a cutting flower. They come in a huge variety of shades, most of the older varieties are usually very fragrant, and have exquisitely formed, pointed buds. Their long flowering season made them popular for planting in public parks and with florists or flower arrangers.

Bush roses are available in a huge range of shades; the newer ones sometimes have unfortunate names, such as *R.* Marry Me, probably chosen for commercial reasons. (In cases where there is also a plant breeder's name, the cultivar name is not shown in quotation marks.) Choice is really a question of flower colour and form. There are two excellent white varieties— *R.* Iceberg, which flowers continuously well into winter but its blooms are supported by thin "necks" so tend to hang downwards and *R.* Margaret Merril, whose elegant, white flowers have a satin sheen and an exceptional fragrance.

Ground-cover or patio roses

This new group comprises roses that sit somewhere between a miniature and a floribunda rose in character, but they are robust with charming, rosette flowers and neat, bushy growth. These roses are all hardy and repeat-flower well.

Some roses in this group grow to over 3 m (10 ft.) in height, for example *R. wichurana*, with single, white flowers and oval, dark red hips or *R.* × *jacksonii* 'Max Graf' with deep silver-pink flowers. Most of us now have smaller gardens, so patio roses may more suitable. Some can also be grown as low hedges, for instance the dwarf polyanthus *R.* 'Baby Faurax', with small, lavender-purple flowers at 30 cm (1 ft.); *R.* 'Mevrouw Nathalie Nypels', with medium rose-pink flowers at 60 cm (2 ft.); *R.* 'Yvonne Rabier' with fragrant, double white flowers at 1 m (3 ft. 3 in.).

Standard roses

These are invaluable for giving height or drama to a planting, above shorter plants or in formal beds. They may also be planted as specimens in a lawn or alongside a path. Weeping standards are less easy to use, often looking unnatural and conspicuous in the garden. Both types of standard rose need a firm support, in the form of a stout stake to prevent wind rock at the roots. All are propagated by being budded (see pages 310–312) on to rootstock stems that are about 1.2 m (4 ft.) tall. Weeping standards are budded on to a 1.5 m (5 ft.) stem. If a uniform effect is wanted, avoid planting different cultivars together because their habits or outlines will vary.

Wild roses

Wild roses are fine, robust shrub roses; they usually display elegant growth, neat foliage, simple flowers and colourful hips and vary enormously in the amount of space they take up. Some, such as *R. spinosissima* (Scottish or burnet rose) grow to only 90 cm (3 ft.) while others, such as *R. moyesii*, with large flagon-shaped hips, grow to 3 m (10 ft.) and spread to 2.5 m (8 ft.). These roses flower only once in a season, but the flowers are often followed in early autumn by very attractive hips, provided that no deadheading has been carried out. The larger wild roses need careful placing, either at the back of a deep border, as a focal point or as single specimens in wilder areas or long grass, where they can display their natural shape.

Choosing a Rose

Use the following criteria to help you make your choice from the huge range of roses available. Check these details in a reliable nursery catalogue or gardening encyclopedia.

- Height and spread—the eventual size of the rose should be appropriate to the given space, otherwise you may have problems keeping it pruned to fit.
- Length of flowering—unless the blooms are really spectacular, choose species or cultivars that flower either continuously or recurrently over the season rather than in a single flush. If you are planning to include the roses in borders that should last from spring to summer, the roses need to be colourful for as long as possible so, however beguiling, avoid the once-flowering varieties.
- Main flowering time—roses can begin flowering from late spring onwards, although most flower in early summer.
- Colour of blooms—although rose flowers come in many hues, the majority are in shades of pink. There are many reds and whites, and a good number of purples and oranges, as well as some unusual shades such as brown or lilac.
- Foliage—this varies enormously in size, shape and texture. Some leaves have an attractive glaucous or blue hue, others are reddish, but most rose foliage is in varying shades of green.
- Disease-resistance—roses are notorious for attracting fungal diseases such as black spot, rose powdery mildew, rust, or downy mildew. Aphids attack roses, usually in late spring and early summer. The leaf-rolling sawfly can cause unsightly foliage from late spring onwards, but does not seriously damage the plants; caterpillars can cause unsightly and ragged leaves by their feeding habits (see also pages 314–334). If disease is a problem, it is crucial to maintain the healthy development of roses by spraying them with a fungicide in early spring or whenever the first new leaves appear. Then continue this spraying every two weeks until midsummer, as well as collecting or picking off and burning any diseased foliage (which harbours the spores). Many rose catalogues indicate which roses are less prone to disease.

Recommended Roses

The list of garden-worthy roses is almost endless, but here are my preferences for each category of rose.

Name	Flower colour	Type of rose
Autumn colour or hips		
R. 'Blanche Double de Coubert'	Pure white	Rugosa
R. 'Geranium'	Clear red	*moyesii* hybrid
R. glauca	Deep pink	Shrub
R. 'Moonlight'	Pale yellow, fading to white	Hybrid musk
R. 'Sealing Wax'	Deep pink	*moyesii* hybrid
R. virginiana	Cerise pink	Shrub
Bush roses		
R. 'Doris Tysterman'	Light orange	Hybrid tea
R. Fragrant Cloud	Coral red	Hybrid tea
R. Iceberg	Clear white	Floribunda
R. Margaret Merril	Blush pink	Floribunda
R. 'Rosemary Rose'	Cerise-crimson	Floribunda
Ground-cover roses		
R. Grouse	Soft pink	Ground cover
R. Kent	White	Shrub/ground cover
R. 'Nozomi'	Pale pink	Climbing miniature
R. Snow Carpet	Creamy white	Ground cover
R. Swany	Pure white	Ground cover
Hedging roses		
R. 'Felicia'	Pale pink	Hybrid musk
R. 'Fru Dagmar Hastrup'	Rose pink	Rugosa
R. 'Mevrouw Nathalie Nypels'	Rose pink	Polyantha
R. 'Roseraie de l'Haÿ'	Purple crimson	Rugosa
Shrub roses		
R. 'Blanche Double de Coubert'	Pure white	Rugosa
R. 'Buff Beauty'	Pale apricot	Hybrid musk
R. 'Charles de Mills'	Purple-crimson	Gallica
R. 'Fantin Latour'	Blush pink	Centifolia
R. 'Perle d'Or'	Pale peach	Polyantha
Shade and north walls		
R. 'Cornelia'	Apricot-pink	Hybrid musk
R. 'Scharlachglut'	Scarlet-crimson	Gallica
R. 'The Fairy'	Pink	Polyantha
R. 'Zéphirine Drouhin'	Cerise pink	Bourbon
Standard roses		
R. 'Albéric Barbier'	Cream	Grafted rambler
R. 'Albertine'	Copper-pink	Grafted rambler
R. 'New Dawn'	Pale pink	Grafted climbing/rambler
R. 'Phyllis Bide'	Pale peach blend	Grafted rambler
R. 'White Pet'	Pinkish-white	Grafted polyantha

Caring for Roses

Although roses have been grown since ancient times, often in fairly inhospitable climates and conditions, they will give of their best only if they are suited to their environment. I have found them happier on heavy clay than on the sandy soil in my current garden. Your roses should be with you for a long time, so it is worthwhile planting them properly.

Soil sickness

If new roses are to be planted in a site where others have grown for some time, it is vital to change the soil to avoid rose sickness. New roses planted in the old soil will not necessarily die, but will sulk and fail to put on new, healthy growth. Rose sickness has still not been completely explained, but is probably a combination of the exhaustion of trace elements in the soil, the build-up of root diseases, and attack by minute eelworms.

The simplest way of changing the soil is to swap it with some in another part of the garden, such as the vegetable garden. Remove the old soil, digging out a hole approximately 60 cm (2 ft.) across and deep for each new plant and fill it with fresh garden soil mixed with plenty of well-rotted organic matter. The discarded, rose-sick soil can be used safely in other parts of the garden.

Roses should be planted as soon as possible. If they are bare-rooted plants, the delivery package should not be left unopened for longer than a week. With a containerized or container-grown rose, knock it out of the pot, disturbing the roots as little as possible, then ease the root ball into a hole just large enough to accommodate it, and once filled in, tread in firmly. Water is essential to a newly planted rose, so for the first fourteen days water each day until the rose looks really well settled.

Planting a rose

For bare-rooted and containerized plants, if the ground is waterlogged or frost-bound, heel them in—which means covering the roots lightly with soil as a temporary protective measure—using a cardboard box or container filled with soil or compost. Keep them out of the frost and wind, keeping the roots just damp. Try to plant the roses as soon as conditions allow.

- The ground should be well prepared in advance, dug deeply and manured with well-rotted farmyard manure or compost. Never use fresh dung or allow the roots to come into contact with any sort of manure.

- If the roots are at all dry, immerse in a bucket of water for an hour or so before planting.

- Dig a hole large enough to spread the roots out evenly. Make up a mixture of one part soil, one part compost and two handfuls of bonemeal.

- If necessary, trim any long roots by cutting them off with secateurs, leaving those with fine root hairs, which take up any available moisture from the soil.

- Place the rose in the planting hole, with the graft union (the visible point of union between the top growth and the rootstock) about 5 cm (2 in.) below soil level. This makes the root ball secure and encourages rooting from the base of the shoots rather than suckering from the rootstock below the graft union.

- Replace the soil in two or three stages. Shake the plant gently as you infill with soil so that the soil filters between the roots. To avoid windrock (which will hinder the roots from establishing firmly in the soil), tread in the soil very firmly as you go.

- If a rose needs support, such as a large container-grown rose or one that has been

moved from elsewhere in the garden, place a stout cane or a post in position into the base of the hole before planting, to avoid damaging the roots. Once the rose has been planted, tie it into the post securely, but not too tightly, which would cause the stem to rub and chafe.

- After planting, water thoroughly to settle the soil around the roots and apply a good layer of mulch over the planting area.

- Top dress with rose fertilizer and mulch.

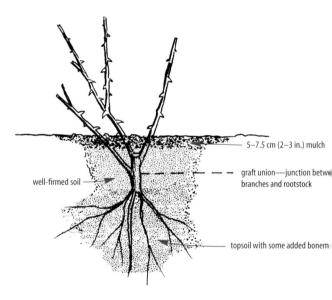

well-firmed soil

5–7.5 cm (2–3 in.) mulch

graft union—junction betwe branches and rootstock

topsoil with some added bonem

Aftercare of roses

Once roses are established, they demand only a moderate amount of maintenance. A sprinkling of organic fertilizer in autumn; a liberal mulch of well-rotted garden compost in early spring; and an annual prune (see pages 282–285) will be sufficient for most species.

Deadheading, widely practiced to keep the plant looking fresh and to encourage blooming, should be carried out weekly during the flowering season. However, if the plant is being grown for hips following the flowers, avoid deadheading to allow hips to form in late summer. Using secateurs, remove the entire, spent flower shoot at a point just above a leaf or new shoot on the stem.

Remember that if the roses are prone to pests and disease, it is vital to start spraying against them early in the spring, before a single aphid, black spot or touch of mildew has a chance to appear. Continue spraying with a proprietory rose spray fortnightly during the growing season.

Climbing Plants and Wall Shrubs

The opportunity to include some climbing plants in your garden should not be missed, since they constitute a crucial element in creating its vertical structure. Many do not take up much space, making them especially valuable in small gardens; they bring colour, scent and year-round interest.

Climbers and wall shrubs can be grown against walls, fences or freestanding screens, and climbers trained over arches, arbours and pergolas. Some climbers may be grown through trees and over hedges or used as ground cover over banks.

Freestanding supports, such as cane tripods or more ornamental obelisks, for climbers can be placed seasonally within borders to give height and opportunities for displaying *Clematis*, *Lathyrus odorata* (sweet pea) or the scarlet-flowered *Phaseolus coccineus* (runner bean). Timber, trellis or metal tripods or frames can also be useful foils for climbers.

Climbing plants generally require more maintenance than shrubs, because many of them need to be trained to supports by regular tying-in of new shoots. To keep them to the desired shape and size and to encourage flowering, they also require regular pruning (see pages 285–287).

Climbers against Buildings

Climbers have an unfair reputation for making walls damp. The only circumstance where this might occur is when dead leaves build up between the plant and the wall close to the ground, eventually bridging the damp-proof course and hindering air circulation. In practice the opposite is true; climbers tend to protect walls and keep off rain. However, very vigorous climbers will, if not pruned regularly, invade the roof space and provide mice with easy access. From an aesthetic point of view, climbers enhance a building by softening bare expanses of wall but they should not be encouraged to grow across tile-hung walls because they can creep underneath tiles and lift them.

climber growing against a wall

wall would normally be dry above the damp-proof course, but here it is damp due to a build-up of decaying leaves and humus

damp-proof course is designed to prevent damp rising above this point—the ground should be at least 15 cm (6 in.) below this.

any build-up of leaves should be cleaned out annually

Buildings and walls actually provide a choice position for more tender and exotic climbers and wall shrubs that would not normally thrive in the open garden. These plants can be tricked into flowering as if they were in a warmer climate: south and west-facing walls have the best aspects, although more shady, north- and east-facing aspects still give a degree of protection. House walls have the advantage of exuding heat from within the property, which helps more tender species to thrive.

Deciding Where to Plant Climbers

- Choose each climber and wall shrub to suit the intended planting site—the soil, drainage, quality or strength of the light (few plants do well in deep shade) and exposure to wind.
- Match the plant to the available space, by researching its speed of growth and eventual height and spread. If the space is cramped, the climber or wall shrub will probably need to be pruned hard, which will destroy the natural outline and impact of the plant.
- The colour of the wall or backcloth is also often overlooked—a red brick wall might kill the colour of a strongly pink rose, whereas a stone or cream-painted wall would enhance it.
- Many climbers recommended in books for cold or shady walls will be even happier on south- or west-facing walls.
- Unless you are lucky enough to have wall nails and wires already in place, it would be wise also to consider if some form of support can be fixed to the wall, or if some other support structure is needed in the garden (see pages 169–174).

How Plants Climb

Some plants have a natural climbing habit; others need help. In the wild, for instance, *Wisteria* will climb to the top of a tree and flower only when it has reached the top. In our gardens, we use man-made structures to persuade the plant to flower at a much lower height. Understanding how your plants climb will influence your choice of both plant and type of support.

Twining plants

Lonicera (honeysuckle), *Wisteria* and other twiners climb by means of their stems, which twist and spiral around any vertical support, whether pole, wire or the stem of another plant, to find their way up. They can be persuaded to grow at a slight angle, but if the support is angled more than 30° off the vertical, the plant is likely to wander and search for a more vertical support.

Tendril climbers

This group, which includes *Passiflora* (passion flower) and *Vitis* (grape vine), will often climb horizontally as well as vertically. They all have tendrils, which may be modified stems (*Passiflora*), leaves (*Cobaea scandens*) or leaf stalks (*Clematis montana*), to grab hold of whatever support is available. They are usually trained against trellis or wires, but the supports should never be fixed tight against a wall or fence.

Most climbers will follow support wires, so a pattern like this should encourage a plant to give good coverage of a wall.

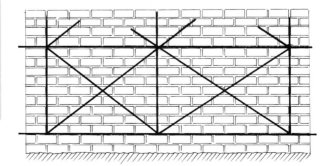

Clinging plants

Hedera (ivy), *Parthenocissus* (Virginia creeper) and *Hydrangea anomala* subsp. *petiolaris* are among the self-clinging climbers. They attach themselves by aerial roots (ivy) or small, sucker-like pads (*Parthenocissus*) to walls, fences or tree trunks and need no other support. However, young plants take several months to cling naturally, so you can speed things up by sticking their stems to the wall with all-weather tape.

Never grow clinging climbers on fences, wooden cladding or on house walls which are rendered or which have lime mortar joints (old walls). If these climbers have to be removed later, they may dislodge large areas of rendering or the soft mortar joints. Sucker pads also leave behind marks that are difficult to remove. If you do have to remove a self-clinging climber, sever the stem through the base and leave the top growth in place for some months to die off. The plant can then be pulled off easily.

Scrambling climbers

Some climbing plants have no means to attach themselves naturally; in the wild, these plants depend on their long shoots being supported by other plants or features such as rocks or boulders. As they grow, newer shoots scramble over the lower, often dead, stems forming a loose shrub. In the garden, these climbers have to be tied to supports to achieve a greater height and spread. Climbing and rambler roses need to be training against wires or trellis, with their stems carefully tied in with garden twine, whereas *Hedera* (ivy) or *Trachelospermum jasminoides* (star jasmine) will scramble of their own accord, perhaps being helped by training them against the wall in the desired direction in their first formative years.

Wall shrubs

Garrya elliptica and *Pyracantha* (firethorn) are classed as wall shrubs—essentially, shrubs with pliable branches that may be trained against a wall on wires or trellis. Often, they grow taller in this situation than in the open garden, because they are sheltered from the elements.

Climbing Habits

- **Twining**—*Actinidia, Akebia, Humulus, Jasminum officinale, Lonicera, Wisteria*
- **Tendril**—*Campsis, Clematis, Cobaea scandens, Eccremocarpus, Ipomoea, Passiflora, Vitis*
- **Clinging**—*Hedera, Hydrangea anomala* subsp. *petiolaris, Parthenocissus*
- **Scrambling**—*Euonymus, Jasminum nudiflorum, Solanum laxum, Trachelospermum*
- **Wall shrub**—*Abelia, Abutilon, Aloysia, Camellia, Carpenteria, Ceanothus, Fremontodendron, Garrya, Itea, Magnolia, Phygelius, Piptanthus, Pyracantha, Rosa, Viburnum*

Types of Support

It is important to match the climbing plant to a support that suits its habit and mature size, to avoid problems as it becomes established. There are many types of support now available, in timber, metal and plastic, some more decorative than others, but take care to install one that will support the weight of the mature plant.

Myriads of preconstructed, climber supports are available to gardeners, many of them advertized in gardening magazines or catalogues. However enticing the illustrations, be aware that it is difficult to imagine how the scale of the object will relate to your property until it is actually on site. Too often an arbour or summerhouse is smaller than anticipated, or the proportions are wrong. Try to choose proportions and materials appropriate to your house and the garden—or have a support custom made.

Wires

Unless you are using a self-clinging climber, wires or trellis will be needed to train it against a wall. This will usually entail fixing horizontal, vertical, and

Vine eyes can be used to fix trellis to masonry or timber and are available in different sizes; some are fixed using plastic wall plugs for a secure fit.

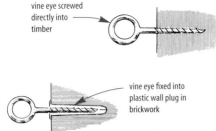

vine eye screwed directly into timber

vine eye fixed into plastic wall plug in brickwork

wire

This steel wedge may either be pushed into mortar joints while they are still soft or be banged in later. Horizontal or vertical wires may be threaded through them, depending on the angle at which the wedges are inserted.

steel wedge

soft lead strap can be gently wrapped around the stem of a climber

hardened steel shaft is banged into a mortar joint

A lead-headed clout nail is ideal for getting self-clinging climbers started on walls.

sometimes diagonal wires. Galvanized wire generally lasts longer and is less obvious than plastic-coated wire; it is available in a range of thicknesses. The horizontal wires and fixing nails should run in line with the mortar joints, and be spaced about 60 cm (2 ft.) apart.

Use heavy-duty vine eyes to fix wires to walls or fences. Depending on the type, these are either hammered directly into the mortar course of a wall, or screwed into plastic wall plugs. You must use a new fixing eye each time the wire changes direction, but some intermediate fixing eyes will be needed to support long runs. Thicker wire should be used for heavy climbers like *Vitis* and *Wisteria*.

Where thinner wire is being used for lightweight climbers such as large-flowered *Clematis* cultivars or *Actinida kolomikta*, lead-strapped wall, or "clout", nails can be used. These are usually hammered into the mortar joints (or into timber) and the lead strap wrapped around the wire, but these are not nearly as robust as vine eyes.

Wall- or fence-mounted trellis

This is available in plastic-coated steel, plastic or timber, and must be strong enough for the job in hand. Pressure-treated timber weathers well and usually looks best. It can be fixed permanently into position on brick walls using a variety of fixings, all of which must leave a gap of about 5 cm (2 in.) between the trellis and the wall. Use spacers when fixing supporting battens to allow space for the plant to climb freely all the way around the supports.

Trellis is often a better option than wires on rendered walls because it requires less drilling (**left**). It is also easily fixed to a fence, especially if the fence has horizontal rails (**right**).

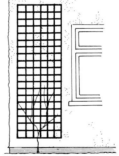

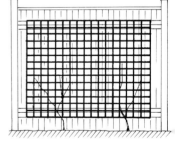

On rendered walls and on fences, trellis can instead be hung on strong hooks. This means that at any time in the future the trellis, complete with the entwined climber, can be carefully unhooked and laid out on the ground while the wall or fence is redecorated or repaired. Care must be taken so that the main stems are not snapped in the process. Some climbers will obviously need cutting back before this can be undertaken.

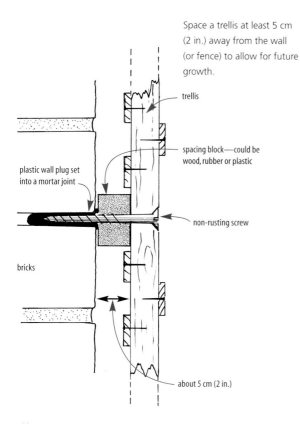

Space a trellis at least 5 cm (2 in.) away from the wall (or fence) to allow for future growth.

trellis

spacing block—could be wood, rubber or plastic

plastic wall plug set into a mortar joint

non-rusting screw

bricks

about 5 cm (2 in.)

Freestanding trellis

This is usually mounted on strong posts. It must be robust enough, if necessary, to support heavy, rampant climbers and to withstand strong winds. This can sometimes be achieved by fixing two trellis panels to the posts (one on each side) as well as using extra-thick posts, perhaps 100 mm (4 in.) square. Pressure-treated posts may be fixed directly into concrete. Once a climber has become established, it is difficult to disentangle it to treat or paint the structure, so the trellis must be thoroughly treated against decay when it is installed.

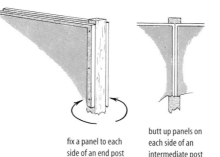

Trellis panels may be fixed to both sides of a support post to make a robust screen, but the posts must be fixed very firmly into the ground to carry the extra weight and withstand the additional pressure from winds.

fix a panel to each side of an end post

butt up panels on each side of an intermediate post

The most effective way to make wooden trellis invisible once the plants have begun to mature is to paint it a dark green or even black before it is installed. It will look smart until the climbers are established, then will appear to merge into the foliage.

Infill trellis

This can be made of metal or timber and is used to fill in the sides of arbours, pergolas, and arches. Most infill trellis comes in the form of small panels, so

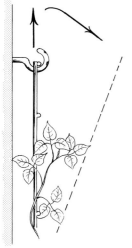

Some of the more robust trellises (particularly plastic-coated steel types) can be hung on heavy-duty hooks so each can be unhooked, together with the plant, when the fence or wall needs maintenance.

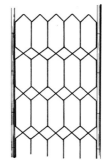

Metal infill trellis for iron structures (**right**)

Wooden infill trellis for wooden structures (**far right**)

relatively lightweight material tends to be used—
heavy trellis would look too clumsy.

Pergolas

These structures should always lead somewhere, to
another area of the garden, to a vista or even to a
focal point such as an urn or a statue. They are
usually constructed from timber because they need to
support the weight of plant growth.

The uprights should be sufficiently strong, 10–15 cm
(4–6 in.) minimum width, and be set wide enough
apart to allow a person to walk through without
being attacked from both sides by any plant stems.
They should also always be set back from the edge
of a lawn or paving by at least 15 cm (6 in.) to allow
the climbers to grow out as well as up. Crossbeams
must be high enough above the ground to allow the
plants to hang down. The crossbeams also need to
be sufficiently sturdy to carry the plants, but for a
visual effect are often set too far apart. The distance
should be no more than 1 m (3 ft. 3 in.). If necessary,
wires or wire netting (which quickly rusts and
becomes almost invisible) may be stretched between
the crossbeams to bridge the gap.

For a pergola or an arbour, it is important to select
climbers that will provide the appropriate density of
shade, for example *Vitis coignetiae* for heavy shade or
Clematis macropetala for light shade. Next to a path or
lawn, avoid very prickly climbers such as roses,
which could scratch passers-by. Include some scented
plants such as jasmines and honeysuckles, especially
over an arbour where people may linger or sit.

Arches

Most preconstructed arches are reasonably robust
since they are designed to support plants. Rustic
arches must be pre-treated against decay for the same
reasons as wooden trellis. Plastic-coated steel arches
are very durable, but the plastic coating may
deteriorate over several years leading to corrosion of
the underlying frame. Well-primed and painted steel
or aluminium may last longer. A climber can be
planted against each of the four uprights of an arch,
but in this case check that the plants will not grow
too large and overwhelm each other and the arch—
one or two vigorous plants may be sufficient.

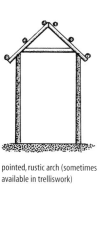

rounded metal arch
(sometimes available
in timber)

pointed, rustic arch (sometimes
available in trelliswork)

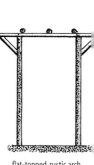

flat-topped, rustic arch

A pergola must be at least 2.1 m
(7 ft.) tall, with its posts set well back
from the edge of paving, paths or a
lawn, to allow for plant growth.

Obelisks

These are freestanding columns, tripods or "wigwams" made from various materials. Columnar obelisks are usually made in the same way as metal arches. Many wigwams or tripods are made from woven willow or some other rustic material that is likely to decay after a few years, so these are more suitable for lightweight, annual climbers. You can make your own simple wigwam by inserting garden canes, at intervals in a circle, into the soil and then gathering them together at the top and tying them with garden twine. More intricate, basket-woven tripods are particularly suitable for the kitchen garden.

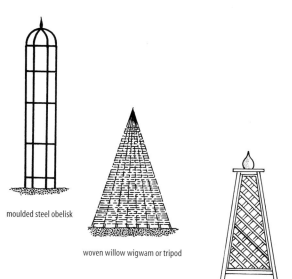

moulded steel obelisk

woven willow wigwam or tripod

timber and trelliswork obelisk

Catenary

In this type of support, fairly thick ropes are hung horizontally, in festoons or swags, between stout upright posts. The ropes are often arranged in two or three rows, one above the other, with the lowest being at least 2.1 m (7 ft.) above the ground. Posts may be several meters or feet apart. When constructing a catenary, it is important to achieve even swags between the posts. To do this:

- Use stout posts.

- On level ground, the tops of the posts should be level.

- If the catenary is on a slope, the posts should be stepped at regular intervals of height to follow the slope.

- Make sure that the ropes' fixings are horizontal.

- Check that the "festoon", or degree of slack, between each set of posts is the same as the next.

- Do not plant climbers with stems that will become rigid with age, for example, *Wisteria*, because they will distort the natural, loose curve of the rope.

Rope catenary on level ground

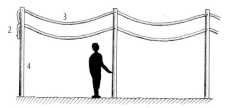

1 posts are drilled through horizontally and rope is pinned by a screw to prevent it from sliding through the hole

2 ends of the ropes are clamped down on to the posts

3 ropes must be adjusted before being pinned, so that they all hang down evenly

4 stout, pressure-treated posts may be round, square, hexagonal or octagonal

Rope catenary on a slope

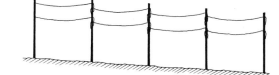

There are two ways to achieve this stepped effect on a catenary that is following a slope. Treat each bay individually, fitting lengths of rope that extend only for one bay.

Alternatively, in every post, drill two holes for each row of rope, making sure that the lower hole on one post is level with the upper hole on the next post.

Feed the rope through the upper hole in each post, then lace it through the lower hole before running it on to the next post.

Do not run ropes parallel to the slope because they will not hang or loop evenly. Instead, they will hang unevenly because of gravity.

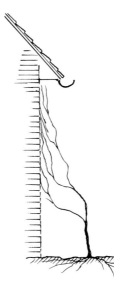

Planting a climber away from the wall, out of the shadow of the roof overhang, will ensure that it receives sufficient moisture.

Supports for Climbers

Make sure that you choose an appropriate support for the habit of the climbing plant.

Wall trellis

Freestanding trellis

Pergola

Arch

Obelisk

Catenary

Planting Climbers

As a general rule, it is worthwhile taking more trouble when planting a climbing plant than when working in open ground. The soil at the base of walls, particularly house walls overhung by tiled roofs, is often dry because rain does not reach this area, so your climber may find it difficult to establish. Consider planting the climber at some distance, say 30–60 cm (1–2 ft.), out from the wall, where it will benefit from rainfall, and training the plant back towards it. Alternatively, install a method of watering or irrigation such as a "leaky pipe" system.

Double-check the soil pH; although the natural soil may be lime-free, building rubble—which does contain lime—is not uncommon in soil near the house. The soil may need removing and replacing before *Lonicera* (honeysuckle), which needs a good, loam soil and plenty of moisture, and other lime-hating climbers can thrive. Keep vigorous climbers away from rainwater pipes or gutters because they may force the pipes from the wall.

Climbers and wall shrubs will be denied light at their bases if they are planted at the back of a border with other shrubs planted in front of them. If you can afford the space, a narrow service path adjacent to the climbers, but behind the shrub border, will allow light and access.

Below: Vigorous climbers should be kept well clear of drainpipes.

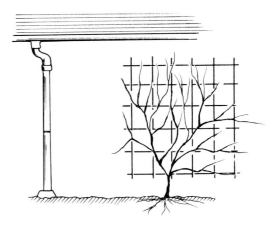

A narrow service path between the climbers and the rest of the border will allow you to get to the plant to prune and train it, and the growth at the base of the climber to receive some sunlight.

Planting technique

The value of correct planting of climbers cannot be overstated. The principles are the same, whether for sites by arches, walls, pillars or pergolas.

- Prepare the ground deeply and thoroughly before planting, incorporating well-rotted manure or fertilizer plus a handful of bonemeal for each.

- Dig each planting hole to a depth and width a little larger than the plant's rootball.

- Spread out the roots in a fan shape away from the wall or support.

- Plant firmly at the appropriate depth, firming in so that the soil mark on the stem is at ground level.

- Water in well and mulch around the base of the plant to help keep the soil moist.

- Use a garden cane to guide the climber toward the support or wall; it can be removed once the plant is established.

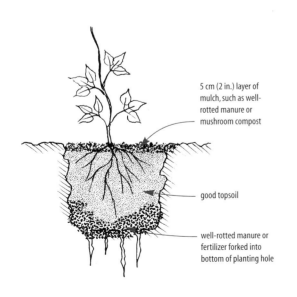

5 cm (2 in.) layer of mulch, such as well-rotted manure or mushroom compost

good topsoil

well-rotted manure or fertilizer forked into bottom of planting hole

Using Climbers in the Garden

- When choosing plants for pillars, tripods or arches, the influence of aspect does not really arise but for planting by walls, the aspect can be critical.
- Planting an early-flowering and a later-flowering climber through a host plant will extend the flowering season from late spring to early autumn.
- Some climbers can be trained as freestanding shrubs. *Hedera* (ivy) and *Hydrangea anomala* subsp. *petiolaris* may be pruned back or grown through the support of a wire frame to take a place in the shrubbery or mixed border.
- Some climbers like company to help them perform and can be persuaded to clothe dead trees or even thread their way through mature trees and large shrubs, provided that the climber is not sufficiently prolific to swamp or destroy the host plant.
- Beware using ivy to climb through healthy trees; when it reaches the top of a tree, it tends to spread out and smother or suffocate other foliage.
- *Clematis* twining through a climbing rose or a large *Vitis vinifera* 'Purpurea' (purple vine) looks happier and more natural than when forced through netting or trellis. They also look beautiful when draped downwards, hanging from parapets or retaining walls.
- More fragile plants which twine or climb by means of tendrils, such as *Eccremocarpus scaber* (Chilean glory vine), *Ipomoea tricolor* (annual morning glory) or *Akebia quinata* (chocolate vine), must explore through the firmer branches of other plants that are strong enough to support their growth.
- Wall shrubs with a stronger personality, such as the evergreen *Ceanothus* or upright

Fremontodendron perform best as a solo plant.

- An evergreen wall shrub such as *Carpenteria californica* or *Itea ilicifolia* will provide structure throughout the year.

- Plants with a well-defined leaf pattern, such as *Vitis coignetiae* with huge leaves that turn orange and crimson in the autumn, are far more striking against a wall than the amorphous foliage of a climber like *Solanum crispum* (Chilean potato tree).

- Some climbers such as ivy or *Clematis* can wind between shrubs as ground cover.

- Climbers can be used for their foliage— evergreen or deciduous—or their flowers or for both. As the amount of wall space is usually limited, and climbers will be few, it is critical to make discriminating choices for texture and outline or form.

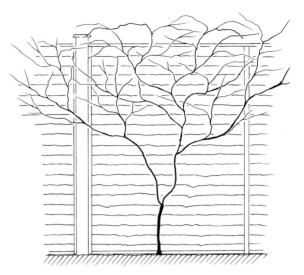

Nearly all climbing plants naturally grow like this—all at the top and very little at the base. They cannot therefore be relied upon to screen the bottom part of a fence or wall, although if the lateral shoots are regularly trained horizontally, they can be encouraged to put on more growth lower down.

Maintaining Climbers and Wall Shrubs

Unless you enjoy spending time up a ladder, maintenance must also be considered before you make a choice. Some climbers, such as rambler roses, grow and spread alarmingly quickly, and the new, lateral shoots need regular tying in. *Wisteria* needs its stems to be cut back to two or three buds twice a year, to encourage it to flower. Some *Clematis* need to be cut back annually to several centimetres (inches) above ground, and the old growth needs to be cleared away from its support. Some pruning will be necessary for most climbers and wall shrubs (see pages 285–287).

Climbers and wall shrubs often become leggy and unfurnished at the base, either because the growth is drawn up to the light or because they are incorrectly trained upwards instead of along the wall space. If you train the lateral, or side, branches horizontally

each growing season, it prompts them to break new flowering shoots along their lengths.

Attaching climbers to their supports

Whatever material you use to train the plants into their supports must be durable and relatively invisible. It must also not be liable to cut into the stems. Among the products commonly available are various twines and soft strings (not always long-lasting), fairly thin, plastic-covered wire and galvanized wire. More recent products such as plastic slot-through ties, foam ties and dark brown, stretch plastic are also useful. Natural-coloured twine is usually the best because it is easy to use, inexpensive, hardly noticeable when the plants is growing, and is easy to cut loose when necessary. Wire tends to cut into plant stems without this being noticeable until the plant has been strangled.

In all cases, the material must be tied or wound, rather like a figure-of-eight, around the stem and support, then knotted. Take care not to tie so tightly that it will strangle and cut into the stem as it thickens in the following weeks or months. It is easy to forget to do so, but try to check ties and occasionally loosen them every year. Climbers with stems that thicken rapidly, for example, *Wisteria*, need regular attention, since strangulation can result in the sudden death of quite large branches.

Annual Climbers

Until long-term climbers become established, annual climbers are useful as temporary infill. Climbing runner beans or *Ipomoea* (morning glory) are easy to grow. Climbing nasturtiums such as *Tropaeolum peregrinum* are particularly successful through trellis or willow basket-weave tripods; they are easily pulled out and discarded when flowering is finished.

Climbing and Rambler Roses

Roses are one of the most popular flowering climbers. Some catalogues differentiate between rambler and climbing roses, which is helpful since their growth rates and eventual sizes vary. Ramblers are much more vigorous, sending out long stems, often up to 8 m (25 ft.), so they need a strong support and plenty of room. They do well trained up through old trees, provided that the tree is able to support the weight of the rose, or to hide unsightly buildings. Ramblers are also suitable for pergolas, where they can be trained across wire or wire mesh to give coverage between the uprights. During the growing season, the new stems of ramblers are very flexible because the sap is still rising; they need to be trained in at this stage, otherwise once they are older and more woody, they may snap at the joints.

Climbers for walls and arches tend to be more refined of habit, due to the lack of space; several shrub or bush roses could also be used as climbers. Climbing roses usually take up a wall space of about 3–4 m (10–12 ft.) whereas ramblers, particularly *R. filipes* 'Kiftsgate', can grow to 11 m (35 ft.) or more and may engulf a small building.

Climbers and ramblers also vary in their flowering habit—some flowers face up to the sun so that their stamens cannot be seen from below, while other have trusses which bow down ready to be admired. You may need to be patient—some strong ramblers take up to three years to flower. There is a huge range of colours to choose from in rose blooms—from whites and creams, mustards through canary-yellow to lemons, shades of red from cherry through cerise to crisp, deep scarlets. The greatest variety is in pinks— from soft pink and salmons through to bluish- and darker pinks—so it is more difficult to decide.

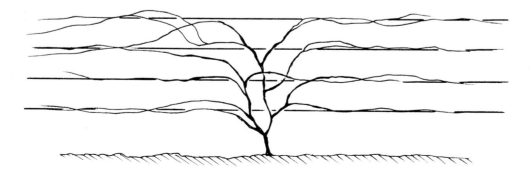

If the lateral stems of a climbing rose are tied in horizontally to wires, they will produce new flowering shoots all along their lengths.

Recommended Rambler Roses

R. 'Albéric Barbier'
A delightfully muddled flower when open and excellent, glossy foliage; suitable for arches and pergolas.

R. 'Albertine'
Famous old rambler with vigorous growth and masses of double, apricot or coppery pink flowers that unfortunately tend to hold on until the end of the summer looking like messy, brown paper shreds; good for arches and pergolas.

R. 'Bobbie James'
Creamy-white, semi-double flowers with a musk scent.

R. 'Emily Gray'
Soft yellow blooms; suitable for shady and cold walls and arches and pergolas.

R. 'Francis E. Lester'
Single, white blooms flushed with pink; good for training into trees.

R. filipes 'Kiftsgate'
So vigorous it would be unwise to recommend it. It can overwhelm a small house.

R. 'New Dawn'
Much-loved, pale pink, shapely and perfumed blooms; suitable for growing up walls.

R. 'Paul's Himalayan Musk'
Very rampant, with scented, very pale pink flowers; suitable for training into trees.

R. 'Rambling Rector'
White flowers; suitable for training into trees.

R. 'Seagull'
White flowers; good for training into trees.

R. 'Veilchenblau'
Scented, large clusters of semi-double, violet-purple flowers that fade to a bluish-lilac; suitable for training into a tree.

R. 'Wedding Day'
Yellow, pointed buds and very fragrant blooms.

Recommended Climbing Roses

White flowers

R. 'Blanche Double de Coubert'
Rugosa rose with spreading habit and white flowers; good on shady or cold walls.

R. 'Madame Alfred Carrière'
Noisette climbing rose, with double, white flushed soft pink flowers; grows well on a cold and shady wall.

R. **Swan Lake**
Perfectly formed, white blooms with a pinkish tinge.

Yellow flowers

R. 'Alchymist'
Double, yellowish-orange flowers that pale with age and have a strong scent.

R. 'Alister Stella Gray'
A heavily scented, noisette climbing rose, with long arching stems; shapely, light yellow flowers with strong yellow centres,

fading to cream, with a long flowering season.

R. banksiae 'Lutea'
Soft yellow flowers; good for clothing walls.

R. 'Climbing Lady Hillingdon'
Outstanding climbing tea rose, combining shapely, apricot-yellow flowers with healthy, plum-coloured shoots and grey-green leaves.

R. 'Gloire de Dijon'
Dates from 1853; has large, tea-scented flowers of pale, buff-orange; some repeat-flowering.

R. 'Golden Showers'
Modern climber with deep golden-yellow, ragged flowers and dark, glossy leaves and relatively thornless stems.

R. 'Goldfinch'
Has scented flowers of golden–yellow and primrose, with richly coloured anthers.

R. 'Maigold'
Semi-double, copper-yellow blooms and glossy, mid-green foliage.

R. 'Mermaid'
Useful for a cold, shady wall, with its almost evergreen foliage and continuous production of single, pale yellow flowers. Has very savage thorns, making it difficult to train.

Red flowers

R. 'Allen Chandler'
Sturdy and healthy, with large, semi-single, brilliant red flowers, set off by golden stamens.

R. 'Guinée'
Highly scented, deep maroon-red flowers.

R. 'Souvenir du Docteur Jamain'
Delicious, wine-red blooms; needs careful placing away from burning sun so that it can mature to its full beauty.

Pink flowers

R. 'Bantry Bay'
Light pink, semi-double, profuse blooms all season.

R. 'François Juranville'
Spectacular, pink blooms; when in full flush, it is superior to 'Albertine' with which it is often confused.

R. 'Madame Grégoire Staechelin'
Deep pearl pink, richly scented flowers with splashes of carmine.

R. 'Zéphirine Drouhin'
Bourbon rose with thornless, lax stems and cerise-pink flowers; good for shady, cold walls.

Clematis

This climber is often used as a partner for a rose, either to extend the flowering season or to intensify a spectacular effect by flowering at the same time as the rose. Clematis does not strangle the host plant because it gently twists its leaf stalks (petioles) around the nearest support—be it a rose stem, trellis or wicker wigwam—in order to climb.

C. alpina
Has single, nodding, lantern-like flowers followed by fluffy seedheads.

C. armandii
Has large, lobed, glossy, evergreen leaves and waxy, white flowers.

C. cirrhosa var. *balearica*
An evergreen; it is lovely in winter when it bears scented, bell-shaped, ivory flowers, which contrast against the bronze-shaded foliage.

C. macropetala
Has semi-double, nodding, deep lavender-blue flowers in early summer.

C. 'Madame Julia Correvon'
Luxuriant climber with wine-red flowers with twisted petals.

C. montana
This species and its cultivars are the most vigorous; in fact, the weight of a mature plant in full foliage has been responsible more than once for bringing down telephone wires and disturbing roof tiles.

C. montana var. *rubens*
Has leaves tinged purple when young and soft rosy red flowers; it is scented and needs plenty of space.

C. 'Niobe'
Has small, deep red flowers with golden stamens.

C. tibetana var. *vernayi* 'Orange Peel'
Has finely cut, grey-green foliage which complements the unique, nodding, waxy yellow flowers.

C. 'Vyvyan Pennell'
One of the large-flowering cultivars; it has good double, violet-blue flowers, shaded crimson, in early summer that are followed by single flowers in late summer.

Hedera (ivy)

Since they thrive on north and east aspects, are self clinging, with their leaf shape and colour contributing far more than is usually recognized, the various forms of *Hedera* (ivy) are very useful. Ivy leaves colour well when in full sun, but tend to revert back to plain green in shade.

H. canariensis 'Gloire de Marengo' (formerly *H. canariensis* 'Variegata') Has large, shield-like, olive-green leaves with silver and white edging—very ornamental and will enliven a dark corner.

H. colchica 'Sulphur Heart' (Persian ivy)
Has longer, oval leaves with an irregular, central splash of yellow—another brightly variegated ivy for a dark corner.

H. helix cultivars
These have much smaller, sharply pointed leaves; *H. helix* 'Glacier' has white leaf margins that turn pink in winter.

Lonicera (honeysuckle)
Climbers in the honeysuckle family are natural twiners that are best allowed to ramble over a pergola, arch or outhouse, or through trees. Since the honeysuckle originated in light woodland, the roots benefit from some shade.

L. × brownii 'Dropmore Scarlet'
Showy but without scent, having bright scarlet, tubular flowers from midsummer until early autumn.

L. japonica cultivars
These flower on the current season's wood and tend to be very prolific.
L. japonica 'Halliana' has pale green leaves and very sweetly scented flowers; it easily covers 4 m (12 ft.) in height and spread.

L. periclymenum 'Belgica'
Flowers in early summer on the previous season's wood.

L. periclymenum 'Serotina'
Flowers in late summer.

L. × tellmanniana
Has no scent, but glowing, yellowish-orange flowers.

Wisteria
Wisterias are the most admired of all deciduous climbers, but it is not generally known that there are several different species. Make sure that whichever wisteria you buy, it has been grafted rather than raised from seed, otherwise it will be years before it flowers.

W. floribunda
Japanese species, with stems that twine in a clockwise direction; has fragrant blue, purple or white flowers carried in slender hanging racemes, or flowerheads, that are about 20 cm (8 in.) long.

W. sinensis
Chinese wisteria, with stems that twine in an anticlockwise direction; flowers with 20–30 cm (8–12 in.) long racemes in white, lilac or dark purple.

Recommended Climbers

Actinidia kolomikta
An unusual, slender and elegant climber with large, heart-shaped leaves that are green when young, then develop cream and pink variegation; needs full sun.

Akebia quinata
A vigorous, twining climber for a sunny, warm aspect. Small, deep maroon flowers in spring are followed by fleshy, chocolate-coloured fruits.

Campsis grandiflora
Spectacular, vigorous, twining plant with orange, trumpet-shaped flowers and good, yellow autumn colouring.

Recommended Climbers (continued)

Euonymus fortunei 'Silver Queen'
Has silver-variegated, green leaves and grows either as dense ground cover or a self-clinging scrambler.

Humulus lupulus 'Aureus'
Best in full sun; has deeply lobed, soft yellow leaves and will quickly cover a fence or trellis.

Hydrangea anomala subsp. *petiolaris*
Slow-growing at first; has medium-sized, vivid green leaves and is smothered in flat heads of white flowers in midsummer. Its brownish-red, leafless stems are still attractive in winter.

Jasminum nudiflorum
Produces bright yellow flowers on bare stems in winter.

Jasminum officinale
Twiner with sweetly scented, white flowers in summer.

Parthenocissus quinquefolia
Partially self-clinging climber with vine-like foliage which turns to dazzling red or crimson in autumn.

Solanum crispum 'Glasnevin'
Scrambler with clusters of rich blue flowers that last all summer.

Vitis coignetiae and *V. vinifera* 'Purpurea'
These climbers have few equals for the brilliant shades of their foliage; they can be trained over walls, fences and pergolas and outhouses.

Recommended Wall Shrubs

Wall shrubs have an important role in furnishing lower levels of boundaries or internal divisions, and linking the house to the garden. There are possibilities not mentioned here, but the suggestions given are all reliable performers. Many tender species can be used because of the protection a wall offers, not only those classed as climbers or wall shrubs. Be careful to match any plant to the aspect and soil. Also, try alternating deciduous climbers with evergreen wall shrubs, to maintain interest through the year.

Ceanothus 'Autumnal Blue'
Has evergreen foliage and is a relatively hardy hybrid, with smaller, dark green leaves that set off its china-blue flowers.

Ceanothus 'Cascade'
Has powder-blue flowers on arching sprays.

Ceanothus 'Puget Blue'
Has glossier foliage and bright blue flowers in late spring and early summer.

Fremontodendron 'California Glory'
Forms a stiff, upright plant and bears yellow flowers over a long period.

Magnolia grandiflora 'Exmouth' and
M. grandiflora 'Goliath'
Best on a sunny, warm aspect. They have wonderfully polished, evergreen leaves and large, richly scented, creamy "goblets", mainly in summer but occasionally at other times. Give these shrubs plenty of space, because after about ten years they will reach the height of an average roof.

Piptanthus nepalensis
Evergreen shrub requiring little or no sun; has large, bright lemon flowers in spring.

Project 3

Making a garden is a gradually evolving process, so now you should be ready to plan and implement the structural planting, including boundary and internal hedges. Study the plan drawn for Project 2.

Work Out Where to Place Structural Planting

Imagine that you are walking through the flat space, and try to include vertical elements such as trees and shrubs, which will help relate the vertical façade of the house and nearby buildings to the horizontal plane of the garden.

- Draw these structural elements, and any hedging, in on your plan or on an overlay to it.

- Then consider all the options, such as evergreen or deciduous, height and spread, and plant numbers (whether a single plant or a group of the same plant). Refer to the tables in this chapter or make your own choice of plants.

- It may help you either to raise your plan up to your eye level or to crouch down and look at it as if you were on the same level as the ground. In this way, you can feel how the inclusion of structural plants has broken up the proportions of the garden, making it relate more easily to the size of the human frame.

Make Plant Lists

For each area of the garden, prepare lists of the plants you need to obtain or buy and plant, with notes on the conditions they need and their eventual heights and spreads, for each of the main structural groups, i.e.
– trees
– shrubs, including boundary or hedging plants
– roses
–climbers and wall shrubs.

- At this stage, you will need to calculate how many plants will be needed for each area— check the spacing required between hedging plants and add up how many you will need.

- For each plant on your list, enter the botanical name and number of plants required, e.g.

Trees:
  Betula utulis   1
  Prunus serrula   3

If you are using the same plant in more than one site or grouping, note the number of plants in each grouping, as in the formulas below. This will remind you that you have separate groups of some plants. Put a separate column at the end of your list so that the totals for each plant can be added up, e.g.

Shrubs and hedging
  Choisya ternata 'Aztec Pearl'   3 + 2 = 5
  Lavandula 'Hidcote'   22
  Viburnum tinus   3 + 2 + 5 = 10
Roses
  R. gallica 'Versicolor'   3 + 5 = 8

- If you are ordering most of the plants from one nursery or garden centre, it will help if you make up your plant list in the same order as on their website or in their catalogue.

- Indicate the plant names and their planting positions on your plan.

- In most cases, you will have a specific variety of plant in mind, so include on your order the words "No substitutes unless previously agreed". This should prevent the supplier from giving you an alternative plant which you may not want.

PLANT LIST

Structural Planting

—Trees   Total

	Total
Acer griseum 1	1
Arbutus unedo (standard/matching) 1 + 1	2
Clerodendrum trichotomum var. fargesii (standard) 1	1
Crataegus orientalis 1	1
Ginkgo biloba 1	1
Sorbus aucuparia 'Aspleniifolia' 1	1
	7

— Additional to order

Tree stakes   7

Tree ties   7

— Shrubs and Hedging

	Total
Berberis thunbergii 'Atropurpurea Nana' 3 + 7 + 7	17
Buxus sempervirens (balls) 16	16
Philadelphus 'Belle Etoile' 1	1
Rhamnus 'Argenteovariegata' 5 + 5	10
Viburnum plicatum f. tomentosum 'Mariesii' 1	1
	45

— Climbers and Wall Shrubs

	Total
Rosa 'Climbing Lady Hillingdon' 1	1
Vitis coignetiae 1	1
Trachelospermum asiaticum 1 + 1	2
	4

Here is an example of a plant list for structural planting, including some accessories supplied by the nursery.

Make Up a Planting Schedule

As you have read through this chapter, you may have had more ideas about your garden layout and how you are going to progress. Some plants need particular conditions such as a good loam or acid soil.

Perhaps your climbers may be under the eaves of your house and will need a trickle irrigation system to prevent the soil from drying out, or wires and wall nails or vine eyes to help them climb. The ground may require preparation for planting trees or boundary and internal hedges, and you may have to protect the new plants from deer, rabbits and other animals. This may mean buying compost, supports, stakes, tree ties and netting.

- Make up a planting schedule for each area (or border) of your garden.

- So that you can move ahead quickly once the plants arrive, make up a list to help remind you of any additional purchases to be made before the planting takes place, and relate this back to the areas on your plan. Check your plant list to make sure that you haven't missed out any item that cannot be provided by the plant suppliers.

Updating Your Garden Plan

- Block in the scheduled new plantings on your simple plan. Remember this plan is for your own records so although it should be neat and legible, it does not need to be work of art.

- Draw freehand circles for any trees and shrubs (a single circle for a single specimen, and several interlinked circles to represent a group of the same type of plant).

- Try to draw the freehand circles to show roughly the amount of space that the mature plants will take up in the garden.

- Use a 'V' to represent a climber, and a 'V' with a half circle drawn round it to indicate a wall shrub.

Now you will see how the planting in your garden begins to take shape. Be prepared to spend time preparing the soil to give the plants a good start in life and they should serve you well for many years.

greenhouse and new timber compost bins (5) and site for bonfire

Crataegus/Ilex (hawthorn/holly) hedge—ivy allowed to proliferate so hedge becomes semi-evergreen

new *Acer griseum*/1

structure planting of *Berberis* 'Dart's Red Lady'/7

Robinia pseudoacacia 'Frisia'

Rear Garden

new *Crataegus orientalis*/1 **3**

New *Clerodenrum trichotomum* var. *fargesii*/1—grown as standard (star plant)

relocated yew (*Taxus baccata* 'Fastigiata') **4**

structure planting of *Berberis* 'Dart's Red Lady'/3+7

New *Arbutus unedo*/2 (standards) **7**

new *Viburnum plicatum* f. *tomentosum* 'Mariesii'/1 (star plant)

existing bed

new paved path and ramp to summerhouse

yew hedge (*Taxus baccata*)

new *Philadelphus* 'Belle Etoile'/1 (star plant)

new *Buxus sempervirens*/16 (clipped into balls) **6**

realigned bed

lawn—rejuvenated through scarifying, spiking, treating with mosskiller and fertilizer

realigned bed

stone path

realigned bed

5

proposed kitchen garden

new summerhouse—with tiled roof and rendered and painted walls **2**

new *Rhamnus alaternus* 'Argenteovariegata'/10—trained into columns

new *Sorbus aucuparia*/1

apple tree

Cupressus hedge, to be tightly clipped

Acer negundo (maple)

new terrace of reclaimed brick **1**

new steps, landing and French windows from living room to garden

new corrugated, clear perspex roof on potting shed

stone wall revealed after removal of ivy

narrow beds widened to allow more space for planting

The existing garden layout proved difficult to alter, but both hard landscaping and planting were changed to be in tune with owner's needs.

new *Buxus sempervirens*/28 (box hedge)

new *Cotinus* 'Grace'/1

new *Taxus baccata* 'Fastigiata/2

new *Ceanothus* 'Concha'/1 (star plant)

new *Lyonothamnus floribundus* subsp. *aspleniifolius* /1 **14**

new climbers— *Trachelospermum asiaticum*/2

new *Philadelphus* 'Belle Etoile'/1 (star plant)

12

12

new pool and fountain **13**

new *Taxus baccata* 'Fastigiata'/3

new *Prunus serrula*/1

new *Amelanchier* 'Ballerina'/1

new *Ginkgo biloba*/1 **10**

double-stemmed silver birch

Sorbus (mountain ash)

new *Buxus sempervirens*/7 (box hedge)

new *Taxus baccata* 'Fastigiata'

red-leaved *Acer*

new *Corylopsis pauciflora*/1

8

11

11

11

9

new brick edge to border

Prunus 'Kanzan'

new *Buxus sempervirens*/7 (box hedge)

new *Buxus sempervirens*/14 (clipped into balls)

new *Betula albosinensis* var. *septentrionalis*/3

new *Amelanchier* 'Ballerina'/1

new *Sorbus aucuparia*/1

new gravel path system

new, multistemmed *Betula utilis*/1

existing pool

Front Garden

North

0   5   10m

Updated Plan of the Rear Garden

Certain elements, such as the paved central pathway set at an angle, would have been expensive to lift and re-lay at right angles to the house; the vegetable garden seemed suited to its original position, so both were allowed to remain. Despite facing northeast, in summer this part of the garden seemed to be in sun from noon until early evening; the focus of the herbaceous planting, to be decided on later, would be on plants that bloom during the summer months. The following major changes were made:

1 A new terrace was necessary for outdoor living, so reclaimed bricks to match the house bricks were used, laid in a basket-weave pattern.
2 As a focal point to be viewed across the length of the garden, a custom-made, circular summerhouse was built against the backdrop of the neighbour's hedge.
3 An unusual hawthorn (*Crataegus orientalis*), chosen for its rather glaucous foliage and large, orange hips in autumn, was planted at the opposite end of the garden to the summerhouse as a focal point.
4 Other trees are planted at strategic points to give height and vertical interest. An upright yew tree was moved to a new position to divert attention from a change in the roof pitch of neighbouring buildings.
5 As structural planting and for year-round interest, the variegated and fast-growing *Rhamnus alaternus* 'Argenteovariegata' was staked and clipped into columns so that the light-edged foliage would show up against the yew hedge behind.
6 *Buxus sempervirens* (box) balls are used to delineate the long paths.
7 Two standard *Arbutus unedo* (strawberry tree) punctuate the left-hand bed, where eventually a doorway will be made through to the building behind.

The occasional star plant was added to give interest at specific times of year. These include *Philadelphus* 'Belle Etoile', grown for its scented, white flowers; *Clerodendrum trichotomum* var. *fargesii*, grown for creamy, scented flowers in late summer; and the horizontally spreading *Viburnum plicatum* f. *tomentosum* 'Mariesii', which may eventually get too large for the space.

Updated Plan of the Front Garden

There was an opportunity here to create several different areas of interest. In the lower area, topsoil was brought in to build up the beds, and informal gravel paths were laid between to create a woodland garden. The following major changes were made:

8 Immediately to the left of the entrance gate, a white garden was proposed; since most friends visit in the evening, white flowering plants would show up well and many would be scented. Although the shrubs and perennials were not yet decided for the white garden, two *Taxus baccata* 'Fastigiata' (fastigiate yews) and a low *Buxus sempervirens* (box) hedge edging the border were planted there to give structure.
9 In the lower woodland area, winding gravel paths were made between the newly created beds, several new trees and shrubs having been planted to give structure, height and shade.
10 A semi-mature *Ginkgo biloba* was planted to screen the view from the garden of the telegraph pole on the opposite side of the road.
11 Clipped box balls were used extensively along the wide gravel path and at the entrance to the paved terrace. These help to connect the upper and lower areas and reduce the width of the path. Low box hedges accentuated the short flights of steps.
12 The terrace borders were widened to allow for more planting, a *Ceanothus* 'Concha' and a *Philadelphus* 'Belle Etoile' being added as star plants.
13 An ornamental pool with small, triple fountains was built on the terrace, to cut out the noise of occasional traffic from the nearby country road.
14 To hide the downpipe beside the front porch, an unusual evergreen tree, *Lyonothamnus floribundus* subsp. *aspleniifolius*, was planted, in the hope that it would not get too large!

Above: Structural planting—beds containing shrub roses with varied underplanting are edged with low box hedging to create a formal entrance to this country garden. Taller, clipped, evergreen shrubs beyond provide a link with the trees behind.

Above: Structural planting—of these evergreen shrubs, the glossy, light-reflective and larger leaves of *Magnolia grandiflora* contrast with the smaller, neat foliage of the *Buxus* (box) hedge. The box is carefully clipped to a "batter" so that the top of the hedge is narrower than the base, allowing light to reach the bases of the plants.

Above: Silver foliage—*Artemisia absinthium* 'Lambrook Silver' is a useful clump-forming, evergreen perennial cultivated for its mass of ferny, aromatic foliage. It needs well-drained, fertile soil in a sunny position.

Right: Glossy foliage—*Magnolia grandiflora* bears long, dark evergreen leaves with russet, velvety undersides. In favourable conditions, this large tree or shrub produces stately, fragrant flowers.

Above: Corrugated foliage—these large, evergreen leaves belong to *Eriobotrya japonica*; it is a tree normally grown as a shrub outside its native environment, which benefits from the protection of a warm wall.

Below: Four upright conifers provide vertical accents to indicate a change of direction in the curved grass path.

Left: Pleaching trees—pleached trees often need training in their formative years; use bamboo canes to define the required shape. When choosing or ordering trees to be pleached, make sure that all the stems are straight and of a similar height and diameter.

Left: Pleaching trees—the soft green foliage of this "hedge on stilts" makes a foil for the rendered and painted wall behind. The lateral branches are clipped annually in late summer.

Above: Trees or hedging plants may be trained to form an arch by tying young branches into pliable bamboo canes. This *Taxus baccata* (yew) arch will give a glimpse of the kitchen garden and a well-dressed scarecrow.

Above: Interesting bark is an asset often overlooked when selecting a tree. Many trees have coloured, marbled or peeling bark, such as this *Acer griseum*.

Above: Sandhill Farm House—the white-stemmed silver birch, *Betula utilis* var. *jacquemontii*, is scrubbed with warm, slightly soapy water and a pot scourer every Easter to remove any old, shaggy, brown, peeling bark.

Above: Each season brings its own excitement. In spring, silver-birch catkins droop elegantly from a tree and are set off by fresh green foliage. The tree can attract over two hundred species of insects and wild life.

Above: In autumn, foliage plays a special part. Several varieties of *Acer* (maple) provide brilliant colours, particularly on acid soil. *Cornus* and *Cotinus* are among other spectacular performers in the autumn.

Above: Summer flowers are the highlight of the gardening year, on shrubs as with other plants. Choose them for their colour, form, size and, in the case of roses, their fragrance and length of performance. Roses may be once-, repeat- or continuous-flowering.

Above: Winter colour—at Sandhill Farm House, *Cornus* (dogwood) is cut back to within 10 cm (4 in.) from the main stem in spring, to regenerate colourful new growth for the following season.

Above: Winter colour—the glowing stems of *Cornus sanguinea* 'Midwinter Fire' and the ghostly branches of *Rubus cockburnianus* 'Golden Vale' brighten up cold winter days and bring the woodland garden at Sandhill Farm House to life.

Above: Clipped "bun" shapes provide a subtle tapestry effect. The occasional exuberance of artichokes or grasses add drama to the scene.

Above: Evergreen shrubs with rounded forms are easy on the eye and provide structure. The early flowers of *Rhododendron* 'Ima-shojo', a dwarf evergreen azalea, live up to its reputation.

Above: Many shrubs are star attractions in a woodland setting, such as this evergreen *Kalmia latifolia*. It prefers an acid soil and flowers from late spring to midsummer.

Above: Berries bring late interest to some shrubs and trees. *Clerodendrum trichotomum* var. *fargesii* has strongly scented, creamy white flowers followed by bright berries and colourful calyces in early autumn.

Above: Although seldom considered for their hips, larger species roses such as *Rosa moyesii* 'Geranium' are striking in early autumn; here the rose is combined with the half-hardy *Canna indica*.

Right: Climbers bring another planting dimension to the garden, like this combination of *Actinidia kolomikta* and *Wisteria sinensis*. Before deciding on a particular climber, consider how the plant can be attached to the wall, and how the flower and foliage colour will show up against it.

Above: *Hedera* (ivy) can be quickly trained over metal supports to form vertical accents in a border. Sometimes wire netting is needed to infill any gaps; when covered, the ivy can be clipped over in spring to keep it dense and to shape.

Above: Climbers can sometimes be used to good effect as trailing plants. Wire netting has been fixed on to this low retaining wall as a support for *Clematis* 'Elizabeth'.

Above: Trained over the roof of a terrace in a sunny or warm climate, *Vitis vinifera* (grape vine) will produce edible fruits as well as look decorative.

Above: A quintessential English scene. Roses and *Nepeta* (catmint) clothe a garden building; the doors and roof timbers are painted in a subtle, co-ordinating shade of blue-grey.

Chapter 4

Planning New Plantings: Herbaceous Plants

Plants are for most people by far the most exciting part of making a garden—the thrill of choosing them, deciding where and how to plant them so that they will grow well, followed by the pleasure of seeing them perform or the disappointment if they don't! Most gardeners start by experimenting with growing or caring for herbaceous plants, so are most familiar with these. Although they are more transient than the structural plants, they are equally important in the garden. Herbaceous plants include herbaceous perennials, often referred to simply as "perennials", bulbs, alpines and rock plants, ferns, ornamental grasses and bamboos, water and bog plants, and annuals and half-hardies. You will also learn about fruit and vegetables and planting in containers.

The same principles that apply to choosing trees and shrubs also apply to non-structural, herbaceous plants. Study what plants grow well in your area before making a choice and select plants that suit the conditions in your garden. Consider aesthetic points including the plant's height and spread, foliage and flowers, seasons of interest, and any special characteristics. Structural plants are valued for their outline and other architectural qualities whereas, for instance, flowers may be the most important feature of herbaceous plantings.

Planting in Layers

Planting in layers means growing herbaceous perennials, annuals and bulbs beneath and between shrubs. Climbers may twine up through a supporting host shrub or small tree, provided that they do not stifle the host plant. For instance, *Clematis macropetala* (downy clematis), an early-flowering, species clematis, has deep, nodding, lavender-blue flowers. It is ideal for threading through a greyish green-leaved shrub such as *Phlomis fruticosa* (Jerusalem sage) and will double its interest seen against the shrub foliage in late spring.

Primula Gold Laced Group or *Viola* 'Irish Molly' could be underplanted beneath the same *Phlomis*—

both are low-growing and undemanding, so will not crowd out the lower shrub branches, be invasive or take too much out of the soil. Bare soil under deciduous shrubs can be used to display bulbs and early-flowering perennials, making the bed come alive in spring before the shrub foliage appears. By planting in layers, you will gradually transform your borders into an ongoing performance of small but pleasurable incidents.

Herbaceous Perennials

Traditional herbaceous borders, once an integral part of the classic English garden that provided a kaleidoscope of colour in the main growing season, have over recent times gradually declined in popularity. Often seen against a backdrop of yew hedging, the true herbaceous border required a high level of maintenance, for example of staking and weeding, yet was resplendent really only for about three months out of twelve, in summer.

In the majority of gardens, the herbaceous border then gave way to the mixed border, where shrubs provide the permanent structure against which the flowering herbaceous plants—or the "pretties" as they are sometimes disparagingly called—are shown off. Average proportions in a mixed planting should be about one-third of herbaceous plants to two-thirds of shrubs or, depending on the desired effect, one-third of shrubs to two-thirds of herbaceous plants. Bulbs such as *Tulipa* and *Narcissus* (daffodil) may be used between the herbaceous plants, with annuals such as *Cleome* or *Cosmos* sown to fill in the gaps until the shrub planting has matured. In this way, the beauty of a border may be extended from one season to another, from winter through spring to summer and autumn.

Recently there has been a move to use mainly summer-flowering perennials, often combined with grasses, to provide a show from early summer through to autumn. In this type of planting, the foliage is best not cut down until the spring, otherwise the area will look bare during winter.

Form and Texture of Leaves

When we decorate our homes or choose our clothes, most of us are aware of the value of combining different textures and forms. We may contrast knobbly cotton or wool fabric with flimsy voile, or smooth, shiny satin with matt velvet and may mix boxy shapes with fluid silhouettes or patterns of different sizes and shapes. We rarely carry this through to our choice of plants, yet form and texture are the most important aspects if the foliage is to be effective in a planting. Herbaceous perennials display an infinite variety of leaves—do not miss the opportunity to develop an interesting interplay between leaf shape, size and texture when planning perennial plantings.

The textural quality of a leaf is far from purely ornamental—it has evolved through a need for the plant to protect itself against the vagaries of nature, often to deflect intense sunlight or to decrease the rate of evaporation. Shiny foliage can become intensely hot in bright, summer sunshine, whereas the grey foliage of many Mediterranean plants, such as *Phlomis fruticosa* (Jerusalem sage), has felted surfaces that filter the sunlight. Some plants have matt or light-absorbent foliage, others have shiny, light-reflective leaves.

Many perennials, such as *Geranium*, have unspectacular leaves and a comfortable, rounded shape; unless punctuated by a more eye-catching or dramatic partner such as prickly *Eryngium* or spiky *Digitalis* (foxglove) and *Verbascum*, the effect would be bland and boring. The spiky fans of *Libertia peregrinans* foliage and pairs of deeply pleated, bronze-tinted leaves of *Rodgersia pinnata*, although less dangerous, give drama to a border and brighten up the rounded shapes of roses or other shrubs or hummocks of other perennials. Varied heights also spice up horizontal mats, such as those formed by *Dianthus*

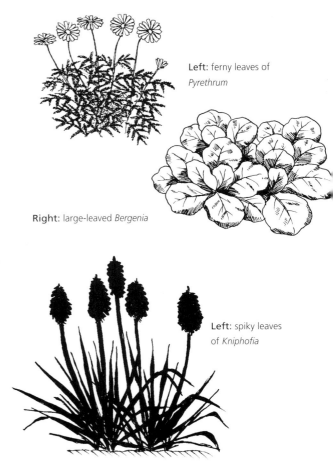

Left: ferny leaves of *Pyrethrum*

Right: large-leaved *Bergenia*

Left: spiky leaves of *Kniphofia*

(garden pink) or *Ajuga reptans*. Lacy leaves, such as those of *Dicentra formosa*, will lighten a bed.

The large, plain leaves of plants such as evergreen *Bergenia cordifolia* ground the rest of the planting. Simple, rounded leaves, such as those of *Nepeta × faassenii*, are necessary to provide cohesion and act as a foil to more striking plants.

Too many forms and textures of foliage can conflict, but occasionally interspersing arresting elements with larger groupings of a more relaxed shape creates interest among herbaceous plantings. Subconsciously, contrasting qualities create in us a psychological tension that contributes to our overall enjoyment of a garden planting.

The tactile quality of herbaceous perennials is also often overlooked, but who could resist stroking the large, felted leaves of *Salvia argentea* or *Stachys byzantina* (lambs' ears) as you pass. Children too become more interested in plants when these qualities are pointed out. Other plants, such as the prickly *Acanthus spinosus* or the spiky *Eryngium variifolium*, warn us to stand clear.

Coarse-leaved plants

Try contrasting fine or delicate leaves, such as the ferny foliage of *Dicentra spectabilis*, by going to the opposite end of the spectrum and choosing as its companion a plant with coarsely textured leaves. Coarse leaves can also create a boldly architectural element to a planting. Try *Acanthus*, *Rheum palmatum* or *Veratrum viride*, with its intriguingly pleated basal leaves. Repeating these coarse-leaved plants occasionally through the border will give drama and rhythm.

Gunnera manicata
  The huge, puckered foliage has jagged edges and resembles gigantic rhubarb; the leaves eventually grow large enough to shelter children or small adults. The flowers that appear in late spring and early summer consist of brownish-green, cone-like spikes. *Gunnera* enjoys moisture, so thrives and reflects well beside water. The foliage should be cut off to the base in autumn, the crown packed with straw, the cut leaves inverted over this and held in place by stones, to protect the crown from frost in the winter.

Heuchera micrantha var. *diversifolia* 'Palace Purple'
  Much smaller, but with a similar outline to *Rodgersia podophylla*, the rich, deep red, hairy and divided foliage is effective in larger groups towards the front of a border, and is useful as a colour contrast.

Rheum palmatum
  If *Gunnera* is too large for your garden, a smaller but similar effect can be achieved with the moisture-loving ornamental rhubarb. Its young foliage is a deep, beetroot red, and is followed by tall, cream, rhubarb-type flower spikes. The cultivar *R.* 'Ace of Hearts' is slightly smaller and has heart-shaped foliage.

Rodgersia podophylla
  The heavily incised, sculptural leaves with a leathery, bronze effect is very distinctive. The plant enjoys damp soil, and contrasts well with ferns and hostas.

Prickly plants

The primary reason for prickles, thorns or spikes is to protect plants from marauders, usually grazing animals. In a garden, these plants can act as a cornerstone to the edge of the borders, preventing people, children and dogs from taking shortcuts or vandalizing plants. Many shrubs such as the prickly *Mahonia aquifolium* and *Berberis julianae* are useful for this task, but there are also several equally aggressive herbaceous plants that serve the same purpose. Most prickly plants cope well with dry conditions and associate pleasingly with more pliant grasses.

Acanthus spinosus
  Prickly mauve flower spires reminiscent of foxgloves, set off by dark green, divided leaves, make this species one of the most statuesque perennials. It can be invasive; it has a long taproot that tends to break off at the base when being dug out, which makes it difficult to eradicate.

Echinops ritro
> This is a handsome plant with elegant, prickly foliage and spherical, steel-blue flowerheads.

Eryngium × oliverianum and *E. variifolium*
> Various forms of sea holly that form prickly rosettes from stout stems and deeply cut leaves. *E. variifolium* has conspicuously veined, evergreen foliage and grey-blue flowers with interesting, white collars.

Onopordum acanthium
> Tall biennial boasting jagged leaves and pink flowers; dramatic near the back of the border. May be treated as a perennial because it will self-seed and replace itself every year.

Silybum marianum
> The biennial thistle is attractive when young, but quickly grows into a mature thug. Marbled, rosette leaves and thistle-like flowers. Like *Onopordum acanthium*, may be treated as a perennial because it self-seeds and replaces itself every year.

Glossy-leaved plants

The combination of shiny or smooth-leaved, light-reflective foliage together with matt or light-absorbent foliage is equally important in the choice of shrubs and herbaceous plants. When using herbaceous plants as ground cover, such foliage contrasts are particularly effective.

Arum italicum 'Pictum'
> Has curiously marbled, creamy-veined, and elongated, heart-shaped foliage. It dies down in summer before producing stalks of fat, vibrant orange berries.

Asarum europaeum
> Has rounded, gleaming, dark green leaves, and would form a pleasing combination with the finely cut foliage of *Corydalis flexuosa*.

Bergenia 'Bressingham White'
> Has large, rounded, glossy leaves and is ideal for accentuating corners of borders or as ground cover.

Waldsteinia ternata
> Produces trailing mats of glossy, tripartate foliage, which turns purplish in autumn. It makes excellent weed-suppressing ground cover at the base of a hedge. The small, bright yellow flowers in mid- and late spring are a bonus.

Felted plants

These very individual plants are the most tactile of plants. They are ideal for showing off other plant textures and patterns, their silvery leaves standing out well against green, red or yellow foliage. Because of their Mediterranean origins, they appreciate dry, sunny sites, quick-drying soil, good drainage and maximum exposure to light.

The fine, downy covering on the leaves not only protects the plants from heat, but also reduces the amount of green chlorophyll manufactured by the leaves and therefore the plant's ability to photosynthesize (make energy from light).

As well as in borders, felted-leaved plants look handsome when planted in gravel, which acts like a blanket mulch and reduces evaporation from the soil. If the plants self-seed, it is also easy to weed out any that are unwanted.

Artemisia ludoviciana
> Has dainty, silver, divided foliage; once established, tends to wander and can then be difficult to remove.

Artemisia 'Powis Castle'
> Has a more delicate, lacy texture of leaf than *Artemisia ludoviciana* and provides gentle, uniting contrasts. The soft pinks, purples and magentas of roses stand out against an underplanting of this artemisia's silvery foliage.

Salvia viridis
> One of the many felted-leaved sages, with conspicuous, purple flowers in summer.

Verbascum olympicum
> This spiky mullein has tall, golden flower spikes that dominate almost any border.

Using Colour in the Garden

Most of us crave plenty of colour in our gardens, but we rarely compose plantings with proper care. Consider each part of your garden—the location, such as a hedge or wall, and aspect, such as sun or shade—to decide how the backdrop may influence your choice. If your garden is small, consisting perhaps of an area of lawn or paving surrounded by planting beds, give each bed its own identity, according to whether it is in sun or shade. In a larger garden, the space could be divided up into a series of garden "rooms", each with its own colour scheme in the planting.

Try not to use a scattergun approach, using the same plant in the different areas, but instead keep a different planting palette for each area. If each area of the garden has its own individuality, the overall effect will not be boring or repetitive.

Key Points for Choosing Perennials for Colour

- As with all plants, don't forget to check that the plant is suited to the conditions in your garden.
- Choose herbaceous perennials that will be most colourful at the time of year when you want the planting to be at its beautiful peak.
- Perhaps use early spring perennials near the kitchen or back door—they will brighten up your entrance into the garden and remind you that summer is not far off.
- Concentrate summer flowers around your terrace or patio, where you can enjoy them while entertaining. If you entertain mostly in the evenings, choose pale colours, which show up well in the dusk.
- Consider whether you want the effect to be harmonious, tranquil or dramatic when composing your colour groupings, and choose your colours accordingly.
- Take account of the amount of light and shade or variations in light level that affect the planting site—they will affect both what perennials will thrive and whether their flowers will look their best.
- Consider the backdrop to your planting, be it wall, hedge, fence or shrubs, since it will affect how the colour of the perennials is perceived.
- Avoid combining shrubs and herbaceous plants with similar leaf shapes and shades of green—much foliage is a fairly deep mid-green. The border will look leaden and heavy.

Before being seduced by something in flower at your local nursery, consider the plant at all moments of its life—is it really going to provide what you need once the relatively brief flowering period is past?

Some herbaceous plants have very pretty early flowers but coarse leaves—perfectly acceptable when at the back of border against a wall, but not worthy of closer examination near the front of a border.

How light affects our perception of colour

Climate and sunlight varies in different countries and localities and greatly influences how we see colours. In hot, dry and often arid areas, the strength of the sun demands the strongest colour schemes. Reds and oranges seem more vibrant, especially if combined with a clash of purple, but pastel shades look washed out. By evening, when the sun has diminished in strength, paler shades become luminous.

In cooler climates, the light has a blue tinge, which brings life to pastel shades, especially in early morning or evening. Bright colours look strong around noon, but appear to dull down later in the day when softer shades of pale colours seem to come forth. In any climate, it is interesting to sit in the garden and observe how our perception of a particular flower colour changes according to the time of day and available light.

The Colour Spectrum

Colour and our appreciation of it is a huge and fascinating subject but, in considering the colours of herbaceous perennials, it is easiest to divide the colour themes into four separate categories. These can be:

- Hot or sunshine colours—bright yellows, oranges and reds

- Cool or pastel colours—pale pinks, blues, creamy whites, and perhaps some silvers

- Complementary colours—those which are opposite to each other in the colour spectrum or wheel, such as orange and blue, yellow and purple, or red and green

- Single colours—whites, yellows, blues, pinks or reds.

Cool colours

These are the pastel shades—pinks, pale blues, lavenders, mauves, lemons and creams—that show up so well in the blue-tinged light of the Northern Hemisphere. The cool colour border is the epitome of what is perceived as the English-garden style. These colours usually work well in shade or sun, although in a hot, sunny area the pastel shades may fade out and instead a stronger colour will be needed to compensate.

- Silver-leaved plants such as *Artemisia ludoviciana*, *Ballota pseudodictamnus* and *Stachys byzantina* are elegant foils for the cool shades of flowers.

- Avoid using too much white—far from being a "nothing" colour, it can be very strong in the garden, dazzling in bright sunlight. Beware of creating a spotty effect by using it sporadically.

- Pale hues may be used to influence the perspective of the garden; they tend to appear more distant than hot colours. If planted at the far ends or corners of beds, they seem to recede into the landscape, making the garden seem larger than it is.

- Many flowers in paler tints are highly scented, so selecting plants with this additional quality may help you to narrow down your choice.

Hot colours

These are the warm, "sunshine" hues that are in close proximity or merge into each other in the colour spectrum. Red merges into yellow to produce orange; yellow into blue to make green; blue into red to create purple or violet.

- Pastels and silvery greys look out of place in the hot-colour border. Even glaucous, green foliage can destroy the dramatic impact.

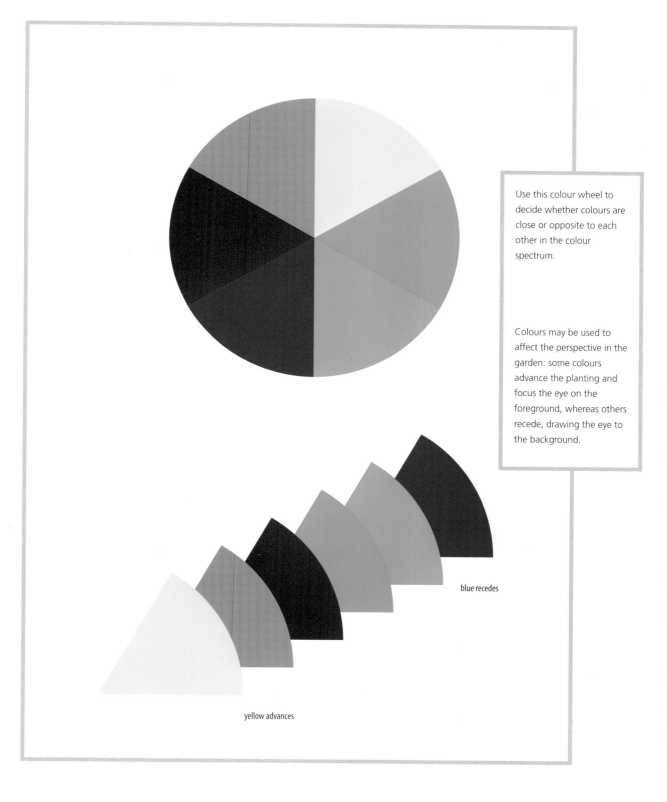

Use this colour wheel to decide whether colours are close or opposite to each other in the colour spectrum.

Colours may be used to affect the perspective in the garden: some colours advance the planting and focus the eye on the foreground, whereas others recede, drawing the eye to the background.

blue recedes

yellow advances

Hot colours

Neutral greenery

Cool colours

- Combine the perennial flowers with plum, purple or brownish foliage. Try shrubs such as *Acer palmatum* 'Bloodgood', *Berberis thunbergii* f. *atropurpurea*, *Cotinus coggygria* 'Notcutt's Variety' or *Weigela florida* 'Foliis Purpureis' or the foliage of perennials such as *Actaea, Canna, Euphorbia, Heuchera, Lobelia cardinalis* or *Ophiopogon planiscapus* 'Nigrescens'.

- Set against this foliage, use architectural perennials such as *Kniphofia* 'Royal Standard', whose flowers have citron-yellow bases and scarlet tips, or *Verbascum olympicum*, with its rosettes of felted, long, grey leaves and yellow flower spikes.

- Add the flat-topped flowers of *Achillea* 'Coronation Gold', vivid red dahlias such as *D.* 'Bishop of Llandaff', the tawny orange blooms of *Rudbeckia hirta* or even brilliantly hued nasturtiums.

- For hot foliage and flowers, try *Lysimachia ciliata* 'Firecracker' with mahogany leaves and modest yellow flowers. It can become rather invasive when established.

- For maximum impact, use the paler shades—lemons and yellows—at either end of a border, and build up through oranges to bright reds and scarlets in the centre.

- Position the hot border where it will be viewed at noon or in early afternoon; the vibrant tints lose their strength as daylight fades; in the low evening light, it will be hard to distinguish hot flower colours from the surrounding foliage.

- Hot hues may be used to alter the apparent perspective; they will seem closer than paler shades, so may be used to foreshorten a view, draw the eye, or bring an area forward.

Complementary colours

Through contemporary art and fashion, complementary colours, previously considered vulgar, have become highly accepted. In hot countries or where there is strong sunlight, a good contrast always draws the attention. Use tints that are opposite each other on the colour wheel, such as purple against yellow, red with green, or blue against orange. Since they share no pigment, juxtaposing two opposite hues has the effect of exaggerating or intensifying each, for better or worse.

Using opposite colours in gardens is a fairly recent phenomenon because previously gardeners tended to "play it safe". The exposure of gardening through the media has changed all this and we are now more adventurous with our use of colour.

Single colours

Every colour has unlimited variations of shade, and it is often helpful to use a decorator's paint colour chart as a reminder of the possible range of tones of one colour, for instance from pale to dark yellows or pale to purplish blues. Paint charts may also inspire you to experiment with colour schemes. Even in single colour plantings, a dash of another shade, such as blue in a mainly yellow scheme or bright pink in a white grouping, adds drama to the overall effect.

White—the most emulated single-colour garden is the white garden at Sissinghurst in Kent, England. This was the creation of Vita Sackville-West, who understood the importance both of seeing the simple freshness of white flowers against silver, spring green or white-variegated foliage and of how foliage was necessary as a foil to white flowers.

- Dark yew hedging can be a very elegant, rather stark, backdrop to white flowers.

- Mix white-flowered perennials with dark red-leaved *Sambucus nigra* f. *porphyrophylla* 'Guincho Purple' or dark green-leaved *Viburnum tinus*.

- One other single colour, such as yellow, blue or pink, may be used as a contrast to enliven the whites.

- Other pale perennials, for example *Achillea*, *Campanula* or the bluish-pink *Dianthus* 'Inchmery' may be used sparingly to lift the white scheme.

Yellow—there is probably a wider range of yellow plants than in any other shade or hue—cool tones vary from pale lemon veering towards lime green and warmer tones range from bright yellows through to golds, oranges and apricots.

- Pale yellows are best seen against fresh green foliage that will accentuate the greenish tones of the yellow.

- Brighter yellows or stronger oranges may need silver foliage, such as that of the slightly glaucous-leaved, tall *Macleaya cordata* (plume poppy), or bronze foliage, like that of the feathery *Foeniculum vulgare* 'Purpureum', to cool them down.

- In a shady situation, ferns provide a good, low-level foil to yellow flowers.

Red—there are two types of red tones or hues and neither type is as successful combined with the other as when used by itself. The blazing scarlet tones that work in the hot border contain a certain amount of yellow or copper.

- To make a red border glow, use perennials, such as the upright *Kniphofia* or the mat-forming *Monarda* 'Cambridge Scarlet' with its aromatic foliage, among shrubs such as the coppery purple-leaved *Corylus maxima* 'Purpurea' or the very dark purple-leaved *Physocarpus opulifolius* 'Diabolo': the dark contrast intensifies the brightness of red blooms.

– Cooler-toned crimson reds contain a certain amount of blue or purple, making them reminiscent of claret or burgundy.

– Red can be overdone, making the garden look heavy unless the wine shades are accentuated or lifted with yellows, the jagged, silver leaves of *Cynara cardunculus* or the dove-grey foliage of *Rosa glauca*.

– Shorter, paler or darker plants such as *Dianthus* or *Dicentra* can be used to ground the planting.

Blue—this is rarely used in a single colour scheme, possibly because in a bluish-toned natural light the blue is intensified until it appears cold. In full sunlight, bluish tones can appear washed out so that they seem almost to disappear; in shade, they retain their intensity. Much green foliage has a bluish tone, so the leaves may seem to merge with blue flowers. However, there is a wide range of flower in the blue spectrum, from palest lilac or lavender through to mid-blue and purple.

– The upright spikes of *Aconitum* 'Spark's Variety' contrast well with the huge, heart-shaped leaves of *Hosta sieboldiana* or the silvery *Artemisia absinthium* 'Lambrook Silver'.

– Handsome spires of blue delphiniums give height to a planting.

– *Geranium* 'Johnson's Blue' or the pale blue-flowered *G. pratense* 'Mrs Kendall Clark', with their rounded shapes, may be used in groups to provide a link between other more upright clumps or plants.

– Using the occasional touch of yellow, such as the frothy lemon flowers of *Alchemilla mollis* or the paler flowers of *Sisyrinchium striatum*, will lighten up a restricted purple or blue palette.

Care of Herbaceous Perennials

Unlike shrubs, perennials do not need pruning, but still need careful tending if they are to grow well. Planting is usually most successful if done in the autumn, while there is still some warmth in the soil, or in the spring, once the soil begins to warm up again. Planting in winter, when the plant is confined to cold and often damp soil before it can get its roots down and begin to put on growth, often leads to an early death.

Buying a plant

Choose a good specimen by making sure that there is some healthy, active growth on the plant, that no weeds are present on top of the compost and that there are no signs of pests, which might mean bringing an unwelcome stranger into your garden. You should also check that the plant is not pot-bound: if the roots do not have enough growing space in the pot, they will become twisted and tangled and circle the root ball, a condition from which they may sulk or never recover. Look for roots growing out of the bottom of the pot.

Herbaceous perennials are rarely effective when planted singly, so buy enough plants to set out in groups of three, five, seven or nine for maximum impact. Generally, the nursery or garden centre will have raised the plant carefully, so plant it as soon as possible rather than leave it lying out in the open until you feel inspired.

Planting perennials

Make a planting hole slightly larger than the size of the pot or root ball; if the soil is dry, soak the planting hole before planting. If the plant pot itself is dry, soak it well in a basin or bucket of water, allowing the root ball to take up plenty of moisture. Depending on the state of your soil, you may need to enrich it by mixing in some well-rotted compost and a slow-release fertilizer; this will get the plants off to a good start.

Before taking each plant out of its pot, remove any old or withered leaves. Knock out the plant and, if necessary, gently tease out the roots. Plant the perennial, with the root ball surface at the same level as it was in the pot, and tread it in carefully but firmly, to bring the roots into contact with the new soil. Finally, water it in well.

Taller plants, such as *Delphinium*, may need staking at planting or just when the plant begins to put on a growth spurt. Staking should be as discreet as possible—it is the plant you want to show off, not the support.

Deadhead perennials regularly to keep them flowering and encourage a second flush later in the season. Cut the flower spikes down to just above a leaf or new shoot.

Tall or floppy perennials may need to be staked at the beginning of the growing season; the emerging foliage will hide the supports as it grows.

Maintenance of perennials

Particularly when newly planted, and in hot, dry conditions, regular watering may be necessary. It is preferable to do this in early morning or in the evening, when loss of moisture during transpiration from the leaves is less likely.

To keep most flowering plants performing over a long period, they need regular deadheading. In the case of perennials, this usually means cutting out the spent stem right to the base of the plant. This will encourage new shoots to form and will help the plant to bulk up.

Most herbaceous perennials need to be cut back to their bases annually. It is debatable whether this is best done at the end of the season, known as the "back end" of the season, or at the start of the next growing season. Tender plants may benefit from the protection from frost afforded by leaving the dying foliage intact until spring. Also, as in the case of plants such as *Verbena bonariensis*, the overwintering seedheads are appreciated by birds.

Tender or borderline-hardy perennials may be protected over cold winters by a wigwam of bracken or straw, pegged or tied down to keep it in place, or by a covering of fleece or bubble wrap. Make sure that air can still circulate around the plant, otherwise the plant may "damp off", or rot.

Provided that the soil is in good order, herbaceous plants generally need no feeding other than a good mulch of well-rotted manure or compost spread over the beds in autumn—frosts over winter will soon break this up and worms will carry it down into the soil, improving its texture and soil structure. If some plants look slightly starved—yellowing of the leaves (chlorosis) may indicate this—a handful of fertilizer or bonemeal spread around the plant and watered in, or a liquid foliar feed, should improve the situation.

Recommended Herbaceous Perennials

There are so many different plants available that it is difficult to make a choice, but most plants will thrive only if they are given similar conditions to those where they originated in the wild. Most of the perennials in this list have many different cultivars too numerous to mention here, so it is up to you to research the best one for your colour scheme.

Dry, shaded soils

Aconitum
Aquilegia
Centranthus
Digitalis
Euphorbia amygdaloides var. *robbiae*
Geranium
Helleborus
Lamium
Persicaria
Symphytum
Tellima
Tiarella
Waldsteinia

Dry soils in sun

Acaena
Acanthus
Agapanthus
Alchemilla
Artemisia
Ballota
Centranthus
Dianthus
Echinops
Erigeron
Eryngium
Erysimum (biennial, but self-seeds)
Euphorbia
Gaura

Kniphofia
Macleaya
Nepeta
Onopordum (biennial, but self-seeds)
Origanum
Osteospermum
Papaver
Penstemon
Rudbeckia
Salvia
Sedum
Stachys
Thymus
Verbascum
Verbena

Deep, moist soils

Actaea
Astilbe
Astrantia
Caltha
Convallaria
Darmera
Eupatorium
Filipendula
Gentiana
Geum
Gunnera
Hemerocallis
Hosta
Iris germanica (use as a spiky perennial)
Ligularia
Monarda
Persicaria
Primula
Pulmonaria
Rheum
Rodgersia
Sanguisorba
Smilacina
Thalictrum

Tricyrtis
Trollius
Zantedeschia

Handsome foliage

Acanthus
Anemone japonica
Angelica
Aralia
Aruncus
Bergenia
Cirsium rivulare 'Atropurpureum'
Crambe
Cynara
Filipendula
Foeniculum
Gunnera
Hosta
Inula
Ligularia
Macleaya
Onopordum (biennial, but self-seeds)
Paeonia
Persicaria polymorpha
Rheum
Rodgersia
Sedum telephium 'Matrona'

In addition to spring bulbs, there are many other bulbs, such as cyclamen and lilies, available that perform at other times of the year, as well as newer cultivars of the old favourites. It is possible to use bulbs to bring interest to the garden in every month of the year. Autumn-flowering bulbs help to bring a garden to a lively close at the end of the season, and associate well with berries and autumn foliage. Some autumn bulbs, for example *Colchicum*, are more or less leafless when flowering, so low-growing silver or grey plants make good foils for the flowers.

Both spring and autumn bulbs flower when there is little else on show, so you could ignore carefully planned colour schemes and experiment with gaudy tulips or cerise-flowered cyclamen. The latter are striking when grown through the black, grass-like perennial *Ophiopogon planiscapus* 'Nigrescens'. Early-flowering crocuses, the spikes of *Camassia quamash*, and the dark *Tulipa* 'Queen of Night' are invaluable bulbs to start the flowering season.

There are many other varieties and cultivars of bulbs other than those listed here and it is worth seeking out a reliable supplier, with a well-illustrated catalogue, to help you make your choice. Buying bulbs from a garden centre may be less successful because you are unlikely to know how long they have been in stock, especially when it gets towards the end of the retail season and the bulbs start to dry out and shrivel.

Bulbs in the Garden

Any garden, new or existing, can be transformed by investing in bulbs. The vibrant flower colours of the very early bulbs enliven a dull time of the year when our jaded spirits eagerly await spring. Many traditional bulbs, such as *Crocus*, *Hyacinthus* and *Tulipa* give superb value, but there is a gradual but continual shift towards more unusual bulbs, such as *Allium*, *Camassia* and *Erythronium*.

Eranthis and *Galanthus*

Flowering in mid- or late winter, among the earliest bulbs are the golden yellow *Eranthis* (winter aconite) and double or single *Galanthus* (snowdrop). Winter aconites prefer sun or dappled shade, perhaps at the base of a hedge, whereas snowdrops may be grown in shade or partial sunshine. They look good in borders, in rough grass, or in light woodland where they emerge before the leaf canopy of the deciduous trees casts deep shade.

What is a Bulb?

A true bulb consists of fleshy "scales" (modified leaves) wrapped round a growing point, as in an onion; typical examples are bulbous *Iris*, *Narcissus* and *Tulipa*. True bulbs also may have overlapping scales, like *Lilium*. Other types of bulbous plant are also commonly referred to as bulbs.

- Corms are formed from swollen underground stems—such as *Crocosmia* and *Gladiolus*.
- Tubers may be either modified starchy stems, as in *Cyclamen*, or swollen sections of root—for example, *Dahlia*.
- Rhizomes are swollen horizontal stems, as in some *Iris*.

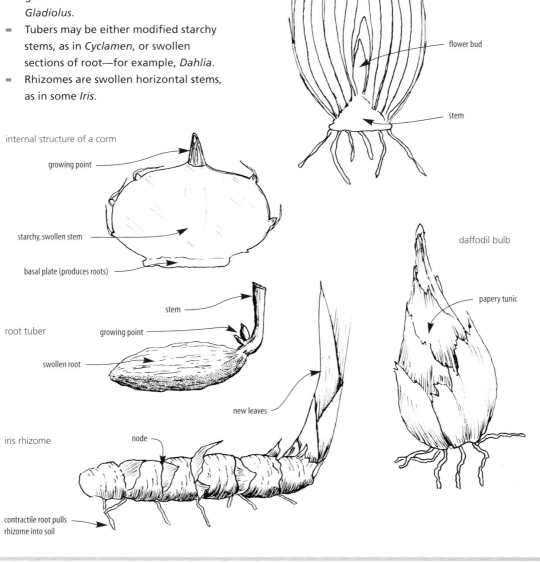

internal structure of a bulb

fleshy leaves

flower bud

stem

internal structure of a corm

growing point

starchy, swollen stem

basal plate (produces roots)

daffodil bulb

papery tunic

root tuber

stem

growing point

swollen root

new leaves

iris rhizome

node

contractile root pulls rhizome into soil

Most spring bulbs are available from bulb growers from the end of summer, after a seasonal drying-off period. However, winter aconites and snowdrops do not respond well to such treatment and are best bought and planted "in the green". This means that they are lifted during or immediately after flowering, are split up or divided by gently separating the congested clumps, then replanted in groups of ten to fifteen or twenty.

Do not plant them too deeply, but at the same level in the soil as they were before. This is indicated by the "soil mark", that is where the main stem changes from white (because it was buried and received no natural light) to green. Firm in the plants gently and water them after planting; allow the foliage to die off or decay naturally.

The more unusual *Galanthus* have recently become collectors' items. Over 150 cultivars and varieties are recorded and high prices are paid for the some, such as *G.* 'S. Arnott' or *G.* 'Magnet'. Most gardeners are content with the simpler, single-flowered (*G. nivalis*) or double-flowered (*G. nivalis* f. *pleniflorus* 'Flore Pleno') snowdrops, which bulk up quickly, are effective when left to naturalize, and at their best planted in groups.

Hyacinthus

Usually forced as indoor plants, *Hyacinthus orientalis* and its cultivars are also excellent for bedding or borders, where their early, scented flowers give unexpected pleasure. When forced indoors, they bloom in mid- to late winter; outdoors, they perform in early to mid-spring. Old favourites for forcing, such as the white-flowered *H. orientalis* 'L'Innocence' and blue-flowered 'King of the Blues' or 'Delft Blue', are usually the most fragrant. For earliest indoor flowering, choose prepared bulbs, which are specially treated to bloom early. Plant the bulbs directly on arrival in early autumn, then keep them cool in darkness, and they will bloom indoors by Christmas or soon after.

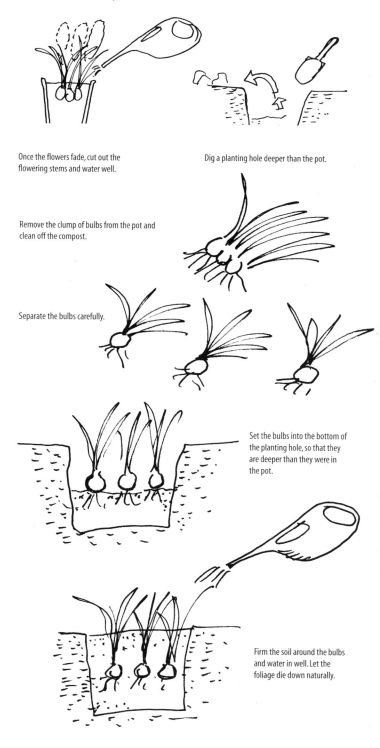

Planting out indoor hyacinth bulbs

Once the flowers fade, cut out the flowering stems and water well.

Remove the clump of bulbs from the pot and clean off the compost.

Separate the bulbs carefully.

Dig a planting hole deeper than the pot.

Set the bulbs into the bottom of the planting hole, so that they are deeper than they were in the pot.

Firm the soil around the bulbs and water in well. Let the foliage die down naturally.

Avoid the temptation to buy the largest and most expensive size, around 18 cm (7 in.), of bulb; the flower spikes often become top heavy and need elaborate staking. It is better to use medium-sized bulbs, about 15 cm (6 in.), because the blooms will look more natural. Outdoor hyacinths do not usually need staking, but when indoor varieties are brought into our homes, they respond to the heat by growing too quickly and keeling over.

Perhaps preferable to staking is the almost invisible method of keeping the flowers upright by inserting a short length of stiff wire through the top of the hollow flowering stalk. Make sure that the wire is long enough to pierce deep into the bulb itself. After the indoor bulbs have finished flowering, they may be planted in a border, perhaps to grow through evergreen ground cover, such as *Stachys byzantina*, that will cover their rather thick stalks.

Outdoor hyacinths may be grown very successfully in containers or in borders where they will flower in spring. Plant them in informal groups of five or seven, with the tops of the bulbs about 5 cm (2 in.) below the surface of the soil. Their foliage will take time to die off after flowering: place them under deciduous shrubs so that the bulbs will receive light before the shrub foliage appears. Alternatively, put them near the front of a border among low-growing, herbaceous foliage plants which will act as foils to the hyacinth flower spikes.

Crocus

Crocuses provide a striking effect in lawns, at the edge of beds and borders or in a gravel garden. Avoid large-flowered cultivars, which are more suited to making a show in public open spaces: instead choose from the smaller, spring-flowering, species crocuses.

Crocuses open to reveal the true beauty of their inner petals only in full sun, so need to be placed carefully. Plant them about 5 cm (2 in.) below the soil surface in large groups of fifteen or more. Perhaps choose a

site in grass at the base of and around the roots of a tree where their dying foliage will not be mown off too soon after they have flowered. If left undisturbed, and provided that mice do not discover them, crocuses thrive in any soil and multiply rapidly.

The first to bloom in early spring are *C. chrysanthus* 'Zwanenburg Bronze', with golden yellow flowers that have contrasting bronze exteriors, and *C. tommasinianus* 'Barr's Purple', with silver-lilac, outer petals and an amethyst-violet interior. *C. chrysanthus* 'Snow Bunting' is the best white and *C. chrysanthus* 'Blue Pearl' an excellent blue.

Autumn crocuses flower in early to mid-autumn and are also versatile and excellent for naturalizing in sunny, well-drained soil. The lilac-purple and conspicuously veined *C. sativus* (saffron crocus which has red-orange stamens prized by cooks) and *C. speciosus* in bright violet-blue are a fresh delight when most garden plants have faded.

Mice and birds are fond of crocus bulbs. Planting the bulbs at the edges of gravel paths seems to help to deter mice; the bulbs also appreciate the drainage provided by the gravel. Birds may be deterred by stringing black cotton through twigs above the crocuses, or by sticking thin florist's wire into the ground between the bulbs—the birds cannot then get sufficiently close to peck at the crocus stamens.

Narcissus

Daffodils are usually the next bulbs to flower after crocuses, and for the uninitiated there is a quite bewildering choice. Slightly shorter species and cultivars, up to about 20 cm (8 in.) tall, usually look better in borders. At the time of their flowering, from early to late spring, there is little else to compete for attention. If the bulbs are planted near the rear of a border, possibly against a wall, they will be displayed effectively. The emerging leaves of other plants will hide the dying foliage and the bulbs are less likely to be disturbed if the soil is dug over in autumn.

Try the scented *N. cyclamineus* cultivars such as 'February Gold', with lemon flowers that have orange-yellow frilled trumpets, white-flowered 'Jenny' or 'Jetfire', with clear yellow blooms that have orange cups. These are about 30 cm (12 in.) tall, should flower in early or mid-spring, and bulk up well, if the foliage is allowed to die off naturally.

Slightly later but equally decorative, robust and also scented are *N.* 'Hawera', which is 20 cm (8 in.) tall with two or more pendent, soft yellow flowers to a stem, or *N.* 'Thalia', a 30 cm (12 in.) tall, snow-white multiflowered cultivar.

For the front of the border or tucked in among other plants, miniature or species narcissi can be useful. *N.* 'Tête-à-Tête' is only 15 cm (6 in.) tall and has small, butter-yellow trumpets. *N.* 'Rip Van Winkle' has dwarf, double, yellow flowers. *N.* 'W.P. Milner' has flowers that are a pale sulphur-yellow, changing to creamy white.

Many of the older, larger varieties and cultivars of narcissi, such as the trumpet *N.* 'King Alfred', tend to look coarse in a garden setting and are best when naturalized in rough grass, perhaps in an orchard. There are many large-cupped, golden yellow narcissi, but there are some about 35 cm (14 in.) tall and slightly more refined in their colours.

Examples are *N.* 'Mount Hood', with creamy white flowers; *N.* 'Barrett Browning', with flowers that have a white skirt of petals (perianth) and orange-red crown (corona); *N.* 'Actaea' or *N. poeticus* var. *recurvus* (pheasant eye narcissus), both with white perianths and yellow or deep red eyes in the flowers. The latter is the last to flower and very fragrant.

Tulipa

Simultaneously with, or soon after, the narcissi flowering, tulips bring a kaleidoscope of colours to borders, although as an investment they are short-lived and do not bulk up in temperate-climate gardens. When grown in the wild in Turkey or other mountainous Mediterranean countries, the bulbs are baked and ripened by the sun after flowering. In cooler regions where this does not happen, some tulips will fail to perform the following year, whether they are left in the soil, where they sometimes rot off or shatter, or whether they are lifted and kept dry for replanting next season. Some gardeners treat tulips as annuals, lifting and discarding them after flowering, and buying them in afresh every season.

The Dutch tulip enthusiasts of the 17th century introduced a classification system based on flowering times, which is still is use today, with additional divisions to include groups of new hybrids with similar characteristics. Some of the main groups are listed below. Two other types of tulips also worth growing are Parrot tulips, with curled and twisted petals reminiscent of early Dutch flower paintings, and Viridiflora tulips, such as *T.* 'Spring Green', whose ivory petals have a delicate feathering of green.

Species tulips

The earliest varieties to flower, from early to mid-spring, are the single-flowered, short-stemmed tulips, which are ideal for tubs, terraces and borders. Look for varieties such as these, some with mottled leaves and in bright colours:

- *T. fosteriana*
- *T. greigii*
- *T. kaufmanniana*
- *T. linifolia*, a beautifully formed scarlet flower
- *T. praestans*, multiflowered in orange red.

Single- or double-flowered early tulips

The main tulip season extends from mid-spring to the end of late spring, beginning with single- or double-flowered early varieties and cultivars, such as:

- *T.* 'Couleur Cardinal', 30 cm (12 in.) tall, single and a most remarkable, scarlet-shaded, plum flower

- *T.* 'Generaal de Wet', 40 cm (16 in.) tall, single, with orange, fragrant blooms

- *T.* 'Peach Blossom', the old favourite, is 25 cm (10 in.) tall, with double, deep rose, flushed-white flowers.

Triumph tulips

These flower slightly later than most tulips, such as *T.* 'Abu Hassan', which is 45 cm (18 in.) tall and has a dark mahogany flower with a narrow, yellow edge to the petals. Among the most uncommon and beautiful are the fringed tulips, with exotically fringed petals, for example:

- *T.* 'Negrita', a glowing purple violet

- *T.* 'Passionale', lilac-purple.

As they mature, both tend to flop a little, so are best planted near low shrubs that may support them.

Single- and double-flowered late tulips

Flowering towards the end of late spring, these tulips provide a brilliant range of different colours. Among the best and varying in height are:

- *T.* 'Angélique', a double, pale pink flower in pale and dark shades

- *T.* 'Maureen', a single, fragrant flower in marble-white.

Lily-flowering tulips

Single-flowered with strong stems and elegantly pointed petals, lily-flowering tulips also perform towards the end of late spring. They are about 45 cm (18 in.) tall, and are some of the best tulips for planting in borders.

- *T.* 'West Point' has a fragrant, primrose-yellow bloom.

- *T.* 'White Triumphator' has a pure white flower.

Colchicum

These are also known erroneously as autumn crocuses. They thrive in any soil but need deep planting—at least 15 cm (6 in.). Plant *Colchicum* corms in late summer or early autumn. Big, rather coarse leaves follow their large, striking flowers, so plant them at the base of a mature shrub or where the foliage will not intrude. *C. autumnale* 'Album' soon brightens up and contrasts with evergreen shrubs.

Summer- and Autumn-flowering Bulbs

There are many other bulbs available to the gardener to enliven borders, sunny or shady areas, woodland or wildflower meadows. They range from the stately spires of *Fritillaria persica* to the low-growing *Muscari armeniacum* (grape hyacinth), which associates so well with the herbaceous perennial *Alchemilla mollis*. Once the *Muscari* have flowered, the soft leaves of the *Alchemilla* emerge.

Allium
A wide range of these ornamental onions is available, with spherical, pendent or flat-topped flowerheads, some extremely large. They look excellent with roses or among shrubs. Plant them in autumn.

Camassia
The blue or white flowers are produced in late spring or early summer on long, strong stems. The tall plants naturalize readily in grassland. The bulbs of *C. quamash* (formerly *C. esculenta*, which means "edible") were dug up and eaten by American Indians.

Cardiocrinum

An enormous plant, closely related to the lily. It grows to 2 m (6½ ft.) tall, with large leaves that demand about 1 m (3 ft.) of space, but it is then exhausted so it dies. It may be propagated from offsets found around the spent parent.

Crocosmia

Produces vivid red, orange or yellow flowers in late summer and forms a new corm each year to replace the old one. There are a number of excellent cultivars, many available from better nurseries as potted plants.

Cyclamen

Species flower in autumn, winter or spring. *C. hederifolium* has silvery green leaves that look rather like ivy.

Eucomis

An unusual member of the lily family (Liliaceae), often called the pineapple flower. Flowers are very striking: white, green or pinkish. They are effective in pots and will last for several weeks in good conditions.

Galtonia

Only *G. candicans* is widely available; it is a stately plant, rather like a giant snowdrop.

Gladiolus

As well as the tall gladioli usually seen in florists' shops, there are more delicate plants, such as *G.* 'The Bride', which has white, starry flowers with greenish blotches. Gladioli may be grown in pots, but may need staking.

Iris

There are a huge number of bulbous and rhizomatous irises, in all sorts of sizes and colours, and for different conditions. A few of the best are *I. ensata*, *I. foetidissima*, *I. germanica*, *I.* 'Jane Phillips', *I. pallida*, *I. pseudacorus* and *I. sibirica*. The early-flowering *I. danfordiae* seems to thrive and flower in most situations except shade, but enjoys being baked by the sun so is useful in dry, sunny areas.

Ixia

The South African corn lily should be planted in spring for flowering in early to midsummer. They are 30–45 cm (12–18 in.) tall, with starry flowers in red, white, purple, pink or yellow on dense spikes. Not reliably hardy.

Lilium

There are 80 or so known species of this group of hardy, summer flowerers. Good drainage is essential—if it is not available, grow them in in pots, tipping them out and plunging them into soil when the flowering stems are about 15 cm (6 in.) tall. They also like adequate moisture. Plant lilies in mid-autumn or soon after. Some are not lime-tolerant and cannot grow on alkaline soils—use ericaceous potting compost instead. The bulbs may be propagated from scales if the basal plate is intact.

Nerine

N. bowdenii is the only truly hardy variety and needs a warm, protected site. The bulb needs to be baked in summer, so plant it just below the soil surface.

Sternbergia
A crocus-like plant, but in the case of
S. lutea with yellow, goblet-shaped flowers.
They must be planted immediately after
purchase, in early autumn.

Triteleia
The variety *T. laxa* has funnel-shaped, blue
flowers. Needs a sunny position, with
good drainage—perhaps at the front of
the border, with gritty soil worked in.

Zantedeschia
The arum lily, with funnel-like spathes, is
good in pots as well as the garden. It likes
a rich soil with plenty of moisture.
A number of new cultivars, such as
Z. aethiopica 'Green Goddess', are now
generally available.

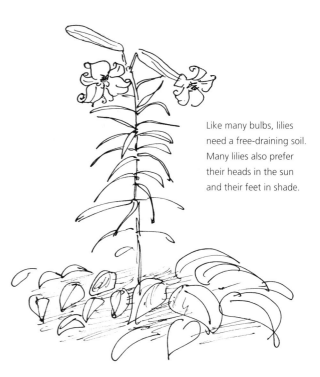

Like many bulbs, lilies
need a free-draining soil.
Many lilies also prefer
their heads in the sun
and their feet in shade.

Cultivation of Bulbs

The basic rule of planting bulbs is to do so when
they are dormant: for spring-flowering bulbs, this
will be in early autumn. Most summer-flowering
bulbs are on sale from late winter and may be
planted as soon as they are bought or kept in a cool
place until the soil warms up a little in early or mid-
spring. The exceptions are lilies, which should be
planted as soon as they become available, in the
autumn or early spring, because their root growth
begins early on. Autumn-flowering bulbs should be
planted from late summer onwards.

As a general rule, plant bulbs, corms and tubers at
about their own depth in heavy soil, and up to twice
their depth in light sandy soil or very dry places. In
heavy or damp soils, bed the bulbs on a layer of sand
to improve the drainage. Even the smallest bulbs
should have at least 5 cm (2 in.) of soil above them.
Make sure you plant them the right way up: look for
the dormant buds and make sure that they point
upwards. If planting rhizomes, for instance of irises,
plant them just below the soil surface, allowing the
uppermost surfaces to be exposed to the sun, and
keep them free of manure which might make them
rot off. Plant summer-flowering bulbs in pots in a
soil-based potting mix.

Try not to mix spring- and summer-flowering bulbs
in the same area as autumn-flowerers: their growth
cycles are diametrically opposed and they need
different treatment. During summer, the autumn- and
winter-flowerers are dormant and need the warmth
of the sun and dry conditions to ripen their bulbs,
while the summer-flowerers need moisture as long as
they are in active growth.

General care
The aim should be to provide the right conditions for
healthy flowering growth so that the bulb can build
up as large a reserve of food as possible, which it will
need to produce flowering shoots in the next growing
season. Bulbs generally require a well-drained soil

enriched with much sand and humus, an alkaline or chalky one being preferable to acid soil. Most bulbs will grow happily in grass, provided that it is not cut until the leaves of the latest-flowering bulbs have died down. The soil should be kept on the dry side during the summer months.

Other than these requirements, most bulbs are undemanding in their needs. Spent flowerheads and stems may be removed, but the leaves should be left to wither until they can easily be pulled from the bulb. As they die, the energy in the leaves is taken back into the bulb and is stored as starch to feed the bulb until the next growing season. Do not follow the out-of-date technique of tying up the dying leaves neatly in bundles; this hinders the food-storage process.

Congested clumps of bulbs should be lifted and divided after flowering to keep them healthy.

Iris rhizomes may be divided, with a knife or by hand, into sections each with at least one good bud.

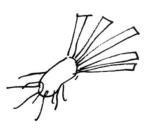

Cut down the leaves to about 15 cm (6 in.).

Replant each division so that the rhizome shows slightly above the soil.

Although it is not really necessary to feed bulbs, doing so will help to improve their performance. Use feeds with an N:P:K: (Nitrogen:Phosphate:Potash) ratio of approximately 15:15:30. Apply the feed when the bulbs are coming into growth at the beginning of the growing season. For smaller bulbs, two or three applications at two-weekly intervals are sufficient. Scatter the fertilizer on the soil around the plants; it will be carried down by rain or by watering. For large bulbs such as lilies, feed weekly right through the growing and flowering period with a liquid feed. Summer-flowering bulbs in pots should be kept watered and given a liquid feed every 14 days.

Bulb problems

Slugs, snails, caterpillars, and lily beetles are the most frequent pests of bulbous plants. Hand picking is the best method of removal, but not always feasible or pleasant. Signs of virus infection are yellowish-streaked leaves, splashes of discoloration or distorted growth. Virus diseases are mostly incurable: burn any infected plants to stop the disease spreading. Fungal disease is often the result of poor cultivation, for instance grey mould (botrytis) occurs in damp, still air and on overcrowded plants. See Chapter 5 (pages 314–335) for details of individual pests and diseases.

Alpine and Rock-garden Plants

There is a distinction between alpine and rock-garden plants. True alpines grow above the tree line in the wild, are able to cope with low temperatures and cold winds, are low-growing and usually flower in spring. They respond well to full sun and do not like to be damp. In their native habitats, they seek out water by developing deep roots, which also lock them into the soil or rocks. Rock-garden plants are easier to grow than alpines and are simply small, slow-growing plants suited to well-drained, small spaces. Their flowering periods usually extend well into summer and autumn.

Making a Rock Garden

Rock gardens were very popular in the middle of the last century, but have recently fallen out of favour; too often they were used as a way of disposing of building rubble. However, rock gardens can be particularly suitable solutions for sloping or precipitous sites and creating a miniature mountain scene can give tremendous satisfaction. For an authentic setting, choose a place free from shade and clear of overhanging trees. The main ingredients are rocks, soil, and plants.

Rocks

Garden centres often sell naturally weathered rocks or boulders, but these tend to be small and unconvincing, so it is better to seek out a local quarry. Their rocks will be appropriate to your locality and will be larger, so may be used to create a more realistic outcrop. All the rocks should be of a single type, whether slate, sandstone or granite.

Set the rocks into a gently sloping bank by cutting into it, or mark out the boundaries of a flat site with string and sand. To look natural, it is important that the "strata lines" run horizontally and that the rocks are partially buried so that they appear to grow out of the soil. Even on a flat site, the rocks should appear to emerge naturally through the soil, so some soil contouring may be necessary.

A narrow channel may be left for a stream, with the water cascading over the rocks; however, this is a more complicated procedure and you may need to employ experienced builders to achieve a successful result. You will also need a pump to circulate the water supply.

Soil

Good drainage is vital for establishing alpine and rock-garden plants, so impoverished, well-drained, gravelly soil is an ideal base. Make planting pockets by using a mixture of weed-free topsoil with an

A rocky terrace looks best with all the strata lines running the same way.

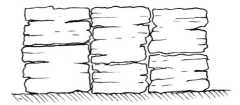

Building up rocks on top of one another creates extra height.

Terracing the rocks and leaning them backwards slightly allows rainwater to run off their surfaces into the pockets of soil; it also looks more natural.

Planting a Trough

- A miniature version of a rock garden or scree bed may be created in troughs or sinks. Find a trough in farmyards or junk shops if possible, or use the reconstituted or fibre-glass versions available from garden centres. Scrub out the container with mild disinfectant before beginning to plant it up.

- Set it up on the ground or raise it up on legs made from stones or bricks.

- Make sure that there are adequate drainage holes, and place the sink in its intended position before planting up so that it is not too heavy to lift. Spread a very thick layer of drainage crocks or pebbles to cover the bottom of the sink.

- Fill the trough with a potting mixture. The mixture should not be too heavy, so use a compost based on peat, or a peat-substitute, which is lighter than a loam-based mix. A good mix is one of 50% peat, 25% grit and 25% loam; add a handful of slow-release fertilizer per bucket of compost. This mixture will allow good growth and drainage.

- Place a group of small rocks, or old pieces of rugged tree bark, strategically on the surface of the potting mixture for added interest.

- Since sinks and troughs are relatively low in comparison with their width, it seems natural to plant them with low plants; tall plants tend to look out of proportion.

- When planting, make a hole in the compost using a plastic pot that is the same size as the root ball of the plant. Then tip the plant out of its pot, insert it into the prepared space, and firm.

- Add a 2.5 cm (1 in.) layer of grit as a mulch to conserve moisture and suppress weeds.

- All alpine plants must be protected from winter wet, otherwise they will rot and die. Drive a small stick into each corner of the sink or trough and balance a pane of glass, or clear PVC, on top. The glass must not touch the plants, so leave a gap of 15 cm (6 in.) between them and the glass. Make sure that the plants receive plenty of ventilation.

equal bulk of grit, then add peat substitute equivalent to half the amount of topsoil and grit. Make sure that this mix contains no fertilizer because alpine plants dislike overfeeding. Use a trowel or dibber to plant, checking that the cracks and crevices are well filled and that the plants are pressed firmly into the soil before they are watered in.

Once the area is planted, spread a layer of coarse grit or chippings to act as a mulch and keep down weeds. This top dressing of gravel also prevents the crowns of the plants from becoming too damp and rotting off. If a scree effect is required, mulch the area between the rocks with matching gravel.

Plants

For the rock garden, some dwarf conifers and shrubs will be needed; choose conifers whose outline—whether upright, horizontal or rounded—will balance and enhance the rock formation. Add some structural shrubs, such as small forms of early-flowering *Daphne* or azalea types of *Rhododendron*.

Bulbs may be included for early spring and autumn colour, but try to choose species that may be found naturally in this type of landscape. *Crocus chrysanthus*, for example, is a good choice, rather than the larger, cultivated hybrids, which would be out of scale in this type of garden.

Some alpine and rock-garden plants prefer acid conditions, others neutral or alkaline soil, so select plants appropriate to the soil of your garden. Smaller specimens will be easier to squeeze into the soil pockets.

There is an enormous range of attractive alpine and rock-garden plants; many are commonly available. Included in the recommendations below are some choice and unusual varieties and cultivars—you may not find them easily, but the search is worthwhile.

Recommended Rock-garden Plants

Berberis × *stenophylla* 'Corallina Compacta'
   A neat, rounded, miniature shrub. Coral-red buds open to orange-yellow flowers.

Campanula poscharskyana 'Stella'
   Deep mauve, starry flowers, trailing habit.

Cerastium alpinum
   Silver foliage, small flowers, trailing habit. Good ground cover for a dry, sunny situation.

Convolvulus sabatius
   Blue flowers on trailing stems.

Corydalis cheilanthifolia
   Bronze, evergreen, ferny foliage and yellow flowers.

Dianthus alpinus
   Vigorous plant with pink flowers that have dark red rings.

Erodium 'County Park'
   Mauve flowers all summer.

Geranium cinereum
   Bright pink flowers.

Helianthemum 'Annabel'
   Double, pink flowers.

Iris cristata 'Alba'
   Small flowers; needs good drainage.

Lewisia cotyledon Sunset Group
   Rosettes of fleshy leaves, pink, orange or red flowers, 15 cm (6 in.) tall.

Lithodora diffusa
   Brilliant blue flowers, trailing habit.

Origanum microphyllum
   Whorls of pale pink flowers.

Phlox douglasii 'Crackerjack'
   Deep magenta flowers.

Primula 'Lady Greer'
   Small heads of soft yellow flowers.

Saxifraga 'Alba'
   Tiny, green rosettes forming a dome; small, white flowers in spring.

Sedum album 'Coral Carpet'
   Coral-pink foliage, pink flowers.

Sempervivum arachnoideum subsp. *tomentosum*
   Silvery, cobwebbed rosettes, deep pink flowers.

Sisyrinchium idahoense blue
   Lavender-blue flower with yellow eye.

Tanacetum haradjanii
   Lovely, grey, ferny foliage.

Thymus pulegioides 'Archer's Gold'
   Mat-forming, yellow foliage.

Veronica peduncularis 'Georgia Blue'
    Dark green foliage; very pretty, bright blue
    flowers.

Viola cornuta
    Lovely, soft lavender-blue flowers over
    a long period.

Viola riviniana Purpurea Group
    Deep purple-black foliage, lavender
    flowers.

Zauschneria californica 'Western Hills'
    Grey-green foliage, orange-red flowers in
    early autumn.

Ferns

Ferns are some of the loveliest of growing things and also among the oldest. They have dominated our vegetation since long before the dinosaur. Their diversity and intricacy of form is fascinating. Although they do not produce flowers, these age-old plants can be highly decorative. The often architectural foliage may be evergreen or deciduous. They vary in size from small and dainty ferns, only a few centimetres or inches tall, to massive, dominant species such as the dramatic *Dicksonia antarctica* (tree fern) from New Zealand. Many ferns are native to Britain; in Victorian times, ferns almost had a cult following. Families would set out on fern forays, returning with prize specimens dug up from the countryside—which is unacceptable behaviour today. The trophies were then planted in the garden or, if air pollution was bad, in cool conditions under glass.

For a natural effect, smaller ferns should be planted in staggered groups of three, five or in larger, uneven numbers. Alternatively, use individual, larger plants, such as the elegant *Polystichum setiferum*, to make a single but show-stopping statement. Place ferns near a path or the front of a border so that the intriguing, new fronds may be admired as they unfurl. You could also combine two or three different types of leaf form. For instance, combine the simple, glossy, evergreen blade of *Asplenium scolopendrium* with the delicate, deeply divided fronds of *Athyrium filix-femina* and the stiff, glossy, leathery ones of *Polystichum aculeatum*. For dramatic effect, consider *Dicksonia antarctica*, with fronds that will eventually reach 1.8 m (6 ft.) long emerging from a thick trunk.

Ferns associate well with other shade-loving plants with handsome foliage, such as *Hosta*, *Pulmonaria*, *Rheum* and *Rodgersia*. Other good companion plants are small, early-spring bulbs such as *Galanthus* and species *Narcissus*; the unfurling fern fronds hide the dying bulb foliage in late spring.

Botany of Ferns

The life cycle of a fern is different from most garden plants, and you are more likely to grow them well if you understand their basic structure.

- The vital part of the fern is the rootstock, which contains the meristem (growing point). Rootstocks, sometimes referred to as rhizomes, vary. They sometimes remain as compact tufts, while others creep, expanding or colonizing at, or just below, soil level.

- The actual roots are fine and much branched and remain in the upper soil level.

- The leaf, or part that is most decorative, is known as the frond. The blade of the frond either extends to soil level, as in *Athyrium filix-femina*, or is supported by a stem, as in *Blechnum spicant* or *Dryopteris*. The fronds may be entire or simple, as with *Woodwardia fimbriata* (chain fern), or divided in one of several degrees of complexity, such as *Polystichum setiferum* 'Divisilobum Laxum'.

- Ferns reproduce by means of fruiting bodies called sori. These clusters of tiny capsules are produced on the undersides of fertile fronds in an asexual stage of reproduction. They contain spores, which are similar to seeds but have no embryos. The spore germinates in moist soil in the sexual stage of reproduction to form a flat, green mass of cells known as the prothallus, which produces male and female organs. In the moisture film in the soil, the mobile, male organ releases spermatozoa to fertilize the female organ; once combined, they begin to produce the first tiny fronds from the prothallus.

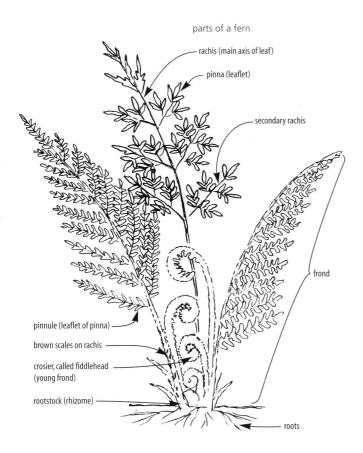

parts of a fern

rachis (main axis of leaf)

pinna (leaflet)

secondary rachis

frond

pinnule (leaflet of pinna)

brown scales on rachis

crosier, called fiddlehead (young frond)

rootstock (rhizome)

roots

Cultivating Ferns

To grow ferns successfully, it is helpful to understand their preferred conditions. In their natural habitats, they grow in the shade of light woodland, amid an undisturbed layer of decaying leaf litter, or in shady nooks and crevices. The soil in these habitats generally has an open structure, free drainage, and high humus content. Most ferns need a fairly damp situation, but there are a few that can cope with dry soil. Above all, they are shallow-rooting plants that like a stable root environment and resent being disturbed.

Contrary to general opinion, ferns do not require acid soil, but do grow best in conditions that replicate the sheltered, dappled or full shade of their wild habitats. Most ferns (particularly the larger types with delicate fronds) dislike high winds, which can bruise them and dry out the soil. Avoid siting them in strong sunlight—the fronds become scorched or bleached and new growth shrivels up.

Some ferns tolerate dry shade such as at the bases of walls, provided that they are well watered during the first season; other ferns are adapted to living on rock-faces or colonizing man-made walls. Some exotic species such as *Cyathea australis* are hardy in sheltered areas with mild or no frosts. They will often grow where little else will flourish, particularly in damp or shady places.

Planting ferns

When planting, treat most ferns as herbaceous perennials, but there are a few other points to consider.

- Dig over the soil deeply and incorporate plenty of well-rotted organic material to increase its moisture retentiveness. Dryness at the roots will cause shrunken, brownish fronds or even death.

- Plant in early autumn, which allows the roots to settle in the soil before winter, or in the spring when the roots are coming into growth.

- Plant ferns in their final resting place because they take time to become established—digging them up and moving them about later will set them back.

- Light, sandy soil should be given additional humus and a thick mulch of leaves or shredded bark to retain the soil's moisture.

Maintenance

As with herbaceous perennials, active growth stops in autumn, but the top-growth will survive mild frosts. Hard, sudden frost may result in blackened fronds. If a hard winter is expected, more tender species may be packed with leaf mould, litter, or any form of deep mulch to protect the crowns.

Several species such as *Asplenium scolopendrium* are evergreen or retain their fronds to protect next season's emerging furls. Once the danger of frost is past, the previous year's evergreen fronds should be carefully cut hard back to allow the curious and very decorative, new fronds to be seen. Delay in cutting back the old fronds in spring may result in damage to the emerging fronds.

Choosing Ferns

For the beginner, selecting ferns can be rather bewildering. If you are new to growing ferns, it is wise to begin with a small collection so that you can study their different habits and see how they grow. Studying ferns in the wild—under trees or in crevices of walls—will give you an idea of the various shapes and sizes of ferns and the conditions they prefer.

Several specialist fern nurseries produce very good-value fern collections for different situations or effect, such as for dry shade or damp soil, as evergreens or for flower arrangers. Gradually other, more unusual ferns may be added to your garden. Often young ferns have not developed their true characteristics so before planting them, make sure

that you find out the amount of space they will need when mature.

Ferns to Start a Collection

Adiantum pedatum
  Maidenhair fern has delicate fronds borne on thin, shiny, black stems.

Asplenium scolopendrium
  The hart's tongue fern has long, tongue-shaped, evergreen, bright green fronds, which have beautifully crimped margins. There are many forms. They contrast attractively with the more matt, deeply fingered foliage and apple-green flowers of *Helleborus foetidus*. Tolerates dry and alkaline (limy) soils.

Athyrium filix-femina
  Lady fern has fine, lacy fronds; it has small, medium-sized, and large forms.

Dryopteris filix-mas
  Buckler fern has tall, upright, feathery fronds.

Matteuccia struthiopteris
  Fronds of the ostrich fern are pinnate (with lots of leaflets) and grow in a large, vase-like cluster around a stout base. Tolerates alkaline (limy) soils.

Osmunda regalis
  Tall, lance-shaped fronds of the royal fern are produced from massive rhizomes. Suited to water gardens.

Polystichum setiferum
  Distinctive shield fern has lance-shaped, arching fronds. Tolerates dry soils.

Recommended Ferns

Small ferns, 8–30 cm (3–12 in.) tall

Asplenium adiantum-nigrum black spleenwort
Asplenium ceterach rusty-back fern
Asplenium ruta-muraria wall rue
Asplenium scolopendrium Marginatum Group
    'Irregulare' hart's tongue fern
Asplenium trichomanes maidenhair
    spleenwort
Athyrium filix-femina lady fern
Blechnum penna-marina hard fern
Polypodium vulgare common polypody
Polystichum setiferum 'Congestum' soft
    shield fern
Polystichum tsussimense Korean rock fern

Medium-sized ferns, 30—60 cm (12—24 in.) tall

Adiantum pedatum maidenhair fern
Athyrium filix-femina 'Vernoniae' lady fern
Dryopteris filix-mas 'Linearis' male fern
Onoclea sensibilis sensitive fern
Polypodium vulgare common polypody
Polystichum aculeatum (some forms) prickly
    shield fern
Woodwardia radicans chain fern

Larger ferns, over 60 cm (24 in.) tall

Blechnum chilense red fern
Dryopteris wallichiana
Polystichum aculeatum (some forms) prickly
    shield fern

Lime-loving ferns

Asplenium ceterach rusty-back fern
Asplenium trichomanes maidenhair
    spleenwort
Asplenium viride green spleenwort

Dryopteris affinis golden male fern
Gymnocarpium robertianum limestone
    polypody
Polypodium vulgare southern polypody
Polystichum aculeatum prickly shield fern

Ferns tolerant of dry conditions

Adiantum aleuticum (and other hardy forms)
    maidenhair fern
Cyrtomium fortunei
Dryopteris (most forms) buckler fern
Polypodium vulgare southern polypody

Ornamental Grasses and Bamboos

Partly as a result of the pioneering work done by
Piet Oudolf, the Dutch designer and nurseryman,
and other Dutch and Belgian growers, grasses have
had a surge in popularity in recent years. The number
of species available to gardeners has gradually
increased as more have been collected from various
parts of the world.

Grasses range from herbaceous or evergreen
perennials to annuals. Some have evolved with
variegated and otherwise coloured foliage. Their
handsome leaves, long seasons of interest, and
distinctive, often tactile flowers provide a dramatic
contrast to shrubs and perennials, especially in early
autumn. They may be used in mixed borders, in lawns
as solitary specimens, by water and in containers.

Flowerheads of grasses vary enormously, some being
silky and very graceful, while others are so subtle
that they are almost unnoticeable. The greatest
variety of flowers is found in the true grasses, which
offer a huge wealth of floral beauty, with tremendous
variations in size, form, arrangement and texture.
Usually the flowerhead, or inflorescence, consists of

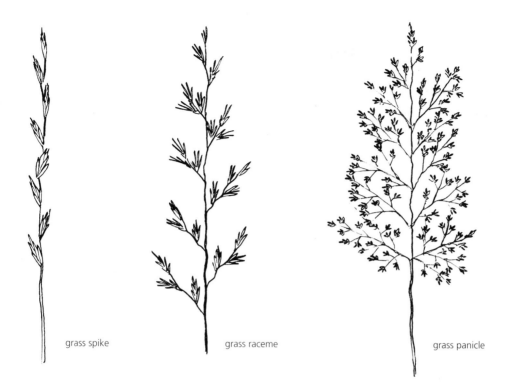

grass spike   grass raceme   grass panicle

a number of tiny flowers combined into a spikelet; spikelets fall into three categories—spike, raceme, or panicle.

A spike is an inflorescence with spikelets attached directly to the main stem (axis) without stalks, and are usually quite tight and narrow. When the spikelets have short stalks attached to the axis, the inflorescence is called a raceme and also tends to be fairly narrow. Panicles, the glorious plumes and open heads associated with many grasses, occur where the spikelets carried on stalks are themselves held on branches from the axis.

Bamboos are infrequent and unpredictable in the event of flowering, and when they do the flowers are very inconspicuous; some may die after flowering, but this is not always the case. Sedges produce generally insignificant flower spikes, and rushes, although useful in extremely wet conditions, also have a paltry flower.

What is a Grass?

Understanding the different families' characteristics will help you to identify whether a plant is a true grass, sedge or rush.

True grasses

- True grasses belong to the family Poaceae (formerly known as Gramineae); bamboos now also belong to the Poaceae, but were previously classified under Bambuseae.
- Stem of all true grasses, and this includes bamboos, is known as a culm.
- Culms are cylindrical, are hollow and have swollen joints called nodes.
- Leaves alternate along the length of the culms; they have straight veins running parallel to the leaf margins.

What is a Grass? (continued)

Sedges

- Sedges belong to the Cyperaceae family.
- Stems lack nodes, are solid with centres filled with pith, and are distinctly angular (triangular in cross-section).
- Leaves are wrapped around the shoots in three ranks.

Rushes

- These plants are from the small Juncaceae family.
- Stems are cylindrical, generally solid and without nodes.
- Pointed leaves usually arise from the soil and wrap tightly around the stems.

Mood or Purpose

Atmosphere in a garden is difficult to describe because our responses are emotional and personal. The presence of grasses seems to evoke a more passionate reaction than that of other plants; this mood is created by the choice of grasses as well as their arrangement. Planted informally in loose groups or in drifts, they are associated with excitement or nostalgia and are reminiscent of the countryside and a feeling of wild nature. Whether planted as specimens or as a group in a border, their leaves and inflorescences swaying in the wind bring the drama of movement into the garden.

Used as ground cover, possibly next to a path, the lower-growing grasses emphasize the directional flow of the path, giving a calming effect. When used in mixed borders, grasses create a flimsy, filmy mood. The flowers vary from dainty, cloud-like sprays to silky tassels that beg to be touched. Children in particular find them irresistible.

Many grasses have very distinctive characteristics, suggesting a diverse range of uses within our gardens. In association with other garden features or plants, they may have a significant impact on their surroundings, so need to be chosen either as specimen plants, as ground cover, or to merge with other planting. Many are tough, easy, low-maintenance plants and ideal for the contemporary garden, while others can be highly invasive and therefore high-maintenance. A little research to select the most suitable variety for your garden will pay dividends in the future.

- As companion planting, grasses offer sharp contrasts when their narrow stems and foliage break up the stiffer and more rounded outlines of other plants.

- To show bluish, grey or variegated grasses and their flowers at their best, choose a dark, uncluttered backdrop with mainly green foliage to act as a foil.

- Some of the more rampant, lower-growing grasses are useful for stabilizing soil on banks because their rhizomes soon knit together and prevent erosion.

- Grasses are also appropriate for gravelled areas—choose varieties with a distinctive characteristic, such as impressive flowers or variegated leaves, to act as a focal point and contrast with the gravel or pea shingle.

- Use the tall bamboos to prove screening or an internal division—plant them in a straight row or a double, staggered row, depending on the required density of the screen.

- For shady or dark areas, the combination of yellow- and green-striped grasses with golden-foliaged shrubs, such as *Philadelphus coronarius* 'Aureus' or *Sambucus nigra* 'Aurea', will furnish a sunny effect.

Shape and Size

There are numerous grasses and bamboos chosen for their strong and distinct, upright outlines, but others contribute by forming loose mounds, by weaving through the spaces between contrasting plant groups, or when used singly as an impressive focal point. Several grasses, such as *Cortaderia* (pampas grass), form enormous, tall clumps and need to be planted singly to remain in scale with other plantings in the garden. Some, like the blue fescue *Festuca glauca*, are only 15 cm (6 in.) tall, while *Miscanthus sacchariflorus* grows up to 2.4 m (8 ft.).

Grasses have two main forms of growth habit; some form clumps or tufts and some have a carpeting habit, spreading vigorously by underground, creeping stems or rhizomes. Since many spreading grasses can be invasive, be sure to use a grass that remains naturally in a clump.

Colour

Few foliage plants can match grasses with their range of foliage and stem colours. The long, narrow leaves vary from silvery white-edged, bluish or grey blades though to strong yellows, buffs, reds and bronzes, not to mention the medley of greens, sometimes striped or variegated or flecked with striking markings. Stem colour varies from green through to cream, bronze, red or striped. Avoid creating a restless effect by not using too many different varieties in one space; instead, plant them singly, in repetitive groupings, or in naturalistic drifts.

Season of Interest

Like corn in a field, most grasses mature later in the year, coming into their own when most shrubs and perennials have ceased to excite. In late summer, it is hard to provide new interest in the garden, but some grasses perform by changing hue in autumn. They will then persist, bringing life to the garden, through the winter until being cut back in the following spring.

Key Criteria for Choosing Grasses

- Mood or purpose
- Shape and size
- Colour
- Season of interest; autumnal effects

Cultivating Grasses

Generally, grasses are easy plants to grow, but like all plants they have their preferences as to soil type, moisture level and light levels. Soil preferences of grasses vary from damp to dry conditions, but most are content with average, well-drained soils; avoid really wet or waterlogged soils, as well as soils that tend to dry out. Most grasses need a sunny aspect, but a few will tolerate shade.

Buy the plants from a reliable nursery or supplier, to make sure that the plant is healthy. Since they form part of the permanent planting scheme, it is worth getting them off to a good start by preparing the soil well for planting.

- Plant in mid-spring when the soil is warming up and is not too damp.

- Place the root ball at the same depth as in the pot, with the crown or growth buds at soil level—they resent being planted too deeply.

- Avoid disturbing the root ball as you firm in the soil around it.

- Be conscientious about watering regularly until the new roots are established.

The plants will need an annual tidy up, removing any dead or untidy leaves rather than complete defoliation. Cut down dead flowering stems completely in autumn or, if the decorative winter stems or silhouettes are wanted, in early spring. Dead or damaged foliage will protect the crown of the plant during winter. If tips of leaves are damaged by winter frosts, cut away only spoilt leaves in early spring, to avoiding damaging emerging new shoots.

The foliage of most ornamental grasses should be left undisturbed until late winter, when they should be trimmed down or combed through with a small hand fork to remove dead foliage. The treatment you choose will depend on the plant—some such as *Anemanthele lessoniana* need attention only every two or three years.

Divide clumps when they become congested, or control invasive species, in late autumn or early spring when the growth is less active. Use a sharp spade to dig a trench around the roots, then with the spade or a sharp knife divide the plant up into manageable sizes, perhaps leaving the reduced parent plant in situ and replanting or potting on the spare divisions for use elsewhere.

Grasses may be propagated by division, which is easier than raising them from seed because this takes many years to produce a mature specimen. Once a plant is established, prise apart the rootstock with a spade or two forks placed back-to-back. Certain species such as *Deschampsia*, *Pennisetum* and some of the sedges can become nuisances if allowed to self-seed, but the timely removal of the seedheads should prevent this.

Recommended Grasses

Ground cover in shade

Carex morrowii 'Variegata'
Dark green leaves with a discreet, white margin, which gives the plant a distinctive crispness.

Deschampsia cespitosa
Cloud-like flowerheads above neat clumps of arching, slender leaves.

Ground cover in sun

Festuca gautieri
Dark, evergreen grass, forms dense, spreading mats irresistible to touch.

Helictotrichon sempervirens
Balls of stiff, blue-grey leaves. Flowers mature to a straw hue and are held well above the foliage.

Molinia caerulea
Long, straight flower stems of distinctive form rise well clear of the neat, basal clump of foliage in late summer.

Pennisetum species
Useful, dome-shaped plants covered in long, rabbit's tail-like flowerheads in late summer—very tactile.

Grasses for mass planting on banks

Calamagrostis × *acutiflora* 'Karl Foerster'
Comes into growth in early spring and continues to perform until well into winter. Flower stems rise in early summer from coarse clump of rich green leaves.

Carex pendula
Slow-growing, evergreen plant for cool, shady sites. Upright, broad, leathery leaves and graceful, pendent flowerheads.

Miscanthus sinensis
Most cultivars are stiffly upright, clump-forming grasses with feathery inflorescences borne in autumn.

Panicum virgatum
Upright growth habit with exciting autumn colour. Large, wide flowerheads create a misty, light effect when planted in a mass.

Pennisetum orientale
Violet-pink flower spikes with a very long flowering season.

Grasses for colour contrast

Arundo donax var. *versicolor*
Variegated with spectacular, cream-margined and striped leaves. Frost-tender.

Elymus hispidus
Narrow, intensely blue leaves.

Festuca
Many blue and bluish-grey colours of leaves, held stiffly like needles.

Hakonechloa macra 'Aureola'
Dramatic, yellow, lax, arching foliage.

Helictotrichon sempervirens
Stiff, blue-grey leaves.

Imperata cylindrica 'Rubra'
Mid-green leaves start out with dark red tips, the colour gradually spreading throughout the whole leaf as the summer progresses.

Leymus arenarius
Bluish-green strappy leaves that roll up when conditions become dry.

Milium effusum 'Aureum'
Soft yellow leaves in all parts in sun, but if there is not enough light its colour will fade to pale green.

Miscanthus sinensis 'Zebrinus'
Horizontal bands of variegation.

Molinia caerulea subsp. *caerulea* 'Variegata'
Cream-variegated, light green leaves.

Panicum virgatum 'Heavy Metal'
Distinguished, grey–green coloration.

Phalaris arundinacea var. *picta* 'Picta'
Longitudinally striped, white and pale green leaves.

Uncinia rubra
Reddish-bronze, tough foliage.

Growing Bamboos

Bamboos are a distinct group of grasses with woody culms, known as canes. Oriental in mood, they impart a grace and elegance to their surroundings. Bamboos have long been used in gardens for various purposes, but they are particularly suitable for contemporary spaces. They work well with decking, while taller varieties may be used for screening or to soften the harsh lines of buildings.

Lower-growing species provide excellent ground cover and are also useful on sloping ground. Bamboos with variegated leaves light up a dark, dank area. These plants are reliable performers and require little maintenance. Evergreen varieties retain their fine, delicate leaves under the most hostile of conditions.

Most varieties prefer light to deep shade. Once established, they survive in sun or shade and will tolerate periods of drought, although in severe cold or very hot summers the plants may die. Bamboos thrive on a good, moist but well-drained soil; they resent very dry areas and severe alkalinity.

Height is a crucial factor when selecting a bamboo—they range from lofty, overhanging plants that are effective against the backdrop of a coniferous hedge—provided that they are planted some distance out to avoid dry soil—to highly invasive, low-growing grasses that can be allowed to colonize difficult areas such as slopes, banks or shade under trees or hedges—provided that there is some moisture in the soil. These plants are fast-growing and most spread, so need to be sited carefully; some varieties produce underground shoots that appear over 4.5 m (15 ft.) away, piercing their way through tarmac or paving.

Bamboo foliage may be in shades from light to dark green, as well as variegated in some varieties. However, bamboos are mostly grown for the tints of their stems, which range from light gold through dark green to a rich black. The flowers are usually insignificant, but some bamboos produce plumes of sulphur-yellow flowers in very hot summers. The plants often die after flowering.

Bamboos are planted in much the same way as other grasses. The soil needs careful preparation, with plenty of well-rotted organic material dug in to enrich the soil and improve its moisture retentiveness. The upright canes should be thoroughly firmed in, otherwise they may rock in the wind and prevent the roots from establishing a grip in the soil.

Key Criteria for Choosing Bamboos

- Mood or function
- Site
- Shape, height and size
- Colour, especially of stems
- Seasons of interest

Recommended Bamboos

Fargesia murielae
Attractive, medium-height bamboo that slowly expands to rounded clumps of pale green foliage; the young stems age to grey-blue.

Fargesia nitida
Forms a wide clump of numerous, slim, purple-black stems. Long and very narrow leaves bestow a delicate quality.

Phyllostachys aurea
Elegant, overhanging bamboo with golden stems. Spreading habit, so needs plenty of space to grow.

Phyllostachys nigra
Similar to *P. aurea*, but with stems that age from dark green to rich black.

Pleioblastus viridistriatus
Hardy golden bamboo so strikingly variegated with bright green streaks that it makes a spectacular plant for the larger garden. To achieve the best colour, cut down the plant in early spring to make room for the rapidly emerging, new shoots.

Sasa palmata
Usually chosen for its beautiful, broad leaves; generally spreads to cover a wide area, so not for small gardens.

Sedges

Sedges evolved much earlier than grasses, yet both families possess many similar characteristics. Although often thought of as grasses, sedges are perennial, evergreen herbs. This family consists of some 35 members, mainly from New Zealand where they form an essential component of the woodland floor. Apart from a few exceptions, they grow in sunny, moist situations and are especially suited as low-growing ground cover.

Some species and cultivars possess coloured foliage, the best-known being *Carex elata* 'Aurea'. Many sedges form clumps of arching leaves that are best appreciated as a single specimen. Unlike most grasses, they should not be cut back in spring because it is difficult to distinguish between dead and living leaves.

Useful Sedges

Carex buchananii
Forms a stiffly upright plant with narrow, cylindrical foliage that curves at the tip. Showy, red-brown leaves colour best in full sun.

Carex buchananii 'Viridis'
A pleasing, pale green version of C. *buchananii*.

Carex comans bronze
A neat, mop-headed form with warm brown leaves, which sometimes look dead.

Carex elata 'Aurea'
Hummock-forming with striking, bright yellow, green-margined leaves; best in partial shade where the full hue of the variegation can develop without becoming bleached.

Carex hachijoensis
Evergreen, with distinct, centre-striped leaves.

Carex hachijoensis 'Variegata'
Distinct, centre white-striped leaves.

Carex oshimensis 'Evergold'
Distinct, yellow stripe in the centre of each leaf.

Cyperus eragrostis
Graceful foliage and umbrella-like, straw-yellow inflorescences.

Schoenoplectus lacustris
Brown, grassy foliage; spreads by creeping rhizomes.

Rushes

These comprise a small family of around nine species, few of which are of interest to gardeners. The most striking feature of the true rush is its cylindrical, pointed leaves. They prefer a moist situation. A couple of garden-worthy rushes are:

- *Juncus effusus* f. *spiralis*—has curious, dark-green leaves, which curl tightly upwards like corkscrews

- *Luzula sylvatica* 'Marginata'—low-growing, with broad, glossy, dark green leaves.

Water-garden Plants

These plants divide into two different types: the first are true aquatics, such as *Nymphaea* (water lily), and the second are plants that thrive in damp soil or boggy conditions, such as *Iris laevigata* (hardy water iris), also known as marginal aquatics. All water-garden plants appreciate sun and should not be planted too close together or under trees. Since they are not short of moisture, they prefer intense light to mature and flower freely.

Most aquatics are best planted in spring when the weather becomes warmer and when plant growth is just beginning. Summer is too late because the plants will be in active growth and will find it difficult to adapt to a new position.

Planting is done either in plastic-mesh baskets, which rest on the bottom or on a shelf in the pond, or directly into a layer of soil and gravel spread over the base of the pool. Perimeter or bog planting may be kept in place until it is established by stacking rolled-up turves along the edge of the planting shelves—this also helps to retain the soil on the shelf.

Almost all water-garden plants should be propagated by division. This is best done in spring when the water is warming up and days become longer. It allows newly divided plants to put on new growth in time for flowering and to become established before their first winter. Divide or transplant water-garden plants on a humid day and keep the rootstocks covered with damp sacking to prevent them from drying out. Use rubber gloves to avoid getting stains on your hands.

Recommended Water- or Bog-garden Plants

For very shallow water and mud

Caltha palustris
  The marsh marigold is the best plant for the water's edge.

Caltha palustris 'Plena'
  A more dwarf plant and with a more compact habit.

Mimulus cardinalis
  Flowers are brilliant orange-scarlet or in shades of red or yellow.

Myosotis scorpioides
  The water forget-me-not is a useful filler for gaps between other plants.

For shallow water 5–15 cm (2–6 in.) deep

Iris laevigata
  Best of all hardy water irises.

For water 15–30 cm (6–12 in.) deep

Acorus gramineus 'Variegatus'
  The sweet flag is variegated, with a lot of colour in its iris-like, young leaves.

Pontederia cordata
  Pickerel weed is one of the very few blue-flowered aquatics for late summer; it makes big clumps.

Zantedeschia aethiopica
  The arum lily is a superb water-garden plant with bold, glossy foliage and elegant, white blooms.

For water 30 cm (12 in.) deep

Aponogeton distachyos
  Cape pondweed or water hawthorn has waxy white, sweetly scented flowers that rest on the surface among the floating leaves.

Butomus umbellatus
  This flowering rush is tall, slender and looks beautiful.

Nymphaea

The aristocrats of the water garden, water lilies, are all gross feeders and have strong, white roots that can penetrate a clay pond, causing leakage. Water lilies are also fussy about the depth of water above them, so choose an appropriate variety for the depth of your pool. Most garden centres supply special open-mesh baskets that can be lined with turf, laid soil-side down and turf-side up, then filled with heavy loam or a mixture of loam and compost.

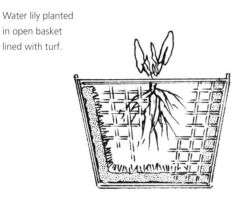

Water lily planted in open basket lined with turf.

Plant each water lily as firmly as possible, with the growing point and tip of the rhizome just showing. Then slide the basket into the water so that it rests either just below the surface of the water or with no more than 25 cm (10 in.) of water above the crown. This may require supporting the basket on bricks for several months until the top-growth is sufficiently developed.

Water lilies may be divided by cutting their rhizomes into sections, and then submerging the repotted sections in shallow water until they develop dormant buds. These buds will eventually break to make new plants.

Recommended *Nymphaea*

For very shallow water, up to 15 cm (6 in.) deep, in small bowls, sinks, troughs or other containers

N. 'Pygmaea Helvola'
  Has beautiful, yellow flowers and foliage that is heavily mottled with rich brown.

For water up to 23–60 cm (9–24 in.) deep

N. 'Froebelii'
  An old favourite and very popular, with abundant, crimson flowers and neat foliage.

N. 'Laydeckeri Lilacea'
  Neat and free-flowering, light mauve-pink blooms.

For water up to 90 cm (3 ft.) deep.

N. 'James Brydon'
  The best all-purpose water lily; tolerant of various depths of water and a little shade. Produces huge, globular flowers of a rich rose-pink and handsome, round, dark leaves.

N. 'Marliacea Chromatella'
  Has large, soft yellow flowers, with handsomely marbled foliage; will thrive even in partial shade.

N. 'William Falconer'
  Flowers are the darkest crimson of all; dark and handsome leaves.

> ## Recommended *Nymphaea* (continued)
>
> **For water up to 1.2 m (4 ft.) deep**
>
> *N.* 'Escarboucle'
> Popular because of its large, rich red flowers and reliability, and therefore scarce.
>
> **Vigorous types for large ponds**
>
> *N.* 'Gladstoneana'
> Huge, vigorous plant with enormous, white flowers that have fine, golden centres. Best in very deep water—in shallow water, the big leaves become overcrowded.
>
> *N.* 'Marliacea Carnea' and *N.* 'Marliacea Rosea'
> Two similar flowers of delicate, pale pink; now the most common lilies in general cultivation.

Annuals and Half-hardy Perennials

The popularity of mixed border planting—using shrubs and herbaceous plants together—has emerged largely because the combination of plants extends the flowering season but, by late summer and early autumn, it is hard to keep an mixed display going. Plants such as *Lupinus* and *Papaver orientale* (perennial poppy) are tired, have finished flowering and will be running to seed. Cutting them hard back may result in an occasional flower spike, but growth will not be as strong and may well leave a gap in the border.

New plants from seed pods or seedheads often will not come true; producing seed weakens the plant and may inhibit flowering of the parent plant in the following year. Other very vigorous flowerers, such as violas, can cover almost 50 cm (20 in.) in the first year of being planted, but will literally flower themselves to death. In late summer, they begin to look straggly and tired. Cut them back hard, give them a bucketful of water and, in a few weeks, they will recover but will inevitably leave some gaps.

Annuals, which have only one season of flowering, and half-hardy perennials, which are raised or overwintered in the greenhouse, are invaluable for filling spaces that appear within borders and will add another three or four months of interest.

Biennials resemble annuals in dying after they have flowered and produced ripe seed, but differ in the time they take to do this. Although they have a lifespan extending over at least part of two years, it is necessary to renew them from seed annually if the flowers are to be enjoyed every year. Examples of biennials are *Lunaria annua* (honesty), *Myosotis sylvatica* (forget-me-not) and *Verbascum bombyciferum*. There are numerous plants that, although not truly biennial, are treated as such because they then produce the best and most reliable results.

Raising Annuals from Seed

Annuals can be bought as seedling plants from local suppliers if the price is reasonable. However, it is easy and inexpensive to sow seed directly into the ground where you want them to flower (which will avoid them suffering from the short adjustment period that usually follows transplanting).

Annuals usually flower six to ten weeks after sowing, but the seed packets will show specific sowing and flowering times. A drawback may be that seed suppliers frequently provide only packets of mixed colours, which may ruin your carefully planned colour combinations. Suppliers with a mail-order service often have a wider range. Get hold of two or three good seed catalogues and spend a cold, winter afternoon by the fire making up an order.

When choosing from the huge range of seed available, concentrate on those varieties that develop quickly, avoiding slower-growing annuals such as *Antirrhinum* (snapdragon), *Erysimum* (wallflower) and *Scabious*, as well as perennials and biennials.

How to sow seed of annuals

- Sow in late spring after any danger of frost has passed; keep sowing batches at intervals to keep the show going.

- Mark out the area you want to cover with sand and broadcast sow within this plot. Alternatively, mark out a series of lines at a diagonal to the path or edge of a border— diagonal lines will create an effect that is more natural than if you use parallel lines.

- Sowing along marked-out lines will allow you to tell when the first true leaves of the seedlings emerge—and whether the seedling is of a choice annual or a weed!

- Avoid sowing too many different varieties in one area—one or two blocks of colour are more effective than a frantic kaleidoscope.

- Stagger the varieties according to any differences in eventual height, so that one annual will not block another from view.

An alternative is to sow seed in trays indoors and germinate them on a cool windowsill, or in a porch or other naturally well-lit space. Using a watering can with a fine nozzle so as not to disturb the fine, emerging seedlings, water daily to stop the compost drying out.

Some seed will benefit from the seed tray being covered with a sheet of clear glass; remove the glass to allow air to circulate as soon as the first seedlings appear. When they are large enough to handle, prick out the seedlings either into pots or into position in your border.

Aftercare

- Unless it rains, water seedbeds twice a week, soaking the ground to a depth of several centimetres or inches. The roots will go deep to seek water, making the plants stronger.

- Usually, seedlings begin to show through in seven to ten days.

- When the first pairs of true leaves appear, thin out the seedlings. Be brutal, leaving only one good plant every 8–10 cm (3–4 in.). This will stop the seedlings competing with each other and allow those remaining to grow strong and straight.

- Once they have filled out, thin out the seedling plants again to about 30 cm (12 in.) apart. Dig out the surplus carefully with a hand fork and, if possible, transplant them elsewhere immediately.

- Avoid pest damage by taking precautions to scare off marauding birds, protect from cats, or deter slugs.

Plug plants

Several suppliers now promote "plug" or "starter" seedling plants, which are raised in a special growing medium in fibrous pots. They need to be inserted in their pots straight into the soil within a day or two of arrival, otherwise they may deteriorate and die.

Recommended Annuals

Several different cultivars and varieties are available of each recommended plant, so look through the catalogues until you find the best one for your purpose.

Ammi majus
> White lace flower, often used as a substitute for Queen Anne's lace; carries umbels of tiny, white flowers. Self-seeds once established.

Calendula officinalis
> Common marigold, with brilliant orange, edible flowers.

Cosmos bipinnatus
> Lacy foliage and silky flowers give an airy touch from midsummer to the first frost. Good for cutting.

Eschscholzia californica
> California poppy, with satiny, orange flowers and silvery blue, ferny foliage. Flowers close at night.

Helianthus
> Sunflowers are mostly tall plants with the central boss of dark seeds surrounded by a "sunburst" of petals. Dwarf cultivars are now available that are only 60–90 cm (2–3 ft.) tall.

Moluccella laevis
> Bells of Ireland have spikes of large, bright green flowers that turn a creamy white when dried.

Nicotiana
> Tobacco plants are available in various heights and flower colours; the tallest is *N.* 'Only the Lonely', with thick stalks and heavily scented, pendulous, white flowers.

Nigella
> Love-in-a-mist has soft blue petals that highlight the central, papery seed capsule; this turns a reddish-maroon when ripe. Blooms throughout the summer until the autumn frosts.

Tagetes
> African or French marigold groups are striking plants, ideal for bedding, edging and containers.

Tropaeolum majus
> Nasturtiums have colourful flowers for bedding or containers; the flowers and leaves are edible. This species has a climbing habit, but there are some bushy *Tropaeolum* species.

Half-hardy Perennials

In semi-tropical areas such as California, around the Mediterranean or in the very mildest areas of Britain, many beautiful, tender perennial plants grow healthily outside all year round. In cooler areas prone to frosts, these plants are described as half-hardies. They need to be treated like annuals and raised or overwintered in a greenhouse or under cover, being planted out only when all danger of frost has passed. Many are handsome foliage plants, such as *Canna* and *Ricinus* (castor oil plant), which provide drama in the border when other perennials are beginning to flag. Other half-hardies, such as dahlias, are grown mainly for their flowers.

In Britain, half-hardies were very popular as bedding-out plants in Victorian times, when most estates had plenty of both glasshouses and gardeners. The Victorians revelled in the fashionable, exotic touch they gave to gardens. Today half-hardies are used in most gardens to prolong the flowering season, because they give their main show and provide colour from late summer through to the early winter.

Growing half-hardies

To allow enough time for half-hardies to develop from the dormant plant of the previous year to full flowering size within the next growing season, most need to be grown on in the greenhouse. In early summer, search for grown-on and potted-up plants to buy at good nurseries, garden centres or local farmers' markets. The half-hardies may be planted out in early summer when they are already at a reasonable size.

Perhaps place them in an area of bare soil where earlier flowering plants have been cut back. Plant them in the same way as perennials, allowing plenty of space for them to develop to their full height and spread. Taller varieties may need staking—do this immediately so that, as the plant develops, its foliage will grow through and hide any unsightly canes or garden twine.

Maintenance of half-hardies

- Half-hardies grow quickly and are often rather tall so, to keep them flowering through the growing season, they need a weekly or fortnightly feed with a tomato fertilizer (to promote flowers rather than foliage) and regular watering.

- Check stakes and ties regularly and re-stake them, if vigorous growth makes this necessary.

- Deadhead regularly, once or twice per week.

- Immediately after the first frosts, when the foliage is limp and black, lift the rootstocks with a fork. Trim off the old foliage, leaving about 10 cm (4 in.) of stalk, then box them up in old, moist potting soil so that the tubers or rhizomes remain plump and do not dry out.

- Store in an airy, but frost-free place, such as a cellar or below greenhouse shelving.

- Check them occasionally, and water sparingly, until new growth appears in spring.

- Then pot up the half-hardies and place them in a conservatory or cool greenhouse to bring them on until they are ready to be planted out in the garden again.

Recommended Half-hardies

Begonia 'Flamboyant'
    Single, dark scarlet flowers.

Brugmansia
    Large, pendent, trumpet–like flowers and fairly large leaves. Highly poisonous.

Canna iridiflora
    Cherry-pink flowers and large, purple-rimmed leaves.

Canna 'Phasion'
    Striped, variegated, pink leaves.

Canna 'Striata'
    Yellow and green striped leaves.

Canna 'Wyoming'
    Orange flowers.

Dahlia 'Bishop of Llandaff '
    Single, red flowers and purple-green leaves.

Dahlia 'David Howard'
    Apricot flower with dark leaves.

Dahlia 'Fascination'
    Shocking-pink flowers and dark leaves.

Recommended Half-hardies (continued)

Dahlia 'Moonfire'
  Single, yellow flowers and dark leaves.

Dahlia 'Pearl of Heemstede'
  Clear pink flowers.

Dahlia 'Roxy'
  Shocking-pink flowers.

Ricinus communis 'Carmencita'
  Gigantic, deeply lobed, dark red leaves on
  very tall plants. Tropical in appearance
  and useful at the back of a border.

The Kitchen Garden

Growing and eating your own vegetables and fruit is always a delight, and even in a small garden there is the opportunity to grow something edible. Path edgings of wild strawberries, wooden or metal tripods supporting runner beans or gourds, apples and pears trained against sunny walls, or clumps of brightly coloured ruby chard may all be included without the need or space for a particularly designated productive area. It is fun to experiment, so use your imagination and give your garden an individual touch by doing something unexpected.

If you do have enough space, it is very satisfying to devote a larger area to growing crops, although if you do decide to do so, be prepared to devote some time to them—edible crops require more regular care than ornamental plants. Recently, there has been a revival of the smaller kitchen garden, or "potager", a smaller space where produce is grown either in geometric rows, perhaps within low box hedges, or in random, informal areas abounding with marigolds or nasturtiums. A useful and decorative herb garden may be interspersed with mop-head, standard roses, clipped bay trees or a small cooling fountain—pretty as well as functional.

Soil Preparation

For crops in a kitchen garden to thrive, the soil must be of a decent depth, well-drained and fertile, so lots of organic matter will need to be added annually. The soil should also be of a fine consistency and devoid of large lumps and stones.

A poor clay topsoil can fairly quickly—in a matter of months over a winter season—be converted to decent soil by adding well-rotted manure, grit and organic mushroom compost. On thin top soil over chalk or sand, where the subsoil cannot be broken up and integrated, it is better to make raised beds with timber boards. This also might give the best results if you have really heavy clay.

For a successfully productive vegetable garden, topsoil should be at least 20 cm (8 in.) deep, but if possible increase it to 30–45cm (12–18 in.) to allow deep-rooting crops such as carrots to thrive.

Prepare the ground in the autumn or winter. If making the kitchen garden out of a previously uncultivated area, skim off the grass or use a rotavator to break up the soil, then spread a thick layer of well-rotted organic matter or manure. Frost will soon break this up and worms will take it down into the soil below. Get rid of all annual and perennial weeds before adding manure.

The growing area may be set out as in the rest of the garden, but it is easier to maintain and pick produce if the beds are fairly narrow. A width of up to 1.2 m (4 ft.) will allow you to reach the centre of each bed from either side without leaving footprints or getting your feet dirty. It also avoids any risk of compacting the soil and harming its structure. If there are any walls in the plot, they may be used to support espalier-trained top fruit or climbing beans.

Crop Rotation

In planning your kitchen garden, aim to have at least four different beds or areas, so that you can move different types of crop annually from one bed to another. This as called "crop rotation" and has several benefits. If the same crop is grown in the same soil year after year, pests and diseases tend to build up; rotating the crop avoids this.

Different crops require varying amounts of nutrients and trace elements from the soil. Moving groups of vegetables with similar nutrient requirements around a plot in regular order will make the most efficient use of the nutrients and avoid the soil becoming impoverished, especially if you want to grow vegetables with minimum applications of fertilizer. Four beds may be used for a four-year crop rotation.

Year 1
Bed 1—potatoes, followed by leeks, lettuce or salad crops for the winter.

Bed 2—mostly root vegetables, such as beetroot (beets), carrots, garlic, onions, parsnips and shallots and parsley and sweetcorn. If carrots follow garlic, there should be no risk of carrot fly.

Bed 3—brassicas such as broccoli, cabbage, cauliflower, kale, oriental salad crops, radishes and rocket.

Bed 4—legumes, for example peas and beans, and cucurbits such as courgettes (zucchini).

Years 2, 3 and 4
Move your crops around the beds in regular rotation over the next three years—this will also help to avoid rust and other fungal diseases.

Protecting the Crops

For early or tender crops, some protection from the elements will be necessary. Before sowing seeds or planting out seedlings, lay down and secure a sheet of plastic over the soil for two to three weeks to warm up the soil. There are also many types of cloche available, which may be used to create a mini-greenhouse effect for your seeds or young plants while keeping birds and the elements at bay.

Some plants such as broccoli or cabbage may need to be netted against insect pests such as the cabbage white butterfly. Alternatively, you could try companion planting—sowing one crop next to another as protection from pests to help attract pollinators and avoid using chemicals. For example, grow onions with carrots to mask the scent of either crop from the onion or carrot fly or use *Tagetes patula* (French marigold) to deter whitefly.

Feeding and Watering Crops

If the soil is healthy and has been well prepared, little feeding should be necessary since the roots will go down to find the nutrients and trace elements. Watering will be vital during the summer months; it is a good idea to have a garden tap nearby that may be attached to a sprinkler or trickle irrigation system.

Leaf and Salad Vegetables

Some of the easiest and most lush vegetables to be grown include cabbages, Brussels sprouts, curly kale, spinach, lettuce, rocket (arugula), watercress and land cress. All are decorative, delectable and a welcome relief from the ready-made and often monotonous "designer" salads so popular in supermarkets, where the shelf life may deplete their rich vitamin content.

Podded Vegetables

This small but highly nutritional group of vegetables, sometimes called legumes, include several scrambling or climbing varieties that are useful also for their decorative effect. Many peas, broad, runner or French beans (green or snap beans) have showy flowers or interesting, streaked or purple pods, although the latter disappointingly lose their colour when cooked.

Most podded vegetables need some form of support, such as garden canes and twine, tripods, or even a wooden arch or hazel tunnel.

Bulb, Stem and Root Vegetables

These are the kitchen staples, mostly with their edible parts hidden underground. They include garlic, onions, carrots, beetroot (beets), parsnips, leeks and potatoes. During the Second World War in Britain, carrots and beetroot were grown instead of bedding plants in public parks; the ferny, reddish, deeply veined foliage was very attractive and needed little maintenance. There are also now many cultivars of "connoisseur" potatoes, such as 'Edzell Blue' or 'Pink Fir Apple', which have been rescued from the past. They look interesting and taste delicious.

Fruiting and Flowering Vegetables

Dramatic and showy, these are the most colourful of vegetables. Many of them belong to the cucumber family and originate from Central and South America. Tomatoes, sweetcorn, pumpkins, squashes and gourds, courgettes (zucchini), marrows and cucumbers all fall into this section. Many are suitable for growing in containers or pots. Globe artichokes or cardoons, with their grey, sculptured leaves, are striking in any border. Aubergines (eggplant), bell peppers and chillies take about five months to yield a crop and since some of these are tender, may be best grown in a cool greenhouse in a cooler climate.

Misfits

Asparagus is grown from crowns or roots; the female plant bearing tiny red berries among ferny, late summer foliage, the male version producing fatter spears. Hybrids are now available that produce only male plants. Asparagus takes up a lot of space in the garden because it needs to be planted in rows 1.2 m (4 ft.) wide, giving room for two rows of plants. Leave 90 cm (3 ft.) between the beds. Asparagus likes freedraining, sandy soil, so add grit to the asparagus trench if you are on heavy clay, giving a high-nitrogen feed in early summer to encourage the ferns.

Asparagus can be grown from seed, but you will need to wait for more than three years to get a decent harvest. Instead buy one-year-old crowns, which should crop within two years. As a rough guide, ten established plants should yield about 3 kg (7 lb.) of spears over a six-year period, for up to twenty years. To build up your stock, do not harvest the spears in the first year after planting, and take only a few in the following year.

Rhubarb (*Rheum × hybridum*) is the vegetable that wants to be a fruit and nobody quite knows which category to put it in! Each rhubarb crown takes time to settle down and when established takes up quite a bit of space, about 90 cm (3 ft.). It will grow on any kind of soil, including an acid one, provided that it is rich in nutrients and freedraining. The planting site also needs to be open and located away from overhanging trees.

Plants will need to be divided every five or so years to avoid them becoming congested. However, rhubarb is little trouble and may be forced into producing tender, early stems by covering it with straw, an upturned, cardboard box or a specialized, terracotta rhubarb forcer.

Recommended Vegetables

Note: U.S. cultivars are given after the semi-colons in this listing, e.g. 'Bonanza' and 'Raab' are U.S. broccolis.

Leaf and salad vegetables

Broccoli 'Romanesco', 'White Sprouting'; 'Bonanza', 'Raab'

Brussels sprouts 'Noisette', 'Peer Gynt', 'Rusine'; 'Jade Cross E Hybrid', 'Tasty Nuggets'

Cabbage 'January King' (Savoy), 'Palinius' (Dutch white), 'Ruby Ball' (red); 'Earliana', Salad Delight' (red)

Chicory 'Chioggia' (red; leafy type)

Curly kale 'Nero di Toscana', 'Pentland Brig', 'Thousandhead'; 'Dwarf Blue Curled Scotch', 'Red Russian' (purple-red leaves)

Lettuce
  Loose leaf types—'Salad Bowl'; 'Green Ice', Royal Oak Leaf'
  Crisphead types—'Windermere'; 'Cardinale', 'Summertime'
  Cos types—'English Cos'; 'Parris Island Cos', 'Romaine'
  Butterhead types—'All the Year Round', 'Tom Thumb'; 'Buttercrunch', 'Mantilia'

Rocket (arugula) 'Salad Rocket'; 'Roquette'

Sorrel 'Buckler-leaf'

Spinach 'Secundo', 'Sigmaleaf'; 'Bloomsdale Long Standing, 'Walter'

Swiss chard (leaf beet) 'Bright Lights', 'Rhubarb Chard'; 'Heirloom Joseph's Coat Chard'

Podded vegetables

Broad beans 'Express', 'The Sutton' (dwarf)

Climbing French beans (green or snap beans) 'Pros Gitana' (green pods), 'Radar', 'Royalty' (purple pods), 'Sungold' (yellow pods), 'Tendergreen'; 'King of the Early'

Mangetout (snow) peas 'Oregon Sugar Pod; 'Roma', 'Super Sugar Snap'

Peas 'Feltham First' (early); 'Hurst Greenshaft' (maincrop), 'Knight'

Runner (pole) bean 'Achievement' (red flowers), 'Kelvedon Marvel'; 'Blue Lake'

Bulb and stem vegetables

Asparagus 'Connover's Colossal'; 'First Edition Long Keeping', 'Premium Jersey Knight'

Celeriac 'Monarch'

Celery 'Celebrity'

Kohl rabi 'Purple Vienna'

Leeks 'Autumn Mammoth', 'Bleu de Solaise', 'Cortina'; 'Albinstar, 'Premium Jersey Knight'

Rhubarb 'Timperley Early','Victoria'

Shallots 'Giant Yellow Improved', 'Pikant'; French shallot sets

Root vegetables

Beetroot (beet) 'Boltardy', 'Bulls Blood'; 'Chioggia striped beets', 'Monopoly'

Carrot 'Autumn King', 'Early Nantes'

Jerusalem artichoke 'Fuseau'

Parsnip 'Avon Resistor'; 'Tender and True'

Potatoes (sold as seed potatoes) 'Charlotte', 'Desiree' (second early), 'Duke of York', 'Edzell Blue', 'Epicure' (first early), 'Pink Fir Apple' (salad); 'Caribe', 'Colorful All Blue', 'Gold Rush'

Recommended Vegetables (continued)

Radish 'French Breakfast'; 'Flamboyant'

Swede 'Marian'; 'Market Express'

Turnip 'Golden Ball'

Fruiting and flowering vegetables

Cauliflower 'Calabrese Comet', 'Jerome' (winter), 'Pentland Brig', 'Snow Crown' (summer)

Courgette (zucchini) 'Ambassador' (green), 'De Nice à Front Rond' (round, pale green), 'Gold Rush' (yellow)

Marrow 'Long Green Trailing'

Pumpkin 'Autumn Gold'

Squash 'Buttermilk', 'Little Gem', 'Turk's Turban'

Aubergine (eggplant) 'Moneymaker'

Cucumber 'Burpless Tasty Green'

Sweetcorn 'Sundance'

Globe artichoke 'Green Globe', 'Vert de Laon'

Tomatoes 'Alicante', 'Gardener's Delight', 'Sungold'

Herbs

Many herbs, such as *Thymus* species or *Salvia officinalis* (sage), do not need to be banished to the kitchen garden, but can be grown in windowboxes or borders. Ever since medieval times, when their flavouring properties were used to disguise the taste of rotting meat, herbs have been vital in cooking. Depending on their type, they may be treated as annuals or as shrubs. Many of them have pretty, edible flowers. They keep their shape and productivity best if continually picked or trimmed for cooking or for use in salads or cool summer drinks.

Not all herbs disappear at the end of the season. Several shrubby perennial herbs may be used either in the kitchen garden, in borders, as single specimens or in pots. They all require sun and are useful for giving structure or long-term interest to the kitchen or herb garden.

Laurus nobilis (bay), which has leaves so useful for flavouring soups and stews whether fresh or dried, may either be left to its natural shape or clipped into a pyramid or ball. The aromatic *Rosmarinus officinalis* may also be clipped; there are prostrate or spreading cultivars such as *R. officinalis* 'Severn Sea', or the more upright variety, *R. officinalis* 'Miss Jessopp's Upright'. Rosemary is often a short-lived plant, but when overgrown it may be cut back hard in mid-spring. The variegated forms of *Salvia officinalis* are more decorative than the plain green version, but the taste is the same—the leaves should be dried and stored in airtight jars for kitchen use.

Some varieties of *Thymus* have a dense creeping habit, others form tiny, rounded bushes. The creeping thymes are ideal in cracks in paving or in gravel beds. The flowers and foliages of the many different species provide useful contrasts and have the added virtue of attracting butterflies and bees. The leaves may be used fresh or dried.

Soft Fruit and Vines

These plants vary from the tiniest alpine strawberry, often used as a decorative edging and flowering continually throughout the summer, to the taller raspberries, black- or redcurrants and grape vines, which take up much more space and require annual pruning to fruit well. As well as the usual bush form, gooseberries may be supplied by specialist nurseries as standards—delicious and decorative.

Try some of the more unusual soft fruits, such as tayberries or loganberries. Vines can be fun to grow, although not all varieties produce edible grapes. Since they have handsome, deciduous leaves that often colour well in the autumn, they may be trained against walls, through arches and along pergolas. In warmer areas, experiment with the more exotic fruits, such as passionflower (*Passiflora* species) or kiwi fruit (*Actinidia deliciosa*).

All soft berrying fruit is attractive to birds, so needs to be netted or grown in fruit cages, usually constructed from netting suspended over a metal or wooden frame, to protect the crop until it is ready to pick. Always allow plenty of space, as for a shrub, between each plant when planting: some may crop very heavily, and the laden branches may become weighed down. Space is also needed for picking.

Ample water is vital to produce good crops—if the water supply is irregular, the flowers may not set properly in spring or the fruits will not swell fully later in the year. You may therefore wish to install a simple, automated or trickle irrigation system or at least a nearby garden tap to make watering the plants easier.

Recommended Soft Fruits and Vines

Raspberries (*Rubus idaeus*) 'Glen Moy',
  'Malling Jewel' (both summer-fruiting),
  'Autumn Bliss' (autumn-fruiting)

Blackberries (*Rubus fruticosus*) 'Ashton Cross',
  'Oregon Thornless', 'Oregon Thornless'

Strawberries (*Fragaria* × *ananassa*)
  'Cambridge Favourite', 'Cambridge Late
  Fine'

Alpine strawberries (*Fragaria vesca*)
  'Alexandra', 'Baron Solemacher'

Blackcurrants (*Ribes nigrum*) 'Ben Sarek',
  'Boskoop Giant'

Redcurrants (*Ribes rubrum*) 'Jonkheer van
  Tets', 'Red Lake'

Whitecurrants (*Ribes rubrum*) 'Versailles
  Blanche'

Gooseberries (*Ribes uva-crispa*) 'Careless',
  'Leveller'

Grapes (*Vitis* species) 'Brandt' (black),
  'Madeleine Silvaner' (white)

Tree, or Top, Fruit

Great pleasure can be derived from growing top fruit. Some trees, such as apples (*Malus domestica*) and pears (*Pyrus communis* cultivars), provide the bonus of spring blossom, while the fig (*Ficus carica*) has splendidly architectural foliage as well as delicious fruits. Even in a small garden, two or three fruit trees can be very rewarding. But many fruits are a long-term investment—the trees will take several years to become established, so it is worth choosing any cultivar carefully. Plant and care for them as for other trees, except for pruning. Pruning tree fruits is described in pages 287–291 and is important to maintain good fruit production.

Choosing the most suitable fruit tree

This can be a daunting task for those new to growing top fruit. There are many specialist growers and you will find that they offer a more interesting and larger range than is available from most garden centres. If possible, try to find a local nursery, since climatic conditions may govern what you can grow.

Some specialist nurseries hold occasional tasting and pruning days.

Fruit trees are grafted on to a range of different rootstocks, which determine the eventual size of the fruiting trees. Rootstocks tend to have numerical names and are categorized according to the size of the mature tree that they will support. Different rootstocks are available in countries across the world, and are chosen for their suitability to the local climate and conditions, such as soil and prevalence of diseases.

If you intend to pick the fruit, the tree size governs whether you need a ladder, so take care to select a rootstock that will produce an appropriately sized tree. In Britain, rootstocks range from M27 to M25. M27 is extremely dwarfing, 1.5–2 m (5–6½ ft.), and suitable for dwarf pyramids or "stepover" trees. M25 is very vigorous, producing trees over 4.5 m (15 ft.) tall for standard or half-standard trees.

Although a few fruit trees are self-fertile, the vast majority is not. This means that a tree fruit usually needs a second tree of a different variety of the same fruit to cross-pollinate it. Furthermore, for successful pollination, the flowering times of the two trees need to overlap. Lack of attention to this fact when choosing and planting trees may result in no fruit. If you are lucky enough to have neighbours that grow fruit trees of a suitable variety in their garden, you may find that their trees cross-pollinate yours.

Fruit trees are supplied as container-grown, containerized or open-ground (also called bare-rooted) plants. Most nurseries supply open-ground specimens from early winter to early spring. Be sure to order in good time because stocks are often limited. As with all trees and shrubs, the early care of a tree fruit will affect its vigour and eventual performance, so follow these principles when caring for a new plant.

- Check the soil regularly and water in dry conditions.

- Discourage fruiting in young trees in their first year by removing the blossom or fruitlets.

- Prune off any shoots growing from the base below the graft union (where the rootstock is united with the tree fruit), and in early spring remove any unwanted or crossing branches.

- Each spring, clear an area with about a 90 cm (3 ft.) diameter around the base of each tree and mulch with well-rotted compost or manure.

- Feed the trees annually in early spring, before growth begins, with a general-purpose fertilizer.

- After the first year, prune the tree appropriately for its type and required shape, to keep it fruiting well (see pages 287–291).

Recommended Tree Fruits

Apples (*Malus domestica*)
    Dessert—'Egremont Russet',
    'George Cave', 'Orléans Reinette'
    Cooking—'Bramley's Seedling',
    'Cox's Pomona', 'Howgate Wonder'

Pears (*Pyrus communis*) 'Beurre Hardy',
    'Conference', 'Doyenne du Comice'

Plums (*Prunus domestica*) 'Czar', 'Victoria'

Sweet cherries (*Prunus avium*) 'Early Rivers'
    (black fruit), 'Stella' (dark red fruit)

Figs (*Ficus carica*) 'Brown Turkey'

Black mulberries (*Morus nigra*) 'Wellington'

Medlars (*Mespilus germanica*) 'Nottingham'

Quince (*Cydonia oblonga*) 'Vranja', 'Meech's Prolific', 'Lusitanica'

Recommended Nuts

Almonds (*Prunus dulcis*) 'Macrocarpa'

Cobnuts (*Corylus avellana*) 'Cosford Cob'

Filberts (*Corylus maxima*) 'Kentish Cob', 'Purpurea' (purple leaves)

Walnuts (*Juglans regia*) 'Broadview' (self fertile), 'Buccaneer' (self fertile)

Nuts

Nut trees or nut hedges make an unusual alternative to fruit trees—have a nuttery as opposed to an orchard. Walnuts and almonds are useful as specimen trees. Almonds usually are the first fruit trees to bear blossom each year, the pale pink blossom standing out prettily against a clear blue, spring sky.

Walnut trees grow quickly, but often refuse to crop for the first twenty years unless several are planted together to aid pollination. Cobnuts and filberts, both types of hazel, have long, decorative catkins to be followed, if squirrels allow, by heavy crops of edible nuts.

Hazel also makes a good informal hedge; it is best in sun or partial shade in a damp, loamy soil. When the plants are four or five years old, they will benefit from some of the oldest stems being cut out or coppiced at the base in late winter, which encourages them to produce new shoots.

Plant in mid-autumn and water until trees are well established and mulch well. Squirrels are the chief pest of all nut trees, but it is almost impossible to deter them.

Growing Plants in Containers

Pots and containers make it possible to grow plants where gardening in beds or borders is not feasible, such as on terraces and decking or in courtyards and roof gardens. Planted containers may also act as puntuation points to accentuate other plantings. They can allow you to grow outdoors in the summer a range of plants that may in winter need the protection of a conservatory or greenhouse.

Traditionally, plants were grown in containers because they needed to be easily moved. In Italy, for instance, orange and lemon trees were important features of any summer garden, but in winter they required protection in a covered orangery or special, slightly heated building. Visiting an Italian garden before the *limonaia*, or citrus trees, are set out means missing part of the garden's charm. Plants in pots are an integral part of any classical scheme. When using containers in your own garden, avoid a random and ill-assorted collection of pots. Plan simultaneously each one of the containers—its type, where it should be placed, and what will be planted in it.

Container gardening can be very fulfilling. A few pots in strategic places, such as near the front or back door or as a focal point at the turning point or end of a path, where the plants can easily be admired, can bring these areas to life.

Successful Container Plants

These are the key factors to consider when growing plants in containers:

- Style and size of container
- Compost
- Drainage
- Watering
- Feeding
- Deadheading.

Choosing the Container

When choosing a container, the first consideration should be to select a style compatible with the character of the house and its surroundings. Since they are comparatively light, contemporary aluminium vessels may be perfect on a roof terrace, a basement patio or in a modern setting, but would detract from the appeal of an old-world, country cottage or stately mansion. Most containers should be a foil for plants, so choose a simple design without distracting or elaborate embellishment.

Use containers that have a natural affinity with their surroundings, such as clay, copper or lead, wood or stone, or seek out materials that simulate them, such as reconstituted stone, fibreglass, or good-quality plastic. Fibreglass pots and others may be painted in self-colours or stripes to give an individual touch. Less usual containers include old chimney pots, old wheelbarrows or hollowed-out tree trunks.

Old, ceramic kitchen sinks or troughs may be used to show off alpine plants, which are not easily grown in most open soils; simulate a mountain or scree landscape by using small rocks, stones or gravel to set them off. (See also pages 215–219.)

Size of pot

Containers work well in groups of several different sizes. They may be graded with the largest—perhaps a single one—at the rear and smaller ones, which are easier to move or to alter the planting, in front. If decorative designs or shapes are wanted, it is often best to use plain shapes at the back, placing the more decorative ones in front.

Consider the scale of the property and where the container is to be sited. A single, large pot makes a more impressive statement than several smaller ones, the latter being more prone to being knocked over accidentally. Place large pots in a permanent position because they are very heavy to move once planted.

The size of pot will govern what can be grown in it. The majority of larger plants do not like to have their roots cramped, so give them enough space to develop without becoming pot bound. *Camellia*, *Ilex* (holly), some *Magnolia* species, *Phormium* and many other larger plants are particularly effective in larger pots. Herbaceous plants, half-hardies and bulbs may be grown in smaller containers.

All pots to be left outdoors should be frost proof, and should contain hardy plants. Smaller ones may be moved indoors and out, according to the changing seasons.

Composts for containers

Pot-grown plants are totally dependent upon you for all their daily needs. Get your plants off to a good start by investing in good-quality compost. Do not stint on the compost because, unlike garden soil, it will not contain worms and other soil organisms to keep it healthy. Choosing the right compost is vital. It must be well-drained, yet hold on to a reasonable amount of moisture, and should be well supplied with nutrients, as well as having a pH that suits the plants that will be growing in it.

Sterilized, soil-based composts, such as the John Innes range in Britain, have been developed to support a wide range of potted plants. They have now been joined by a variety of soil-less composts. There are some differences between them.

- Soil-based composts are based on loam, whereas soil-less composts are founded on peat or peat-substitutes which contain humus.

- Soil-based compost tends to be heavy and can become compacted and difficult to water.

- Soil-less composts are light but tend to dry out quickly—once very dry, they do not easily absorb water.

- Soil-based composts, thanks to an element of clay, retain a wide range of nutrients better than soil-less ones and are therefore ideal for plants that are expected to live in a container for many years. Soil-less composts are more generally used for annual flowers and vegetables (often sold in growing-bags) or for some of the more exotic houseplants. A good compromise is to create a 50/50 mix of the two.

Both types of compost come in varying degrees of nutritional value, ones of moderate nutritional value being best for young plants, with high-nutrition mixes mostly being used for mature plants. The composts are relatively cheap and lightweight and promote the rapid growth that is ideal for these types of plants. However, they tend to run out of food fairly quickly and in time will oxidize away. The major considerations when choosing your compost will depend on whether you are planting the container for the short or long term.

Short-term plantings

Soil-less composts based largely on humus or fibrous material, with added nutrients, are widely used for bedding plants, annuals or crops in transit to a permanent site in the kitchen garden or flower border.

Long-term plantings

These include shrubs, shrubby houseplants, climbers or any plant expected to grow in the container for several years, even though it may need to be repotted during that time. Soil-based potting composts are better for these plants, because the clay which forms part of the loam can hold on to the nutrients for quite a long time. In addition to these benefits, soil-based composts are considerably heavier than soil-less ones and therefore offer the plant greater root stability.

If a long-term plant prefers a high humus content, mix together soil-based and soil-less composts in a 50/50 ratio. Some ferns and rainforest plants also prefer a light, humus-rich compost. Most of these plants are able to survive for many years in this growing media.

Water-retentive gel

There are several forms of this gel on the market; the most popular come in lightweight granules. Once incorporated into composts, before planting, they absorb water, swell up and become heavier. The plant can then tap into this reserve because the compost gradually takes back the water if it dries out. Gels are particularly useful in hanging baskets, which dry out quickly. Use the granules only in the recommended quantities to avoid the compost becoming spongy.

Drainage

All containers must have drainage holes and something to prevent the compost from washing out.

Traditionally, pieces of broken clay pot (crocks) have been placed over the holes in the bottom of a pot to maintain free drainage. This technique—or something similar—works well for plants that are watered from above, but it is useless where plants are stood on irrigation matting, sand or some other medium to take up water from the bottom.

In commerce, fibrous material such as sphagnum moss or osmunda fibre is often used instead of crocks. The advantage of sphagnum moss is that although it allows free drainage it can also absorb and transport water back up into the pot from, say, a sand bench or irrigation mat. The pots stand on a generous layer of the moss, with some of the moss forced through the drainage holes to make contact with the damp sand and act as wicks.

- Patio pots watered from above should be stood on small "feet" so that water drains freely away.

- Rainwater (as opposed to alkaline tap water) should be used on potted houseplants and, more especially, on any pot-grown plant that needs an acid, or ericaceous, compost (with a low pH).

- It is easy to overwater pot-grown plants. Always test the necessity for watering by feeling the compost with your finger to see how dry it is.

- Install an irrigation system of thin, plastic piping leading off to each pot. Black piping is barely noticeable and the system may be linked to a timed valve that is fixed to a garden tap. Nutrients may also be supplied in this way.

- To give a continuous display, many flowering plants such as *Pelargonium* (geranium) or *Nicotiana* (tobacco plant) need regular watering. Most plants resent standing in water, but some moisture-lovers such as *Hydrangea* may benefit if the pot stands in a large, water-filled saucer. The compost and plant can then draw up water as it is needed, by capillary action.

Feeding

A number of slow-release, compound (inorganic) fertilizers are available as granules. They release their nutrients over a period of several weeks or months, every time the plant is watered. Some are specially formulated to feed trees and shrubs, others to feed lawns. They are especially useful for trees and shrubs growing long term in containers. Always check the

ingredients in the analysis on the packet. You may also need to add trace elements because they are not always incorporated in the formula; these are best if watered on.

Many pot-grown plants benefit from a fortnightly dose of liquid fertilizer to promote flowering. Use any tomato feed or another high-nitrogen fertilizer, to promote production of flowers rather than foliage.

Deadheading

Regular deadheading increases the flowering potential of most plants, but is essential for many pot-grown half-hardies. This should be carried out twice a week during the growing season.

Planting in Containers

Before planting, soak porous containers thoroughly so that they do not absorb the moisture from the compost. Choose the potting medium carefully and check that it is compatible with what is to be grown. Acid-loving plants such as *Acer palmatum* (Japanese maples) or heathers (*Calluna* and *Erica* species) may not appreciate an alkaline, garden clay but will thrive in a pot filled with acid (ericaceous) or peat-based compost. Place a layer of broken crocks—broken pots, stones, pebbles or even pieces of polystyrene— at the bottom for drainage.

Plant in the usual way, taking extra care to firm in the soil around each plant. Water thoroughly but gently, using a watering can with a rose or long spout to avoid disturbing the soil or damaging the plants. Finish off the planting by pouring a thin layer, about 0.5–1.25 cm (¼–½ in.) of fine gravel or pea shingle on top of the compost. This helps to keep moisture in and also discourages weeds.

Choosing Plants for Pots

With a myriad of plants to choose from, it is easy to be over-ambitious. As with borders, use the same principles to choose plants. For instance, look for different leaf shapes and textures; choose flower colours that will contrast with or complement each other; avoid using too many species of plant. Simple but well-considered groupings, with repeats of plants, are usually the most effective.

Always make sure that all the plants destined for one container are compatible. They should like the same soil pH and texture and amount of water. There is no point in planting a drought-tolerant species, such a *Lavandula* or *Rosmarinus*, in the same pot as a moisture-loving *Hydrangea* or *Astilbe*—one or the other will soon cease to thrive.

Maintenance

Although some plants will survive for long periods without water, most require regular watering. In hot weather, watering will need to be more frequent—sometimes twice daily, preferably in early morning and evening— than in cooler weather. The amount of water and liquid feed for container plantings may be easily controlled by using an automatic system connected between tap and hose. The required feed is then distributed to the plants evenly and regularly.

Pests and diseases should be treated in the same way as on plants in open ground. Regular inspection should be carried out, perhaps when watering, to spot early stages of infestation or infection. Smearing the rims of your pots with grease such as Vaseline, or placing a length of copper tape just outside and beneath each rim really does deter slugs and snails, but even this technique is not foolproof.

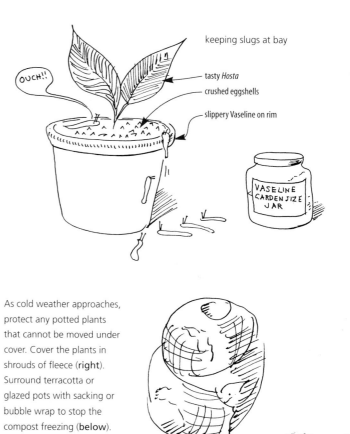

keeping slugs at bay

tasty *Hosta*
crushed eggshells
slippery Vaseline on rim

OUCH!!

VASELINE GARDEN SIZE JAR

As cold weather approaches, protect any potted plants that cannot be moved under cover. Cover the plants in shrouds of fleece (**right**). Surround terracotta or glazed pots with sacking or bubble wrap to stop the compost freezing (**below**). Move the pots to a sheltered position.

Project 4

Now that you are aware of the huge diversity of decorative plants and what can be achieved with them, you are ready to plan and implement the in-fill planting of the garden, probably the most creative and enjoyable part of making a garden. Follow the steps below to make sure you get the best out of the large choice of plants at your local nursery or garden centre.

Start a Photographic File

Whenever you can, take photographs of plants that appeal to you and illustrate your style, whether they are in garden centres or public, botanical or neighbours' gardens. Take care to record vital information about the plant in a notebook—you will need to refer back to it later. Here are some points to guide you:

- Take photographs with a good SLR (single-lens reflex) or digital camera, capable of taking both close-up and more general shots. Usually 200 ASA film is best.

- Take photographs of the overall plant shape, to show its form.

- Take close-ups of any interesting features, e.g. leaves, buds, flowers, fruit, stems, seedheads or bark.

- Note the following information:
  - Location—you may wish to return later
  - Time and date
  - Full botanical name—visiting gardens where plants are labelled will save time on research and prevent identification errors
  - Climatic and soil conditions e.g. sunny, damp or waterlogged.

- It is useful to transfer your notes to the back of the photographs or the digital image files.

- Store photographs in labelled folders or boxes rather than random packages. Consider sorting them by feature, e.g. autumn colours or ground cover, or plant type, e.g. trees, shrubs.

- Keep a stock of cuttings from garden magazines as a further source of pictures and information.

You could make up photocards like this, to keep in a file that may be added to as you spot more plants that you like.

Sedum spectabile

Herbaceous perennial

Common name: iceplant

Height: 45 cm (18 in)

Spread: 45 cm (18 in)

Soil: any well-drained, fe...
adequate moisture in sum...

Hardiness: 4

Notes: flowers in dense du...
dry stems; appear in l...
grey-green succulent...
well; attracts bees an...

Prunus mume

Small, deciduous tree

Common name: Japanese apricot

Height: 2.5 m (8 ft)

Spread: 1.5 m (5 ft)

Soil: any moist, but well-drained, fertile soil;
full sun

Hardiness: 4

Notes: delightful, small tree with green, young
shoots and single, almond-scented, pink
flowers in early spring. Needs little pruning
apart from dead, diseased or damaged wood.

Compile a Plant Groupings Portfolio

Completing these for different sites or effects in your garden will help to plan your plantings, as well as increase your knowledge of plants and their requirements. For each situation, choose between three and six suitable plants. If you find it difficult to make a selection, list all the possible plants, then use our lists or a catalogue to research the plants' needs, which in turn will restrict your choice. Then consider form, size and texture of foliage as well as the more ephemeral flowers. The objective is to create an effective planting combination.

Record the "vital statistics" of each plant (see template, opposite, and examples on following pages) so that you compile a full record of the plants intended for each grouping. You could also attach photographs or images of the plant clipped from magazines, or cross-refer to your photographic files. Possible categories for a grouping might be:

- Dry shade

- Moist shade

- Dry, sunny site

- Windy situation

- North walls

- Winter interest

- Ornamental stems or bark

- Autumn colour

- Thrives on chalk

- Thrives by the coast

- Attracts butterflies and bees

- Lime-free or acidic soil.

You may find it useful to record synonyms, out-of-date Latin names that are still well-known or commonly used, and to list books or websites in which you found most information on the plant.

When recording the height and spread of a plant, choose an appropriate scale of years. For example, for a perennial, note height and spread at two years, five years and 10 years. For a tree, indicate five years, 10 years and 20 years. Assume average growing conditions in your area.

You could also add notes at the end of the profile sheet on any important miscellaneous information or add cross-referencing; for example, *Taxus baccata* (English yew) may be included in groupings for a mixed border and for hedging.

Botanical name

Plant family   **Common name/s**

Synonym/s   **Origin and native habitat**

Useful references

Description
Foliage, flower, fruit and stem

Period of Interest   **Form, height and spread**

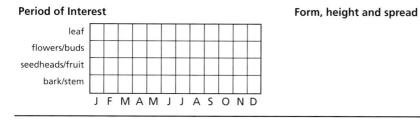

leaf
flowers/buds
seedheads/fruit
bark/stem

J F M A M J J A S O N D

Cultivation notes
Soil and moisture
Aspect
Maintenance
Propagation

                                         Hardiness

Design notes

Complementary plants

Alternatives

Meaning of botanical name

Notes

Botanical Name	*Ilex aquifolium* 'Pyramidalis'		
Plant Family	Aquifoliaceae	**AGM**	H4
Synonym	None known	**Common Name**	Common holly / English holly
Origin	West and South Europe, North Africa, W. Asia	**Availability**	26 suppliers
Native Habitat	Mixed woodlands as an under storey to large, deciduous trees such as oak.		

DESCRIPTION

A narrowly conical, upright, female shrub or small tree with variable growth.

Leaves Narrow, elliptical, bright green leaves about 6–8cm long.

Flowers/Buds In May and June, small, fragrant, waxy-white, four-petalled flowers appear in clusters in the leaf axils. Male and female flowers are carried on separate trees. One male has to be planted for every six females to ensure pollination.

Fruit/Seedhead Produces abundant, bright red, spherical berries, that, if ingested, can cause mild stomach upset. Berries ripen in late autumn or early winter and often last till spring. Each contains up to four black seeds.

Bark/Stem Has a yellow-green stem.

PERIOD OF INTEREST

	J	F	M	A	M	J	J	A	S	O	N	D	**Form**	**Height & Spread (m)**
Leaves	▓	▓	▓	▓	▓	▓	▓	▓	▓	▓	▓	▓	Narrow conical	**10/20 yrs** Height 6m Spread 5m
Flowers/Buds					▓	▓								
Seedheads/Fruit									▓	▓	▓			**2/5yrs**
Bark/Stem														Height 2m

CULTIVATION

Soil & Moisture Moist but well drained, moderately fertile, humus-rich soil.   **Hardiness** Fully hardy (−15°C/5°F)

Aspect Full sun or partial shade

Maintenance & Pruning Planting or transplanting is best done in late winter or early spring. Prune freestanding trees in the early years only. Clip formally grown plants in summer; trim hedges in spring. After pruning, apply a well-rotted mulch, about 5–7cm deep, around the base of the tree.

Propagation Take cuttings with heels in late summer: plant in a shady cold frame, transplant after a year, then grow on for a further year or two before setting in a permanent site.

Problems & Drawbacks Young shoots are susceptible to aphids; scale insects and leaf miners may be a problem on evergreen species. Sometimes suffers from phytophthora root rot.

DESIGN & ASSOCIATED PLANTING

Design Use

(1) Makes a fine garden hedge, an effective barrier against cold winds and noise.

(2) Fine specimen for a woodland garden.

Complementary Plants

(1) Viburnum x bodnantense 'Dawn' – Upright, deciduous shrub with ovate to oblong, toothed, dark green leaves. Heavily scented tubular, dark pink flowers, ageing to white, borne on bare wood, over a long period from late autumn to spring. Fully hardy. Will add a softness to the planting, whilst extending the flowering interest and introducing scent into the planting scheme. Same planting conditions as above. Fully hardy, AGM H4. Height 3m, spread 2m.

(2) Mahonia japonica – Erect shrub with stout, upright branches and pinnate, dark green leaves with sharply toothed, ovate-oblong to lance-shaped leaflets. Fragrant, pale yellow flowers are produced in arching, then spreading, racemes from late autumn to early spring, followed by ovoid, blue-purple berries. Flowers give a good colour contrast with the red berries and has complementary, spiky leaves. Fully hardy. Same soil as above. AGM H4. Height 2m, spread 3m.

Alternatives

(1) Ilex aquifolium 'J.C. van Tol' – broad, female tree with dark purple stems and elliptic, puckered, almost entire, dark green leaves. Bears abundant, bright red berries. Self fertile. Height 6m, spread 4m. Fully hardy. Same soil conditions as above. AGM H4

(2) Ilex x altaclerensis 'Camelliifolia' – large, conical, female tree or shrub with purple-tinged stems, elliptic to oblong, deep green leaves and scarlet berries. Frost hardy. Height 14m, spread 12–15m. Same soil conditions as above. AGM H3

Meaning/Origin of Botanical Name Ilex : Holly. From the Latin name for the holm oak (Quercus ilex).
aquifolium : classical name for holly.
'Pyramidalis': "pyramid-shaped".

Notes Valuable food source for insects and birds, particularly in the winter.

Ilex aquifolium 'Pyramidalis'
Kew Gardens
October 2004

An example of a completed Plant Groupings Portfolio entry. As the sheets build up, you will have your own information file on your favourite plants, and notes on what other plants may be used with them to enhance the effect.

Update your Garden Plan

As you develop your ideas for planting or install new borders and plantings, mark them on your garden plan in the correct positions, or make separate planting plans for larger beds and borders.

Decide on the trees, structural shrubs and climbers first, then follow with the decorative planting, usually the herbaceous perennials, annuals, or half-hardies. Use your Plant Groupings Portfolio to plan groupings. Arrange the perennials in groups around the structural planting, thinking about shape, texture, height, and colour, and where possible, scent. Around the perimeter of your border, use your plants to emphasize the outline. Remember to give each plant space to grow to its full potential—although there may be plenty of bare earth showing in the early stages, the plants will soon fill out and eventually there will be little soil on view or for weeds to invade.

The Red Border

The new planting in this bed was inspired by the bronze, red and buff tones of the brick wall behind. Despite facing northeast, this border is particularly prominent during the summer, when the family are using the nearby terrace. Most of the shrubs are deciduous because this border is intended to peak during summer and early autumn, so there is less need for structural planting. The red border provides an ongoing display of colour from early summer through to the first frost, when the cannas and dahlias are lifted to overwinter under cover.

The plan opposite shows the main plantings; other herbaceous plants, including bulbs, were used to in-fill to create a lush border. The main points to note are:

1   The fastigiate yew (*Taxus baccata* 'Fastigiata') was moved to this bed to disguise the change in roof pitch behind.

2   The existing evergreen camellia was retained—although the pink flowers are not strictly according to the colour scheme, they appear early, before the other shrubs and perennials begin to perform, and are a welcome relief after the winter.

3   An unusual shrub, *Clerodendrum trichotomum* var. *fargesii*, which has cream, very fragrant flowers enclosed in maroon calyces in late summer is grown as a standard tree. It was used as a pivot to mark where the border changes direction and to hold the eye from travelling beyond the garden.

4   The only climbers used are *Rosa* 'Meg' and *R.* 'Climbing Lady Hillingdon' whose scented, apricot-yellow tones blend well with the brick wall, together with the ivy, *Hedera colchica* 'Sulphur Heart', which provides a bright backdrop during winter and a refuge for birds.

5   Evergreen shrubs are the bright yellow-fruiting *Photinia davidiana* var. *undulata* 'Fructu Luteo', whose older leaves turn bright red in autumn; *Salvia officinalis* 'Purpurascens', useful and near the kitchen for picking; and the semi-evergreen *Berberis thunbergii* f. *atropurpurea* 'Dart's Red Lady', which is clipped and used to accentuate corners, although it can prove difficult to restrict its size.

6   Other deciduous shrubs, selected for their varying leaf colour and shapes, set off the herbaceous planting.

7   A range of herbaceous plants, chosen partly for their leaf colour and partly for their flowers in sunshine colours of scarlet, orange and gold, are interspersed with bulbs, such as the glowing red *Tulipa* 'Couleur Cardinal' and the scented *T.* 'Generaal de Wet'.

8   For summer impact, the golden yellow, highly scented lily, *Lilium regale* Golden Splendor Group, is planted in groups of three.

9   Flowering extends into autumn with the addition of tall, red-flowered *Canna indica* and the dark-leaved *Dahlia* 'Bishop of Llandaff'.

10 Evergreen *Bergenia* 'Eric Smith', named after the famous plantsman, is a real aristocrat with sumptuous, glowing red-bronze foliage in winter. Two groups of it were used to define the corners of the border, where eventually there will be an entrance through the barn.

11 Other herbaceous plants that might be included in the red border are:

Achillea siberica 'Summerwine'

Achillea 'Walther Funcke'

Astrantia maxima

Crocosmia 'Lucifer'

Echinacea purpurea 'Kim's Knee High'

Potentilla 'Gibson's Scarlet'

Detailed planting plans for the Red Border in the rear garden

Shrubs & climbers

Herbaceous perennials

Berberis thunbergii f. atropurpurea 'Dart's Red Lady'/5

Clerodendrum trichotomum var. fargesii (standard)/1

Rosa 'Buff Beauty'/3

Taxus baccata 'Fastigiata'/1 (relocated)

Sambucus nigra 'Gerda'/1

Salvia officinalis 'Purpurascens'/3

Hedera colchica 'Sulphur Heart'/1

Symphoricarpos orbiculatus 'Foliis Variegatis'/1

Diervilla sessilifolia/1

Berberis thunbergii f. atropurpurea/1

Rosa 'Climbing Lady Hillingdon'/1

Berberis thunbergii f. atropurpurea/1

Photinia davidiana var. undulata 'Fructu Luteo'/1

Hedera colchica 'Sulphur Heart'/1

Cotinus coggygria **Golden Spirit**/1

Physocarpus opulifolius 'Diabolo'/1

Rosa 'Meg'/1

Existing Camellia (pink)/1

Berberis thunbergii f. atropurpurea 'Dart's Red Lady'/3

Sedum spectabile/3

Hemerocallis 'Stella de Oro'/5

Lonicera tellmanniana/1

Cirsium rivulare/3

Echinacea 'Purpurea'/7

Dahlia 'Bishop of Llandaff'/5

Canna indica/3

Geum pentapetalum 'Prinses Juliana'/5+5

Sedum 'Bertram Anderson'/5

Kniphofia 'Toffee Nosed'/5+5

Geum pentapetalum 'Prinses Juliana'/5

Canna indica/3

Lobelia cardinalis 'Queen Victoria'/3

Canna indica/3

Dahlia 'Bishop of Llandaff'/5

Bergenia 'Eric Smith'/3+3

Lobelia cardinalis 'Queen Victoria'/3

Heuchera 'Cherries Jubilee'/5

This is the plan for replanting the bed that runs along the side wall of the rear garden at Sandhill Farm House (see detailed caption opposite).

North

0   5m

The White Border

As you enter the garden through the arch in the tall beech hedge, the luminous white border and the multistemmed silver birch, *Betula utilis*, opposite, form the first impression of the front garden. I am too busy to entertain much during the day, most of my friends coming for an informal supper, so the main theme here is white and silver, shades which stand out as dusk approaches. Many of the pale-coloured plants are highly fragrant to attract butterflies and moths—a lovely bonus.

The main shrubs and climbers are supported by herbaceous perennials and climbers. In making a white border, often too many plants with green foliage and white flowers are included, making it predominately a green border with white flowers. To avoid this, and to achieve a luminous effect, plants with white flowers and silver foliage are used. Also often forgotten are the many differing shades of white—from the pure whites to greenish, pink, yellow or creamy whites. For an effective white border, settle on one of these tones and carry the theme through. For example, the bulb *Camassia leichtlinii* subsp. *leichtlinii* 'Alba Plena' would be assumed to have white flowers—in fact they are parchment cream, and look dirty when placed next to a pure white flower.

At present, with so many bulbs to plant annually and the roses to deadhead, the White Garden is very labour-intensive, but it does create an instant impact for about nine months of the year, which is asking a lot from a small space. Points to note are:

1   The structural backdrop to the flowering plants is provided by two upright yews, *Taxus baccata* 'Fastigiata', which stand as sentinels, and the boundary to the border of a glowing, light-evergreen hedge of box, *Buxus microphylla* 'Faulkner'.

2   The mainstay of the border relies on groups of *Rosa* Iceberg, which continue flowering here until early winter. The rose blooms tend to hang down on a fairly thin "neck", or stem; perhaps a more floriferous variety, such as *Rosa* 'Margaret Merrill' despite its having a shorter flowering season, should have been chosen instead.

3   Against the warm backdrop of the stone wall is *Rosa* 'Cooperi', a gift and a vigorous rambler that is quickly covering almost the entire wall. It is a thug to prune, but intertwines with *Clematis* 'Alba Luxurians', which has white-tinted mauve flowers, to extend the season of interest. Also against the wall are two choice *Carpenteria californica*, whose large, white flowers with golden anthers light up the space in midsummer.

4   Herbaceous plants include the ultimate white border plant, the outstanding *Lysimachia ephemerum*, which has metallic-blue foliage setting off its upright, white, candle-like, long-lasting flowers. Beneath the roses, the early-flowering *Pulmonaria* 'Sissinghurst White' serves as ground cover without interfering with the roses' growth. The richly clove-scented *Dianthus* 'Mrs Sinkins', again with glaucous leaves, comes into play later, in early summer. Silver-leaved *Artemisia* 'Powis Castle' threads through the other plantings, giving rhythm and cohesion to the overall effect.

5   In trying to achieve a dramatic effect in a fairly small space, bulbs and annuals are invaluable. The season begins with the early flowering snowdrop, *Galanthus* 'S. Arnott' emerging through the foliage of the *Pulmonaria*, followed by the snow-white, pendent flowers of *Narcissus* 'Thalia' emerging beneath the stone wall.

Then tulips take over—first, the single early *Tulipa* 'Diana'; the glamorous *T.* 'Garden Party', a rare diversion from the controlled colour spectrum, with white petals that glow carmine around the edges; the pure white single late *T.* 'Maureen'; the elegant, upstanding, lily-flowering *T.* 'White Triumphator'; finally, the much remarked upon *T.* 'Spring Green', which has an ivory-white, feathered green flower that links in with both the foliage and flowers of the border.

I realise I should treat this abundance of tulips as annuals and lift them every year, but sometimes I forget and am surprised at how many reappear unscathed for a second showing, largely because of the light, sandy soil.

6   As the season draws on, the *Agapanthus africanus* 'Albus', the heavily scented *Lilium regale* and annuals such as the white-flowering snapdragon, *Antirrhinum hispanicum* 'Avalanche', continue flowering throughout the summer.

Detailed planting plans for the White Border in the front garden

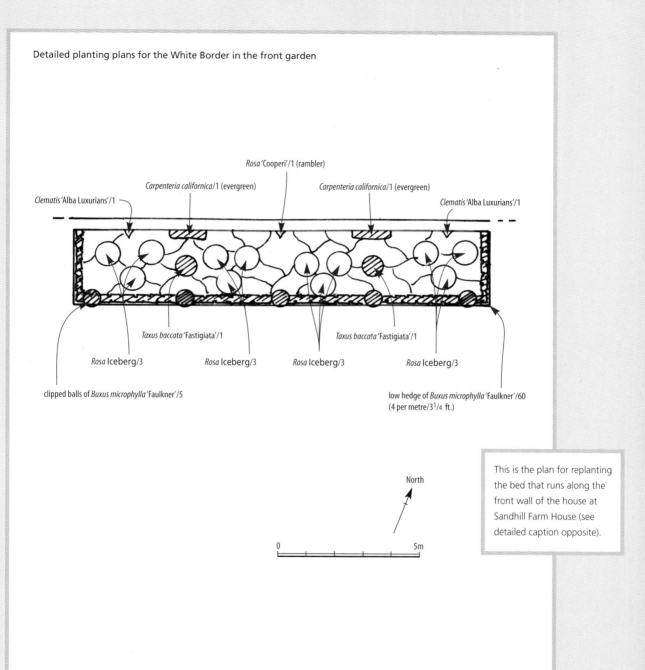

Rosa 'Cooperi'/1 (rambler)

Carpenteria californica/1 (evergreen)

Carpenteria californica/1 (evergreen)

Clematis 'Alba Luxurians'/1

Clematis 'Alba Luxurians'/1

Taxus baccata 'Fastigiata'/1

Taxus baccata 'Fastigiata'/1

Rosa Iceberg/3

Rosa Iceberg/3

Rosa Iceberg/3

Rosa Iceberg/3

clipped balls of *Buxus microphylla* 'Faulkner'/5

low hedge of *Buxus microphylla* 'Faulkner'/60
(4 per metre/3¹/₄ ft.)

North

0　　　　　　　　5m

This is the plan for replanting the bed that runs along the front wall of the house at Sandhill Farm House (see detailed caption opposite).

Above: Herbaceous plants should be chosen as much for their leaves as for their flowers. The large, white-veined foliage of *Brunnera* 'Jack Frost' brings interest and a touch of lightness to a cool, shady area.

Above: Delicate, ferny foliage in bluish-grey is in short supply. *Dicentra formosa alba* is a low, spreading perennial suited to a shady border or woodland edge.

Above: To contrast with the rounded shapes of most plants, use upright or spiky leaves. *Iris pseudacorus* 'Variegata' needs deep, acid, moist soil in sun or light shade.

Above: The large leaves of *Rodgersia podophylla* are purplish-bronze when young, and give textural interest near water or when it is naturalized at a woodland margin.

Above: Many taller perennial plants need staking. There are several different types of metal supports available, but all need to be placed over the plant in early summer so that the foliage growth will hide the supports later.

Above: Hazel twigs or pea sticks blend in naturally so as to be almost unnoticeable. To make them sturdier, their pliable tops can be bent over and tied together.

Above: In a traditional herbaceous border, billowing plants soon knit together as the summer progresses. Frothy yellow flowers of *Alchemilla mollis*, beloved of flower arrangers, grow through *Geranium* 'Ann Folkard'; both are trouble-free plants.

Right: In colder areas, or for frost-tender plants, a protective wigwam can be made from bracken held in place by garden canes. This makeshift structure still allows air to circulate and keeps the plant healthy.

Left: Until devastated by birds, a few perennial plants provide vivid berries. *Arum italicum* subsp. *italicum* 'Marmoratum' is a tuberous perennial with arrow-shaped, glossy, dark green leaves from winter to late spring, followed by these spikes of orange-red berries.

Left: To make a big impact at the edge of paths or borders, trickle bulbs of *Muscari* (grape hyacinth) into a shallow trench, then cover them with soil, rather than attempting to plant them singly.

Above: At Stoneacre, Kent in Britain, a double band of grape hyacinths flank either side of the path and continue as an edging as the path changes direction. The spent flower heads are removed to prevent this rather invasive bulb from seeding around.

Left: In cooler climates, dahlia tubers of cultivars such as *Dahlia* 'Moonshine' can be potted up and wintered under cover, then brought out, when the foliage has emerged, to be planted in borders in late spring.

Above: When overcrowded, *Iris germanica* may cease to flower. The rhizomes need to be dug up, the older part discarded, and the newer growth with young leaves replanted. Plant the rhizomes in a fan-shaped formation, so they sit on the soil surface and are baked by the sun.

Left: Autumn-flowering bulbs prolong the flowering season. The flowers of *Colchicum autumnale* look well against a carpet of the evergreen shrub, *Pachysandra terminalis* 'Variegata'.

Right: The enormous range of tulips now available makes it difficult to choose. This fine triumph tulip, *Tulipa* 'Couleur Cardinal', flowers in late spring and is suitable for most garden situations.

Above: Shallow stone troughs, placed on the ground or raised up on stone columns, allow alpines to be grown. Group the plants to contrast their shapes and foliage.

Above: The popularity of grasses and the range of varieties now available have revolutionized traditional planting. They are a bonus in late summer when much of the perennial planting is beginning to die back.

Above: Cutting back grasses—most ornamental grasses need little care, other than an annual shearing over or "combing" in early spring to remove dead foliage.

Above: Cutting back grasses—a clump of *Pennisetum*, after shearing over. A clump of this size could be split up into three plants, using two forks placed back to back to prise the tough crown apart.

Above: Taller varieties of bamboo quickly provide a dense screen, but can be invasive. Cut out the older culms (stems) in spring, using them either for staking other plants or bent into low hoops to form an edging to a border.

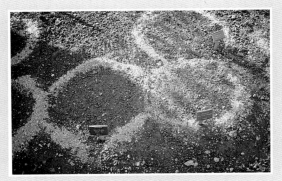

Above: Sowing seeds—for an informal effect, mark out a rough circle with sand, then sow the seeds in straight lines within this circle. The lines will help you distinguish your seedlings from weeds.

Above: Sowing seeds—group several circles together, each sown with one variety, to create natural drifts in a border. Mark each sown area with the plant name, date sown, and the seed supplier (in case the seed doesn't perform as expected).

Right: Successful wildflower meadows depend on poor or infertile soil, non-aggressive or weak grass growth, and a flower mix that is suited to the local soil.

Above: In a kitchen garden, a painted arbour provides a focal point and a place to relax while deciding what to pick. A small growing plot can supply the average family with vegetables, salad crops and soft fruit that are much superior to bought offerings.

Right: In a kitchen garden, utilizing the space to be as productive and healthy as possible can produce an attractive combination of plants.

Above: As well as crop protection, wicker cloches have a variety of uses. They allow light and air to the plants, look decorative, are inexpensive and easily stored.

Chapter 5

Caring for Plants

Now that you have invested time, effort, and probably money in putting all the major elements of your garden into place, it is time to consider what care and maintenance will be needed to keep the plants healthy so that they perform well in the future.

Some people are said to have green fingers. They seem to be able to grow plants without any specialist or technical knowledge. The rest of us find that some inside knowledge of what plants need to survive is very useful, if not essential, to avoid expensive disappointments. For example, a basic understanding of the life cycle of a plant might help us to alter its growing conditions in order to achieve better results.

It also helps to understand the reasons behind the pruning and propagation techniques, why occasionally things do not go according to plan and how to rectify matters. This first section of this chapter therefore covers the basic structure of plants and how they grow and develop.

One of the major tasks in caring for a garden is pruning. The basics have already been covered when discussing renovation of woody plants, but to maximize their potential you will also need to learn more about how to prune them to keep them in shape. You will also find advice on pruning popular plants such as roses, clematis and apple trees.

Very few experienced gardeners spend much money on buying plants. Although they all love plants, they obtain that unusual perennial or prized, scented shrub by swapping seeds or growing plants from cuttings given to them by other keen gardeners. The satisfaction of growing your own stock is enormous, and the various methods of propagation are dealt with later in the chapter.

Plant health is also important to gardeners—there is no point in maintaining a garden or growing plants unless they do well. To get the best out of them, you need to understand how to keep them healthy. The section in this chapter on common pests and diseases will help you to identify and control any problems before they get out of hand.

Once you have mastered the essentials in these major areas of plant care, you may be amazed at what you can achieve by putting theory into practice while caring for your garden.

How Plants Work

Plants grow and develop by combining sunlight, carbon dioxide (from the air) and water to produce sugars and energy; they are highly efficient biochemical processors. You only have to look at a tree to see what this process, called photosynthesis, can create over the years. Leaves trap the sunlight, roots take in water and nutrients and stems transport water and sugars in solution to the various parts of the plant to feed its growth.

A plant is a complex organism made up of different parts—roots, stems, leaves, flowers, and seeds. Each part plays a vital role in the biological cycle of fertilization, germination, feeding, growth and reproduction. It is a mutual dependency network. If any part breaks down, the whole system may collapse and if the problem is not solved, the plant will eventually die.

Roots

It helps to be familiar with the various parts of a root and know what a healthy root system should look like. While it is not often possible to inspect roots when they are deep underground, you can easily inspect those growing in a pot. Take a small, but well-established, potted plant and knock the root ball out of its pot.

Do this by holding the potted plant in the palm of one hand and place the fingers of your other hand over the surface of the soil either side of the stem. Turn the plant upside down and tap the rim of the

Plant Groups

Most flowering plants fall into into two classes—monocotyledons and eudicotyledons, previously known as dicotyledons. (The Magnoliaceae family used to be included in dicotyledons, but now form their own, the magnoliids.) All the examples in the following text on plant botany are based on eudicotyledonous plants, since most plants you will use are likely to fall into this group.

Bulbs, which consist of a compressed stem at the base (basal plate) and a series of concentric leaves around the growing point, are all monocotyledons; they are not seen in dicotyledonous families, unlike tubers, corms and rhizomes.

Monocotyledons have:

- Only one seed leaf in each mature seed
- Fibrous roots, as in grasses
- Strappy-shaped leaves, with parallel veins
- Flower parts, e.g. petals, stamens, in threes
- Petals and sepals that look the same, collectively known as tepals.

Dicotyledons have:

- Two seed leaves in each mature seed
- Often, a taproot (one main root with others branching off it)
- Broad leaves, with reticulate (web-like) veins
- Flower parts, e.g. petals, stamens, in fours or fives
- Distinctly separate petals and sepals.

pot firmly down on the edge of a bench or wall. The impact should loosen the root ball so that you can simply lift off the pot and expose the many roots that will be visible around the edge of the root ball.

You will see that many of the roots are white and branching perhaps with one or two thicker brown ones near the top. At or near the tip of each root, you may just be able to see a white, fuzzy mass of root hairs. These are usually only just visible with the naked eye, but are one of the most important parts of a root. Replace the pot, turn it the right way up, and tap the pot and plant down on to the bench to settle it back into the pot.

Basic root structure

It is only at its very tip that a root grows in length, and it is in this region that root hairs develop. The hairs are only one cell thick. They take in water and soluble mineral nutrients and play a vital part in the plant's nutrition. Root hairs are very fragile and do not survive for long but as one dies off, another grows below, and the root tip extends.

The wall of the root hair acts as a semi-permeable membrane, allowing only water and dissolved mineral salts to pass from the soil (a low-salt concentration) through into the root hair (a high-salt concentration). Under normal circumstances, the concentration of mineral salts in solution within the root hair is greater than that within the surrounding soil moisture.

For many plants, the root system becomes permanent. It thickens with age to form the plant's means of anchorage in the soil, as well as a route through which water and nutrients can pass, eventually reaching the stem.

Water and mineral salts in solution, collected by the root hairs, passes from cell to cell, across the cortex (the bulk tissue) until they reach the xylem transport vessels, made of tube-like cells. They then travel up the xylem vessels into the stems and other parts of the plant. The salts end up in the phloem transport vessels, which conduct the salts to the rest of the plant. The phloem vessels also bring to the roots sugars made by the plant in the leaves during photosynthesis. Both xylem and phloem are formed from cambium (active growth) tissue.

root tip—typical longitudinal section

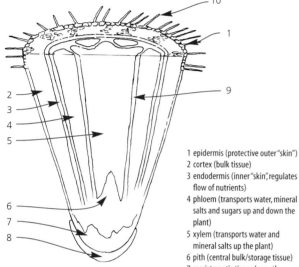

1 epidermis (protective outer "skin")
2 cortex (bulk tissue)
3 endodermis (inner "skin", regulates flow of nutrients)
4 phloem (transports water, mineral salts and sugars up and down the plant)
5 xylem (transports water and mineral salts up the plant)
6 pith (central bulk/storage tissue)
7 meristematic tissue (growth tissue—length)
8 root cap (protective sheath)
9 cambium (growth tissue—girth)
10 root hairs (take up water and dissolved mineral salts from soil)

root tip—typical cross-section

Key Points Affecting Root Care

Overfeeding

Plants shouldn't be overfed. If too much fertilizer is watered in around a plant, the salt concentration around the outside of the root hairs could become higher than that within, and suck out water from the roots. This process is called reverse osmosis. The immediate symptom would be wilting. Drenching the plant roots with water to flush through excess fertilizer could help, but only if the soil or compost is well drained.

Damaged roots

When fibrous roots are damaged or pruned, they will usually regrow. Adding soft humus, fibre or peat can speed up this growth by providing a good balance around the roots of air and moisture. As soon as new root hairs develop, the plant can once again take in water and nutrients. It is often better to delay feeding a new plant for a while until its roots have developed, rather than include fertilizer along with the humus or fibre.

Waterlogging

If, as a result of overwatering and poor compost, air is excluded from around the roots, then root hairs and other parts of the root may die and again cause wilting. If the situation cannot be quickly rectified, it may be possible to remove pieces of the stem and put them in water to recover (which they should do without the faulty root). Then decide how best to propagate the plant (for example from cuttings, budding or grafting).

Key Points Affecting Root Care (continued)

Anchorage

For most plants, the root system provides anchorage in the soil. Many trees, for example, have a long taproot for stability. Should the taproot be damaged in its early years, several less penetrating roots may develop in place of it. This could mean that when the tree is subjected to high winds, it might blow over. Never trim the taproot before planting a tree unless it is seriously damaged.

Some trees, notably *Eucalyptus*, need to be planted in their permanent positions when very young. If they are grown in a pot for any length of time (say two years), they may never develop a deep root in the open ground.

Different types of root

Some plants have thickened roots, or root tubers—for example *Dahlia*. Some are treated as vegetables, for example carrots and parsnips. These roots store food and allow the plant to overwinter in the ground and survive cold conditions.

Many tropical plants, such as *Monstera deliciosa*, develop aerial roots from their stems that can absorb moisture from the air—ideal in humid jungles. As you have already seen (see pages 168–169), some plants use aerial roots as a means of support to climb towards the light. Aquatic plants have roots that function in water, with no soil.

Many plants may be propagated from root cuttings. Others, such as fruit trees, can be grafted on to a host root (stock or rootstock) of another plant, so that they can either develop greater vigour or have their natural vigour restricted. Both methods of propagation are described later (see pages 306–312).

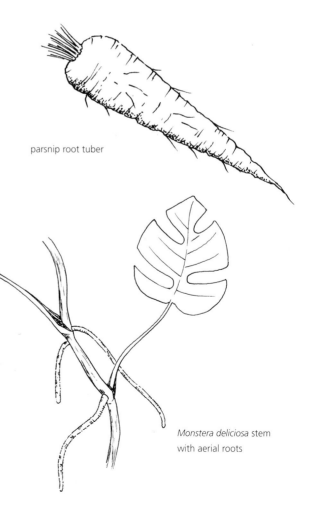

parsnip root tuber

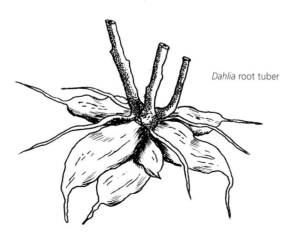

Dahlia root tuber

Monstera deliciosa stem with aerial roots

Stems

A knowledge of how stems are structured both inside and out will help you to understand how the plant:

- grows

- supports its leaves

- flowers and fruits

- might be pruned or propagated successfully.

There are two main types of stem—woody and herbaceous. Woody stems build up layers of hard, dead tissue containing a substance called lignin, year on year, to form a permanent framework, as with trees and shrubs. Herbaceous stems are soft and many—but not all—die back to a permanent crown of shoots in winter.

External features of a stem

To be successful at pruning or various propagation techniques, you will need to be familiar with the external appearance of stems and any relevant features. Take any length of stem, whether or not it has leaves.

If your piece of stem includes the tip, you will see that your stem ends with a bud (or buds). This is the terminal, or apical, bud(s). As you work your way down the stem, you will find other buds (and perhaps young shoots), placed not entirely randomly but at specific, slightly swollen "joints". The joints are called nodes. Leaves, stems, flowers and even roots can emerge from the nodes, so they are important features when it comes to taking cuttings or pruning a plant is correctly. Buds occur in various arrangements along the stem: they may be opposite (arranged in facing pairs), alternate (spaced singly on alternate sides) or arranged spirally.

The relatively smooth stem between nodes is the internode. Along each internode, you may see tiny

pores called lenticels. These often allow the passage of gases through the epidermis (the relatively thick, outer skin or bark) of the stem.

If you take another stem that is relatively soft and obviously in growth, you will see not a bud at the tip (unless it is a flower bud), but a green shoot with tiny leaves developing. Almost invisible to the naked eye on the stem tip is a cluster of cells, called the growing tip, or meristem; the cells multiply rapidly to produce new growth.

opposite buds on horse chestnut stem

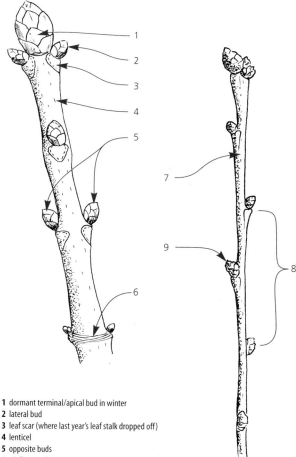

1 dormant terminal/apical bud in winter
2 lateral bud
3 leaf scar (where last year's leaf stalk dropped off)
4 lenticel
5 opposite buds
6 girdle or scale scars (location of previous terminal bud)
7 epidermis (outer "skin" or bark)
8 internode
9 node (joint)

spiral buds on oak stem

Internal structure of a stem

Inside a stem, the bulk of the tissue is starchy storage tissue, often called ground tissue, and there are three main, other types of tissue, which originate in the roots. The xylem transport tissue is formed like a series of tubes through which water can travel from the roots to the rest of the plant. In a tree, this tissue builds up over many years to form the main part of the woody trunk.

At the outer edges of the xylem tubes are layers of actively dividing growth cells, called the cambium. On the outsides of these lies the phloem—more transport tissue arranged into vessels that conduct nutrients both up and down the stem. The cambium and phloem are close to the surface of the stem—just beneath the epidermis.

Key Points Affecting Stem Care

Pruning stems

When a plant is pruned, the portion of stem remaining on the plant must end in a bud or node. If a length of internode is left without a bud at the top, the stem will die back to the next node and provide an opportunity for disease to enter the plant.

Damaged growing tips

Sucking insects, such as aphids, can easily damage the meristem. This then severely distorts the subsequent growth from the meristem, whether it is leaves, stems or flowers. The damage may be permanent by the time it is spotted by the human eye (see also pest control, pages 314–335).

young shoot—longitudinal section

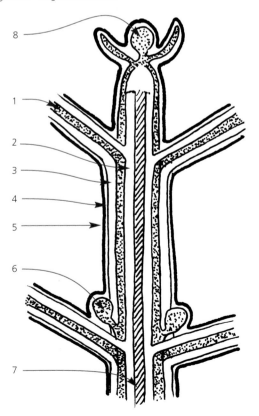

internal structure of a eudicotyledonous stem

1 cambium (growth tissue—girth)
2 xylem (transports water and mineral salts from roots)
3 phloem (transports water, minerals salts and sugars up and down the plant)
4 cortex (outer bulk/storage tissue)
5 epidermis (outer, protective "skin")
6 lateral bud
7 pith (central bulk/storage tissue)
8 shoot meristem (growth tissue—length)
9 endodermis (regulates flow of nutrients)

mature stem—cross-section

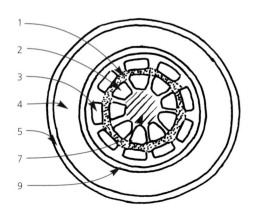

Propagation

The meristem on the growing tip is usually free from plant viruses, so in recent years, this part of the plant has been used to develop test-tube techniques of propagation (micropropagation) to produce virus-free plant stocks.

Training stems

Plant ties can damage a stem. Phloem tissue is so close to the outside of a stem that strangulation by a wire or plant tie may prevent nutrients from travelling any farther up that stem (water will continue to flow through the xylem). The result can be fatal for the upper portion of the stem. Sick-looking, but not wilting, foliage beyond the point of strangulation is usually the first sign that something is wrong; there may just be time to correct the situation by checking and loosening all ties.

If the stems of a fast-growing climber like *Wisteria* are trained through vine eyes or any other kind of fixing which cannot be loosened from time to time (**below left**), they can be easily strangulated as they grow (**below right**).

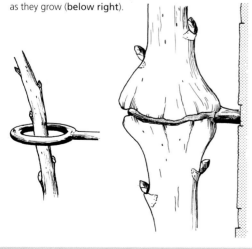

Different types of stem

While all stems perform the same overall functions, of support for the leaves and flowers and as conduits for water and nutrients, some are modified quite substantially and it helps if you are familiar with them.

Corms are thickened stems and, although they resemble bulbs, they are formed of solid, starchy tissue, with buds around the outside, protected by papery scale leaves. Corms also serve as a food store, allowing the plant to survive over winter. Often tiny corms, called cormlets, form in clusters around the base. Examples include *Crocus* and *Gladiolus*.

Rhizomes are horizontal stems, sometimes thickened and growing below or along the surface of the ground. Common examples are *Iris pseudacorus* (flag iris) and *Elymus repens* (couch grass).

aerial or terminal shoot

Iris rhizome

node

horizontal, swollen stem, or rhizome

lateral swollen stem, or rhizome

A stolon is a shoot or stem that grows across the surface of the soil, forming roots as it goes. Good examples are the strawberry runner and *Ranunculus repens* (creeping buttercup).

Ranunculus repens sends out roots and shoots from the nodes of its creeping stolons.

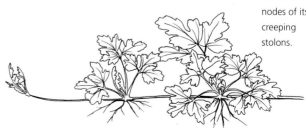

potato plant

aerial stem and leaves

fleshy stem, or rhizome
(often underground)

stem tuber with eyes, or buds

A stem tuber is a swollen stem that stores food (often starch), usually underground. A potato is a stem tuber: potato "eyes" are actually buds on the stem.

Some lilies have large buds, called bulbils, on their stems in the axils of leaves, which will, if planted, eventually develop into large, flowering bulbs.

cross-section through a eudicotyledonous leaf

1 stoma (pore through which gases, mainly oxygen and carbon dioxide, enter and leave plant)
2 spongy parenchyma (cells with air spaces to allow passage of gases)
3 epidermis (protective "skin")
4 collenchyma (strengthening cells in leaf veins)

5 veins, or vascular bundles (of xylem and phloem transport tissue)
6 cuticle (waxy, waterproof, protective layer)
7 palisade parenchyma (contain most of chlorophyll, main site of photosynthesis)

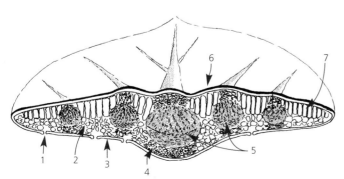

Leaves

The leaf is the "factory" that produces the energy that is necessary for plant growth. It is where CO_2 (carbon dioxide), H_2O (water), sunlight and chlorophyll (the green element within leaves and stems) come together to produce carbohydrates. This photosynthesis process also releases oxygen as a by-product during daylight hours.

It is useful to be familiar with the various parts of a leaf so that you can understand how they function. Leaves often display telltale symptoms if there is something wrong with the plant. The size, shape and colour of leaves are extremely variable, but the way in which all leaves function is basically similar.

Most of the internal detail of leaves is too small to see with the naked eye, but the diagram (below left) will give you a good idea of what the inside of a typical eudicotyledonous leaf looks like.

Leaf colour

Chlorophyll gives leaves their green colour. Some plants that have yellow or variegated leaves may have less chlorophyll and therefore be less vigorous than completely green plants. Variegation (particularly yellow or white streaks or flecks) can sometimes be the result of a viral infection.

Autumn colour is due, in part, to an accumulation of impurities within the leaf and a reduction in the amount of chlorophyll just before leaf fall (called dehiscence). Plants that regularly lose their leaves in winter are termed deciduous. Those that keep leaves in winter are termed evergreen, but even these often lose old leaves during midsummer.

Most leaves that sustain any physical damage are unable to repair themselves and so remain in a damaged state until they eventually fall. Seriously damaged leaves ought to be removed because they are vulnerable to disease.

Light

Light-sensitive cells, called palisade cells, are arranged mostly in the upper half of the leaf and are shaped to trap the maximum amount of light possible for photosynthesis. Some plants, such as *Pelargonium*, need very bright conditions to succeed, while others, like *Aspidistra*, are happy in very poor light. It follows that plants that are naturally tolerant of very poor light are especially useful in gardens where there is a lot of deep shade.

Most leaves can re-orientate themselves to face the sun (or light), even though their stems may have been retrained, for example when climbing plants are tied up to a support. The petiole (leaf stalk) of a water lily leaf can extend in quite a short period of time, if the plant is suddenly placed in deeper water.

Moisture control

The leaves control the amount of water in a plant. Water vapour enters a leaf, and gases enter and leave, through "pores" called stomata, most of which are situated in the underside of the leaf. When the aperture of the stoma is fully open, the exchange of gases is greatest; the aperture is smallest when the plant is wilting.

When the stomata are fully open on a warm, breezy day, a large amount of water vapour leaves the leaf and creates a pull on the water travelling up the xylem transport tissues from the roots. This process is called transpiration and will obviously be less on a dull, still day.

Veins

These are made up from xylem, cambium and phloem tissue. Xylem and phloem transport water and nutrients throughout the leaf and connect with the same tissues in the stem. They also give a leaf its rigidity. The cambium layer, as in other parts of the plant, contains growth cells and can play a part in propagation of a plant from leaf cuttings.

Epidermis

Both surfaces of a leaf are protected by an epidermis. The top surface may also possess extensions of epidermal cells that form hairs, which may protect the plant from hot sun or act as a defence. In other cases, the top surface of the leaf may be protected by a thick, waxy cuticle, as in for example *Camellia*. Many drought-tolerant plants have leaves that are protected by a very thick cuticle or dense hairs, both of which help to reduce excessive water loss.

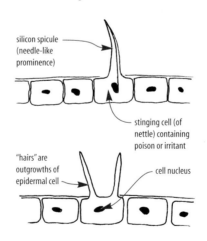

silicon spicule (needle-like prominence)

stinging cell (of nettle) containing poison or irritant

"hairs" are outgrowths of epidermal cell

cell nucleus

In some plants, for example *Urtica dioica* (stinging nettle), leaf hairs contain silica, which makes them brittle so that they break when brushed against, and exude a toxin.

In other cases, the hairs protect the plant from the sun in hot climates.

stoma, or pore

guard cells

epidermal cells

These stomata, situated on the lower epidermis of a eudicotyledonous leaf, are controlled by pairs of sausage-shaped guard cells. When the guard cells are turgid and full of water, they pull the stoma fully open (**left**). When the guard cells are flaccid, with less water in them, they allow the stoma to become partly closed (**right**).

Many soft leaves that have a thin cuticle can absorb a certain amount of very dilute, liquid plant food through their surface, applied as a spray (foliar feeding). This might be done, for instance, when the plant's roots are not functioning properly.

Unusual leaves

Some plants have few or no leaves and rely upon stems for their leaf functions. The leaves of *Mimosa pudica* (sensitive plant) collapse when touched and recover slowly, as special cells gradually become turgid again.

A small, insect-eating plant called *Drosera rotundifolia* (sundew), native to some boggy areas of northern Europe, has leaves that have sticky hairs on the upper surface. When insects becomes trapped by one of these hairs, the plants gradually close the leaves around the prey and dissolve it.

Strictly speaking, a bulb is a leaf modification, usually growing under or on the surface of the ground. If you were to cut open an onion bulb, you would see that it is composed mainly of thickened leaves enclosing a bud or embryo shoot—possibly even an embryo flower. *Hyacinth* and *Tulipa* are two examples of bulbs.

Flowers

Flowers are often the most attractive or distinctive part of the plant. Much of plant classification is based upon flower structure. A knowledge of flower parts and how they function is helpful should you decide to carry out some artificial fertilization, either to assist fruit setting or to create new cultivars of your own. It will also help you with plant identification and understanding botanical plant descriptions.

Flowers enable a plant to perform sexual reproduction, whereas reproduction by corms, bulbs, rhizomes, rooting stems or stolons and roots is termed asexual or vegetative.

Many flowers contain both male and female parts and are hermaphrodite. Some plants, such as cucumbers, have separate male and female flowers on each plant. Other species have separate female and male plants (the latter therefore bearing no seed); examples of these include most *Ilex* (holly) and some *Skimmia* species.

Flowers can occur singly or in clusters, in various arrangements. A head of flowers is called an inflorescence. There is such a huge diversity in flower forms (and accompanying terminology) that the following can form only an introduction.

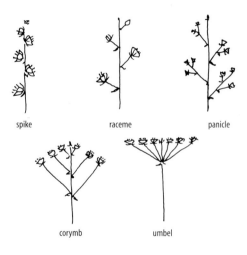

spike   raceme   panicle

corymb   umbel

Main Divisions of Garden Plants

Garden plants fall into two main groups of garden plants, depending on what type of seeds they have.

- Conophyta (previously called gymnosperms) have "naked" seeds that are not enclosed in an ovary. This group includes conifers. The plants tend to have cones and somewhat insignificant flowers.

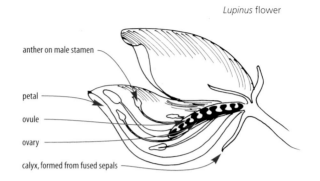
Lupinus flower

anther on male stamen

petal

ovule

ovary

calyx, formed from fused sepals

- Anthophyta (previously called angiosperms) produce seeds within an ovary. This group encompasses the vast majority of ornamental flowering plants, so the structure of the flower discussed in the text relates to anthophyta.
- Some other plants, such as ferns, *Ginkgo*, mosses and funghi belong to other groups.

Typical structure of a flower

Most eudicotyledonous flowers have all the following parts, which may be larger or smaller according to the species. Some details differ in monocotyledonous plants. In a number of cases, plant breeding has produced flowers that have an extra whorl of petals at the expense of stamens and perhaps other vital organs.

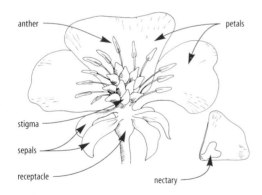
Ranunculus repens (buttercup) flower

anther

petals

stigma

sepals

receptacle

nectary

- Receptacle: an often swollen part at the top of the flower stalk that holds the flower and, like the flower stalk, is usually green.

- Sepals protect the flower while it is in bud and, collectively, are called the calyx. Although usually green and somewhat insignificant, some plants have very conspicuous sepals (often termed bracts). *Poinsettia* "flowers" are actually red or cream bracts; *Clematis* have sepals in a whole range of colours.

- Petals normally occur just inside the sepals and are often brightly coloured—principally to attract insects and birds for pollination. Most petals have a pattern of lines on them (guide lines) that help to lead insects to the centre of the flower. Collectively, petals are known as the corolla. In monocotyledons, the petals and sepals look very similar and are referred to collectively as the tepals.

- The nectary lies at the base of many (but not all) petals. A wide variety of insects find this an attractive source of energy and may visit the flower for this prize even if the petals are not be highly developed. It is during the struggle to get at the nectar that insects unwittingly pollinate the flower—the whole purpose of the exercise!

- The stamens are the male part of the flower. Each stamen usually is comprised of a filament (stalk) and an anther which, when ripe, produces pollen grains. The length of the filament varies considerably depending upon the arrangement of the organs within the flower.

anther

filament

cross-section through anther

pollen sac containing pollen grains

- The carpel is the female part of a flower and is made up of a style, stigma and ovary. The ovary is at the base and contains one or more ovules, which in turn each contain an ovum (egg). A short style (stalk) extends from the ovary and supports the stigma. When the stigma ripens, it usually becomes sticky in order to trap pollen grains.

stigma

style

Pollination

This is the transfer of pollen from anthers on to the stigma. It may occur naturally:

- merely by vibration within the same flower

- on a different flower on the same plant (self-pollination)

- between flowers on different plants (cross-pollination).

Pollination may be carried out by all types of insects, birds, other animals such as bats, the wind or even by human intervention.

Pollination by humans is done in a bid to create a new cultivar and is usually carried out under strictly controlled conditions, for example in a greenhouse. There is some evidence that spraying water on to the flowers of crops like tomatoes and beans (preferably not in hot sunshine) aids pollination through vibration and therefore produces a heavier crop.

F1 Hybrids

This term applies to plants, mainly vegetables and annuals such as in *Petunia*, that have been cross-pollinated under controlled conditions from parents of a known pedigree to produce a crop of "super" flowers or vegetables with 100% uniformity in their characteristics. It is important to realize that seeds produced in the open garden from F1 hybrid flowers could be the result of uncontrolled cross-pollination. They are unlikely to produce many, if any, plants with exactly the same characteristics as the much-admired F1 parents.

Fertilization

A grain of pollen can fertilize only a flower of the same species and in suitable climatic conditions. Before fertilization occurs, the pollen grain grows a tube down the style and into the ovary and an ovule. If fertilization—fusion of the ovum and male cells from the pollen to form an embryo—is successful, the ovule eventually becomes a seed. The ovary is then, botanically, termed a fruit—whether it is a pea pod containing lots of seeds, or a juicy cherry with just one seed (stone).

If you look into the centre of a strawberry flower, you will just be able to recognize the cone-shaped cluster of carpels as the infant strawberry. Each carpel is topped by a tiny stigma waiting to be pollinated and fertilized. As soon as each carpel has been fertilized, it develops a fleshy exterior, swelling up in the process. All these swollen carpels together form the strawberry, a compound fruit.

Sometimes, if conditions are poor, for example too cold or too wet, a number of carpels may remain unfertilized and therefore fail to swell up, leading to a disfigured fruit. In other species, this problem might result in a poor overall crop, with only a limited number of fruits forming.

Care of Flowers

Removing fading flowers—deadheading—from some plants before they have had time to develop seeds often encourages a plant to continue flowering. This applies mainly to flowers like *Viola* (pansy and viola) and possibly *Pelargonium*.

Ripening fruit gives off a gas called ethylene (sometimes used commercially to speed up the ripening of bananas). It also speeds up the ripening of a flower, so that a vase of flowers next to a bowl of apples is likely to deteriorate more quickly than flowers in a well-ventilated room without fruit. Flowers bought from a grocery store may therefore have a shorter life than those bought from a florist's shop.

Fruits and Seeds

Seeds are important in gardening for three main reasons:

- Propagation—growing plants from seeds is one of the main methods of raising plants

- Ornamental—there are thousands of seeds and fruits that are very decorative, and extend the interest of a plant beyond the flowering season

- Wildlife—seeds and fruits are attractive to birds, insects and animals, and can therefore be used to attract a greater range of creatures into the garden.

Most plants reproduce themselves sexually, by seed. The seed contains the plant's future, so it is important to understand how the seed might be spread, its survival technique of dormancy and subsequent, successful germination. Like the birth of a baby, germination is one of the most vulnerable moments in a plant's life.

Methods of seed dispersal

- Mechanical—many ripe fruits and seeds split to release the seeds, which simply drop to the ground. Some seedpods "explode" when shaken or touched, often throwing their seeds over great distances. Examples include the weed *Cardamine hirsuta* (hairy bittercress), *Impatiens* (wild balsam) and perhaps most spectacular of all, *Ecballium elaterium* (squirting cucumber) from the Mediterranean.

- On animal fur—some seeds have burrs or hooks that readily attach themselves to animal fur (and human clothing) until they are brushed off. Examples include *Dipsacus* (teasel), and *Galium aparine* (goosegrass or cleaver).

- By wind—many seeds have hairs, wings or some other arrangement that enables them to travel great distances through the air. Examples are *Taraxacum officinalis* (dandelion), *Chamerion angustifolium* (rosebay willowherb) and various trees which have winged fruits, for example *Acer* (maple or sycamore).

- As the diet of birds and animals—if eaten, seeds are seldom totally destroyed during digestion and so are excreted, often many miles from where they were ingested.

- By water—the seeds of some aquatic and marginal plants float and may therefore travel great distances down rivers and even across the oceans.

Seed storage

Seeds must be stored somewhere cool and dry. Never keep them in a plastic bag for the lack of air creates the perfect environment for moulds to attack the seeds. Even then, they will gradually deteriorate—lose viability—over a period of months or years. Seeds of wheat and barley are reputed to remain viable for many years whereas those of *Delphinium* may lose 50% viability within the first 6–8 months.

Some seeds from cool climates can be stored for many years if frozen, but this treatment might well damage or kill seeds from warmer parts of the world. Sometimes instructions on the packet will indicate how particular seeds should be stored; it helps to date all your seeds and seed packets so that you know how old they are.

Seed dormancy

Many seeds require a period of dormancy before they will germinate. Sometimes special conditions are needed to bring this dormancy to an end. Some seeds from cold regions of the world may require a period of very low temperatures, simulating winter, before they will germinate. In practice, it may mean freezing some seeds (notably various alpines and conifers) before they will germinate.

Cactus seeds sometimes contain a chemical inhibitor that has to be washed away by substantial rainfall before germination can take place, thus ensuring that the seedling has enough moisture to develop properly. These seeds need to be watered copiously to get them started.

Some seeds, such as those of legumes (peas and beans), that have very hard seed coats may be nicked carefully or sandpapered so they can more easily absorb water. Soaking the seeds in water for an hour or two will assist this process, but they should never be left in water for any length of time. They will try to germinate anaerobically (without air), produce alcohol in the process, and eventually die.

Other seeds, such as those of *Banksia*, need to be activated by chemicals in smoke of bush fires. It is therefore important that you follow all the instructions for germination on the seed packet.

Germination

At the moment dormancy comes to an end, the seeds will begin to germinate. This nearly always begins by the seeds taking in water. Once this happens, nothing must hinder the process until the young

plant has developed a root system that is good enough to support continued growth. Plants are highly vulnerable when emerging from a seed; if they are denied moisture at this time and during the subsequent hours and days, they will most probably die. This point is especially important to remember when raising a lawn from seed.

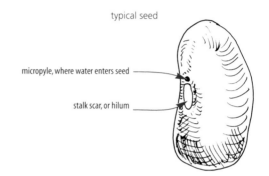

typical seed

micropyle, where water enters seed

stalk scar, or hilum

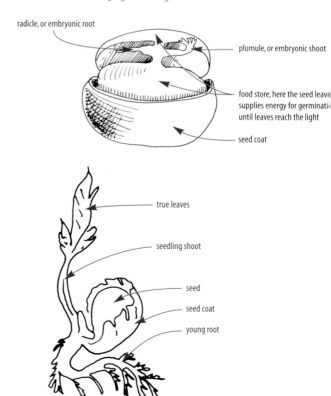

cross-section through germinating seed

radicle, or embryonic root

plumule, or embryonic shoot

food store, here the seed leaves supplies energy for germination until leaves reach the light

seed coat

true leaves

seedling shoot

seed

seed coat

young root

Ways of Germination

Seeds germinate in two slightly different ways, called epigeal and hypogeal germination.

- Epigeal germination means that the leaves that you first see above ground are not the true leaves, but cotyledons (seed leaves). Seed leaves are very simple, rounded leaves; there may be one or two. True leaves, typical of the plant, soon appear above the seed leaves.
- In hypogeal germination, the cotyledons remain in the seed or below ground so the first leaves to appear above ground are the true leaves. However, in some cases it is juvenile foliage and remains so for many weeks, possibly months, before developing a mature, more familiar leaf shape. Two examples are *Passiflora* (passionflower) and *Eucalyptus gunnii*.

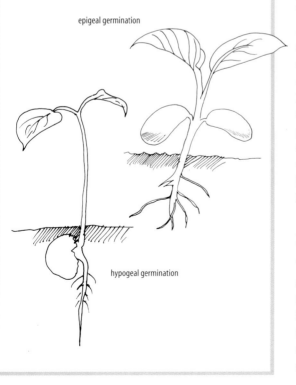

epigeal germination

hypogeal germination

Critical factors for germination

- Air and moisture—seeds take in water through the micropyle (tiny opening at the end of the stalk scar) but germination needs to be "aerobic" i.e. there must be oxygen present too, so that conditions are suitable for sustained growth of the radicle (young root).

- Temperature—seeds from hot regions of the world may require temperatures of 20–30°C (68–86°F) to germinate, whereas those from cool temperate zones will often germinate at 7°C (45°F). So it helps to know which part of the world seeds have come from.

- Light—many seeds prefer not to be buried deeply and to have some light; lettuce seeds germinate best if they are barely covered. Conversely, the seeds of *Nigella* (Love-in-a-mist) germinate best in total darkness.

Light and Growth

Most plant stems naturally grow towards light (positively phototropic), while roots tend to grow away from light (negatively phototropic). Plants of course need natural daylight for healthy growth. This light contains a good balance of blue and red light so, if you are planning to use extra light in your greenhouse or indoors for your houseplants, you must use an appropriate light source. Either mercury-vapour or blended mercury-vapour lamps are suitable, but not ordinary, tungsten-filament light bulbs, which have insufficient blue light for healthy plant growth.

Light and Flowering

You may have noticed that potted *Chrysanthemum* plants are available in flower all year round, even though they would normally flower only in late summer or in autumn. This feat is achieved by growers changing the length of day inside their greenhouses to make the chrysanthemums think it is always autumn! To do this, they shorten the day length in summer using blackouts, and lengthen days in winter by using red, tungsten-filament lamps. This manipulation of the light affects only flowering, not growth.

Pruning

Plants of all kinds seem to grow successfully in the wild without any need for control from man, so why prune? In the wild, life is a ruthless free-for-all and a case of survival of the fittest, but by contrast the garden is an artificial community where each plant is given an equal opportunity. If left to nature, many of the trees, shrubs, climbers and conifers grown in our gardens would grow far too large for the given space; they might also not perform well.

In the garden, pruning is as much a basic gardening technique as it is a form of art, and trimming at the right time and in the right way controls growth, shapes plants, keeps them healthy, and encourages flowers and fruits to form. The only way that some plants can be kept in proportion for many years is by occasional or regular pruning.

You might think that dwarf or slow-growing plants are the answer to this problem, but no plant stops growing until it dies—if a slow-growing plant lives long enough, it too might exceed its allocated space.

You have already learned the basics of pruning in order to rejuvenate the existing plants in the garden before undertaking any new planting (see Chapter 2, pages 76–85), but once all the planting is in place, you will need to continue pruning. Some of this will be essential, for the reasons already discussed in Chapter 2, but you may also begin pruning for performance. By pruning appropriately each year, you should maintain the plants you have renovated as well as new plantings.

Although it will not be possible to cover the specific routine pruning of every plant here, there are some widely grown plants that require special attention.

Reasons for Pruning

As a rule of thumb, never prune plants without good reason.

- To remove damaged, diseased, crossing or dead material, enabling the rest of the plant to remain healthy.
- To keep the plant relatively young and vigorous, so that it continues to produce healthy stems, foliage and, where appropriate, to maximize performance in flowering and fruiting.
- To maintain an attractive shape, especially in the formative years or if the plant is being grown as a specimen.
- To remove suckers or surplus stems growing from the roots, but away from the main plant. These can take over if not removed.
- To keep rampant plants within limits.
- To clip plants into a required shape, for example trimming hedges and topiary, or train them into ornamental or space-saving forms such as fruit fans.
- To undertake regular, gentle pruning of evergreens to maintain foliage cover.
- To cut hard back some plants grown for ornamental stems and foliage.
- To maintain the shape of fastigiate plants.
- To deadhead or divert the plant's energy away from seed production into further flowering and growth.
- To rejuvenate neglected plants.

These are roses, clematis and several other climbing plants, and fruit trees. Advice on pruning these plants is covered in more detail in the following pages.

Basic rules

If you need to prune any plants that are not mentioned here, you should first consider whether the plant needs pruning (see "Reasons for Pruning" box). Some basic principles can be applied—first, decide why you are growing the plant, for example for foliage, flowers or fruit, and work out:

- Is the most desirable growth produced on new or old branches?

- Does the best growth appear on the tips of stems or farther back on older branches?

- When does the best growth appear?

The answers to these questions will dictate your timings or how and when you prune the plant to obtain optimum performance. For example, you will not want to prune off old or the previous year's stems if these are the ones that will produce flowers and fruit in the current year. A fairly simple rule of thumb is to prune flowering shrubs that flower before midsummer immediately after flowering, and prune ones that flower later in the year in the autumn or early spring. Observing the growth pattern of a plant should help you to prune it to obtain its best potential.

You could also consult one of the helpful, specialist books on pruning for advice on individual species. Remember that flowers, fruit and stems all thrive best without much competition, and the object of pruning is to give them the best chance. In many cases, you may not need to carry out any pruning at all!

Renewal Pruning

As a plant grows old, the flow of sap becomes less effective because it has to work its way through an increasingly complex and woody system of branches. Leaves, flowers and fruits tend to become smaller (but sometimes more numerous). Removing some of the branches every few years will invigorate the plant.

The one-third/two-thirds, or renewal, method of pruning is especially useful for pruning deciduous shrubs and is a simple and safe way of keeping a shrub relatively young. It is usually carried out every year during the winter or very early spring, or in early summer for spring-flowering plants.

Starting with the oldest wood, cut out about one-third of the shrub, taking each branch down to within three or four buds from the base. The remaining two-thirds are left largely unpruned, except for the removal of dead flowerheads, dead or dying growth and so on. If you always cut out the oldest wood, eventually none of the branches will be older than three years.

The newest shoots may not flower in their first year, but the older shoots should have regained their flowering cycle by the second year. Avoid hard pruning on very old shrubs that have never previously been pruned.

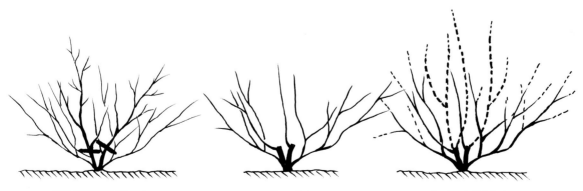

shrub before renewal pruning   after pruning   new growth anticipated in following year

Shrubs suitable for renewal pruning

Abelia

Berberis thunbergii

Ceratostigma

Deutzia

Escallonia

Forsythia

Hydrangea (mophead and lacecap)

Hypericum

Kerria

Kolkwitzia

Leycesteria

Philadelphus

Physocarpus

Potentilla

Ribes

Rubus

Sambucus

Spiraea

Weigela

Pruning Architectural Plants

Shrubs that are grown for their handsome shapes, like *Aralia*, *Fatsia*, *Magnolia*, *Acer palmatum* (Japanese maples) and shrubby *Paeonia* (tree peonies), are seldom pruned because most forms of pruning could ruin their outlines.

However, it may become necessary occasionally to remove a complete branch in order to improve the overall balance. The plant could well respond by producing extra branches, some of which may eventually also need removing. The least disruptive way of doing this is to rub out unwanted new shoots with your thumb as soon as they appear, which is less likely to trigger a response than waiting to prune them out once they have developed further.

Pruning Roses

In the wild, roses produce strong, new shoots from near the bases of the plants in each growing season. In subsequent years, the secondary or lateral growth from these shoots becomes progressively weaker. As more new shoots appear, the food taken in by the roots is directed to the newest growth and the original shoots are gradually starved out, eventually dying and falling to the ground as dead wood.

The purpose of rose pruning is to short-circuit the rather long-winded, natural process, by cutting away the old, worn-out shoots and so encourage production of vigorous, disease-free, new growth as well as the optimum number of flowers for the rose concerned.

Regular deadheading, or the removal of spent blooms, is crucial so that the plant's energy goes into producing new flowers instead of the spent flowerheads developing into fruits or hips. The exception to this rule is when you are growing a particular type of rose, such as the sweet briar and rugosa roses, for their colourful, late-summer and autumn hips.

A typically overcrowded bush rose at the end of the growing season.

For healthy roses, hygiene is important, which means disposing of all prunings and fallen leaves to avoid any spread of fungal diseases, such as black spot. Burn or discard the material, but don't add them to the compost heap.

When choosing where to cut, buds of roses should be carefully selected to produce shoots that will grow in the most desirable direction, keeping the centre of the plant open. Hard frosts may damage these young shoots, so delay pruning until after the hardest frosts.

within three or four healthy buds of the old wood. This may be quite close to ground level in the case of young bushes, but perhaps at 60 cm (2 ft.) or more on old bushes because of their more extensive permanent framework.

The same method of pruning may be adopted for standard and half-standard bush roses. Cut fairly hard back to a point where all the branches join the main vertical stem. Some gardeners advocate a less harsh approach, cutting shoots back by no more than two-thirds each spring.

Cut back to buds that point in the direction a new shoot is needed.

Fairly hard pruning results in vigorous, new growth the following spring and summer. Aim to keep the centre of the bush as open as possible. Pruning of floribunda roses is similar, but possibly less harsh.

Shrub roses

Prune out up to one-third of the oldest shoots and shorten the rest by about half, in early spring before new shoots appear. This will open up the bushes, allowing in more light and air, and will help to keep the bushes vigorous. It will also stimulate production of new shoots, many of which will flower during early summer.

Bush roses

Hybrid tea and floribunda roses differ slightly in their growth habits. Floribundas usually produce more densely branched bushes than hybrid teas; floribundas also bear their blooms in clusters, whereas hybrid teas produce flowers on single stems. Both are pruned in the spring in a similar way.

First, weak and diseased branches are removed, then all the previous season's growth is cut hard back to

Climbing roses

Most of these originate from bush roses and climb by way of an old and often gnarled main stem. The success of a climbing rose relies on maintaining its permanent framework of branches, as well as annually training in some of the vigorous, new shoots. These often grow from the old branches and will also produce flowers.

Apart from the removal of dead and diseased wood, the current season's growth is cut back fairly hard to two to three buds or 15 cm (6 in), retaining a few branches to extend or replace part of the permanent framework. This pruning often stimulates the production of strong, new shoots from near the base of the plant; if there are any suitable shoots, these

Climbing roses

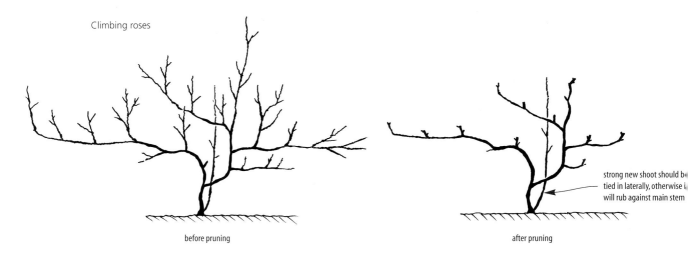

strong new shoot should be
tied in laterally, otherwise it
will rub against main stem

before pruning   after pruning

can be tied in and trained to replace some of the
oldest framework branches.

Examples of roses that may be pruned in this way
include: *R.* 'Bantry Bay', *R.* 'Danse du Feu', *R.* 'Golden
Showers', *R.* 'Mermaid', and *R.* 'Zéphirine Drouhin'.

Rambler roses
In most cases, the growth and performance of these
is quite different from that of climbers. During the
summer, a crop of long (sometimes almost thornless)
stems grow from an established basal clump of older
branches. Some of these new branches reach a length
of 1.8 m (6 ft.) or so by the end of the summer.

The following spring or early summer, clusters of
flowers emerge from many of the buds along these
stems and a few may continue to flower well into the
summer. At the same time, a new crop of branches
will appear at the base.

As soon as the older branches have finished
flowering, cut them hard back to the bare main stem
and train the new shoots up in their place. Some old
stems may be cut back less hard to produce extra
young shoots. Apart from the basal clump, no part of
the plant should ever be more than two years old.

The following winter, all the new shoots will be
ready to tie on to wires or a trellis. Most, if not all,

This rambler rose in early summer has
older shoots, which have just finished
flowering (dead flowers and leaves
omitted for clarity), together with a
crop of new shoots. Now is the time
to cut the older stems hard back.

The following winter, all the young
shoots that remain after summer
pruning should be tied in to form
a new framework.

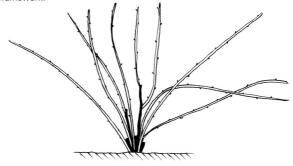

should produce a crop of flowers early next summer before they too are cut back. Such vigorous growth places a great demand on the soil's store of nutrients so feed during early summer.

Roses are sometimes grown in different forms, such as pillars, weeping umbrella standards and even as ground cover. Before pruning these, you will need to identify which type they are—climbers or ramblers.

Pruning Climbers

Climbing plants often become a tangle of growth, making it very difficult to see which branch goes where. On some occasions, you will need to prune out some old branches while retaining others.

Before cutting what you think is an old branch or stem, shake it and pull it gently so that you can follow it through the plant. It is all too easy to cut what you thought was an old stem, only to discover afterwards that you have removed a mass of new growth.

Pruning *Clematis*

There are three widely recognized groups of *Clematis*, and nursery catalogues nearly always state which group a particular clematis belongs to. They are divided into groups so that their mode of growth and therefore the pruning can be easily identified.

If the plant is pruned in the wrong way, it could mean that all the flowering shoots for the coming season are cut off when they should have been left on.

Pruning Group 1

Some examples of climbers in this group are *Clematis alpina*, *C. armandii*, *C. cirrhosa* and *C. montana*. Since these flower in the spring or early summer, on shoots produced during the previous year, all this growth

must not be cut back until the end of the growing season or during the winter. Tie in the growths and wait to prune until after flowering. Then, the oldest shoots should be removed or shortened, and any dead material cut out.

Once the plant has become old and extensive (and often too large and inaccessible to prune), limit pruning to the removal of any shoots that have grown where they are not wanted. Clematis of this type will live and flower for many years without any significant pruning.

Pruning Group 2

Clematis 'Barbara Jackman', *C. henryi*, *C.* 'Lasurstern', *C.* 'Marie Boisselot' are all large-flowered types and belong in this pruning group. These clematis also flower on growth made the previous year, but the flowers may not appear until late summer and continue until the autumn. Some flowers are also produced on the current season's growth. During this time the plant will be producing new shoots for the next year, without stimulation from any pruning.

Any pruning is best done during the winter and consists mainly of removing dead wood, weak shoots and a general thinning out. After three or four years, large sections can be cut hard back in the early spring to generate some completely new growth.

Pruning Group 3

Clematis in this group, such as *C.* 'Hagley Hybrid', *C.* 'Jackmanii', *C. tangutica* and *C.* 'Ville de Lyon', are among the latest to flower. They produce flowers mainly on growth made during that year.

They are easy to prune because virtually all the current season's growth may be cut hard back, almost to ground level, in late winter or early spring. This gives the plant a fresh start each spring and keeps it reasonably neat. A few of the previous year's shoots may be retained so they can produce some earlier flowers.

Pruning *Jasminum*

Jasminum nudiflorum (winter jasmine) and *J. officinale* (summer jasmine) both flower on the previous year's growth, although the latter may take longer to produce flowers.

They are both pruned after flowering in the spring by cutting hard back any shoots that have flowered. Both develop a framework of older branches, parts of which may be replaced from time to time by taking some new shoots and tying them in, to fill up the space left by removal of some of the older shoots.

Pruning *Lonicera*

Prune *Lonicera japonica* and other honeysuckles in the spring, by cutting out some of the oldest shoots and tying in new ones. Alternatively, well-established plants may be clipped over with shears but a good clean out of dead and old wood, using secateurs (pruners) is advisable every few years. Honeysuckle is naturally untidy and will usually become bare at the base.

Pruning *Solanum*

Both *Solanum crispum* and *S. laxum* develop a permanent, woody framework of branches from which vigorous, new shoots grow. Flowers are always produced on the new season's growth.

Cut back the most recent growth each spring—and possibly, in mild localities, at intervals during the summer—to stimulate as much new growth as possible. Never cut hard back into old wood since this may not be able to recover.

Pruning Vines

Several species of vines, including both ornamental and fruiting species of *Vitis*, are commonly used to cover walls, fences and pergolas. They are all pruned in a similar way. Vines gradually develop a gnarled system of branches that are usually trained along wires. Each spring, long, vigorous shoots develop from various points along these branches and, by the end of the summer, may produce bunches of grapes.

During the winter, and before the sap begins to rise in the spring, cut these long branches back to within two or three buds of the old branch. A few of them could be kept to train in and extend the permanent framework. Bleeding of sap from the wounds, depleting the plant's energy, may occur if the main pruning is delayed until spring, although when the plant breaks into leaf the flow of sap may be taken up by the developing growth.

When winter-pruning vines, cut each lateral stem, or sideshoot, above an outward-facing bud to within 2 or 3 buds from the main stem.

If growth is very strong, removal of surplus new growth or some light pruning may become necessary during the early summer, otherwise the fruits that are produced may be numerous, but very small and less likely to ripen. Cuts made to remove surplus branches at this time of year will bleed, dripping sap on to the soil below.

Pruning Wisteria

These beautiful but rampant climbers will live to a great age if properly pruned and trained. Left to themselves, they develop a dense and twisted system of branches, a mixture of very old and relatively new growth, which if left unpruned will sap the plant of energy rather than directing it into flowering. An old and neglected wisteria may require several years of careful pruning before it comes back into flower. Cold spring frosts may also damage the flowers.

Summer pruning is needed to restrain growth and also to maintain the stubby spur system on which the flowers develop, emerging from buds clustered on short spurs close to the main stem and from some of the previous season's growth. At the same time, many vigorous, new shoots grow from other points along the main stems and continue to develop all summer. Pruning is often done in two stages.

Summer pruning

Initially, the main growths should be tied in or placed to cover the allotted space until a framework is built up. Thereafter it will be necessary to control the stems forming the framework to prevent them from becoming twisted together. The lateral growths from the main stems should be spur-pruned annually, but in order to promote freer and better flower-bud formation, this should be carried out in two stages.

Carry out the first stage during midsummer, or about two months after flowering: any stems that are needed to cover more wall space, especially on young plants, should be tied in and cut to the required length. Prune sideshoots and long trailing growths, or laterals, back to 15 cm (6 in.), or to about five or six leaves, from a main branch.

Winter and spring pruning

Carry out the second stage of pruning during midwinter, and once the leaves have fallen, so that you can see what you are doing. Those branches that were left longer at the summer pruning to preserve the maximum number of flower buds, may be cut back or shortened again to two buds or 7.5 cm (3 in.).

The main reason for growing wisteria is for its flowers, so it is important to avoid removing potential flower buds during routine pruning. For that reason, the main pruning may be delayed until early spring when the difference between leaf and

flower buds becomes apparent. If you do this, be warned—as the flower buds become increasingly obvious they also become very fragile, so be careful not to knock the buds off.

Flower buds swell to become fatter and more rounded than the smaller, more slender leaf buds. Those clustered on the short spurs should not be pruned out. Other buds form close to the base of relatively young stems, often on those that arose during the previous summer.

Tying in branches

Do not tie in *Wisteria* branches tightly. The stems thicken very quickly and can become strangled by ties, eventually causing the whole of that branch to die. Check and loosen all ties regularly. All this requires a considerable amount of ladder work. Large specimens may grow up to 10 m (30 ft.) high against the wall of a house, but unless the plant is pruned regularly, the whippy, lateral growths will become unmanageable and there will be few or no flowers.

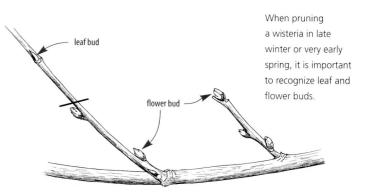

leaf bud

flower bud

When pruning a wisteria in late winter or very early spring, it is important to recognize leaf and flower buds.

Pruning Fruit Trees

These trees are decorative as well as productive, their bare branches creating in winter satisfying patterns against the sky. Sustaining productivity and appearance requires efficient and regular pruning and training. For the first few years after planting, formative pruning will be needed to ensure a balanced shape.

Once flowering and cropping begins, an annual pruning routine may be started, usually around midsummer, to persuade the tree to produce more fruit and less surplus growth. The objective is to have a well-maintained tree that is an asset to your garden and will produce high-quality fruit crops.

Most fruit trees do not develop new fruit buds on new stems until the end of the second summer. These then subsequently flower and fruit in the third year. The older, small knobbly fruit spurs elsewhere in the tree usually fruit year after year.

Pruning Apples and Pears

A combination of operations is involved in pruning an apple or pear tree, which may be grown as several different forms. Dwarf bush apple trees, grown on a stem of 60 cm (2 ft.), are usually grown on M9 or M26 rootstocks and are useful where space is limited. The larger bush, with a stem of 60–90 cm (2–3 ft.) is readily produced on rootstocks such as MM106 for apples and Quince A for pears. Both have main branches arising fairly closely together to form the head, and are probably the most easily managed for fruit picking.

Half-standards or standards are trees with a stem of 1.2 or 1.8 m.(4 or 6 ft.), from which the branches arise to form a large head. These trees are grown on vigorous rootstocks and are suitable only for orchards where there is plenty of room; they are usually too large for small gardens. A spindle bush is a cone-shaped tree with a single, vertical stem.The sideshoots are tied down, which induces the tree to form fruit buds and so the trees start to fruit earlier.

There are also restricted tree forms. Cordons have a single, straight stem, which has short fruiting spurs all along its length; it is usually grown at an oblique angle, with the sideshoots restricted by summer pruning. Cordons are excellent for the small garden because several trees may be grown in a relatively small area.

Fan trees are trained flat against a wall or fence, with branches radiating from a short trunk like the ribs of a fan. Espaliers are have a central, vertical, main stem with pairs of horizontal branches (tiers) arising more or less opposite each other and growing out at right angles on each side of the main stem. Espalier trees usually consist of two or three tiers, but they may have more.

Pyramids or dwarf pyramids have a main stem from which, from a little higher than 30 cm (1 ft.) from ground level, branches of gradually diminishing lengths radiate at intervals.

Renovation pruning

Do this during the winter when all the branches are bare (this is when most pruning is carried out). If you take a good look at your tree, you are probably faced with many branches, some of them thick, old and woody. As with many other trees and shrubs, the oldest wood of apple and pear trees will be dark in colour and rather knobbly, whereas new wood will be much paler and straighter. The most recent branches will be about pencil thickness, smooth and pale in colour and quite straight.

There will probably also be small, twiggy clusters of buds, often growing directly from the older branches but also from the bases of some of the more recent stems. These are clusters of fruit buds on fruiting "spurs". It is quite easy to tell the difference between fruit and leaf buds—fruit buds are rounder and fatter. If an apple tree doesn't have these spurs, it is a "tip-bearer" and needs to be pruned slightly differently, as below.

- First take out any dead, diseased or damaged branches right back to a healthy branch, using a saw to cut thicker branches.

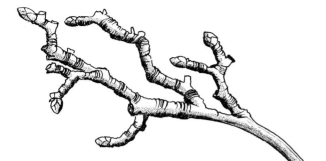

This fruiting spur has been producing fruit for many years. Your pruning should encourage the formation of new spurs, as well as preserving a good many of the older ones.

One-year-old wood

This section grew last summer. Next summer, the terminal bud will produce a new length of stem, the lateral buds will each produce a leaf, and new buds will form in the leaf axils and may become fruit buds.

Two-year-old wood

This section of the stem grew during the summer of the previous year. Last summer it produced leaves and initiated the buds you see here, many of which are fruit buds. Some could go on to develop new fruiting spurs over the next few years.

- If any branches cross one another or touch, remove them completely.

- Keep the centre of the tree fairly open to allow air and light through to the fruits.

- Try to avoid cutting out fruit buds, although that might be unavoidable.

- Tidy up the edges of any large, sawn cuts, using a sharp pruning knife.

Then look more closely at how the tree has been growing. The straightest, thinnest shoots were probably produced during the most recent summer; they are classed as one-year-old shoots. Some will be quite long and come directly off a much thicker branch while others, rather shorter and less vigorous, will grow directly out from the tips of slightly thicker, older shoots; these shoots are known as extension growths.

The thicker sections immediately beneath the extension growths are likely to be two years old and may have formed some fruit buds down towards their bases. No two trees are the same—some may have lots of new growth and few flower buds while others could show the reverse condition. You should aim for a good balance between the two.

- Cut back the most vigorous one-year-old shoots to half their length (wherever they occur).

- Then cut back all the two-year-old shoots, again to half their length.

- Retain any shoot that is well placed to become part of the tree's main framework of branches. For example, a shoot that can be used to replace some of the damaged or diseased branches you removed earlier.

- Less vigorous one-year-old shoots may be cut back harder, but leave the very weakest unpruned.

- Cut hard back (to within two or three buds of the base) most of the shoots that have borne fruit this year. This will stimulate new, strong, one-year-old shoots for future cropping.

- On the remaining fruited shoots, you may be less harsh and cut them back to just above where they have fruited. This will encourage them to develop more complex fruiting spurs.

- Finally, check over all the old, knobbly fruiting spurs and thin out or remove any that appear cluttered. This is called spur pruning and will reduce the number of flowers, but improve the size and quality of fruits from the remaining spurs.

Tip-bearing Trees

Some apple trees have fruit buds only at the ends of their branches. Examples of tip bearers include *Malus* 'Cornish Gilliflower', *M.* 'Irish Peach', *M.* 'Tydeman's Early Worcester' and *M.* 'Worcester Pearmain'. There are a few tip-bearing pears also, for example *M.* 'Jargonelle' or *M.* 'Merton Pride'.

Tip bearers require a different form of pruning to spur bearers. After pruning the initial dead, diseased, crossing and dying growth, a large proportion of the laterals on tip bearers should not be pruned. Only the strongest laterals are pruned, to three or four buds. Leave a good number of shoots unpruned until they have fruited, then cut these fairly hard back by about one-third to stimulate new extension growth and the production of more tip-bearing laterals.

Some apple trees are partial tip bearers and do have some fruiting spurs, for example *M.* 'Bramley's Seedling', *M.* 'Blenheim Orange', *M.* 'Discovery', *M.* 'Epicure', *M.* 'Golden Noble', *M.* 'Lord Lambourne', *M.* 'St. Edmund's Pippin'.

The renovation pruning outcome

Your renovation pruning will have removed very few of the fruit buds that had already formed on the lower half of two-year-old shoots and they should go on to fruit next summer. It will also have left the lower half of one-year-old shoots to develop new fruit buds; some of the stronger shoots will form fruit buds during the next summer and fruit in the following year. Your hard pruning should also result in the production of new shoots next season.

Routine pruning

This is less drastic than renovation pruning. For trees grown in the open, typically the bush, standard and spindle forms, winter pruning should be applied. Established trees that are cropping well should be pruned only lightly. This means cutting the laterals and branch leaders down to 15–20 cm (6–10 in.) just above a downward- or outward-facing bud.

Restricted-form fruit trees are pruned in the summer, the purpose being to inhibit their growth—necessary because they are grown in a confined or limited space. Summer pruning checks growth and allows light and air on to the wood and on the fruit, helping to promote fruit buds for next year and to improve the colour of existing fruits.

If repeated annually, this process should make sure that the tree has some fruiting potential each year, rather than producing fruit every other year (a common phenomenon called biennial bearing).

Summer pruning of trained trees

In the case of trained forms of apple and pear trees, such as cordon, espalier, fan, pillar and step-over trees, growth and fruit production has to be on a limited scale. This is because the trees are relatively small overall.

To preserve the limits of this growth and retain the special shapes of these trees, shorten some of the new growth in the middle of the summer. Other than this, winter pruning is much the same as for larger trees except that there will be a heavier emphasis on training and shaping.

Pear trees

The winter pruning of pears is slightly simpler than for apples. Pears tend to have more fruiting spurs. Spur thinning is therefore important to keep up the quality of the fruits, but each year it is important also to do some hard pruning, as for apples, to stimulate the formation of new spurs.

Prunus Fruit Trees

Prunus domestica (plum) trees usually fruit at the base of one-year-old stems and along most older stems. Pruning is therefore usually limited to the removal of excess growth, as well as dead and damaged material. *Prunus* is very susceptible to the airborne disease silver leaf, so pruning must be done during the summer immediately after fruiting: it also avoids the risk of rising sap bleeding from wounds.

Plums can grow very strongly, so trained trees, for instance a fan, pyramid or spindle, will need more rigorous pruning to make sure that the form of the tree is not lost. Pruning of *P. avium* (sweet cherry) and *P. cerasus* (acid cherry) is much the same as for plums.

P. persica (peach) and *P. persica* var. *nectarina* (nectarine) also fruit on one-year-old wood. Once a shoot has borne fruit, it should be cut back to a growth bud (not a flower bud) to stimulate a new shoot. Again, any pruning must be carried out during the summer because of the risk of silver leaf disease.

Plant Propagation

Plant propagation is probably one of the most exciting, enjoyable and rewarding aspects of gardening. It covers such a wide range of activities that some degree of success is possible for every one.

Most plants can reproduce themselves in some way or another. Quite often, all that is needed is a helping hand and nature will do the rest. Some plants require a higher degree of skill, but with patience and the appropriate method most plants may be propagated successfully.

Methods of Propagation

The following methods of propagation start with the most straightforward and progress to the more difficult.

- Seeds
- Division
- Bulb propagation
- Layering
- Cuttings
- Budding
- Grafting

Plants from Seeds

As we have seen, seeds have ways of making sure that they germinate at the best time for seedlings to survive, and in sufficient levels of water, oxygen, warmth and light. Virtually all seeds need sustained moisture throughout germination and for their subsequent development. Drying out halfway through, or just after, germination can prove fatal.

So that the seedlings can establish themselves and grow into healthy plants, nearly all seeds need to be in contact with soil at the time of germination. In practical terms, this means providing them with suitable compost or a seedbed and also suitable climatic conditions.

Buying seed

Most seeds are reliable and have useful growing information on the packet—the seed company's reputation depends upon good results. Seeds that are likely to deteriorate quickly in the atmosphere are often packed in airtight, foil packets. After some of the seeds have been used, make sure that the packet is re-sealed as tightly as possible in case further sowings are needed.

Many hardy flowers, vegetables, trees and shrubs will germinate and grow outdoors in quite low temperatures of 8–10°C (46–50°F), but there are many other plants from a warmer climate that need higher temperatures to germinate. These are achievable only under glass in cool climates. It is therefore important to read the instructions on the seed packet regarding temperature.

Collecting your own seeds

Many plants will come "true", or exactly replicate the parent plant, from seed, especially trees, shrubs and many conifers but others, like those raised from seeds of F1 hybrids, may not. Plants produce either dry or fleshy seeds.

Many dry seeds are held in seed pods or capsules. Gather the seedheads as they are beginning to ripen (usually when brown and papery) and lay them out on a greenhouse bench for two or three weeks. Here, they can fully ripen and dry and then split open to release the seeds.

"Exploding" seed pods, such as those of *Lunaria* (honesty), have to be placed in cardboard boxes with lids or in sealed paper bags, until they have burst and expelled the seeds. Once the seeds have dried, separate them from their pods or capsules, and clean out any remaining chaff, before storing them in a cool, dry, dark place in labelled paper packets.

Fleshy seeds (berries) turn colour and perhaps soften when ripe. Separate these seeds from their flesh by crushing them with a flat piece of wood, then wash them in a bucket of water. Any useless seeds are likely to float to the top, so you can discard those. Set the washed seeds out on a bench to dry.

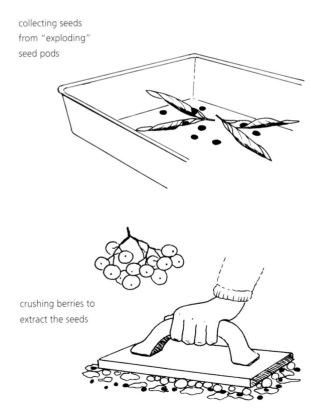

collecting seeds from "exploding" seed pods

crushing berries to extract the seeds

Stratification

Many seeds from berries have a very hard seed coat (testa), which will not readily absorb moisture. In the autumn, place alternate layers of sharp sand and seeds into a well-drained pot, finally topping off with a good layer of sand and, as protection from birds and to keep in moisture, some fine gravel. Stand it outdoors somewhere cold for the winter so that it freezes and thaws a few times, which should help to soften the seed coats and break the seeds' dormancy.

In spring, you may sow the stratified seeds outdoors in rows, where they should eventually germinate. They are best left in situ until the following autumn. This technique obviously only applies to fully hardy plants like *Berberis*, *Cotoneaster*, *Crataegus*, *Rosa*, and so on.

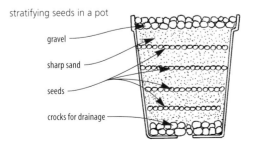

stratifying seeds in a pot

gravel

sharp sand

seeds

crocks for drainage

When to sow

In many climates, the natural light is often too poor in winter to support plant growth. This is the main reason why most outdoor plants stop growing in the autumn (although roots may continue to develop) and why it is more usual to sow seeds in spring and summer. However, seeds vary greatly in their requirements, so always follow the instructions on the seed packet where available.

If you intend to sow in the very early spring (perhaps in a greenhouse) when the light is still relatively poor, some artificial lighting may need to be used for the first few weeks to start off the growth cycle. Weak seedlings seldom go on to produce sturdy plants, so it is often better to delay sowing until there is an abundance of natural light. There are, however, some hardy flower and vegetable crops, such as *Erysimum* (wallflowers) and cabbages, that will germinate and grow quite normally, although slowly, during the autumn, winter and early spring.

Seed Depth

As a general rule, cover the seed to a depth of twice its greatest thickness. *Begonia* seeds are dust-like, so a very fine covering of only 1 mm may be all that is necessary—if any at all. A pea seed might be covered by 1 cm (½ in.) of soil or compost. As always there are exceptions: lettuce seeds prefer little or no cover and *Nigella* seeds require slightly more.

Sowing seeds outdoors

Seeds of most hardy plants may be sown outdoors and, once the soil has warmed up and frosts have passed, seeds of many less hardy plants.

Random, or broadcast, sowing can create serious maintenance difficulties, so most seeds, especially of vegetables, are sown in rows to make weed control and harvesting easier. With straight rows, it is easy to distinguish between weeds and seedlings even when they are at the first leaf stage.

Preparing a Seedbed

- Choose an area that is flat and fairly level; an appreciable slope could mean that seeds get washed away in the rain. The soil should be neither rock hard nor boggy.
- Clear the ground of weeds and large stones.
- Dig over or cultivate the soil (see "Cultivating the Soil", pages 97–100).
- Tread up and down the soil, in rows and using your heels, before raking it over again. Repeat this twice so that the seedbed is flat, smooth, and firm all over.
- After raking, the seedbed should have a fine, crumbly layer, about 2.5 cm (1 in.) deep, on the surface of the soil that can be easily raked. This is known as a fine tilth.
- On sticky clay, allow several weeks to elapse between the various operations, waiting for dry weather to work the final tilth.
- Seedling development could be improved by raking some phosphorous fertilizer into the tilth a week or so before sowing.

To make a straight row, stretch a string line tightly along the ground between two pegs and use another peg to create a small gulley, or "drill". Alternatively, large seeds may be sown individually alongside this string without drawing a drill. For very shallow drills and for tiny seeds, draw the end of a garden cane along the string line.

The corner of a draw hoe is ideal for creating shallow drills.

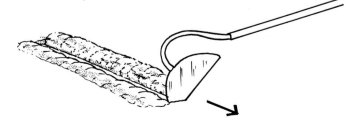

Some seeds, such as pea seeds, are large enough to sow singly at a sensible spacing. Tip smaller seeds into the palm of one hand and distribute them as thinly as possible along the drill, using your thumb and index finger to sow a pinch at a time. The easiest way to do this is to stand astride the line, bend over, and gradually work backwards.

Always put any unused seeds back into the packet for making further sowings in the future. Label each end of the row, noting the crop and the date sown. Once the seeds are covered, it will be difficult to see exactly where the row is. The string line should now be removed.

The most effective way of covering the seeds is to bend over, cupping your hands so that your fingers are touching the soil either side of the drill. Draw them backwards so that your closed fingers act as a sort of ploughshare, pulling the soil evenly back over the seeds from both sides.

Finally, go over the filled-in drill, using the soles of your feet as if walking on a tightrope, and firm the soil on top of the seeds. If for any reason, such as appearance, you need to rake the soil afterwards, do so lightly and along—not across—the rows so that the seeds are not dragged sideways.

If weeds germinate before the crop, it should be possible to hoe lightly between the rows without disturbing the seeds. Where some initial protection is needed from the elements, especially for half-hardy annuals, cloches may be set up over the rows. Several will be needed to cover an entire seed row.

Pots or trays?

There are slight differences between the pots and seed trays, but both need to be clean. The latter may be washed or scrubbed in a sink or bowl of hot water and detergent. Especially dirty containers could be soaked overnight in a bleach solution and thoroughly rinsed afterwards, but beware of getting bleach on your clothes.

Use one of the many seed composts available, whether loam-based or soil-less. They are all sterile, contain no weeds or pests, and are freedraining, unlike most garden soils. Never fill your pots or seed trays with garden soil.

When only a small number of seedlings are wanted, a pot diameter of about 7.5 cm (3 in.) is probably large enough. Some form of drainage material will be needed in the bottom. It is unnecessary in trays because they have plenty of drainage holes.

If a large number of seeds of one plant is needed, use an entire seed tray. Otherwise, sow seeds of several different plants in rows or batches into a prepared seed tray. The drawback with this method is that the seeds will probably germinate at different rates and some seedlings may have to be moved out before others. This can be very disruptive for those seedlings that are not yet ready, so leave plenty of space between the rows or batches.

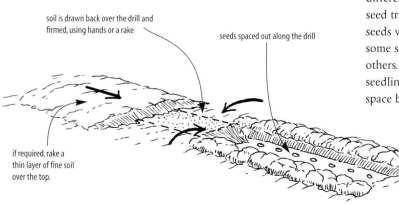

soil is drawn back over the drill and firmed, using hands or a rake

seeds spaced out along the drill

if required, rake a thin layer of fine soil over the top.

Sowing seeds in containers

- Fill the container loosely to the brim with compost.

- Take a small block or circle of wood or the smooth underside of a small clay pot—whichever is appropriate—and compact the compost until it is about 1 cm (½ in.) below the rim of the pot and perfectly smooth.

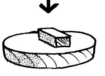

Use a presser to firm the loose compost to create a level surface and a watering rim.

Sow seeds thinly over the surface.

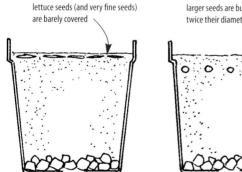

lettuce seeds (and very fine seeds) are barely covered

larger seeds are buried to up to twice their diameters

- Large seeds can be pressed individually into the surface and covered with more compost. Finer seeds may be scattered thinly and evenly over the surface and covered by a fine sifting of compost.

- Water seeds by standing the container in a tray of water so that the compost soaks up water. Do not water from above with a watering can because this might dislodge the seeds or cause them to float to the surface.

- Do not forget to label the container.

- Place the container in a greenhouse, cold frame or under a pane of glass. Turn the pane of glass carefully each day so that condensation does not cause problems by dripping on to the germinating seeds.

- If the seeds are destined to germinate outdoors—possibly over many weeks—place a layer of 3 mm (⅛ in.) shingle or gravel on top of the compost to prevent rainwater from disturbing the seeds.

Damping off

A number of fungal diseases can attack seedlings at soil level and kill them off. Poor air circulation, too much moisture (especially from condensation), and overcrowding can all encourage disease. Thinner sowing, better air circulation, less condensation, and the use of a broad-spectrum fungicide may all help to minimize the problem.

Pricking out seedlings

Soon after germination, seedlings need to be separated and moved into a more spacious container with new compost. It would be risky to put such tiny plants straight out into the garden. The best time to do this is when the first true leaves have just begun to appear, after the cotyledons, or seed leaves. At this stage, the root is still quite small and easy to transplant. The longer you delay pricking out, the more of a setback the seedlings are likely to suffer.

- Before transplanting, prepare the new container. It should be a pot or tray of lightly firmed, potting or seed compost.

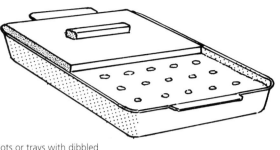

Prepare pots or trays with dibbled holes in the compost.

- Make a hole or holes with a plastic or wooden dibber—a small stick, about 1 cm (½ in.) thick and bluntly pointed at one end—or a pencil.

- Take any small, flat instrument, such as a knife, spatula or widger, and prise out a section of compost complete with a cluster of seedlings.

- Take hold of one seedling by its cotyledons and gently ease it away from the rest. Never hold a seedling by the fragile stem; it will die. Lower the root into the dibbled hole, not covering the stem, and use the dibber and one finger to push in the compost gently from either side so that the seedling is held firm.

- The pot or tray must be gently watered afterwards, preferably from overhead to settle in the seedling.

- Small plants will need protecting from slugs and the elements with glass or plastic cloches.

- Eventually, the seedlings will develop into young plants that can go into larger pots or straight into the garden.

Never prick out root crops like carrots and parsnips because their roots would be damaged and not develop properly. Root crops should be sown where they are to crop, the seedlings thinned within the row, and the thinnings disposed of.

Division

This is another easy form of propagation but is only suitable for those plants that grow as a clump. This includes most herbaceous perennials, for example *Delphinium*, *Lupinus* and *Monarda* as well as some grasses, bamboos and certain bulbous plants. The base of the clump, or crown, is pulled or cut apart to produce several individual plants, each with its own root system.

This is normally done during autumn or winter when the plants are dormant; many will have died back to

Carefully separate out individual seedlings from a clump.

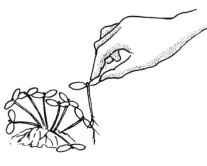

make holes in the compost with a dibber

seedling is carefully lowered into hole

dibber is used to press compost carefully back around the roots

ground level. It is good practice to dig up, divide and replant herbaceous plants every 3–5 years so that vigour and flowering is maintained.

With a garden fork, begin by digging up the clump, which will probably have quite shallow roots. The clump usually may be split up into several pieces by inserting two garden forks back to back and prising them apart. If the clump is very dense or congested, you may need to use a large knife to cut up the clump. Once the entire clump has been split up, it is easy to separate out individual plantlets. Make sure that each plantlet has some healthy buds and a good number of roots.

pull handles of forks apart to prise apart clump

In many cases, the best plants are to be found around the outside of a clump because these will be the youngest and most vigorous. Those in the centre generally will be old and not worth keeping. Take care to plant the plantlets at the same depth as they were when attached to the main plant.

Bulb Propagation

Most bulbs are easily propagated by either division or seeds. Seed of most genera germinates best when fresh. If sown in the early autumn of the year in which it ripens, and kept outside, much of it will germinate the following spring. Some species require a cold period to stimulate germination, while some, including *Lilium*, have more complex requirements, so that germination if often delayed for about a year.

Division of a bulb is necessary where especially good forms are to be increased or where seed is unobtainable. The many different methods of division depends on the type of bulb.

Bulblets

Bulblets are simply small bulbs that develop around the main bulb, in the case of *Galanthus* (snowdrop) and *Narcissus* (daffodil), or are divisions, usually called offsets, of the main bulb itself. Each of these may be separated from the main bulb and planted individually, and will become mature bulbs and probably produce flowers in about three years.

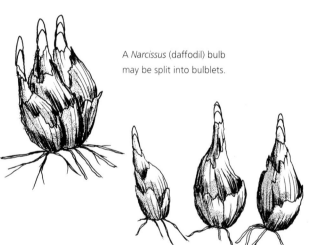

A *Narcissus* (daffodil) bulb may be split into bulblets.

In most cases, this technique is carried out during the summer once all the foliage has died back. With bulblets of *Galanthus* (snowdrop), it is best done immediately after flowering.

Bulbils

Bulbils are tiny, almost black bulbs that form in the leaf axils of some lilies. Remove them gently during the summer and store them somewhere cool, in dry peat, until the following spring. Then line them out in trays of cutting compost made from equal parts of sharp sand and peat or humus.

Water and feed the bulbils like any other lily bulb and leave them to develop over the next few years. They should be large enough to flower in three years.

Scales

The scales of lily bulbs are usually detached by gently breaking them off from the parent bulb in the early spring, before the bulbs begin to sprout. It is important to retain a small part of the basal plate on each scale, since this is where the new bulblets and roots are produced.

The scales should be set in loose, peaty soil or cutting compost, with the tip of the scale just above the soil, in rows into pots or trays and placed either on a heated propagation bench or in a cold frame. Watering should be sparing at first, but should be increased once bulblets and roots begin to form at the base of each scale.

Layering

Layering is a form of propagation just waiting to happen and one of the easiest to perform without any risk to the parent plant. It exploits the fact that most branches or stems that come into contact with the ground can easily be encouraged to root and therefore produce a new plant. Many plants do this naturally.

Rubus fruticosus (blackberry) colonizes its territory by sending out long shoots that root from the tips as soon as they touch the ground; other plants that often root from their branches or stems include *Hedera* (ivy), *Prunus laurocerasus* (laurel) and *Rhododendron*, as well as strawberry runners.

Young branches are much more likely to root than old ones, but even these could take several months to root. There are several simple operations that you can carry out to speed up rooting and extend the range of plants that can be propagated by layering.

Layering a shrub

If a young branch of a shrub is close to the ground and supple enough to bend, there is a good chance it can be encouraged to root—it may already have done so. Roots tend to form most readily at, or

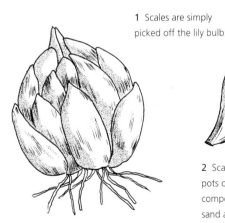

1 Scales are simply picked off the lily bulb.

2 Scales are inserted into pots or trays of cutting compost (equal parts sharp sand and peat or humus).

3 Scales eventually develop roots and bulblets.

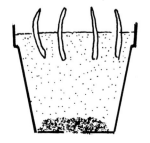

4 Young bulbs eventually begin to develop their own leaves and reach flowering size in about three years.

around, nodes on the stem, where cambium activity (cell division) is greatest. This activity may be accelerated by layering of the stem.

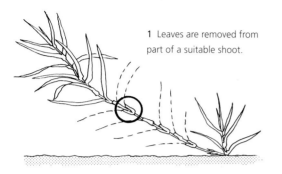

1 Leaves are removed from part of a suitable shoot.

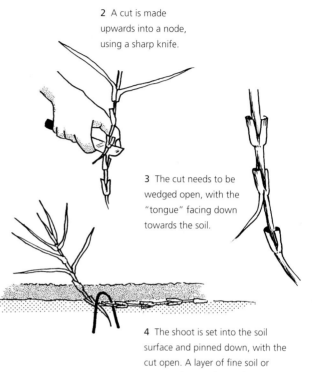

2 A cut is made upwards into a node, using a sharp knife.

3 The cut needs to be wedged open, with the "tongue" facing down towards the soil.

4 The shoot is set into the soil surface and pinned down, with the cut open. A layer of fine soil or compost is spread over the top; avoid using acid soil or compost.

- Although layering may be carried out at any time of the year, best results are obtained during spring and summer.

- Choose a young vigorous shoot with several leaves and sideshoots.

- Strip the leaves from the shoot for about 10–30 cm (4–12 in.) behind the growing tip, where it will touch the soil.

- Bring the stem down to the ground and mark its position on the soil. Bend the stem at right angles, cutting partway through the stem where it will touch the soil.

- Wedge open the cut with a small stone.

- Peg the wounded part of the stem down into some soft soil, using a piece of thin wire bent into the shape of a staple.

- Eventually, after two or three months, roots should develop, providing you with a new young plantlet.

- Detach the plantlet from the parent shrub, with secateurs.

Layering a climber
Most climbing plants may be layered in the same way as shrubs, by cutting the stem and pegging it down. It may still take several months for a good root system to develop.

Layering herbaceous plants
A similar technique may be used on *Dianthus* (border carnations and pinks), but because the stems are relatively soft, rooting should be quicker.

Plants like strawberries and the houseplant *Chlorophytum comosum* (spider plant) naturally produce plantlets on the end of stems or runners. These may be encouraged to root by weighing them down with a small stone or pegging down with a piece of bent wire or cleft wood in pots of soil or directly into garden soil without the need for any "surgery".

Air layering

As well as outdoor garden plants, there are also many indoor plants that may be air-layered very successfully. *Ficus elastica* (rubber plant) often grows tall and leggy, but by air layering it approximately 23 cm (9 in.) from the top of the stem, a new, vigorous plant may be easily created.

- With a sharp knife, cut any vertical stem, up and under a node.

- Open out the cut carefully by bending the stem and stuffing it with some damp sphagnum moss (available from a florist). The cut surfaces could be smeared with a little hormone rooting compound.

- Then wrap more moss right around the wounded part of the stem.

- Encase the moss in clear plastic, such as kitchen film or a piece of plastic bag, and secure it to the stem, top and bottom, with "twist-it" ties.

- The stem may need strapping to a cane for support.

- After several weeks, roots should be visible just under the plastic, indicating that the new plant is ready to be detached, with a sharp knife or secateurs, and potted up.

During the rooting period, the plant may remain in its normal position. Quite often, the parent plant responds to the removal of the rooted air layer by producing several, new sideshoots and developing into a bushier specimen. It is worth trying air layering on a whole range of plants that tend to be leggy, for example *Rhododendron* and some other garden shrubs.

Taking Cuttings

The propagation techniques discussed thus far have been relatively safe, with little risk of failure. When you remove part of a plant and try to encourage root growth without the aid of a "safety net", the situation is different. Virtually all stems, leaves and roots have

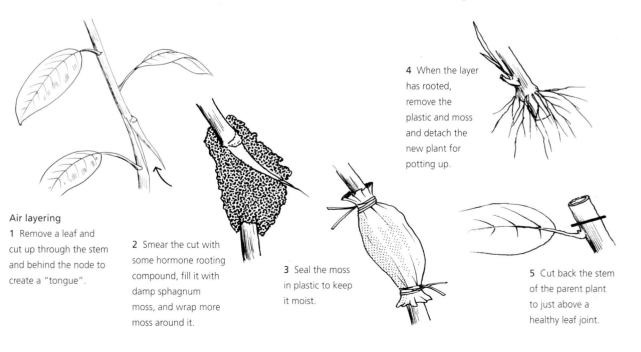

Air layering

1 Remove a leaf and cut up through the stem and behind the node to create a "tongue".

2 Smear the cut with some hormone rooting compound, fill it with damp sphagnum moss, and wrap more moss around it.

3 Seal the moss in plastic to keep it moist.

4 When the layer has rooted, remove the plastic and moss and detach the new plant for potting up.

5 Cut back the stem of the parent plant to just above a healthy leaf joint.

a good supply of cambium, or meristematic tissue, which will generate roots and therefore has the potential for a new plant, if it can be kept alive long enough in the right conditions.

Timing can be crucial for taking cuttings, which is why hardwood cuttings, usually taken in the autumn when the plant stem has matured, is generally considered the easiest method. Softwood and semi-ripe cuttings are less predictable and sometimes several attempts need to be made before the cuttings respond and begin to adapt and grow.

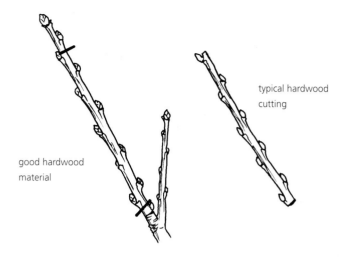

typical hardwood cutting

good hardwood material

Types of Cuttings

In increasing order of difficulty:
- Hardwood cuttings
- Heel cuttings
- Root cuttings
- Leaf cuttings
- Leaf-bud cuttings
- Semi-ripe cuttings
- Softwood cuttings

Hardwood Cuttings

The cuttings with the least risk of failure are taken from mature, hardened shoots and are called hardwood cuttings. There are many trees and shrubs that, with very little preparation, can produce roots from these cuttings.

It is crucial to choose the right material. Experiment with plants such as *Cornus alba*, *Deutzia*, *Forsythia*, *Ribes*, *Weigela* and black- and redcurrants. This technique could also be used on some evergreens such as *Buxus* or *Sarcococca*.

Choose a parent, or stock, plant that has been growing reasonably vigorously and healthily during the summer. By the early autumn, all the current year's shoots—those mainly around the outside of the plant that have just finished growing—will have

matured and hardened. Ideally, they should be reasonably smooth and straight. By leaf-fall, they will be ready for "harvesting".

- Use sharp secateurs to remove shoots about 30 cm (12 in.) long.

- Then remove the top 2.5 cm (1 in.) or so, making sure that each cutting ends neatly at the top and bottom with a node (bud).

- Check that all the cut branches on the parent plants are neatly pruned back to a node.

- Garden soil in moist shade is the ideal place for these cuttings, not a greenhouse. Make a slit in the ground with a spade and push the cuttings into it by about half their length (making sure they are the right way up!) and about 6 cm (2½ in.) apart.

- If there are several rows, make sure that they are wide enough apart for you and a hoe to travel between them.

- Use your foot to push soil firmly up against the cuttings and to close the slit. Insert a label securely so that you will remember what cuttings you have taken.

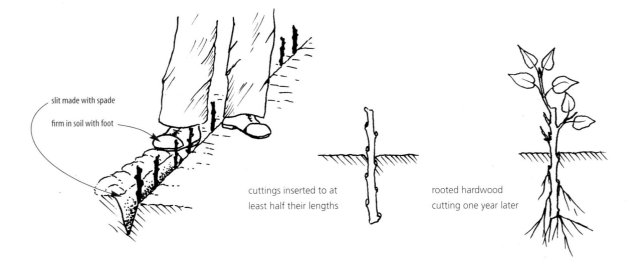

slit made with spade

firm in soil with foot

cuttings inserted to at least half their lengths

rooted hardwood cutting one year later

- The cuttings can stay there all winter and through the following spring and summer. Several of them should sprout in the spring, developing small branches during the summer. Never let them dry out, because they will be developing their root systems.

- In the following autumn, dig up the rooted cuttings and plant them elsewhere.

Your degree of success will depend upon both the plant species—some are harder to root this way than others—and the condition of the material used, but in general the results should build your confidence to move on to other techniques.

Softwood Cuttings

"Soft", or immature, unripe, wood or shoot material, is likely to wilt within a couple of hours: the challenge is to keep the cutting alive long enough for it to grow its own roots. This need not be as difficult as it sounds.

Many soft cuttings may be rooted in water on a bright windowsill, but difficulties may lie ahead with acclimatizing the new, waterbound root system to living in compost. In general, it is preferable to root cuttings in a specialized cutting compost rather than first in water.

Spring and summer are the obvious times to take softwood cuttings, before the stems begin to harden and rooting becomes slower.

Which plants to choose?
Almost any plant, indoors or out, which produces some soft, actively growing shoots can be propagated from softwood cuttings. This includes most pot-grown plants, many shrubs, some climbers and a few trees. For specific detail on individual plants, consult a propagation manual. As with so many aspects of gardening, there are quite a few exceptions and peculiarities, and some plants are simply temperamental.

Environment
In many cases, the cutting needs to be provided with what amounts to an intensive care unit, ideally a bright, well-ventilated greenhouse with automatic misting nozzles that will continually coat the leaves with a thin film of moisture. The bench on which the pots and trays of cuttings stand might have soil-warming cables to supply "bottom heat" to the cuttings to stimulate rooting; these are usually set into sand spread over a large, well-drained, tray

bench. This set-up will ensure that the cutting has a cool top, through evaporation and misting, and a warm base: a contrast that is likely to produce the best possible results.

propagating bench

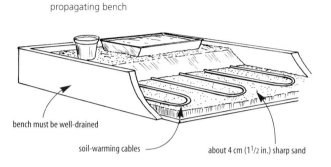

bench must be well-drained

soil-warming cables

about 4 cm (1¹/₂ in.) sharp sand

All this can be expensive, so a more modest approach is either to use a greenhouse without mist and less ventilation, a heated propagator, or a large box with a pane of glass over the top.

If soil-warming cables are used with little ventilation, there is the possibility that the entire cutting could heat up. Frequent overhead manual spraying and misting can be helpful.

Cuttings may also be inserted in a pot of compost with a plastic bag (or a cut-off plastic bottle) placed over the top. While this can work reasonably well, it is often a race between roots starting to grow and a fungus destroying the leaves.

Taking the cuttings

A typical softwood cutting is about 10 cm (4 in.) long, but the precise length depends on the growth rate of the parent plant; cuttings of fast-growing plants such as *Cornus* (dogwood) often being as long as 12.5 cm (5 in.).

- The parent plant needs to be healthy and producing reasonably vigorous growth, although the strongest shoots are not always the most suitable. Very often, sideshoots from halfway down the plant are more suitable than shoots right at the top, because the cuttings will tend to shoot in each of the leaf axils.

- Use a clean and very sharp knife or blade to take the cuttings, to lessen the risk of disease entering the wound and preserve the ability of the cutting to root.

- The growing tip of each cutting must be intact, and the cutting should have a node at its base.

- Cuttings that have flower buds are less desirable and successful than those that have not, because energy will be diverted to forming flowers rather than roots.

- It is unwise to bury leaves of cuttings because they can rot and make the cutting fail, so the lower leaves must be carefully cut off, not pulled off, with a sharp knife or blade.

- As soon as cuttings have been removed from the plant, they should be placed in a moist plastic bag, so that they do not loose any moisture before they are inserted into compost.

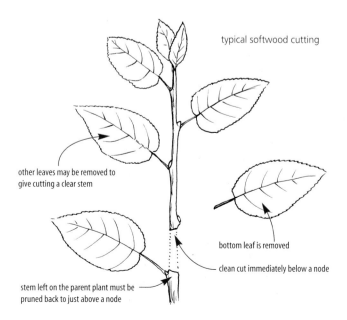

typical softwood cutting

other leaves may be removed to give cutting a clear stem

bottom leaf is removed

clean cut immediately below a node

stem left on the parent plant must be pruned back to just above a node

Preparing the pot

The base of a cutting needs air and moisture. A 50/50 mixture of moss peat or fibre and washed, sharp sand (horticultural grade) will provide this. Nutrients are normally not added because cuttings are moved on soon after rooting. Should this be delayed, then cuttings may usually be given a foliar feed.

Clay pots produce the best results, mainly because the clay allows the passage of some air. If cuttings are inserted around the edge of the pot against the clay, they may root more successfully than they would in a plastic pot or tray.

Inserting the cuttings

- Fill the pot to the top loosely with compost.

- Rooting hormones: there is evidence that the use of hormone powder, gel or liquids can speed up rooting, but it is less certain that these additives can make a cutting root that would not have otherwise done so. The base of the cutting is usually dipped in the product before being inserted in the compost; always read the instructions supplied with the product, and look at the "sell-by" date, if given; failure with hormone rooting compound is often the result of it being out-of-date and losing its efficacy.

- The compost should be soft enough for you simply to push the prepared cuttings into it but if not, use a dibber or pencil to make holes first.

- Insert the cuttings; they are often inserted to half their length, perhaps getting two nodes rather than one in the compost. Cuttings may be placed anywhere within a plastic pot, but preferably around the outside of a clay one.

- Avoid overcrowding the cuttings, although it is almost inevitable that their leaves will touch.

- Once all the cuttings have been inserted into the compost, grasp the pot in both hands and tap it firmly down on the bench two or three times to settle the compost. Also use your finger to firm the compost gently between the cuttings.

- Finally, water carefully from above, label, and place the cuttings in your propagation unit.

cuttings inserted around the edge of a clay pot

Caring for softwood cuttings

Pick off all dead and diseased leaves as soon as they develop, otherwise fungal infection will appear and spread rapidly to healthy tissue. A broad-spectrum fungicide can be useful.

How long will they take to root?

Every gardener wants to know this! Most books and seed packets are over-optimistic: many plants take as long as eight weeks to root, but ready-rooting plants such as *Fuchsia*, *Impatiens*, *Hydrangea* and *Pelargonium* may root within five weeks or even less. There are so many variables that it is impossible to be precise. It has nothing to do with green fingers!

It is sometimes difficult to tell, just by its appearance, whether or not a cutting has rooted. The fact that wilting has ceased is always an encouraging early sign. Quite often, new leaves begin to appear and the cuttings seem very firm within the pot.

The only sure way to tell is to turn the pot upside down and gently tap out the soil ball. Any roots should be immediately visible around the outside. It may also be apparent that some cuttings have plenty of roots and others have none. In this case, it is usually best to disentangle the rooted ones and pot them up. The unrooted ones may either be re-inserted or thrown away.

Semi-ripe Cuttings

If softwood cuttings were not successful in the early summer, or if suitable facilities were not available, a second chance of propagating many plants (mostly shrubs) is offered by semi-ripe cuttings.

From about midsummer onwards, the shoots of many plants begin to harden, leaving only their tips soft enough to wilt. Cuttings taken at this stage do not need as exacting conditions as softwood cuttings. There are many shrubs, for instance *Berberis*, *Laurus*, *Pieris* and several conifers, which may be raised from semi-ripe cuttings in a cool, lightly shaded greenhouse, or cold frame out of the hot sun. In many cases, semi-ripe cuttings may be more successful than softwood cuttings.

Taking the cuttings

Semi-ripe cuttings are taken from current season's growth; the length of cutting will depend on the size of shoots available. Some *Berberis* cuttings could be 15 cm (6 in.) long, but *Pieris* cuttings will probably be shorter. *Calluna* and *Erica* (heather) cuttings, commonly rooted from mid- to late summer, will be shorter still at perhaps only 7.5 cm (3 in.) long. Prepare the cuttings as for softwood cuttings.

- As before, the base of the cutting must end with a node.

- If the top of the shoot is very soft, it may be cut back to a firm node or left untrimmed.

- The bottom third or half of each cutting should be stripped of leaves.

- If you use a cold frame, you can insert cuttings either directly into well-drained, gritty soil or compost in open ground or put them in trays or pots and place these in the cold frame.

- Use a dibber to make holes deep enough to insert each cutting to about half its length.

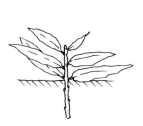

Pieris semi-ripe cutting material, about 10 cm (4 in.) long

prepared *Pieris* cutting in cuttings bed outdoors

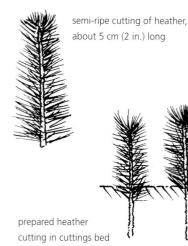

semi-ripe cutting of heather, about 5 cm (2 in.) long

prepared heather cutting in cuttings bed

- Be sure to firm the compost around each cutting with your fingers, and label.

- Water in the cuttings from above. You will not need to keep the leaves misted with water.

Rooting the cuttings

Many of the cuttings will have rooted by the winter, but some will take longer. Soil-warming cables are likely to speed up rooting, as might the use of rooting hormones, especially for conifer cuttings. As always, some plants are easier to propagate this way than others; some heather nurseries root all their cuttings in late summer into cold frames. It is inexpensive and quite reliable.

Heel Cuttings

Many conifers and some shrubs, such as *Azara* or *Viburnum tinus* that have only small shoots may be taken with a "heel". The heel helps to prevent a rather soft, semi-ripe cutting from rotting at the base. Conifer heel cuttings are best taken from bushy branches fairly close to the base of the plant, rather than from vigorous shoots near the top.

- Carefully tear the cutting from a branch so that it comes away with a heel of bark and older wood at the base.

- Shorten or trim the heel of bark with a sharp knife and flick out the tiny wedge of old wood with the tip of the knife.

- Do not forget to trim back the parent plant to a healthy node because taking heel cuttings can be quite damaging.

- Insert the cuttings and root them in the same way as for semi-ripe cuttings.

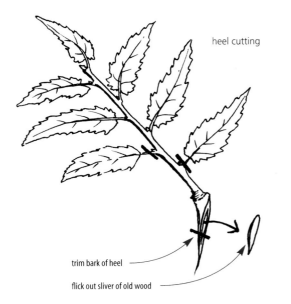

heel cutting

trim bark of heel

flick out sliver of old wood

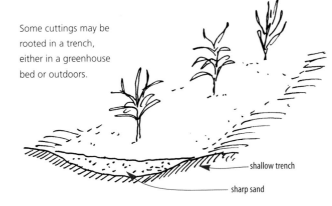

Some cuttings may be rooted in a trench, either in a greenhouse bed or outdoors.

shallow trench

sharp sand

Root Cuttings

Plants to use for root cuttings include *Acanthus, Aralia, Papaver orientale, Phlox paniculata, Primula denticulata, Rhus typhina,* as well as *Ceanothus* and *Romneya;* the last two require some bottom heat. The best time to take root cuttings is in midwinter.

- Dig up the parent plant and remove a few of the roots that are about the thickness of a pencil. Plants like *Phlox* have relatively thin roots, so use the thickest. Never use all the roots. Leave plenty of fibrous roots and a few larger ones on the parent plant so that, once replanted, it can continue to grow.

- When taking cuttings, always make a straight cut at the top and a slant at the bottom so that you know which way up to plant them.

- Collect the roots in a moist plastic bag until ready to plant.

Preparation of root cuttings

It will be midwinter, so a greenhouse is probably the best place to work.

- Lay the thicker roots out on a bench with their bottom ends towards you.

- Chop them into sections about 5 cm (2 in.) long, cutting the top ends straight across and the bottom ends with a slanting cut.

- Using a fungicide to dust the cut ends of the cuttings will reduce the risk of rotting.

- Using a dibber, push the cuttings into a deep tray or a pot of cutting compost so that the flat, top ends are flush with the surface. If the tray is not very deep, it may be necessary to insert the cuttings at an angle.

- Top-dress with grit or fine gravel.

Thick root cuttings may be inserted vertically into a pot of compost so that the top, cut surfaces are flush with the compost.

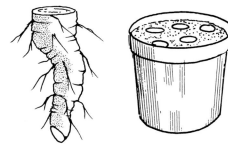

- Thin cuttings of similar lengths may be laid horizontally on the surface and lightly covered with about 5 mm (¼ in.) of compost, which must then be firmed.

- Place the labelled cuttings to root outdoors in a cold frame or in trays in a cool greenhouse.

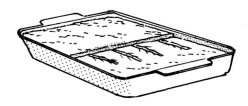

Thin root cuttings are laid horizontally in a tray of compost and lightly covered.

Plantlets should appear in the spring and continue to develop during the summer. Cutting compost has little nutritional value, so the plantlets will need feeding throughout the summer. They can be dug up and planted out in the following autumn.

Leaf Cuttings

The plants most commonly propagated from leaf cuttings include several popular houseplants. The best time of year to do this is in spring and summer.

Peperomia and Saintpaulia

Remove mature, healthy leaves, complete with their leaf stalks (petiole), from the plant with a very sharp, clean knife or razor blade. Using a dibber, insert these around the edge of a clay pot that is filled with moist cutting compost, so that virtually the entire petiole of each cutting is buried. Use your fingers to firm each cutting and water from above.

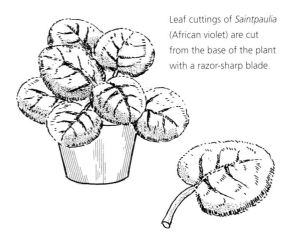

Leaf cuttings of *Saintpaulia* (African violet) are cut from the base of the plant with a razor-sharp blade.

A dibber is used to make holes in a pot of compost.

If possible, leaves should hardly touch within the pot.

Sansevieria and Streptocarpus

Remove a complete leaf and lay it on the bench with its base pointing towards you. Using a sharp knife, cut it across into sections 8–50 mm (½—2 in.) long. Carefully push each of these sections, with the uppermost section to the top, into a slit in the compost, so that it is half buried, and then firm it in with your finger. Allow enough space between the cuttings for them not to touch.

The long leaves of *Sansevieria* may provide several leaf cuttings. You may cut straight across the leaf, or at angles to create chevrons, which make it easy to tell which way up the leaf cuttings should go into the compost.

discard tip

chevron-shaped leaf cutting is inserted so it "points" downwards

straight sections made by cutting at 5 cm (2 in.) intervals

make sure cuttings are the right way up—cuts made nearer the base of the parent leaf should be in compost

The variegated *Sansevieria* will produce only green plants from a variegated cutting. The best way to reproduce a variegated plant is by division.

Begonia rex

Cut off a healthy leaf and lay it flat on a bench with its petiole towards you. The cuttings may be prepared in one of two ways.

The first method involves cuttings out rectangular sections of leaf, each about 2.5 cm (1 in.) across and 5 cm (2 in.) long, with a thick vein running vertically through the centre. Make these rectangles slightly narrower towards the bases so that you can remember which way up they should go. Make a slit in a tray or pot of cutting compost and insert each section to about half its length, with the narrower end downwards. Make sure that the cuttings do not touch, and firm them with your finger.

If using the second method, lay a leaf upside-down on the bench. With a very sharp knife, score across several of the largest veins. Carefully place the leaf the right way up on a tray of firmed, moist cutting compost. Weigh down each cut with a small stone. Alternatively, fix the leaf in position with staples of thin wire pushed over the veins, through the leaf and down into the compost, so that all the cut surfaces are in contact with the compost.

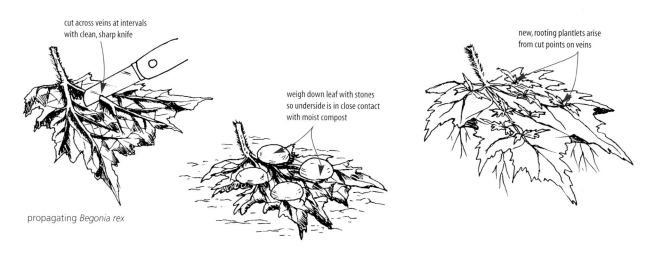

cut across veins at intervals with clean, sharp knife

weigh down leaf with stones so underside is in close contact with moist compost

new, rooting plantlets arise from cut points on veins

propagating *Begonia rex*

Rooting leaf cuttings

All these cuttings need a warm, humid atmosphere, either in a greenhouse or indoors. As long as the glass is turned regularly to minimize condensation, a box with a glass top and some soil-warming cables would be suitable. If you are using a heated propagator, open the vents if you see condensation building up on the lid. It may take several weeks for tiny, rooted plants to develop at the bases of the leaves or sections. Eventually they will be large enough to handle and pot on.

Leaf-bud cuttings

This is a technique that may be used to root cuttings from quite a wide range of plants, including *Camellia*, *Clematis*, *Dracaena*, *Ficus elastica*, *Hedera*, *Mahonia* and *Passiflora*. It involves using just one leaf and its bud, so is ideal where cutting material is very limited.

The best time of year varies according to the plant. For houseplants like *Dracaena* and *Ficus*, it may be at any time during spring and summer. For *Clematis* and *Passiflora*, cuttings are best taken from soft, spring growth. The best time for leaf-bud cuttings of *Camellia* is late summer and of *Mahonia*, autumn. The technique for taking leaf-bud cuttings from all these plants is much the same.

– Take a stem of current year's growth and cut it into sections about 5 cm (2 in.) long, so that each section has a leaf and bud at the top and a bare length of stem below. Very large leaves may be rolled up, secured with an elastic band, and supported with a split cane, to prevent them from overbalancing.

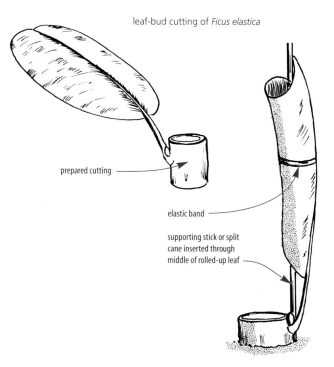

leaf-bud cutting of *Ficus elastica*

prepared cutting

elastic band

supporting stick or split cane inserted through middle of rolled-up leaf

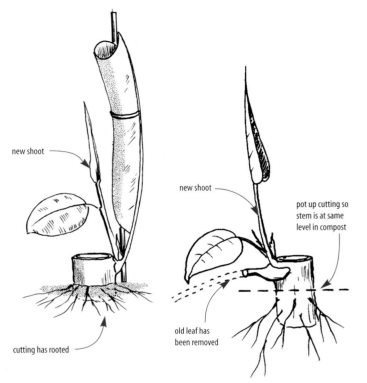

new shoot

cutting has rooted

new shoot

old leaf has been removed

pot up cutting so stem is at same level in compost

- Take a length of stem that grew and ripened during the previous summer and cut it into sections about 5 cm (2 in.) long, using sharp secateurs. Each section must have a bud at the top; if there are two opposite buds, carefully pinch one out.

- Push each section into a pot or tray of compost so that the bud is just touching the compost.

- Place the vine eyes in a warm greenhouse and keep moist. Quite soon, shoots will appear, but it will be some time (probably well into the spring) before enough roots grow to enable you to dig them out and pot them up.

vine eye with bud at the top

vine eye inserted so bud sits on surface of compost

vine eye produces shoot before there are many roots

- Dip the base of the stem into some rooting hormone compound.

- Push the cuttings into a pot or tray of compost, so that each leaf is just touching the compost.

- Firm the cuttings in thoroughly; this is important since their only anchorage is a short length of stem.

- In all cases, provide warm, moist conditions with bottom heat. The woodier plants could take several weeks to root.

Vine Eyes

This is a common method of propagating all ornamental and edible vines (*Vitis*). The best time of year to do this is midwinter. The principle is much the same as for leaf-bud cuttings (see above), except that there is no leaf.

Budding and Grafting

Some plants we grow would not achieve their shape, height, vigour or cropping if they were not grafted or budded on to the rootstock of another plant.

Ornamental roses would often be too weak to grow successfully if they were not budded on to the rootstock of a particularly strong-growing rose. Weeping *Cotoneaster* plants would not weep, but simply spread across the ground, if they were not grafted on to a more vigorous, upright-growing *Cotoneaster*. Most fruit trees, especially apples, are grafted on to rootstocks to keep them dwarf, give them added vigour, help them to tolerate poor soil conditions, and so on.

You normally will purchase plants that have already been budded or grafted, so it is unlikely that you would need to carry out these operations yourself. However, you might wish to try it out, so here is a brief description of what is involved in budding and grafting.

Although different in technique, budding and grafting are biologically similar processes. They both involve the use of two plants—a host plant to provide roots together with a length of stem, called the stock or rootstock, and a piece of another plant, called the scion, which has certain desirable features but performs better on the roots of another plant.

Both budding and grafting are designed to bring together the cambium (meristematic or growth tissue) of the two plants so that they join and create a strong union. New xylem and phloem develop to ensure that water and nutrients can flow from one side of the joint to the other. A successful union will mean that the new plant goes on to grow, flower and fruit for the length of a normal life span.

Sometimes the rootstock will grow suckers from buds below the graft union. If these are not removed as soon as they appear, they will often grow very rapidly and eventually, over the years, swamp and overcome the scion.

Budding

This is carried out during the summer when many modern roses are budded on to the roots of various wild roses. The wild roses give the cultivar extra vigour and, in the case of standards and half standards, a good, straight stem.

Several small slivers of wood, each containing a bud, are taken from the cultivar (the ornamental rose). These "buds" are inserted under the bark of the

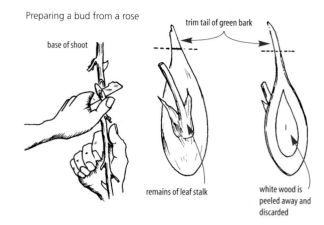

Preparing a bud from a rose

base of shoot — trim tail of green bark — remains of leaf stalk — white wood is peeled away and discarded

Remove a length from a vigorous, flowering shoot, about 30 cm (12 in.) long. Cut off all the leaves so a small part of each leaf stalk remains. Using a clean, sharp knife, scoop out a bud, together with a sliver of stem and the leaf stalk.

Preparing the rootstock for budding

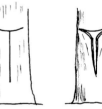

T-shaped cut scored into bark, about 10 cm (4 in.) above soil level

flaps of bark opened out to expose green cambium beneath

bud slotted into cut so leaf stalk points upwards and top of bud is flush with top of cut (trim the top of the bud if needed)

bud-graft bound with grafting tape to keep it in place. All of cut is covered with tape to prevent it drying out

rootstock, either at ground level (for a bush rose) or partway up a straight stem (for standard roses). Tree fruits and some ornamental trees may also be budded in this way.

Grafting

Grafting is used for a wide range of trees and shrubs. Unlike budding, it is carried out during winter or the very early spring. The reasons for doing it are much the same as for budding, but a portion of stem rather than just a bud is joined to the rootstock. The stock and scion are cut to match each other, so that the two surfaces can lock together and eventually form a strong union. It is almost like joinery or carpentry and takes quite a high level of skill and practice to achieve good results.

Occasionally grafts fail, and mature branches break loose in rough weather, but this is nearly always due to a poor union at the outset and not a gradual deterioration of the graft.

A saddle graft is often used for *Rhododendron* or surface-rooting, woodland shrubs.

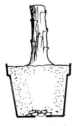

pot-grown rootstock cut down to 30–37.5 cm (12–15 in.) stem

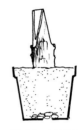

stem cut away on two sides to produce wedge-shaped "saddle"

scion taken from another plant, about 10 cm (4 in.) long

base of shoot cut up the centre, to same length as cuts on rootstock, and opened out

scion fitted precisely over saddle of rootstock so the cambium layers, just beneath the bark, are aligned

if the scion stem is slimmer than the rootstock stem, line up one side of the scion and rootstock so the cambium of both aligns

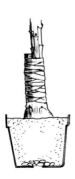

entire graft is bound with tape to secure it, and keep it moist, until the cambiums unite

A whip-and-tongue graft is often used for apple trees. Once fitted together, the graft may be bound with raffia.

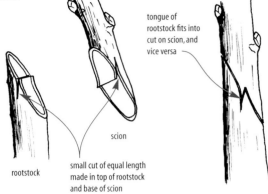

tongue of rootstock fits into cut on scion, and vice versa

scion

rootstock

small cut of equal length made in top of rootstock and base of scion

Greenhouse Management

If you have the boon of a greenhouse, it is important to keep it well maintained to avoid problems and use it to its best potential. There are many different types now available, such as octagonal or multisided, lean-to or ornamental. The main construction material is either non-rusting aluminium alloy (now largely replacing the original cast-iron types) or cedarwood, which has an advantage over other materials because it is a slow conductor of heat—but it may need painting or treating every two or three years.

Modern conveniences such as double glazing and automated ventilation and heating systems make greenhouse management much easier than ever before. However, it will need a thorough cleaning every year.

Hygiene

During the winter, or whenever the greenhouse has few plants in it or is least active, the entire structure—glass and framework—should be washed down with soapy water to which a little disinfectant should be added. Pay particular attention to nooks and crannies where tiny pests might be hiding. Also any old pots and boxes should be cleared out.

Shelves and staging should be treated similarily at the same time, at a period between crops when the house is least full or active. Keeping to a good hygiene routine will also avoid the spread of diseases that could affect successful propagation and plant growth.

It is vital to keep a greenhouse clean and free from dead and decaying material, most of which can harbour pests and fungal diseases. Seedlings and cuttings are especially vulnerable to infection. Keep the greenhouse tidy and brush up spilt compost as you work.

Climate Control

A well-equipped greenhouse can create and maintain a wide range of conditions. Where only one crop is being grown, it is easy to establish the appropriate levels of humidity, light and temperature, but problems arise when plants demanding different conditions are grown together.

There may be seedlings, which are vulnerable to fungal infections in high humidity, growing next to bromeliads, which do need high humidity, and *Ficus benjamina*, which can become infested with red spider mite if kept in a dry atmosphere.

Large greenhouses may be partitioned to create more than one microclimate, but it may not be possible to accommodate a wide range of plants at the same time in a small greenhouse.

Humidity

Minimum use of water in a greenhouse will produce a very dry atmosphere. On the other hand, frequent, manual damping down of the floor and benches as well as growing plants on constantly moist irrigation benches will help to raise the humidity. This may be increased further by spraying water over the plants in a fine mist, but preferably not in bright sunlight as the foliage may suffer from shock.

Temperature

If heating has been installed in the greenhouse, a thermostat connected to the heat source is essential to keep an even temperature. The temperature may be lowered by opening the greenhouse vents or louvres, but care is needed when the outside air is cold. Although inexpensive, paraffin and oil heaters tend to give off gases that can be injurious to some plants, so are best avoided.

Many plants drop their leaves if they experience marked or sudden changes in temperature. In particular, *Croton* species, some *Ficus* and *Mimosa pudica* (sensitive plant) specimens should never be too close to the door.

Light

Hot summer sun can scorch plants inside the greenhouse, but levels of light may be decreased by the use of shading blinds or a shade paint wash. Any external, greenhouse shade paint or wash will need to be removed in autumn and reapplied in the following summer.

Difficulties sometimes arise when there is insufficient light for rapidly growing seedlings in the early spring. Artificial lighting can make significant improvements to plant growth and can also be effective in controlling the flowering of some potted plants. Supplementary lighting is easy to install and inexpensive to run, but may need to be linked to a timer or a device that turns it on and off according to the light levels within the greenhouse.

Feeding Greenhouse Plants

Feeding plants in a greenhouse is much the same as for plants elsewhere in the garden, except that the levels and frequency may need to be a little higher. This is because many of the plants will grow more rapidly than they would outdoors and because the compost in the pots will contain a limited amount of nutrients.

As you would expect, the kind of plant food required depends upon what the plants are being grown for. If foliage is the main attraction, then a high-nitrogen fertilizer might be required during the summer. Flowers or fruits will respond better to relatively high levels of potash.

Pest and Disease Control

A greenhouse is a controlled and enclosed environment so allows more options for controlling pests and diseases. Some pesticides may be administered in the form of smokes, which are particularly penetrating and can reach into every crevice in the greenhouse frame or structure.

Biological controls, which exploit pest predators, may be used under glass. They can be very effective at controlling, for example, whitefly, which might have otherwise become resistant to a range of chemical pesticides.

In most greenhouses, a wide range of plants grow together and so the instructions for any chemical control must be read carefully, to check if any plant within the greenhouse could be harmed. Ring the changes in your use of chemicals, so that resistance is less likely to develop over a period of time.

Pests and Diseases

Prevention is usually better than cure. In most cases, avoiding a problem and being well prepared are the most successful ways to protect your plants. Organic gardening practices, such as using disease-resistant cultivars or physical barriers against some pests and not sowing some crops until the threat of a pest or disease has passed, may avoid the need for any chemical intervention.

Either way, to keep your plants relatively free from pests and diseases, you will need to decide:

- Whether you are dealing with a pest or a disease (often fungal)

- Which pests are your friends and which are foes

- At what point, in the life cycle of the pest or disease, should you take action to eliminate the problem most effectively

- How much damage you are prepared to tolerate before taking action

- Is the action really justified?

For example, if roses are grown purely as a cut-flower crop and not in the ornamental border, is it really worth spraying a fungicide against black spot every week? Usually only the lower leaves are affected, leaving the upper leaves and flowers untouched. Any infected, fallen leaves should be cleared up and burned. Instead of spraying everything in sight, take sensible precautions to minimize a problem.

Understanding a little about common pests and diseases is the best way to help your plants avoid or recover from attacks. If you can recognize problems early on, you should be able to deal with them swiftly and prevent the plants from suffering too much harm.

Chemicals have long been used by professional and amateur gardeners to combat garden diseases and dispose of pests, but these are now considered controversial and many have been withdrawn for reasons of stringent health and safety control.

Many gardeners prefer to use natural methods, employing substances and techniques derived from the biochemistry and ecology of the garden and its wildlife, so experiment and choose whichever method you prefer.

Plant Problems

There are many reasons why a plant might look sick and not all of them are due to pests or diseases. Possible causes might be:

- Incorrect watering
- Nutritional deficiencies
- Sudden changes in temperature
- Insufficient light
- Seasonal growth changes
- Physical damage, for instance from heavy rain, hail, winds or frost
- Pests
- Diseases
- Viruses.

Types of Disease

There are many diseases specific to individual plants or groups of plants, but many common diseases of garden plants fall into one of a few main types. You can learn to recognize what type a disease may be from observing certain basic characteristics.

Fungal infections

These include downy and powdery mildews, leaf spots and rusts. Most are transmitted by air-borne spores landing on the outer surface of the plant, which then enter the plant through a wound, natural opening or even by penetrating the plant's external protective barriers. The spores "germinate" to produce a network of filaments (mycelium), which is usually white or grey and just visible to the eye. This whitish bloom gives a mildewed appearance to leaves, stems and fruits.

In powdery mildew, the filaments are external to the host plant and push minute suckers into the sap to extract food. In downy mildew, the fungus filaments are found inside the plant.

Spores can overwinter in the soil or remain on infected debris so good hygiene is required to

minimize future attacks. Treatment is generally to cut out and destroy infected parts, and in some cases, sprays may be used.

Viruses

These organisms are invisible to the eye, although the damage caused is not. They are systemic, meaning that they invade every part of the plant even though only one part of the plant may show any symptoms. Once in a plant, viruses are there for good—all the year round—being spread by sap-sucking insects, physical injury, animals brushing past, on knives used in propagation and during pruning. Seeds from these plants are also likely to be infected. So the only option with an infected plant is usually to dispose of it, or burn it; don't add it to the compost heap because the virus will survive to be spread around the garden.

Bacterial rots and cankers

Again, the organisms are not visible to the eye, but their effects on plant tissue are quite often dramatic. They may give plants an unpleasant smell, with a sticky and often regular, seasonal mass oozing from the stems and spreading the condition. Injury to the stems (mainly of trees and shrubs) could make the plant susceptible to infection.

Physical Control of Diseases

It is possible to avoid or control some diseases without the use of chemicals. In some cases, due to increasingly stringent health and safety legislation, there are no longer any chemical controls available to the amateur gardener. Preventative measures are therefore vital.

- Remove any diseased or dead leaves and stems as soon as they appear.

- Where it is practical, isolate diseased plants from healthy ones until they regain their vigour.

- Improve air circulation by opening greenhouse

vents, removing cold frame covers on mild days, and pruning trees and shrubs to create open systems of branches. This may also slow down the spread of fungal diseases.

- Avoid the excessive use of nitrogenous fertilizer, especially during late summer and autumn.

- Don't overwater potted plants.

- Improve soil drainage.

- Purchase only strong, healthy plants.

Chemical Control of Diseases

When preventative measures do not succeed, chemical control may become necessary, if it is available. Most chemicals used against plant diseases are termed fungicides. Most are sprayed on to the plant, but a few are dusted on. The majority remains on the surface and may therefore wash off after a while, but there are some systemic fungicides, which are absorbed by the plant and inoculate it for a period of time.

Types of Pest

The range of plant-damaging pests is considerable and far more diverse than that of diseases. Knowing how pests live and reproduce will help you determine how best to control or eradicate them.

Some pests, like aphids (greenfly and blackfly), have a life cycle that produces sap-sucking creatures at almost every stage (except for the egg stage). Sap-suckers are detrimental not only because they feed off the plant's main source of energy but also because they transmit diseases from plant to plant. The plant is therefore at constant risk from attack and protection may be difficult.

Butterflies and moths, on the other hand, will cause damage only during the caterpillar or grub stage,

which may span only a short and very specific period of just a few days or weeks. If you find out when this is likely to be, you can prepare yourself to do something about it.

Damage to a rose leaf caused by the leaf-cutter bee rarely affects the health or vigour of the plant.

Many flies and beetles are relatively harmless as adults, but pests in the larval stage. The adult crane fly (also known as daddy-long-legs) does not attack plants, but its grubs, called leatherjackets, eat the roots of grass and other plants during autumn and winter. The grubs of the click beetle, known as wireworms, also eat roots and root crops—again, mainly in autumn and winter.

Larger garden predators

Most of us, particularly those who live in the country, have problems with some of the local wildlife. As with smaller invaders, prevention is preferable to cure.

If in the early stages of making a garden the entire property is fenced off, either to keep family pets such as dogs within bounds, or to keep out unwelcome animals, much anguish will be avoided. It is worth consulting your local pest control officer, but too often there is little that can be done legally in Britain to eradicate a problem in the garden. With little or no hunting and few predators, many unwelcome animals are free to multiply as fast as the food supply will permit. Keeping domestic animals such as dogs or cats helps to control rodent pests.

Chemicals and Safety

- Use chemicals as a last resort and always with safety in mind.
- ALWAYS READ AND FOLLOW THE INSTRUCTIONS ON THE LABEL.
- Always wear protective clothing to cover exposed skin and goggles and breathing masks when handling concentrated chemicals. For safety's sake, avoid breathing in dilute spray, dusts or smokes even if they are approved products—they may later be banned.
- Check that any product you use on food crops is designed for edible crops and is safe.
- Mix chemicals up carefully—if you are mixing a solution for use in a sprayer, partly fill the sprayer with water and add the concentrate, wearing rubber gloves. Refill the measuring cup with water several times, each time emptying it into the sprayer, before finally topping up the sprayer with more water to the required level.
- After using chemical sprays, thoroughly wash out the sprayer and all its parts, disposing of the residue safely.
- Do not spray or dust on windy days to avoid the chemical drifting on to other plants or parts of the garden.
- Some chemicals can harm pets or beneficial insects such as fish in ponds or bees. READ THE LABEL TO CHECK.
- Observe clearance periods for food crops and do not harvest crops while the chemical is still active.

Non-chemical Pest Controls

The main area where organic and "chemical" gardening differ is in pest control. There are specific organic, or non-chemical, measures to be used against many pests (see following pages), but in organic gardening you need to try to avoid problems before they happen, taking every opportunity to outwit pests. There are many general principles that you may apply to keep them at bay. These include:

- Using carefully placed physical barriers to prevent a pest from reaching the plant. For instance, a 45 cm (18 in.) tall barrier of fleece or fine mesh around a crop of carrots will prevent attack from the low-flying carrot fly. If the adult cannot reach the carrots, she cannot lay her eggs, and so there will be no maggot-like larvae to tunnel into the roots and spoil the crop.

- Separating infected plants from healthy ones until all danger from infection has passed, which may take a full growing season.

- Delaying the sowing of certain crops until the danger of infection or attack has passed, such as carrots, which are best sown after early summer when the risk of carrot fly is over.

- Setting traps and hand picking off pests such as slugs. Whether filled with beer or stale milk, traps work well in keeping the local slug and snail population down—particularly if you add a sprinkling of porridge oats! Make sure that the uppermost 2.5 cm (1 in.) of the beaker protrudes

a slug trap

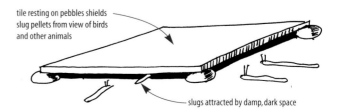

tile resting on pebbles shields slug pellets from view of birds and other animals

slugs attracted by damp, dark space

above the soil surface, so that you don't inadvertently trap beneficial insects such as ground beetles.

- Growing certain plants alongside others to distract or repel pests. For example, grow alternate rows of onions and carrots in your vegetable plot. The smell of the carrots helps to mask the presence of the onions (making them less likely to be attacked by onion fly), while the smell of the onions decreases the likelihood of the carrot fly detecting the carrots.

- Selecting cultivars that are resistant to certain pests (see "Organic gardening", pages 335–336).

- Horticultural fleece, if used with care at the appropriate time of year, may keep many pests at bay. Cover newly planted rows with fleece and keep it anchored, removing the fleece only for routine maintenance such as watering and weeding. Brassicas raised in this way should be free from their most common pests, including aphids, cabbage root fly and caterpillars.

Positioning and maintaining traps and barriers takes some expense and time, but usually less than that taken up by applying chemicals.

Biological control

This occurs naturally in the garden with birds, frogs and toads, hedgehogs, ladybirds and insects such as centipedes feeding on creatures that the gardener regards as pests. Often, this can keep the pest population down to tolerable levels and there is no need for further measures.

However, in the enclosed environment of a greenhouse or conservatory, predators or parasites, often insects, may be introduced quite successfully on infested plants to eradicate specific pests, including aphids, mealybugs, red spider mites and certain scale insects. The parasitic wasp *Encarsia formosa* will eventually destroy whitefly.

Biological controls are also available for use against slugs, caterpillars, leatherjackets and vine weevils. These may be used on pests both out in the garden and in the greenhouse. Imported predators are used outdoors mostly to attack soil-borne pests, but this often requires very specific conditions to be successful. Advertisements in gardening journals are usually the best way of locating supplies of specific predators for biological control.

Never use biological and chemical controls together. Biological controls can be very useful; they may not kill all the pests but will keep them down to a tolerable level. Do not be tempted to "finish off" the application with a chemical—this would kill the biological agent too.

Biological controls are, on the whole, considerably more expensive than the chemical alternatives. When you consider that many pests are now showing resistance to commonly used insecticides, and that some exotic plants may respond badly if sprayed with a pesticide, biological controls seem more appealing. They are also, in some cases, self-perpetuating and so regular applications need not be made.

Gardeners' Friends

- Centipedes are gingery brown, slightly flattened creatures that eat many small organisms, including some plant pests. You can distinguish them from millipede pests because centipedes have only one pair of legs on each body segment. Centipedes each have a pair of quite prominent feelers, move over the soil very quickly and measure between 2.5–5 cm (1–2 in.) in length.

centipede

- Lacewings are small, emerald-green flies with relatively large, green, lacy wings. They are beneficial insects because they feed on greenfly during spring and summer and overwinter indoors, but are susceptible to several insecticides.

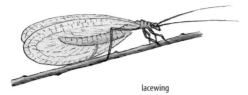

lacewing

- Ladybirds are well-known beneficial insects; both the adults and the larvae feed on a wide range of small pests, including aphids, mealybugs, red spider mites, and scale insects. They may be introduced into a greenhouse as a biological pest control.

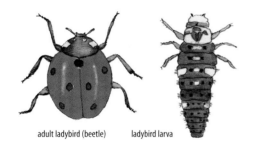

adult ladybird (beetle)   ladybird larva

Chemical Pest Controls

These are also known as inorganic controls, or pesticides, and are best used only as a last resort, although there are not many organic options available when it comes to controlling fungal or bacterial infections. All chemicals used on plants are subject to very strict controls and should be considered safe only if used strictly in accordance with the instructions. Most pesticides fall into two main categories.

- Contact pesticides deposit a chemical on the surfaces of the plant, either as a dilute spray, a powder or dust, or when used in greenhouses as a smoke. They either kill the pest immediately on contact or poison the surface over which they are likely to crawl. Rain or irrigation eventually washes off many of these chemicals.

- Systemic pesticides come in a liquid form. The chemical is absorbed by the plant either through its leaves or through the roots, and it spreads throughout the plant, poisoning the sap and anything that sucks the sap or eats the leaves and stems. These chemicals remain effective for a fairly limited time. They are to be avoided, or used with great care, on edible crops.

Both types of chemical are available, separately or sometimes combined, for pest and disease control.

Looking for Trouble

It is good practice to inspect your plants regularly so that any changes are noticed and you can deal with any problems early on. If the change is marked, it would suggest that the problem has taken quite a hold, and you may be too late to stop the plant suffering a check in growth or more severe harm.

One of the most common foes of gardeners are slugs and snails, because of the speed with which they chomp on our plants. Typical signs are holes between the veins, as on this *Iris* leaf.

When checking plants, look carefully at their leaves, buds, or stems—sometimes it might be worth using a powerful magnifying glass. Buds and first symptoms are frequently very small. Most revealing are the undersides of leaves, but problems may have occurred at the roots, in which case you might have to dig

Common Symptoms and their Possible Causes

Symptom	Possible cause
Twisted and distorted growing tips and flower buds	Aphids, midges, thrips, and other small sap-sucking insects, seen clustered around the growing tip. Fungal infection, often showing as a white deposit or mildew over the shoot. Fumes from hormone lawn weedkillers (especially 24–D) following warm summer weather. No pest or disease evident. Severe fluctuations in weather conditions, especially temperature. Again, no pest or disease evident.
Leaves with pieces missing, especially round the edges	Caterpillars usually create irregularly shaped gaps, with just a few holes appearing in the centre of the leaf. If the damage is mainly at the top of the plant near the tips, the caterpillars are probably still around. If the damage is farther down the stem, with unaffected foliage higher up, the caterpillars may have been and gone. Birds may rip away large portions of leaf or complete leaves. Damage is not as neat as caterpillar damage, but is less common. Leaf-cutting bees cut out small, semi-circular pieces from edges of leaves, especially fully formed leaves. By the time they are noticed, the pest will probably have departed. Slugs and snails. Unlike the previous examples, the holes appear mainly within the body of the leaf and less so around the edges. Some holes may not go right through the leaf and those closest to the ground are most affected. There may also be some silvery or slimy trails. Flea beetles and thrips. Leaves may be peppered with lots of tiny holes.
Leaves are discoloured or blotched	Red spider mite. A serious infestation (mostly on the undersides) causes leaves to turn slightly bronze. Tiny red mites and some fine webbing are usually just visible. Mildews and moulds (fungal). A white, or sometimes black, covering on the top or lower surfaces of leaves (and stems). Leaves may also produce yellow patches. Viruses. Yellow streaking in the leaves, with distortion and poor development. Rust (fungal). Rust-coloured spots or pustules all over the leaves.
Unexplained wilting, yellowing and withering of stems and soft stems rotting at ground level	Fungal infection at ground level or in the roots. Grubs eating the stems and roots. Root aphids. Severe overwatering and poor drainage. A dangerously high concentration of inorganic fertilizer.
Distorted flowers and stunted, deformed growth	A virus. Look out for yellow streaking in distorted leaves.
Small, white, fluffy blobs on stems and in the leaf axils	Woolly aphid—common on some fruit trees. Mealybug—common along the mature or woody stems of many trees, shrubs and house plants. Scale insect—more scaly than fluffy, hugging the bark of mature stems in many trees, shrubs and houseplants.
Swellings on stems, leaves or fruit	A small grub inside the swelling (produced by a moth or fly). Fungal infection—no other visible symptom. Bacterium—no other visible symptom.
Fruit with brown patches or other discoloration on the surface	Mostly fungal infections. A grey mould or a whitish "bloom" often accompanies the discoloration. Blossom end rot of tomatoes. A physiological disorder where the blossom end of the fruit develops a dark patch, due to erratic watering. Easy to correct in time for newly developing fruits.

down or turn the plant out of its pot. Areas you might examine include:

- Growing tips and soft stems—always the most vulnerable places, where damage can occur long before you are aware of it. Damaged cells may distort the developing leaves or flowers. Some fungal infections and many sucking insects start at these points.

- Young leaves—attract sucking insects or fungal infections. Pieces missing suggest that something has been eating them.

- Mature leaves—there may be pieces of leaf missing, particularly on the undersides. You might see small creatures moving about, such as the vine weevil. The leaves may have changed colour or have developed unusual markings.

- Stems which mature and harden—they become less vulnerable to attack (except in some trees), but problems can occur so these must be inspected too.

- Roots—the least likely place to look for infection, unless the plant looks sick or is wilting. Root-vegetable crops are, however, very vulnerable.

- Flowers—damage here is sometimes visible, although you may have to search deep inside the flowerhead to find any bugs. Many of the damaging creatures, including birds, will probably have already departed the scene of the crime.

- Fruits—imperfections are sometimes the result of earlier infections or infestations. Pests and diseases can often be found both on the insides and the outsides of fruits.

A–Z of Common Pests and Diseases

A number of pests and diseases affect a wide range of plants, but many have specialized forms, which vary slightly and which attack specific plants. To find more detailed information on these and their controls, you need to consult a specialist book on pests and diseases.

Aphids

These are one of the most widespread pests, capable of attacking almost any kind of plant by sucking sap from the shoots, buds and leaves, causing permanent distortion. A sugary secretion from the aphids (called honey dew) often makes the leaf surfaces sticky and is colonized by a harmless, black fungus, or sooty mould. Ants are often attracted by honey dew; they even "farm" aphids, protecting them from predators in exchange for feeding on the honey dew.

Aphids are usually green, yellow, brown or black, although other colours may be found; they are generally 2 mm long, but conifer aphids are larger. During the summer, a female aphid can give birth to live young without mating, so it takes only one aphid to start an infestation. Many aphids can fly and most overwinter as eggs but may be killed off in severe winters. They also transmit some viruses as they feed on plant sap. Aphids on indoor plants may not go into a dormant, or egg, stage, so may need controlling at most times of year.

winged and wingless aphids

Control:

- Where eggs occur on woody stems, particularly those of fruit trees, destroy them with a winter tar oil wash; but protect any plants growing underneath from the wash.

- Aphids on actively growing soft tissue may be killed by means of various contact and systemic insecticides. Ring the changes from time to time to ensure that the pest does not build up a resistance to one particular product and apply the insecticide at regular intervals to treat subsequent generations as they hatch from the eggs. Systemic insecticides are especially useful, being specific to aphids and not harming other insects including bees. Pyrethrin and Derris are two useful organic compounds.

Badgers and foxes

No known miracle solutions can be recommended here. Badgers may dig up and wreck lawns and borders, but are protected by law in Britain. Foxes may damage the appearance of plants by urinating on precious shrubs such as *Buxus* (box) balls, but have the advantage of being predators on the rabbit population.

Blackleg

This disease is caused by various, soil-borne fungi and is encouraged by poor hygiene and badly drained compost. It affects cuttings: just before or during rooting, the cuttings may quite suddenly start to look sick and wilt and under the compost or soil, the stems will have turned black and mushy.

Control:

- Clean pots and well-drained, sterile compost minimizes the problem.

- Dipping the ends of cuttings in a hormone rooting powder that has been combined with a fungicide will also offer some protection.

blackleg on a *Pelargonium* cutting

Black spot or brown or grey leaf spot

These are caused by various bacteria and fungi. Bacterial spots are angular with yellow edges, whereas fungal spots have concentric zones and areas of tiny, fungal fruiting bodies. Most leaf spots do not cause serious problems and may only develop on plants that are in poor condition.

Control:

- Remove and burn all infected leaves and improve the plant's growing conditions by, for example, moving it to a position where there is better air circulation.

- Spray with a suitable fungicide for fungal leaf spots.

Capsid bugs

These pale green insects, about 6 mm (¼ in.) long, suck sap from the growing tips and flower buds of many plants, causing severe distortion and many small holes in the leaves. They are active throughout the spring and summer.

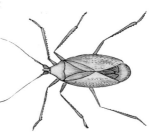

common green capsid bug

Control:
A number of insecticides are effective. Spraying should begin as soon as the first symptoms appear, and then be continued at intervals throughout the summer.

Caterpillars
Caterpillars are part of the life cycle of moths and butterflies. Together with a wide range of grubs, they seriously damage plants by eating leaves and shoots. At a specific time of the year, the adult insects lay eggs on or near the host plant. Most caterpillars are active during late spring and summer, but they are often damaging to plants for a relatively short period, while they are in a transitional stage between the egg and the pupa, or chrysalis. Most caterpillars are specific to just one or two plants, so it does not necessarily follow that a different species next to the affected one will be attacked.

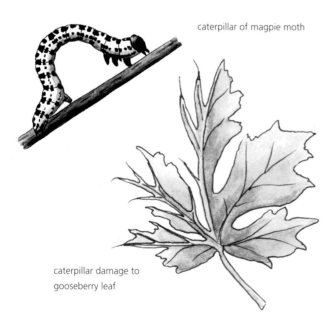

caterpillar of magpie moth

caterpillar damage to gooseberry leaf

Control:
- The use of a systemic insecticide just before an expected attack often works well, but there are several contact insecticides that can also be useful once the attack has begun.

- On food crops, where the infestation is not widespread, hand picking the pests is an option.

Chafer grubs
These plump, white grubs are about 25 mm (1 in.) long with a brown head. They are found half-curled up in soil in considerable numbers during the late summer and winter, when they eat the roots of plants, especially grass. They can kill off large patches of lawn by spring and also attract the attention of foxes and badgers who may dig up a lawn in order to find them!

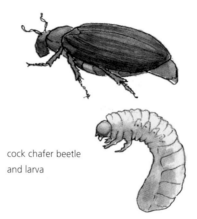

cock chafer beetle and larva

Chafer grubs are the larvae of cock chafers, or maybugs, which are on the wing and fly into security lights during early and midsummer. They inject their eggs into the lawn or into soil close to other plants, especially vegetable crops.

Control:
- If found during digging, chafer grubs may be picked out and destroyed.

- Chemical control of the older grubs (late on in the winter and early spring) is not easy, but some insecticides watered into the soil may be effective if used early on.

- A soil-borne roundworm, or nematode—*Steinernema carpocapsae*—may be introduced by watering it into warm, moist soil during late summer. The nematode paralyzes the grubs and eventually destroys them.

Chipmunks and squirrels

These animals do their damage by digging round the roots of plant, particularly during winter. The roots are then exposed to freezing temperatures and can easily die. Fencing off is unsatisfactory because the animals can climb. They seem to be less prone to digging up bulbs such as *Crocus* if the bulbs are planted in coarse grit or gravel, but perhaps they are simply lazy.

Cows, sheep and horses

These animals are not usually a problem when kept in surrounding fields, but they may lean over fences to sample nearby garden shrubs. Some plants, such as *Rhododendron* or *Taxus* (yew) can be toxic, so make sure that these plants are well out of reach.

Damping off

Infected seedlings may collapse and die in patches. A white fungal growth can often be seen on the surface of the soil or compost and dark patches near the bases of the stems. Sometimes a whole tray or pot of seedlings can be destroyed within just a few days. Poorly drained, unsterilised compost, a stagnant, humid atmosphere, and dense sowing encourage this fungal disease.

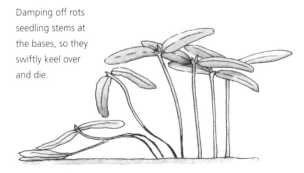

Damping off rots seedling stems at the bases, so they swiftly keel over and die.

Control:

- The use of sterile, well-drained compost, clean containers, the constant removal of dead and diseased material, good ventilation, and thin, well spaced-out sowings will help to avoid serious infection.

- Seeds can be dusted with a copper-based fungicide to provide a good level of protection.

- A copper-based fungicide may be watered on to the compost or soil at the time of sowing, as well as at intervals afterwards.

- Avoid watering seeds with water from a waterbutt; use tap water.

Deer

As the urban sprawl continues to expand, it creates a perfect environment for the increasing proliferation of deer. Especially during winter, deer will consume the stems and foliage of almost any tree or shrub; they are partial to the prickliest of hollies and to roses.

Control:

- Various materials may be hung on wire, or spread near favoured plants, to act as deterrents. These include: human hair—the more unwashed the better; cloths dipped in creosote; lion dung.

- Human urine may be used as a deterrent spray.

- If space and terrain allow, deer fencing may be the best answer. This is commonly available as polypropylene mesh in two gauges—lightweight and heavy duty—and is virtually invisible. The material is pulled tight from tree to tree or post to post with spans of over 6 m (20 ft.) between trees being possible. Deer have very poor vision and perception of depth; since the barrier comes with netting, posts and all other accessories in black, the deer cannot judge where it starts or stops and will beat a path round it rather than attempt to jump over it.

Downy mildew

Leaves develop yellowish patches on the upper surfaces and on the undersides greyish-white fungal growth. Eventually, the patches will spread and the leaves wither and die. Downy mildew is more common in cool, damp, overcrowded conditions. Young, soft plants growing in humid conditions are the most vulnerable.

downy mildew
on leaves

Control:

- Remove all infected tissue and improve air circulation or humidity.

- Make sure that outdoor crops are not planted too close and maintain good weed control.

- Several fungicides will eradicate the disease, but the damage may have already been done. Preventative spraying with a copper fungicide early in the season and at intervals thereafter is the best course of action.

Earthworms

The benefits of earthworms (which include aerating the soil and improving soil drainage and fertility) far outweigh the problem of unsightly worm casts on the surface of a fine lawn. Therefore, think twice before trying to eliminate worms from a lawn. Only a few types of earthworm produce casts. They appear over quite a short period and can be brushed away into the grass once they have dried out.

Control:

- If the problem becomes severe, worms may be attracted up to the surface with Mowrah meal or permanganate of potash. Both are usually watered in. Once on the surface, the worms may be swept up and moved elsewhere—these treatments seldom actually kill the worms.

- In extreme cases, worms may be killed using the same products that control leatherjackets and chafer grubs.

Fairy rings

This is a fungus for which there is no real cure. The fungus starts as a strongly green patch of grass with a paler centre. As it spreads outwards and the green patch becomes a ring (often many metres or yards across), the paler area in the centre gradually recovers to make the green ring look more like a water stain on a piece of cloth. The fungus does destroy some of the grass, and then releases nitrogen, which gives rise to the darker green ring. Some fairy rings are reputed to be more than 100 years old, by which time they can be quite extensive.

Control:

- The use of fertilizers may keep the grass green either side of a fairy ring, but it is seldom sufficient to mask the symptoms completely.

- If the ring is spotted very early on while it is still quite small, it is usually possible to dig out all the infected soil. The soil should be taken out, to at least 15 cm (6 in.) beyond the ring and to a depth of about 30 cm (12 in.), and replaced with clean soil.

Fireblight

This is a seriously harmful bacterium and, in Britain, the disease should be reported to DEFRA (Department for Environment, Food and Rural Affairs). It affects *Cotoneaster*, *Crataegus* (hawthorn), *Malus* (apple), *Pyrus* (pear), *Sorbus* (mountain ash) and several other members of the Rosaceae family.

Fireblight causes wilted leaves and staining under the bark, as on this *Pyracantha*.

the leaves, usually during the summer. Bad attacks can severely disfigure or kill young plants.

Control:

- Light infestations may often be overcome by rapid growth, so make as many sowings as possible in warm, humid weather, when the plants are less likely to dry out.

- Insecticidal dusts or sprays usually provide good control, but since attacks are unpredictable it is difficult to know when to implement any preventative treatment.

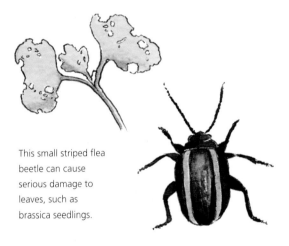

This small striped flea beetle can cause serious damage to leaves, such as brassica seedlings.

During the spring and summer, isolated blossoms and the tips of new shoots suddenly turn black and wilt—almost as if they have been burned in a fire. The wood just beneath the bark along infected branches appears a reddish-brown and sunken cankers may appear. During the winter, bacterial ooze seeps from cracks in the bark and this can spread the disease with the help of birds and insects. In severe cases, the shrub or tree can be killed.

Control:
Cut back at least 60 cm (2 ft.) into healthy wood; burn all infected material and sterilize the pruning tools. Badly infected plants should be carefully dug up and burned.

Flea beetles
Tiny beetles, mostly shiny black, can often be found along rows of seedlings, especially in the kitchen garden; when disturbed they jump (hence their name). They mostly attack soft low-growing plants, including many vegetables such as potatoes, *Erysimum* (wallflower) and sometimes *Fuchsia*, but also some older plants. The beetles make lots of tiny holes in

Foxes (see Badgers)

Fusarium wilt
Fusarium is a soil-borne fungus that invades the conductive tissue (particularly xylem vessels) of plants and blocks them. This causes the plant to wilt, giving the impression that watering is needed. The plant does not recover when watered and, if the stems are cut open, brown staining may be seen running through the conductive tissue.

Different strains of the fungus tend to be fairly specific to certain plants, but a wide range of plants may be affected. Cool, damp conditions can

section of stem
showing staining
typical of fusarium wilt

fusarium wilt on
tomato plant

Grey mould

Botrytis cinerea is one of the most common fungi, living on dead and live tissue. It is recognizable by the grey, fuzzy mould that grows on dead leaves, shoots, petals and fallen fruits. Spores spread through air and water and circulate everywhere, ready to germinate whenever conditions are favourable in summer or winter. High humidity, poor hygiene and overcrowded plants all encourage the spread of the disease, which persists for many weeks in the soil or on dead tissue.

grey mould on grapes

sometimes cause a fluffy growth (mycelium) of creeping, whitish-grey filaments growing from infected stems. Soft plants may die quickly but woody plants survive longer, although they too eventually die. The spores of the fungus can survive in the soil for several years.

Fusarium can kill off large patches of lawn, especially when the grass remains wet during the spring and autumn. The blades of grass collapse and become enveloped in the mycelium, which spreads very quickly through moisture on the blades of grass.

Control:

- There is no chemical control. Remove and destroy infected plants as soon as the disease has been diagnosed. Dig out and replace infected soil or avoid growing the same type of plant in the same place for at least 5 years.

- Grass can be particularly susceptible if has been given generous amounts of nitrogen. The use of high-nitrogen feeds should be restricted or stopped at the end of the summer and not resumed until well into the following spring. Precautionary treatment using a systemic fungicide may offer some protection if used at the beginning of more vulnerable periods.

The fungus also produces small, black, seed-like "sclerotia", or resting bodies, which can lie dormant for several weeks until conditions are right for them to spring into life and continue the infection.

The fungus enters a healthy plant through wounds and any part of a plant, especially soft tissue, can become infected. As the infection spreads, so plant tissue dies and becomes mushy, causing the plant to collapse and eventually die.

Control:

- Meticulous hygiene, cutting or picking off dead and diseased tissue and spraying with a suitable fungicide all help to minimize infection.

- Weak plants are more susceptible, so try to improve cultural conditions such as light and air circulation.

Honey fungus

This fungus attacks trees and shrubs although it has the potential to attack any plant in open ground. It lives on dead wood lying on the ground and in old stumps and spreads out through the soil at a depth of about 20 cm (8 in.) by means of rhizomorphs. These resemble thin, dark roots and seek the roots of a susceptible, living plant. The fungus then invades the plant and may eventually kill it, thus adding to the amount of host dead tissue.

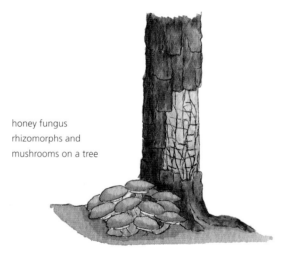

honey fungus rhizomorphs and mushrooms on a tree

The most typical symptom of honey fungus is the sudden death of isolated branches, often in full leaf, during summer months. In winter, it is particularly noticeable on evergreens. The dead leaves usually remain hanging on the branches while the rest of the plant appears healthy. Gradually, over several years, more branches die off until eventually the whole plant is killed.

Large trees may be affected for many years, yet not completely die. Privet hedge is especially susceptible; a section of it may be completely dead, with a section either side looking sick. As each year passes, the dead portion spreads until the entire hedge is affected.

Thick, flattened rhizomorphs may usually be found under the bark of diseased trees and shrubs, close to ground level, giving the fungus its other common name of bootlace fungus. A thick, white mycelium, giving off a strong, mushroom-like smell, will also be present. Honey-coloured mushrooms, or fruiting bodies, often appear in clusters around the base, or a short way up the stem, of an infected plant during the late summer or autumn. These produce white spores that can spread the infection.

Control:

- Remove and burn all old infected wood and stumps.

- Avoid replacing a plant with the same species in the same place and keep all other plants in the vicinity growing strongly.

- There is some evidence that putting a vertical barrier of thick PVC, about 40 cm (16 in.) into the ground, to encircle a plant's roots completely, may prevent the fungus from reaching it. This is useful when planting a new, choice specimen into an area suspected of infection. Dig out old soil from within the enclosure and replace it with clean, sterilized soil.

Leaf miners

The larvae of several types of fly are termed leaf miners, because they tunnel their way between the upper and lower surfaces of leaves, creating telltale trails of destruction. If you hold an affected leaf up to the light, the bugs may be clearly seen in these passages. After feeding, they pupate inside the leaf. Although many leaves may be disfigured, it is unusual for an attack to kill the plant. *Ilex* (holly) and *Chrysanthemum* are susceptible.

Control:

- Pick off and burn all infected leaves.

- Use a systemic insecticide; this is most effective if it can be timed to work in a preventative way, such as immediately before the larvae pupate.

leaf miner on *Chrysanthemum*

Control:

– The same as for chafer grubs.

– In addition, place a black, plastic sheet over a lawn at night to bring the grubs to the surface; they may then be gathered up for disposal.

Mealybugs

This pest attacks many plants, both indoors and out. Cacti are especially vulnerable. Mealybugs are small, soft, greyish-white insects that are usually found in the axils of leaves and in other crevices. They exude a whitish, waxy substance that protects both the feeding adults and their eggs.

Leatherjackets

These are the larvae of the crane fly, or daddy-long-legs. During summer, the adult flies lay their eggs just under the surface of the soil, in much the same way as cock chafers. The grubs are about 2.5cm (1 in.) long, soft, brown and leathery, with no legs. They feed on the roots of young plants, especially of grass—by the spring, large areas of a lawn may be killed. Grubs in a lawn attract large numbers of starlings, which then spoil the lawn as they dig up the grubs.

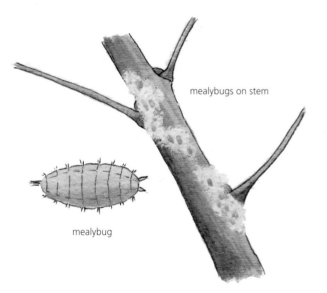

mealybugs on stem

mealybug

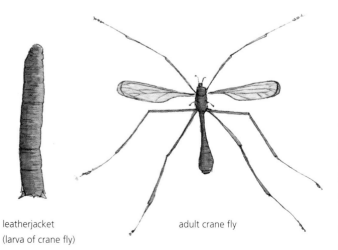

leatherjacket
(larva of crane fly)

adult crane fly

Their sap sucking can eventually weaken and disfigure a plant, while unsightly but harmless sooty moulds may develop over some of the sticky leaves. Indoor species of mealybug can remain active all the year round.

Control:

– If only a few bugs are present, a soft cloth and some insecticidal soap used with rubber gloves can be used to wipe them away.

- A specific type of ladybird may be introduced as a biological control under glass.

- Alternatively, an insecticide may be used in conjunction with some insecticidal soap, which will help to dissolve the waxy substance and make the pest more vulnerable to the insecticide.

Millipedes

These smooth, mostly grey metallic, segmented creatures with many tiny legs are often confused with centipedes—millipedes have two pairs of legs on each body segment. They feed on decaying vegetation and attack the lower stems and underground parts, including tubers, of many ornamental plants and vegetables. Eventually, they eat their way right through stems, with detrimental consequences.

Control:

Although difficult to control with pesticides, millipedes are unlikely to become a serious problem as long as decaying vegetation and surface compost is cleared away.

millipede

Moles

These can quickly wreck lawns and borders; they use the same, regular routes so soon after you clear mole-hills away, new ones will appear. There are various remedies and appliances for disposing of moles, but most have limited success unless a mole trap is used. Even the services of a professional mole-catcher may not provide a long-term solution, but it may be worth trying some of the controls mentioned below.

Control:

- Commercial remedies or deterrents such as burying a sonic mole bleeper or a stereo down the mole hole seem to have little or no effect.

- Placing fishbones, moth balls or lion urine down the holes are recommended by some sufferers.

- Mole traps can be effective, although they may be considered cruel.

Powdery mildew

Unlike downy mildew, which appears mostly on the undersides of leaves, this fungus is a white, powdery mildew that first develops on upper leaf surfaces. It then spreads to other parts of the plant, including stems and fruits. Diseased leaves become yellow and distorted and some affected fruits may develop cracks in their skin.

Powdery mildew is more prevalent in a warm, dry season, particularly on plants growing on a light soil with insufficient spacing between them. Badly infected plants often die back, but recover in the following spring. This disease is encouraged by a combination of dry soil and a humid atmosphere, so may not occur every year.

powdery mildew
on apple leaves

Control:

- Especially at the end of the season, remove infected tissue and as a preventative measure, just before an expected attack, spray with a suitable fungicide, such as a sulphur mix.

- Grow plant cultivars that are disease-resistant.

Rabbits

These can be very destructive, especially during winter months when they quickly "ring" a tree or shrub—eating the bark right around the stem or trunk and exposing the living cambium, which then causes the stem to die.

Control:

- As rabbits now often live under shrubs instead of burrowing (when ferrets could be used down the burrows), rabbit traps may be an answer; bait them with a supply of lettuce leaves or carrots freshly sliced to expose the sweet, inner cores and check the traps daily.

- Sink chicken wire into the ground to a depth of about 20 cm (8 in.) as a barrier around the garden boundary or selected planted areas.

- A gamekeeper, friend with an air rifle, or a hunting dog is a more drastic measure.

Raccoons

These have the infuriating habit of digging up newly planted perennials and leaving them lying on the soil so they dry out.

Control:

- Sprinkling black pepper or garlic powder on the soil around newly planted perennials—buy it in the industrial size—is recommended by the gardener Tracy DiSabato-Aust. Remember to replace it after it rains.

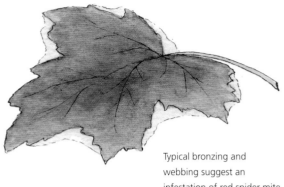

Typical bronzing and webbing suggest an infestation of red spider mite on the underside of this leaf.

Red spider mite

Various strains of this small, red, spider-like pest can cause damage to a wide range of indoor and outdoor plants. As the name suggests, this pest is a spider-like creature and produces a fine web, enabling it to move around the plant and on air currents between plants. It is barely visible to the naked eye, but may be seen under a magnifying glass, often in great numbers, moving around on the undersides of leaves.

The mites lay eggs and can be very persistent. In the garden, they are active throughout the summer and early autumn, but indoors remain active all year round. The mites suck the plant sap and the most common symptom is the resulting yellowing or bronzing of the leaves, which sometimes dry up and fall off.

Control:

- Indoors, under glass, affected plants must be isolated from healthy ones. Provided that the infestation is at an early stage, a predatory mite (*Phytoseiulus persimilis*) may be introduced to give good control.

- Alternatively, indoors or outside, use a systemic insecticide; several applications may be needed to kill all newly hatched mites.

- There is some evidence that the pest is deterred by regular demisting of indoor plants and keeping the humidity high. However, these conditions could encourage certain fungal infections to move in.

Red thread

This is another fungus that spreads under similar circumstances as fusarium and also destroys patches of grass. The mycelium appears especially during the winter and early spring and looks like pink or red webbing spreading between the blades of grass. Grass may be particularly susceptible to this disease if it has been fed with generous amounts of nitrogen.

Control:

- Control is difficult, as for fusarium, but a systemic fungicide can sometimes prove effective in limiting the damage.

- The use of high-nitrogen feeds should be restricted or stopped at the end of the summer and not resumed until well into the following spring when plants are in growth.

Rusts

The name for these distinctive, fungal diseases derives from the raised, rust-coloured pustules, seen mostly on leaves, which eventually rupture to give off spores. Rusts affect plants that are weak and in poor health, growing in poor soil conditions or receiving too much nitrogen and insufficient potash. Dead and diseased leaves, persistent high humidity, stagnant air and dry soil all encourage the growth of rust fungi, particularly during spring and summer. There is a link with excessive nitrogen and a potash deficiency in the soil.

Control:

- Spray with Bordeaux mixture and repeat two or three weeks later.

- Remove all diseased leaves and burn them.

- Do not leave diseased plants to overwinter in the ground.

- Control weeds such as groundsel, which are hosts to the disease.

- Grow resistant varieties.

Scale insects

These sap-sucking pests have scaly shields and occur often on the undersides of leaves and along stems. Eggs are laid under the protection of these scales and eventually the young nymphs move out in search of new feeding sites. They do not move far and soon create their own scaly shields under which they remain, feeding and breeding.

Although they are unsightly, it takes a great number of scale insects to have any significant impact on the health of a large plant. Sooner or later, however, the plant becomes weakened and may lose leaves. Most of this pest's activity outdoors takes place in summer, but indoors the pest is active most of the time. Bay trees tend to be prone to scale insect.

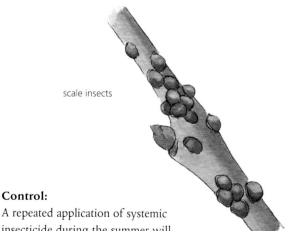

scale insects

Control:

A repeated application of systemic insecticide during the summer will gradually kill off the pest. Many of the old, dead scales may remain; wipe them off by hand, using a damp cloth.

Slugs and snails

Probably the best-known garden pest, this needs no description. Damage is mostly to the leaves—holes are eaten into them, both in the centre and around

snail

slug

the edges—but stems, flowers and fruits are also attacked.

Control:

- There are too many well-documented deterrents to mention all of them here. Some organic methods include beer traps, hand-picking at night, barriers such as copper bands, and smearing grease around the top of a pot containing a susceptible plant.

- Plants that are very prone to attack from slugs and snails may be protected to some extent by placing a mulch barrier all around the base of each plant. The most effective materials are cocoa shells and pine needles.

- There are also various types of slug bait and pellets. Some are poisonous to pets and other animals.

- Many slugs, but not snails, shelter just beneath the soil surface during the day. These are susceptible to a type of nematode called *Phasmarhabditis hermaphrodita*, which may be watered into soil that is warm and moist, yet well drained, in the spring or autumn. The nematode penetrates the slug's body and releases a fatal bacterium. This control can be very

effective for several weeks and significantly reduce slug, not snail, numbers.

Squirrels (see Chipmunks)

Verticillium wilt

This soil-borne fungus causes leaves to wilt on one branch at a time: the affected leaves often have yellow or brown discoloration between the veins. Once all the leaves on a branch are affected, the entire stem dies. This branch-by-branch process can progress for several years on a large shrub before the plant is killed. The tissue beneath the bark on an infected branch has brown or purple streaks, mainly towards the base of the stem or plant. Roots where the infection started also have a discoloured central core.

Control:

There is no cure. It is pointless cutting off dead branches, but if you do, then sterilize the pruning tools. Plants should be dug up, including all the roots, and burned. Avoid putting the same type of plant back in the same soil. Changing the soil in that area might help avoid re-infection.

verticillium wilt on tomato leaves

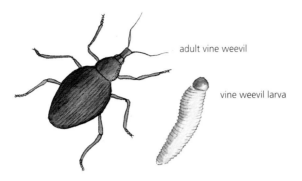

adult vine weevil

vine weevil larva

Vine weevil

Despite its name, this pest attacks a wide range of plants. Pot-grown plants are particularly vulnerable because the bug is often carried in prepared composts, but it also occurs in open ground. The adult weevil is a dark brown, hard-bodied, slow-moving beetle that is about 8–9 mm ($^3/_5$ in.) long. During the spring and summer the adult beetle feeds at night on leaves, cutting notches from around the leaf margin, hence its nickname, "the ticket collector".

Many eggs are laid during the summer and the resulting grubs (creamy white, slightly curled and legless) bury their way into the soil and feed on the roots. As the roots are eaten away, so the plant becomes stunted, wilts and may eventually die. Most of this damage occurs between the autumn and the spring.

Control:

- Chemical control in the form of an insecticidal soil drench may have some effect on the grubs, although it is not always successful.

- A more promising approach is to water in a specific nematode (*Steinernema carpocapsae*), which can destroy the young grubs, under the right conditions.

- Alternatively, the adult beetles may be hand picked at night or sprayed with an insecticide during a warm summer evening.

- For pot-grown plants, try knocking them out of their pot, shaking out all the soil and grubs, then repot the plants into new, sterile compost.

Whitefly

Aptly named, these flies are white and quite conspicuous as they fly from one plant to another, laying eggs. Like aphids, whiteflies suck sap from the leaves and soft stems and exude a sticky substance that encourages a sooty mould to grow on some leaf surfaces. The sooty mould is harmless and may be easily washed off. Under glass, whitefly are active all year round, but only during the spring, summer and autumn in the garden.

Control:

- Chemical controls may prove ineffective since whiteflies are now resistant to several of the commonly used insecticides. As with aphids, if chemical control is to be effective, it should be carried out at regular intervals to catch the various generations as they hatch from the eggs.

- Under glass, biological control using the parasitic wasp, *Encarsia formosa*, may be highly successful, but only if introduced early on in the infestation.

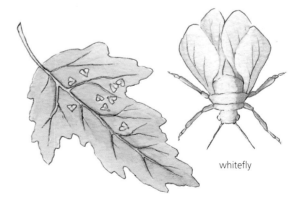

whitefly

Organic Gardening

The damage caused by using chemicals in gardens is now well documented and the use of alternative organic methods is well worth trying to put into practice. The interpretation of "organic" in gardening varies from simply avoiding using chemical pesticides wherever possible to being truly organic. This involves proscribing any chemical pesticides or fertilizers and focusing strongly on overall health and soil fertility.

Although initially organic gardening may seem to be a more trouble-ridden way of raising and growing plants, the garden will gradually settle into the new regime and you will be rewarded with healthier plants and increased wildlife. Vegetables and fruit from the garden will taste better.

Key Considerations

Gardening organically does require more thought; instead of relying on insecticides, fungicides and so forth, take time to plan what to grow and how you can best nurture it so that pests, diseases and other problems will not arise.

- If you are starting with a piece of rough ground or a weed-ridden plot, the initial clearance will need to be done without weedkillers, which will invariably take longer than chemical treatment.

- A composting system is a vital tool to any organic gardener, providing plenty of nourishment for the plants, as well as a valuable soil conditioner. Compost improves the soil's structure and its ability to retain moisture and any nutrients.

- The resistance of plants to disease and pests varies. A quick look through a selection of seed catalogues may indicate which varieties and cultivars are generally resilient.

- Although the appearance, texture and taste (of an edible crop) of plants are of utmost importance to any gardener, it makes sense to choose plants that can best avoid or cope with an attack. Always record your own observations.

- Make sure that each plant is suited to its site. For an organic gardener this is especially important. A well-adapted, vigorous plant is always better equipped to fight off pests and diseases. It might also rapidly produce replacement growth if it does suffer an attack. A plant that is struggling in an unsuitable site will never do well.

- There are simple and easily applied fertilizers that may be used by organic gardeners as well as garden compost, such as pelleted chicken manure and comfrey liquid. Do not use chicken manure when it is fresh since it will scorch the plants; put it on the compost heap to degrade for a season.

Although it is possible to garden organically in one area and use pesticides in another, it is easier and more satisfactory to avoid using chemicals or fertilizers completely. You can then allow a larger area to become properly balanced, with a larger number of naturally occurring parasites and predators to ward off pests.

Pros of Going Organic

- Edible crops, the grass in the garden, flowers and other plants are all free from harmful chemical residues, so if children or adults use the garden, they are not at risk from pesticides, fungicides or herbicides.

- Within a short time of giving up artificial fertilizers and pesticides, even a small garden will begin to act as a valuable oasis to a wider range of wildlife. In the absence of pesticides, many creatures can feed, live and breed more easily and also benefit the garden. There may be a few that are not welcome, but butterflies, hedgehogs, frogs, toads, newts and a whole host of beneficial insects are more likely to appear. Hedgehogs eat slugs; some birds feed on pests such as aphids, caterpillars and snails; predatory larvae of the hoverfly, lacewing and ladybird consume vast numbers of aphids.

- Organic gardeners are also less inclined to be wasteful and more inclined to recycle wherever possible; there is no doubt that this is of huge benefit to the environment as a whole.

- More and more companies are stocking organic gardening products, plants and seeds; it is undoubtedly the way forward for the future.

Cons of Going Organic

- Organic gardening may take up more time.

- The initial clearance of a site may be much more time-consuming when carried out organically.

- Organic gardeners usually spend more time tending their plants and checking them for pests and diseases but, in the process, other things will be noticed that need attention.

Planning for the Future

Lifestyles, circumstances and families are apt to change suddenly or unexpectedly, which may affect our available time and desire to garden. For instance, in their early gardening years, working couples with children will have less time than a couple who have taken early retirement. Similarly, it is sad to see keen, older gardeners struggle to maintain a garden when they are no longer able to be as active.

Although it may be hard to hold our enthusiasm in check, there is little point in over-developing a garden so that it becomes a chore instead of a pleasure. Gardening and the appearance of your garden should, if approached wisely, be scaled to something that you can achieve and enjoy.

Try to be realistic in what can be achieved, either by carrying out the work yourself or by employing someone to help you to do the heavier, or less skilled, work. Younger gardeners may be wise not to develop their gardens fully until more time or money is available, whereas cutting down on weeding by turning some borders over to grass may help the older generation. Reducing a vegetable or soft-fruit plot keeps the garden under control while still providing enjoyment.

Project 5

Now that you have created your garden and have learned how plants work and what they need to grow healthily, you should be able really to enjoy your time there, whether you are working, relaxing or showing it off to friends. Perhaps you might even open it occasionally under one of the "Open Garden" schemes that exist in many countries as well as Britain. However, in working through this book you will have realized that the garden is never static, and that maintaining its appearance and health is an ongoing process.

Try to get into the routine of making regular observations about your outdoor space, considering not only the plants but also routine maintenance tasks such as clearing gutters of autumn leaves or spiking and scarifying the lawn. As well as continuing to keep a note of your own activities and observations in your Garden Log (see Project 2), you might find it useful to keep some additional records.

Keep Pruning and Propagation Notes

For this, you will need a separate notebook in addition to your Garden Log. Perhaps the front half could be devoted to pruning and the rear half to propagating, although sometimes you will propagate from the prunings of a plant, for example you could use spring prunings of *Cornus* for cuttings. It should be fascinating, in the future, to look back on what you have done, and when and how.

By keeping a detailed record, you will be able to judge your success rate, and if needed consider other methods or timings that may be more successful. The simplest way of keeping these observations is to have your diary or notebook easily accessible, perhaps in the kitchen or potting shed, or even on a table beside your bed.

Keep a Plant List

I try to keep an up-to-date list of all the plants in the garden on my computer, arranged in lists according to where and when they were planted. If I move a plant from one area to another, remove it or if it dies, or if I add new plants, I can also easily change the plant list on the computer. Soon I hope to be able to give these plant lists out to garden visitors so that they can perhaps discover a plant that they haven't seen before.

On the following two pages are some suggested headings for your notes on Pruning and Propagation.

Pruning Notes

Month: _____

Plant	Date pruned	How pruned	Follow-up needed/when	Comments/Results

Propagation Notes

Month: _____

Method	Parent plant	Material taken/date	Germination/ rooting date	Success rate	Prick out/pot up date	Pot on/plant out date	Yield	Comments

Above: A Japanese-style "cloud" treatment is an interesting method of pruning mature box. Once the "clouds" have been defined, any unwanted shoots appearing on the stems should be removed.

Right: Open wounds caused through careless or bad pruning can encourage fungal diseases.

Right: Fruit trees can be trained into various shapes, such as this pyramid pear supported by a metal frame. The soil at the base should be kept clear, to avoid competition from other plants.

Above: Attaching climbers to a wall: wire stretched across at 60–90 cm (2–3 ft.) intervals is kept in place with vine eyes, or wall nails. Use garden twine to tie in plant stems, in front of the wire so that it will not cut into the stems as they mature.

Right: The young, pliable stems of roses can be trained against wires to form an impenetrable barrier. To keep them under control, prune out some of the older stems annually in spring or late autumn.

Above: When training a *Ficus* (fig) against a wall, first cut out any surplus or unwanted growths, then tie in each branch evenly to the supporting wires spread across the wall.

Above: Potting up seedlings—plant each seedling in a small pot and top up with compost to a level slightly below the rim to allow for watering. Label each plant.

Above: Potting up seedlings—firm each plant in so that the roots make contact with the soil. As a finishing touch, spread a fine layer of grit over the surface to keep moisture in and to deter weeds.

Above: Dividing rootstocks—lift and split up the rootstock of a congested plant, such as this *Primula*, without damaging the roots, by inserting two forks back to back. Spread a plastic sheet on the ground to avoid making a mess.

Above: Dividing rootstocks—take each piece of rootstock and pull the rooted sections gently apart, trim up their roots, then cut off any dead or damaged leaves before replanting them individually. Remember to water them in.

Above: Dividing bulbs—after digging them up, clumps of bulbs can be divided by gently pulling them apart. Sometimes a garden knife will be needed to cut through tangled roots.

Above: Dividing bulbs—after splitting them up, replant each bulb in a prepared hole. Give each sufficient space for the roots to be spread out, then infill with compost or garden soil. Firm up and water in.

Above: Some garden insects are beneficial. In spring, bees are busy pollinating *Crocus chrysanthus* 'Blue Pearl' and other early-flowering plants.

Above: Unless protected by netting, cloches or fleece, newly planted brassicas can quickly be destroyed by pigeons. Use wire hoops to keep the netting from coming into contact with the plants.

Above: Hostas are particularly prone to damage by slugs. Spreading sharp grit around the base of the plant is an environmentally friendly way of deterring these pests.

Above: If you care for your plants and protect them from pests and diseases, using scrupulous hygiene, regular watering and careful pruning, you will be rewarded with lush, healthy growth.

Right: As well as dissuading unwanted intruders, a scarecrow can be fun to make and provide a decorative element in the kitchen garden.

What to Do When in the Garden

All experienced or trained gardeners work to a routine, carrying out certain tasks regularly or at appropriate times of year to prevent any part of the garden from getting out of control. How much time will be needed to maintain your garden depends greatly on its current state. A newly planted, virgin site may need much care during the first three years, or until it becomes established. The workload will ease off as plants mature and give more coverage. In a neglected or overgrown garden, the first year or so may require maximum effort to restore it to order.

This section may be used as a reminder of most of the tasks you might need to carry out to care for your plants, but you may find it useful to make up your own garden "calendar" or diary, which relates to the particular plants that you have in the garden.

Regular Chores

Looking after any garden is a time-consuming task. Although the amount of work involved will depend largely on the size, style and state of your garden, there are a few key areas which are always on view and which need regular attention. It is important to learn to work to a routine, which will help you use time efficiently and keep crucial areas in order.

Approach to the Garden

We often walk or drive up to the house without noticing how the entrance appears to the outside world or to occasional visitors. Familiarity often leads us to neglect obvious tasks, often noticing them only when returning from holiday or after a long absence. Part of our weekly or fortnightly routine should extend beyond our own property to make sure that it is always well maintained and welcoming. Regular maintenance of entrances, paths, driveways and steps should include:

- picking up any rubbish left by passersby

- sweeping up any accumulation of leaves

- mowing untidy verges

- keeping paths weed free, otherwise they will detract from the general appearance

- regularly raking gravel or shingle paths

- topping up loose material, such as gravel, every year or two because it tends to sink in or disappear over time

- keeping boundary fences in good repair.

In winter months, brick or stone paths and steps tend to become mossy or covered with green algae, which makes them slippery. Spray paths and steps with an algae remover. Two thorough applications are usually all that is necessary.

Weed Suppression

Time spent on this usually most labour-intensive gardening chore, may be reduced by beginning weeding early in the season. Weeding may be done by hand or with a small hand fork, but it saves time to use a specific, systemic product. Systemic weedkillers are absorbed both by the leaves and the roots and are effective against a wide range of established and germinating weeds, and since they lie on the soil, prevent regrowth for several months.

- The first application should take place as soon as weeds begin to appear, usually when the weather begins to warm up in early spring.

- Later applications will be needed in early summer and perhaps autumn.

- Be very careful—in addition to remaining on the surface as a deterrent, systemic weedkillers will also maim any growing plant. Even the lightest wind may cause the spray to drift on to plants at the edges of paths, leaving unsightly, pale spots on the foliage. Make sure that any nearby plants are loosely covered with sacking or plastic sheeting to prevent the chemical drifting on to them.

- Gravel or shingle usually needs to be drenched so that the spray will filter to the surface below, but with brick or stone paths, the spray needs to be applied only to the joints or cracks where weeds take hold.

- Systemic weedkillers are expensive, so avoid unnecessary spraying.

Lawns and Grass Edges

Lawns tend to set off the rest of the planting, so need to be well maintained with a regular regime during the growing season. (See also "Lawn maintenance", pages 63–76.)

- Mow lawns at least once per week during the active growing season.

- Re-adjust the height of the blades on cylinder mowers as the seasons progress. Shaving the lawn too closely early on will result in bare patches later.

- Regular edging once or twice a month gives grass verges and lawns a manicured appearance.

- The overall appearance of your lawn will also be governed by the work you put into it at the beginning and end of the season, on tasks such as spiking or aerating, scarifying and spreading lawn fertilizer.

Areas of longer grass need less regular attention, but ought to be cut before they are flattened by wet weather and wind, making cutting very much harder.

Borders

Most occasional maintenance is usually taken up with the borders. The variety and amount of tasks will depend to some extent on the plants in the border and their individual needs, but there are general points to bear in mind.

- It is wise to check borders weekly to prevent weeds from seeding in them. In the growing season, weeds can appear overnight.

- Remember that weeds lurk under foliage.

- A mulch will act as a weed suppressant for part of the year, but by late summer worms will have taken much of it into the soil. Weed more actively during the summer and early autumn.

- Weeding may be done by hand picking or with a trowel, fork or hoe—whichever suits you and your garden. Remember that disturbance of the soil cover during summer months or dry weather will allow moisture to evaporate, so avoid cultivating the soil in very hot weather.

- Deadheading and cutting back spent foliage or flowers may be carried out at the same time as undertaking weeding.

- From time to time, check staking of herbaceous perennials.

Shrubs and Trees

Normally, maintenance pruning or reshaping should be carried out either early in the season—if the plant has flowered before midsummer—or in the late summer or autumn—if the plant flowers later. To improve a plant's appearance, or to show off the surrounding plants or views, you may also wish to cut or remove the occasional branch during the main growing season.

- Remember to check on the plant's period of flowering before pruning, in order to avoid removing next year's flowering stems.

- Roses will need weekly deadheading.

- Check tree stakes regularly to make sure that they are secure and not too tight.

Climbers

Climbers tend to grow rapidly, so frequent checking, every two weeks or so, will be necessary.

- Tie in new growth while it is still pliable.

- Add or replace missing wall wires. This is vital to establish a good framework.

Hedges

Depending on the speed of growth of the hedging plants, all hedges need regular maintenance. An untidy hedge can detract from an otherwise immaculate garden.

- Trim *Ligustrum* (privet) every six weeks.

- *Taxus baccata* (yew) or *Fagus* (beech) grows more slowly, only needing thorough clipping with shears or hedge cutters every year, usually in early summer.

Midwinter

General Tips

Gutters—Check they are not clogged. Put any leaves cleaned out of them in a leaf-mould bin to rot down.

Leaves—Remove dead leaves from under hedges and shrubs, otherwise slugs and snails will take shelter there.

Christmas trees—Shred and compost them.

Snow warning—Be ready to brush snow from evergreen shrubs and conifers because the weight can weigh down and damage their branches.

Seeds—Write off for catalogues and place orders.

Bulbs, corms and tubers—Check stored stock for signs of rot or deterioration. Remove diseased bulbs and sprinkle others with sulphur powder to prevent disease setting in.

Flower Garden

Roses—Plant bare-rooted roses (see page 165). To avoid risk of disease, never plant new roses where old roses have been removed unless the soil has been replaced down to 60 cm (2 ft.) and reconditioned.

Annual climbers—Pinch out the tips of seedlings raised from autumn sowings to encourage sideshoots to form and make bushy plants.

Shrubs—Move any shrubs that have outgrown their position or are not where you want them. To avoid root damage, lift established plants with as large a root ball as possible. Dig a trench around the plant, gradually cut into the root ball and ease some hessian underneath. Attach the hessian to a pole to make lifting the shrub easier, lift it and place into the new planting hole, stake it securely and water in well once firmed in (see also pages 86–87).

Wisteria—Carry out winter pruning, cutting back longer branches to two buds or 7.5 cm (3 in.), but taking care to preserve the flower buds (see pages 286–287).

Cuttings—Take hardwood cuttings of shrubs (see pages 301–302).

Containers—Stand planted patio pots up on feet to improve drainage and prevent waterlogging. Protect pots in very cold spells with wraps (see page 247) and move them to a sheltered position.

Fruit Garden

Currant bushes—Shorten each sideshoot on red- and whitecurrants to just one bud. Remove any old stems crowding the centre of the bush.

New fruit plants—Plant new tree fruits and bushes. Bare-rooted plants, available by mail order from specialist fruit growers, offer the best value. Raspberries and other cane fruits may also be planted now.

Vegetable Garden

Early rhubarb—Place buckets or forcing jars over dormant clumps of rhubarb, packing them with straw to encourage new stems to form.

Soil—To aerate the soil, dig over bare areas (see pages 97–100), forking in plenty of compost or rotted manure to improve soil structure.

Potatoes—Order seed potatoes now for early spring delivery.

Greenhouse

Amaryllis or *Hippeastrum*—Plant bulbs in pots in free-draining compost and place them in a warm position, such as on a shelf over a radiator. This will encourage strong root development and earlier flowering.

Hyacinthus—Provide support for developing flower spikes by tying them to short canes. Alternatively, push a length of thick wire down the centre of each flower stem into the bulb.

Roof, gutters and water butts—Wash down the greenhouse roof to remove grime and let in more light. Clean leaves and other debris out of gutters and empty and clean water butts.

Lawns

Repairs—Prepare worn areas of grass for sowing (see pages 66–68). Lawns may also be levelled—if the soil is heavy and the ground really wet, use boards to tread on to avoid compacting the soil.

Frost—Remember not to tread on the lawn if it is frozen.

Late Winter

General Tips

Ties—Check stakes and ties, whether on trees, standard roses, climbers and wall shrubs, to make sure that they are secure. Use extra ties if necessary. Use garden twine or brown or black plastic, rather than wire, which can cut into the stem. If any ties are cutting into plant stems, loosen them and insert a small length of hose or other protective packing between the twine and stem.

Order—Send off for onion and shallot sets.

Flower Garden

Alpines—Cover any early-flowering alpines, like *Lewisia*; place a sheet of glass resting on canes over each plant to protect the flowers from rain and snow and to prevent the crown from rotting.

Bulbs and half-hardies—Order stock of *Canna*, *Dahlia*, *Eucomis* and other summer-flowering bulbs, corms and tubers, as well as half-hardies, for additional summer colour.

Borders—Before the spring bulbs start emerging, lightly fork over the soil in mixed borders. This improves surface drainage and prevents moss growth. Finish off by spreading a mulch of manure or compost to discourage weeds.

Roses—Continue planting bare-rooted roses. Delay pruning (see pages 282–285) until late in the month in mild areas or in early spring in colder districts. If the plants are pruned too early, a warm spell may encourage new growth that is susceptible to spring frosts.

Clematis—Prune large-flowered clematis in Pruning Group 2: removing dead wood, weak shoots and generally thinning out (see page 285).

Fruit Garden

Blackcurrants—On large bushes, cut out about a quarter of the oldest shoots at their base. This relieves congestion, improves air circulation through and encourages productive new growth.

Fruit trees—Prune damaged or diseased branches, as well as badly growing or crossing stems, on apple and pear trees. Aim to keep the centre of the tree open to let in light and air.

Vegetable Garden

Soil—Cover beds with cloches, fleece or sheet plastic to warm up the ground before making early sowings.

Harvest—Brussels sprouts, cabbage, cauliflowers, leeks and parsnips should be cropped while they are still at their best, and before pigeons or other pests attack them.

Potatoes—When seed potatoes arrive, set them out to "chit" to accelerate early growth. Put the seed potatoes, nose end uppermost, in cardboard trays or egg boxes. Keep in a cool, light room indoors until the shoots develop and reach about 5 cm (2 in.). Plant them out immediately or after all risk of frost has passed.

Greenhouse

Hyacinthus—Once the blooms of indoor bulbs have started to fade, separate the clump of bulbs and plant outdoors in the border (see page 209).

Lawns

Worm casts—If there are any, scatter these with a birch broom on dry days.

Mowing—Late in the month, the lawn might need a first cut, provided that it is dry.

Early Spring

General Tips

Fertilizer—Sprinkle a general fertilizer around trees, shrubs and along base of hedges. This is especially important for establishing growth on recently planted stock.

Mulch—Spread garden compost around the base of fruit trees, shrubs and roses to stop weeds and unwanted grass. Avoid piling the mulch up against the stems because this could cause rot.

Flower Garden

Galanthus—While they are still in leaf but once the flowers are fading, divide up any congested clumps of snowdrops (see page 341).

Lilium—Provided the ground is not frozen, plant out the bulbs in well-prepared soil. On heavy soils, plant them on a deep layer of grit or gravel or grow them in pots. They prefer partial shade with the top-growth in sun and roots in shade.

Perennials—Lift and divide established or congested clumps to increase your stock and encourage flowering (see pages 296–297). On light soils, this may also be done in autumn.

Roses—Plant new, bare-rooted or container-grown roses in borders. Roses may be pruned (see pages 282–285) in colder districts.

Clematis—Prune out last year's growth from summer-flowering varieties that blossom on the current season's growth before growth begins again, for example *C.* 'Etoile.Violette'. Cut any tangled, old stems down to a pair of new shoots near ground level, or to 10 cm (4 in.), as soon as possible before new growth begins.

Prune mature, large-flowered clematis from Pruning Group 2, cutting some large sections hard back in the early spring to generate new growth (see page 285).

Shrubs—General pruning may be done now. The main objective is to control growth, improve the shape of the plant and prevent it from becoming straggly. Cut out a few older stems to allow air to circulate. Shorten new growth. Delay pruning tender and silver-foliaged plants until spring frosts are over.

Jasminum—Trim winter-flowering jasmines (see page 286), tying in any new shoots that you want to retain.

Cornus (dogwood) or *Salix* (willow)—Bare winter stems should be pruned back to their bases, so that new young shoots will provide colour for next winter.

Fruit Garden

Tree planting—Finish planting bare-rooted tree fruits. Container-grown trees may be planted out at any time of year.

Figs—Prune out any old branches from wall-trained fig trees.

Vegetable Garden

Parsley—Sow in pots (see page 295) for seedlings to be planted out later in the year.

Chives—Divide clumps to encourage strong growth.

Seeds—Sow seed of beetroot (beets), broad beans, Brussels sprouts, leeks, hardy peas, radishes and summer cabbages outdoors (see pages 293–294) in warm areas or, in colder regions, under cloches.

Shallots—Plant out shallot sets, spacing them at 15 cm (6 in.) intervals in rows 30 cm (12 in.) apart.

Onions—Plant sets out into a firm seedbed when the weather is warmer.

Potatoes—Continue to chit potatoes, as in late winter. Earlier varieties (first earlies) may be planted out now, but delay planting a month if you are in a cold climate.

Greenhouse

Dahlia—Plant tubers in pots of compost to encourage growth of new shoots. Shoots may also be used as cuttings.

Lawns

Edges—neaten the line of the edges with a half-moon cutter.

Mowing—Cut when dry; mower blades should be set higher for the first few cuts.

Aerating—Spike with a garden fork to improve drainage. Lawn sand or sandy compost should be brushed into the holes.

Mid-spring

General Tips

Slugs and snails alert!—Protect newly emerging shoots of vulnerable perennials, such as *Hosta* and *Lupinus*. Trap slugs under grapefruit skins and remove the slugs daily or sprinkle sand, grit, crushed eggshells or vermiculite around choice plants. If you do use slug pellets, cover them with a tile resting on pebbles to prevent access by birds and animals and scatter them sparingly, not in heaps.

Flower Garden

Soil—Prepare the soil in areas where summer bedding will be planted out towards the end of late spring.

Pruning—Prune all silver-foliaged and tender shrubs. Prune hard back tall, old stems on *Buddleja davidii* and *Leycesteria formosa* before growth begins again. Other shrubs that respond well to hard pruning include *Sambucus nigra* 'Aurea' (golden-leaved elder), *Cotinus coggygria* (smoke bush), and *Corylus* 'Purpurea' (purple hazel), which will then produce fresh, young growth with brighter and larger leaves.

Layering—Pin down with wire on to the soil low-growing branches of *Magnolia* and *Rhododendron* to produce new plants. Make a small cut in the stem where it is buried and tie the shoot tip to a cane for support. The plant will then root at the point at which it is in contact with the ground. (See also pages 298–299.)

Hydrangea—Prune off the old flowerheads from mophead types. Cut back to a strong pair of buds.

Dahlia—Start tubers into growth in large pots to plant outdoors in late spring.

Lavandula—Rooted heel cuttings may be planted out in the garden, once all danger of frost has passed.

Seedlings and plug plants—Mail orders will be delivered during mid- and late spring and need opening immediately. Any delay can cause leaves to yellow and rot to set in. Do not over-water them or you may drown the plant roots.

Hardy annuals—Finish sowing hardy annuals outdoors (see page 233) in mid- and late spring. Later sowings will result in later blooms.

Containers—Smear rims of pots with grease or ring them with copper tape to deter slugs (see page 247).

Fruit Garden

Gooseberries—Prune out long stems to open up the centre of the bush and make future picking easier.

Vegetable Garden

Potatoes—If you have space, grow an early, second main crop and salad variety to give you a continuous supply. Remember to earth up the stems regularly to stop daylight reaching the tubers, which turns them green. Potatoes need lots of water when they are growing fast, so make sure that irrigation is at hand. A trickle irrigation system linked to a water butt can work well.

Lettuce—Sow seeds little and often. A short row every fortnight through spring and summer will ensure a continual supply.

Seed—Continue to sow outdoors beetroot (beets), broad beans, Brussels sprouts, cabbage, cauliflower, carrots, kohlrabi, leaf beet, leeks, parsnips, peas, radish, spinach, spring onions and turnips.

Onions—Last chance to plant out sets and shallots.

Greenhouse

Tomatoes—Sow now to raise plants for growing in unheated greenhouses or planting outdoors in early summer.

Herb cuttings—Tip out pots of well-rooted cuttings that were taken last summer and pot them up separately.

Lawns

Equipment—Check the mower is in good working order, ready to give lawns their first cut of the season. Send the mower for servicing or repairing, if necessary, and get the blades sharpened ready for the growing season.

New lawns—Sow seed or turf new areas of lawn, selecting the seed mix or turf according to locality, wear and tear and desired appearance (see pages 66–69).

Mowing—Established lawns may be cut with blades at medium height.

Feeding—High-nitrogen fertilizer may be applied towards the end of the month (see pages 74–75).

Late Spring

General Tips

Watering—Regularly water newly planted fruit trees, roses and shrubs.

Late frosts—Keep sheets of fleece handy to throw over plants at night if a late ground frost threatens.

Flower Garden

Weeding—Hoe borders once a week to prevent weed seedlings from establishing.

Perennials—Buy tender, young plants and summer bedding from nurseries and garden centres. Pot on into 7.5 cm (3 in.) pots and grow on in warm, bright conditions indoors, ready for planting out at the end of the month. Acclimatize the plants gradually to cooler outdoor conditions before planting them out. In colder districts, wait till early summer to avoid losing the plants to frost and cold weather.

Seedlings and plug plants—Mail orders delivered this month need opening immediately. Any delay can cause leaves to yellow and rot to set in. Do not over-water or you may drown the plants.

Hardy annuals—Finish sowing hardy annuals outdoors (see page 233).

Supports—Place support frames over tall perennials, or those with a floppy habit. Use metal frames, hazel twigs or peasticks, link stakes, or garden canes. Emerging foliage will hide the supports as it grows up and through. For safety, remember to put eye guards on top of any canes.

Pruning—Prune tender and silver-foliaged shrubs once spring frosts are over.

Dahlia—Plant tubers outdoors in late spring.

Vegetable Garden

Peas—Push twiggy supports into the soil along rows of peas, to give support as they grow.

Potatoes—Continue to earth them up and water them regularly.

Rhubarb—Harvest any early stems that have been forced under jars. Grip each firmly at the base and then pull it sharply away from the crown, or parent plant.

Seeds—Sow seed outdoors (see pages 293–294) of beetroot (beets), Brussels sprouts, cauliflower, courgettes (zucchini), dwarf French beans, endive, kale, kohlrabi, lettuce, marrows, peas, radish, ridge cucumbers, runner beans, spinach, sprouting broccoli, summer and Savoy cabbages, swede, sweetcorn and turnips.

Greenhouse

Seeds—Continue sowing summer bedding plants. Thin out those in trays, or prick them out individually into pots.

Tomatoes—Plant young tomato plants out in beds or growing bags.

Pest control—Watch out for pests. Treat immediately with conventional pesticides or use biological control agents (see page 318) for red spider mite, whitefly, and other pests.

Vines—Pinch out the tips of shoots, two leaves beyond a developing fruit truss, to produce more growth.

Lawns

Mowing—Cut the grass at least once a week.

Feeding—Poorly growing areas may be treated with sulphate of ammonia.

Weeds—Tackle these individually, either weeding them out by hand or applying a spot weedkiller on a dry day, when the soil is moist.

Scarifying—If not completed in autumn, remove dead grass and moss with a scarifier or wire, spring-tined rake.

Early Summer

General Tips

Ponds—Twist blanket weed out of ponds with a long stick.

Flower Garden

Perennials—Give a boost to new plantings by watering them in with liquid fertilizer.

Shrubs—Prune flowering shrubs such as *Berberis*, *Forsythia*, *Philadelphus* or *Weigela* as soon as flowers have faded. Cut back any shoots that have carried flowers, shortening them to shape the shrub and control its size and vigour. On mature plants, remove two or three older stems completely to allow air and light to circulate. Remember to keep standing back to check the plant's outline.

Clematis—Prune mature species clematis of Pruning Group 1 after flowering (see page 285).

Bulbs—Remove yellowing foliage of spring-flowering bulbs, such as *Narcissus* (daffodil) and *Tulipa*. Pick off any developing seedheads. Where bulbs are naturalized in lawns, leave them for at least six weeks after flowering before mowing the grass.

Lilium—Potted lilies will be growing quickly now. Plant out in borders or containers. As their flowers become top heavy, they will need some support. Push canes into the soil or into the compost around the edge of the pot and link them with twine, to provide support.

Iris—Once irises have finished flowering, congested clumps may be lifted, divided (see page 215) and replanted. Reduce the leaves by cutting them across horizontally by half to reduce moisture loss and stress on the plant and replant them, so that the rhizomes rest on the soil surface.

Primula—Dig up large clumps now and divide into individual plants, each with leaves and roots (see page 341). Replant into newly prepared soil.

Annuals—Thin out seedlings of hardy annuals sown directly into borders.

Fruit Garden

Cane fruits—Tie new canes of raspberries and blackberries on to support wires as they grow. Separate them from last year's shoots, which will flower and fruit this summer.

Soft fruit—Spread nets over currants and strawberries to prevent birds from stripping off all the fruits.

Vegetable Garden

Onions—Start harvesting from autumn-planted sets.

Potatoes—Continue earthing up the rows as the plants grow.

Tomatoes—plant out tomato plants outdoors, in growing bags or beds.

Seedlings—Thin out rows of vegetable seedlings from earlier sowings, such as beetroot (beets), lettuce and radish. Leave the seedlings spaced as indicated on seed packets. Water the row to settle the soil back around the remaining roots. (Root vegetables cannot be pricked out; thinnings will not root.)

Seeds—Continue sowing vegetable crops in batches.

Greenhouse

Shading—Paint greenhouses with shade paint or put roller blinds or shade netting in place to reduce the heat of the sun.

Potting—As soon as cuttings taken earlier in the season have produced a good root system, or plants have outgrown their pots, pot them into a slightly larger pot. Try and use the same type of compost as they were potted in before. Don't overfill with compost, but leave sufficient space at the top of the pot for watering.

Lawns

Mowing—Mow at least once a week. Lower cutting height if growth is too fast, but watch out that this does not create bald patches on uneven lawns.

Watering—Water well in drought conditions unless there are hosepipe bans.

Midsummer

General Tips

Hedges—Regularly trim fast-growing hedges such as *Ligustrum* (privet).

Weeds—Be ruthless with strong, problem weeds, removing any flowering stems before they have a chance to set seed. Remove the weeds by hand, digging deeply to get out every piece of root, or use chemical treatments.

Flower Garden

Clematis—Prune mature species clematis of Pruning Group 1 after flowering (see page 285).

Perennials—Cut away faded flowers of vigorous, clumping perennials (for example, of *Delphinium*, *Doronicum* and *Lupinus*) after flowering. Early deadheading encourages a second flush of flowers late in the season. Cut each flower spike down to just above a new shoot or leaf. Water each plant with a generous liquid feed to encourage fresh growth.

Biennials—*Campanula* (Canterbury bells), *Dianthus barbatus* (sweet William), *Digitalis* (foxglove), and *Myosotis* (forget-me-not) should be sown as soon as fresh seed is available.

Chrysanthemum—Encourage shoots to branch out and carry more blooms by pinching out shoot tips from early to midsummer. This technique is called stopping.

Cuttings—Take cuttings from non-flowering shoots on many shrubs and climbers.

Aquilegia—Cut down flower stems after they have flowered, unless you want to save the seeds.

Fruit Garden

Fan-trained fruit—Unwanted shoots should be cut out from *Prunus domestica* (plum) and *Prunus armeniaca* (apricot) to maintain the shape.

Figs—Prune out the tips after the fifth leaf of any unwanted sideshoots on fig trees, or remove them completely.

Cordon gooseberries and currants—Sideshoots should be pruned back to approximately five leaves or 10 cm (4 in.).

Bush gooseberries—Prune back the main shoots and sideshoots to five leaves.

Apples—Some heavy fruits will drop off naturally, but if trees look overladen, pick off some of the crop by hand. Remove any small, damaged or diseased fruits to leave those remaining 10 cm (4 in.) apart. Finish summer pruning the sideshoots on trained apple trees (see page 290).

Vegetable Garden

Watering—Flowering crops and any carrying fruits or pods, such as runner beans, need regular watering. So too do moisture-lovers such as celery.

Onions—Finish harvesting from autumn-planted sets. Water summer crops well if weather is dry, to maintain the yield.

Sweetcorn—Plant out pot-grown sweetcorn in blocks, not rows, so that they are able to cross-fertilize (the pollen is carried by wind from plant to plant). Space them about 45 cm (18 in.) apart each way.

Potatoes—Check early crops to assess the crop size. Leave them to develop further if the potatoes are too small. Continue to earth up if necessary, and water the rows every week to boost yields.

Tomatoes—Pinch out any sideshoots regularly and tie the leading shoot to its support as it grows. Feed plants weekly with a high-potash tomato fertilizer and never let them go short of water.

Leaf crops—Crops such as endive, kohlrabi, radish and spring cabbage may be sown until the middle of the month.

Winter crops—Sow spinach and other winter crops from now until early autumn.

Herbs—Take cuttings of sage, parsley and thyme.

Harvest—Beetroot (beets) and other root crops are sweetest while they are still young and tender.

Greenhouse

Watering—All potted plants need a daily check for watering. Use a full-strength liquid fertilizer once a fortnight or a diluted one more often.

Ventilation—Open vents, louvres and doors every morning, but close them again on cool evenings.

Damping down—Hose the greenhouse floor every morning on hot days to increase humidity. The plants will love this and it also helps to discourage red spider mite.

Growing Bags—Never let crops in growing bags go short of water. Standing bags on gravel trays or on reservoirs with wicks through the bases of the bags can prevent them from drying out.

Pests—Continue to use biological pest controls against red spider mite and whitefly .

Cuttings—Pot on rooted cuttings of *Argyranthemum*, *Fuchsia*, *Pelargonium* and other plants, as soon as the roots have filled their pots. Take softwood cuttings of *Fuchsia*, *Pelargonium* and tender perennials: they will root quickly at this time of year.

Lawns

Mowing—Continue to cut at least once a week—or twice if the grass is growing fast. Finish by cutting the edges neatly with a lawn edger. Mix the clippings into the compost heap, but only if no weedkiller has been applied recently.

Feed—A summer fertilizer may be applied as long as no other has been used in the previous month or so.

Late Summer

General Tips

Weeding—Hoe gravel paths, then apply a residual path weedkiller to keep the area weed-free.

Water—Top up sunken levels in garden ponds.

Hedges—Conifers can become tall and annoy neighbours by cutting out their light. Be considerate and cut their tops down to a maximum of 3 m (10 ft.).

Flower Garden

Roses—Deadhead roses regularly, cutting off the flowers just above the uppermost sideshoot. Semi-ripe stem cuttings (see page 305) may be taken.

Lilium—Tie tall lily stems to canes for support. Watch out for bright scarlet lily beetles and their larvae. Pick the beetles off by hand and destroy them immediately; they will eat the blooms.

Lavendula—Once the flowers have passed their best, trim the bushes lightly to remove the old blooms and shoot tips. Do not cut back heavily into the old wood because it will not regrow.

Flowers for drying—Cut everlasting flowers such as *Achillea* and *Helichrysum*, as well as grasses like *Pennisetum*, when they are at their peak. Hang them upside-down in a warm, airy position to dry naturally, ready for decorative arrangements.

Wisteria—Shorten long, wispy shoots and sideshoots back to about five or six leaves from the main framework (see page 287). Drench soil with high-potash fertilizer to improve flowering. The wisteria will need to be pruned again in midwinter, but pruning now will curb its desire to climb and will encourage flower production.

Shrubs—Water *Camellia* and *Rhododendron* during the summer while they are developing their flower buds for next spring's display. Shortage of water now can lead to bud drop next year.

Bulbs—Order from suppliers for autumn planting.

Containers—Stand pots on gravel trays topped up with water. They will gradually absorb moisture so the compost doesn't dry out. Alternatively, use an automatic trickle-watering system, linked to an outside tap and controlled by a timer, to water the pots each day.

Fruit Garden

Strawberries—Peg down runners from new plants into the soil or into pots of compost to root. Shear off the foliage just above the crown of each plant and clear away any debris.

Raspberries—Pick the last crop, then prune the stems that have fruited of summer cultivars down to soil level. Tie in most new shoots, about 10–15 cm (4–6 in.) apart and remove surplus ones to avoid overcrowding.

Vegetable Garden

Runner beans—Pinch out the tips of the plants when they reach the tops of their supports.

Leeks—Transplant to their final positions, when the stalks are about the thickness of a pencil.

Potatoes—If conditions are hot and humid, spray potato crops overhead with fungicide to avoid potato blight, or install trickle irrigation, possibly from a waterbutt, between the rows.

Seeds—Sow directly outdoors winter crops, such as Chinese cabbage, endive, kohlrabi, lettuce, radish, spring cabbage, turnips and winter spinach.

Courgettes—Pick small and tender courgettes (zucchini) regularly, cutting them off at the base with a sharp knife. If they are left on the plant, they will grow too large to be tasty. Wear gloves if your hands are particularly sensitive to their hairy leaves and stalks.

Watering—Continue regular watering of flowering crops, or any carrying fruits or pods such as runner beans, potatoes, and moisture-lovers such as celery.

Greenhouse

Shading—If you use blinds, make sure that your plants are well shaded on hot days to avoid scorching the plants.

Watering and ventilation—Keep watering, ventilating, and damping down the greenhouse, daily if necessary.

Lawns

Mowing—Set the mower blades higher and cut grass longer in hot, dry weather since it will not grow so actively. Cut twice a week.

Watering—Use a sprinkler regularly, if possible.

Weeds—Spot treat and dig out weeds; fill the holes with gritty compost. Rake grass seed into any bare patches (see page 65).

Early Autumn

General Tips

Conifers and hedges—Time for a final trim.

Ponds—Cut down marginal plants once they are past their best.

Flower Garden

Perennials—Move rooted softwood cuttings of *Fuchsia*, *Pelargonium* and other tender perennials to a windowsill or a cold frame to grow on over winter.

Bulbs—Begin planting early-flowering spring bulbs such as *Muscari* (grape hyacinth) and *Narcissus*, making sure that you place them at the correct depth.

Hardy annuals—Sow now (see page 233) for early blooms next summer.

Roses—Prune flowered stems and remove any suckers at the bases of rambler roses. Roses on their own roots do not throw up unwanted suckers. Take hardwood cuttings (see pages 301–302)—ramblers always grow well from these cuttings and so do many old-fashioned roses and floribundas. Pick off all rose leaves infected with black spot and burn them, together with any that have fallen to the ground below. This good hygiene removes the source of infection that harbours black spot from one year to the next.

Lavandula—Take heel cuttings (see page 306) of lavender. They may be rooted in a sheltered bed outdoors or in a sandy soil in a cold frame—make a shallow trench and sprinkle it with plenty of sharp sand before inserting the cuttings.

Deadhead—Removing spent heads from bedding plants encourages them to produce more flowers.

Cuttings—Semi-ripe cuttings (see page 305) may be taken from perennials and a wide range of shrubs.

Fruit Garden

Raspberries—Cut down autumn-fruited canes of raspberries and tie in new ones.

Vegetable Garden

Onions—Lift and lay out on the soil to dry and ripen in the sun.

Apples—Pick fruits of early-ripening cultivars.

Harvesting—Gather tomatoes, potatoes, sweetcorn and salad crops.

Japanese onion and garlic—Buy sets to plant out after harvesting others.

Celery—Earth up trench to blanch the stems.

Brussels sprouts—Draw soil up around the stems to give them support as they become increasingly top-heavy with sprouts.

Spinach—Sow winter crops now while soil is still warm.

Greenhouse

Cuttings—Take softwood cuttings (see pages 302–305) from tender bedding plants.

Potting up—Pot up any well-rooted seedlings and cuttings taken during late summer.

Pests—Treat plants in pots with nematodes to control vine weevil (see page 334).

Watering—Bring dormant plants like *Cyclamen* back into growth by watering sparingly.

Hardy annuals—Sow seed of *Calendula* (English or pot marigold) and others in pots, for early spring colour.

Light—Improve light levels in the greenhouse by removing the shading.

Lawns

Mowing—Raise the height of mower blades slightly.

Top dressing—Apply a mixture of loam, peat and sand; proportions vary according to soil.

Feed—Apply an autumn feed (see pages 74–75)

Seed—Prepare ground (see pages 66–67) to sow grass seed or lay new turf during mid-autumn.

Mid-autumn

Flower Garden

Annuals—Lift dead plants and compost them.

Bulbs—Continue to plant *Narcissus* and early-flowering bulbs. Lift and store half-hardy bulbs such as *Gladiolus*.

Dahlia* and *Canna—Cut down the foliage after frost blackens the leaves. Lift and store the tubers.

Perennials—On light soils, lift and divide established or congested clumps to increase your stock and encourage flowering (see pages 296–297). Divide established plants after they have finished flowering. Old foliage of *Helleborus orientalis* (Christmas rose) should be cut back to allow emerging flowering stems to show through.

Shrubs and trees—New deciduous trees and shrubs may be planted (see pages 149–150).

Fruit Garden

Cuttings—Take hardwood cuttings (see page 301) of red-, white- and blackcurrants and of gooseberries.

Vegetable Garden

Winter lettuce and brassicas—Remove any leaves that show signs of infection.

Spinach—For a winter crop, put cloches over late spinach sowings to protect them from frost.

Soil—Dig over any bare areas (see page 97), to allow the soil to be broken up by winter frosts.

Harvest—Gather root crops such as parsnips.

Lawns

Turf—Lay turves for a new lawn or sow seeds (see pages 66–69).

Mowing—Again raise height, if necessary, of mower blades when cutting established grass.

Brush and rake—Keep the lawn free of falling leaves. Scarify with spring-tined rake to remove dead matter (thatch) from the grass. Apply proprietary mosskiller, if necessary and wait three weeks until the moss is completely dead—it will turn black— before raking it out.

Feeding—Apply an autumn lawn fertilizer, if not done in the previous month.

Weeding—Weedkillers may be used, if necessary.

Late Autumn

General Tips

Hedges—Container-grown evergreens and conifers planted now will get a really good start in life, so complete new hedging projects as soon as possible. Bare-rooted plants are cheaper, but need to be planted immediately after arrival.

Fences and trellis—Before the arrival of destructive, strong winds, repair weak or broken fencing, to avoid permanent damage.

Frost—Keep a few sheets of fleece handy to throw over tender plants or containers if there is a sudden frost. This will give some temporary protection until you have time to pot them up or dry them off for next season.

Flower Garden

Borders—Any perennials that have been affected by frost or are now past their best may be cut right down to just above soil level; clear away the remains and add them to the compost heap. New growth will develop from below ground next spring.

Bulbs—Plant tulips for spring. This is your last chance to plant spring-flowering bulbs. If border space isn't quite prepared, plant them in large pots instead. The bulbs may be planted out to fill gaps later when space is available.

Roses—Plant bare-rooted specimens at the end of the month (see pages 165–166).

Containers—Move pots to a sheltered position. Surround terracotta or glazed pots in sacking or bubble wrap to prevent the compost from freezing and the pots from cracking.

Fruit Garden

Tree fruits—Female winter moths will be climbing up fruit trees looking for a crevice to overwinter; stop them by tightly wrapping grease bands around stems and greasing stakes.

Blackberries—Prune canes that have carried fruit this year down to soil level and tie new canes that will fruit next year into place.

Apples—Continue to pick apples as soon as they are ripe. Fruits from some cultivars may be eaten straight from the tree, while those from other cultivars are best stored for a time in a cold place until they have reached perfection.

Vegetable Garden

Seeds—Early varieties of broad beans should be sown now.

Garlic—Plant out selected strains of garlic cloves.

Onion—Plant selected onion sets to give a crop from early to midsummer.

Greenhouse

Bulbs in bowls—Finish planting up bowls of spring–flowering bulbs, including *Crocus*, dwarf *Iris*, *Narcissus* and *Tulipa*, as well as pots of *Lilium*. Then place them in a cool area to develop, covered for protection from heavy rain and to keep out the light.

Lettuce—Obtain a continuous supply of crops for harvesting through the autumn months and into winter by planting hardy lettuces in growing bags, pots or borders.

Lawns

Mowing—This will probably be the final cut, if it is dry enough.

Scarifying—Remove dead grass and moss with a scarifier or wire, spring-tined rake.

Early Winter

General Tips

Leaves—Finish clearing up autumn leaves.

Cold frames and cloches—Wash these, cleaning the glass, or PVC, inside and out. The greenhouse may be cleaned out now as well.

Water—Turn off the mains water supply to outside taps and pipework to prevent them from freezing and suffering cracks.

Hoses—clean and store away all hoses and any irrigation equipment.

Tools—Wipe metal parts of garden spades and forks with an oily rag to prevent them from rusting over winter. Sharpen cutting tools such as secateurs (pruners).

Christmas shopping—Add any new books or tools that you want to your shopping list.

Flower Garden

Convallaria (lily-of-the-valley)—Plant rhizomes in drifts under deciduous shrubs, or in pots in a greenhouse to ensure earlier blooms.

Roses—Collect any fallen leaves around roses to stop them spreading black spot. Plant bare-rooted specimens (see pages 165–166).

Pruning—Standard roses and taller shrubs may be damaged by wind rocking their stems (windrock) and loosening their roots. Prevent windrock by shortening long stems, cutting them back by about half. Full pruning should wait until early spring. Check and replace worn stakes and ties.

Trees and shrubs—Continue planting container-grown evergreens and hedging while soil conditions still allow.

Fruit Garden

New planting—Order any new fruit trees from specialist growers to plant this winter. Young trees are the cheapest to buy and may be trained to any form required. Consider the rootstock (see page 242) on which the fruit tree is growing before you buy because this will determine the vigour and ultimate size of the tree.

Vegetable Garden

Rhubarb—Lift and divide (see pages 296–297) large clumps of rhubarb, or plant new cultivars in well-manured soil.

Celery—Continue to earth up the stems.

Harvest—Brussels sprouts, cabbage, carrots, cauliflower, leeks, parsnips, radish, swedes, turnips and other crops.

Carrots—Store any carrots that are not needed immediately. Twist off the foliage, then stack the roots in containers, with layers of compost between each layer.

Compost—Spent or unharvested crops should be pulled up and added to the compost heap.

Greenhouse

Cyclamen—Gradually increase watering of cyclamen tubers brought back into growth after their summer rest. Feed weekly and grow on under cool conditions.

Lilium—Finish planting lily bulbs in large pots and keep them in the greenhouse to develop.

Amaryllis **or** *Hippeastrum*—Buy bulbs to grow for indoor displays. Plants saved from last year benefit from a cool period before being brought indoors to bloom.

Watering—Most plants require very little watering at this time of year. Check plants individually and water sparingly only when required, making sure that the compost never dries out completely.

Dahlia **and** *Canna*—Keep the tubers in frost-free conditions and check for signs of rotting or dehydration. Soak in tepid water for a few hours if they are shrivelling, then lay them out to dry before putting them back in store.

Insulation—Lining the greenhouse with UV-resistant bubble wrap will reduce heat loss and help to protect plants. Pin it to a wooden framework or attach it to a metal one. Cheaper material will become brittle and tend to deteriorate in sunlight.

Heaters—Use a max-min. thermometer to check day- and night-time temperatures.

Lawns

Drainage—Aerate badly drained areas with a spiked roller, or hollow-tined fork (see page 74).

Mowing—Grass may still be cut during a dry period, if it is still growing strongly.

Plant Hardiness Zones

In the United Kingdom, plant hardiness is generally described in terms of relative hardiness. A plant may be fully hardy, frost-hardy, half-hardy or frost-tender. In other parts of the world however, hardiness is often more complex because of the wide variety of climates. Often, plant hardiness zones are used. These zones are a guide to help you decide which plants will grow in your locality.

United States and Canada

Based on weather records throughout North America, temperature zones have been created and mapped (see page 366). The United States Department of Agriculture (USDA) hardiness zone map, which was last updated in 1990 (based on weather records from 1974–1986), is generally considered the standard measure of plant hardiness throughout much of the United States. The Canadian government's agriculture department has issued a similar map for Canada. The USDA plant hardiness map divides North America into eleven hardiness zones. Zone 1 is the coldest; zone 11 is the warmest, and comprises a tropical area found only in Hawaii and southernmost Florida. Generally, the colder zones are found at higher latitudes and higher elevations.

If you live outside North America, you can roughly translate the USDA hardiness zones by finding out how low the temperatures can reach in your area. Use the chart on page 366 to find your corresponding zone.

The Problem with Plant Hardiness Zones

The average minimum temperature is not the only factor in determining whether a plant will survive in your garden. Soil types, rainfall, daytime temperatures, day length, wind, humidity and heat also play their roles. For example, although Austin, Texas and Portland, Oregon are in the same zone (8), the local climates are dramatically different. Even

within a city, a street, or a spot protected by a warm wall in your own garden, there may be microclimates that affect how plants grow. The zones are a good starting point, but you still need to determine for yourself what will and won't work in your garden.

Sunset and American Horticultural Society Maps

Gardeners in the western United States more often use a 24-zone climate system created 40 years ago by *Sunset* magazine. The *Sunset* zone maps, which cover 13 Western states factor in not only winter minimum temperatures, but also summer highs, lengths of growing seasons, humidity, and rainfall patterns, to provide a more accurate picture of what will grow there. If you live in the western United States, you may find that nurseries, garden centres, and other western gardeners usually refer to the *Sunset* climate zones rather than the USDA plant hardiness zones.

The American Horticultural Society (AHS) has issued a Plant Heat-Zone Map. The aim of this map is to indicate to gardeners if a plant cannot survive in a location. This advice is based on the high temperatures in the area rather than the cold temperatures. There is currently an effort to mark all plants with not just the USDA and Sunset zones, but also the AHS heat zones.

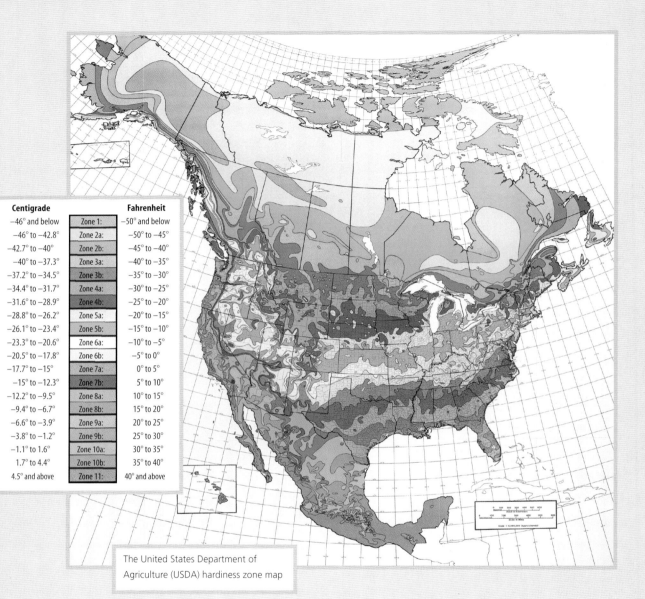

Centigrade		Fahrenheit
−46° and below	Zone 1:	−50° and below
−46° to −42.8°	Zone 2a:	−50° to −45°
−42.7° to −40°	Zone 2b:	−45° to −40°
−40° to −37.3°	Zone 3a:	−40° to −35°
−37.2° to −34.5°	Zone 3b:	−35° to −30°
−34.4° to −31.7°	Zone 4a:	−30° to −25°
−31.6° to −28.9°	Zone 4b:	−25° to −20°
−28.8° to −26.2°	Zone 5a:	−20° to −15°
−26.1° to −23.4°	Zone 5b:	−15° to −10°
−23.3° to −20.6°	Zone 6a:	−10° to −5°
−20.5° to −17.8°	Zone 6b:	−5° to 0°
−17.7° to −15°	Zone 7a:	0° to 5°
−15° to −12.3°	Zone 7b:	5° to 10°
−12.2° to −9.5°	Zone 8a:	10° to 15°
−9.4° to −6.7°	Zone 8b:	15° to 20°
−6.6° to −3.9°	Zone 9a:	20° to 25°
−3.8° to −1.2°	Zone 9b:	25° to 30°
−1.1° to 1.6°	Zone 10a:	30° to 35°
1.7° to 4.4°	Zone 10b:	35° to 40°
4.5° and above	Zone 11:	40° and above

The United States Department of Agriculture (USDA) hardiness zone map

Index

Page numbers in *italic* type refer to photographs.